A Slave Who Would Be King

Oral Tradition and Archaeology of the Recent Past in the Upper Senegal River Basin

Jeffrey H. Altschul, Ibrahima Thiaw
and Gerald Wait

Archaeopress Archaeology

Archaeopress Publishing Ltd
Summertown Pavillion
18-24 Middle Way
Oxford OX2 7LG

www.archaeopress.com

ISBN 978 1 78491 351 9
ISBN 978 1 78491 352 6 (e-Pdf)

© Archaeopress and the authors 2016

Front cover: The village of Bamabarayading seen at sunset
Back cover: SRI Nexus and IFAN fieldwork team at the conclusion of the field investigations in the exploration camp at Sabodala

All rights reserved. No part of this book may be reproduced, in any form or by any means, electronic, mechanical, photocopying or otherwise, without the prior written permission of the copyright owners.

This book is available direct from Archaeopress or from our website www.archaeopress.com

Contents

List of Figures and Tables v

List of Tables ix

Acknowledgements x

Chapter 1: Introduction 1
    Methodology 1
    Regulatory Framework of the SCHP 1
    International Regulatory Framework 1
    Senegalese Regulatory Framework 3
    Site Significance 3
    Project Chronology and Summary Results 4
    Report Organization 5

Chapter 2: Environment and Culture History in Southeastern Senegal 6
    Environmental Setting 6
    Geologic Background 7
    Cultural Setting 9
        Paleolithic Assemblages 9
        Neolithic Assemblages 12
        The Iron Age and Historical Period 12
    Ethnography of Southeastern Senegal 13
    Research Questions 14
        Paleolithic 14
        Neolithic 15
        The Iron Age and Historical Periods 15

Chapter 3: Village Histories and Ethnography within the Oromin Sabodala Concession 16
    Objectives and Methodology 16
    Culture History and Affiliation in the OJVG Concession 18
        Phase 1: The Time of the Bassari 20
        Phase 2: The Soumare Soninke Period 20
        Phase 3: The Cissokho Lineage Period 20
    Village Histories and Settlement Dynamics 22
    Society and Social Organization 27
        Malinke Society 31
        Peul Society 31
        Chieftaincy 31
        Merchants 32
        Healers 33
        Endogamous Craft Specialists 33
            Blacksmiths and Potters 33
            Griots 33
        Slave Descendants 34
    Cultural Heritage 34
        Public Ceremonies and Festivals 34
        Sacred Sites 35
        Industrial Mining and Local Community: Opportunities and Concerns 39
    Conclusion 39

Chapter 4: Archaeological Field Methods 41
    Pedestrian-Survey Methodology 41
    Detailed Site Mapping 44
    Site Test Excavations 46
    Summary 47

Chapter 5: Archaeological Survey and Test-Excavation Results 48
Material Culture and Features 48
Material Culture 48
Feature Types and Functions 50
Site Types 50
Resource-Processing Sites 54
Field Houses 56
Site 129 57
Site 133 57
Site 155 58
Farmsteads 59
Site 11 61
Site 78 64
Site 79 64
Site 147 65
Site 149 67
Site 151 68
Hamlets and Villages 71
Hamlets (Example Site 77, with Site 153, and Site 130) 75
Site 77, with 153 75
Site 130 82
Villages (Example Sites 71, 123, and 156) 87
Site 71 87
Site 123 95
Site 156 99
Polity Centers 102
Sites 8, 9, 10, 11, 78, and 79 108
Ideological/Sacred Sites 118
Site 1 118
Site 157 122
Excavation of Feature 1 124
Excavation of Feature 3 124
Discussion of Site Settlement Types and Distribution 127

Chapter 6: Artifact Analyses 129
Ceramic Sampling and Analysis Procedures 129
Method for Analyzing Body Sherds 129
Plain Sherds 130
Slip 130
Plastic Impression 130
Subtractive Motifs 130
Twine Impressions 130
Cord-Wrapped Stick 130
Carved Wood Roulette 130
Incision 133
Channeling 133
Other subtractive motifs 133
Additive Motifs 133
Multiple Attributes and Unidentified Motifs 135
Method for Analyzing Rim Sherds 135
Rim Attributes and Morphology 135
Simple Rims 135
Everted Rims 135
Collared Rims 135
Other Rims 138
Results of Ceramic Analysis 138
Small Finds 141
Conclusion 143
Lithic Analysis 144

ii

    Field Collection Strategy and Analytical Procedures 144
    Results 146
        Lithic Tools from Test Excavations 147
        Lithic Material from Surface Contexts 147
        Debris 147
        Flakes 147
        Cores 150
        Handaxes 150
        Milling Implements 152
        Grinding Slabs 152
        Pestles 152
        Pierres à Cupules 153
        Traces of Wear on Milling Implements 153
        Hammerstones 155
        Axes 155
        Miscellaneous 156
    Conclusions 156

Chapter 7: Geoarchaeological Investigations 158
    Introduction 158
    Preliminary Buried-Site Model 158
    Methods 158
        Field Methods 158
        Laboratory Methods 166
    Results 168
        Backhoe Trenching 168
            Proposed Freshwater-Reservoir Area 168
            Proposed Haul-Road Alignment 180
    Summary and Discussion 180
        Buried-Site Probability 182
        Association of Landforms and Archaeological Sites 183
    Conclusions 184

Chapter 8: Where Are the Sites, and Why Are They There? A Methodological Exercise in Archaeological Predictive Modeling 194
    The History of Predictive Modeling 194
    Inductive versus Deductive Models 196
    The SCHP Predictive Models 199
        Buried-Sites Model 199
        Surface-Sites Model 199
        Combined-Sensitivity Map 201
        Summary 204
    Why Are Sites Located Where They Are? The Case for Agent-Based Modeling 205
    Conclusions 207

Chapter 9: Settlement Dynamics in Beledougou in the Second Millennium A.D. 208
    Beledougou in Context 208
        Continuity in Settlement 210
    Settlement Dynamics 210
    Masato: The Archaeology of a West African Polity Centre 213
    Sabodala and Internal Frontiers 214
    The Past Living in the Present 214

Chapter 10: Summary 216
    Significance Evaluations 216
    Sacred and Traditional Resources 216
    Archaeological Sites 217
    Impact Analysis 221

Appendix A: Gazetteer of Sites 224

Appendix B: Gazetteer of Features and Sites 241

Appendix C: Ceramic Decorative Techniques **252**

Appendix D: Ceramic Rim Sherd Data **255**

References Cited **263**

Agricultural-Soil Productivity of the Oromin Joint Venture Group **272**

Concession, Senegal **272**

    Introduction 272

    Methods 272

    Field Methods 273

    Analytical Methods 279

    Results 280

        Evaluation of Agricultural-Soil Productivity for the OJVG Concession 280

    Agricultural Management in Mamakhono 285

    Traditional Malinké Agriculture 286

    Agricultural Field Study 295

    Assessment of Mining Effects on Agricultural Systems 307

        OJVG Concession 307

        Mamakhono 309

        Summary and Recommendations 309

References Cited **31**

List of Figures and Tables

Figure 1.1. The OJVG concession. 2
Figure 2.1. Hydrology map of the project area. 8
Figure 2.2. Known Neolithic sites in Senegal (after Guitat 1970). 10
Figure 2.3. Known sites in Senegal, including Neolithic and Paleolithic sites (after Ravisé 1975). 11
Figure 3.1. Map of villages in OJVG concession. 17
Figure 3.2. Map showing polities around the OJVG concession. 20
Figure 3.3. Schematic time line for the villages in the OJVG concession. 26
Figure 3.4. 1926 map, scale 1:200,000. 27
Figure 3.5. 1933 map. 28
Figure 3.6. 1957 map. 29
Figure 3.7. Historic map of 1960. 30
Figure 3.8. Locations of known sacred and archaeological sites as of May 2009 38
Figure 4.1. Terrain in the Oromin Joint Venture Group concession. 43
Figure 4.2. Visibility with wet-season grass 44
Figure 4.3. Survey crew at work. 44
Figure 4.4. Institut Français d'Afrique Noire Fiche de Prospection. 45
Figure 4.5. In-camp artifact processing. 45
Figure 4.6. Global Positioning System recording. 46
Figure 4.7. Sample excavation unit at Site 156. 47
Figure 5.1. Map of all sites in the OJVG concession. 49
Figure 5.2. Legend for all GIS-generated site maps. 50
Figure 5.3. A currently occupied domestic hut with foundation stones. 51
Figure 5.4. A current storage hut with foundation stones. 51
Figure 5.5. A typical 'rock alignment,' or cairn; Feature 4 from Site 156. 52
Figure 5.6. A typical rock square or rectangle from Site 156. 52
Figure 5.7. Map showing all resource-processing sites. 53
Figure 5.8. Acheulean biface tools. 54
Figure 5.9. Map of all field house sites. 55
Figure 5.10. Site 129. 56
Figure 5.11. Site 133. 57
Figure 5.12. Feature 1 at Site 155, a stone circle. 58
Figure 5.13. Feature 3 at Site 155. 59
Figure 5.14. Map of the farmsteads discovered during the surveys. 60
Figure 5.15. GIS-generated map of Site 11. 61
Figure 5.16. Feature 1 at Site 11. 62
Figure 5.17. Feature 2 at Site 11. 62
Figure 5.18. Feature 4 at Site 11. 63
Figure 5.19. Feature 8 at Site 11. 63
Figure 5.20. Feature 1 at Site 147. 64
Figure 5.21. Feature 8 at Site 147. 65
Figure 5.22. GIS-generated map of Site 147. 66
Figure 5.23. GIS-generated map of Site 149. 67
Figure 5.24. Map of Feature 3 at Site 149. 68
Figure 5.25. Map of Feature 2 at Site 149. 69
Figure 5.26. Feature 2 at Site 149. 69
Figure 5.27. Feature 4 at Site 149. 70
Figure 5.28. Feature 3 under excavation. Note buried inverted pottery vessel to right of photo board. .. 70
Figure 5.29. Feature 5 at Site 149. 71
Figure 5.30. GIS-generated map of Site 151. 72
Figure 5.31. Feature 2 at Site 151. 73
Figure 5.32. Feature 6 at Site 151. 73
Figure 5.33. Map of all hamlets, villages, and polity centers in the OJVG concession. 74
Figure 5.34. GIS-generated map of Site 77 showing the three loci. 76
Figure 5.35. Feature 1 at Site 77. 77
Figure 5.36. Feature 2 at Site 77. 77
Figure 5.37. Feature 3 at Site 77. 78
Figure 5.38. Feature 2 at Site 153. 78
Figure 5.39. Feature 5 at Site 77. 79
Figure 5.40. Feature 1 at Site 153. 79
Figure 5.41. Feature 1 at Site 153. 80
Figure 5.42. Mapping a feature at Site 77. 80
Figure 5.43. Recording a feature at Site 77. 81
Figure 5.44. Archaeological feature (Site 77) with current farmstead in background. 81
Figure 5.45. GIS-generated map of 130. 82
Figure 5.46. Record drawing of Feature 6 at Site 130. 83

Figure 5.47. Record drawing of Feature 111 at Site 130. 84
Figure 5.48. Feature 7 at Site 130, a rock alignment. 84
Figure 5.49. Feature 12 at Site 130. 85
Figure 5.50. Beginning mapping Feature 6 at Site 130. 85
Figure 5.51. Feature 7 at Site 130, subsquare. 86
Figure 5.52. Feature 1 at Site 130 prior to cleaning and recording. 86
Figure 5.53. Feature 12 at Site 130 prior to cleaning. 87
Figure 5.54. GIS-generated site map of Site 71. 88
Figure 5.55. Feature 37 at Site 71. 89
Figure 5.56. Feature 78 at Site 71. 89
Figure 5.57. Feature 97, a subrectangular stone platform. 90
Figure 5.58. Feature 86, a possible burial. 90
Figure 5.59. Feature 101 at Site 71. 91
Figure 5.60. Feature 100 at Site 71. 91
Figure 5.61. Feature 3 at Site 71. 92
Figure 5.62. Feature 8 at Site 71. 92
Figure 5.63. Feature 30 at Site 71. 93
Figure 5.64. Feature 4 at Site 71. 93
Figure 5.65. Feature 20 rock alignment at Site 71. 94
Figure 5.66. Feature 2 at Site 71, a rectangular stone platform. 94
Figure 5.67. GIS-generated map of Site 123. 95
Figure 5.68. Enclosure, Site 123. 96
Figure 5.69. The enclosure wall at Site 123. 96
Figure 5.70. Site 123 enclosure wall 97
Figure 5.71. Stone circle inside the enclosure wall at Site 123. 97
Figure 5.72. Sun-square stone outside enclosure wall at Site 123. 98
Figure 5.73. GIS-generated map of Site 156. 100
Figure 5.74. Record drawings of features at Site 156. 101
Figure 5.75. Feature 26 at Site 156. 101
Figure 5.76. (*a*) Map and (*b*) excavated section of Feature 6, Site 156. 102
Figure 5.77. Feature 5 at Site 156. 103
Figure 5.78. Feature 10 at Site 156. 103
Figure 5.79. Feature 14 at Site 156. 104
Figure 5.80. Feature 19 at Site 156. Note second hut circle in the background. 104
Figure 5.81. Feature 20 at Site 156. 105
Figure 5.82. Feature 56 at Site 156. 105
Figure 5.83. A stone circle at Makhana Site 24. 106
Figure 5.84. A large oval feature at Makhana Site 24. 107
Figure 5.85. An oval stone feature at Makhana Site 24, identified by one informant as a burial. 107
Figure 5.86. GIS-generated map of Site 8 109
Figure 5.87. GIS-generated map of Sites 9 and 10. 110
Figure 5.88. 2009 panorama of the southwest corner of the enclosure at Site 8. 111
Figure 5.89. Overall map of enclosure at Site 8 111
Figure 5.90. Map of Feature 57 at Site 8, the putative mosque. 112
Figure 5.91. Map of Feature 49 at Site 8, a putative burial. Profile A-A not reproduced here. 112
Figure 5.92. Feature 49 at Site 8, a putative burial, prior to excavation. 113
Figure 5.93. Feature 62 at Site 8, a putative burial. 113
Figure 5.94. Feature 61, the enclosure wall in foreground with putative mosque 113
Figure 5.95. Putative mosque Feature 57 after cleaning. 114
Figure 5.96. Excavated section through west wall of putative mosque Feature 57. 114
Figure 5.97. Enclosure wall Feature 61 in process of excavation. 115
Figure 5.98. Enclosure wall Feature 61 during course of excavation. 115
Figure 5.99. Excavated section through the enclosure wall of Feature 61 at Site 8. 116
Figure 5.100. Feature 5 at Site 9 prior to excavation. 116
Figure 5.101. Feature 7 at Site 8, a stone circle, prior to excavation. 117
Figure 5.102. Feature 5 at Site 9 after excavation. 117
Figure 5.103. Feature 7 at Site 8 after cleaning, with rammed clay floor clearly visible. 118
Figure 5.104. GIS-generated map of Site 1. 119
Figure 5.105. Scale drawing of the initial cluster of cup/cupules at Site 1. 120
Figure 5.106. The cup marks at Site 1 on the summit of the hill. 120
Figure 5.107. Features 9–11 at Site 1. 121
Figure 5.108. Feature 47. Note the size of the 'cup mark.' 121
Figure 5.109. GIS-generated map of Site 157. 122
Figure 5.110. Feature 1 at Site 157, *tumulus pierre*. 123
Figure 5.111. Feature 9 at Site 157, *tumulus pierre*. 124
Figure 5.112. Feature 3 at Site 157, *tumulus pierre*. 125
Figure 5.113. Feature 5 at Site 157, *tumulus pierre*. 125
Figure 5.114. Feature 6 at Site 157, *tumulus pierre*. 126
Figure 5.115. Scale map of Feature 1, pre-excavation. 126

Figure	Page
Figure 5.116. Scale drawing of Feature 3 during excavation.	127
Figure 5.117. Graphical presentation of percentages of the site in each site type.	128
Figure 6.1. Subtractive decorative techniques, twine impression (TW)	131
Figure 6.2. Subtractive decorative techniques, sabot and cord-wrapped stick	131
Figure 6.3. Subtractive decorative technique: carved wooden roulette (CWR)	132
Figure 6.5. Subtractive decorative techniques	133
Figure 6.6. Subtractive decorative techniques	134
Figure 6.7. Subtractive decorative techniques	134
Figure 6.8. Everted rim types.	136
Figure 6.9. Major rim classes in the SCHP collection.	137
Figure 6.10. Simple rim types.	137
Figure 6.11. Collared rim types.	138
Figure 6.12. Frequency of plain and decorated body sherds in the SCHP collection.	138
Figure 6.13. Frequency of plain and decorated body sherds from test excavations.	139
Figure 6.14. Rim morphology and decorative techniques documented in the SCHP collection.	139
Figure 6.15. Rim morphology and decoration techniques documented at Site 8, Masato.	140
Figure 6.16. Possible ritual vessel fragments 142.	141
Figure 6.17. Small finds from the SCHP collection.	141
Figure 6.18. Small finds from the SCHP collection.	142
Figure 6.19. Lithic tools from the SCHP collection.	149
Figure 6.20. Centripetal bifacial cores from the SCHP collection.	150
Figure 6.21. Centripetal unifacialcores from the SCHP collection.	150
Figure 6.22. Handaxes from the SCHP collection	151
Figure 6.23. Acheulean handaxes.	152
Figure 6.24. Milling implements from the SCHP collection.	153
Figure 6.25. *Pierre à cupules* from Site 137.	154
Figure 6.26. *Pierre à cupules* from Site 71.	154
Figure 6.27. Hammerstone from Site 233.	155
Figure 6.28. Examples of axes from the SCHP collection	155
Figure 6.29. Partially polished axe from Site 294.	156
Figure 7.1. Laterite exposed on an old geomorphic surface in the western part of the Oromin Joint Venture Group concession	159
Figure 7.2. Laterite exposed on an old geomorphic surface in the northern part of the Oromin Joint Venture Group concession,.	159
Figure 7.3. Road cut showing laterite on a road south-southwest of Maka Madina.	160
Figure 7.4. Close-up of laterite exposed in a road cut on a road south-southwest of Maka Madinal.	160
Figure 7.5. Hilly terrain in the Masato area.	161
Figure 7.6. Hilly terrain in the southern portion of the concession,south-southeast of Kunemba.	161
Figure 7.7. Buried-site-probability map for the proposed freshwater-reservoir area.	162
Figure 7.8. Aerial photograph of the proposed freshwater-reservoir area t	163
Figure 7.9. Idealized valley cross section showing Ruhe's slope elements.	164
Figure 7.10. Locations of backhoe trenches in the proposed freshwater-reservoir area.	165
Figure 7.11. Backhoe excavation of Backhoe Trench 6	167
Figure 7.12. Backhoe excavation of Backhoe Trench 11 in the proposed haul-road alignment.	167
Figure 7.13. Photograph of geoarchaeology crew members screening fill from a backhoe trench.	168
Figure 7.14. Channel of an intermittent stream during thedry season in the proposed freshwater-reservoir area.	169
Figure 7.15. Stratigraphy of the T0 terrace fill exposed in the creek bank in the proposed freshwater-reservoir area.	170
Figure 7.16. Profile of Backhoe Trench 2 in the proposed freshwater-reservoir area.	172
Figure 7.17. Profile of Backhoe Trench 3 in the proposed freshwater-reservoir area	173
Figure 7.18. Profile of Backhoe Trench 6 in the proposed freshwater-reservoir area.	173
Figure 7.19. West view of a remnant of T1 terrace in the proposed freshwater-reservoir area, west of Backhoe Trench 5.	174
Figure 7.20. Profile of Backhoe Trench 4 in the proposed freshwater-reservoir area	174
Figure 7.21. Profile of Backhoe Trench 1 in the proposed freshwater-reservoir area.	175
Figure 7.22. East overview of the proposed tailings-reservoir area from a hilltop.	176
Figure 7.23. Location of Backhoe Trench 9 on the T0 terrace (floodplain), in the proposed tailings-reservoir area.	176
Figure 7.24. Channel of an intermittent stream in the proposed tailings-reservoir area (near Backhoe Trench 9)	177
Figure 7.25. Profile of Backhoe Trench 9 in the proposed tailings-reservoir area	177
Figure 7.26. Profile of Backhoe Trench 7 in the proposed tailings-reservoir area.	178
Figure 7.27. Location of Backhoe Trench 8 on the T1 terrace, in the proposed tailings-reservoir area.	178
Figure 7.28. Profile of Backhoe Trench 8 in the proposed tailings-reservoir area.	179
Figure 7.29. Profile of Backhoe Trench 10 in the proposed tailings-reservoir area	179
Figure 7.30. Profile of Backhoe Trench 11 in the proposed tailings-reservoir area.	180
Figure 7.31. Profile of Backhoe Trench 12 in the alignment of the proposed haul road	181
Figure 7.32. Profile of Backhoe Trench 13 in the alignment of the proposed haul road	181
Figure 7.33. Buried sherd in the bank of a small, ephemeral stream northwest of Kunemba.	183
Figure 7.34. Close-up view of the buried sherd (see Figure 7.33) in the bank of a small, ephemeral stream.	184
Figure 7.35. Distribution of sites, differentiated by site type.	191
Figure 7.36. Distribution of sites	192
Figure 7.37. Bar graph of site frequency and site type for different landforms	193
Figure 8.1. Surface-sites predictive model.	201
Figure 8.2. Mine development plan superimposed on the combined high-sensitivity zones	202

Figure 9.1. The geopolitical context of Beledougou. 209
Figure 9.2. Abandoned field houses and (*c*) stone-circle foundations for an 'archaeological' hut at Wassa in 2009 211
Figure 9.3. Bambarayading, from the approach road... 212
Figure 10.1. Archaeological sites within the areas of direct impact (ADI). 220
Figure 10.2. Traditional sacred properties within the areas of direct impact (ADI). 223

Agricultural-Soil Productivity of the Oromin Joint Venture Group

Figure 1. Map of agricultural fields for a 2-year period (2008–2009) 274
Figure 2. Locations of agricultural fields and field controls in the Mamakhono area 275
Figure 3. Map of Fields 9/10 and the Field 10 control, ... 276
Figure 4. Mamadou Cisse (*left*) and Amy Colle Seck (*right*) collecting soil samples from an agricultural field. 277
Figure 5. Massal Diagne collecting unsaturated hydraulic-conductivity data from an agricultural field............................ 277
Figure 6. Mamakhono Chief Boucary Cissokho with family and local farmers.. 278
Figure 7. Map of soil types in the Oromin Joint Venture Group concession 281
Figure 8. White sorghum in gravelly soil at Field 13.. 288
Figure 9. Ground white sorghum in a calabas (or gourd) bowl.. 288
Figure 10. Maize in Fields 9/10 in 2009 289
Figure 11. Rice field in the northeast arm of the proposed freshwater reservoir. 289
Figure 12. Common crops in the project area: 290
Figure 13. Field 8, a mango orchard near Mamakhono 291
Figure 14. Close-up view of abundant mangos growing in Field 8 291
Figure 16. Conical iron tip of a digging stick used in planting... 292
Figure 15. A hoe (dabo) such as this is one of the main farming implements 292
Figure 17. Elevated drying rack made of wooden posts, bamboo, and thatch... 293
Figure 18. Drying rack made of wooden poles and bamboo 293
Figure 19. Typical agricultural field house made of bamboo and thatch 294
Figure 20. Field 10 on the T0 terrace (floodplain), with maize-crop residue and tree stumps 295
Figure 21. Bamboo-and-post fencing around Field 10 295
Figure 22. Field 9 on the T1 terrace, with maize residue.. 296
Figure 23. Field 9 control in a grassland-woodland vegetation community. 296
Figure 24. Field 5, a field on the T1 terrace with numerous tree stumps. 297
Figure 25. Field 5 control on the T1 terrace, in an area dominated by bamboo 297
Figure 26. Field 6 on the T0 terrace (floodplain), with sorghum-crop residue and numerous tree stumps........................ 298
Figure 27. Field 6 control, with thick, grassy vegetation.. 298
Figure 28. Field 7 on a T1 foot slope, a landscape position where runoff is concentrated. 299
Figure 29. Field 7 control on a similar T1 foot slope (see Figure 28), south of Field 7 299
Figure 30. Histograms of organic carbon, nitrogen, carbon-to-nitrogen ratios, and available phosphorus 304
Figure 31. Histograms of calcium, potassium, magnesium, and sodium for all fields versus all controls 305
Figure 32. Histograms of soil hydraulic properties. 306
Figure 33. Map of the Oromin Joint Venture Group concession with agricultural land (2008 and 2009).......................... 308

List of Tables

Table 3.1. Questionnaire	18
Table 3.2. Schedule of Activities	19
Table 3.3. Village Settlement History	24
Table 3.4. Sacred Sites	36
Table 4.1. Sites Selected for Detailed Mapping	46
Table 5.1. Number and Percentages of Sites for Each Type of Site	48
Table 6.1. Small Finds from Survey and Test Excavations	143
Table 6.2. All Lithic Artifacts	145
Table 6.3. Distribution of Lithic Surface Collection, by Type of Blank	148
Table 6.4. Lithic Tools per Site	148
Table 6.5. Raw Material Distribution within Different Classes of Grinding Equipment	152
Table 6.6. Distribution of Wear Types on Different Classes of Milling Stones	154
Table 6.7. Raw Materials Used to Manufacture Axes	156
Table 7.1. Dominant Geomorphic Processes and Expected Artifact Densities for Different Slope Elements	164
Table 7.2. Summary of Locational and Geomorphological Information for Backhoe Trenches	166
Table 7.3. Summary of Locational and Geomorphological Information for Backhoe Trenches	169
Table 7.4. Soil Chemical Properties for Soil Profiles in Backhoe Trenches 1–6	170
Table 7.5. Particle-Size Distributions, Textural Class, and Geometric Means for Soil Profiles in Backhoe Trenches 1–6	171
Table 7.6. Association of Diagnostic Subsurface Horizons for Different Geomorphic Surfaces in the Proposed Freshwater-Reservoir	182
Table 7.7. Summary of Sites Found during Geoarchaeological Survey of Stream Channels, Subsurface Exposures	185
Table 8.1. Means and Standard Deviations of Elevation, Slope, and Runoff Accumulation, by Sensitivity Class	201
Table 8.2. Comparison of Model Predictions for the Test Sample and Survey Results	204
Table 8.3. Comparison of Model Predictions for Residential Site Types and Survey Results	204
Table 8.4. Means and Standard Deviations of Elevation, Slope, and Runoff Accumulation	204
Table 10.1. Significance of Archaeological Site Classes for the OJVG Concession	219
Table 10.2. Archaeological Sites In the Areas of Direct Impact (ADI)	221
Table 10.3. Sacred Sites in the Areas of Direct Impact	222
Table C.1. Body Sherd Decorative Techniques from the SCHP Collection	252
Table C.2. Body Sherd Decorative Techniques from Tested Sites	254
Table D.1. Rim Sherd Data from the SCHP Collection	255
Table D.2. Rim Sherd Data from Tested Sites	262

Agricultural-Soil Productivity of the Oromin Joint Venture Group

Table 1. Soil properties that may indicate soil degradation caused by cultivation	273
Table 2. General characteristics of soils in the Oromin Concession (key for Figure 4).	282
Table 3. Area (hectares) of soil map units and agricultural land (years 2008 and 2009) for each village.	283
Table 4. Malinke terms for soils, crops, other agricultural terms, landforms, and animals.	287
Table 5. GPS coordinates, summary of last crops in each agricultural field, and vegetation in field controls.	294
Table 6. Chemical soil properties of fields and field controls.	300
Table 7. Particle-size distributions, textural class, and geometric means of fields and field controls.	301
Table 8. Chemical soil properties for soil profiles in backhoe trenches 1-6.	302
Table 9. Particle-size distributions, textural class, and geometric means for soil profiles in backhoe trenches 1-6.	303
Table 10. Unsaturated hydraulic conductivity and modeled hydraulic soil properties for fields and field controls.	307

Acknowledgements

Dr Jeffrey Altschul (SRI) was the Principal Investigator for the project. The fieldwork and analyses were led by Drs Ibrahima Thiaw (IFAN) and Gerry Wait (Nexus Heritage), assisted by Drs Bradley Vierra, Jeff Homburg, Diane Douglas, and Scott Kremkau all of SRI (USA). The field archaeological team consisted of Massamba Lame, Jidere Balde, Michel Waly Diouf, Ami Collé Seck, Demba Kébé, Massal Diagne and, Mamoudou Diallo. The study of Agricultural-Soil Productivity of the Oromin Joint Venture Group Concession, Senegal was by Dr Jeffrey Homburg and Gora Bèye. We also benefitted from discussions and interpretations with Jenny Wong of Wild Resources (UK) and Mark Vendrig then of SRK Consulting. Maria Molina and the production staff of SRI assisted with the editing the text and drafting many of the figures.

Chapter 1

Introduction

The Sabodala Cultural Heritage Program (SCHP) was designed to comply with the Terms of Reference (ToR) for the Environmental and Social Impact Assessment (ESIA) for the Sabodala Gold Mining Project (Vendrig and James 2008). Located in the upper Senegal River Valley of eastern Senegal, the gold mine will be developed by the Oromin Joint Venture Group (OJVG) in a 230-km^2 area, herein termed the OJVG concession (Figure 1.1). The ToR identified a series of specialist baseline studies for the ESIA, including one for 'archaeology and cultural heritage.' For the latter, the ToR outlined the study's objectives as:

> The primary objective of the Archaeology and Cultural Heritage specialist study is to identify, map and describe significant archaeological and cultural resources/spaces in the concession area and surrounding areas affected by the proposed mining project. A protocol for dealing with new archaeological sites in the project area will be developed, along with the relevant legal framework for the project design to remain in compliance with national legal standards and World Bank guidelines. The specialist should ensure that the specialist study undertaken meets or exceeds any relevant requirements of the World Bank Group Guidelines and/or Senegal legislation. Canadian Heritage Conservation Act: http://www.qp.gov.bc.ca/statreg/stat/h/96187_01.htm [Vendrig and James 2008:73].

Methodology

- Description of the baseline archaeological and cultural environment of the study area
- Description of the significance of any finds in a national context
- Summary of the relevant legal framework (national legal standards and World Bank guidelines) for archaeology sites in Senegal that could affect compliance of the project design
- Provide suggestions for dealing with any new archaeology sites that may be discovered during the proposed mining project.

In March 2009, Statistical Research, Inc. (SRI), a comprehensive cultural resource management (CRM) firm based in the USA, was awarded a contract from SRK Consulting (SRK) to complete the specialist baseline study for archaeology and cultural heritage for the Sabodala gold mine ESIA. SRI served as the prime contractor for the study, which it performed in partnership with the Institut Fondamental d'Afrique Noire (IFAN), based in Dakar, Senegal, and Nexus Heritage from the UK. The principal investigators for the SCHP were Dr. Jeffrey Altschul (SRI), Dr. Ibrahima Thiaw (IFAN), and Dr. Gerald Wait (Nexus Heritage).

Regulatory Framework of the SCHP

Several international conventions, charters, and policies provide guidelines for assessing impacts of projects funded by the WB and the International Finance Corporation (IFC) on environmental and cultural resources. Below, we summarize these guidelines as they pertain to the Sabodala gold mine as well as Senegalese regulations developed to help protect cultural resources.

International Regulatory Framework

The international regulatory framework for environmental impact assessment is well known at a strategic level, but less developed in terms of project implementation. The principal conventions and guidance are:

- United Nations Educational, Scientific and Cultural Organization (UNESCO) World Heritage Convention (1972)
- World Bank Operational Policy/Bank Procedure (OP/BP) 4.11—Physical Cultural Resources
- International Finance Corporation's Performance Standards on Social and Environmental Sustainability (2006), especially Performance Standard 8: Cultural Heritage
- International Finance Corporation Operational Policies (e.g., OP4.01) (1998)
- The Equator Principles (2006)

In the last 40 years, standards of 'best practice' have developed, particularly in North America and Europe, with regard to the identification, protection, and management of cultural heritage sites and resources. These standards are generally at a project-specific level and serve to support implementation of the international guidance and conventions, such as the UNESCO World Heritage Convention, the IFC's Performance Standards and Operational Policies, and the Equator Principles, which are strategic in nature and provide little practical guidance.

UNESCO has published a series of Conventions, Declarations, and Recommendations applicable to cultural heritage projects. Senegal is a signatory to

FIGURE 1.1. THE OJVG CONCESSION.

UNESCO and the UNESCO Conventions and ordinarily uses those conventions as if they were national legislation. The principle relevant instruments are:

- UNESCO Convention Concerning the Protection of World Cultural and Natural Heritage (1973)
- UNESCO Convention on the Safeguarding of the Intangible Cultural Heritage (Paris 2003)
- UNESCO Operational Guidelines for the Implementation of the World Heritage Convention (2005)
- UNESCO Recommendation on International Principles Applicable to Archaeological Excavations (1956)
- UNESCO Declaration Concerning the Intentional Destruction of Cultural Heritage (2003)
- UNESCO Recommendation on the Safeguarding of Traditional Culture and Folklore (1989)
- UNESCO Recommendation for the Protection of Movable Cultural Property (1978)
- UNESCO Recommendation Concerning the Safeguarding and Contemporary Role of Historic Areas (1976)
- UNESCO Recommendation Concerning the Safeguarding of Beauty and Character of Landscapes and Sites (1962)

The International Council on Monuments and Sites—ICOMOS—is an international nongovernmental organization of professionals dedicated to the conservation of the world's historic monuments and sites. ICOMOS works for the conservation and protection of cultural heritage places. It is the only global non-government organization of its kind, dedicated to promoting the application of theory, methods, and scientific techniques to the conservation of the architectural and archaeological heritage. ICOMOS has published a number of charters, of which the following are most pertinent:

- ICOMOS Charter for the Protection and Management of the Archaeological Heritage (1990; the Lausanne Charter)
- ICOMOS The Burra Charter: The Australia ICOMOS charter for the conservation of places of cultural significance (1999)
- ICOMOS Charter—Principles for the analysis, conservation, and structural restoration of architectural heritage (2003)
- ICOMOS Charter on the Built Vernacular Heritage (Mexico, 1999)
- ICOMOS International Charter for the conservation and restoration of monuments and sites (Venice Charter; 1964)

By following these UNESCO conventions and ICOMOS Charters, the SCHP will be in accord with international best practice.

The World Bank Operational Policy/Bank Procedure (OP/BN) 4.11 Physical Cultural Resources set out standards for the treatment of cultural heritage resources in projects financed by the WB (see Goodland and Webb 1987). The trend at the WB has been to shift the treatment of heritage sites/resources from a condition of funding to a component of the Environmental Assessment (EA) process. The WB balances EA costs to the project applicant against need for sufficient information by national regulatory agencies/departments to make informed decisions about the known and potential impacts of a project. The presence of a known or potential World Heritage site may have serious implications for a project—sites of lesser significance would have lesser implications that the proponent could managed through the mitigation/compensation plans arising from an EA. The process also highlights the risk of discovery of significant heritage sites or resources in later stages of project design, or worse, project implementation where costs of mitigation can be very disruptive—a project applicant and the WB, IFC, and other major banking institutions will want to minimize risk, which means acquiring appropriate levels of information.

In practice, WB compliance requires implementing a variety of technical studies that identify the physical cultural resources at risk for project impact. Such studies typically include (among others) documentary research, analysis of aerial photographs, archaeological surveys, geophysical surveys, geoarchaeological surveys, ethnographic research, etc. To determine the studies to include in the baseline study, the proponent, in consultation with the WB, relies heavily on professionals to assess the amount of information available for an area. The less studied an area, the more intensive the baseline surveys.

Following the baseline studies to identify cultural resources, the proponent may need to undertake additional work to evaluate the resources in terms of their scientific and cultural importance. Test excavations are often required to determine the age of sites, their nature (e.g., settlement versus industrial versus agricultural sites), their rarity (a common site type versus a rare site type), and their degree of preservation. Proponents also may use test excavations to determine the depth, extent, nature, and density of buried artifacts and features within the site.

The extent to which site testing is required is again a function of professional judgment based upon the level of background knowledge available—what constitutes 'sufficient' information to allow informed regulatory decisions is not an absolute. In parallel to providing sufficient information to regulators, this process also allows project applicants to seek appropriate funding to manage cultural resource risk throughout a project. This final stage is to complete a CRM plan, which specifies how significant cultural resources will be adequately mitigated so that the proponent is eligible for WB funding. Typically, cultural resource mitigation involves avoidance or the excavation of archaeological or historical cultural properties, followed by analysis and publication or presentation. Compensation for impacts within a mining zone is another mitigation option, particularly for traditional or intangible resources, by means of interpretive presentation of heritage resources.

Senegalese Regulatory Framework

The principal Senegalese heritage legislation is Law 71 of 12 January 1971. This is divided into 4 parts:

Part 1 regulates, in Articles 1–12, the listing, preservation, and refurbishment of historic buildings and properties.

Part 2 concerns archaeological excavations and discoveries in Articles 13–21. For example, Article 13 includes a provision for archaeological excavations to be authorized by the government. Other articles address the issue of the ownership of discovered artifacts, including chance-finds (Article 21). Article 20 requires archaeological discoveries to be reported to the appropriate government agency.

Part 3 (Articles 22–27) provides for penalties that may be applied in the event of actions contravening the other Articles, including financial fines or imprisonment up to 6 months.

Part 4 (Articles 28–30) provides for a Historic Buildings commission with duties of advice.

This legislation is, by comparison with most industrialized countries, relatively weak. Senegal, however, is a signatory to UNESCO and the UNESCO Conventions; the country ordinarily uses those conventions as if they were national legislation.

Site Significance

As described in the previous section the ESIA process requires OJVG to identify and evaluate cultural resources in the OJVG concession. Cultural resources can have scientific and traditional value. Local communities often place traditional values on places that symbolize their history and culture. Such places can be burial grounds, traditional medicinal plants, hunting grounds, churches, mosques, markets, and so forth. Although diverse, all traditional resources share the fact that they are part of an ongoing cultural system. In addition to physical locations, local communities may have significant intangible resources that are critical to maintaining their place in the world. Areas where spirits live or witches hide may appear to be nothing more than natural hills and valleys, but their disturbance will bring on real problems to the living (Altschul 2008; Smith and Akagawa 2009).

Archaeological and historical sites are generally considered important for their scientific information. There are exceptions, such as Thiaw (2003) documented on Gorée Island with regard to the use of archaeological sites to convey the place of the slave trade in Senegalese culture. For the most part, however, to determine the importance of an archaeological site, we must place it in context. How rare is it? What can it tell us that we don't already know?

One approach to compliance with regard to traditional and intangible properties is to create a list of these resources and try to minimize impacts to them. We have found that unless one can avoid all such resources, a better approach to compliance is to view these properties as part of a system. Our strategy is to work with local leaders and elders to ensure that the system is maintained regardless of the outcome to any individual property. For example, all cultural systems must pass on norms of acceptable behavior to the next generation. Often, stories that teach these norms are embedded in the natural environment, such as a tree struck by lightning, which is said to be the burned corpse of a man who disrespected the animals that he killed. It may not be possible to save the tree, but we may be able to work with the community to either save another endangered place that embodies the same story or to provide the local community with a place within the concession to create a similar story. Consultation is the key to a successful outcome.

We have also found that it is imperative that any mitigation strategy include all traditional and intangible resources. In this manner, we are not continually reopening negotiations over complex issues.

Archaeological and historical sites are generally considered important for their scientific information. There are exceptions, such as Thiaw (2003) documented on Gorée Island with regard to the use of archaeological sites to convey the place of the slave trade in Senegalese culture. For the most part, however, to determine the importance of an archaeological site, we must place it in context. How rare is it? What can it tell us that we don't already know?

The OJVG concession is located in the upper Senegal River Valley, which we took as the appropriate geographic context for the SCHP. As a first step in the ESIA process, we reviewed what was known about the environment, archaeology, ethnography, and history of the region based on published and unpublished sources. From this overview, we developed a series of research questions to guide site evaluation. These questions will be refined in consultation with the peer reviewers, as necessary as we develop management plans for significant resources affected by the project.

Project Chronology and Summary Results

- **Reconnaissance Survey and ESIA Workshop.** In February 2009, Altschul and Thiaw, together with Dr. Masamba Lane of IFAN, attended a workshop in Dakar with Senegalese government officials and representatives of SRK to finalize the ToR for ESIA. Altschul and Thiaw then spent several days at the project site, documenting the existence of archeological sites and the range of site types.
- **Ethnographic Fieldwork.** Between April 28 to May 17, 2009, Thiaw and Wait conducted ethnographic research at the 10 villages in the OJVG concession. Fieldwork focused on identifying sacred and traditional sites, documenting village histories, assessing the ethnic composition of village residents, their social position, traditional beliefs, and traditional economy. Fieldwork resulted in the identification of 46 sacred sites and 49 archaeological sites (Wait et al. 2009).
- **Predictive Model.** In June 2009, SRK authorized the creation of surface and subsurface predictive models of archaeological site location. These models were completed in September and used in the in the mine development plan.
- **Reconnaissance Geoarchaeological Survey.** Geoarchaeological fieldwork led by Dr. Jeffrey Homburg was to begin in November 2009. However, the fieldwork was aborted due to unrelated matters related to geological explorations of the gold deposit. Homburg and Dr. Diane Douglas of SRI were able to make a reconnaissance visit of the area and recorded a number of archaeological sites.
- **Archaeological Monitoring.** To ensure that mine exploration activities were not affecting archaeological sites, a monitoring program was begun in January 2010 (Altschul and Douglas 2010). Between January 18 and February 24, Thiaw and Massal Diagne performed two sessions of archaeological monitoring during which they recorded 64 archaeological sites (Thiaw et al. 2010a, 2010b).
- **Archaeological Investigations and Agricultural Study.** Between February 26 and March 31, the proposed areas of direct impact (ADI) for the gold mine were intensively surveyed. Additionally, geoarchaeological studies, focused primarily on the ADI, were conducted. Combining the intensive survey with monitoring and reconnaissance surveys, we recorded 251 archaeological sites in the OJVG concession. Seventeen sites were subjected to detailed recording, and test excavations were performed at 6 sites. Beyond archaeological studies, Homburg, in collaboration with Gora Beyé, completed a study of agricultural soil quality.

- **End-of-Field Report**. In April 2010, SRI, IFAN, and Nexus Heritage compiled the results of the intensive archaeological survey of the ADI and the agricultural study into an end-of-fieldwork report (Wait et al. 2010).
- **Baseline Reports**. At the end of July 2010, the SCHP submitted draft reports on the archaeological and ethnographic studies (this volume) as well as the study of agricultural soils (Homburg and Beyé 2010). The 251 archaeological sites were classified into 7 site types, each of which was evaluated in terms of its scientific and traditional value at local, country, and regional levels. Of the 251 sites, 66 will be disturbed either completely or partially by the current mine plan. In addition to the 46 traditional sites identified, 3 will be disturbed. Recommendations were then offered for the CRM plan as well as for the long-term management of cultural resources in the OJVG concession.

Report Organization

This report documents the results of baseline archaeological and cultural heritage studies in support of the ESIA for the Sabodala gold mine. It is organized into 10 chapters. Following this introduction, the results of background and archival research are presented in Chapter 2 in the form of a cultural historical framework. We also present the research questions that guided the evaluation of the archaeological sites documented as part of the project. Chapter 3 is devoted to the ethnographic component. Here, we present our methods as well as the results of the sacred sites survey. We also describe the social structure that prevails in the villages and how that structure affects village life. Intangible resources, such as festivals and dances, are discussed. Field and analytical methods for survey and test excavations are the subjects of Chapter 4, whereas the results of archaeological fieldwork are presented in Chapter 5. Fieldwork resulted in the collection of a relatively large artifact assemblage, which is described and compared with other regional collections in Chapter 6. In Chapter 7, we present the methods and results of the geoarchaeological investigations, which allow us to conclude that buried cultural deposits, if they exist, are restricted to small parts of the OJVG concession. We undertake a methodological examination of predictive modeling as it was used in the SCHP in Chapter 8. Settlement dynamics are explored in Chapter 9 which when combined with our interpretation of site and feature function forms the basis for site type evaluations. We conclude in Chapter 10 with an evaluation of sites in terms of their scientific and cultural significance and offer recommendations on the appropriate treatment of sites that will be affected by the development of the mine as well as on long-term management of the OJVG concession's cultural resources.

Acknowledgements

Dr Jeffrey Altschul (SRI) was the Principal Investigator for the project. The fieldwork and analyses were led by Drs Ibrahima Thiaw (IFAN) and Gerry Wait (Nexus Heritage), assisted by Drs Bradley Vierra, Jeff Homberg and Diane Douglas, and Scott Kremkau all of SRI (USA). The field archaeological team consisted of Massamba Lame, Jidere Balde, Michel Waly Diouf, Ami Collé Seck, Demba Kébé, Massal Diagne and, Mamoudou Diallo. The study of Agricultural-Soil Productivity of the Oromin Joint Venture Group Concession, Senegal was by Jeffrey A. Homburg and Gora Bèye. We also benefited from discussions and interpretations with Jenny Wong of Wild Resources (UK) and Dr Mark Vendrig then of SLR Consulting.

Chapter 2

Environment and Culture History in Southeastern Senegal

The archaeological research focuses on the OJVG concession that covers 230 km² in southeastern Senegal in the upper Senegal and Gambia River drainages. The study is significant, as our knowledge of the prehistory and history of the upper Senegal region is extremely limited, and the cultural resources in the region are in jeopardy from increased development. With the exception of the Canal du Cayor Project in the mid-1990s, studies assessing the impact of development programs on archaeological and cultural resources have been extremely rare in Senegal (Consortium SNC-Lavallin/BCEOM 1996). Yet, in the last two decades, archaeologists, historians, sociologists, and anthropologists have documented the destruction of large numbers of archaeological and cultural resources as a result of development projects (Bocoum 2008; Thiaw 2007, 2008). Senegal is not alone. The lack of protection for cultural resources in developing countries has been the norm (Naffe et al. 2008). The Sabodala Cultural Heritage Project is a step in the direction of correcting this situation.

In this chapter, we present the state of knowledge about the prehistory and history of the upper Senegal River Valley prior to this project. We note that the oldest Stone Age industries in Senegal were recorded in the upper Senegal region, and human settlement has been continuous there until historical times. Whereas most of Senegal lies in the Senegalo-Mauritanian sedimentary basin, the most substantial outcroppings with volcano-sedimentary rock suitable for lithic-tool manufacture mainly occur in the upper Senegal River, in the southeastern region of the country. The outcropping of various geological series, some of which contain gold veins, may have been an incentive for human settlement in the region both in ancient and recent times. Extensive laterization has yielded soils that are highly weathered and contain large amounts of iron and aluminum oxide, making agriculture problematic. These soils, combined with a rugged topography, have confined cultivation largely to the Senegal and Gambia Rivers, their tributaries, and fossil drainages (only 5 percent of lands in some areas) (Bassot 1966; Michel 1973). In spite of its limitations, the upper Senegal region has played a critical role over the past thousand years in the development of trade and the growth of major regional polities, including Ghana, Takrour, Mali, and Sonrai (Bathily 1989; Curtin 1975; Girard 1992; Thiaw 1999). The reasons are simple. The upper Senegal is rich in gold and lies at the crossroads of east-west and north-south trade networks in the Western Sudan. The failure of colonial mining exploration, the abolition of slavery, and the growth of groundnut cultivation in regions adjacent to the Atlantic coast, however, has led to the redeployment of economic activity to the coastal Atlantic region and has plunged the upper Senegal region into its current state of economic lethargy (Thiaw 1999).

We begin with the environmental setting. Next, we outline the culture historical sequence for the last 300,000 years in the upper Senegal River. We then briefly touch on the ethnographic groups that inhabit the region, a subject which is explored in much greater depth in Chapter 3. Following these descriptive sections, we present the research questions that guided our work.

Environmental Setting

The OJVG concession straddles a mountain range that forms the divide between the Gambia River and Falémé River (part of the Senegal River) drainage basins. The mountain range trends north-south and roughly bisects the concession. The concession straddles the Mako volcanic series and the sedimentary rocks of the Dialle-Dalema series and is divided into five main water catchments fed by nonperennial streams (Figure 2.1). Within the concession, elevation ranges from 126 m above mean sea level (MAMSL) to 374 MAMSL; the area is dissected by numerous ravines and washes.

The Senegal and Gambia Rivers both rise in the highlands of Guinea and flow northwest to the Atlantic Ocean. The Senegal River flows along the eastern and northern borders of Senegal, dividing it from Mali and Mauritania. The Gambia River flows through southern Senegal, with its lowest reach contained within the tiny country of The Gambia. Ephemeral streams flow north from the project area merging with the Falémé River, a major tributary of the Senegal River, about 40 km to the northeast on the Senegal-Mali border. Other ephemeral streams flow into the Senegal plains to the west and south before being captured by the Gambia River about 100 km to the southwest of the project area.

Natural vegetation in the project area ranges from dense savannah grasses and shrubs to forest. Fauna in the project area include a variety of rodents, reptiles, birds, and large game: the Niokolo Koba National Park is located nearby, and animals from the park often range into the project area. Land use within the concession includes agriculture

(3.9 percent), mining (0.4 percent), villages (0.2 percent) and pastoralism (95.4 percent); much of the pastoral land is covered in forest.

There are no meteorological stations near the project area, but there are three seasons—a rainy season from June to September; a cool, dry season from October to February; and a hot, dry season from March to June. During the rainy season, downpours and strong southeasterly winds predominate, and average precipitation in the project area is approximately 1,130 mm (44.5 inches). Maximum temperatures during the hot dry season can reach 40°C, and the heat is exacerbated by hot, dry Harmattan winds.

Few paleoclimatic studies have been conducted in the upper Senegal River, requiring us to look further afield for information on how the environment may have changed over time. Thiaw (1999) has synthesized much of this material for the Holocene, which we summarize below.

The late Pleistocene (18,000–13,000 B.P.), termed the Ogolian period in West Africa, was characterized by a hot and dry climate. Rivers shrank in size, and dune formation took place in different parts of the Sahara and Sahel (Sarnthein 1978). Desertification took place and the boundary between the Sahara and the Sahel was 300–400 km south of its current position (Lezine 1989; Michel 1973; Petit-Maire 1991:212).

Beginning around 9000 B.P., the monsoonal pattern improved providing increased rainfall to the region. Populations increased in parts of the Sahara (Brooks 1986; McIntosh and McIntosh 1988; Petite-Maire et al. 1991). Until around 4500 B.P., conditions were generally positive for human use of the region (McIntosh 1993). Thereafter the climate deteriorated, albeit with periodic climatic oscillations, until around 2300 B.P. The next 600 years or so were marked by a hot and dry period that probably led to rapid deterioration of areas supporting human occupation in the Sahara (Brooks 1986, 1993). This period witnessed the earliest occupation of the inland Niger Delta and the middle Senegal River Valley (McIntosh 1995; McIntosh and McIntosh 1980; McIntosh et al. 1992). The last part of the first millennium A.D. witnessed a return to more moderate conditions, leading to the refilling of lakes and recharging of rivers, the larger of which were able to breach dune barriers created during the preceding dry period (Chavane 1985:111–112; Michel 1973:602).

The second millennium A.D. began with a wet period. Humidity and standing water reached a point that discouraged Saharan-based Berber horsemen from raiding the tse tse infested Sahel (Brooks 1956:50). By the beginning of the twelfth century, however, conditions had begun to degrade once more. By 1300–1400 A.D., there is widespread abandonment of mound sites in the Middle Niger River valley and adjacent Mema (McIntosh 1983; McIntosh 1994; Togola 1966).

For the last 500 years, paleoenvironmental reconstructions are aided by historic documents. Portuguese accounts indicate that conditions improved from the fifteenth into the sixteenth century (Daveau 1969). From the sixteenth until the late seventeenth century, traders and explorers noted that the Senegal River was covered with thick stands of trees, mashes, and gallery forests (Chambonneau 1898; Nicholson 1978:102). Thiaw (1999:16) suggests these riverine environments may be due more to floodwaters originating from the upper Senegal River Valley than an increase in local rainfall. Around A.D. 1800, lakes eeding the Senegal River become increasingly desiccated, and gallery forests are replaced by windblown sands. This trend was reversed in the 1870s and 1880s, but rainfall again decreased by 1900 (Nicholson 1978), by which time modern conditions prevailed.

Geologic Background

The OJVG concession is dominated by hills composed of unweathered metabasalts, with local intrusions of subvolcanic dolerite and gabbro sills and dykes, quartz-feldspar porphyry, and unfoliated rhyolite dykes. Gold deposits in the project area are in the Maka mafic volcanic sequence and are located within the west Birimian gold province, host to some of the world's largest gold deposits. These volcanic outcrops, east of the gold deposits, indicate an approximate northeast-southwest striking sequence that dips steeply to the west and northwest. The structural geology indicates that gold deposits are part of a large structural zone known as the Sabodala Shear Zone. Gold mineralization is concentrated in dilational breccia zones within the shear zone—associated with quartz, sericite, and ankerite/siderite veins—and altered zones of orange-colored silica, albite, carbonate, and pyrite. OJVG geologists 'have defined nine gold deposits and 18 promising gold targets within a 22-km-long, 5–8-km wide, northeast-trending structural corridor at the OJVG Concession' (Oromin Explorations, Ltd. 2010).

A major watershed divide runs across the concession, with drainages in the northern and eastern parts of the OJVG concession draining into the Falémé River and, ultimately, into the Senegal River. The rest of the project area drains westward, into the Gambia River. Terrain in the project area is dissected by a number of ephemeral drainages in the upper watershed of these major rivers. All drainages in the OJVG concession flow either intermittently during the rainy season or for brief periods after flashy storm events. A number of Quaternary stream terraces flank the floodplain in these alluvial systems, especially away from the uplands, forming

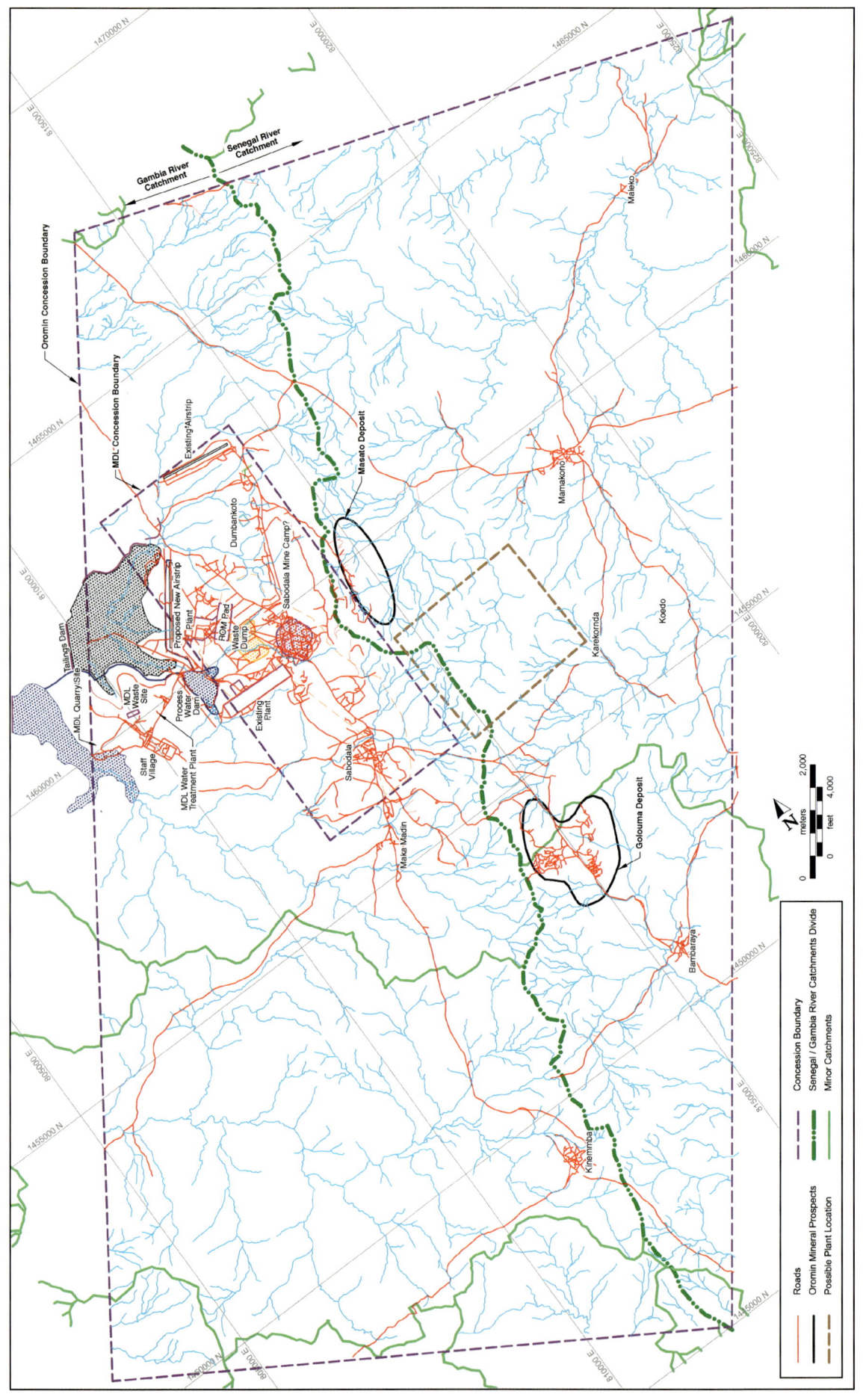

Figure 2.1. Hydrology map of the project area.

stair-step topography adjacent to stream channels. These terraces were formed as a result of cut-and-fill events associated with episodic downcutting that stranded the former floodplains above the new floodplain and thus transformed the former floodplains into terraces. Intervening periods of rapid aggradation are marked by weak to no soil development, and prolonged periods of geomorphic stability are marked by stronger soil development. The youngest alluvial geomorphic surface is on the floodplain, and the older surfaces of terraces are on successively higher landscape positions.

Laterite is widespread in upland areas of the project area (Figures 7.1–7.4), including summits and slopes of hills in upland areas, such as the proposed Masato (Figure 7.5) and Golouma mining areas and south of Kunemba (Figure 7.6). The oldest laterites occur on the hilltops, where they reach thicknesses of about 17 m. These old laterites likely date to the Miocene period. Younger ones are widespread on landforms that likely date to the early to middle Pleistocene period.

No geomorphological or geoarchaeological studies were conducted in the Sabodala region prior to this investigation. The most-detailed work in the region, a study of the Gambia River drainage basin, was conducted by Michel (1973). Although the OJVG concession extends into the upper watershed of the Gambia River, almost all of the impact areas associated with the proposed mining activity are concentrated in the upper watershed of the Senegal and Falémé Rivers.

Cultural Setting

It is ironic that with so much European interest focused on the Atlantic region, the first archaeological find in Senegal was officially recorded in eastern Senegal by Captain Parent, who collected polished hematite axes near Senudebou along the Falémé River in 1846 (Diagne 1978). Throughout the twentieth century, there was a fascination with Acheulean hand axes (Zeltner 1916) and the finely polished Neolithic stone axes of eastern Senegal (Hamy 1901, 1904; Laforgue 1924; Moreau 1900). These finds resulted in the Sabodala region being mentioned in an early regional review on the prehistory of the Sahara and West Africa (Laforgue 1923, 1925). Archaeological research in Senegal, however, only took root after the foundation of IFAN (Institut Français d'Afrique Noire, or French Institute for Black Africa) that was created in 1936. From its headquarters based in Dakar (Senegal), IFAN pioneered research in archaeology, ethnography, history, geology, botany, zoology, and entomology in the French West African colonial empire and even beyond.

In the field of archaeology, Raymond Mauny (1961) published the first synthesis of the massive archaeological database accumulated by IFAN throughout West Africa. Similar regional syntheses were later pursued both in archaeology and close disciplines but were narrowed to the newly established national borders. Guitat (1970) published one of the first maps of known Neolithic sites in Senegal (Figure 2.2). He reported 14 Neolithic sites in eastern Senegal out of a total of 77 known sites nationwide, placing this region in a second position after the Cap Vert peninsula around the capital, Dakar. Later on, Ravisé (1975) published her inventory of Neolithic and Paleolithic sites, reporting more than 200 sites, of which 35 Neolithic sites and 3 Paleolithic sites were recorded in eastern Senegal alone (Figure 2.3).

Extensive survey by Martin and Becker (1970, 1974, 1977a) shifted efforts to later prehistory, covering sites dating to the past two millennia A.D., as they were interested in historical demography. This large-scale inventory of archaeological sites, however, was unsystematic and targeted easily accessed regions along major transportation and fluvial routes. In addition, Martin and Becker's work was largely focused on large-scale sites and therefore emphasized megaliths, earthen tumula, shell middens, and habitation mounds. Building on that work, subsequent surveys and excavations were conducted among habitation mounds in the Senegal River Valley (Bocoum 1986; Deme 2003, Guèye 1998; McIntosh and McIntosh 1993; McIntosh et al. 1992; Thiam 1991; Thilmans and Ravisé 1980), shell mounds along the Atlantic coast (De Sapir 1971; Descamps and Thilmans 1979, 2001; Thilmans and Descamps 1982), and earthen tumuli and megalith sites in west-central Senegambia (Thilmans et al. 1980) and in the Falémé (Thiaw 1999). Although Paleolithic (Camara and Duboscq 1984, 1987, 1990) and Neolithic (Diagne 1978; Lame 1981; Ravisé 1970, 1975) sites continued to be investigated, archaeological research in Senegal after 1970 focuses largely on protohistoric/Iron Age and historical-period sites.

Paleolithic Assemblages

Geological (Bassot 1966), geomorphic (Michel 1973), and archaeological (Descamps 1972) data collected in Senegal over the past decades suggest that southeastern Senegal and, to a lesser extent, the Cap Vert Peninsula, where substantial stone outcroppings suitable for lithic-tool manufacture occur, were the only areas in Senegal suitable for supporting hunter-gatherer populations. A putative Acheulean industry was identified in the Falémé by Zeltner (1916) and later by Corbeil and Mauny (quoted in Ravisé 1975), who collected a cleaver near Djita in the middle Falémé River. Diop (1980) also recovered an Acheulean hand axe near the same site, prompting excavations by Camara and Duboscq (1990). According to the latter, this industry was found in medium alluvial deposits, suggesting an upper Pleistocene occupation dated 130,000 B.P. The earliest evidence of occupation in eastern Senegal, however, was recovered on the lower

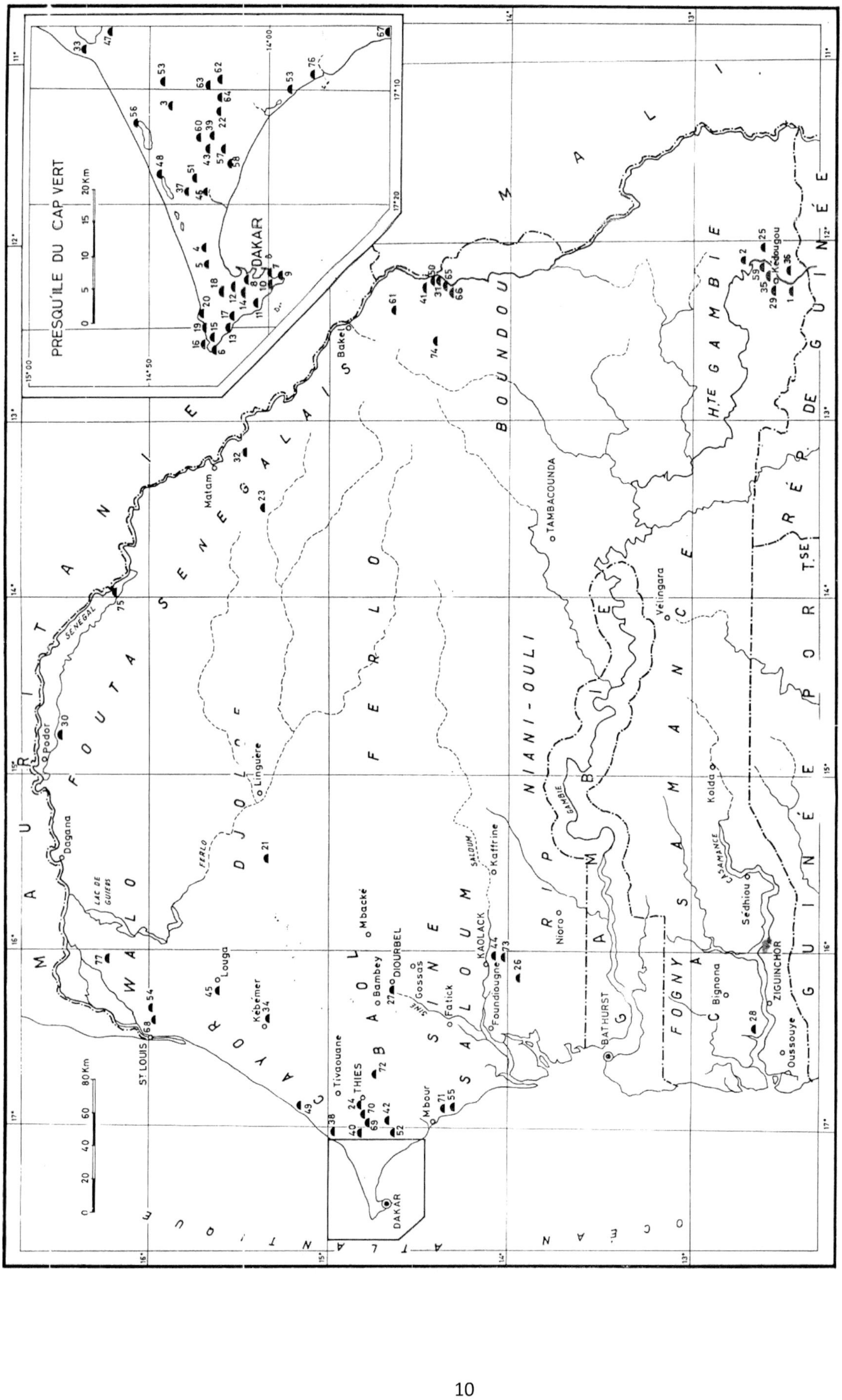

Bulletin de l'IFAN, t. XXXII, série B, nº 4.

Carte des sites néolithiques du Sénégal.

Figure 2.2. Known Neolithic sites in Senegal (after Guitat 1970).

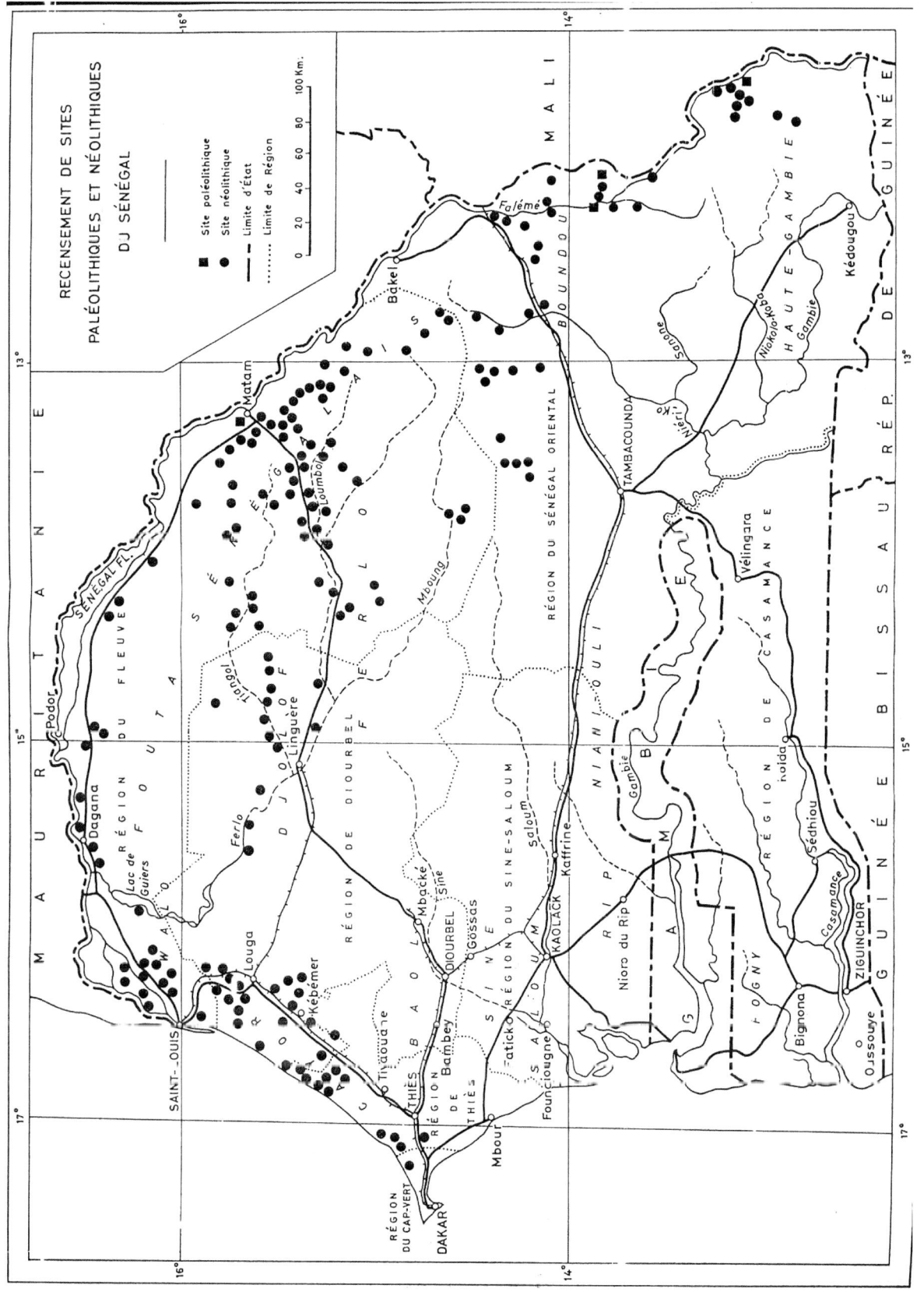

FIGURE 2.3. KNOWN SITES IN SENEGAL, INCLUDING NEOLITHIC AND PALEOLITHIC SITES (AFTER RAVISÉ 1975).

Falémé River at the site of Sansandé, where Acheulean hand axes, side scrapers, Levallois flakes, and cleavers were tentatively attributed to different periods of the Paleolithic between 345,000 and 32,000 B.P., on the basis of geomorphic and oxygen-isotope correlations by Camara and Duboscq (1984, 1987).

The upper Senegal and the Cap Vert Peninsula are known to have hosted the earliest hunter-gatherer populations in Senegal. Descamps (1972) hypothesized that these two regions were separated by a no-man's-land that stretches over 450 km, which remained unoccupied until recent prehistoric times. In recent years, however, a few Paleolithic assemblages were recovered outside these areas and in the middle Senegal River region, in the Ferlo, and along the Atlantic coast (Ravisé 1975). The most likely explanation for this distribution is that the Senegal and Gambia Rivers and their major tributaries that flow from the moist Fuuta Djallon Plateau headwaters in Guinée were active enough when rainfall was abundant to transport heavy gravels and stones suitable for tool manufacture during the Pleistocene and Holocene (Michel 1973).

Although rich in archaeological material, the Paleolithic in Senegal is poorly documented. Most studies are based on small-scale survey and limited excavations. Analysis has been oriented primarily to stone tool typology and correlations of the archaeological record with geological strata and geomorphic land surfaces, which have been interpreted through a context of rapidly changing climatic conditions. No taphonomic analysis has been attempted so far, and little is known on adaptations to the natural environment, subsistence strategies, and patterns of mobility. The extent to which early Paleolithic hunter-gatherers occupied this region and how they adapted to it remain critical questions. Intensive survey and excavations in the upper Senegal region would contribute enormously to our knowledge of Senegalese and African prehistory.

Neolithic Assemblages

Like those of the Paleolithic, Neolithic assemblages in the upper Senegal region have been documented since the early twentieth century (Hamy 1901; Laforgue 1924; Moreau 1900; Zeltner 1916). Over the past decades, many more Neolithic sites have been located in the region (Camara and Duboscq 1984, 1987, 1990) than originally reported by Ravisé (1975). More than 80 Neolithic sites were recorded in the lower Falémé in the 1990s alone (Thiaw 1999). Known Neolithic sites in the region were generally found along the Senegal River banks, its many tributaries, and along fossil drainages. Even with an abundant archaeological record, archaeologists working in the region have focused most of their attention recently on other research topics.

With respect to other regions of Senegal, the Neolithic of the upper Senegal is described as a unique faciés characterized mainly by its finely polished hematite axes. Little is known about the other components of the assemblages, which include a diverse set of stone tools, cordage, and pottery. The Neolithic faciés of the upper Senegal region is known to differ fundamentally from that of the rest of the country. The Neolithic of Khant near the mouth of the Senegal River, for instance, represents a different tradition in a marine and fluvial environment lacking suitable raw material for lithic manufacture. This assemblage, including axes, fishhooks, harpoons, needles, etc., is almost completely made from bone (Ravisé 1970). Other Neolithic traditions identified in Senegal include the microlithic assemblages on the dunes along the northwestern Atlantic region (Lame 1981) and the Neolithic of Bel Air and Cap Manuel in the Cap Vert Peninsula, characterized by its heavy and crude lithic equipment, which includes picks and adzes (Diagne 1978).

Although the description of these different traditions may be significant, their characterization is too broad. Most faciés have been defined on the basis of the material from one or a few sites and focus generally on one category of artifacts. Most importantly, the chronology and possible interactions among the various faciés is barely understood. Almost 30 years ago, Massamba Lame (1981) hypothesized the likelihood of early trade during the Neolithic between the settlers of Diakité, a site located near Thiés in western Senegal less than 100 km from the Atlantic, and the Neolithic settlers of eastern Senegal. Axes and adzes found in Diakité were made out of amphibole, a raw material occurring only in the surrounding regions of the upper Senegal. Similar questions and many others related to trade and culture interactions, subsistence, early food production, and adaptation to an increasingly fragile environment during the Holocene and later prehistory can only be addressed via more systematic survey and excavations and the development of more-refined chronologies.

The Iron Age and Historical Period

The Iron Age in Senegal spans roughly the last 2,000 years. Archaeological evidence from the upper Senegal region for this time period is extremely limited. This region was largely excluded in the extensive surveys of the 1970s by Martin and Becker (1970, 1974, 1977a) who only mentioned slag piles as testimony of the presence of iron users in the upper Senegal. The only comprehensive investigation of Iron Age/historical-period sites was limited to a 50-km segment of the lower Falémé region, located farther north of the OJVG concession (Thiaw 1999). Even so, archaeologists have accumulated evidence from the broader region on cultural interactions and trade over the past 1,500 years. Around A.D. 700–1000, assemblages from both the western lower Falémé (Thiaw 1999) and the middle Senegal River Valley (McIntosh and Bocoum 2000, 2002; McIntosh et al. 1992) underwent important changes affecting pottery manufacture (new ceramic styles; e.g., collared rims, channelling, etc.), trade patterns (expansion of the trans-Saharan trade, imports of trade goods; e.g., copper and beads), and technology (e.g., *disc à cordeler*, spindlewhorls). Materials from the upper Senegal and lower Falémé regions indicate that both were incorporated into the trans-Saharan trade system by A.D. 1000 (Thiaw 1999).

Evidence from the Falémé region also suggests potential connections with the middle and possibly the upper Niger. Thin-walled vessels from the deep levels of Arondo, dated to A.D. 400, remind us of similar vessels recovered in the early deposits of Jenne-Jeno (McIntosh 1995). Surveys in the Falémé region also revealed carved wooden roulette motifs that show striking similarities with other materials in the upper Senegal and Upper Niger River regions (Thiaw 1999).

Stories of gold exploration and mining in eastern Senegal since medieval times soon attracted European explorers to the region in the early phase of transatlantic exploration (Bathily 1989; Boucard 1974; Charpentier 1984; David 1974; Pruneau 1983; Rançon 1894; Thiaw 1999). The Portuguese were the first Europeans who visited the region and may even have considered blowing up the Félu Falls in the fifteenth century to ease their penetration deep into the hinterlands. From the seventeenth century onward, the French established a number of trading outposts along the Senegal and Falémé Rivers to capture gold from the region (Bathily 1989; Thiaw 1999). A diverse assemblage of European trade goods dating to the eighteenth and nineteenth centuries, which included ceramics, glass beads, bottle glass, various metal artifacts, and gunflints, was collected from the lower Falémé. Historical and archaeological evidence gathered in the upper Senegal region indicates that a number of important events occurred there over the past 500 years. These include the expansion of European trade and the construction of trading outposts, the spread of Islam, the establishment of clerical paramountcies (e.g., Bundu) and trade diasporas (e.g., Jakhanke and Malinkés), and the arrival and settlement of Fulani or Peul pastoralists (Thiaw 1999). These new forces completely or partially altered the political, economic, and social systems of the upper Senegal societies.

It must be pointed out, however, that the culture history of the upper Senegal region is largely unknown and is inferred from oral traditions and a few documentary sources limited largely to the eighteenth and nineteenth centuries. Clearly, only the establishment of a detailed cultural historical sequence and well-dated assemblages will throw light on the processes of change involved in these historical events and the extent to which they affected earlier forms of social, political, and economic organization.

Ethnography of Southeastern Senegal

The upper Senegal region is one of the most economically marginal regions in the Senegambia. The southeastern part of the upper Senegal is also characterized by extremely low population densities (5 inhabitants per square kilometer) that contrast with the densely populated Atlantic coastal region. The upper Senegal region is also home to a number of ethnic and linguistic groups (Bassari, Bedik, Konyagui, Badiaranke, Boin, and Bapen) that each include only a few thousand speakers and that constitute some of the most marginalized and endangered communities in modern Senegal (Diouf 2006). The different communities living in this region of Senegal can be grouped into three major linguistic groups: Mande, Tenda, and Peul. These different groups are spread between Senegal, Guinée Bissau, the Republic of Guinée, Mali, and the Gambia.

The Mande group includes the Mandinka, Jakhanke, Jalonke, Xasonke, and the Soninke. These populations may have been part of successive waves of migrations from the upper and inland Niger Delta region subsequent to the military and trade expansion of the Empire of Mali beginning in the thirteenth century A.D. Mande speakers are generally established along the ancient trading routes linking the Bambuk and Buure gold-producing regions and the Gambia (Martin and Becker 1977b:66). It is likely that the arrival and settlement of Mande speakers has pushed the Tenda speakers to the highlands, where they live today.

The Tenda include small communities of Bassari, Bedik, Konyagui, Badiaranke, Boin, and Bapen. These small-scale communities are agriculturists, but a substantial part of their diet also comes from hunting and gathering. Some of them, such as the Bedik and the Bassari, today occupy the hills west of Kédougou. Although some of these communities have converted either to Islam or Christianity, they still practice their 'traditional' religion, and as such, they are particularly attached to their natural environment and forest groves, which host a number of spirits and vital resources for subsistence (Singleton 1982:79). Among the Bassari for instance, certain *rites de passage*, such as initiation rituals, which mark the passage from childhood to adulthood, are still extremely important in the life of the community. Over the past decades, the Tenda country, in particular the Bassari and Bedik communities, has been largely marketed by independent Senegal as a tourist attraction, which is increasingly becoming an important source of revenue for these communities.

The Peul are part of the Pulaar family. They may have arrived in the region as early as the fourteenth or fifteenth centuries, but it is mainly in the seventeenth century that their presence began to be felt (Diallo 1972:34). At this time, they converted en masse to Islam, establishing

Islamic paramountcies in Bundu, Fuuta Jallon, and the middle Senegal River region, which played an important role in the expansion of Islam in the region. Nomad pastoralism is the Peul's main economic pursuit, but over time, some of them have become sedentary pastoralists and agriculturists. The arrival of the Peul in the upper Senegal has also contributed to the marginalization of earlier Tenda settlers.

Both in the past as well as in the present, the relationships between these different groups are extremely complex. They are characterized by conflict, cooperation, and exchange. Over the past centuries, these different communities have not been completely isolated from another. Instead, they intermingled and continue to intermingle in the present. As a result, the cultural frontiers between them have been reshaped with respect to power relations and the development of new ideologies (Islam or Christianity, for instance). These societies and their dynamic social and political histories are explored in greater depth in Chapter 3.

Today, agriculture and pastoralism are the main subsistence activities in the region, with artisanal gold mining another major economic activity. Agriculture is largely dependent on rainfall. The Sabodala region has no perennial streams, and the floodplains that exist are extremely narrow. Although soils are deepest and best suited for agriculture in constrained alluvial settings, soil development also has occurred on plateau-like areas on the tops of hills. In contrast to floodplain agriculture, slash and burn is the most common technique to clear farmland and replenish nutrients lost to crop uptake and erosion. Slash and burn also stimulates fresh grass, clears out thorny vegetation for cattle and goats, and facilitates hunting wild game.

Although today pastoralism is very important, Thiaw (1999) has argued that it is unlikely that such was the case in the more distant past. The climate in West Africa was sufficiently wet that the tsetse fly would have impeded the development of pastoralism until about 500 years ago. Since then, a change to drier conditions and vegetation clearing allowed pastoral groups to settle in the project area.

Artisanal gold mining has been practiced in the hills of Senegal since at least the rise of Islam in West Africa (Thiaw 1999). For the most part, gold mining was an adjunct to other subsistence activities. The gold trade has historically been controlled by North African traders, who maintained the trade routes through the Sahara, together with local brokers and merchants known as Juula, who were generally Soninke or Malinke people. This practice continues today, with much of the gold being bought by traders based in the adjoining country of Mali. Gold mining is practiced through an intricate social organization in which mining is completed by male task groups that sell the excavated 'dirt' to family-based groups, who in turn sluice and process the gold.

The Sabodala region is occupied currently by a variety of ethnic and linguistic groups. Communities of two linguistic groups—Malinke and Peul—dominate the region and exert the greatest influence on social and political institutions (see Altschul, Thiaw, and Wait 2010; Altschul, Thiaw, Wait, Ciolek-Torello, et al. 2010) (this volume). Malinke and Peul societies are typically stratified and are subdivided into three classes: nobles, 'castes,' and slaves. Slavery is outlawed in Senegal today; yet, because status is ascribed, the term 'slave' is still used to refer to descendants of slaves, and master/slave relations have been largely transformed into relations of clientage (Thiaw 1999).

Lands suitable for agriculture are quite restricted and are controlled by the elites who are predominantly of the Cissokho lineage. The agricultural potential of other lands is poor, although they are plentiful; lands poorly suited to agriculture are left to the lower classes. Land is inherited within the lineage, which means it is collective in theory, but in practice, members of the lower classes and junior members of elite classes do not have access to quality land. The result is high mobility among these people, who are constantly in search of better land.

Each village considers the lands within 8–10 km as 'theirs' with regard to agriculture and claim use rights to lands up to 50 km from the village for herding and hunting. Villages tend to be located adjacent to or near agricultural land and in locations where potable water is near the surface and available year-round. Villages are spaced relatively far apart, separated by vast tracts of land of marginal quality for agriculture. Movement is not greatly restricted, and the sociogeographic history of the region is of social groups continually fragmenting and starting new communities.

Research Questions

The previous section outlined our current understanding of the prehistory and history of the upper Senegal River region. Limited archaeological research has been conducted in the area of the OJVG concession. One of the prime objectives of the archaeological component of the project, therefore, was and is to create a more fully developed sense of the events and influences that shaped the cultural evolution of the region. We identify the research questions we were able to address (**emboldened**), and then suggest others as topics for future research when more or better data becomes available.

Paleolithic

1. What is the sequence of lithic technological evolution? Can we define prehistoric cultures on

the basis of assemblages? What other aspects of material culture can be documented for these early cultures?
2. How were Paleolithic cultures distributed in the region? How similar or different are the cultures of the upper Senegal to nearby regions?
3. What were the environments of the upper Senegal during the Paleolithic? What resources would have been available to early hunter-gatherers? How did these cultures adapt to the environment, and how did this change over time?
4. How were early hunter-gatherer communities organized? Were these people nomadic, or did they have a seasonal round? How large were their territories? How large were the individual groups? How many such groups occupied the upper Senegal region?

Neolithic

1. The Neolithic of the upper Senegal is described as a unique faciés; how unique is it, and what makes it so?
2. **Were the Neolithic groups of the upper Senegal trading with the settlers of Diakité? If so, what did they trade?** How was this trade organized?
3. **How important was agriculture to the Neolithic groups? Were these people primarily farmers who keep goats or herders that farmed?** Were there two communities, one of farmers and one of herders? If so, what was the nature of the interaction between these groups?
4. **How insulated were the groups of the upper Senegal from regional events? Were these communities incorporated into larger political entities? If so, what was the impact on the local community?**
5. How did agriculture and herding affect the local environment? Were these Neolithic adaptations viable and sustainable?
6. **What was the nature of Neolithic social structure, and how were households and communities organized?** Did Neolithic people inhabit permanent villages, or did they continue to follow a seasonal round?

The Iron Age and Historical Periods

1. **When were the communities of the upper Senegal and lower Falémé regions incorporated into the trans-Saharan trade system?** How did this process change local culture?
2. What effect did the advent of gold mining have on local culture? **What was the impact of European exploration and colonialization on the communities of the upper Senegal River?** How important was trade with the Europeans? How did increase in trade change the indigenous economy?
3. How was Islam incorporated into local cultures? What is the connection between the arrival of Islam and the arrival and settlement of Fulani or Peul pastoralists?

To address these research questions, we neede to identify archaeological and historical sites and record them sufficiently so that we can assess if they contain data relevant to these questions. Our methods for achieving this goal are outlined in the next section.

Chapter 3

Village Histories and Ethnography within the Oromin Sabodala Concession

Ethnographic meetings and interviews were conducted with members of 11 villages in the Sabodala region of eastern Senegal from April 28 to May 17, 2009. Ten of the villages are located within the OJVG concession (differentiating between Bransan, which is Malinke, and Madina Bransan, which is the adjacent Peul community), whereas Khossanto is located immediately to the southeast (Figure 3.1). An interim report has already been submitted outlining key information recorded during that first phase of the ethnographic research (Wait et al. 2009). This chapter provides a more thorough analysis of ethnographic data collected. Additional information on the study area was gathered from the Archives Nationales du Sénégal (ANS) and other documentary evidence.

The first section of this chapter describes the objectives and methodology of the ethnographic research. Next, we analyze the history and identity of the principal groups historically associated to the area in light of oral traditions collected and available archival and documentary evidence. In the third section, we explore village settlement history to understand site-location preferences, population mobility, and the land tenure system. In a region where land ownership is generally based on first occupancy rights, information on settlement history is key to understanding land tenure system, populations' movements, distribution and access to critical resources, and shifting power relations in time. The fourth section elucidates the nature of Malinke and Peul societies and how those societies affect social relations in the villages. Understanding the history of the chieftaincy, for instance, illuminates the complex socio-political structure of the polity of Beledougou and its surrounding areas. As history is negotiated in the present, these considerations may have profound implications in the present. The fifth section focuses on tangible and intangible aspects of ethnographic cultural heritage section, including the documentation of sacred sites, belief systems and cultural festivals. The sixth section relates villagers concerns about the prospect of the OJVG mine development. The chapter concludes with an overall assessment of social dynamics collected as part of the ethnographic and archival work.

Objectives and Methodology

The goal of the ethnographic research was to collect information relevant to the cultural heritage of the area. More specifically ethnographic fieldwork was designed to gather information on the history and culture of the different villages in the OJVG concession. We sought to determine the identity of the inhabitants, their traditional ways of life, their belief systems and the sites, monuments, material cultures and stories associated with them. Villagers were asked questions about their subsistence activities and their natural environment, artisanal crafts, and what they valued most in their cultural heritage and identity and what they would like to preserve. They were also asked questions about their village's future and how they thought their traditional way of life would be impacted by the expansion of industrial mining within the region (Table 3.1).

The initial meeting in each village was arranged by SRK village liaison Mabo Sidebe or another SRK agent. These meetings followed the social convention of meeting first with the village's chief, who then would arrange for an interview with the villagers. We have no idea how the individuals were selected for these meetings, but they were predominantly Malinke and/or Peul adult males. It is likely that most were relatives, clients, or in the same political faction as the chief. Although different age grades were present, one or a few individuals, generally the chief and a few elders, controlled the speech in these group interviews. Sometimes women were present, but they would only timidly participate in the meeting.

Information collected at these meetings was limited, primarily by the nature of the settings which inhibited some from speaking openly in public. Yet, the information gathered was critical for gauging the social, cultural and political landscape within each village. These meetings were the basis for identifying key informants for further interviews, which occurred in private or semi-private settings. This approach was extremely productive; we were able to follow up on contradictions in narratives both within and between the villages as well as on questions we thought had been insufficiently addressed. In addition to chiefs, griots (professional story-tellers, historians, negotiators), blacksmiths, and healers providing useful information, women yielded critical knowledge in private that they would not have been able to disclose in public. As fieldwork progressed, we started to make connections between the different narratives. The disparity in the number of visits to the various villages (see Table 3.2 for a schedule of activities) in part reflects incomplete narratives obtained in some village requiring multiple visits to complete the stories.

Most interviews were conducted in either Malinke or Peul, which required Drs. Wait and Thiaw to rely on translators provided by SRK. One translator interjected

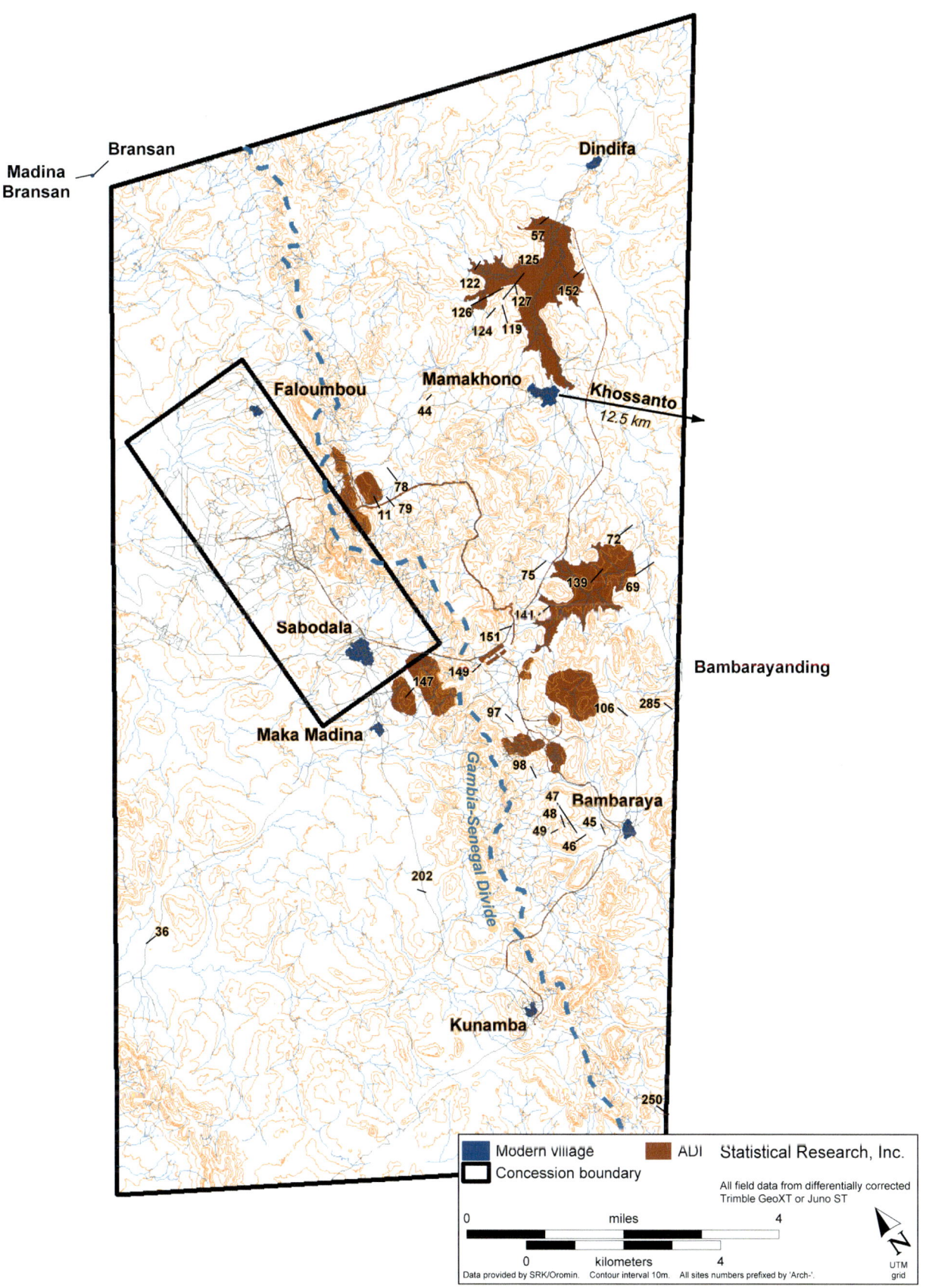

FIGURE 3.1. MAP OF VILLAGES IN OJVG CONCESSION.

TABLE 3.1. QUESTIONNAIRE

Ethnographic Questions: IFAN / SRI-Nexus
1. **Village and date**
2. **Name of chief/key informants**
3. **Self determination and self identification**
    - 3.1. Could you briefly tell us who you are and how your story or your family story have marked your village and community?
    - 3.2. What have you or others have achieved for your village and community that you are the most proud of?
4. **What you value most**
    - 4.1. Can you tell us about:
        - Your village culture
        - your village history
        - your sacred places – cemeteries, other sacred places (and stories about them)
        - historical places (places of the ancestors)
        - environment (animals, plants, and traditional use areas)
        - traditional ways of life (agriculture, herding, mining, etc.)
    - 4.2. What different types of traditional religious/ritual/social sites do you have? Can you show them to us?
    - 4.3. How important is it that you keep your traditional way of life? Will the mine change that? What will be changed for the better? What for the worse?
    - 4.4. What do you want to preserve about your culture? Environment? History? Way of life?
    - 4.5. Where did your village come from / where was the village located before its present location?
    - 4.6. How long has the village been here?
    - 4.7. Is this a 'good' place? Why, or why not?
    - 4.8. What do you value most about yourself as a person – your qualities, strengths and experiences?
    - 4.9. What do you value most about the nature of your identity? What makes your cultural heritage rich?
5. **Envisioning the future**
    - 5.1. If you were ask to imagine the future for your village or community, what would you want the future to be like for your descendents?
    - 5.2. What is the best way to create and maintain a unified identity in your area?
6. **Artisan and craftsmen**
    - 6.1. Who practices? Can we talk to them?
    - 6.2. Pottery making
    - 6.3. Wood-carving
    - 6.4. Blacksmithing
    - 6.5. Weaving
    - 6.6. Leatherworking

---

his own beliefs, which affected the narratives being collected. Fortunately we quickly noticed the problem and requested another translator from the SRK office. Finally, some interviewees spoke French or Wolof, which allowed direct communication with Dr. Thiaw.

In most villages, the interviews were conducted in a relaxed atmosphere in the courtyard of the chiefs' household. In Sabodala, however, there was reluctance to respond to our questions. Even before we began, the chief of this village launched into a diatribe against MDL, the mining company whose current operations have the greatest effect on the village. Although similar complaints were reiterated in most villages, their tone and intensity were unique in Sabodala.

Culture History and Affiliation in the OJVG Concession

The OJVG concession encompasses the historical province of Beledougou, a small-scale Malinke and Peul polity. In the nineteenth and early twentieth centuries, it was bounded by the more centralized polity of Boundou in the north. In the east, southeast and southwest, Beledougou was bounded respectively by the small-scale polities of Sirimana, Dentilia, Badon, and Niocolo (Figure 3.2).

Over the past two centuries, the political boundaries of these small-scale Malinke and Peul polities in the upper Senegal were extremely elastic. In the nineteenth century, they were often exposed to the domination of the more centralized polities of Boundou in the north and Fouta Djallon (modern Guinée) in the south. Both Boundou and Fouta Djallon were theocracies founded by Peul speakers in the eighteenth century, becoming a dominating force in regional politics by the nineteenth century (Barry 1988; Gomez 1992).

Following the expansion of French colonial rule in the region in the late nineteenth and early twentieth centuries, Beledougou and the other small-scale Malinke and Peul polities became incorporated in the Cercle de Kayes, an administrative subdivision which depended on the French Soudan (modern Mali). Later they became integrated in the administration of Senegal depending on the Cercle of *Bakel* and by 1907, on Kédougou, to put a stop to the exactions of both Boundou and Fouta Djallon's chiefs. The chiefs regularly pillaged the villages for the extractions of tax under the umbrella of colonial administration, causing large-scale population movements that largely reshuffled and redistributed geographically the ethnic groups in the area (cf. ANS, Dakar, Sénégal, Etude générale, missions diverses, incursions des gens du Fouta-Djallon [1869–1917], Série D (Affaires politiques et administratives de la colonie du Sénégal), Sous-séries -10D1/006; ANS, Expédition du Niokolo contre les gens du Fouta Djallon [1894], affaire de Lamina [1894–1895], Série D, Sous-séries -10 D1/0010; ANS, Cercle de Kédougou: Rapports trimestriels d'ensemble [2e, 3e, 4e], Sous-séries 2G (Rapports périodiques, mensuels, trimestriels, semestriels et annuels des gouverneurs, administrateurs et chefs de services), -2G 24/51ANS; ANS, Sénégal- Cercles de Kédougou-Rapports mensuels d'ensemble de janvier à décembre), Sous-séries 2G, -2G11/38).

The history and identity of the populations living today in the OJVG concession is largely intertwined with events and processes of the major polities that dominated this region over the past millennium. Oral histories collected during our fieldwork fit largely the broad narratives developed by other scholars working in the region (Bathily 1989; Gomez 1992; Thiaw 1999). The internal coherence of the oral traditions collected coalesces around a three-phase cultural chronology of the study area: a Bassari period, followed by a Soninke period dominated by Soumare lineages, ending with a Malinke period dominated by the Cissokho lineages. A fourth phase marked by the political domination of Boundou and Fouta Djallon and the arrival and settlement of Peul speakers in the region may be recognized; however, we collected little information about these cultural processes. It is only at the third phase, characterized by the arrival and dominance of Malinke Cissokho lineages, that we can identify a consistent structure, coherence, and logic in the narratives.

TABLE 3.2. SCHEDULE OF ACTIVITIES

	Calendar of Meetings/Interviews
25 26/04	Arrive Dakar, work with Jenny Wong + William Hawthorne.
27/04	Meetings IFAN; GW + IT.
28/04	Dakar -> Sabodala.
29/04	Bransan, CH group.
30/04	Workshop for complete social team in Camp.
01/05	CH group—jeep trip ARCH sites.
02/05	Kunamba—entire social team led by Tropica + HVV.
03/05	Mamakhono entire social team led by Tropica + HVV CH see Blacksmith—private interview.
04/05	Bambaraya—entire social team led by Tropica + HVV. Later CH see griot and traditional healers × 2.
05/05	Madina Bransan; CH group.
06/05	Day typing notes in Camp.
07/07	Dindifa—CH group interview. Maka Madina—CH group interview.
08/05	Bambaraya—see Chief—SACR and ARCH sites. Bambarayanding—CH group.
09/05	Khossanto—CH Group. Bransan—SACR and ARCH sites. Blacksmith and Potter.
10/05	Maka Madina—CH single informant.
11/05	Camp—type-up notes.
12/05	Faloumbou—CH Group.
13/05	Kunamba—CH Group (2nd). Bambaraya—interview griot.
14/05	Mamakhono—SACR + ARCH sites with Chief + informant. Sabodala—CH Group (1st).
15/05	Bambaraya Chief—Interview and SACR + ARCH sites.
16/06	Khossanto—Interview griot. Sabodala (2nd).
17/05	Type notes and return to Dakar.

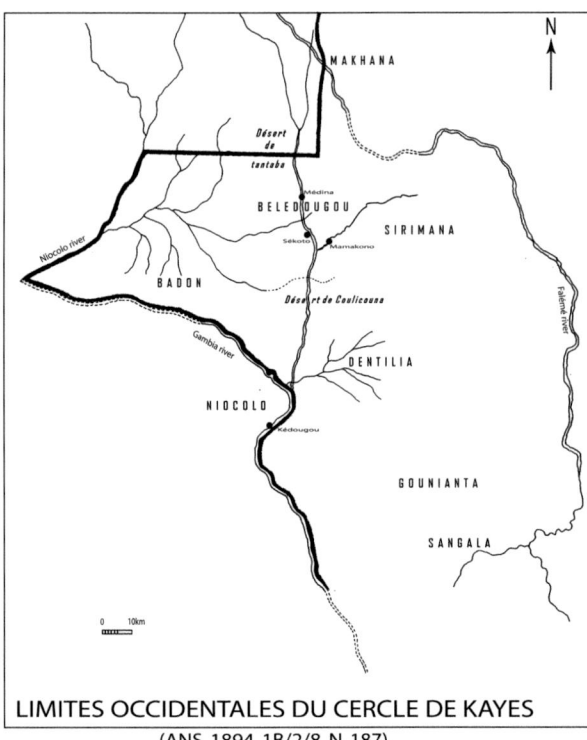

FIGURE 3.2. MAP SHOWING POLITIES AROUND THE OJVG CONCESSION.

Phase 1: The Time of the Bassari

The first phase is characterized by initial settlement of Bassari speakers and possibly other populations of Tenda minorities, which, in addition to the Bassari, included the Bedik, Konyagui, Badiaranke, Boin, and Bapen. No speaker of any of these minorities was interviewed. We were told that one or two Bassari families were present in Sabodala, but these were likely recent migrants who came into the area as a result of the new opportunities brought in by the recent development of industrial gold mining. Today most of these minorities live further south in and around Kédougou. Although local informants referred to some of the abandoned sites we located in the area as Bassari settlements, the chronology and extent of their presence is poorly documented and will not be further discussed.[1]

Phase 2: The Soumare Soninke Period

The second phase of settlement is marked by the arrival of Mande groups, which most likely included Malinke, Jakhanké, Jalonké, Xasonké, and Soninke. Of these subgroups, only Malinke speakers were encountered and interviewed. However, some Malinke speakers with the patronym Soumare were present in a number of villages and were sometimes referred to as descendants of Soninke speakers. The oral traditions recorded in many Malinke villages within the OJVG concession hold that Soumare Soninke families settled in the area prior to the arrival of other Mande subgroups including the Malinke.[2] Similar narratives are well known elsewhere in the upper Senegal River Valley. Soumare Soninke lineages allegedly colonized most of the upper Senegal region in the early first millennium A.D. (Bathily 1989; Thiaw 1999). They progressively moved south, competing with the Siima Soninke families for control of Gajaaga that extended at that time to most of the upper drainage of the Senegal River and Falémé Rivers.

Malinke speakers arrived after the military and trade expansion of the Empire of Mali in the thirteenth century A.D. (Niane 1989). Of the 10 villages included in the study, only Mamakhono, whose members claim that the village has been occupied for 670 years, could date to the Soumare Soninke period.[3] Regional settlement history recorded by other scholars, however, indicates that Malinke speakers generally established villages along the ancient gold-trading and -producing regions of Bambuck and Buure, which are located further east along the Senegal and Falémé River drainages and in the Gambia (Martin and Becker 1977b:66).

Phase 3: The Cissokho Lineage Period

Narratives collected in Mamakhono, Khossanto, and Bambaraya suggest a third phase in regional settlement, characterized by the arrival of Malinke Cissokho lineages. According to oral traditions collected in all 10 villages, Cissokho lineages came from the District or Province of Tomara in modern Mali. They arrived in Beledougou via Marougou on the border of the Falémé River where they may have lived for some time.[4]

Today the majority of village chiefs in the OJVG concession claim descent from Cissokho lineages. They arrived in the region as warriors and were specifically assigned to liberate the province of Beledougou from the despotic domination a slave 'king' or chief named Tobri Sidebe, who allegedly harassed the Soumare landlords and other Malinke populations in the region. The processes through which a slave became king are not too clear. What we do know is that the eighteenth and nineteenth centuries were characterized by the expansion of slavery and the rise of what is known in the Senegambia as *ceddo* regimes. To maintain power, these regimes employed slave armies specialized in war and pillage. In many cases, these slave armies became so powerful that they wrested political control and establish their own dynasties (Barry 1988; Bathily 1989; Roberts 1987; Thiaw 1999).

---

[1] Interview with Dembo Cissokho, chief of Bambaraya.

[2] Group interview in Bransan; group interview in Sabodala.
[3] Group interview in Mamakhono.
[4] Group interview in Mamakhono, Khassanto; interview with Boubou Kanouté in Bambaraya.

Historically, most of the Soninke and Malinke polities in the upper Senegal region were prosperous because of their involvement and experience in trade. In the eighteenth and nineteenth centuries, these merchant communities relied on mercenaries and slave armies that existed throughout the western Sudan to defend their interests (Bathily 1989; Manchuelle 1997; Roberts 1987; Thiaw 1999). They also were heavily invested in slavery; merchants acquired slaves to produce marketable agricultural surpluses (Manchuelle 1997). Senegalese historian Abdoulaye Bathily (1989) pointed out that these polities were political dwarfs, but economic giants.

The context of the narrative situates Tobri Sidebe between the eighteenth and nineteenth centuries, a time that coincides with the birth and growth of two major polities, Boundou and Fouta Djallon. Both polities were founded by Halpulaar or Peul Muslim clerics. It is likely that the ancestors of most Peul speakers in Beledougou, and our study area in particular, arrived in the region at this time.

According the narratives collected throughout the OJVG concession, at some point in the distant past, Beledougou fell under the control of a Peul-speaking slave known as Tobri Sidebe. Historians infer that Peul speakers arrived in the region initially around the fourteenth and fifteenth centuries, but it is not until the eighteenth or nineteenth centuries that their presence became significant (Barry 1988). One widely told story is Tobri gained control over water sources, most particularly a well on which the entire countryside depended. He demanded that the inhabitants pay him gold before being allowed to fetch water from that well.[5] Although the processes through which this slave became so powerful are not clearly understood, the internal structure of this narrative suggest that water and gold were critical resources in the area and, as such, were strictly controlled by those who retained power.

In response to Tobri's exactions, the Soumare appealed to the Cissokho chief of Tomara, Sanga Moussa or Sora Moussa, for help. This leader sent two of his sons Dan Moussa and Dan Sirima to oust Tobri from power. Tradition has it that Dan Moussa was responsible for evicting Tobri, eventually killing him. However, some interviewees indicated that this would not have been possible without the help of his sister Dan Manian. She allegedly seduced Tobri, who married her despite the warnings of his entourage. Dan Manian refused to consummate her marriage unless Tobri revealed to her the secrets of his powers.[6]

This part of the intrigue recalls another popular Malinke story concerning the marriage of the powerful king of Sosso, Soumangourou Kanté, in the thirteenth century to the sister of Sounjata Diata Keita (Niane 1960). Whether the story of the marriage of Tobri and Dan Manian is an anachronism, parts of the narrative apparently have been censured, because aspects are considered taboo. In any case, the traditional account maintains that one night was sufficient for Dan Manian to learn the secret of Tobri's invincibility and help her brothers, but no child was born from their marriage.[7]

Subsequently, Tobri was decapitated and according to the traditions, Dan Moussa Cissokho and his descendents have held the chieftaincy in Beledougou ever since. His brother Dan Sirima and his descendents controlled the chieftaincy in the Sirimana. As for the descendents of Tobri Sidebe, they were banned from the chieftaincy and from intermarrying with members of the Cissokho lineage. They were allowed to live, however, in some of the villages of Beledougou where they had their own neighborhoods. According to Boubou Kanouté, although Tobri's descendents are historically ethnic Peul, they now speak Malinke, as they were absorbed into Malinke culture and society.

Three important conclusions can be drawn from the story of the Peul Tobri Sidebe and his encounter with the Cissokho lineage of Malinke origin. First, some of the Peul speakers in the area are probably descendents of Tobri; their ancestors most likely arrived in the region before members of the Cissokho lineage. Second, Tobri's mystical powers are apparently non-Islamic, and reference to Peul speakers does not seem to be linked to founders of the eighteenth- and nineteenth-century theocracies of Boundou or Fouta Djallon (Barry 1988; Boulègue 1987). Third, traditions collected suggest that the Soumare who were Soninke were already present in the region before the Peul and the Malinke.

One tradition recorded by Marakary Danfakha (1992) holds that upon their victory over Tobri, the Cissokho received from the Soumare the equivalent of the weight of Tobri's skull in gold in exchange for their services. The Cissokho, however, refused to return to their homeland and instead maintained their control over the chieftaincy of Beledougou at the expense of the Soumare. Another version of the narrative holds that 'the Cissokho who rule Beledougou are of the same lineage as Fakoli and are the masters of the Kanté who are griots.'[8] In the epic of Soundjata, Fakoli was a nephew of the powerful blacksmith king of Sosso, Soumangourou Kanté, suggestive of a blacksmith origin for the Cissokho lineage. This inference is consistent with yet another version of the story that states 'the mother of all Cissokho was a blacksmith woman of Mande origin whose name was Kankouba Kanté.'[9] Our informant vigorously objected, however, to the conclusion that the

---

[5] Group interview in Mamakhono; interview with Boubou Kanouté in Bambaraya.
[6] Interview with Boubou Kanouté in Bambaraya.
[7] Interview with Boubou Kanouté in Bambaraya.
[8] Anonymous informant in Bambaraya.
[9] Anonymous informant in Bransan.

ruling Cissokho lineage in Beledougou had a blacksmith origin.

According to one informant (who wished to remain anonymous), 'the Cissokho sacrificed a griot to be able to capture Tobri.'[10] This event allegedly took place in Mamakhono, which was the first inhabited village in the Beledougou. Interestingly, the tradition holds that to this day no griot is allowed to build and live in Mamakhono,[11] a point that we will return to in our analysis of the sociopolitical structure (see below). The control and exercise of power in Mamakhono was apparently a source of profound tensions and jealousy. The ruling Cissokho lineage eventually split into competing families, but they still managed to exclude the Sidibe, who were descendents of Tobri, and the Soumare, who initially enjoyed first settlers' rights.

Since the time of Soundjata and the defeat of Soumangourou in the thirteenth century, no blacksmith or griot (both carry social status implications tat go beyond mere craft skills)has been allowed to rule or be chief in the entire country of the Mande and its dependences (Niane 1960). The Kouroukanfougan charter established by Sundjata defined the specific social and political role assigned to each of the different social categories and identities within the Mande country. It was designed to regulate intergroup relationships within the Mande and its dependencies. In that charter, both griots and blacksmiths were banned from holding political office but could be advisers and clients to the ruling class. The possibility of a blacksmith origin of the Cissokho lineage, therefore, poses problems of historical legitimacy. Similar cases of concealed or identity change have been reported elsewhere in West Africa (Launay 1995).

Several conclusions can be drawn from this analysis of culture history and affiliation that must be fully understood to appreciate the complex modern social relationships that exist in the villages of the Sabodala region. First, the displacement and marginalization of Bassari and other minorities who were the first settlers in the study area by Malinke and Peul speakers has been codified in their placement near the bottom of the social order. Second, the confiscation of political power by the Cissokho ruling lineage from the Soumare still resonates with members of both groups. Third, although the identity and fate of Tobri Sidebe's descendents is unknown, all Peul speakers are treated as though they are responsible for Tobri's excesses. Peul speakers have been excluded from political office since the establishment of the Cissokho ruling lineage in the area, and their status remains relatively low. Fourth, the historical and social legitimacy of the Cissokho ruling lineage remains intact with chiefs of all villages save Bombarayading affiliated with this lineage. Cissokho connections to slavery and/or blacksmithing remain an important component of their social and political power. Fifth, the status and identity of slave descendents and members of endogamous craft specialists including griots and blacksmiths are very ambiguous and entangled with major social and political dramas whose consequences need to be fully appreciated to understand their social roles today.

Village Histories and Settlement Dynamics

Most villages in the OJVG concession have a very shallow history. With the exception of Mamakhono and to a lesser extent Khassanto, local memories on the settlement history in most of the villages rarely extend beyond 100 years. A number of villages within the concession descended from Mamakhono. According to many of the traditions collected, Mamakhono was the first village settled in the Beledougou sometime in the thirteenth century. It was founded by the Soumare, who were Soninke from Marena or Mareka now located in modern Mali. According to various informants, Mamakhono was established by people from a village, now abandoned, located near Masato between Sekhoto and Sabodala. Interestingly, one of the largest complexes of archaeological sites in the area was found near Massato (Arch 08–09). Local laborers on the archaeological field crew claimed that Arch 08 was the home village of Tobri Sidebe, the Peul slave king. In any case the villages of Mamakhono, Medina, and Sekhoto (Arch 44?) are plotted in their current locations on a late-nineteenth-century map (ANS, 1894, 1D, 2/8, N° 187). None of the other currently inhabited villages in the concession are on this map or mentioned in the map notes. Another map printed in 1926 by the Service Géographique du Ministère des Colonies shows Mamakhono, Nion Madina, Ouassa, Maka Madina, and Makhana. Villages like Sabodala and Bambaraya appear in the Afrique Occidentale map of the Dalafi region in 1933. In 1957, Bransan, Faloumbou, Dindifa are plotted on the Carte de l'Afrique de l'Ouest (Dalafi region). Basing the history of village settlement on these maps, however, is problematic. We cannot be sure why some villages are plotted and others are not: Was it because the villages did not exist? Or, was it because the map makers did not know of them or chose not to include them? The fact that oral traditions are consistent in the main with these maps, however, strongly supports the inference that most villages in the Concession were founded in the late nineteenth and into the twentieth centuries (Table 3.3).

This conception of the villagers of the history of their villages can also be shown graphically as in Figure 3.3. Extracts of the principal twentieth-century maps are presented in Figures 3.4–3.7.

In Khossanto, villagers relate that their settlement was founded in the 1800s by Ansoumana Cissokho and one

---
[10] Anonymous informant in Bambaraya.
[11] Group interviews in Mamakhono and in most villages within the Oromin Concession.

of his brothers. They chose to settle there because the site appeared to be very suited for farming (particularly for rice) and hunting.[12]

Bambaraya was founded by one of Dan Moussa's sons, Jankounda Moussa.[13] It is shown on an early-twentieth-century map, which suggests that the village was established in the late nineteenth or early twentieth century. Oral tradition claims that Bambaraya was founded in 1882 by one of Dan Moussa's sons. If correct, then the foundation of Mamakhono could not possibly predate the eighteenth century.

Not all villages in the concession claim to be established by people from Mamakhono. Bransan, which was founded between 1929 and 1931 (informants very in their dating), was founded by people from Nion Madina, a site located just a few hundred meters to the south. Nion Madina was founded by a Malinke named Kharifa Cissokho.[14] Peul speakers came later, creating their own neighborhood known as Madina Bransan. The founder of Madina Bransan is Idy Diallo, and one of his children is still alive. Idy Diallo came from Makhana, which he decided to leave because of a severe drought. Bransan was a good place for farming, pastoralism, and hunting and was located near a ravine where water was plentiful.[15]

It was also by people from Nion Madina, that the village of Maka Madina was initially settled. Its founder was a Peul, Arfa Ibrahima Diallo (although other informants identified the founder as a Malinke: Karfa Cissoko). One of his sons is still alive and claims he was 15 years old when his father died. Arfa Ibrahima Diallo was later joined at this site by a Malinke named Tamba Cissokho, who came from Wassa, where a number of recently abandoned archaeological sites were located (i.e., Arch 38 and Arch 39). Tamba Cissokho was a warrior who 'brought war and devastation into the area.'[16] He has no descendant in the village because his family later migrated to Boundou. Maka Madina was renowned for its large production of maize. Nion Madina was abandoned because of an epidemic known in Pulaar as 'Nianfion' (probably tuberculosis).[17] Our informant said that this disease spread 1 year after the site was settled.

Faloumbou was peopled from Wassa via Dar Salam, located between Maka Madina and Wassa. Wassa is now abandoned but still seasonally visited by nomadic agriculturists and pastoralists. Diamadi Keita founded Faloumbou in 1945. His firstborn child in Faloumbou was Kourou Keita, who is now 60 years old. According to our informants, Wassa was a good site for agriculture, but 'the settlement was ravaged by an epidemic caused by a devil and in which Diamadi Keita lost three of his children.'[18] As a consequence of that epidemic, he decided to relocate in Faloumbou, where he was later joined by Peul families from Makhana. One informant pointed out that 'Peuls always follow when things are nice and well.'[19] The first Peul who came to settle in Faloumbou was Moussa Ding. At that time, 'Faloumbou was reputed as the number one millet (white millet or sorghum) producer in the whole region and that people came from all over the country to purchase grains.'[20]

Sabodala was initially peopled from Niakaféri, an abandoned settlement located just a few hundred meters away. Sabodala was founded by Fali Cissoko, Moussa Soumare, and Fili Cissokho. Although villagers claimed that settlement is 266 years old, the youngest son of Moussa Soumare (one of the founders) is still alive and is 67 years old. Therefore, it is likely that Sabodala is at best a late-nineteenth- or early-twentieth-century settlement. Before Niakaféri, the ancestors of the present occupants of Sabodala claim to have come from Sekhoto, an abandoned settlement (Arch 44?) near Mamakhono. One informant from Mamakhono indicated that Sekhoto was abandoned in 1949.[21]

Our informants pointed out that it was the spirits that instructed founders of Sabodala to migrate south where they would discover a site that would be known to the whole world. 'At that time, there was no Muslim in country.'[22] Our informants in Sabodala said that founders visited the site and placed several fetishes there to protect the lands. Originally, the most important economic activities were farming, pastoralism, and hunting. Hunting was later forbidden by the State (Senegalese government), and the inhabitants progressively converted to artisanal mining. They said that in drought years, artisanal mining allowed villagers to survive until the next season.

Although we do not have an exact date for the foundation of Dindifa, we were told that one of the daughters of the founder was still alive. This village was founded by Makekouta Cissokho, who was originally from Mamakhono. Makekouta, who was a farmer and a pastoralist, decided to resettle in Dindifa because he needed more fertile lands. Dindifa means a 'where one can feed a child.'[23]

Bambarayading was founded in 1974 by Mamadou Tigana and Souleymane Danfakha who were initially from Bambaraya.[24] This is the only village in the concession

---

[12] Group interview in Khassanto.
[13] Interview with Boubou Kanouté in Bambaraya.
[14] Group interview in Bransan.
[15] Group interview in Madina Bransan.
[16] Group interview in Maka Madina.
[17] Interview with Mamadou Aliou Diallo in Maka Madina.
[18] Group interview in Faloumbou.
[19] Group interview in Faloumbou.
[20] Group interview in Faloumbou.
[21] Interview with Saibo Daniokho in Mamakhono.
[22] Group interview in Sabodala.
[23] Group interview in Dindifa.
[24] Group interview in Bambarayading.

Table 3.3. Village Settlement History

Village	Founding, Inhabitants, and Important Historical Events
Bambaraya	**Foundation**: The village was founded in 1882. Bambaraya means millet in Malinké. The village is a place where they came to grow millet. The first inhabitants were Malinke who came from Mamakhono in search of fertile land. **Important historical events remembered:**<ul><li>1980: Measles epidemic caused lots of deaths.</li><li>1984 and 1993: Fire out breaks, which burned down parts of the village.</li><li>Many people have joined the village in search of gold.</li></ul>
Bambarayanding	**Foundation**: The village was founded in 1974. People settled because of the fertile soil. It used to be an agricultural area belonging to Mamakhono. The name means little Bambaraya, because it is close to Bambaraya. The first inhabitants came from Casamance and became Malinkés. **Important historical events remembered:**<ul><li>1964: Water shortage.</li><li>1982: Epidemic of disease, which particularly affected men.</li><li>1984: Epidemic of *Ver de Guinée* (dracunculoses).</li><li>2004: Drought, discovery of large gold deposit (sudden increase in local standard of living).</li><li>2007–2008: Epidemic amongst the livestock.</li></ul>
Bransan	**Foundation**: The village was founded between 1929 and 1931. It was moved as a result of a need for more fertile soil from a site 2 km south of current position. The name is the vernacular name of the tree *Accacia albida*, which was regarded as an important tree by the founder of the village. **Important historical events remembered:**<ul><li>1978: Distribution of food aid under president Senghor.</li><li>1981–1982: Distribution of food aid under president Abdou Diouf.</li><li>1989: Drought, epidemic of *Ver de Guinée* (dracunculoses).</li><li>2001: Distribution of food aid under president Wade.</li><li>2005: Cricket plague.</li></ul>
Dindifa	**Foundation**: The village was founded more than 120 years ago by Malinkés in search of fertile soil, who came from Mamakhono. Dindifa means 'where one can feed a child.' **Important historical events remembered:**<ul><li>1934: Disease outbreak affecting mainly women and children.</li><li>1974: Drought.</li><li>1975: Disease outbreak (measles?).</li><li>1999: Lack of water.</li><li>2004: Drying out of local swamp/ fire burns down 2 concessions.</li><li>2005: Borehole.</li><li>2006: Fire burning harvests.</li><li>2009: Lions attack cattle—22 died.</li></ul>
Faloumbou	**Foundation**: The village was founded in 1945. The chief of the original village had lost 3 of his children and decided to change the site of the village to avoid further deaths. The first inhabitants were Malinkés. **Important historical events remembered:**<ul><li>1797: Drought which caused several families and their herds to move away.</li><li>1985: Measles epidemic.</li><li>2000: Fire which burns down 3 houses.</li><li>2003: Discovery of gold at Faloumbou.</li><li>2005: Arrival of MDL—increase in material wealth in the village.</li><li>2006: Installation of a borehole (women).</li><li>2007: Start of a womens' organization (women).</li></ul>
Khossanto	**Foundation**: The village was founded in the mid-1800s by Ansoumana Cissokho. Before Mama Kono, the ancestors of village founders were Tomara in Mali. On their way from Tomara, two brothers Dan Manian (younger bother) and Dan Sirima (older brother) settled for while in Marougou on the border of the Falémé River. It is the former that would later found the province of Bélédougou, and the later the Sirimana. **Important historical events remembered:**<ul><li>1944: Guimbo Cissokho, first son of village founder, Ansoumana Cissokho passed and was replaced by Sira Boula Cissokho, who was the last 'Chef de Canton' in Khossanto but passed in 1970.</li><li>1957: Two people were asphyxiated in mine.</li><li>1960: Measles epidemic.</li><li>1971: Famine.</li><li>1966 & 2000: Fire decimated over 100 houses in village.</li><li>1984: Earthquake in Guinée was felt in village.</li></ul>

Village	Founding, Inhabitants, and Important Historical Events
Kunamba	**Foundation**: The village, which is also called Makhana (meaning maize) was founded in 1961. Peul people moved from the original Makhana (in a different location) to the current position because the previous location was mountainous, and isolation hampered the marketing of their agricultural produce. Subsequently, villagers from Mamakhono, Bambaraya, and Sabodala joined them. In-migration stopped in 1983. **Important historical events remembered:** • 1981–1984: Period of drought. • 1981–1982: Epidemic of *Ver de Guinée* (dracunculoses).
Madina Bransan	**Foundation**: the village was created in 1929 by people who moved from Makhana in search of water. The first inhabitant was Idy Diallo (Peul) who came from Makhana. **Important historical events remembered:** • 1949: severe drought. • 1979: Drought and epidemic of *Ver de Guinée* (dracunculoses). • 1975: A lion attacked the cattle. • 1984: A very good harvest.
Maka Madina	**Foundation**: The village was founded more then 100 years ago by Karfa Cissoko and others in search of fertile land. Maka Madina means a good maize harvest. The first inhabitants were Malinkés, who were later joined by Peul from Guinea. **Important historical events remembered:** • 1988: Drought and famine in the village. • 1984/85: Discovery of gold at Goulouma and Khobokhokoly—purchase of bicycles, marriages. • 2003: Five people died on gold excavation site.
Mamakhono	**Foundation**: The village was founded around 1340 on a site which had fertile soil, gold and water. The village was founded by two hunters, respectively from Guinee and Mali who met on a hunting trip. Mamakhono is a deformation of the word Makono, which means wait here for me. The first inhabitants were the Soumare from Mali. **Important historical events remembered:** • 1935 and 1975: Food shortage. • 1964: Meningitis epidemic.
Sabodala	**Foundation**: The village was founded more than 100 years ago. The first inhabitants were Malinkés from Sekhoto in search of fertile soil. The Sabodala has a sacred significance that may not be divulged. **Important historical events remembered:** • 1984: Cricket plague and meningitis epidemic. • 1998: Cricket plague. • 2003: Death of several miners in pit. • 2005: Man killed by lightning.

in which the chief is not a member of the Cissokho lineage. Kunamba was founded around 1961 by a nomad Peul named Thierno Doura. Born in Makhana, which is currently abandoned, Doura left Kunamba soon after he arrived for Mako. Kunamba remained unoccupied until around 1981, when a Malinke named Momo Cissokho from Bambaraya re-established the village. He came to Kunamba because it had fertile lands that were suited for agriculture. The current chief of Kunamba came to the site in 1983, two years after Momo Cissokho. He was also originally from Bambaraya, which he decided to leave because his lands were old and infertile.

Although the exact settlement history of the OJVG concession cannot be ascertained, oral narratives allow us to draw a number of inferences.

1. The earliest established sites in the concession were Sekhoto, Nion Madina, Wassa, and Mamakhono. Of these, only Mamakhono is still inhabited. People from Mamakhono probably established some of the currently inhabited villages in the concession, including Bambaraya and Dindifa.

2. Populations are extremely mobile, although the reasons for movement are quite variable. Among our informants, the most common reasons for moving are land shortage, disease, drought, lack of access to water sources, inadequate pasture for cattle, and poor hunting. Although land is plentiful and access to it is free, land suitable for agriculture is quite restricted, and access to it is controlled by powerful families. Within these families elder members monopolize control of good agricultural land at the expense of junior members. Disenfranchised families and junior members of ruling families are constantly in search of better land. Because population density is extremely low, the area has a frontier 'feel' with open opportunities. An analysis of settlement dynamics indicates that movement, although frequent, is generally of short distance. This

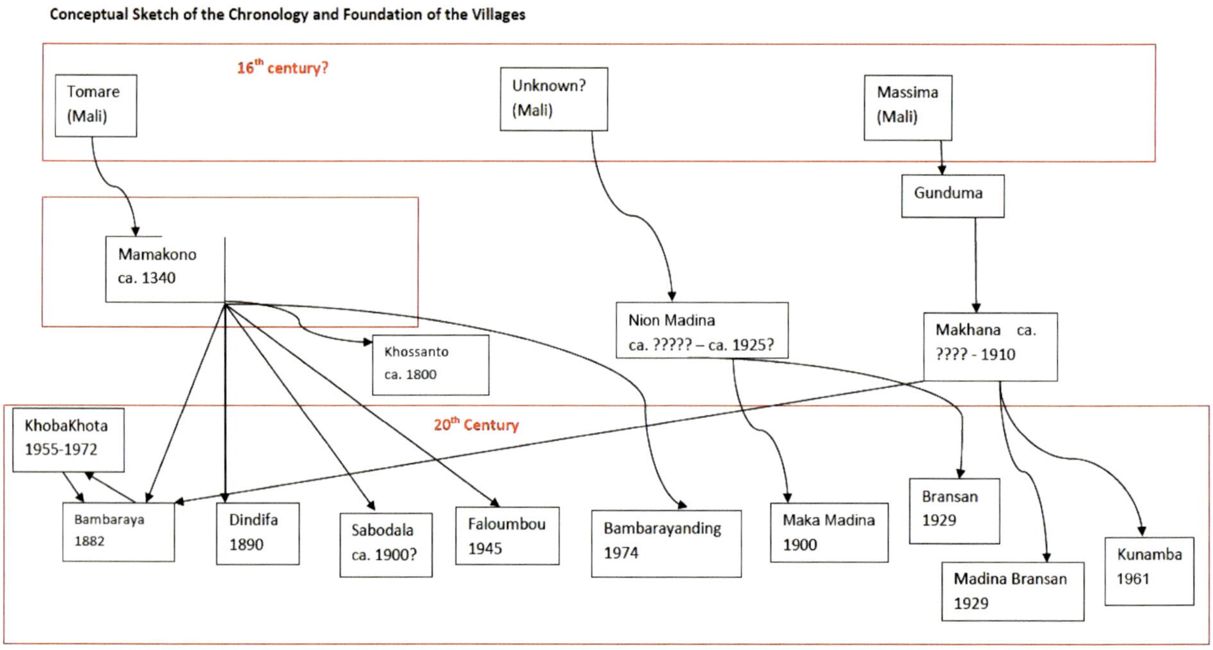

Conceptual Sketch of the Chronology and Foundation of the Villages

FIGURE 3.3. SCHEMATIC TIME LINE FOR THE VILLAGES IN THE OJVG CONCESSION.

pattern recalls what Kopytoff (1987) referred to as 'the internal African frontier,' where migration is a function of micro-sociopolitical processes, such as family disputes, nightmares, witchcraft accusations, etc.

Settlement mobility may have important consequences for the expanding industrial gold mining activities in the region. In a region where population densities are extremely low but where land is plentiful but poorly suited for agriculture, local populations adapt through short-distance migrations. Settlement mobility is not simply an economic adaption. Mobility is also a common strategy in segmentary societies for regulating and resolving social tensions. The expansion of industrial gold mining may result in a more sedentary population, but unless fundamental social change accompanies these shifts, there is no reason to believe that the social tensions inherent in the OJVG villages will abate. Profound social disruption may accompany industrial gold mining activities, therefore, and mechanisms to ameliorate these tensions should be developed in advance.

Residential and population movement also is inherent in nomadic pastoralism, an activity mainly associated Peul speakers. Elsewhere in the region, the seasonal mobility of Peul nomad pastoralists has been a major source of tensions with more sedentary and agriculturist populations. Today, Peul nomad pastoralists referred to as Haga or Aga continue to migrate in and out of the area and are considered by many of our interviewees as largely responsible for the degradation of the natural environment.

3. Like land, water is a critical resource both for human consumption and livestock. As with land, water is a key factor in settlement dynamics and population movement.

4. Epidemics have struck the area periodically over the past couple of centuries. Some of these catastrophes were attributed to supernatural forces. Of particular interest is the concern voiced by various informants that disturbance of abandoned villages and sacred sites can release malevolent forces responsible for epidemics.

5. Settlement dynamics also are a response to historical events. One informant confided that the site of Kobokhoto (ARCH 25) was founded in 1956 by people from Bambaraya. The new settlers were mainly slave descendents who rebelled against their former masters. They ultimately returned to Bambaraya in 1973 when the conflict was resolved.[25]

6. Colonial taxation also may have been a cause of population movements. One narrative recorded in Bambaraya reported that Makhana, a large abandoned site in the area (Arch 24) was founded by Peul speakers. The anonymous informant reported that 'when his grandfather returned from World War 1, the inhabitants of his village were paying taxes to Makhana on which they depended.' It was his grandfather who asked inhabitants of his village to refuse to pay taxes to Makhana. Elsewhere in the upper Senegal region

---

[25] Anonymous informant.

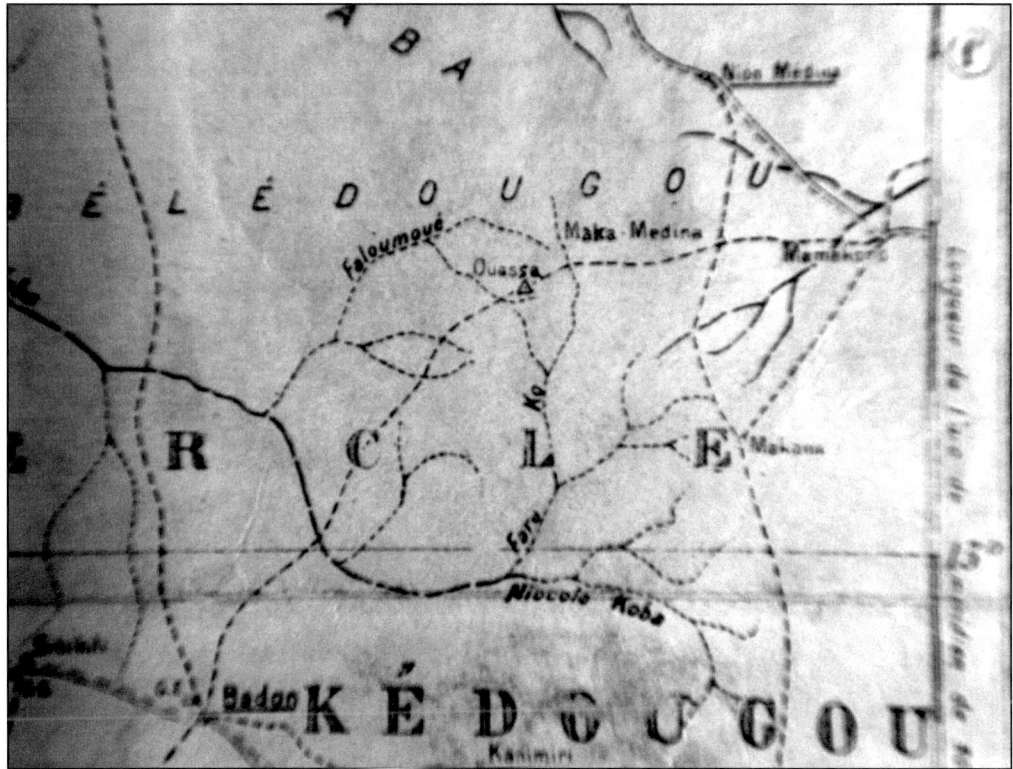

FIGURE 3.4 1926 MAP, SCALE 1:200,000.

(Clark 1994) and in the Senegambia (Searing 2001) such conflicts were reported until 1960 and maybe later in places where colonial and postcolonial administration was weak. Overtaxed populations included a large number of slave descendents and ordinary yeomen. Members of these groups who were World War I and World War II veterans have been important vectors of change. The same anonymous informant indicated that it was his grandfather who 'brought in the area the habits of having breakfast (before there were just two meals: lunch and dinner), washing hands before eating, etc. The rest of Beledougou followed afterwards.'[26]

Society and Social Organization

Like most other Mande and Halpulaar (including Peul and Toucouleurs) societies, Malinke and Peul communities in the Sabodala region are highly stratified and include nobles, endogamous craft specialists and musicians (griots or bards, blacksmiths, potters, wood carvers, etc.), and slaves. In theory, status is ascribed and each of these categories is assigned a specific social role that is passed from one generation to another. The nobles include the aristocracy, clerics, and merchants and freemen. By far, the largest segment of the aristocracy consists of freemen, who are generally powerless peasants that are subject to the exactions and pillages of the nobles. Clerics generally combine their religious activity with trade, which is an important source of revenue. Some clerics also are involved in agriculture, capitalizing at times on their armies of disciples. Agriculture, pastoralism, and war have traditionally been the only acceptable manual activity for freemen. War is not a viable economic activity in the area today, and it is clear from interviews that agriculture and pastoralism are the most important sources of subsistence. Artisanal gold mining is a major source of cash and supplements farming, particularly in years with bad harvests.

Craft specialists are minorities, and their activities are considered unclean. They are generally clients of the freemen, including the aristocracy, and sometimes they assume important functions such as advisers, diplomats, and negotiators at time of conflicts, or during social events, they serve as messengers, entertainers, and the like. In theory, members of the endogamous craft specialists and musicians cannot assume political office. They can, however, accumulate wealth; for some, their proximity to ruling class clients allows them to influence important political decisions. In addition to their craft specialties, members of these minority groups are believed to hold mystical powers, and as such, they are feared. In the past, they could possess slaves, but overall, their activity and behavior are considered socially degrading and therefore they are despised. Recent studies have demonstrated that status and identity of the

[26] Anonymous informant.

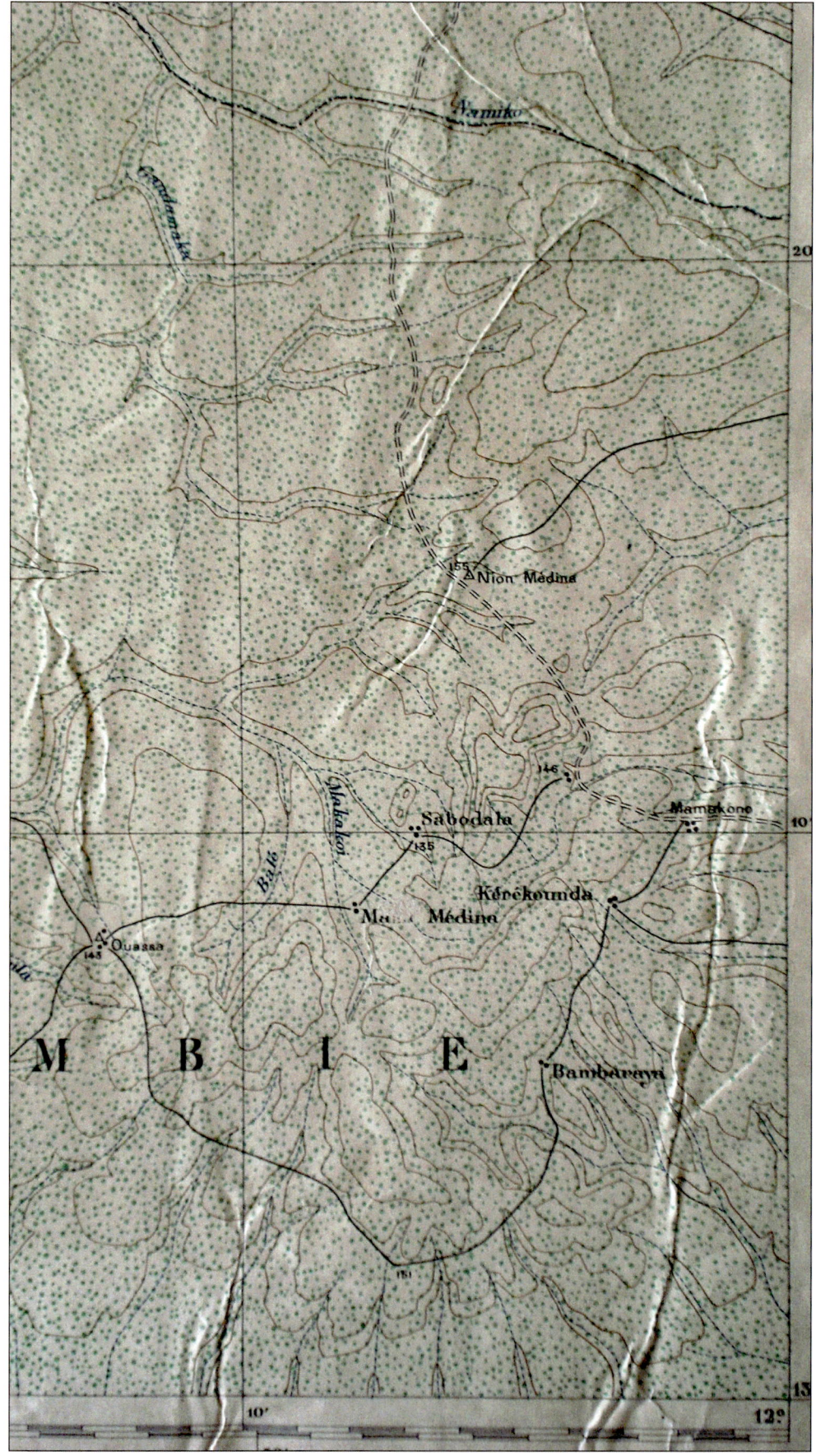

Figure 3.5. 1933 map.

Village Histories and Ethnography within the Oromin Sabodala Concession

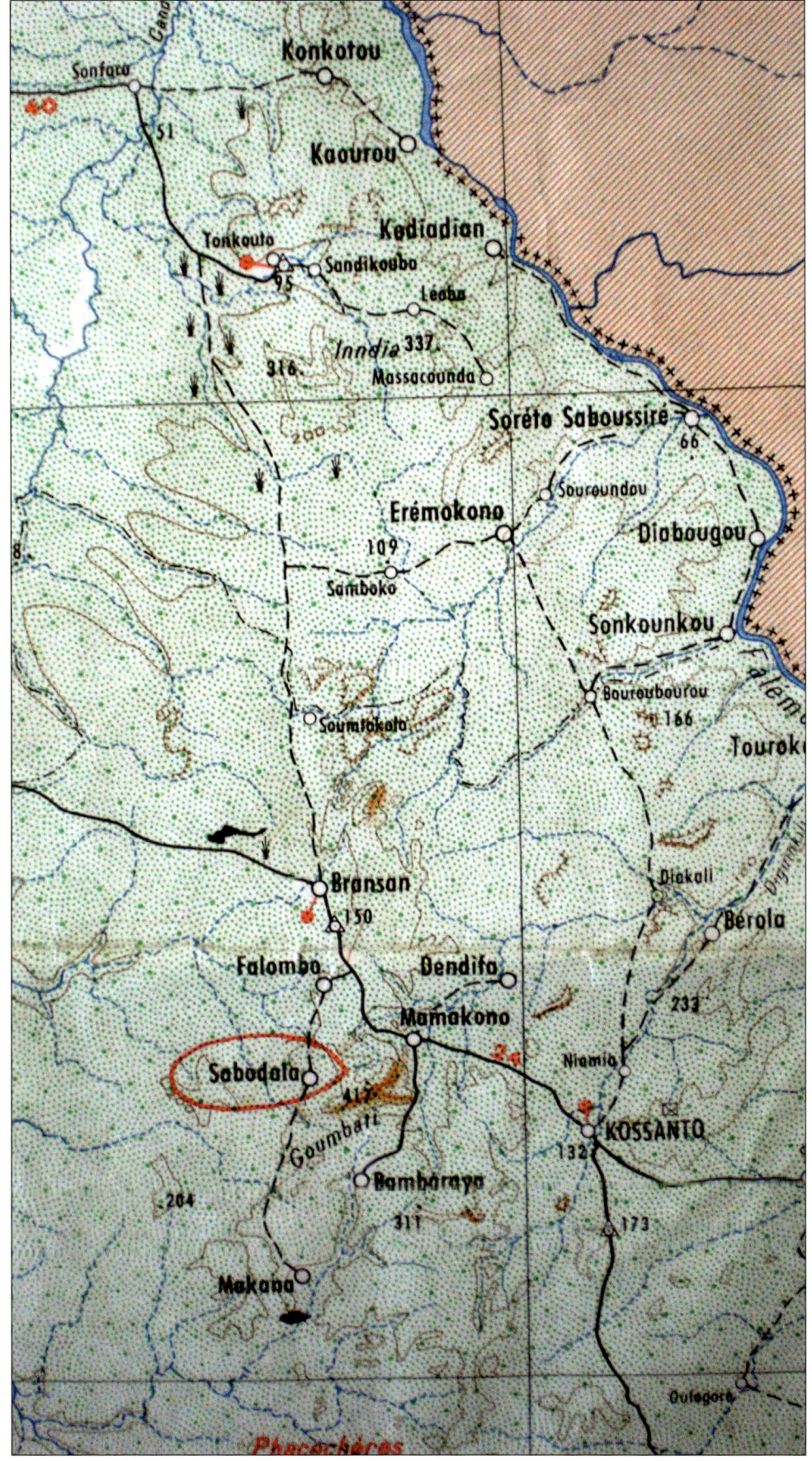

Figure 3.6. 1957 map.

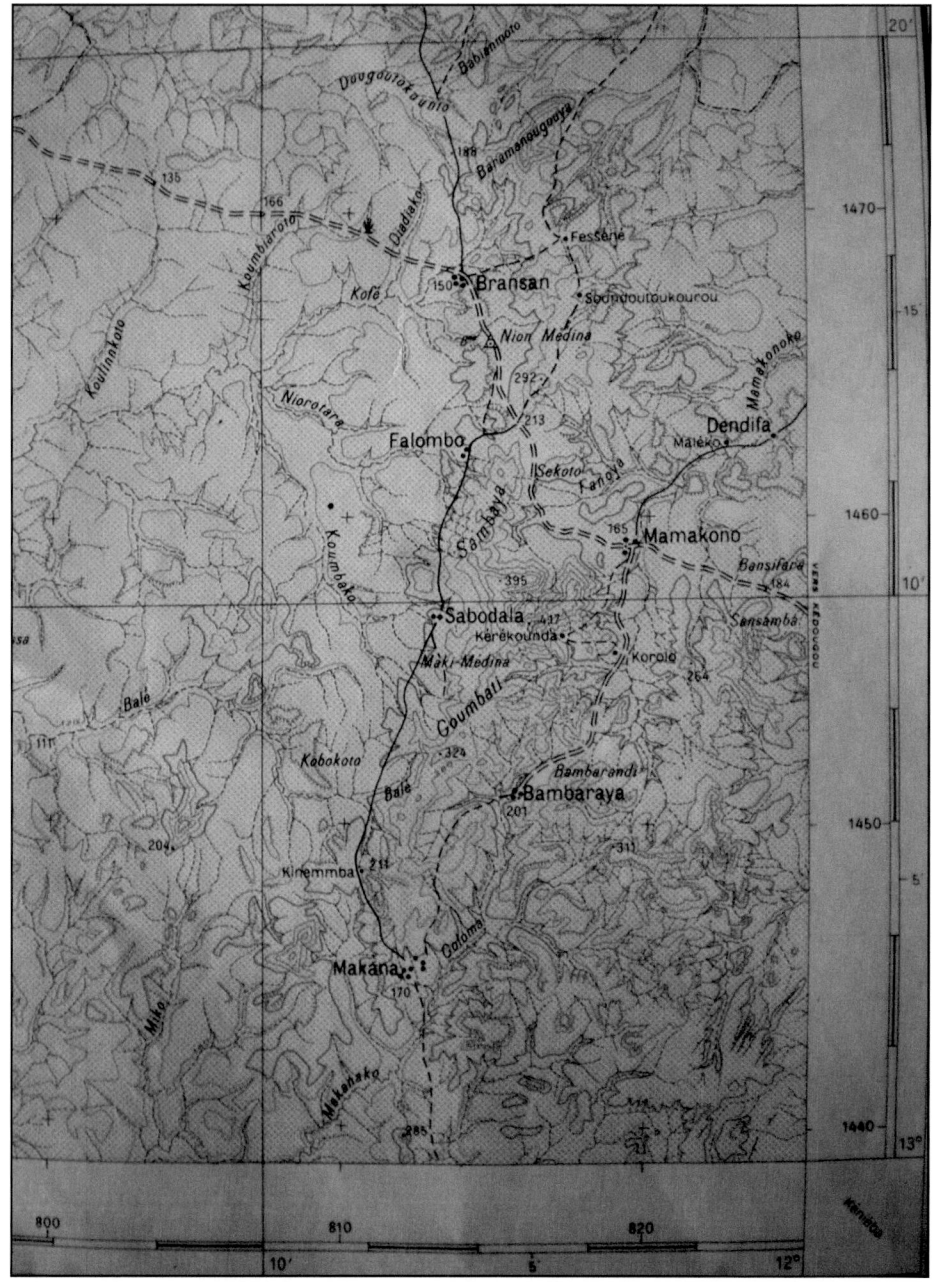

FIGURE 3.7. HISTORIC MAP OF 1960.

endogamous craft specialists are ambiguous (Conrad and Frank 1995). They are feared for their mystical powers and knowledge, adored for their useful skills, and despised for their degrading 'social behavior.' In both Halpulaar and Malinke societies, slaves are at the bottom of the social ladder.

Although there are still nobles, members of 'castes,' and slave descendents in the villages of the OJVG concession, a careful study of the oral traditions collected in the study area during our fieldwork revealed that some of these categories and their social roles have shifted with some being subverted by politically powerful newcomers. In particular, members of the Cissokho lineage now control the chieftaincy of all but one village in concession, removing Peul speakers from these roles and relegating them to 'socially despised' castes.

Yet it is important to remember that both Malinke and Peul are considered foreigners in the upper Senegal region. Although both groups are widely spread across West Africa, the processes responsible for their arrival and the timing of their movements are totally different. A realistic understanding of the social dynamics in the OJVG concession, therefore, must take into account the differing sociocultural and socioeconomic systems of the Malinke and Peul.

Malinke Society

Malinke are a branch of the Mande family, a large group of related peoples in West Africa that speaks one of the many Mande languages. The Malinke are associated with the medieval empire of Mali, whose heartland was located either in modern Mali or modern Guinea. They are agriculturists, merchants, and hunters. They are generally associated with powerful secret societies like *komo, poro,* and the *kankourang,* which in 2008 was placed on UNESCO's Representative List of the Intangible Cultural Heritage of Humanity (UNESCO 1995–2010).

Malinke speakers in the Senegambia are referred to in the literature as western Mande (Niane 1989). They are believed to have arrived in the region initially in the thirteenth century during the military expansion of the empire of Mali (Niane 1989). Subsequent to the colonization of southern and southeastern Senegambia, Malinke merchants established trade diasporas across this region (Brooks 1993). In addition to trade, these Malinke communities were generally Muslims and contributed to the peaceful spread of Islam. Curiously however, Islam seems to be a recent development in the villages of the concession. The relatively recent spread of Islam, combined with the shallow memories characteristic of oral traditions collected during fieldwork, suggests that the peopling of the villages in the concession resulted largely from different historical processes than those commonly admitted by the villagers.

Peul Society

Historically and culturally, Peul (or Fulani or Fulbe) belongs to a larger family referred to in the Senegambia as Halpulaar, which combines Peul and Toucouleur. Peul are generally associated with nomadic pastoralism. Although travelling seasonally with their cattle is an important feature of their lifestyle, some communities like the Toucouleur have adopted a more sedentary way of life, becoming agriculturists. Halpulaar speakers also played a critical role in the spread of Islam in the region. They founded the theocracies of Boundou, Fouta Toro, and Fouta Djallon in the eighteenth century. With the expansion of European colonialism in the region in the second half of the nineteenth century, El Hadj Umar Tall initiated a *jihad* known as *fergo,* which involved a massive movement of population between the middle Senegal Valley, the upper Senegal, and parts of modern Mali (Robinson 1985). The mobility of the Halpulaar and their association with Islam was a major source of conflict with modern sedentary agriculturist communities, who generally practiced local variants of a pan-African religion.

In the historical record of the upper Senegal, Peul speakers arrived in this region initially in the fourteenth or fifteenth century. It was not until the eighteenth and nineteenth centuries, however, that they began to control and organize major political formations in the area, first Boundou and then Fouta Djallon. The story of Tobri Sidebe, the slave king, probably coincides with the rise of Peul or Halpulaar hegemony in the upper Senegal River sometime between the fourteenth and nineteenth centuries.

Over the past five hundred years, Peul migrations across Senegambia completely reshuffled ethnic distribution in this region. From the Inland Niger Delta, they found colonies in the middle Senegal Valley, Fouta Djallon (Guinea), Boundou (Senegal), and parts of Mali and Guinea.

Chieftaincy

Today, all villages in the concession except Bambarayading are ruled by members of the Cissokho lineage. The origin and rise to power of the Cissokho lineage when contextualized, poses a number of problems. First, ethnographic evidence suggests a blacksmith origin for members of the Cissokho lineage that claims to be descended either from Fakoli or from a Mande woman named Kankouba Kanté. Yet, if asked explicitly if Cissokho are blacksmiths, our informants responded 'no.'[27] In addition to a putative blacksmith origin, the Cissokho came to the area to rent their military services to the Soumare. The latter were being harassed by the Peul slave Tobri Sidebe, who at some point controlled the chieftaincy.

The Cissokho lineage ruling class is united in appearance. This unity, however, masks profound divisions that reflect old and recent tensions. At least six factions were identified during the interviews, and each was characterized by its own qualities, stereotypes, and prejudices.[28]

The six families that constitute the Cissokho ruling class are:

1. The Sabakounda family, which is in charge of mystical affairs. They are great farmers and will always harvest even in a bad rainy season. They have the *Baraka,* or luck. They descend from a woman named Saba. Members are generally settled in Sabodala and Dambagoto.
2. The Kamakounda is a warrior family and is the one primarily associated with the chieftaincy. They descend from a woman known as Kama. Members are generally settled in Mamakhono, Bambaraya, and Dindifa. We also know that founders of Bambaraya and Dindifa were originally from Mamakhono, which is the village

---
[27] Anonymous informant from Bransan.
[28] Anonymous informants in Khossanto and in Bambaraya.

mainly associated with chieftaincy. One of our informants pointed out that Mamakhono had an army of bees to defend their territory along with arrows and bows.

3. According to one of our informants, members of the Sandéla family are reputed to be 'trickster and are smart like Peuls.'[29] As such, they are generally considered to be traitors, cheaters, unable to keep a secret, and always go in the opposite direction from others. They descend from a woman named Sandé. Members are generally settled in Khossanto and Bransan.

4. At least three of the families (Sabakounda, Kamakounda, and Sandéla) descend from the same father but have different mothers. Part of the conflicts and tensions within the ruling Cissokho families, therefore, may be due in part to polygamy, a practice that is still common in the region. This version of the narrative refers to these first three families as Sabadingo. Kama (first wife), Sande (second wife) and, Saba (third wife) were all married to one Cissokho chief whose name was Moussa Cissokho. Eventually, chief Moussa Cissokho took a fourth wife named Gnougoulisi Kounda who was a 'beautiful slave woman' given to Kama, the first wife.[30] This marriage gave birth to the fourth family, known as Gnougoulikounda. From that marriage were born 'illegitimate' children, who nonetheless could vie for the chieftaincy as it is transmitted from patriarchal descent. According to our informants, claims over the chieftaincy by this slave descendent family introduced profound tensions within the Cissokho lineage, and even today, some village chiefs within the concession are contested. There are few Gnougoulikounda members in the concession villages, mostly in Bambaraya and Madina-Bérola.

5. Members of the Fouloumboukounda family are believed to be newcomers and according to our informant have a Guinean and Peul origin. Some of them are established in Sabodala and Niakaféri. They are reputed hunters and farmers.

6. Members of the Kantela family are smart but careful. They reportedly work hard not to create problems. Many of them live in Bransan. They are reputed sorcerers and are in charge of the well-being of young men during initiation and of newlywed couples. They also protect the inhabitants of Beledougou against bad witches.

From this analysis, it is clear those relationships within and among the families of the Cissokho lineage are extremely complex. Some of the salient points include:

- It is possible that members of this lineage are from different origins, some from modern Mali and other from Guinea or Senegal.
- It is also possible that this lineage is composed not only of Malinke speakers, but also of Peul speakers. The latter suggests that their outward unity is based mainly on political alliances rather than patriarchal blood line.
- If not all, at least some of these families have connections to slavery and could well be slave descendents. We have documented at least one case of a contested chieftaincy that is probably the result of the chief's linkage to a slave origin.
- The stereotypes associated with each of the major families suggest tensions between them.
- A greater understanding of how these alliances are made and unmade both in the distant past as well as in the present is critical to the success of economic and industrial development in the area.

Merchants

The period beginning in the eighteenth and lasting until the twentieth century was a time of instability in the Senegambia. The expansion of slavery and the slave trade, the continuing spread of Islam, and the establishment of colonial rule and concomitant resistance movements were the regional processes that shaped local histories (Klein 1998). Armies renting their services were common in the region. These armies were generally composed of slaves, who rented their services to the ruling class and merchants. Most Soninke and Malinke polities in the upper Senegal were small scale and dominated by a weak aristocratic class that relied on taxes and a class of Soninke traders, known as Juula (Bathily 1989; Thiaw 1999).

The fortunes accumulated in interregional trade as well as the Saharan and Atlantic trades allowed the Juula merchants, who acted as middlemen along the trade routes, to become major players in regional politics. Yet, during interviews, there were very few individuals who portrayed themselves as Juula merchants. This reflects a major shift in the lifestyle of the Soumare, who constituted the elite class prior to the arrival of the Cissokho lineage.

The redeployment of economic activities to the Atlantic regions and the growth of groundnut cash crop in the second half of the nineteenth and early twentieth centuries ultimately isolated the upper Senegal communities. Initially dependent on Kayes and then Bakel, by 1907 this region was administered from the Cercle of Kédougou. At a lower administrative level, they depended on the Canton of Saraya and later on Khossanto. Instead of peanuts, however, it was artisanal gold mining that grew considerably in the areas of the Falemme and its tributaries, following the abolition of slavery and the development of legitimate trade in late nineteenth

---
[29] Anonymous informant in Khossanto.
[30] Anonymous informant.

and early twentieth centuries (David 1980:38). Today, artisanal gold mining still attracts many people to the Sabodala region from Senegal and the border countries.

Healers

Two healers using traditional medicine were interviewed. Both were from Bambaraya and claimed that they did not inherit their skills and knowledge from their parents. They claimed to have learned from travelers passing through their villages or from their own travels. The diseases they treat include sexually transmitted diseases, stomachache, painful menstruation, cholera, and smallpox. Some of the most useful treatments for these diseases include the following plants: *mokho yiro, tankhan, kaba, jouto, wongo, tousouma,* and *santango*. Both healers said that they could still find a number of useful plants nearby but also pointed out that there were plants for which one needs to travel far from their village.

In some of the other villages we collected contact information of local healers and useful plant names. Unfortunately, we did not have time to interview them. Additional information on healing in the OJVG concession was obtained by Jenny Wong (personal communication 2010) of Wild Resources, Limited.

Endogamous Craft Specialists

Practicing members of the endogamous crafts specialists constitute a small minority in most of the OJVG concession villages. Oral traditions suggest that blacksmiths, potters, griots, and leatherworkers are still present. Woodcarving is handled by blacksmiths; apparently, there are no weavers.

Blacksmiths and Potters

We interviewed three blacksmiths, one from Mamakhono, one from Bransan, and the other from Bambaraya. Only the blacksmith from Mamakhono claimed to be autochthonous to his village. The other two were originally from villages outside of the concession. The patronyms of the blacksmiths interviewed were Camara, Daniakho, and Kanté; no Cissokho blacksmith was encountered or interviewed.

Until recently, blacksmiths were responsible for producing most utilitarian implements, including farming tools and weapons. They also made jewelry and other domestic items. They generally used recycled metal from old cars that are bought from nearby towns like Tambacounda and Kédougou. Increased access to mass-produced iron and plastic items over the past few decades has considerably reduced the economic importance of blacksmiths.

Blacksmiths play other important roles within society. According to one of the blacksmiths interviewed, blacksmiths are messengers and are in charge of organizing public ceremonies such as weddings and funerals. Traditionally, they performed the circumcision of young boys and the excision of young girls. Today, the circumcision of young boys largely takes place at the local health clinic or dispensary. The excision of young girls also has considerably declined following massive media campaigns against the practice. We suspect that this practice is still practiced clandestinely in some villages. Information about excision, however, can only be obtained in private interviews and with experienced fieldworkers, as it is well known by the villagers that it is now an illegal practice.

In the Senegambia, the wives of blacksmiths and griots are commonly potters. Although the number of blacksmiths (3) and griots (2) interviewed was small, this pattern conforms to the practice in different villages of the OJVG concession with one exception; the wives of one blacksmith did not make pottery. Overall, pottery making is weakly developed, and the quality of the products is poor. Most locally made pottery is used in the village where it was made, with the excess sold in nearby markets. Water jars, steamers, and incense burners are the most commonly manufactured items. Growing imports of plastic and metal implements have undoubtedly contributed to the decline of the pottery industry. In the past, blacksmiths and other members of the endogamous craft specialists could sustain themselves with their traditional activity. Today according to Saibo Daniokho,[31] they must also farm and work in artisanal gold mining to feed their families.

Griots

The status and importance of griots in the villages of the OJVG concession are difficult to assess. Griots are known to historians and anthropologists of West Africa as major agents for safeguarding the traditions, history, and memory of the communities where they live. They are musicians, entertainers, advisers, messengers, and porte-parole; they also help settle disputes. In many societies of West Africa, Malinke and Halpulaar in particular, griots are targeted by outsiders to record oral traditions and cultural heritage.

In most Malinke communities, griots are a distinct social category with a relatively high status and visibility in the community. Yet, such does not appear to be the case in the OJVG concession villages. We were expecting to find griots in most of the villages but were surprised and intrigued to learn that most villages did not have one. The only villages where we came across griots were Bambaraya and Khossanto. In Bambaraya, there is a griot

---

[31] Interview with Saibo Daniokho in Mamakhono.

who migrated to the region from Mali about 6 years ago. He told us that he came to area to work in artisanal gold mining but ultimately found himself a nice patron and started to perform as a griot. According to information, there are several griots in Khossanto, but we only found and interviewed one. He told us that his father was the first griot who settled in the village of Khossanto and that he came there as a trader but ultimately became a friend and a client to one of the families and was invited to stay. According to this informant, all other griots in Khossanto have come to the area in the past few years.

Two narratives recorded in the area perhaps best explain the absence of griots in most of the villages in the OJVG concession. The first relates that 'since its foundation, Mamakhono, has been inhabited by a jealous griot spirit that forbids other griots from settling there.'[32] Although we were told in several interviews that even today griots do not dare spend a night in Mamakhono, one informant told us that a griot could spend a night in Mamakhono but could not build and settle there.[33] This informant added that other villages in Beledougou do not have jealous griot spirits and the reason why there are no griots is that they do not want to go there.

Secondly, there is narrative which holds that 'the Cissokho sacrificed a griot to be able to capture Tobri.'[34] The reasons why the Cissokho sacrificed a griot are unclear, but such an action may have been related to tensions between different social classes. Members of endogamous craft specialist groups are, at the same time, despised, feared, and adored (Conrad and Frank 1995). Yet, they maintain a near complete monopoly on their crafts, which in the past were viable sources of revenue (Launay 1995). We may presume that a group that would sacrifice the griot and forbid other griots from settling in the area had the skills and social legitimacy to fill the gap that was caused by the elimination of this specialty.

The Cissokho lineage's connections with the chieftaincy of Beledougou, blacksmithing, slavery, and griots are extremely complex. To make these connections, we need to understand Malinke society and its sociopolitical and socioeconomic structures as well as the historical processes presiding over their migration and settlement in the region. In other parts of the Senegambia, there are cases of egalitarian or segmentary societies without endogamous craft specialists groups. In such societies, everyone can practice a craft without being socially stigmatized because of that activity. Such, however, is not the case in Malinke societies (Tamari 1991).

How, then, did the Cissokho lineage finesse their role as nobles and craft specialists? Despite their limitations, oral traditions yield clues to help us answer this question and in so doing address the enigma surrounding the status of griots in the villages in the OJVG concession. In particular, oral history helps address how villages without griots could handle the social roles and responsibilities entrusted to these specialists in other Malinke and West African societies. The answer has to do with the role and social status of slaves and slave descendents.

The veracity – historical, social, political – of the griots stories is an open question. Conrad's (2008) study of the related Mande epics serves as a reminder that the griots of Sabodala, like the *jeliw* (professional bards) of the Mande preserve epics stories that tie elements of the physical landscape to the explained origins of kinship, political authority, land rights and accesss to ad control of spiritual power. The studies recounted here have barely scratched the surface of this area and much further work may be done.

Slave Descendants

One narrative recorded during fieldwork related that in Tomara (Mali), the purported homeland of the Cissokho lineage, slaves and slave descendents also play drums and are entertainers like the griots. A number of concordant narratives recorded in the villages of the OJVG concession, where there are few or no griots, indicated that slave descendents are mainly the entertainers (including playing drums). Considering that playing drums was and still is a lucrative economic activity, the competition for its control at the beginning of the settlement between slaves and griots makes sense.

The identity of these slave descendants is generally concealed or silenced. There was no reference to such a social category in public interviews. In public, members of this social group referred to themselves as artists. In semi-private and private interviews, we learned that members of this social category constituted a large part of the population of many villages. We were told that the villages with the highest population of slave descendants were Mamakhono, Kunamba, Niamaya, Dialakhotoba, and Khossanto. One informant estimated that at least 50 percent of the population of Mamakhono are slave descendants, and that the large majority of Peul speakers in Kunamba are also slave descendants.[35]

Cultural Heritage

Public Ceremonies and Festivals

The villages of the Sabodala region maintain ceremonies and festivals common to most Malinke societies. In Faloumbou villagers, for instance, said that previously they organized an annual feast after harvest. The feast was held in the village's public space and neighbors

---

[32] Anonymous informant.
[33] Interview with Boubou Kanouté in Bambaraya.
[34] Anonymous informant.

[35] Anonymous informant.

from Bransan and Sabodala were invited to attend. As part of the feast, they organized the 'dance of the chief,' in which the best dancers were rewarded in fictitious imaginary government positions. Villagers said they no longer organize the harvest festival because harvests these days are poor and they cannot afford the cost of the festival.

In all villages in the OJVG concession, the passage from childhood to the maturity is marked by the younger generation taking control of the village's public space or *bera* during *dansa*. To do so, they have to beat the elder generation in a drumming competition in what is tantamount to a *rite de passage*. This competition only takes place on Friday nights during marriage and circumcision ceremonies, and everyone can play and dance. It is only during these *dansa* ceremonies at the *bera* that freemen or nobles can play drums like griots or slaves. This ritual poses two lines of inquiry that need further investigation.

1. Could this ceremony be a re-enactment of an old tradition by a group whose identity has shifted or is concealed?
2. *Dansa* definitely appears to be borrowed from the French word, *danse* or dance. The antiquity of this tradition seems shallow and perhaps suggests an uprooted community seeking to redefine itself.

Initiation ceremonies that are rites of passage marking the entrance of young boys and girls into adulthood are no longer performed today. Traditionally, they accompanied the circumcision of boys and the excision of girls and were organized in a forest grove. During those ceremonies, the *kankourang* (or the masks in charge of the initiation ceremony) came out to ensure the well-being and the protection of the young initiated boys against malevolent spirits and witches. Historically, this event was associated with Malinke speakers and operated as a secret society. Today the masquerade of the *kankourang* is largely abandoned, and circumcision takes place in the local clinic or dispensary. Recently, there have being attempts to revive the *kankourang* masquerade in some villages like Kunamba and Sabodala. However, these are mere performances, and some informants referred to them as theatrical, as they are associated neither with initiation or the forest grove. They are mainly organized as entertainment for tourists or officials, and uninitiated boys, girls, women, and even Peul speakers can participate in these performances as actors or part of the audience, which would have being impossible in a traditional *kankourang* ceremony.

Sacred Sites

Today, Islam is the dominant religion in the villages of the OJVG concession. Like many parts of West Africa, conversion to world religion has not impeded belief in African religion. Although most people claim to be Muslims, African religion is still very strong in most of the villages in the OJVG concession, as evidenced by the type of sacred sites we documented. Indeed, local African religion may have been used to resist the spread of Islam, particularly in the eighteenth and nineteenth centuries, which was marked by the establishment of theocratic regimes in Boundou and Fouta Toro and the *jihad* wars of El Hadj Umar (Robinson 1985) and Mamadou Lamine Drame (Bathily 1970). One tradition collected in the area, for instance, reported that Mamakhono was sacred because it was defended by an army of bees.

We documented 46 sacred places, and another 20 sacred sites were identified but could not be corroborated due to time constraints. Information on the location and nature of each of the 46 sacred sites is presented in Table 3.4; the locations of the known sacred sites are presented in Figure 3.8. (*Note*: Table 3.4 lists sites we were able to visit; in the following text, we also discuss places we were told about during interviews on other subjects and so we were not able to verify location, nature, or the origin myths or other stories about them.)

As the first settlement in the area, we were told that most sacred sites in Deledougou were to be found in Mamakhono. Somewhat surprisingly, the list of sacred sites from Sabodala was the largest of all the villages and includes at least 11 sites. Unfortunately we did not have the time to substantiate this information on the ground and take their GPS coordinates. We believe the interviewees in Sabodala exaggerated their list to heighten OJVG concerns.

Interestingly, Mamakhono shares a number of sacred sites with other settlements. Sougoukoutourou (SACR 26), which features stones on top of a hill that allegedly represent a petrified couple that was put in that state as they mocked the spirits, is shared with Bransan and Dindifa. Mamakhono is also inhabited by a snake named Mamakhono Khoto that it shares with Khossanto.

Most sacred sites include features of the natural environment including water sources, hills, trees, forests, and possible caves (Bransan [SACR-34]). Water sources, such as Defe (SACR-37; near Dindifa) and Leyloumba (SACR-44; near Kunamba), are often associated with bees that should not, according to oral traditions, be disturbed. Other sacred sites are places where initiations were held (e.g., Tiroto near Faloumbou) and places inhabited by spirits (e.g., Koungadji near Faloumbou; Kourouboulougho, Makho Khoto, and Kharoundingkharoma near Khossanto; Findi [SACR-27] Golla-Gola [SACR-28], Bangouraye [SACR-29], Douka-Mansour [SACR-30], and Bambou Lounda near Madina Bransan [SACR-31]); humans should not disturb these places. (*Note*: Tiroto and sites near Khossanto were not visited and are therefore not included on Table 3.4;

TABLE 3.4. SACRED SITES

Site No.	Village	Site Name	UTM Coordinates Unpublished	UTM Coordinates To protect sites	Altitude (m)	Direction from Given Point	Type	Size	Description
SACR-1	Mamakhono				165		cemetery	340-m perimeter	~70 years old.
SACR-2	Mamakhono				161		sacred tree		Sacred tree that holds insects that protect the village population—'bees' will attack enemies of villagers.
SACR-3	Mamakhono				168		sacred tree		Sacred tree on which one can make prayers when one sprinkles some water containing maize flour, and promises that if one succeeds/has prayers answered, one will give a chicken or goat; age ~120 years.
SACR-4	Mamakhono				181		cemetery	260-m perimeter	40 years old.
SACR-5	Mamakhono				156		sacred tree		~80 years old; where women can make prayers due to problems with child, fertility; old man accompanies woman to tree and if she has child, it will be man's namesake.
SACR-6	Faloumbou				170		cemetery	7 ha	~50+ years old.
SACR-7	Faloumbou				167		sacred tree		One which one can make prayers; 100 years old.
SACR-8	Faloumbou				166		sacred tree		One which one can make prayers; 100 years old.
SACR-9	Faloumbou				170		sacred tree		Prayers; 100 years old.
SACR-10	Faloumbou				146		sacred tree		Prayers.
SACR-11	Sabodala				201		cemetery		
SACR-12	Kunamba				217	SE	cemetery	~7 ha	36 years old.
SACR-13	Kunamba				224	NW	sacred place	7 ha	Sacred place between two trees where one goes to pray.
SACR-14	Kunamba				211	W	sacred tree		~25 years old.
SACR-15	Kunamba				202	NE	sacred tree		~30 years old.
SACR-16	Bambaraya				197		sacred place		Ancient and first site of Bambaraya village that was overcome by mud and the population was displaced to rocky (higher) ground.
SACR-17	Bambaraya				191		cemetery		
SACR-18	Bambaraya				194		cemetery		
SACR-19	Bambaraya				195		sacred tree		Tree grows from a root belonging also to a sacred tree situated to the east of Mamakhono.
SACR-20	Bambarayanding				181		cemetery		
SACR-21	Bambaraya				194		sacred tree		
SACR-22	Sabodala				197		cemetery		
SACR-23	Bambaraya				200		sacred tree		In the mosque, there is a tree in which an evil spirit (demon) lives. The demon appears as a white goat, late in the night. If someone has the misfortune of seeing the goat, they will die.
SACR-24	Maka Madina				196		cemetery		Site of ancient cemetery, no longer used; 100 years ago? The villagers were interred here; a sacred tree grows here—if a sick person eats the fruit of this tree they will die.
SACR-25	Maka Madina								
SACR-26	Bransan/Dindifa/Mamakhono	Soungoutoukorou			187		cemetery	250 m	Soungoutoukorou (Young Girl's Rock).
SACR-27	Madina Bransan	Findi							Findi

Site No.	Village	Site Name	UTM Coordinates Unpublished	To protect sites	Altitude (m)	Direction from Given Point	Type	Size	Description
SACR-28	Madina Bransan	Golla Gola						2 ha	Golla Gola
SACR-29	Madina Bransan	Bargouraye							Bangouraye
SACR-30	Madina Bransan	Douka Mansour							Douka Mansour
SACR-31	Madina Bransan	Bambou Lounda							Bambou Lounda
SACR-32	Bransan	Nio Madina						2–3 ha.??	Nio Madina—Former/Ancestral Village.
SACR-33	Bransan	Koumbadial							Koumbadial
SACR-34	Bransan	Goumbougamba							Goumbougamba Cave/Mountain where dragon lives with snakes and hyenas.
SACR-35	Mamakhono/ Dindifa	Nyounguifokhola						2–3 ha??	Nyounguifokhola—former/ancestral village (former village of Sara Mousa) between Dindifa and Lefakhola, some 5–6 km from Mamakhono; 13° 11.986 11° 59.485.
SACR-36	Mamakhono	Hamarayholi							Hamarayholi—sacred place where spirits will throw stones at you.
SACR-37	Mamakhono	Defe						100-m diameter	Défé—sacred stream where water flows at night, with soft sands into which unwary visitor will be trapped.
SACR-38	Mamakhono / Dindifa	Khorowarowoola						4–5 ha??	Khorowarowoola (250-m circle). Sacred area not to be cultivated (but under cultivation—doubt veracity?) also ARCH 21.
SACR-39	Maka Madina	Golon Khono						300 m east-west	Goulounhono—sacred spring in ravine between Oromin Camp and village to east of road.
SACR-40	Maka Madina							100 m, oval	Sacred baobab tree and hill in middle of village; it scares off people who live too close, and fruit on left branch not edible, has humar hair inside the fruit.
SACR-41	Maka Madina	Wassa						1–2 ha	Wassa—ancestral village site (also ARCH 39).
SACR-42	Kunamba							50-m diameter	Sacred tamarinye (tamarind) tree near well.
SACR-43	Bransan	Koumba diallo							Koumba diallo
SACR-44	Kunamba	Loumba (Leyloumba)							Leyloumba—sacred site, a water source in a ravine protected by bees.
SACR-45	Maka Madina								Sacred tamarinye (tamarind) tree near well.
SACR-46	Dindifa	Sekhoto						2–3 ha?	Sekhoto ancestral village also ARCH 44, at n13° 11.626 w12°04.430.

Note: The association between the village(s) and the sites is based on ritual links and not spatial proximity.

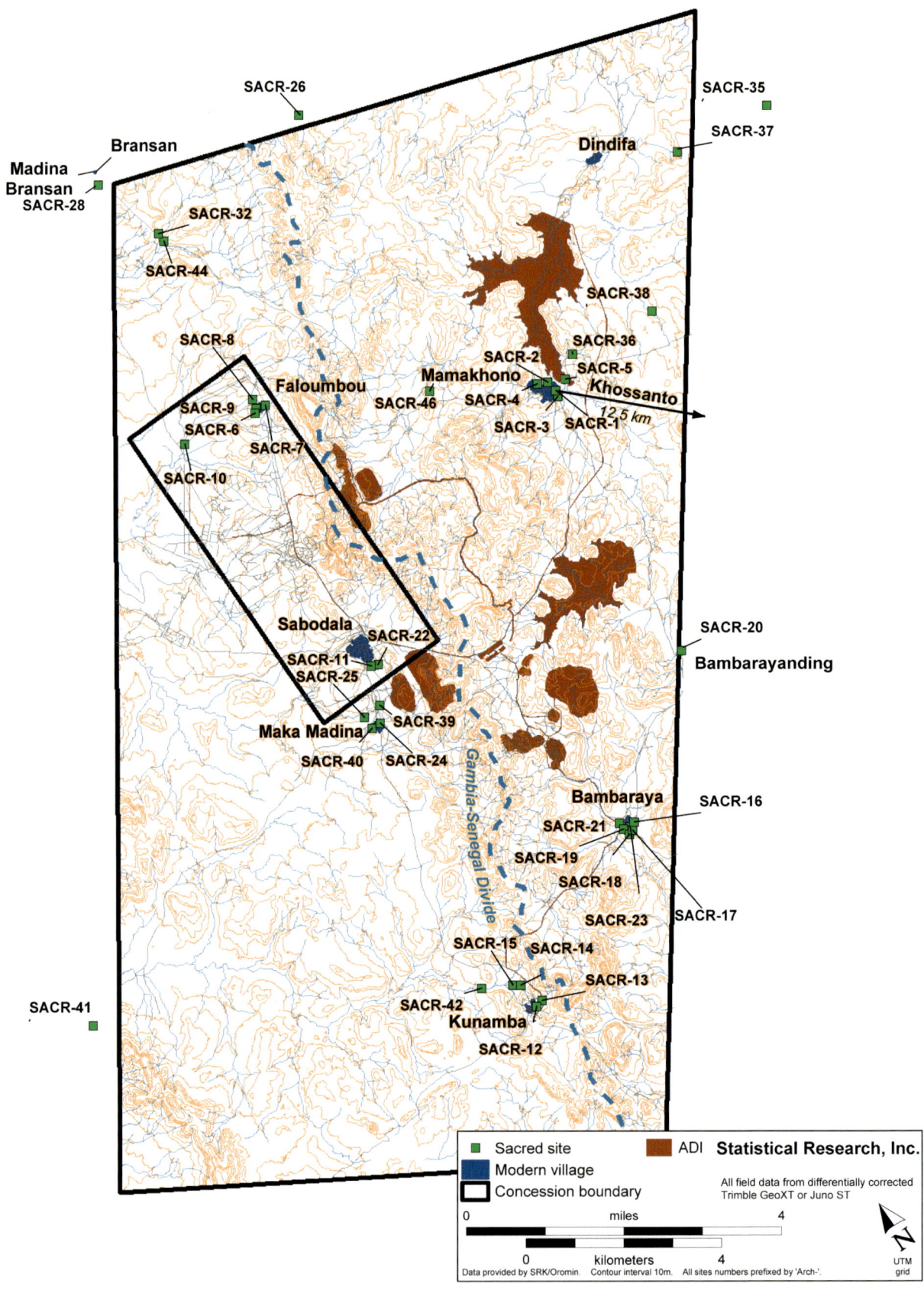

Figure 3.8. Locations of known sacred and archaeological sites as of May 2009. Known sites located outside the concession do not appear on this map.

we were unsure of Tiroto's location and Khossanto is well outside the concession.) Also, there are ravines that should not be crossed (Golon Khono near Maka Madina) and places inhabited by spirits associated with artisanal gold mining (Sora Moussa Niongui Fokhola between Dindifa and Léfakho) (we were unable to visit and verify these sites).

Industrial Mining and Local Community: Opportunities and Concerns

The general sentiment in most of the villages in the OJVG concession is that industrial mining will bring modern lifestyles to the Sabodala region and that will destroy their traditional way of life. Some voice concerns about losing their farmlands and cattle grazing lands. Villagers also worry about air and water pollution and that the chemicals used in industrial mining will spread diseases. Trenches dug by industrial mining are viewed as potentially hazardous to cattle. Finally, there are fears that industrial mining will destroy their sacred sites and expose communities to all sorts of dangers if the proper sacrifices are not performed and alms not offered.

There were also concerns that industrial mining will bring many strangers in the area, which may pose security problems. Some villagers thought that too much competition will exhaust their land, which will render it unproductive. Others thought that it would be difficult for them to succeed in a competitive environment because they are technologically inferior. Some villagers thought that the future of their communities was dark because industrial mining would ultimately expropriate them (deprive them of their proprietary rights) and there was nothing they could do to prevent it but pray for the best.

Even as they voiced their concerns, most interviewees held the view that the course of upcoming changes is hard to predict. They feel that industrial mining will bring new opportunities as well as new challenges to their communities. In terms of opportunities, villagers expect industrial mining to improve aspects of their living conditions, including healthcare, schools, mosques, mills, running water, employments, etc. Many of our interviewees thought that improvements in farming techniques are key to the well-being of their communities.

Conclusion

An analysis of the ethnographic data collected during our fieldwork reveals a region with a complex history with connections to regional and interregional historical events and processes that transcend the boundaries of modern Senegal. As a border region between Senegal, Mali, Guinea, and the Gambia, the study area has a cultural heritage tightly intertwined with this broader region both in the past and present. It is a country of immigration whose peopling can only be better understood in relation to political and economic forces within this broader region. Patterns of population movements were critical for shedding light on old and recent trade and exchange networks, matrimonial and political affiliations and affinities, availability of resources, subsistence strategies, and intra and inter-group competition for access to such resources. The information on population movements and settlement history that was collected was critical to understanding the complex identities of the different societies living within the concession and the memories they retained about themselves or others.

In addition to information on identity, valuable information was also collected on the sociopolitical structure of the different villages within the concession. Historically, both Malinke and Peul societies are highly stratified, and their sociopolitical structure comprises three major subgroups: the nobles, the endogamous artisans and musicians generally referred to as 'castes,' and the slaves. In theory, all these social categories have the same rights and privileges today. Yet, the largest majority of villages' chiefs in the concession bear the patronymic Cissokho that has controlled the chieftaincy since at least the late nineteenth century.

Ethnographic fieldwork revealed that this social stratification still persists in the region, but some identities are either concealed or silenced. Although the categories, nobles, 'castes,' and slaves are known within the villages where we conducted our interviews, the presence of certain categories of population such as slave descendants is not openly acknowledged. Social categories can be identified by the craft a person practices or certain social roles to which he or she is specifically assigned. The status and importance of crafts specialists such as griots also pose a number of conundrums that we will try to elucidate.

Although the oral record that was collected indicates that the region was first occupied by Bassari speakers and then by Soumare lineages of Soninke origin, Cissokho lineages of Malinke origin control power in most of the villages today. Gender roles and age grades appeared as major organizational principles within the villages of the concession, but these too were subject to the forces of change, especially in the course of the last century. When linked to old and present competition for the control of restricted but critical resources, including fertile lands and water and gold sources, these sociopolitical and economic considerations revealed potential tensions both within and between the families, classes, villages, and even ethnic groups and may have profound consequences in any development project in the region.

This review of the results of village and individual interviews carries a close reflection of the processes that Stahl (2001) discusses in the aptly named 'making

History in Banda' (and see also Conrad 2008). It is ineluctably the case that both Soumare and Malinke groups have engaged (and are engaged today) in 'history making' in Sabodala, and our efforts have contributed to the process of fact creation simply because we have recorded and are now publishing some of what we were told, and that we too are unavoidably engaged in affirming some of those stories even where our discussion suggests caution in a too ready acceptance of recently crated historical narratives as being the same as the recently 'lived history' of Sabodala. We return tot hese issues in Chapter 9.

Chapter 4

Archaeological Field Methods

The objective of the archaeological investigations set out in the ToR was to conduct field surveys of the concession area, with particular emphasis on the ADI, to determine whether archaeological sites existed, where they were likely located, and what significance, if any, could be ascribed to them. To achieve this goal, we implemented a sequential survey design. First, we performed reconnaissance surveys to determine whether archaeological sites were present in the area. These reconnaissance surveys continued as an embedded part of the ethnographic fieldwork. Once it was clear that archaeological sites were present in relatively large numbers, we developed a monitoring protocol that required survey prior to ongoing land-disturbing activities. Finally, we performed an intensive survey of the ADI.

Our field methods evolved as the project transpired. Initially, our survey technique was opportunistic: we specifically targeted areas in which we believed sites would be found. Site recording was perfunctory; site locations were recorded by a single Global Positioning System (GPS) reading. A small, grab-bag collection of artifacts was obtained, a few photographs were taken, and a sketch map, generally not to scale, was created. Over time, our methods became more systematic. Survey and site-recording methods were standardized in the monitoring protocols, which were only slightly modified in the intensive survey of the ADI. Chance finds encountered in other parts of the OJVG concession continued to be documented using rudimentary forms, particularly as they were embedded in other activities (e.g., geoarchaeological investigations and agricultural soil studies).

Because so little is known about upper Senegal River basin archaeology, we had very little upon which to base inferences about site and feature chronology, function, and integrity. We were particularly concerned with the stone features, which were ubiquitous in the concession but had not been reported elsewhere in Senegal. We began performing limited test excavations during monitoring, which we then increased during the intensive survey. Only sites in the ADI were selected for excavation, as these are the ones at risk. Although we originally targeted only stone-circle features, by the end of fieldwork, we had decided to test several other feature types, including burial features and a possible mosque.

Early in the project, it became clear that most sites dated toward the end of prehistory and into the early-historical period. Oral histories and ethnographic interviews indicated that this period was characterized by waves of migration of different ethnic groups into and out of the region. In hopes of tying archaeological sites to these migration processes, we wanted to create, or at least to start to develop, a fine-scale ceramic chronology and to characterize, as well as possible, the material culture assemblage. Accordingly, we placed a major effort into the analyses of artifacts collected from the surface of each site and through test excavations.

In this chapter, we describe our field methods, beginning with the survey methods in their most evolved state: those used during the intensive survey of the ADI. Next, we describe the excavation methods used to test features within a select group of sites. Methods used to analyze the artifact collection are described in Chapter 6, and field and analytical methods used in the geoarchaeological study are presented in Chapter 7.

Pedestrian-Survey Methodology

There are two major features of the OJVG concession that archaeologists must contend with during survey. First, the area is hilly (Figure 4.1), making it difficult to survey in straight lines in a systematic fashion. This challenge would be difficult for seasoned crews. It was extremely difficult for us, because one of the SCHP's objectives was the capacity building of archaeological expertise within the country. Crews were composed largely of students with little field experience. Leaders of survey crews, therefore, had to pay careful attention to the spacing of surveyors, with the result that the daily area covered was significantly lower than expected.

The second concern is vegetation. Grass grows thick, tall, and luxuriantly in the Sabodala region, and until the grass is burned, ground visibility is negligible (Figure 4.2). We had originally intended to begin the intensive survey in November 2009. For a variety of reasons unrelated to archaeology, this field season was aborted—a fortunate happenstance, because the villagers had only started burning the brush and visibility was poor. When we returned in March, most of the grass cover had been burned off, so that 90 percent or more of the ADI had good ground visibility. Of course, the trade-off for postponing fieldwork was that the climate was considerably harsher. Temperatures during fieldwork routinely hovered above 40°C, with humidity increasing as the field season wore on.

We used standard archaeological techniques to survey and record sites. Because of good ground visibility, there was no need to systematically probe the surface using shovel tests. Instead, the survey was entirely pedestrian in nature. Survey crews consisted of five archaeologists, led by either Dr. Brad Vierra or Dr. Scott Kremkau, both of SRI. Survey crew members were spaced at 20-m intervals, each walking a straight-line transect checked at regular intervals with a handheld compass. When an artifact or feature was observed, the surveyor notified the crew leader, and all crew members marked their positions on the survey line and converged on the artifact or feature location (Figure 4.3). A general reconnaissance of the area ensued. If the artifact or feature was an isolated occurrence, the crew leader took a GPS recording and plotted the site on satellite-image aerial photographs provided by SRK. If the artifact was rare or temporally diagnostic, it was collected and placed in a plastic bag, with its provenience information written on the outside of the bag and on a scrap of flagging tape that was then placed inside the bag with the artifact. Surveyors then returned to their marked places on their transects, and the survey proceeded.

If more than a few artifacts were found, the area was designated a site. Following criteria established by IFAN, a site minimally consists of clusters of surface artifacts or isolated stone features; in some cases, both artifact scatters and stone features were found in association and were collectively considered to be one site. After a site was declared, the crew leader assembled the materials needed to record the site, while the other crew members determined tentative site boundaries, identified disturbances, and defined the general nature of the site. On small sites, all artifacts and features were marked with flagging pins, and on larger sites, only features, artifact concentrations, and diagnostic or rare artifacts were flagged.

The crew leader and one of the crew members then filled out the IFAN site form (Fiche de Prospection) (Figure 4.4). In the field, site forms were completed by hand, in French; later, each handwritten form was typed into a digital site form and entered into the IFAN database in Dakar. Recorded information included site location, site size and dimensions, surface cultural material, cultural features, topography, site type, natural and human-made impacts to the site, vegetation, hydrology, and soils and minerals.

The locations of the sites were determined by a Garmin eTrex Summit GPS handheld unit with sub-15-m accuracy. All readings were taken using Universal Transverse Mercator (UTM) coordinates. The UTM coordinates were then used to plot each site location on aerial photographs and were verified through visual assessment. For small sites, only a single point near the center of each site was recorded with the GPS. For larger sites, GPS readings were taken for the center of each site and along each site boundary. GPS readings were also taken for feature locations and other noteworthy site characteristics, such as artifact concentrations, midden deposits, disturbances, and stone outcrops. Sketch maps were made of sites with features, though not for sites consisting solely of surface artifacts. Sketch maps were generally not to scale and were designed solely to check computer-generated maps created in the laboratory, using the GPS information for site boundaries and feature locations. Detailed, scaled site maps were only made of the most complicated sites (see below).

The surface-collection strategy balanced speed, space, and effort. Our goal was to collect an adequate number of artifacts to characterize the site collection but not so many as to slow down fieldwork, increase the amount of material to be returned to Dakar, or require more analytical time and effort than we had budgeted. We concentrated on artifacts that were temporally sensitive, mostly decorated ceramics and historical-period glass and metals, as well as those that might be indicative of activities, such as farming implements, hand axes, rim sherds, and slag fragments. Each site was systematically searched for these types of artifacts. For most sites, we collected all artifacts in the targeted categories. For extremely large and dense sites, we set a limit of a few hundred as sufficient.

Artifacts were not provenienced beyond the site level. For the most part, the surfaces of the sites in the OJVG concession are quite dynamic and subject to sheet erosion. The placement of individual artifacts on the surface is largely a function of postdepositional processes and is not easily related to human behavior. We did not believe the investment of time in point-proveniencing artifacts would yield a great research benefit. Each site collection was placed in one or more paper bags, with the site number, date, collectors' initials, and project name (SCHP) written on the bag and on a tag of flagging tap placed inside the bag. Artifacts were returned to camp, where they were washed and cleaned (Figure 4.5) before being rebagged and prepared for transport to IFAN's laboratory in Dakar.

Site recording was thoroughly documented with digital photographs. Individual or multiple photographs were taken of general site locations, features, vegetation, disturbances, and any other noteworthy characteristics.

The survey crews recorded 157 sites using these methods. These sites represent all sites recorded during the reconnaissance survey, ethnographic survey, site monitoring, and intensive archaeological survey of the ADI (some of the sites recorded early in the project had to be re-recorded). The only sites not recorded with these methods were those found during the geoarchaeological/agricultural soils investigations. Although recording

Figure 4.1. Terrain in the Oromin Joint Venture Group concession: (top), view to the north from Site 157; (bottom), view to the west from Masato Site 8.

FIGURE 4.2. VISIBILITY WITH WET-SEASON GRASS.

FIGURE 4.3. SURVEY CREW AT WORK.

during these investigations was not as systematic as the survey-crew recording, every effort was made to obtain a grab-bag collection of artifacts, to record the location of each site with a GPS reading, and to record enough information so that an IFAN site form could be completed in the OJVG field camp; all site information was verified in the field by Dr. Jeffrey Homburg (who recorded 95 sites as part of the geoarchaeological/agricultural soil studies) or by Dr. Ibrahima Thiaw.

Detailed Site Mapping

The decision to create computer-generated site maps from GPS readings was based on the assumption that most of the sites encountered would consist primarily of artifact scatters. We recognized that some of these scatters might contain the remnants of field houses, in the form of stone features, but most of the sites would be relatively simple. Investing large amounts of time to

Archaeological Field Methods

Fiche de Prospection

SENEGAL 2010

N° DU SITE :   NOM DU SITE :   REGION D'ETUDE :

DATE :   CHERCHEUR :

LOCALISATION   FEUILLE TOPOGRAPHIQUE :

PHOTO AERIENNE   position :   km. à   °du point principal

VILLAGE LE PLUS PROCHE :   position :   km à

LONGITUDE :   LATITUDE :

INSTRUCTIONS POUR TROUVER LE SITE

SITUATION LEGALE :   PROPRIETAIRE :

HABITATION :   permanente,   temporaire (mois de),   abandonnée

DEGRE DE PERTURBATION NATURELLE ?
ANTHROPIQUE ?
MENACES IMMINENTES ?

SITUATION GEOGRAPHIQUE
GEOMORPHOLOGIE/TOPOGRAPHIE :

HYDROLOGIE AUX ALENTOURS :

VEGETATION NATURELLE :

UTILISATION :
MINERAI DE FER A PROXIMITE :
SOLS : TEST AHN :   CLASSIFICATION MUNSELL DU SOL:
LOCALISATION ET N° DES ECHANTILLONS DE SOLS :

CARACTERISTIQUES ARCHEOLOGIQUES   ELEVATION ESTIMEE
SUPERFICIE : N-S   E-O   TOTAL EN M²:

DESCRIPTION DU SITE

FIGURE 4.4. INSTITUT FRANÇAIS D'AFRIQUE NOIRE FICHE DE PROSPECTION.

the creation of detailed site maps seemed a poor use of field effort, particularly if doing so lessened the amount of time we could use for test excavations.

Early in the survey, it became clear that some sites were not simple artifact scatters or isolated stone features. Complex sites with good integrity that encompassed multiple features and multiple feature types were encountered. These sites ranged from family farmsteads to the possible centers of small West African polities. Once we defined the seven site types used to describe the survey results (see Chapter 5)—resource processing, field house, farmstead, hamlet, village, polity, and ideological/sacred—we selected examples of each type (except resource-processing sites) to create detailed, scaled maps. Seventeen sites were chosen, all of which are located in the ADI. These sites are listed in Table 4.1.

Detailed site surveys were led by Dr Gerry Wait of Nexus and began the process of detailed site mapping by recording points along the site boundaries, using Trimble GeoXT and GeoXH GPS units (Figure 4.6). These GPS units are more accurate (1–5-m accuracy after correction) than the ones used by the survey crews. The locations and dimensions of all features were also recorded using the GPS units. Scaled drawings, at 1:20 or 1:50 scales, of all or a sample of surface features were then made. Detailed photographs showing site features, topography, vegetation, and disturbances were taken.

Surface collections were taken from each feature and artifact concentration, to augment the earlier grab-bag

FIGURE 4.5. IN-CAMP ARTIFACT PROCESSING.

collection of the whole site. Emphasis remained on temporally or functionally diagnostic material, with particular attention to decorated ceramics, rim sherds, ceramic pipe fragments, tuyere fragments, formal stone tools, and glass and metal artifacts.

Site Test Excavations

Test excavations were performed (led by Drs Vierra, Kremkau, Thiaw and Wait) at six sites, to evaluate site integrity, site function, and site chronology. Excavations occurred at five sites as part of the investigations of the ADI; these sites were Sites 08 and 09 in Masato rock dump, Site 149 in the area of the processing plant, and Sites 156 and 157 on the line of the proposed road from the plant to the reservoir dam, between Mamakhono and Dindifa. The sixth site, Site 69 in Korolo, was excavated as part of archaeological monitoring (Thiaw et al. 2010a).

Excavations focused on features. For the most part, we concentrated on stone circles interpreted as the remnants of huts or storage features. We also tested the possible

TABLE 4.1. SITES SELECTED FOR DETAILED MAPPING

Site Number	Site Type	Location
1	farmstead	Niakifiri
8	polity	Masato
9	polity	Masato
11	farmstead	Masato
71	village	tailing-mine facility
77	hamlet	tailing-mine facility
78	farmstead	Masato
79	farmstead	Masato
129	field house	reservoir
133	field house	reservoir
147	farmstead	Golouma
149	farmstead	processing plant
151	farmstead	road—plant to reservoir dam
153	hamlet	tailing-mine facility
155	field house	road—plant to reservoir dam
156	village	road—plant to reservoir dam
157	ideological/sacred	road—plant to reservoir dam

FIGURE 4.6. GLOBAL POSITIONING SYSTEM RECORDING.

FIGURE 4.7. SAMPLE EXCAVATION UNIT AT SITE 156.

mosque at Site 08 in Masato and a possible burial feature at Site 157.

Excavations were undertaken by the archaeological team, with the assistance of local laborers. We excavated in test pits that were generally 1 m by 1 m or 1 m by 2 m in size (Figure 4.7). At times, the excavation unit conformed to the dimensions of the targeted feature. Test pits were excavated in 10-cm levels or in stratigraphic layers (if these layers were visible), using hand tools (generally trowels). The fill was screened through 0.635-cm (0.25-inch) hardware-cloth mesh. Artifacts were provenienced and bagged by level. Plan maps of test-pit floors, along with stratigraphic profiles of relevant test-pit walls, were drawn. IFAN feature forms (Fiche de Feature) and test-pit-level forms (Fiche de Niveau) were completed, documenting soil, disturbances, cultural features, and artifacts found in each level. Test-pit excavation was documented thoroughly with digital photographs and scaled (1.20) drawings of profiles.

Summary

Archaeological field methods used in the SCHP evolved over time. As we learned more about field conditions, site integrity, site structure, feature types, and surface artifacts, we tailored our methods and approach to the problems at hand. Our chief objective was to document as thoroughly as possible the archaeological sites in the ADI, through survey and excavation. Most of our field efforts were allocated to this task. As time allowed, we placed the sites in a larger regional context by documenting chance finds throughout the concession; although performed at a much lower level of effort, this work provided important information that would not have been otherwise available. In all, 251 sites were recorded, 17 sites were subject to detailed mapping, and test excavations of features at 6 sites were performed. The results of these efforts are presented next, in Chapters 5 and 6.

Chapter 5

Archaeological Survey and Test-Excavation Results

The SCHP investigations resulted in the location and documentation of 251 archaeological sites in the OJVG concession. As field investigations progressed, the team gained an understanding of the variations in site size, numbers and types of features, and numbers and varieties of artifacts, as well as the topographic, vegetative, and hydraulic settings of the sites. We used this information to define seven site types—resource processing, field houses, farmsteads, hamlets, villages, polities, and ideological/sacred—and to classify each of the recorded sites into one of the types (Table 5.1).

In this chapter, we present the archaeological results of the surveys and test excavations undertaken for the SCHP. Archaeological fieldwork occurred between February 2009 and April 2010; archaeological investigations were the focus of or were included in reconnaissance surveys, ethnographic surveys, and archaeological survey and test excavations of the ADI; geoarchaeological investigations; and monitoring activities. Archaeological investigations documented 251 sites; test excavations were conducted at 6 sites—Site 69 in Korolo, Sites 8 and 9 in Masato, Site 149 in the area of the processing plant, and Sites 156 and 157 on the line of the proposed road from the plant to the reservoir dam, between Mamakhono and Dindifa.

We begin with a discussion of the key elements used to define site types: material culture and stone features. Because the objectives and goals driving artifact collection and analysis were discussed in Chapter 4, we focus here on features and, in particular, on one type of feature: stone features. Such features are ubiquitous throughout the OJVG concession. The most common type of stone feature is a stone circle, of which hundreds were recorded in the OJVG concession. Surprisingly, similar features have not been reported previously in the upper Senegal River basin – for example recent investigations by Cameron Gokee (2010) have found stone features on middle Faleme. . After the discussion of stone features, we present the results of the archaeological investigation, by site type. Examples of each type are presented, most of which are drawn from the ADI and were the subjects of detailed recording and mapping efforts; some also had test excavations performed on some of their constituent features (see Chapter 4). We end with a general discussion of settlement distribution in the OJVG concession.

Appendix A provides a list of all sites recorded as part of the SCHP; data on features are presented in Appendix B. Figure 5.1 presents the locations of all sites in the OJVG concession, by site type. A legend for all GIS-generated maps is provided in Figure 5.2. IFAN site forms for each site are deposited in the archive in IFAN. The following section discusses the results of the investigations, making use of the sites that were investigated in more detail.

TABLE 5.1. NUMBER AND PERCENTAGES OF SITES FOR EACH TYPE OF SITE

Site Types	Sites in Types (%)	No. of Sites
1. Resource processing site	45	113
2. Fieldhouse	33	83
3. Farmstead	12.7	32
4a. Hamlet	3	7
4b. Village	2	5
5. Polity center	1	3
6. Sacred site	3	7
Uncategorized	0.3	1
Total	100	251

Material Culture and Features

The surveys revealed that most archaeological sites can be categorized by either or both of two constituent parts: surface artifacts and surface stone features. Each category is discussed below.

Material Culture

Analyses of surface-collected artifacts were designed to provide information regarding site function and temporal use. In Chapter 6, we will describe the methods and results of the artifact analyses. We placed special emphasis on the analysis of ceramics, which make up the bulk of the collection, and lithics; a handful of historical-period material was also analyzed.

Each site was assessed on the basis of artifact quantity, density, and diversity. Sites were categorized from simple to complex material culture collections, with the former characterized by small collections of one or two material classes that were found dispersed evenly and in low densities across the site. More-complex collections exhibited not only more artifacts but greater structure to their spatial distributions. Although there were no formal rules to this assessment, in general, simple collections were associated with sites of limited duration and a restrictive set of activities. Collections of greater complexity were associated with sites of longer duration and multiple activities. At the apex of this continuum were collections consistent with year-round habitations of several hundred people.

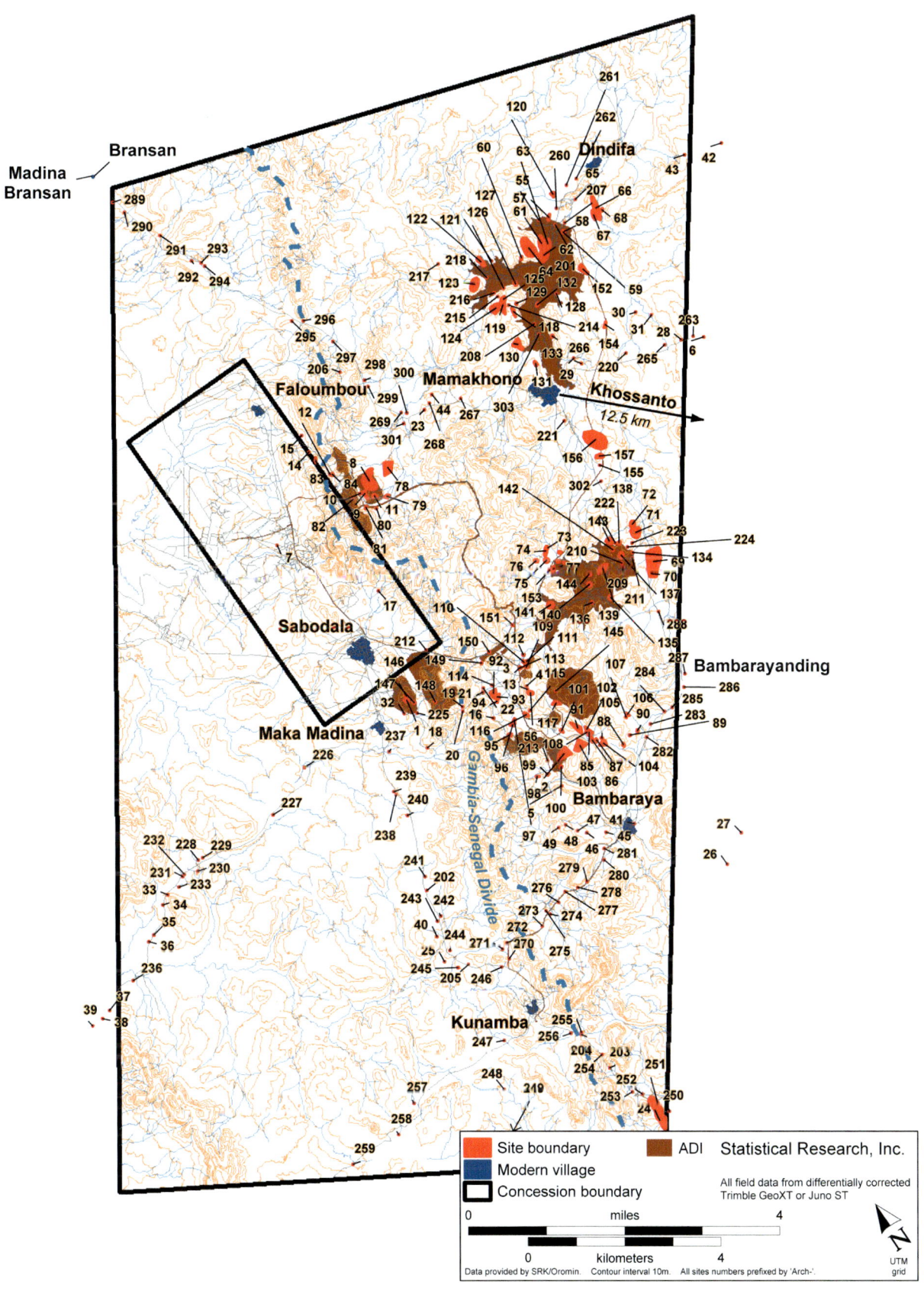

Figure 5.1. Map of all sites in the OJVG concession.

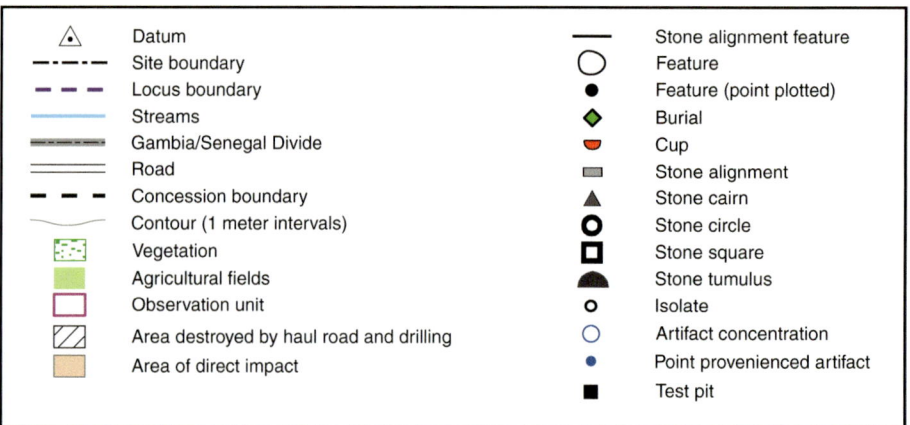

Figure 5.2. Legend for all GIS-generated site maps.

Feature Types and Functions

With the exception of cupules ground into bedrock at Site 1, all other features found in the OJVG concession consisted of features made by placing stone cobbles on or into the ground. In all, 455 stone features were identified and recorded during the field investigations (see Appendix B). We classified these stone features into three types:

1. rings or **circles** of stones,
2. **linear alignments** of stones, and
3. **stone squares**/rectangular arrangements.

Even a cursory observation of the present villages within the concession reveals the most likely interpretation for the rings or circles of stones: these are the typical foundations for the majority of huts. They range from 2 to 5 m in diameter and serve a very wide variety of functions—domestic huts, storage huts, raised granaries, and probably a range of other, less-specific uses, as well (Figures 5.3 and 5.4).

Is seems likely that smaller stone rings are the foundations for storage/granary structures, whereas those more than about 3 m in diameter are more likely to be domestic in nature. It was observed in the field that some stone rings contained quantities of burned daub from walls, and equally, there are circular mounds of burned daub that do not have stone rings but are arguably also hut sites. Modern huts are regularly plastered with a clay-based daub that is not fired; when a site is abandoned, huts are pulled down, and the areas may be burned off as part of the process of returning them to forest or agricultural uses. This abandonment process is likely to be the origin for the burned daub. Daub that has not been accidentally fired would simply 'melt' in the seasonal rains and disappear from the archaeological record.

The next most commonly observed type of feature is the linear arrangement—an alignment or cairn—of stones (Figure 5.5). Again, a variety of functions are discernable in modern contexts. One common function is the clearance cairn, created by clearing fields of larger stones in preparation for agriculture. Domestic sites also include a variety of liner arrangements that form foundations for walls around domestic compounds. Additionally, these cairns may be Islamic burial markers or graves. Such markers are commonly ca. 1–2 m in length and typically less than 1 m in width and are oriented variously east-west through to north-south, more commonly north-south.

The third type of stone feature is a square or rectangular setting (Figure 5.6), which typically may be three to five rows of three to five stones, set closely packed. In the modern-village and field-based crop-processing contexts, these are the bases for crop-drying platforms (especially for sorghum), keeping the harvested plants above the ground level.

Stone features were found in all areas of the OJVG concession. Jeff Homburg (personal communication 2010), whose geoarchaeological investigations took him to all parts of the concession, noted that such features are not found in areas where laterite covers the ground. He also noted that these features are concentrated in the Senegal River drainage and that they dramatically decrease in frequency in the Gambia River drainage to the west.

Site Types

In the following discussion, we first present the defining characteristics of each site type, followed by one or more examples of sites of each type. For the most part, the seven site types represent functional assessments that have been strongly shaped by ethnography. We found strong continuity between ancient and contemporary farming settlement systems. Some of the sites recorded are quite recent, as indicated by some of the local laborers who, in some cases, knew the names of associated villages

Figure 5.3. A currently occupied domestic hut with foundation stones.

Figure 5.4. A current storage hut with foundation stones.

Figure 5.5. A typical 'rock alignment,' or cairn; Feature 4 from Site 156.

Figure 5.6. A typical rock square or rectangle from Site 156.

Archaeological Survey and Test-Excavation Results

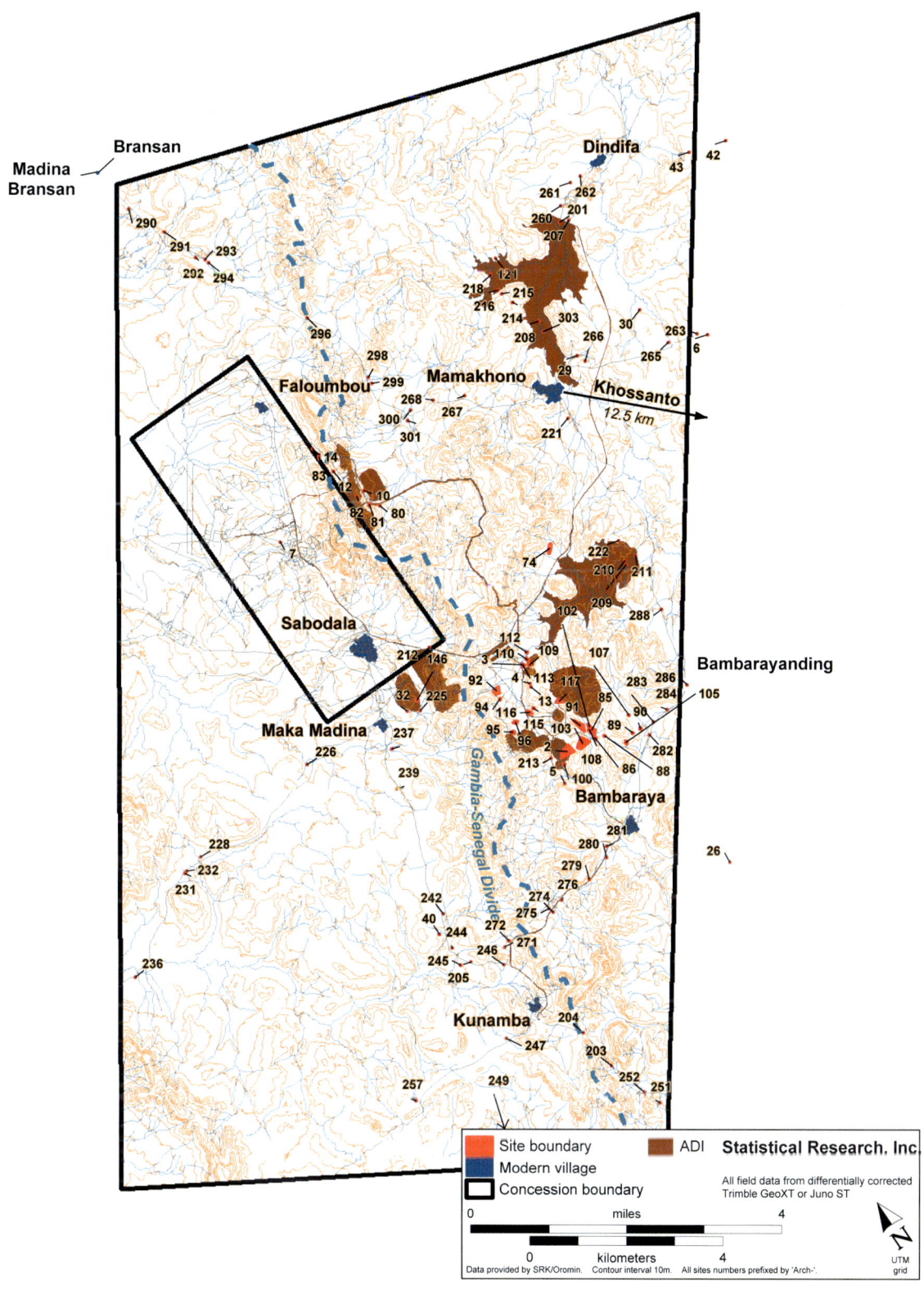

Figure 5.7. Map showing all resource-processing sites.

FIGURE 5.8. ACHEULEAN BIFACE TOOLS.

and of past and present chiefs and where the farmers had moved. As interviews with Mamakhono farmers suggested, an important factor in the placement of field houses is the distance to the village. For fields close to villages, no field house is needed, because villagers can walk to those fields easily. Of course, today, some use bicycles or motorcycles, allowing them to travel farther to their fields without needing a field house, except at critical times during the growing season (especially to keep wild animals from their crops near harvest time).

How far these modern practices extend into the past is unknown. Decorated pottery from field house sites indicates that the modern land-use patterns are of some antiquity. It is important not to be blinded by the present when interpreting the past. We found some sites that have no ethnographic analogies, such as the polities. Further, modern economic practices have been greatly altered by industrialization and globalization. Although ethnography can be very helpful, our goal, in part, is to explain how the past became the present, not to project the present indefinitely into the past.

Resource-Processing Sites

By far, with 113 representatives, more sites were typed as resource-processing sites than any other category (44 percent of the total). These are defined as artifact scatters with no stone features. Resource-processing sites represent a variety of activities associated with short-term resource processing and production. Such activities include hunting, plant gathering, and herding livestock. Many of the artifact scatters were procurement locations, with processing (such as rendering small animals and plants) taking place where people lived (or perhaps field houses). Some initial processing took place for bulky items, but not much. This category might equally be called resource-procurement sites, resource-extraction sites, activity loci, etc. These sites would be expected to be scattered among agricultural fields or in the forest, in proximity to the resources being harvested, processed, and prepared.

Resource-processing sites are found in the higher elevations of the concession (Figure 5.7). Given their ephemeral nature, it is perhaps not too surprising to find that resource-processing sites lie on steeper slopes than any site type with stone circles. Resource-processing sites are found facing all directions, although, in contrast to their more agricultural and domestic counterparts, which face mostly to the east, nearly a third of all resource-processing sites face west.

To a large extent, the resource-processing category is a catchall that includes all sites that could not be classified to a more specific functional class. The diversity of activities, cultures, and time periods represented by sites in this class is supported by the eclectic artifact collections. Resource-processing sites are generally composed of light pottery scatters, often with milling equipment, such as grinding slabs and pestles. The pottery is often very eroded. Rim morphology is generally dominated by simple, open; simple, closed; and short, everted vessels. Twine roulette and slip are the predominant motifs for both rim and body sherds.

Of particular note, we found a number of resource-processing sites dating to the upper and lower Paleolithic (see Chapter 6). Three Acheulean bifaces (Figure 5.8) were collected from Isolates (ISOs, or isolated occurrence of an artifact or feature with any other associated remains) 01 and 06 and Arch 156B. All three artifacts were made of local greenstone, with edge margins that had been worked along both sides. In addition, they all exhibit a heavy geological varnish. Each item was associated with the highest terrace on the laterite

Archaeological Survey and Test-Excavation Results

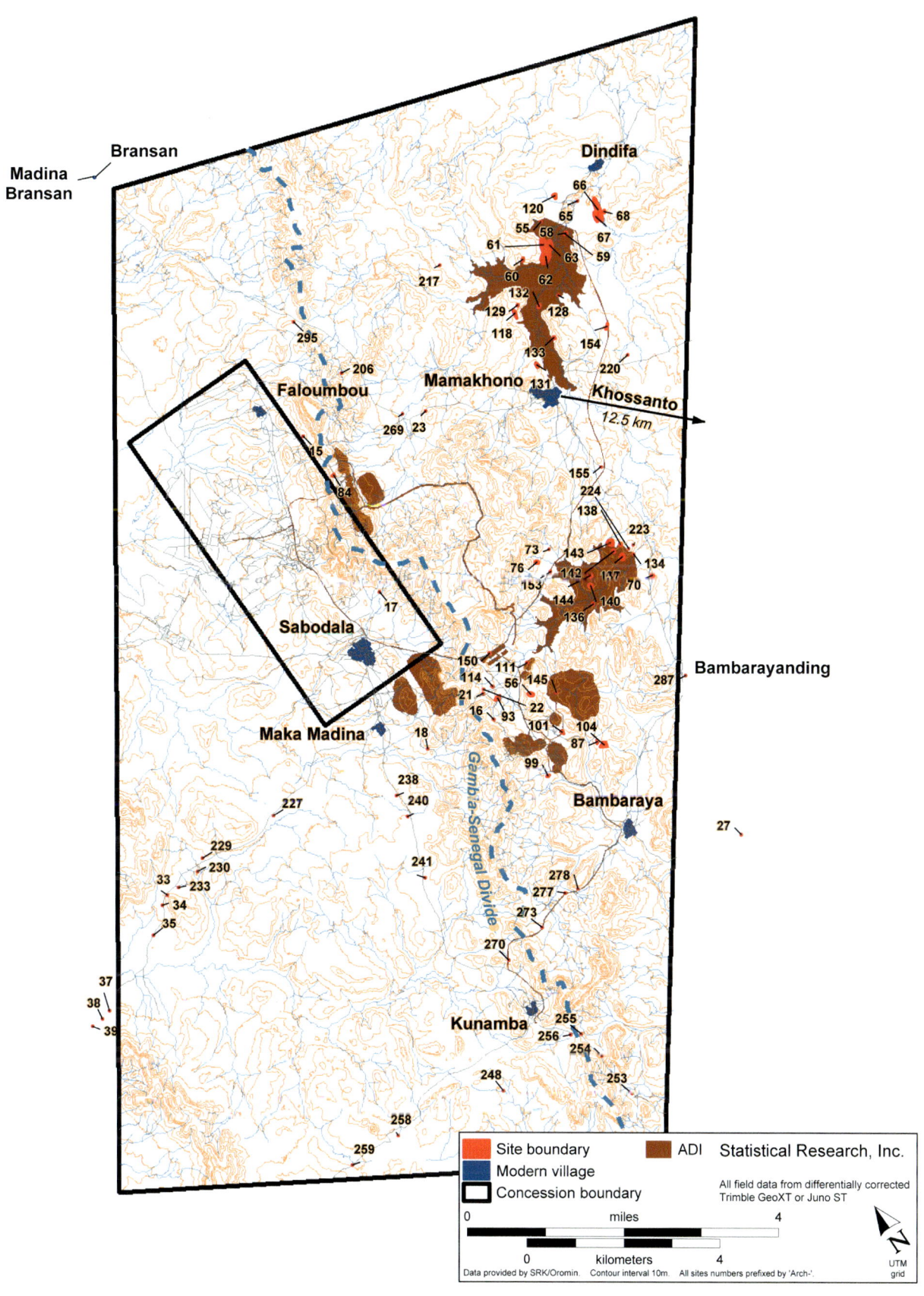

Figure 5.9. Map of all field house sites.

bedrock (or on a nearby slope). The literature suggests that it takes at least 300,000 years for laterite deposits to form (Jeff Homburg, personal communication 2010). If these artifacts are that old, they would be consistent with Camara and Duboscq's (1984) argument that the gravel terraces that contain Acheulean artifacts on the Falémé River date to ca. 200,000–300,000 years ago. The Falémé artifacts are heavily waterworn and were recovered from alluvial deposits. As previously noted, the Sabodala artifacts are made on local greenstone and exhibit heavy geological varnish. Therefore, the Sabodala artifacts were probably associated with a stable land surface. If so, this dichotomy between alluvial and inland contexts could provide insight into the ancient land-use strategies of Senegalensis; that is, typical handaxes from areas with large gravel materials, as opposed to marginally worked bifaces from inland lithic-resource-poor areas. An intensive surface reconnaissance of these upper terraces may provide more examples of this rare stone tool technology.

Field Houses

Artifact scatters with one to five stone features or artifact scatters with more than five stone features but no other type of feature were classified as field houses. Rarely, we classified sites that contained multiple stone features and other types of features as field houses, but only if they could be clearly associated with agricultural activities (e.g., if one of our laborers told us a particular site was a field house or if the site was located in an abandoned field). In all, 83 sites were defined as field houses, representing 33 percent of the total number of sites.

Field houses are critical components of the agricultural system, but they also figure in other activities. For example, today, young boys often camp at field houses just before the harvest, hunting monkeys and other animals that are attracted to the ripening crops. In general, field houses are used seasonally during the growing season, as well as for shorter periods during key times of the season, especially before and during the harvest and processing of crops (e.g., drying crops, hulling, threshing, etc.). As suits their substantial variability in function and duration of use, field houses are characterized by a varied archaeological record. Stone features can represent the remnants of houses, storage facilities, privies, menstrual huts, drying racks, and so on. Field house sites are concentrated on the first terrace, which is the best farmland and not subject to flooding that occurs on the flood plain. Figure 5.9 shows all the field house sites discovered by the surveys. The flood plain was (and is) used, too, but mainly as part of a floodwater-recessing-farming system, to grow such crops as rice.

Three field house sites (Sites 129, 133, and 155) were subject to detailed site mapping. These sites are representative of their class.

Figure 5.10. Site 129.

Site 129

Location in concession: Site 129 is located on the western edge of the freshwater reservoir north of Mamakhono.

Topographic setting: An elevated first-terrace plateau above the floodplain, with ravines immediately adjacent.

Vegetation: Open bush with bamboo.

Hydrology: Adjacent ravines carry runoff, the floodplain is about 100 m.

Modern disturbances: None.

Site description: Two stone circles. Artifacts are spread over about 0.5 ha.

Artifacts: The sample includes ground stone and nondecorated vessel fragments. The sherds are generally very fragmentary and quite eroded, which suggests that occupation could be relatively old but was probably short term.

Site interpretation: The site is interpreted as a field house, one typical of its type in topographic setting, size, and artifacts.

Lying on what will become a relatively high peninsula that extends into the west end of the reservoir, Site 129 consists of two stone circles and an artifact scatter distributed over a little more than half a hectare (Figure 5.10). The rock rings are about 3.5 m in diameter and show good integrity. The site lies on a slightly sloping surface that faces southwest and is located relatively far from water (ca. 350 m to the nearest blue-line feature). Once burned, the site would be conducive to traditional runoff agriculture.

Site 129 is bordered by a field house to the south (Site 118) and a resource-processing site to the west (Site 214). About 300 m to the west are two farmsteads (Sites 119 and 124), and slightly farther to the north are two other farmsteads (Sites 126 and 127). The entire terrace appears to have been favored by traditional agriculturists for runoff agriculture.

Site 133

Location in concession: The site is located immediately adjacent to the eastern edge of the freshwater reservoir north of Mamakhono.

Topographic setting: A second terrace that slopes downward to the west.

Vegetation: Bush and bamboo.

Hydrology: An adjacent ravine and a floodplain to the west.

FIGURE 5.11. SITE 133.

Modern disturbances: None.

Site description: The site consists of a single stone circle of slightly sloping plateau; the circle contains an unusual quantity of stone in its interior.

Artifacts: Artifacts are sparse. The pottery collection is very fragmentary with a predominance of nondecorated vessels. Material from this site could be relatively old, but the presence of a tobacco-pipe fragment suggests that the site was reoccupied in the recent-historical-period past and, therefore, was a palimpsest. It is likely that both occupations were short term.

Site interpretation: The site is interpreted as a field house, with artifacts spread over about 0.1 ha.

Site 133 lies on a terrace along the eastern edge of the freshwater reservoir's southern arm (Figure 5.11). The site is very small, about 1,000 m². Facing south-east, it lies in an open savannah about 150 m from a mapped stream. No modern disturbances exist and site integrity is judged to be very good. The archaeological deposit is composed of a single small stone circle (the diameter is approximately 2.3 m) and a small surface scatter of artifacts.

Site 133 is relatively isolated. The closest site is a field house located about 500 m to the west, adjacent to a stream. Site 130, a hamlet, is the closest residential site; it is located about 1,000 m to the west, on the opposite (western) terrace of the valley.

Site 155

Location in concession: The site is located south of Mamakhono, in the Korolo region.

Topographic setting: A broad, flat Holocene terrace.

Vegetation: Sparse, open bush and grassland.

Hydrology: None nearby.

Modern disturbances: The site is near a footpath but in the trace of a proposed haul road.

Site description: The site consists of three stone circles in a small cluster measuring about 0.25 ha.

Artifacts: Artifacts are sparse. The ceramic collection is dominated by nondecorated, followed by those exhibiting a twisted and rolled twine (Tw6; see Chapter 6) motif, reflecting a possible recent, short-term occupation.

Site interpretation: The site is interpreted as a field house that is typical, except that it is located on a low, flat terrace rather than on the higher, flanking Pleistocene terraces.

Located on the proposed road between the processing plant and the dam site, Site 155 contains three stone circles and a scatter of artifacts. It is located on a flat Holocene terrace adjacent to a low-lying floodplain. At the time of fieldwork, the ground cover had been burned,

Figure 5.12. Feature 1 at Site 155, a stone circle.

FIGURE 5.13. FEATURE 3 AT SITE 155.

and surface visibility at the site was good. The site is in good condition; no disturbances were noted, although a road bends around the site to the south and east.

The stone features consist of circles of similar shapes and sizes (Figures 5.12 and 5.13). Each is circular with a diameter of about 2–3 m. There appears to be little soil development in the area, and we do not believe the features have any significant depth of deposit. There is a relatively sparse scatter of ceramics on the site, dominated by twisted and rolled twine (Tw6; see Chapter 6) and plain vessels (see Chapter 6).

Because it was found on a linear survey of a proposed road, the site context is difficult to infer. A major village and sacred site were found to the north (Sites 156 and 157, respectively), and south there is an uncategorized site (Site 302). No evidence was found, however, to link the field house with the village.

Farmsteads

Farmsteads are sites with 5–10 stone features; they are interpreted as places where nuclear or extended families lived during the growing season. Features at farmsteads include domestic huts and storage, granaries, and a variety of other features. Distributed in a fashion that is similar to that of field houses, farmsteads are located on the first terrace, overlooking alleviated areas. Figure 5.14 shows all the farmsteads discovered during the SCHP field investigations. The numbers and diversities of artifacts and features suggest that farmsteads were year-round residences. It is possible that farmsteads represent an earlier, familial-based settlement system that preceded the development of polities in the area. Such a system would depend on the availability of ample quality agricultural land. Otherwise, individual families would be in such competition with each other for access to quality land that a village- or polity-based system would be necessary to mediate disputes. Although it is theoretically possible that artifacts at farmsteads are earlier than those found on hamlets, villages, or polities, the collected artifacts show no such indications. Instead, it appears that farmsteads are inherent parts of the village- and polity-based system. Ethnographically, as quality land close to villages becomes rare, young men who have little status within a lineage break off and start their own settlement. We suspect that farmsteads reflect this part of the settlement cycle, with the farmstead either abandoned in a relatively short time or developed into a hamlet or village.

We identified 32 farmsteads—13 percent of the total number of sites. Detailed maps were made of 5 farmsteads (Sites 11, 78, 79, 147, 149, and 151); each is discussed below.

A Slave Who Would Be King

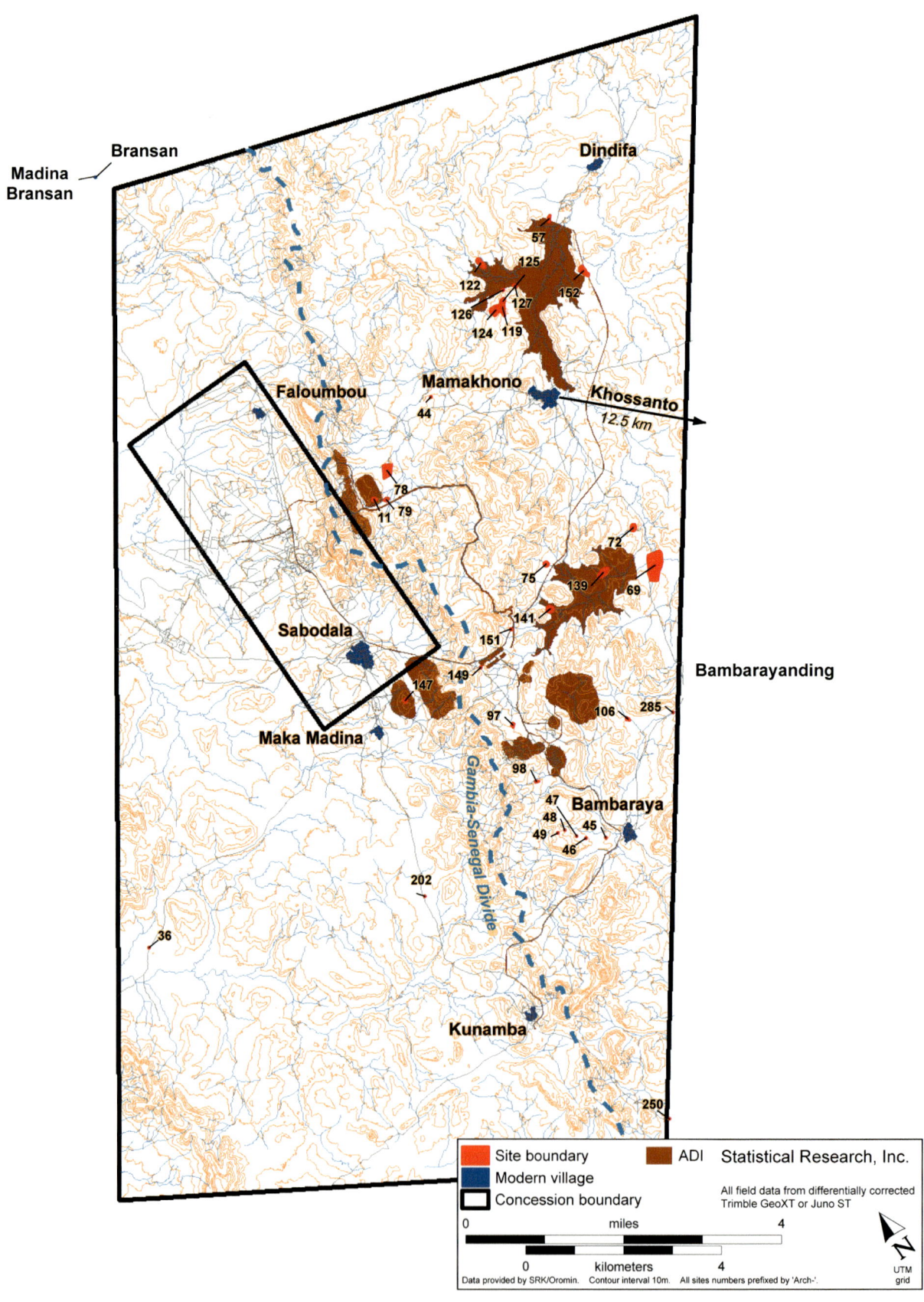

Figure 5.14. Map of the farmsteads discovered during the surveys.

Site 11

Location in concession: Site 11 is located in Masato, to the south of the broad plateau upon which Site 8 is located.

Topographic setting: A low-lying first terrace adjacent to narrow floodplains.

Vegetation: Open bush, with dense stands of bamboo immediately around.

Hydrology: Stream courses in a narrow floodplain are immediately adjacent.

Modern disturbances: A modern track used for mining exploration passes very nearby but has not impacted the site. No other impacts are noted.

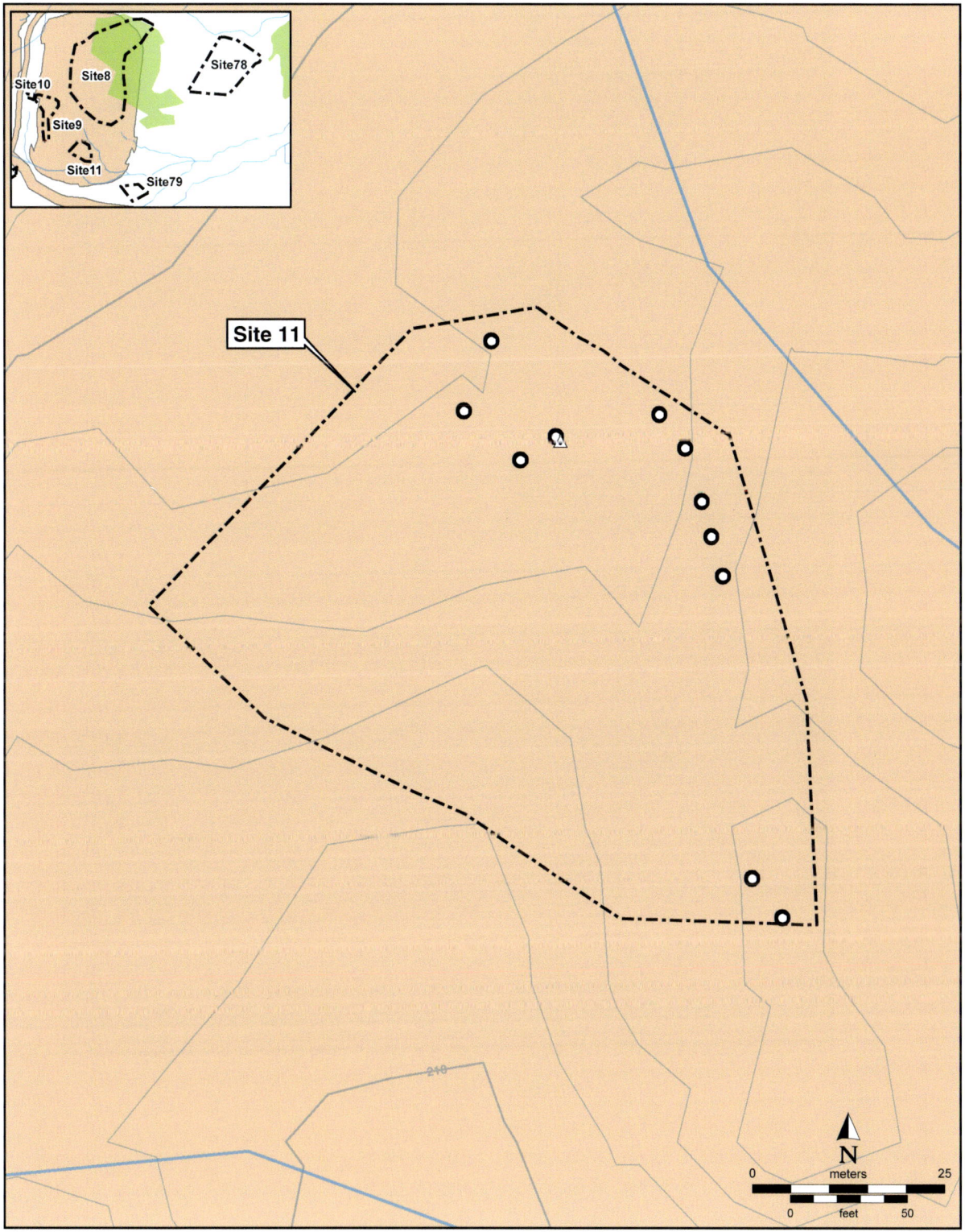

FIGURE 5.15. GIS-GENERATED MAP OF SITE 11.

Figure 5.16. Feature 1 at Site 11.

Figure 5.17. Feature 2 at Site 11.

Site description: Site 11 consists of an elongated cluster of eight stone circles, with an additional three located about 50 m from the main cluster. The features appear in good condition, but nothing is known about the depth of deposits that may be present. The features are all stone circles and are 3–4 m in diameter, several with considerable quantities of burned daub, suggestive of residences.

Artifacts: The collection of artifacts includes quantities of ceramics dominated by slip and tw6 motifs. The rim

FIGURE 5.18. FEATURE 4 AT SITE 11.

assemblage includes only one long-neck jar (E7; see Chapter 6 and Appendix D), which suggests a possible recent-historical-period site.

Site interpretation: Site 11 is interpreted as a farmstead. It is likely part of the larger Masato polity complex but is otherwise a typical example.

Site 11 lies in a low, flat levee between two ephemeral, seasonal streams in the valley south of the major Polity Center of Masato (Figure 5.15 shows Site 11 in association with Sites 8, 9, and 79). The site is relatively small (ca. 1,700 m²) and opens to the southwest, whereas the polity center on the nearby terrace faces exactly the opposite direction. Although the general area has witnessed substantial alterations from mine-exploration activities, Site 11 (and nearby Site 79) has been bypassed by these activities, and site and feature integrity is very good.

The site consists of a surface artifact scatter composed of ceramics and 11 stone circles or hut foundations (Figures 5.16–5.19), such as Feature 8, shown in Figure 5.19.

Like the two nearby farmsteads, Sites 78 and 79 (see below), Site 11 is interpreted as part of the Masato polity complex. Unlike with the polity center, which we believe was for defensive purposes (see below), the key determinant in the location of the farmsteads appears to be proximity to good agricultural land. Although speculative, it seems reasonable to infer that residents of farmsteads may have also had residences within the polity center to which they retreated when the polity was under attack.

FIGURE 5.19. FEATURE 8 AT SITE 11.

Site 78

Location in concession: Site 78 is located to the east of Site 8, in Masato, on the lower slopes of the same plateau, which descends steadily to the east.

Topographic setting: The slightly sloping lower reaches of the plateau, immediately above and adjacent to lower-lying floodplains.

Vegetation: Bush, with occasional stands of bamboo and open grassland nearby.

Hydrology: Watercourses are visible and adjacent to the east and southeast.

Modern disturbances: None.

Site description: Site 78 consists of 12 stone features—4 stone circles and 8 rock alignments—that appear to be the bases for walls or other longer, linear structures. The features appear in good condition, but nothing is known about the depth of deposits that may be present.

Artifacts: Artifacts are sparse. The collection is dominated by simple vessels, long-neck jars, and nondecorated followed by slipped vessels, which suggests a recent-historical-period site.

Site interpretation: Site 78 is interpreted as a farmstead. It is likely to be part of the larger Masato polity complex but is otherwise a typical example.

Located in the valley below the polity center at Masato, Site 78 lies on an elevated terrace overlooking ephemeral streams to the north and east. Surface visibility was excellent during fieldwork, and site integrity appears to be very good, with no disturbances noted.

Facing northeast on sloping terrain, the farmstead consists of a dozen stone features distributed over 32,600 m². Four features are circles that appear to be the remnants of huts, based on their diameters (3+ m) and associated artifacts, especially the ceramics. The remaining eight features are stone alignments that could be walls of structures but are more likely agricultural terraces used to channel runoff and to accumulate sediment for gardens.

Site 79

Location in concession: Site 79 is located southeast of Site 11 and south of Site 8, in Masato.

Topographic setting: First terrace adjacent to lower-lying floodplains.

Vegetation: Open wood/bush, with dense stands of bamboo nearby.

Hydrology: Stream courses are nearby, in the floodplain.

Modern disturbances: None.

Site description: The site is located in open bush vegetation, with some clusters of bamboo that had been burned, but not recently. The site overlooks a lower floodplain, but this has not been used for agriculture for a considerable length of time, judging by the size and density of the bush. The features appear in good condition, but nothing is known about the depth of deposits that may be present.

Figure 5.20. Feature 1 at Site 147.

Artifacts: Artifacts are sparse. The collection is dominated by simple vessels that are generally either plain or slipped, which suggests a recent site.

Site interpretation: Site 79 is interpreted as a farmstead. It is likely to be part of the larger Masato polity complex but is otherwise a typical example.

Site 79 is less than 200 m east of Site 11 and about 700 m south of Site 78. It lies in the same broad alluvial valley as Site 78, and like its northerly neighbor, Site 79 is situated on a terrace facing down the valley (to the northeast) and overlooking ephemeral/seasonal streams to the north and east. The site is open and unprotected.

Site 147

Location in concession: Site 147 is located in the center of the OJVG concession, south of Sabodala and east of the mining exploration camp, in the area known as Niakifiri West.

Topographic setting: An east-west ridge on the upper slopes of the same hill where Site 1 (an ideological/sacred site) is located.

Vegetation: Field relatively recently reverted to wooded bush.

Hydrology: The nearest watercourses are a few hundred meters to the south.

Modern disturbances: None, although mining exploration has occurred less than 100 m to the north.

Site description: Site 147 consists of eight stone circles, in no apparent order. The features appear to be in good condition, but nothing is known about the depth of deposits that may be present. The site is in open low bush (ergo, probably cleared in the last few years but now reverting to bush), on thin soils overlying laterite. The stone circles are smaller (<3 m in diameter) than many that are interpreted as residences but are undisturbed by modern activity.

Artifacts: The sparse artifact collection includes large numbers of nondecorated vessels that are organic tempered, suggesting a recent, seasonal occupation.

Site interpretation: Site 147 is interpreted as a farmstead, although it is in an unusual topographic position, located at a higher elevation and at a greater distance from water than most farmsteads.

Site 147 is located in the hills that form the divide between the Senegal and Gambia River drainages. Its location is unusual for a farmstead: high elevation, relatively far from water, on slopes ranging from flat to 9°. The site has good, but not excellent, integrity, with postdepositional influences from tree growth evident among the features. Site visibility was decent, but twigs and leaves obscured some of the surface (Figures 5.20 and 5.21)

Site 147 is a larger farmstead composed of eight stone circles on a ridge northeast of Site 1 (Figure 5.22). Site 1, which is described below, consists of about 40 cupules. How the two sites are related, if at all, is unknown. The stone circles at Site 147 follow the contour along the side of the hill but are not otherwise placed in any

Figure 5.21. Feature 8 at Site 147.

apparent order. The features consist of stone circles whose morphology and associated artifacts suggest some domestic use, but perhaps not of great intensity or long duration. The surface collection at Site 147 is largely dominated by nondecorated vessels, suggesting a recent-historical-period occupation.

Although the site is classified as a farmstead because of the number of stone circles, it is not at all clear that the site functioned as a residential locus. It is possible that Site 147 is tied to Site 1, with both playing different parts in a ritual. Alternatively, Site 147 may have been a favored agricultural or resource-processing site that was returned to, time and again. Beyond Site 1, the three closest sites to Site 147 are all field houses.

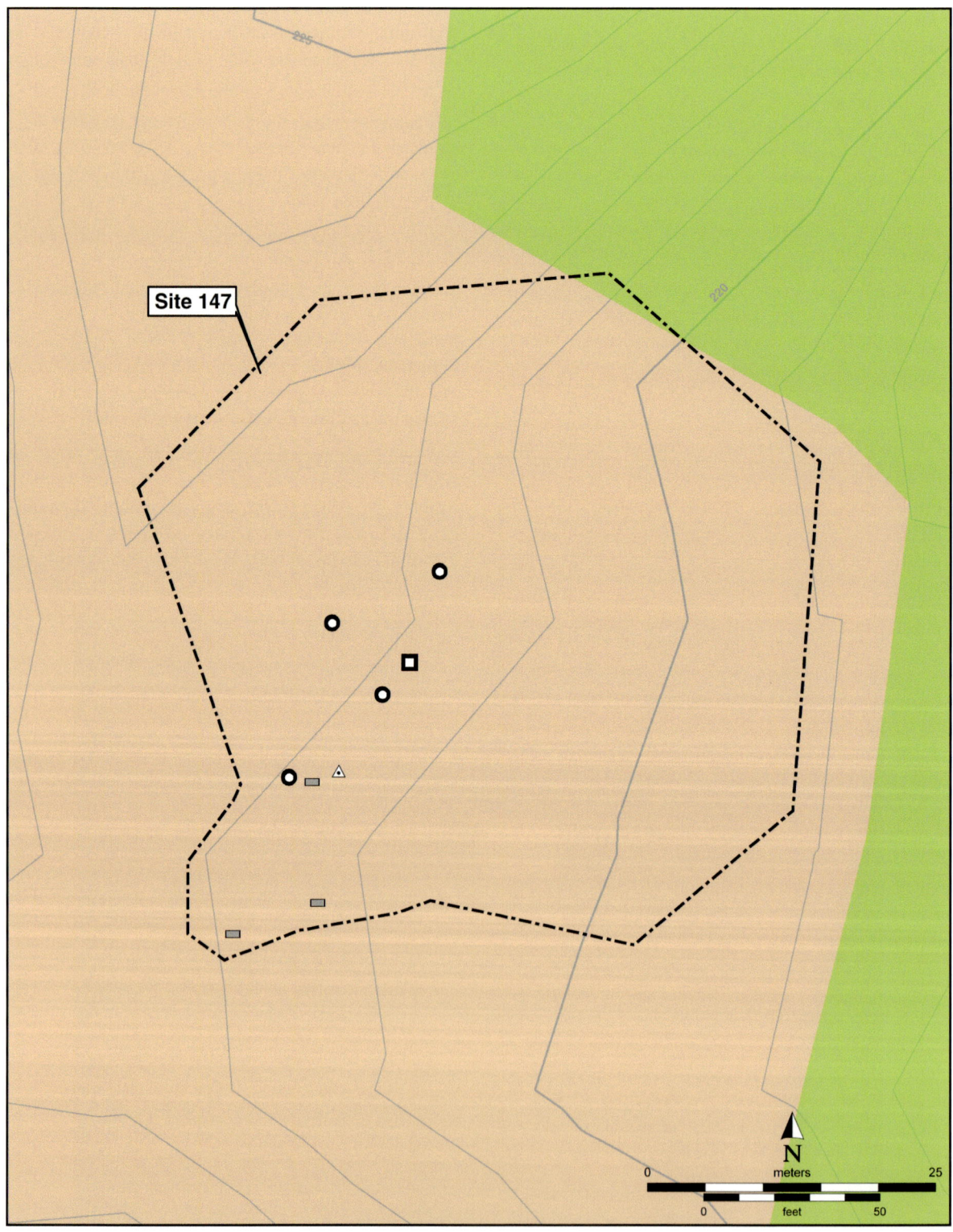

FIGURE 5.22. GIS-GENERATED MAP OF SITE 147.

Site 149

Location in concession: Site 149 is located in the area of the proposed processing plant, near the center of the concession.

Topographic setting: A broad, slightly sloping second to third Pleistocene terrace adjacent to a floodplain to the south.

Vegetation: Sparse, open bush.

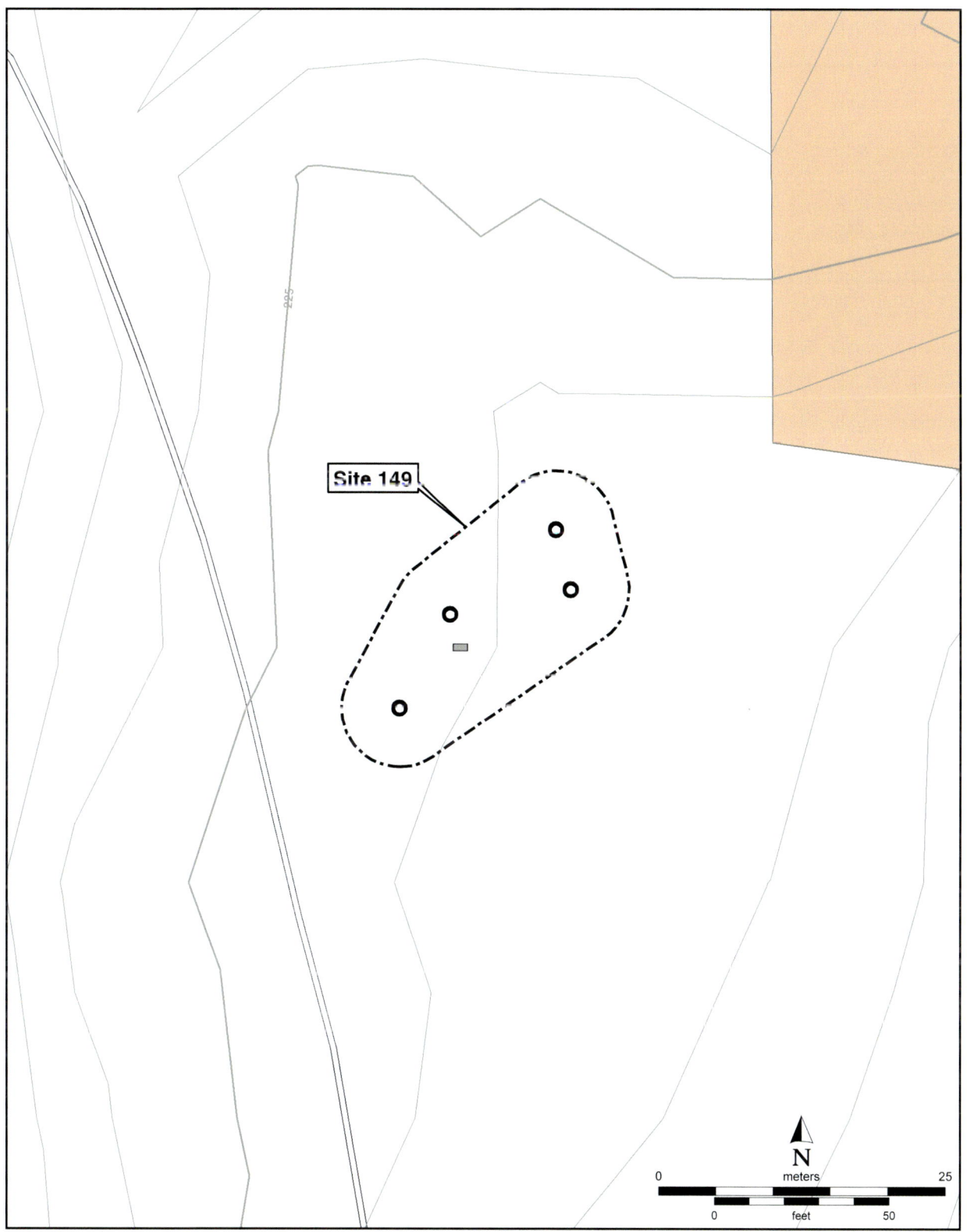

FIGURE 5.23. GIS-GENERATED MAP OF SITE 149.

Hydrology: Ravine to the north.

Modern disturbances: The site is adjacent to a modern road, in the location of a proposed processing plant.

Site description: The site consists of five stone circles (three with quantities of daub). One circle has a substantially complete ceramic bowl buried in the floor of rammed earth. The features appear in good condition, but nothing is known about the depth of deposits that may be present.

Artifacts: Artifacts are sparse. The collection includes pottery that is largely nondecorated. This site also yielded ground stone fragments and tuyere fragments, suggesting metalwork activities.

Site interpretation: The site is interpreted as a farmstead but is on the lower end of the size limit for a farm.

Located on the western edge of a narrow alluvial valley, Site 149 is a small farmstead (covering about 0.4 ha) (Figure 5.23). The site is situated about 1,500 m northeast of Site 147, near the southwest corner of the proposed processing plant. The features at the site are all in good condition. A modern road lies immediately west of the site.

The site consists of four stone-circle features and a scatter of surface artifacts (Figures 5.24–5.29). Features and artifacts are concentrated in a relatively small area; fields, if they existed, would most likely lie to the east of the site. With the exception of Feature 3, the stone circles are generally small (see Figures 5.24 and 5.25). Due to its size, Feature 3 was excavated, revealing an inverted whole vessel (an open bowl with an everted rim that is morphologically likely to date to the late-nineteenth or twentieth century) buried within the rammed-earth floor (this seemed to be the surrounding soil, rammed hard and flat through usage, not a floor constructed of imported materials, which was in good, undisturbed condition) (see Figures 5.24 and 5.28). Feature 3 is interpreted as the remains of a hut, based on its size (nearly 4 m in diameter) and the buried bowl, although artifacts generally on the site were relatively few, consisting only of a small collection of ceramics.

Site 151

Location in concession: The site is in the center of the concession, in the area of Kerekounda, along the proposed haul road from the processing plant to Mamakhono.

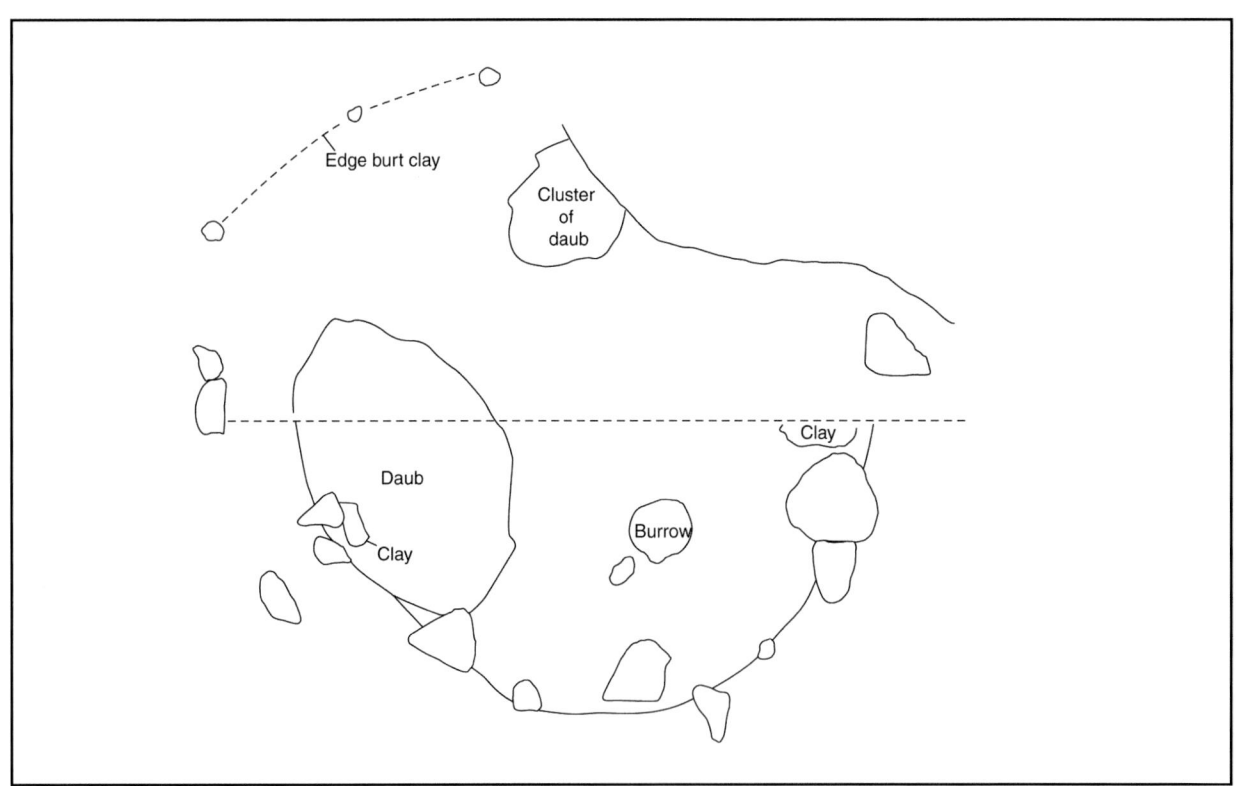

Figure 5.24. Map of Feature 3 at Site 149.

Archaeological Survey and Test-Excavation Results

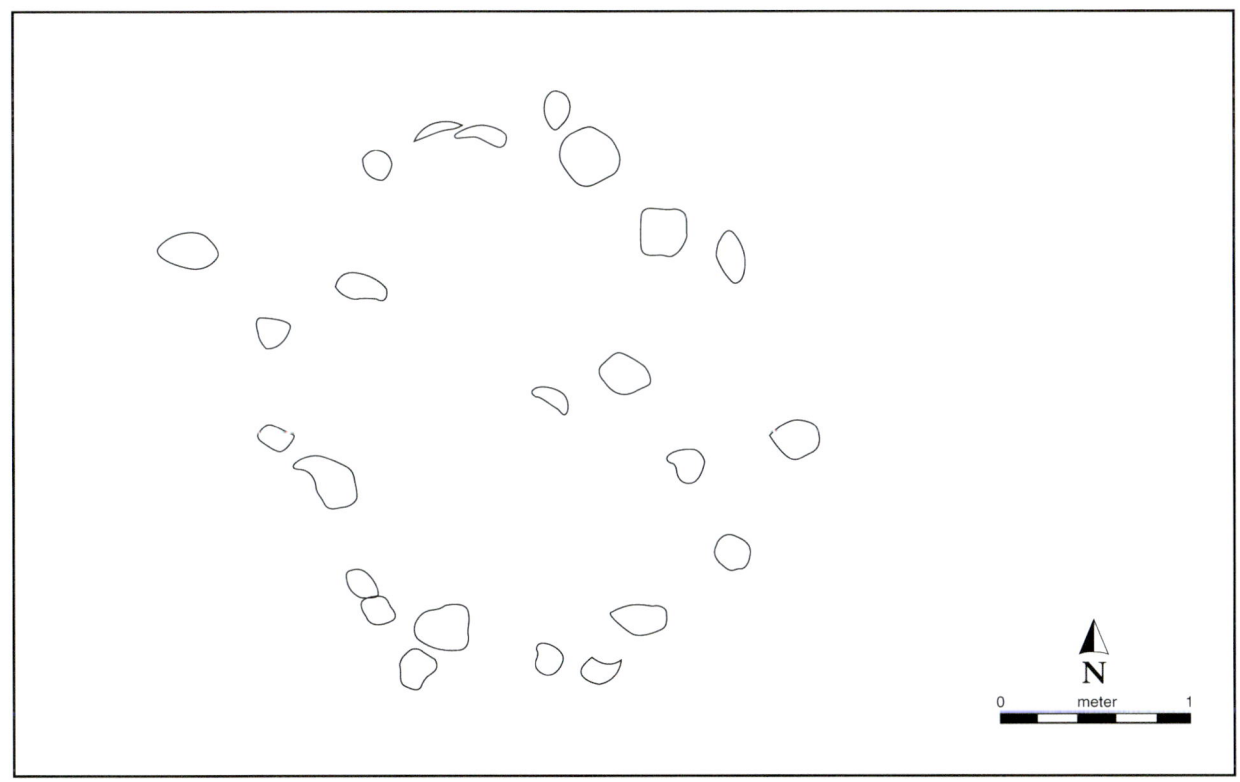

Figure 5.25. Map of Feature 2 at Site 149.

Figure 5.26. Feature 2 at Site 149.

Figure 5.27. Feature 4 at Site 149.

Figure 5.28. Feature 3 under excavation. Note buried inverted pottery vessel to right of photo board.

Archaeological Survey and Test-Excavation Results

Figure 5.29. Feature 5 at Site 149.

Topographic setting: A first-terrace rise between two ravines, with a floodplain adjacent.

Vegetation: Open bush-grassland with few trees.

Hydrology: Ravines to the east and west carry water seasonally.

Modern disturbances: None.

Site description: Site 151 consists of six stone circles, one of which has quantities of daub, not apparently placed in any order or pattern, and a scatter of ceramics. The features appear in good condition, but nothing is known about the depth or integrity of deposits that may be present.

Artifacts: The artifacts are sparse and fragmentary ceramics. Chronology is uncertain.

Site interpretation: The site is interpreted as a farmstead. It is in a common topographic location that is characteristic of farmsteads, generally.

Site 151 is located on the proposed road between the processing plant and the dam site, just before it intersects with the haul road to Masato (Figure 5.30). The site lies in the middle of the same alluvial drainage as Site 149, which is located about 1,000 m to the southwest. The setting is open brush, and currently, site integrity is high.

No other sites were found nearby, probably a function of the linear nature of the survey. We suspect there are other agricultural and residential sites nearby that utilize the drainages of the ephemeral/seasonal streams.

The site is small, only 600 m². Within this area, we found six stone circles dispersed among a scatter of ceramics (Figures 5.31 and 5.32). The stone circles are of the size of modern huts and are interpreted as the remains of residential structures. Daub was associated with one feature and may have formed as the result of accidental burning after the structure was no longer in use.

Figures 5.30 and 5.31 show Features 5 and 2 (both stone circles) at Site 151.

Hamlets and Villages

Several extended families may have lived together in hamlets of 50–100 inhabitants (ca. 10–25 stone features). Hamlets tend to be year-round settlements. Those with access to particularly good agricultural lands and strong leadership may become villages, whereas those that command only marginal lands are probably abandoned within a generation. Hamlets would be expected to have a variety of stone features and a greater density and diversity of artifacts, particularly ceramics, representing the intensity and variety of activities.

A Slave Who Would Be King

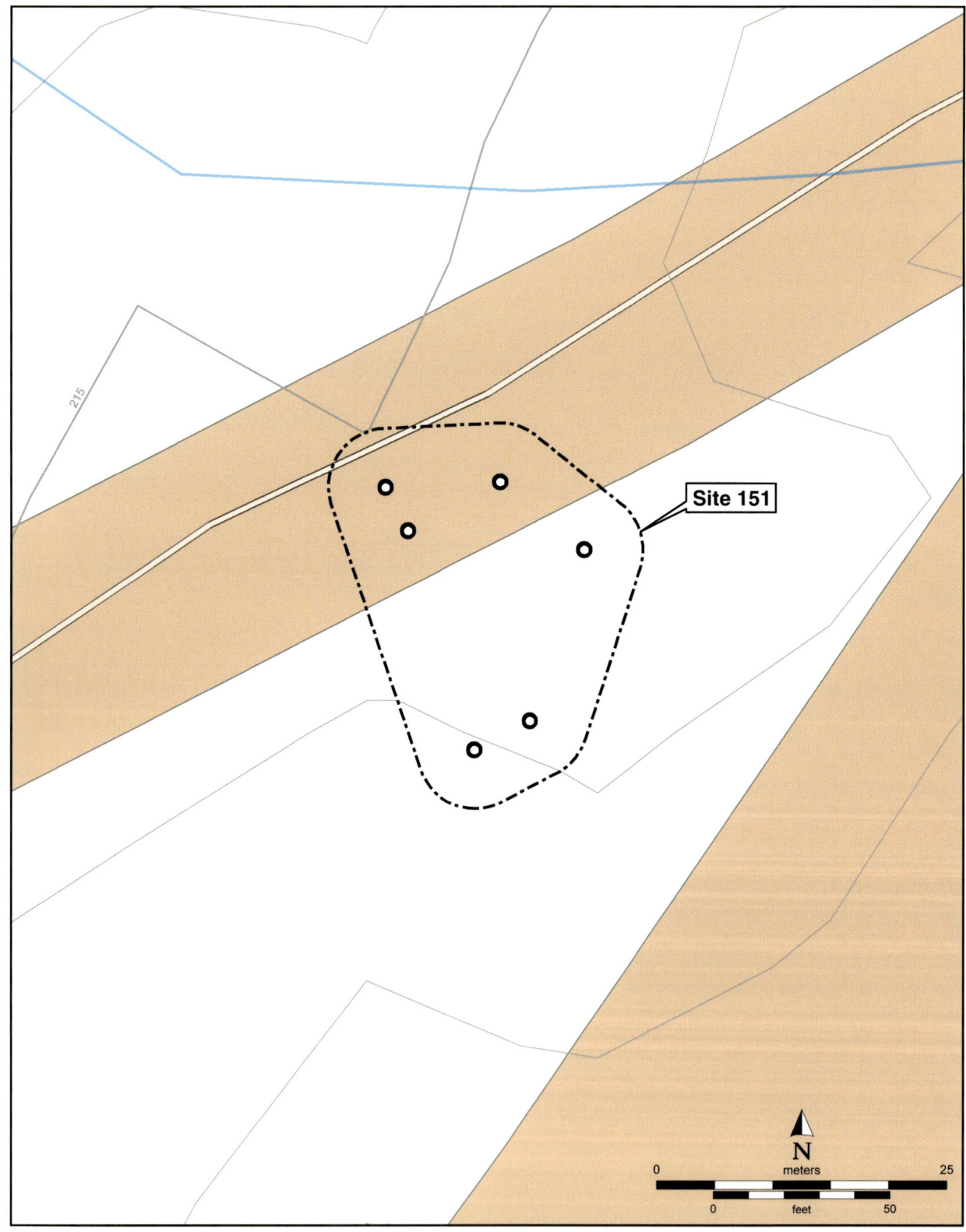

Figure 5.30. GIS-generated map of Site 151.

Archaeological Survey and Test-Excavation Results

Figure 5.31. Feature 2 at Site 151.

Figure 5.32. Feature 6 at Site 151.

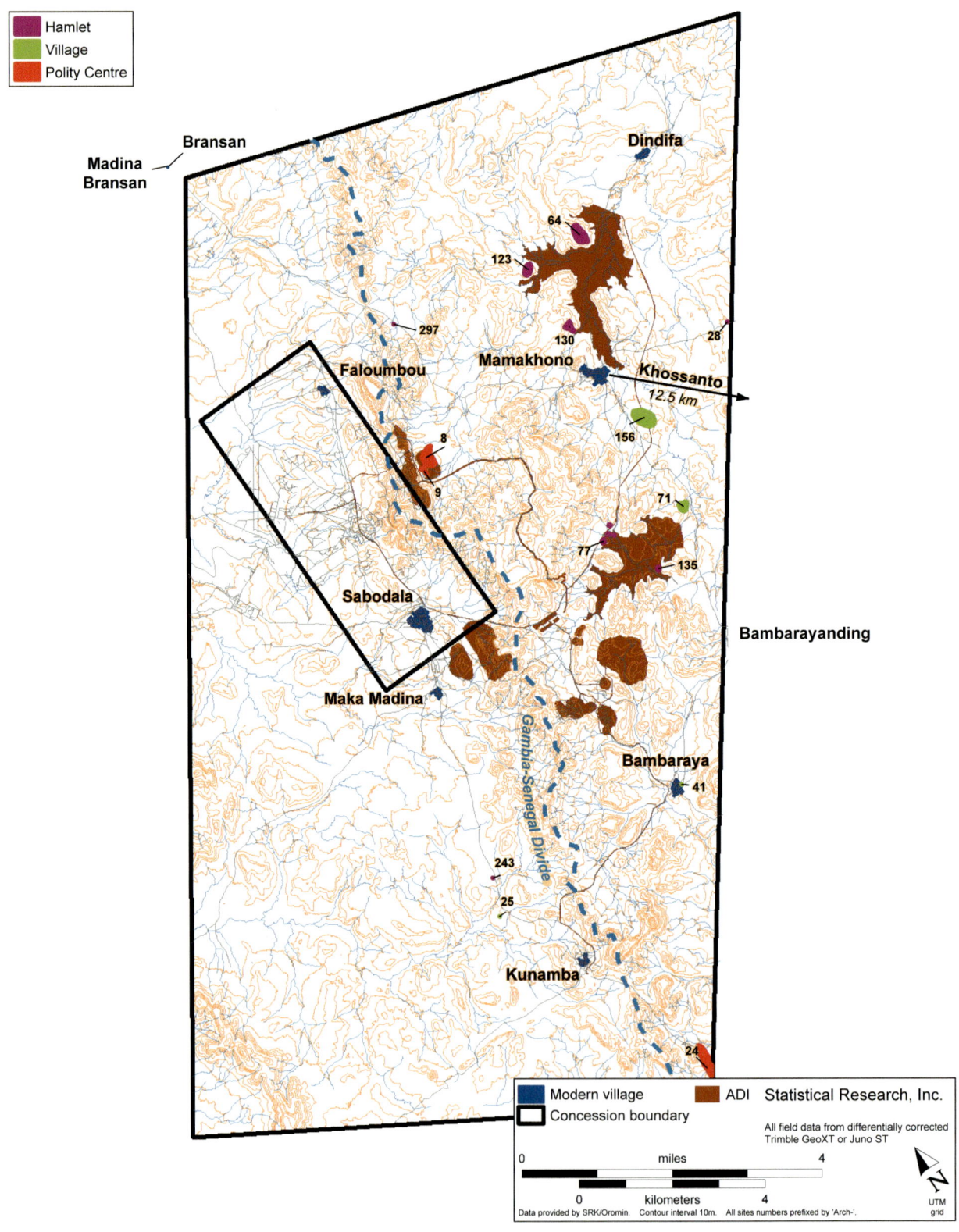

Figure 5.33. Map of all hamlets, villages, and polity centers in the OJVG concession.

With populations numbering in the hundreds and a diversity of economic and social activities, villages are hubs of sociopolitical power for ruling lineages who have subjugated other lineages and disenfranchised individuals. Village sites may contain more than 50 stone features that probably represent house foundations, storage facilities, menstrual huts, unmarried-men's clubs or houses, and so on. Village sites exhibit strong site structure, with different areas of the site characterized by different feature types and with concentrations of features differentially distributed across the site. The artifact assemblages at villages are larger and more diverse and are more likely to include materials imported from some distance, including European trade goods.

We found seven hamlets and five villages in the OJVG concession (4 percent and 2 percent of the total number of sites, respectively). Figure 5.33 shows the hamlets, villages, and polity centers (see below) discovered in the surveys. Hamlets and villages were found at similar elevations that were substantially lower than those of resource-processing sites and much less variable than either field houses or farmsteads. Hamlets and villages also are found on flatter land than were these site types. Interestingly, hamlets and villages are found farther from water than resource-processing sites, field houses, or farmsteads. Archaeological hamlets and villages are also farther from water than modern villages, although they are quite similar to modern villages in other environmental characteristics.

Detailed site maps were created for one hamlet (Site 77 and its outlier, Site 153) and two villages (Sites 71 and 156). Site descriptions for these sites and several other examples are provided below.

Hamlets (Example Site 77, with Site 153, and Site 130)

Site 77, with 153

Location in concession: Site 77 has been divided into three loci (a–c), and to these should be added Site 153, to define one hamlet. Sites 77 and 153 were discovered during different surveys and were recorded as separate sites, but Site 153 is quite close to 77a (the 'a' used to identify the westernmost locus of the site), and the sites are known to have functioned as one community in the recent past.

Topographic setting: A first terrace, with rising ground to the north and floodplains adjacent to the south. Ravines separate the three loci.

Vegetation: Open bush-grassland.

Hydrology: The ravines and floodplain carry water seasonally.

Modern disturbances: The site is bisected by a footpath track that has damaged a few features.

Site description: Sites 77 (a–c) and 153 consist of at least 36 stone circles, about a third of which have quantities of daub. The stone circles are not placed in any apparent order or pattern. A scatter of ceramics is found amongst the stone circles. The features appear in good condition (excepting those crossed by the footpath), but nothing is known about the depth or integrity of deposits that may be present.

Artifacts: For such a recently abandoned settlement, the ceramics are dominated by nondecorated and slipped vessels with amounts of organic material, which confirms the recent character of the occupation. The collection includes glass bottles, probably pharmaceutical, supporting the recent character of the site.

Site interpretation: The site is known from the recent past as the hamlet of Kerekounda. There are former residents from the last phase of occupation (when the settlement originated is not known) who could be consulted to shed light upon function and nature. This direct link makes the site much more important than might otherwise be the case. From a strictly archaeological perspective, the site would probably be interpreted as two large farmsteads with some outlying field houses, but the local informant (Sekho Cissokho) reported that the different loci were family- or lineage-based residential compounds (albeit all were apparently Cissokho), with some other families also present.

Site 77, and its adjacent outlier 153, is possibly the most recent archaeological site that we recorded (Figure 5.34). The surveyors spoke to Sekho Cissokho, whose father was the *propriétaire* for this hamlet, which he called Kerekounda. The hamlet was not abandoned until the later 1990s. Cissokho identified the main part of the hamlet at the westward end of the area, where there are scattered ceramics, with a subsidiary cluster of buildings to the northeast and a handful of field houses in the lower floodplain to the southeast. The occupation areas are on first-terrace levees, with Site 153 and the majority of Site 77 features to the west and two much smaller clusters of features in the central and eastern parts of the site.

The stone features are consistent in size and shape (Figures 5.35–5.40). All are circles measuring about 2 m in diameter that, based on ethnographic interviews, were foundations for huts. The daub found at the site represented burned huts, according to former residents. Artifacts included pottery and glass-bottle fragments.

Site 77/153 is located on the western edge of the Tailing Mine Facility near the modern village of Kerekounda. It represents a short-term attempt to develop a permanent habitation that was unsuccessful. The habitation areas are located on the eastern edge of a small toe slope formed from hills to the west. Field houses are distributed on the toe slope to the west of the hamlet. Based solely on

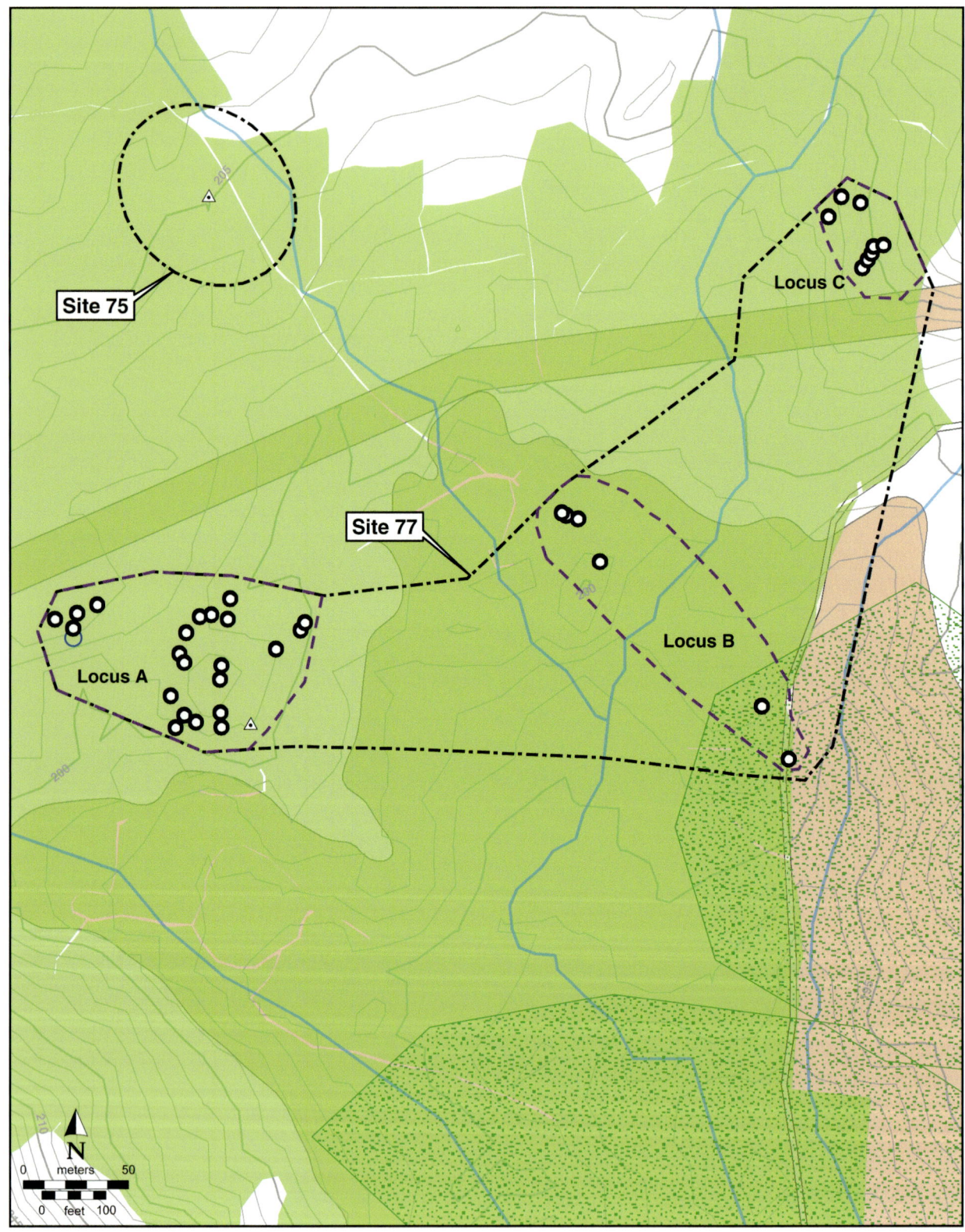

FIGURE 5.34. GIS-GENERATED MAP OF SITE 77 SHOWING THE THREE LOCI.

its topographic position, the site is located in a desirable place from which to pursue traditional agriculture. According to informants, these environmental features were the original draw to the location. Unfortunately for its residents, the fields were not as productive as anticipated.

Figures 5.35–5.40 show Features 1, 2, 3, and 5 at Site 77 and Features 1 and 2 at Site 153; all are typical stone circles.

Archaeological Survey and Test-Excavation Results

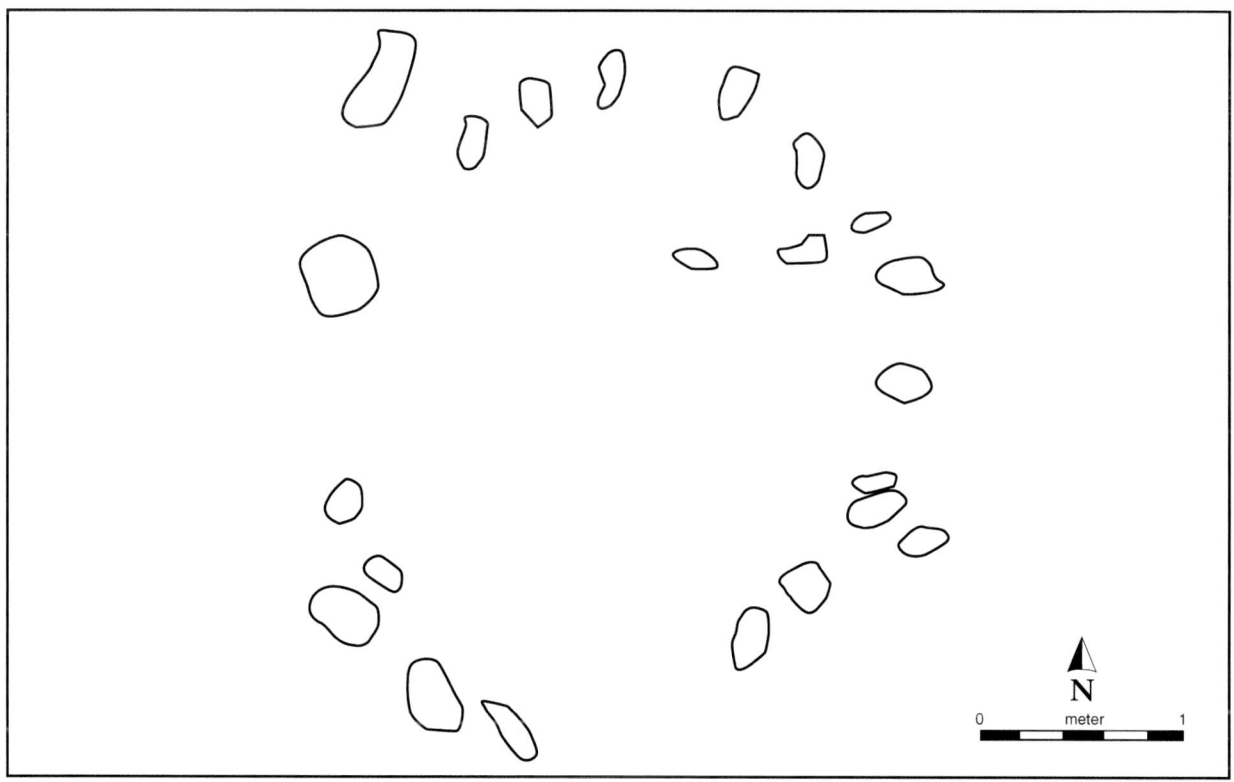

Figure 5.35. Feature 1 at Site 77.

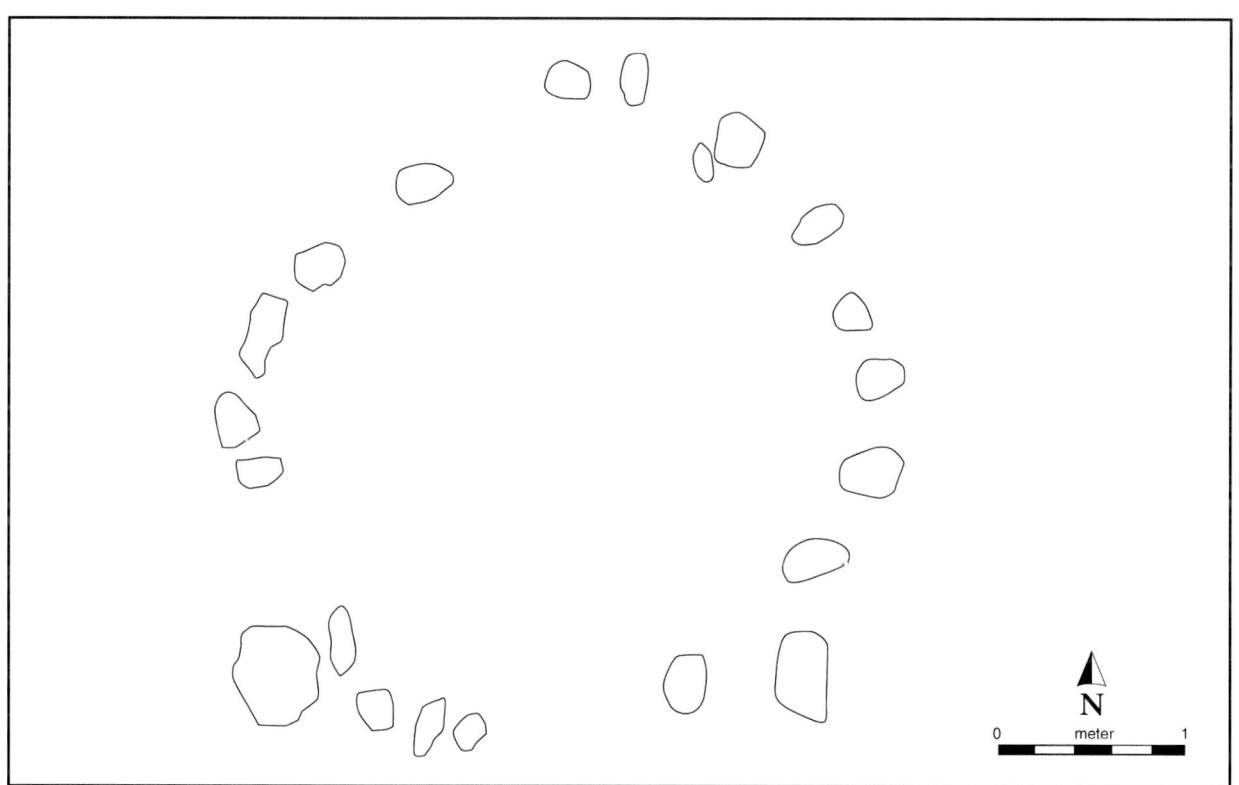

Figure 5.36. Feature 2 at Site 77.

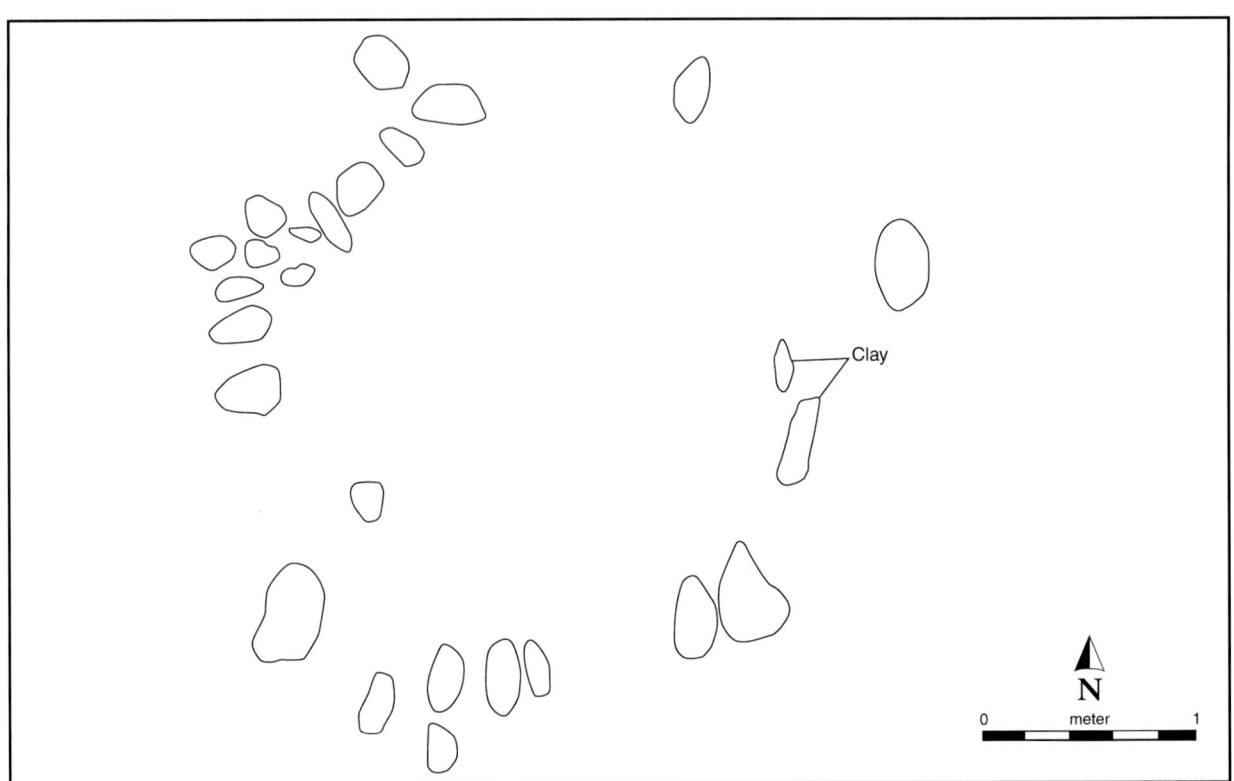

Figure 5.37. Feature 3 at Site 77.

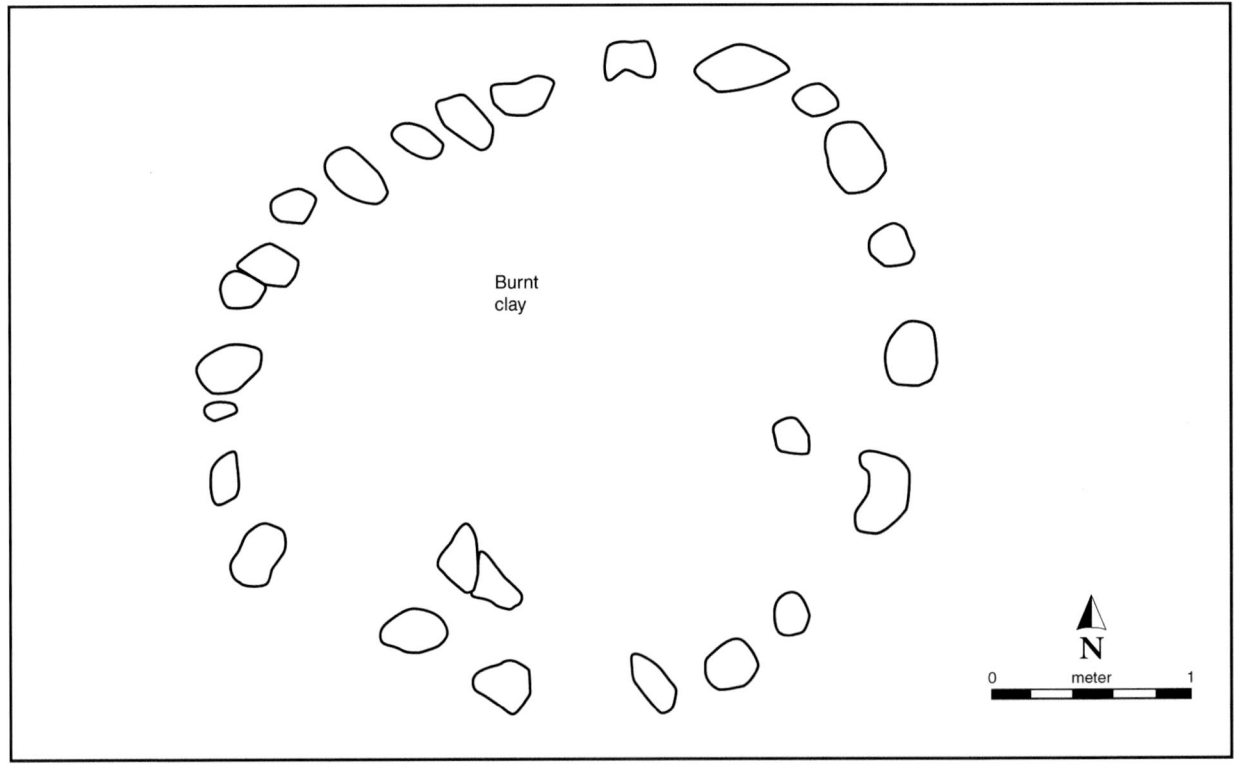

Figure 5.38. Feature 2 at Site 153.

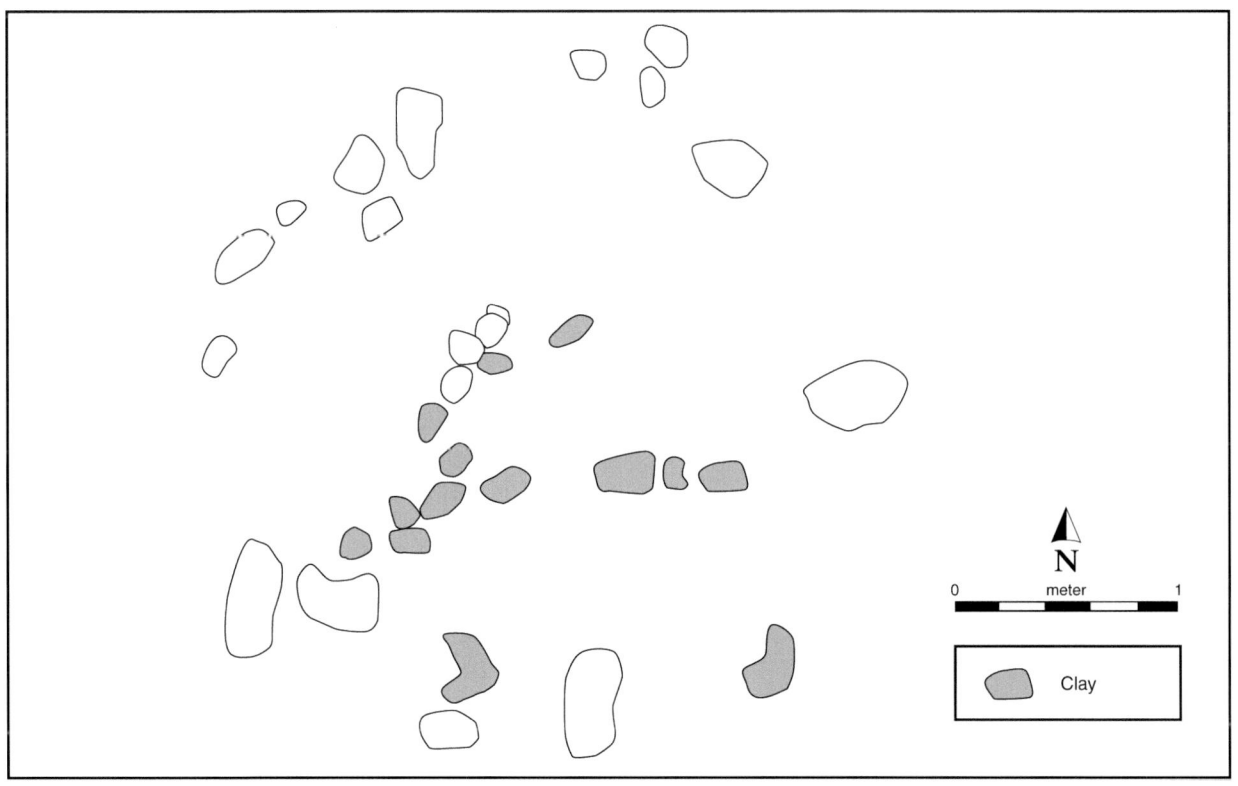

Figure 5.39. Feature 5 at Site 77.

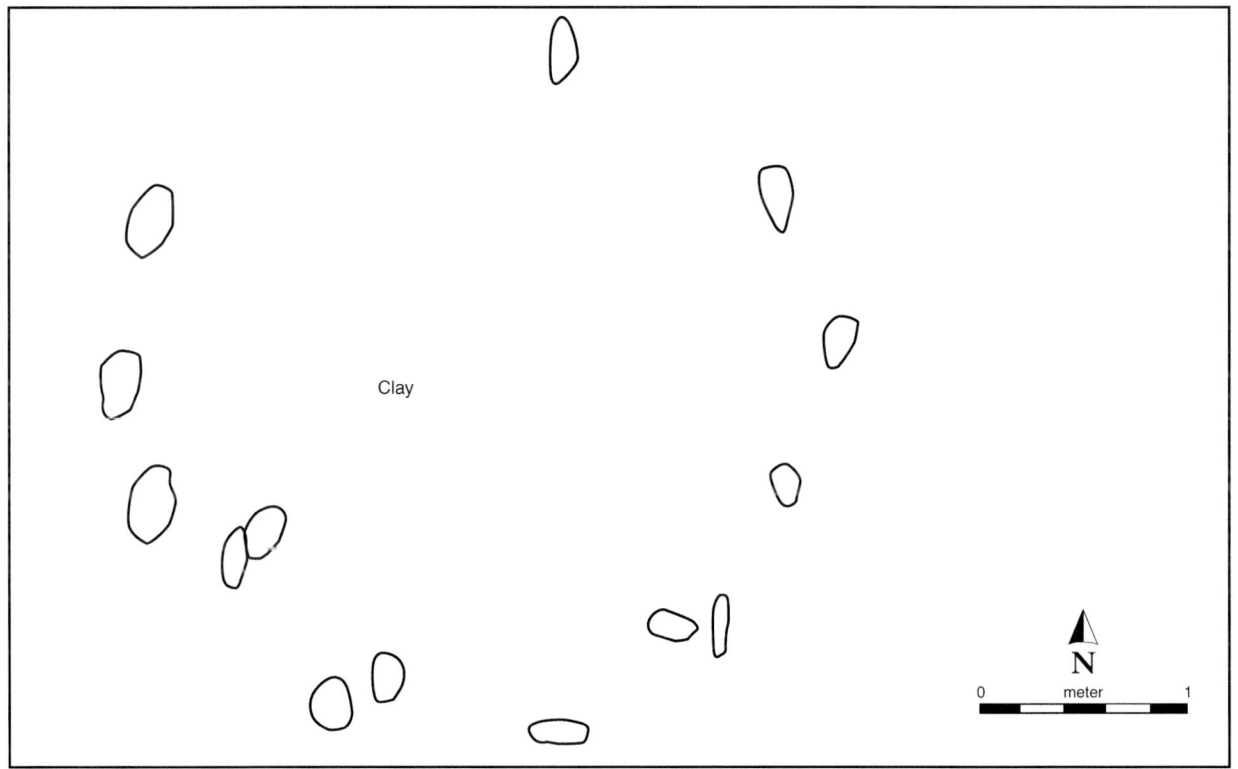

Figure 5.40. Feature 1 at Site 153.

Figures 5.41–5.44 show Feature 1 on Site 153 and various features recorded at the easternmost loci (locus C) of Site 77.

FIGURE 5.41. FEATURE 1 AT SITE 153.

FIGURE 5.42. MAPPING A FEATURE AT SITE 77.

ARCHAEOLOGICAL SURVEY AND TEST-EXCAVATION RESULTS

FIGURE 5.43. RECORDING A FEATURE AT SITE 77.

FIGURE 5.44. ARCHAEOLOGICAL FEATURE (SITE 77) WITH CURRENT FARMSTEAD IN BACKGROUND.

Site 130

Location in concession: Site 130 is located on the western periphery of the freshwater reservoir north of Mamakhono.

Topographic setting: A saddle between two laterite hills, equivalent to a second terrace. Not a defensible position.

Vegetation: Some bush trees and some dense stands of bamboo giving way to open laterite slopes to the east and west.

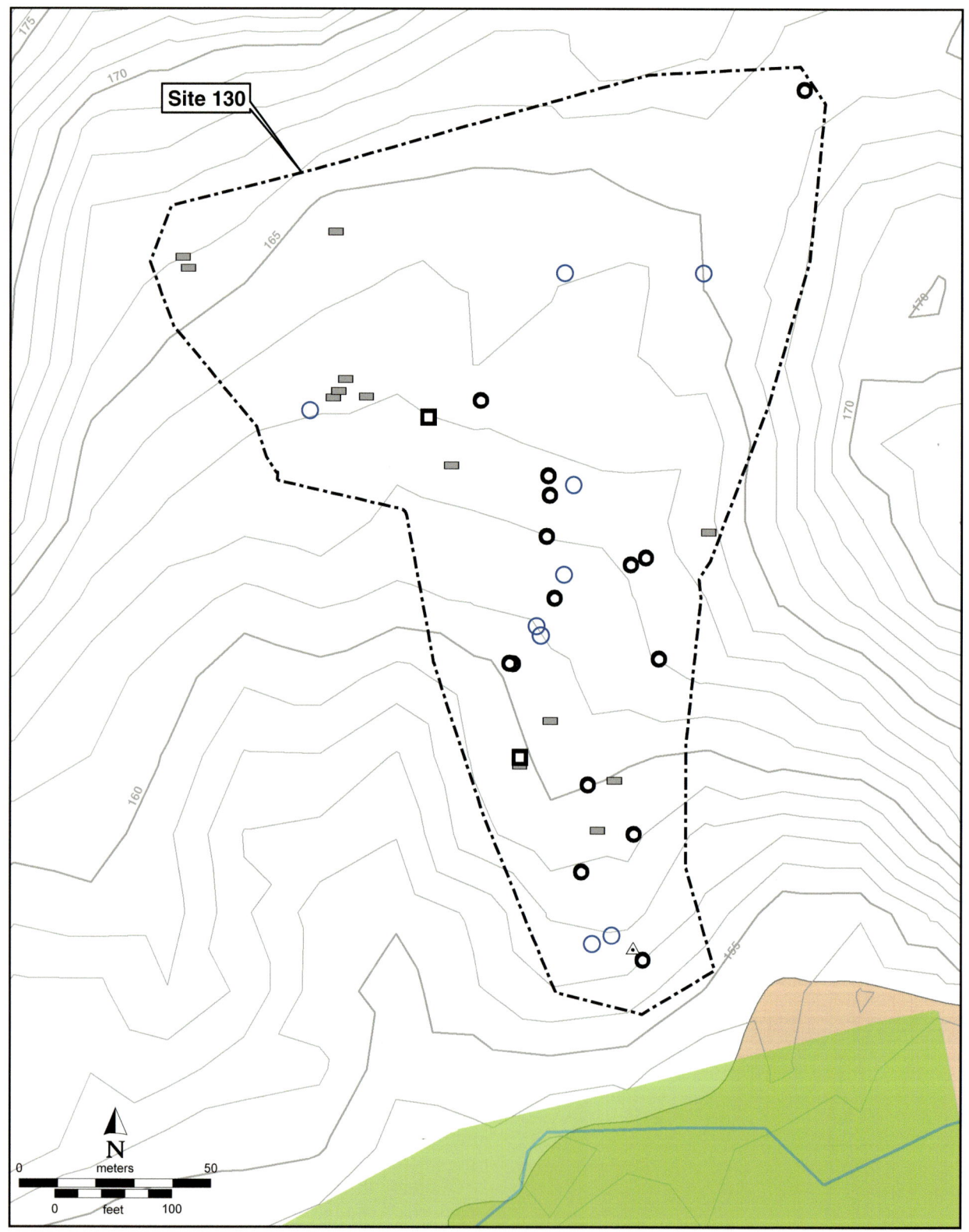

FIGURE 5.45. GIS-GENERATED MAP OF 130.

Hydrology: Above the floodplain to the east, with a ravine to the southwest.

Modern disturbances: None.

Site description: The site has about 30 stone features, of which about a dozen are stone circles and the remainder of which are a variety of squares/rectangles and alignments, the latter being more amorphous than is often the case. There is no apparent organization to the placement of the stone circles or other features. The features appear in good condition, but nothing is known about the depth or integrity of deposits that may be present.

Artifacts: There is an unusually sparse collection of ceramics, plus a very few fragments of ground stone.

Site interpretation: Site 130 is interpreted as a hamlet but has a smaller and more limited artifactual collection than seems normal, although the size and topographic position is common to the type.

Site 130 may be regarded as a typical hamlet in its structures, consisting of at least 30 stone features on a saddle between two laterite hills overlooking a floodplain to the east. The stone circles are apparently randomly scattered across the saddle, sometimes with 50–100 m between features (Figure 5.45), as seen on the site plan. In addition to stone circles, other stone features were identified. A number of square stone features that may have served as granaries or other types of storage facilities were encountered, as well as rock alignments composed of parallel lines of rock. The latter do not appear to be foundations for structures. Alternative functions could include burial markers, ramadas, or elevated storage platforms.

Only a few ceramics were found at the site, which is unusual for a habitation site. The ceramics are dominated by simple vessels—short, everted rims and a handful of collared rims. Although the pottery assemblage is relatively small, the diagnostic presence of collared rims could indicate a late-first- and early-second-millennium occupation, although the production of collared rims continued well after that period, and it is possible that the site dates later. There were a few fragments of ground stone milling querns, but these are smaller in quantity and diversity than at other sites (e.g., Site 71). There is no evidence of site disturbance or any postdepositional process that would account for the meager amount of surface artifacts. It is possible that the site was 'cleaned' when it was abandoned, with the residents taking their material possessions with them. The lack of broken material that would have been left behind suggests that the site was occupied for only a short time.

With hills flanking it to the east and west and lower-lying agricultural land on the floodplain to the south, Site 130 seems ideally placed for a hamlet. The site is relatively isolated, with the closest habitation (Site 123, a village) about 1,500 m to the north. Numerous field houses are found to the north, south, and east, areas that have been

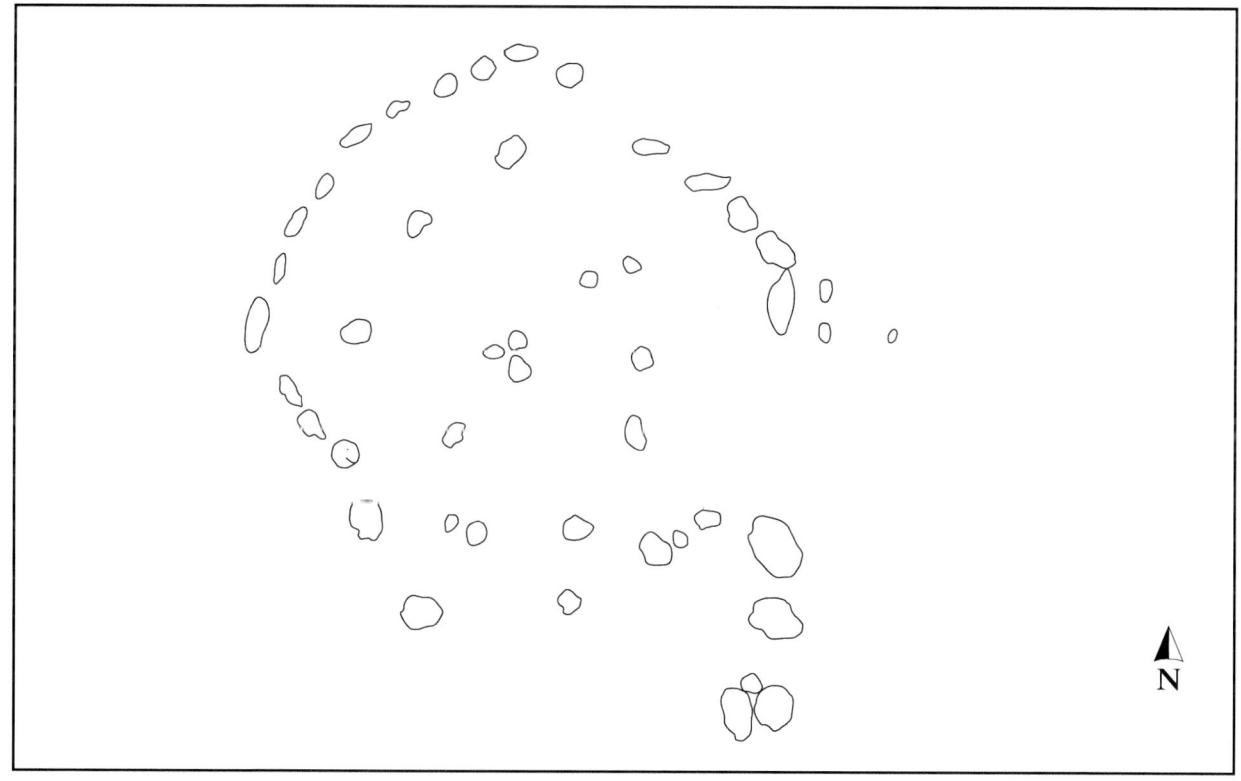

FIGURE 5.46. RECORD DRAWING OF FEATURE 6 AT SITE 130.

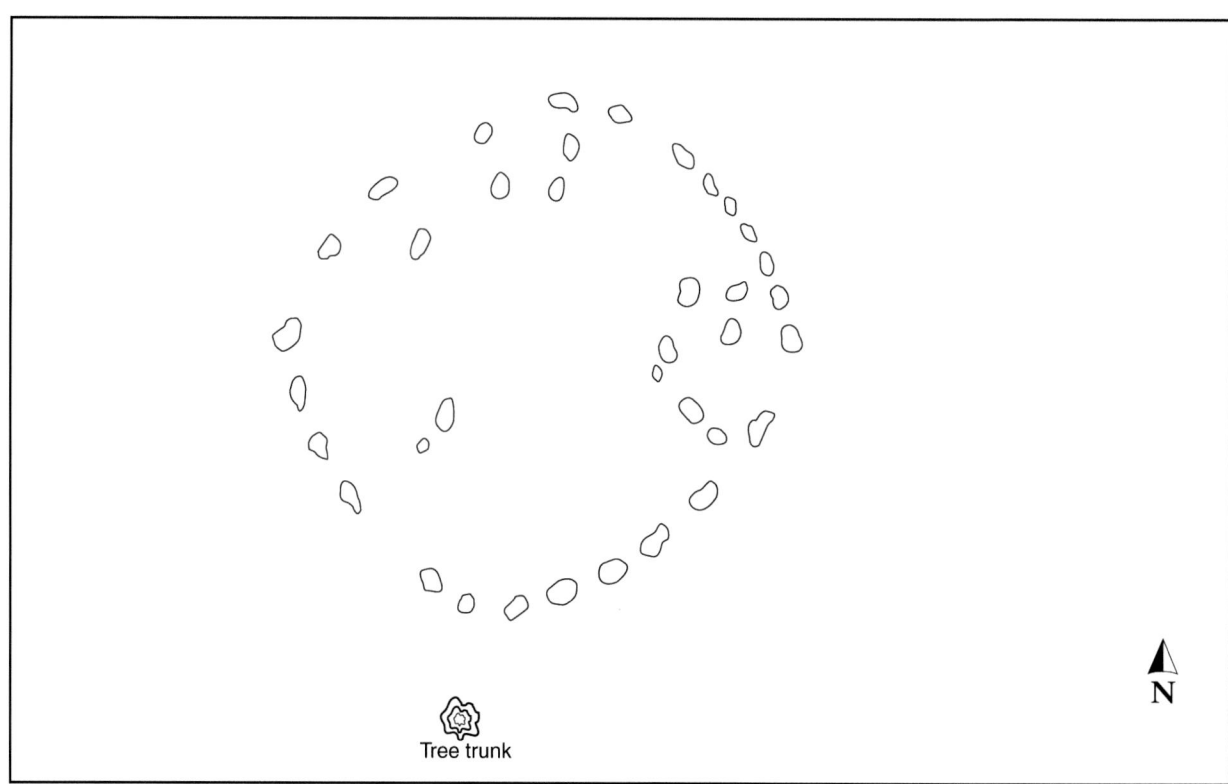

FIGURE 5.47. RECORD DRAWING OF FEATURE 111 AT SITE 130.

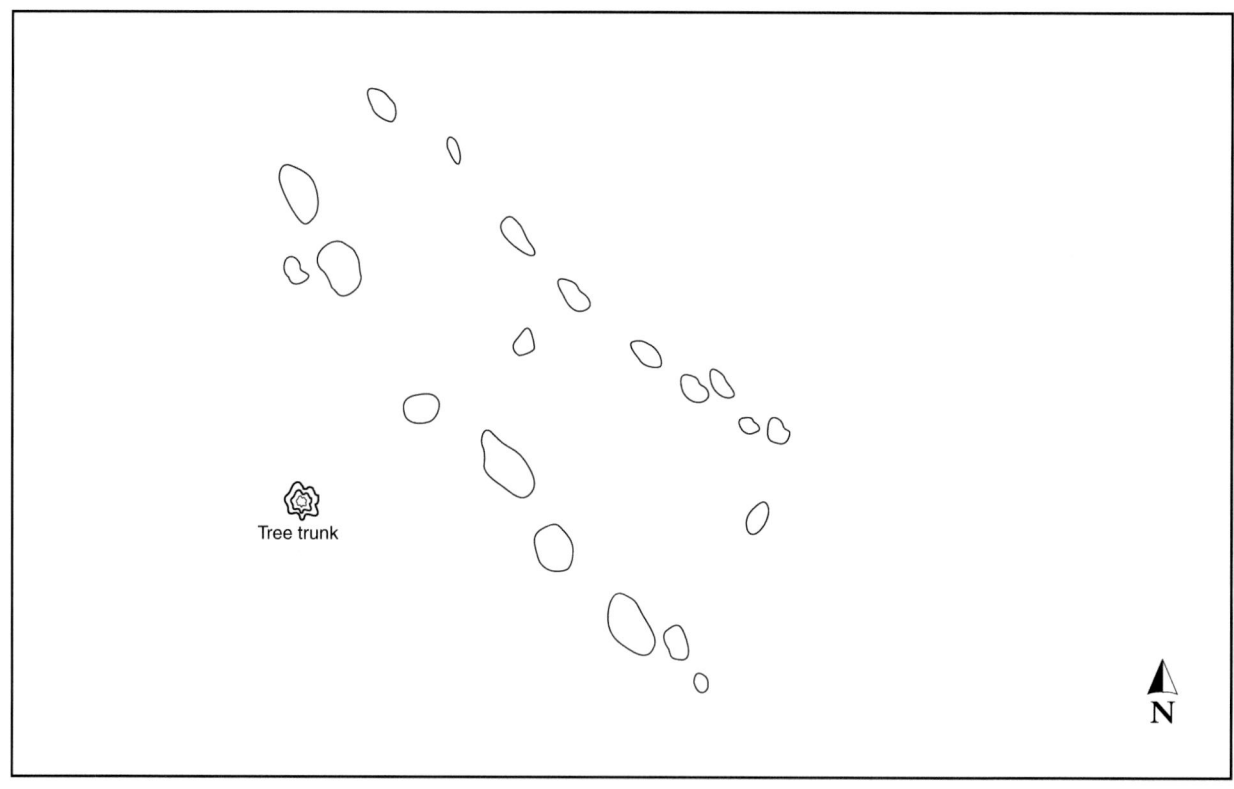

FIGURE 5.48. FEATURE 7 AT SITE 130, A ROCK ALIGNMENT.

surveyed. West of the site was not surveyed, although it, too, appears conducive to runoff agriculture.

Figures 5.46–5.49 show scaled plans of Features 6, 7, 12 and 111 at Site 130.

Figures 5.50–5.53 show Features 1, 6, 7, and 12 at Site 130.

Archaeological Survey and Test-Excavation Results

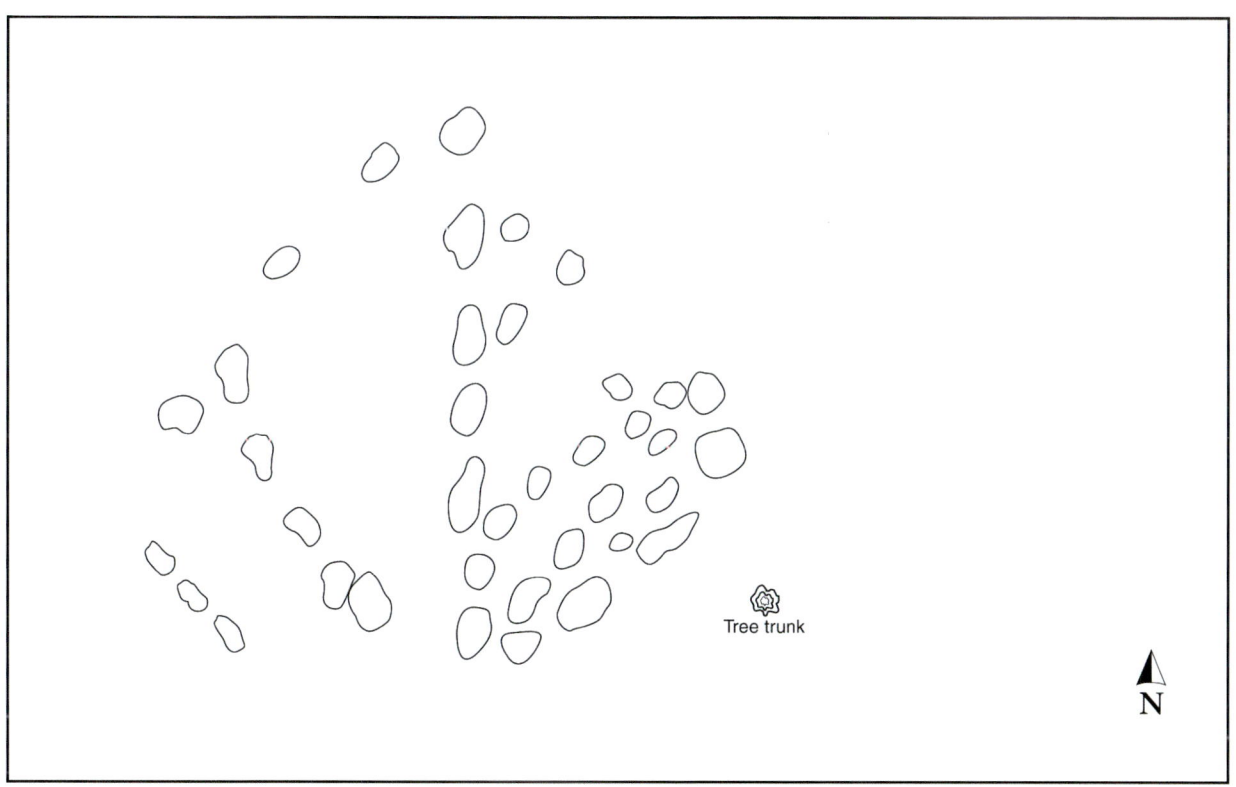

Figure 5.49. Feature 12 at Site 130.

Figure 5.50. Beginning mapping Feature 6 at Site 130, with the higher laterite hill to the east in the background.

Figure 5.51. Feature 7 at Site 130, subsquare.

Figure 5.52. Feature 1 at Site 130 prior to cleaning and recording.

Figure 5.53. Feature 12 at Site 130 prior to cleaning.

Villages (Example Sites 71, 123, and 156)

Site 71

Location in concession: Site 71 is located just east of the dam for the tailings-management facility.

Topographic setting: Site 71 is located on a shallowly sloping terrace plateau below a hill. The site is bisected by two ravines and is adjacent to the floodplain to the east.

Vegetation: Open bush, few trees, with scattered, dense stands of bamboo, especially along the ravines.

Hydrology: The ravines carry seasonal flows, and the stream in the floodplain at the foot of the terrace is a more permanent water source.

Modern disturbances: None.

Site description: The site consists of about 100 features, but many more are likely to be present in the denser bush. The main locus is to the northeast, with a secondary cluster to the southwest, across a ravine (which, on plan, looks like a central open space), which consists solely of rock alignments (possibly burials) and one subrectangular structure. The features appear in good condition, but nothing is known about the depth or integrity of deposits that may be present.

Artifacts: A large collection of ceramics and other finds was assembled from Site 71. The ceramics suggest that the site was occupied until the recent past, but its origination is uncertain. Large numbers of ground stone milling basins were encountered. The pottery collection is dominated by simple vessels, (short, everted) and a handful of long-neck jars. Nondecorated and slipped are the dominant motifs and, combined with glass bottles, including menthe alcohol and possible wine-bottle fragments, suggest a nineteenth-/early-twentieth-century assemblage.

Site interpretation: The site is interpreted as a village because of the number and diversity of features as well as the rich surface-artifact assemblage. The site is not defendable. It is likely to have remained occupied until the relatively recent past, and this postdates Sidebe's site in Masato. The topographic positioning, size, and diversity of artifacts are all common to sites interpreted as villages.

Site 71 covers about 3 ha on a relatively flat plateau divided from a site to the north by a steep-sided ravine and by a shallow draw on the southwestern edge of the site, as depicted in Figure 5.54. Site 71 consists of well over 100 features, of which some 96 were recorded in detail, including stone circles of various sizes, square and rectangular stone platforms, and a very wide variety of stone alignments. On the southern edge of the site, separated from the main locus of stone circles and overlooking low-lying land to the south and west, is a dense cluster of stone alignments, many of which are oriented roughly north-south and are the approximate sizes and shapes of burials. There is an area in the middle of the site that is devoid of features; this is a narrow but quite deep ravine that bisects the plateau on which the site sits.

At Site 71, all the features were recorded using a GPS device and photographed, and a selection were also recorded using scaled drawings, which are presented in Figures 5.55–5.59. Photographs of features are presented in Figures 5.59–5.66. Of particular note, Feature 97 is a typical stone rectangle/square feature, and Features 86 and

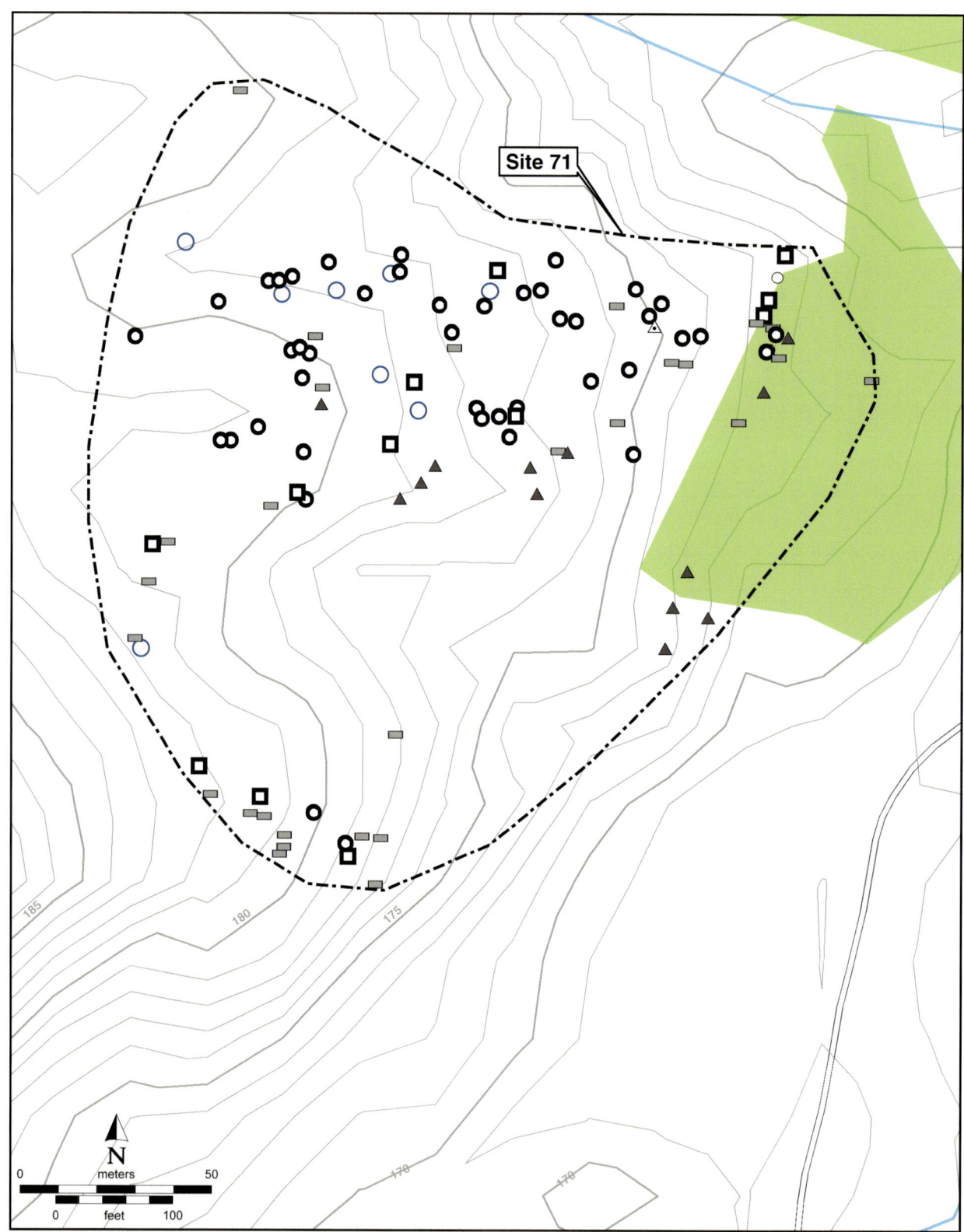

FIGURE 5.54. GIS-GENERATED SITE MAP OF SITE 71.

100 are rock alignments, of the type that might be burials; both are from the cluster of features on the southwest periphery of the site, south of the narrow ravine.

The material culture of Site 71 was characterized by *subactuelle* ceramics associated with European imports, including alcoholic-beverage glass-bottle fragments.

Site 71 is located about 1,500 m east of the modern village of Kerekounda. A dozen field houses and two farmsteads were recorded in the drainage just above the village site. Open in all directions, leaving it vulnerable to attack, Site 71 was clearly placed less for defense than for its proximity to agricultural fields.

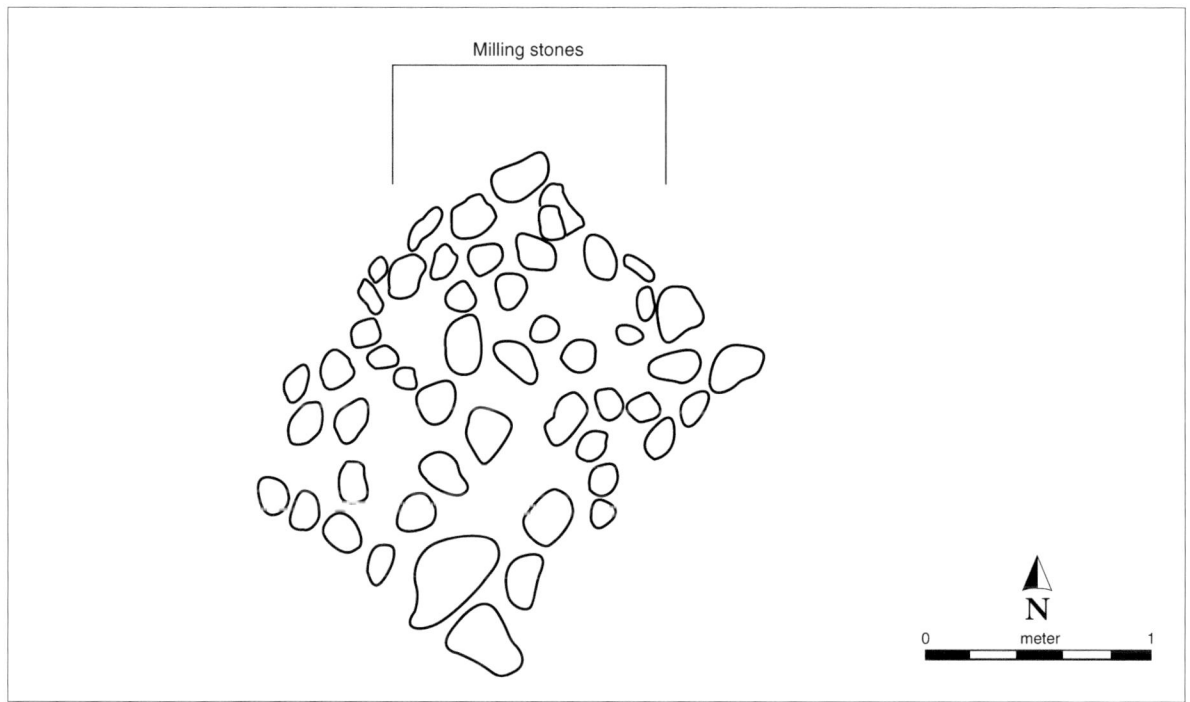

FIGURE 5.55. FEATURE 37 AT SITE 71.

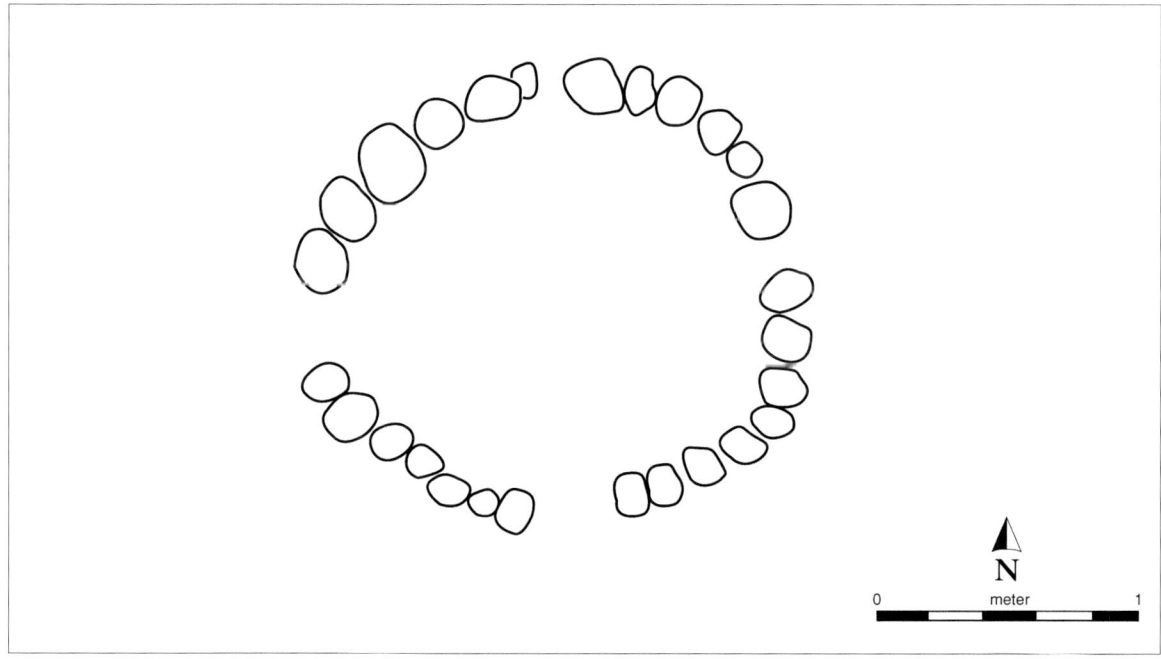

FIGURE 5.56. FEATURE 78 AT SITE 71.

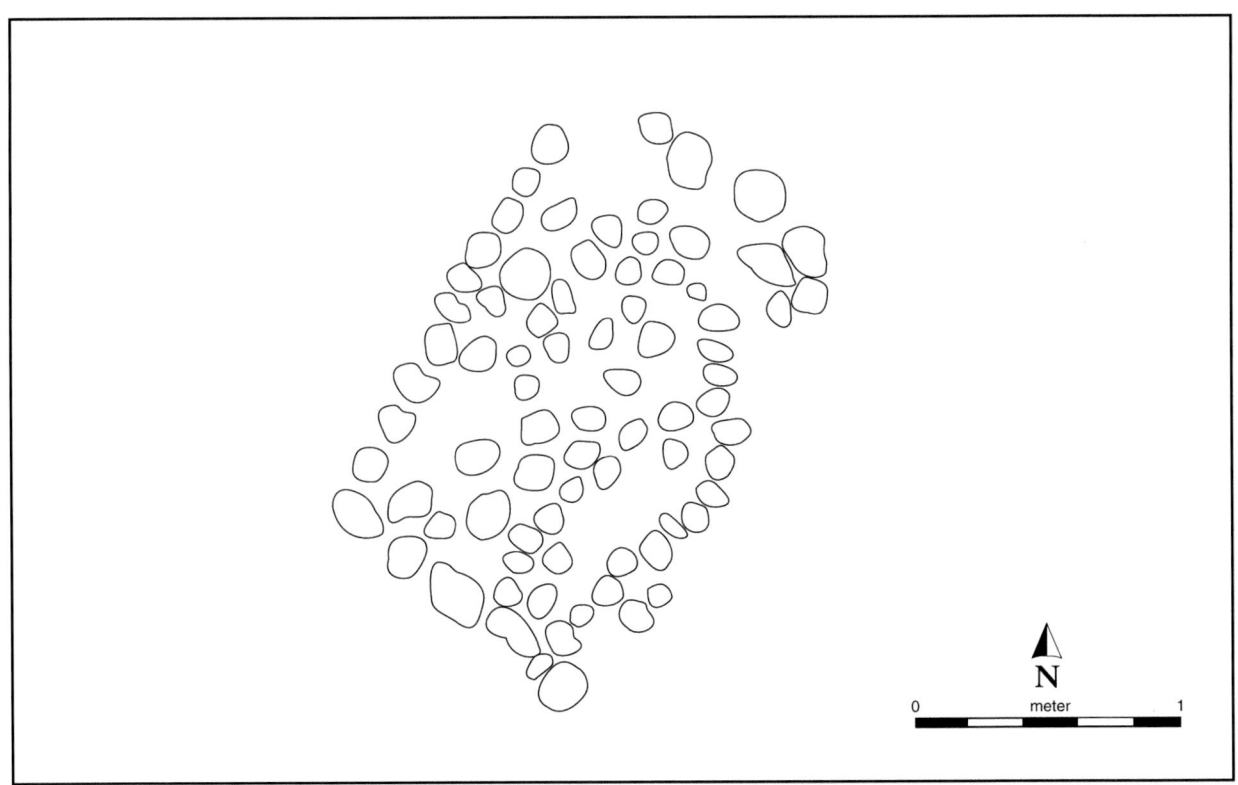

FIGURE 5.57. FEATURE 97, A SUBRECTANGULAR STONE PLATFORM.

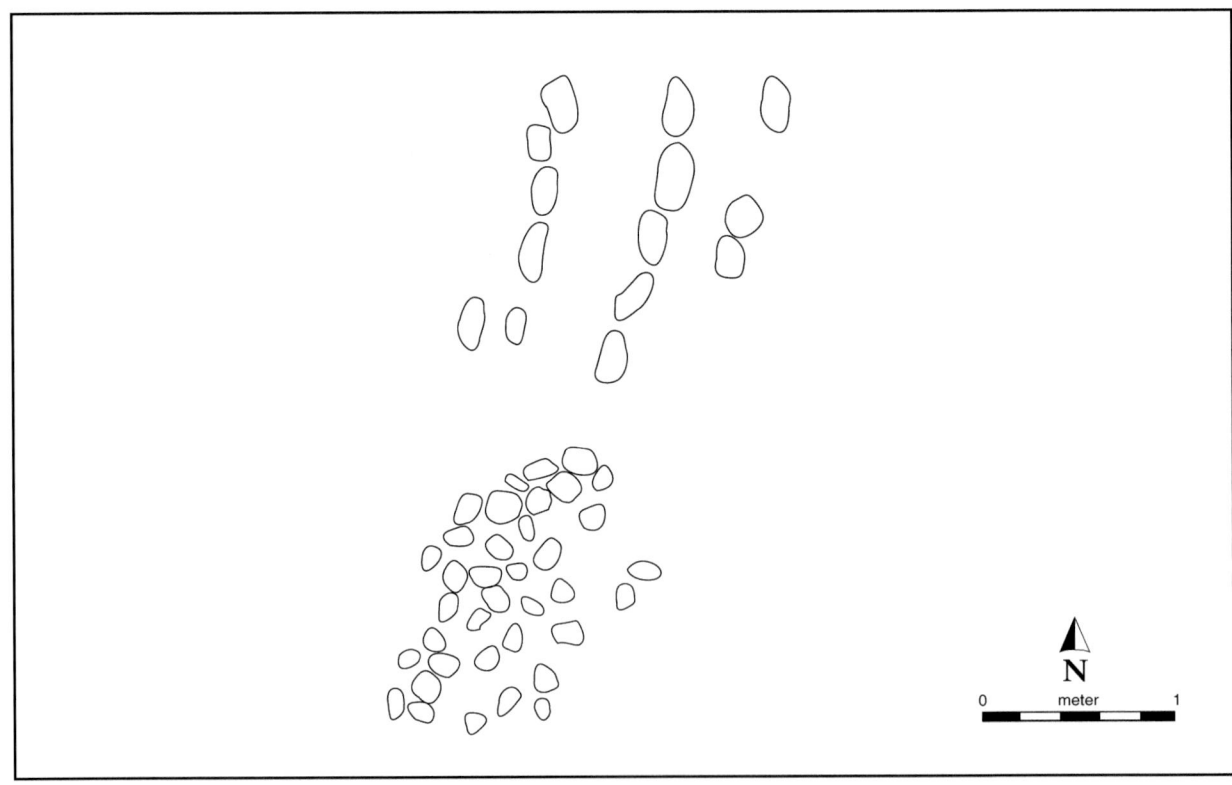

FIGURE 5.58. FEATURE 86, A POSSIBLE BURIAL.

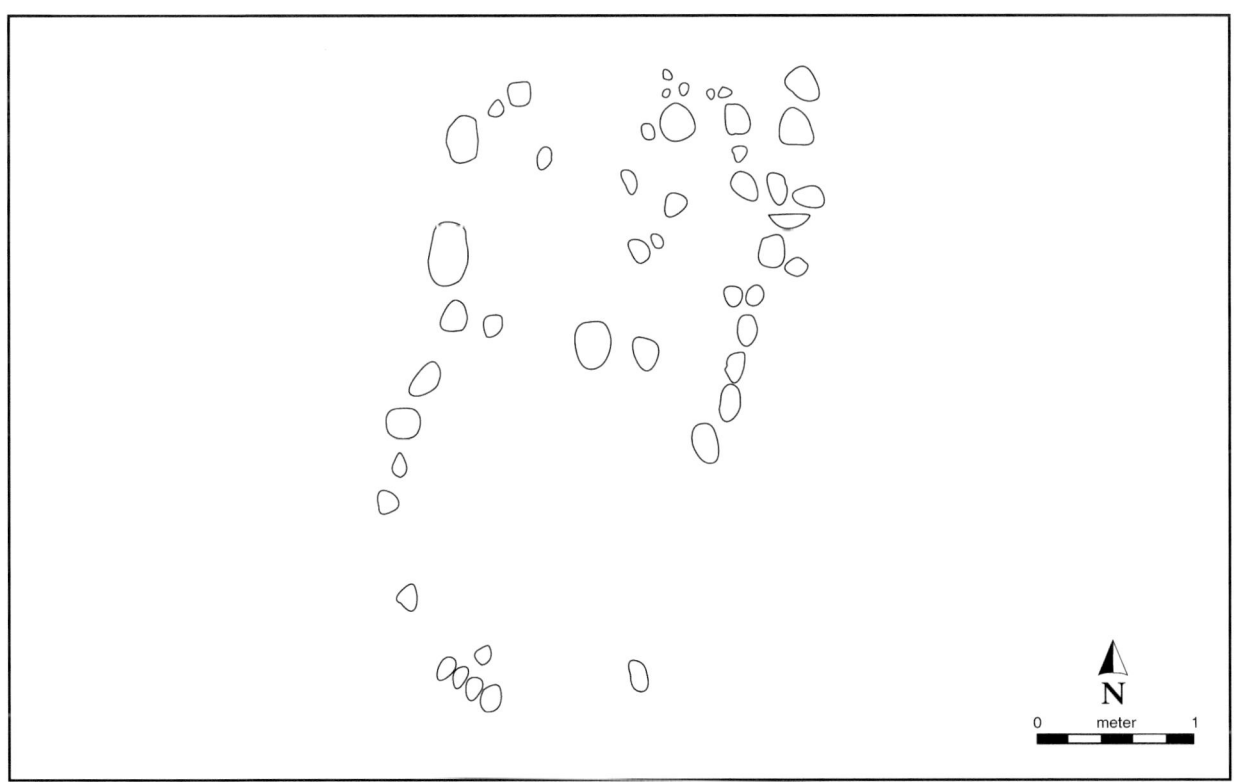

Figure 5.59. Feature 101 at Site 71.

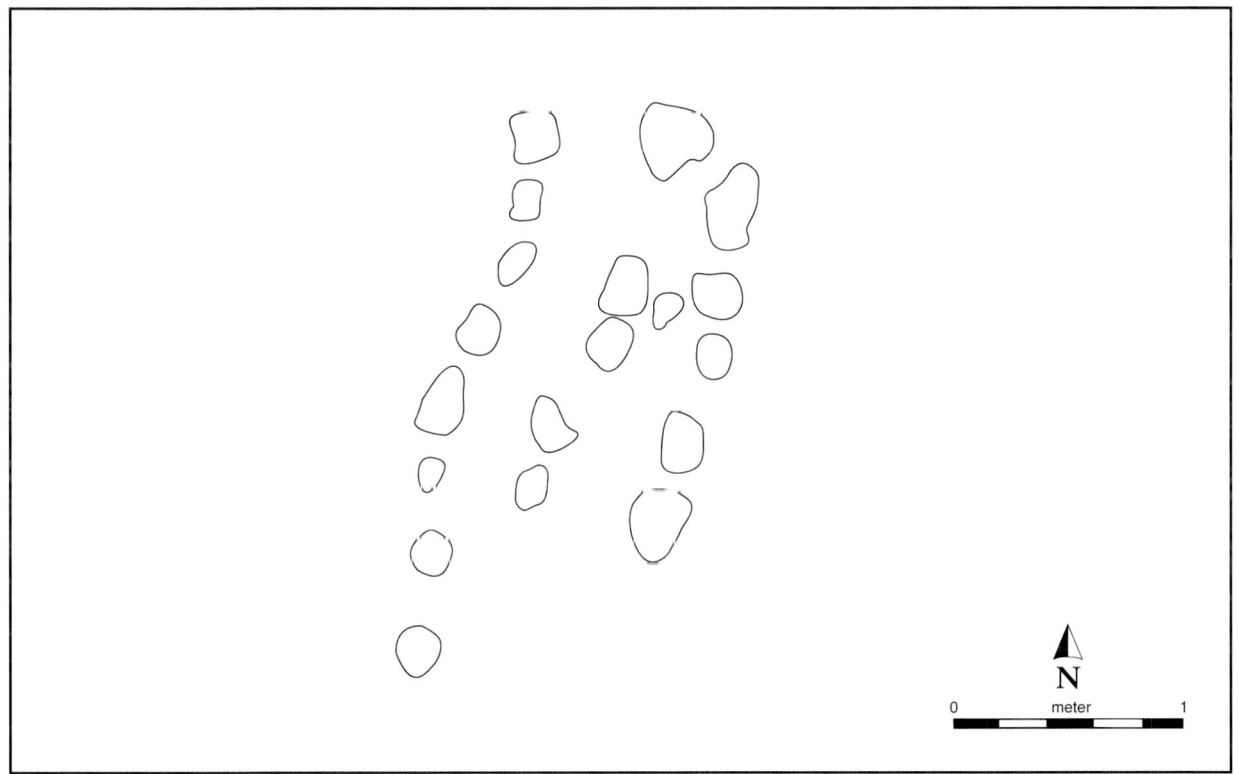

Figure 5.60. Feature 100 at Site 71.

Figure 5.61. Feature 3 at Site 71.

Figure 5.62. Feature 8 at Site 71.

Archaeological Survey and Test-Excavation Results

Figure 5.63. Feature 30 at Site 71.

Figure 5.64. Feature 4 at Site 71.

Figure 5.65. Feature 20 rock alignment at Site 71.

Figure 5.66. Feature 2 at Site 71, a rectangular stone platform.

Site 123

Location in concession: Site 123 is located on the northwestern edge of the freshwater reservoir north of Mamakhono.

Topographic setting: On the crest of a locally prominent second-terrace hill/ridge, overlooking floodplains to the north and south.

Vegetation: The crest of the ridge is largely open laterite, but the western end where the site is located is covered with dense bamboo.

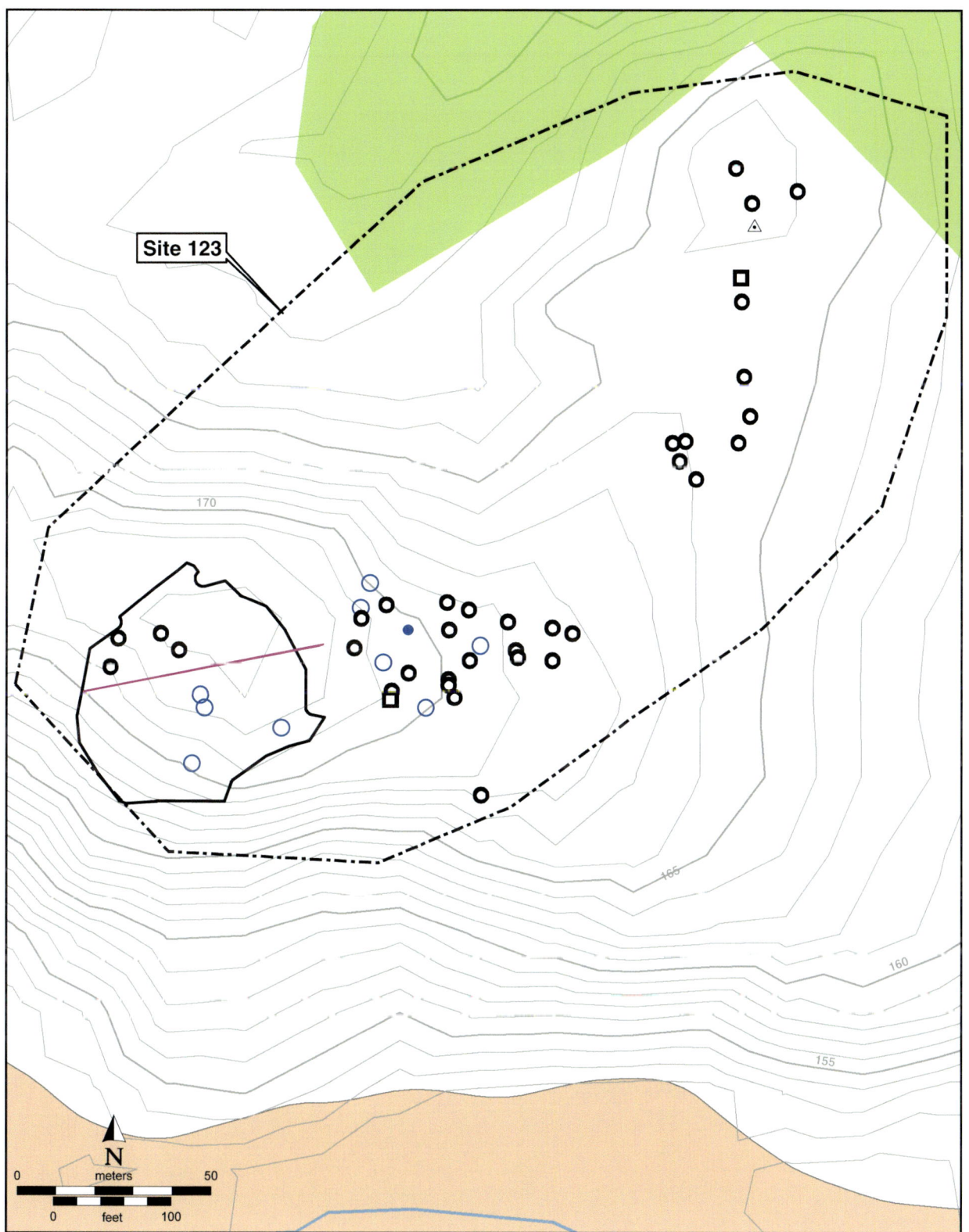

FIGURE 5.67. GIS-GENERATED MAP OF SITE 123.

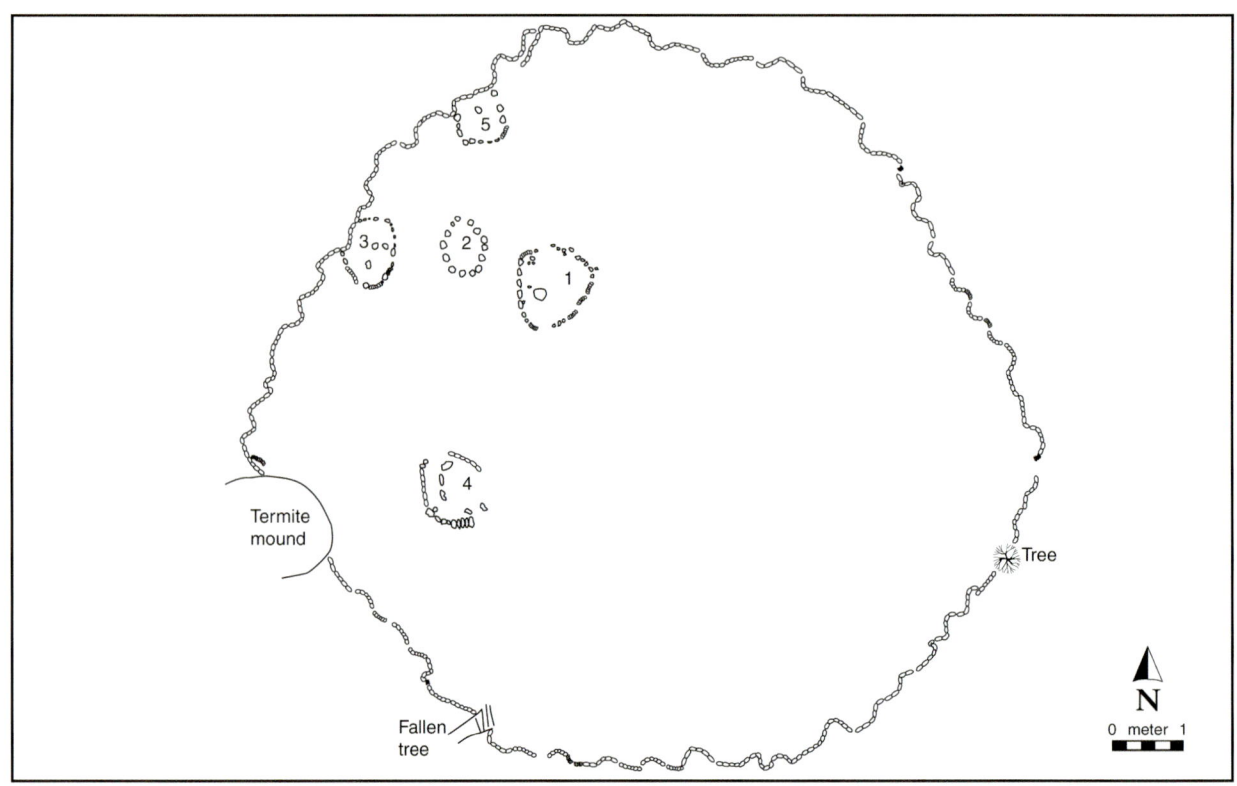

Figure 5.68. Enclosure, Site 123.

Figure 5.69. The enclosure wall at Site 123.

Archaeological Survey and Test-Excavation Results

Figure 5.70. Site 123 enclosure wall. Note 'niches.'

Figure 5.71. Stone circle inside the enclosure wall at Site 123.

Figure 5.72. Sun-square stone outside enclosure wall at Site 123.

Hydrology: Floodplain water to north and south (more accessible to the north).

Modern disturbances: None.

Site description: The site consists of a scatter of stone features (largely stone circles) in an apparent arc, with its 'open' side to the north and, at its western end, a unique circular enclosure. The enclosure is encircled by a very low stone wall or barrier, one stone wide and high. The wall has 'niches' about 60–80 cm wide, 50 cm deep, and spaced at about 2-m intervals for the complete circumference. The enclosure is approximately 60 m in diameter. Inside the enclosure are five stone circles. The interior had a lighter concentration of artifacts, but outside, especially to the east, the artifact scatter was much denser and more variable. The features appear in good condition, but nothing is known about the depth or integrity of deposits that may be present.

Artifacts: The ceramics assemblage is dominated by nondecorated, with slip and twine motifs, suggesting a possible nineteenth-century assemblage. Couscous-steamer fragments and Evian-bottle glass were also collected at this site, confirming the recent character of the occupation.

Site interpretation: The site is interpreted as a village. The number of features might argue for typing it as a hamlet, but the unique enclosure wall certainly denotes a more important purpose than hamlet status might provide. The features and artifacts are typical of village sites, but the enclosure wall is unique.

Site 123 is a most unusual village. It contains 19 identified stone circles, which would suggest it should be classified as a hamlet, but it contains other features, such as a 'niched' enclosure and a strong site structure, that gave us pause and caused us to reclassify Site 123 as a village. The recorded circles are scattered along an east-west ridge (first to second terrace) overlooking the floodplains to the north and west (Figure 5.67). We suspect that there are probably many more to be found, particularly in the dense bamboo that covers the western end of the site. The ridge rises in elevation toward the west, where the flat summit is occupied by a walled enclosure about 40 m in diameter. The enclosure wall is built of upright stone slabs (standing about 30–50 cm high, too low to be functional) placed so as to create niches at about 2-m intervals (Figures 5.68–5.70). Enclosed within the wall are 5 stone circles. In size and shape, the stone circles inside the enclosure are not different from those found on the outside (Figures 5.71 and 5.72). Yet they are clearly separated from other such features. The distances between the 5 circles are much greater than in other feature clusters, and these are the only such features at the summit of the hill. We suspect that their location and layout reflect the relatively high status of those within the enclosure.

In addition to recent *subactuelle* pottery, the artifacts collected at Site 123 include fragments of steamers and Evian-bottle glass that confirm a nineteenth-/twentieth-century assemblage. Site 123, with its niched enclosure wall, is without parallel and is unique in Eastern Senegal. It is in other respects reminiscent of the enclosure at Site 8 at Masato, which lies less than 5 km to the southwest. Of note, Site 8 is only open in the direction of Site 123 (it backs up to hills on the other three sides) and, as will be noted below, was placed in a manner to defend against intruders coming from the northeast. Similarly, Site 123 is situated in a location defendable against people coming from the southwest, who would have had to pass through a narrow passage between two hills to reach the site. Given the distance between the two and their relative positions on the landscape, it is possible that the two were rivals. Alternatively, with the difference in size, one could just as easily argue that the two were aligned, with Site 123 being a 'vassal' village of Site 8.

Although the relationship between the two sites is intriguing, at the moment it consists of little more than speculation; more research on this topic is certainly warranted.

Figures 5.69–5.70 depict the enclosure wall, with its distinctive and unique niches.

Site 156

Location in concession: Site 156 is located 1,500 m south of Mamakhono, along the route of the proposed haul road.

Topographic setting: A broad plain of second terrace, with two small but steep-sided laterite hills, the larger of which is encompassed by Site 156.

Vegetation: Generally open bush, the northeastern part extends into the arable fields of Mamakhono (the green polygons in the map extract).

Hydrology: There are no stream courses in the immediate vicinity.

Modern disturbances: None.

Site description: Site 156 is a large agglomeration of stone circles (about 65) plus some other stone features (squares, alignments, etc.). The stone circles appear to cluster in three to four loci: one to the extreme northeast, one in the center, and a looser locus on the slopes of the flat-topped hill. There are some stone features on the hilltop but no stone circles. Unusually, at this site the stone circles are not only clustered but, in a number of instances, appear conjoined (determining whether this is the case will depend upon close dating of the features, which is unavailable at present). There is no evidence to phase the loci, and they appear otherwise to be very similar. Site 77 (with Site 153) may provide an interpretative parallel for the loci as lineage-based residential complexes. The features appear in good condition. Where sample excavation was undertaken—in both the central locus and on the hilltop, as described above—there are both A and B soil horizons up to 40 cm thick overlying natural geological strata.

Artifacts: The ceramics are largely dominated by nondecorated vessels, followed by twine and other subtractive motifs; we also found a couscous-steamer fragment. In its entirety, the assemblage suggests a recent-historical-period occupation.

Site interpretation: Site 156 is interpreted as a village, on the basis of the number of stone features and also the quantity and diversity of ceramics and stone artifacts. The site is unusual, in that it is not located adjacent to ravines or floodplain.

Site 156 is a large scatter of over 65 stone circles along a flat terrace, plus, at the southeastern end of the site, a hill with a flat summit of about 100 m in diameter (Figure 5.73). The lower hill slopes have several stone rings, whereas the summit has a number of stone squares/rectangles and a dense concentration of sherds. The hill of Site 156 is less than 200 m northeast of an ideological/sacred site (Site 157) composed of more than 20 *tumuli pierre* (see discussion below).

The stone circles at Site 156 are clustered in several distinct loci. This distribution is similar to that described above for Site 77. Ethnographic interviews at the latter site associated the loci with distinct families and/or lineage branches.

All of the features at Site 156 were recorded with a GPS device and photographed; only a few were recorded by scaled drawings (Figure 5.74), and only two were investigated by excavation (Figures 5.75 and 5.76). The stone features represented several types. As usual, most were stone circles interpreted as foundations for huts. We found several circles that were either conjoined or superimposed. The most likely explanation is that these represent sequential houses, although future excavation will be needed to test this hypothesis; it is possible they are contemporary. Other feature types include square and round features whose interiors are covered by a stone pavement; these are most likely granaries or other storage facilities. A few ovoid features covered with rock are interpreted as Islamic burials. These are similar to, but smaller than, the features found at Site 157 (see below).

Figure 5.74 shows scaled plans of 20 of the features at Site 156, including stone circles (the most numerous

A Slave Who Would Be King

feature type), as well as stone squares and rock alignments. Feature 26 is shown at a larger scale in Figure 5.75, followed by plan and excavated sections of Feature 6, a stone square (Figure 5.76).

Figures 5.77 and 5.78 show Features 5 and 10 on the southwestern slopes of the hill in Site 156.

Figures 5.79 and 5.80 show Features 14 and 19, both stone circles (note additional circles behind Feature 19)

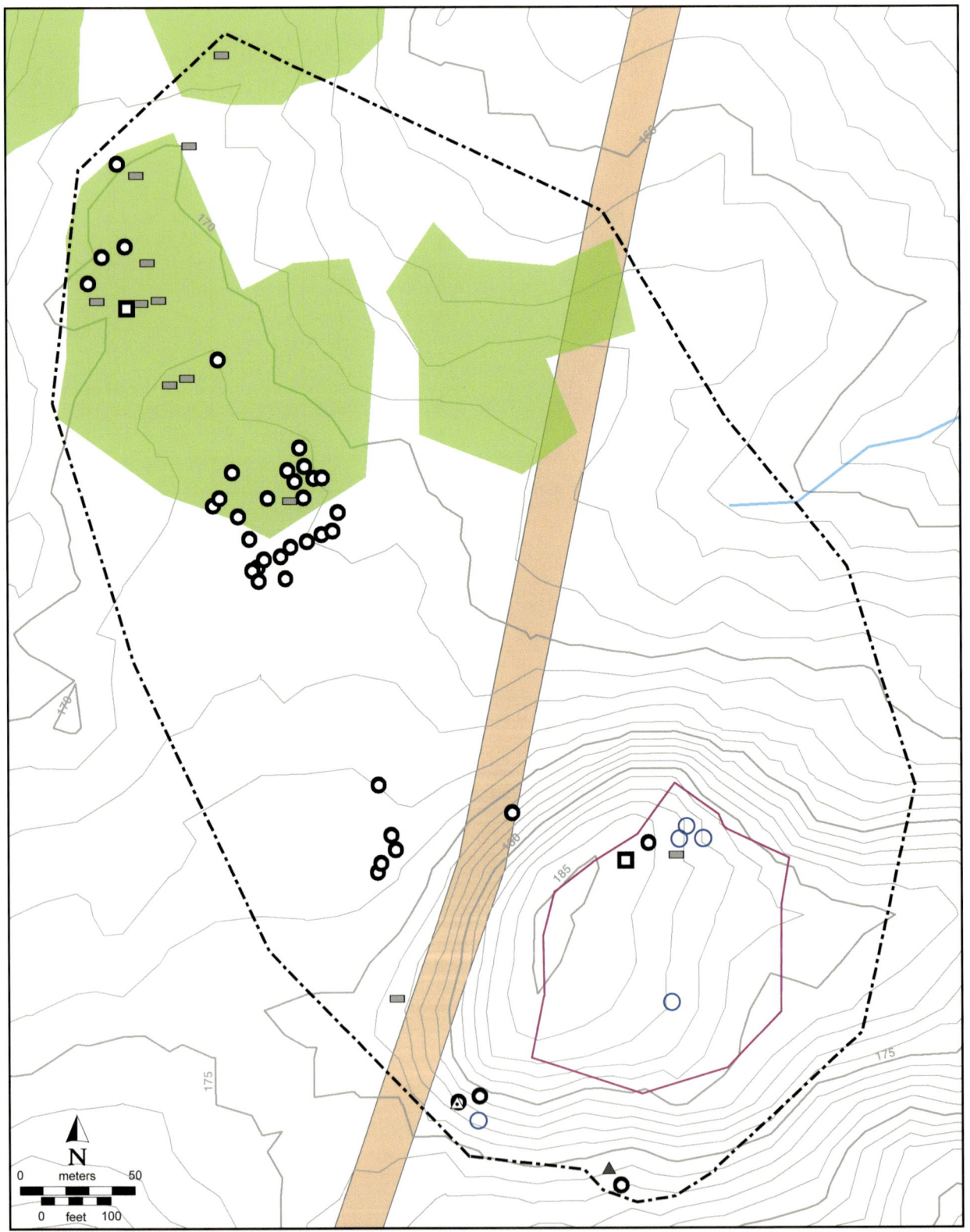

FIGURE 5.73. GIS-GENERATED MAP OF SITE 156.

Archaeological Survey and Test-Excavation Results

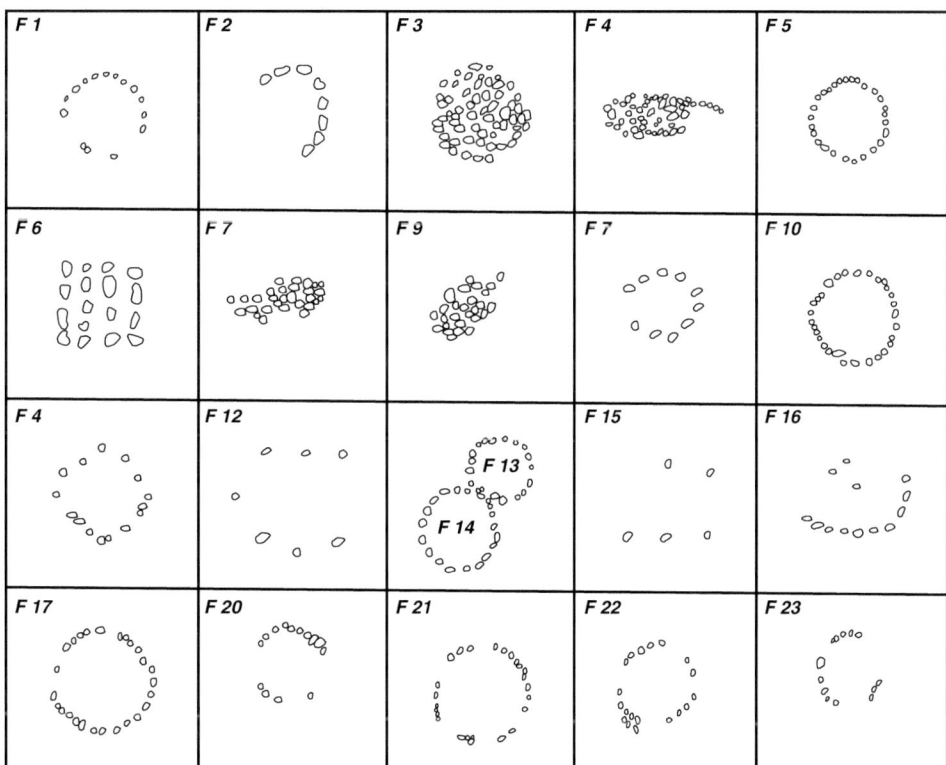

FIGURE 5.74. RECORD DRAWINGS OF FEATURES AT SITE 156.

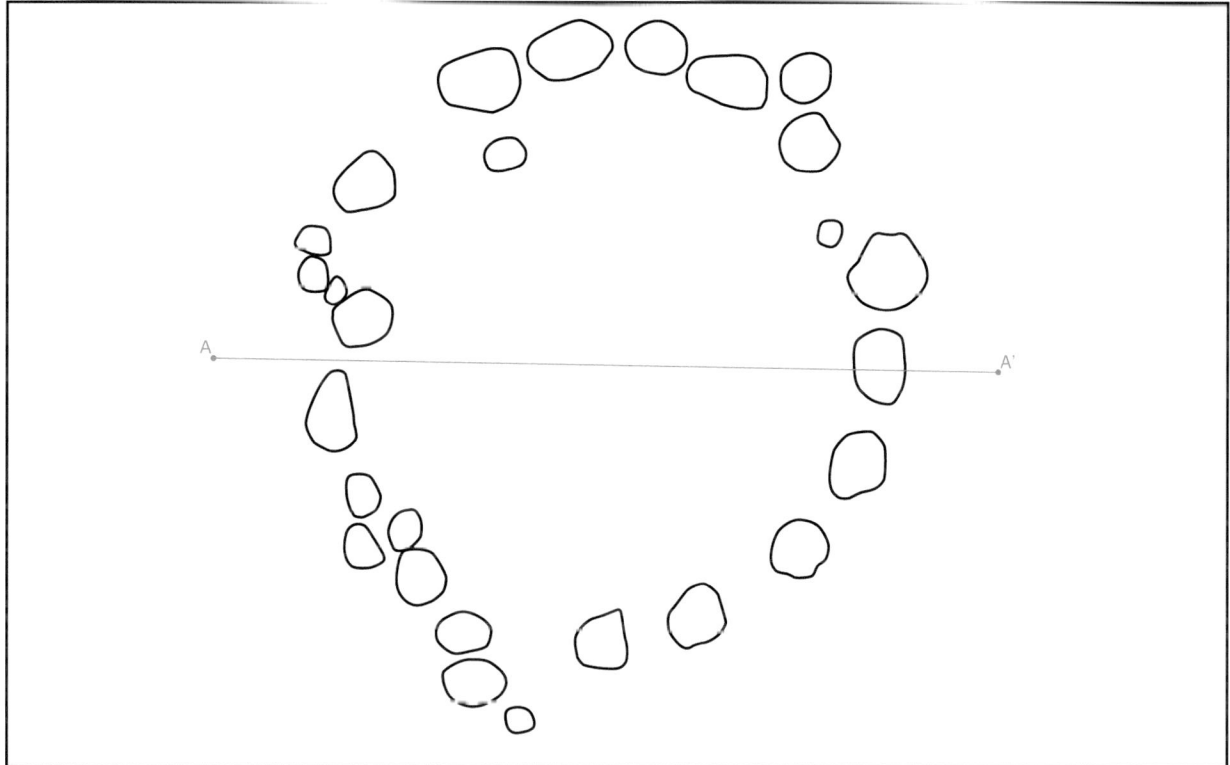

FIGURE 5.75. FEATURE 26 AT SITE 156.

in Site 156; Figure 5.81 shows Feature 20 on the edge of the slope toward the floodplain; and Figure 5.82 shows Feature 56, a small stone square.

At the very top of the hill, we found a concentration of surface artifacts. Analysis identified numerous short, everted and long-neck jars that suggest a post-fifteenth-century occupation. The occupation on top of the plateau could be slightly earlier than the one in the lowlands, which is characterized by more-recent ceramics with organic inclusions.

Site 156 is located halfway between the modern village of Mamakhono and Site 71, another archaeological village site. Today it lies in and among a dense concentration of agricultural fields. Based on the density and diversity of artifacts at Site 156, it would appear to have been relatively long-lived. It certainly lies in an area favored by farmers today.

Polity Centers

At the apex of the settlement system are a pair of villages that may have been seats of small polities. These contained 100 or more stone features, sometimes spread over an area of more than 5 ha. Polity centers exhibit the most complicated site structure of any class in the Sabodala region. For example, the polity near Masato has an enclosure separating the center of the site from the hut clusters outside. Inside the enclosures we found linear rock features, which may be burials; larger, circular stone features, which may represent chiefs' residences; and large, square-shaped foundations, which may be the remnants of mosques or some other community buildings.

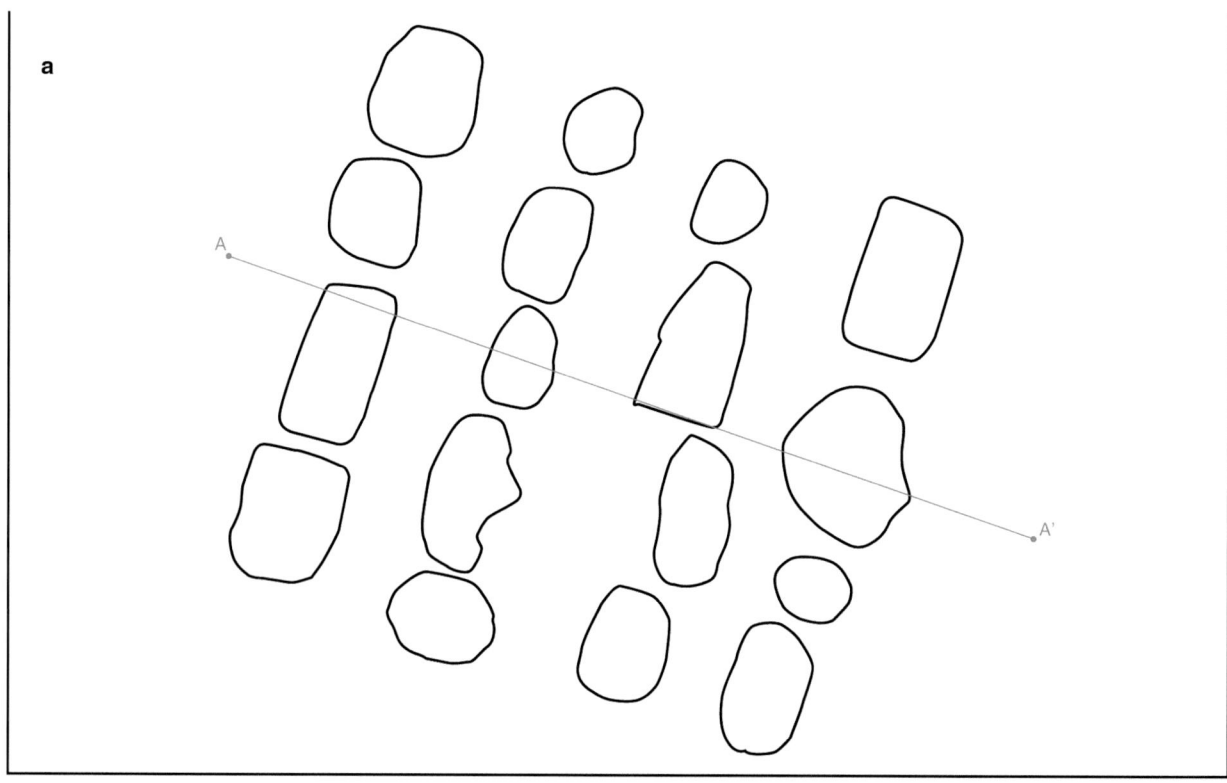

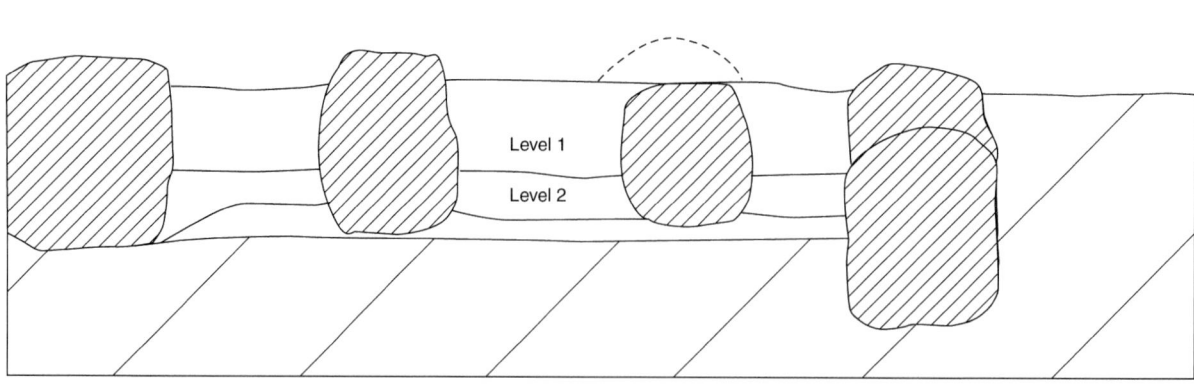

FIGURE 5.76. (A) MAP AND (B) EXCAVATED SECTION OF FEATURE 6, SITE 156.

ARCHAEOLOGICAL SURVEY AND TEST-EXCAVATION RESULTS

FIGURE 5.77. FEATURE 5 AT SITE 156.

FIGURE 5.78. FEATURE 10 AT SITE 156.

Figure 5.79. Feature 14 at Site 156.

Figure 5.80. Feature 19 at Site 156. Note second hut circle in the background.

ARCHAEOLOGICAL SURVEY AND TEST-EXCAVATION RESULTS

FIGURE 5.81. FEATURE 20 AT SITE 156.

FIGURE 5.82. FEATURE 56 AT SITE 156.

Oral tradition and ethnographic informants ascribe the status of polity center to the site in Masato, but these claims need to be verified through archival and archaeological inquiries. If verified, the presence of a late-nineteenth- to early-twentieth-century African polity in the Sabodala region would be of significant scientific and cultural interest. From an archaeological perspective, the village and associated sites would allow the examination of issues of social structure, subsistence, regional dynamics, gender roles, slavery, and the like. Culturally, the site may be of historical or spiritual importance to people in the area. Of particular interest is the possibility that the site may empower lineages that currently have limited access to power and wealth to seek ways of changing their status.

We defined two polities, one in the ADI at Masato and one near the southern boundary of the OJVG concession near Makhana (see Figures 5.1 and 5.33, the map of all sites in the concession and the map of only hamlets, villages, and polity centers). We recorded Site 24 near Makhana as a 'chance find' during the ethnographic survey of 2009. It was not visited again in 2010 because it is located outside the ADI. Consequently, the site was not recorded in detail; there is no scaled site map, nor is there a surface collection from the site. During our brief site reconnaissance, we noted that the site extends for nearly a kilometer. It consists of at least three main areas, or 'neighborhoods,' each containing scores of stone features (Figures 5.83–5.85). Some aspects of the history of Makhana were recorded and are described in the ethnography chapter (see Chapter 3). The key element to mention here is the association of the site and a nearby hill with Sheikh Omer (and/or his mother), which suggests that the site served as a local base during the mid-nineteenth-century *jihad* through Beledougou. On this basis, the site has been classed as a polity center.

The second polity we defined is located within and surrounding the proposed rock dump at Masato. It consists of a polity center (Sites 8–10) and associated residential sites (Sites 11, 78, and 79). The Masato polity is unusual in many regards. First, local members of the crew associated it with the historical figure, Tobri Sidebe, a Peul-speaker that purportedly led a slave mercenary army and gained control of the region in the latter part of the nineteenth century. Second, the site is located 'all wrong,' in terms of environmental attributes—far from water and at a high elevation. It does not border areas of good agricultural land as do all hamlets and villages. Instead, the site location seems to have been selected to make it easily defensible. It is possible that the site location was selected to gain control over artisanal mining in the area. Oral tradition holds that Sidebe's power was related to gold. These traditions also have it that Sidebe controlled a well and that all needed to have his permission to obtain water. To our knowledge, no modern well currently exists in the vicinity of Masato. Jeff Homburg (personal communication 2010) suggested that a well could have existed in the past that has since dried up. Alternatively, Sidebe could have controlled a

FIGURE 5.83. A STONE CIRCLE AT MAKHANA SITE 24.

well located at some distance from his village (e.g., near Site 123). Finally, the story could have no historical merit.

Considerable field effort was invested to create a scaled map of the polity center at Masato. We also conducted more-intensive surface collection of the general site and test excavations of specific features, which were only found at Masato. Below, we present the results of these investigations.

FIGURE 5.84. A LARGE OVAL FEATURE AT MAKHANA SITE 24.

FIGURE 5.85. AN OVAL STONE FEATURE AT MAKHANA SITE 24, IDENTIFIED BY ONE INFORMANT AS A BURIAL.

Sites 8, 9, 10, 11, 78, and 79

Location in concession: The sites are located in Masato, on the eastern slopes of the central spine of hills (or locally, 'mountains') of the concession.

Topographic setting: The sites occupy a broad, gently sloping, elevated plateau, quite high at the western edge (Site 9) and dropping down to the plateau where Site 8 is located and then sloping steadily eastward to debouch upon a first terrace and the floodplain at Site 79. Deep ravines to north and south demarcate the plateau, with Sites 10, 11 and 79 in the valley bottom to the south and floodplains adjacent.

Vegetation: Mostly open bush to the (higher) west, changing to open laterite grassland farther east and reverting to more-densely tree-covered bush with stands of bamboo at Site 79 and in the ravine bottoms to the north and south. The central plateau has a notable collection of very large baobab trees, the largest (possibly the oldest?) located in the center of the Site 8 enclosure.

Hydrology: The plateau is arid, but the north and south ravines carry seasonal flows. Site 79 has floodplains adjacent to the east.

Modern disturbances: Sites 9 and 11 have been damaged by mining exploration—notably Site 9, where two stone circles were largely destroyed by bulldozer pushes.

Site description: The Masato complex is best described as several components or loci. These components were discovered at various times in different phases of work, and the attribution of them all to a single complex was arrived at in analysis, not in the field. Site 9 is the westernmost and consists of 7 stone circles—probably a single-family residential complex. Site 11, to the south, is larger, with 11 stone features, and Site 79 is similarly sized. Site 78 at the lower, eastern end of the plateau, is again slightly smaller, with 8 features. All of these loci contained artifact scatters of ceramics and ground stone milling basins. In the center of the plateau is Site 8, consisting of a subsquare, walled enclosure. Inside the enclosure are a number of stone circles, plus a possible mosque—features suggestive of public space—and a variety of rock alignments interpreted as burials (further description is provided below). Outside the enclosure and scattered over an area of 2–3 ha are an additional 60–70 stone features (the number is uncertain because of dense grass). The features appear to be in good condition. Where sample excavation was undertaken in Site 8, in both the central focus and outside the enclosure, there are both A and B soil horizons up to 40 cm thick overlying natural geological strata.

Artifacts: The ceramics are dominated by long-neck jars and simple vessels with short, everted rims. Most body sherds are undecorated, although a few have twine, other subtractive motifs, slip, and multiple decorations. The presence of small finds, including gunflints and tobacco-pipe fragments of local manufacture and of European origin, suggest a post-fifteenth-century occupation.

Site interpretation: The local traditional story, repeated by Sadio Daniakho of Sabodala, says that this site at Masato was the seat of a polity led by Tobri Sidebe in the late-nineteenth or early-twentieth century. This account is the basis for speculating that Masato is an archaeological example of one of the small West African polities. Further discussion of the ethnographic narrative associated with Tobri Sidebe was presented in Chapter 3.

Site 8 in Masato was visited and recorded in 2009 and again in 2010, when it was surveyed in detail. In 2010, over 60 features were recorded with GPS devices and photographed; many of the features were also recorded by scale drawings (see below), and several were tested by sample excavation (Figure 5.86). Site 9 is considered to be part of Site 8, or perhaps a distinct neighborhood of Site 8, reminiscent of Makhana, and the foci identified at Sites 77 and 157 (Figure 5.87).

The main part of the polity center, Site 8, is located on a broad plateau surrounded by hills on all sides but the northeast. It is largely inaccessible from any direction but the northeast. It commands an excellent view of the drainage below the site.

Site 8 is unique in this area of Eastern Senegal because it contains a suboval enclosure with a possible stone wall that might once have stood to a meter in height (Figures 5.88 and 5.89). This enclosure is about 45 by 50 m in extent and encloses a variety of stone features.

Most notable among these is Feature 57, a stone square approximately 6 m on a side, with a square apse extending from its eastern side (Figure 5.90). Morphologically, this is consistent with stone foundations for a wood-framed mosque. The eastern 'wall' has a central gap, as if for a doorway; other possible doors are in both the north and south walls. Elsewhere to the east is a cluster of stone circles, and to the north, there is a cluster of several dozen small stone alignments, most oriented roughly northeast-southwest or east-west. These were tentatively identified as burials. Features 49 and 62 are two examples that were tested by excavation (Figures 5.91–5.93). Surprisingly, human bone was not found, although the soil conditions are conducive to its preservation (relatively neutral pH) and a few very small bone fragments were found in Feature 49. The placement of the stones in the fill of Feature 49 (see Figure 5.91) is exactly that observed in stone-lined burials in Europe. The fills contained pottery sherds and a very few small fragments of bone and little else. Despite the lack of surviving bone, our interpretation is that these are indeed burials, but if so,

Archaeological Survey and Test-Excavation Results

the bodies must have been removed. This raises further questions that our very limited test excavations are simply unable to answer.

Feature 57, the putative mosque, was recorded by both scaled plans and photography, and then a small sample test pit was excavated through its southern wall.

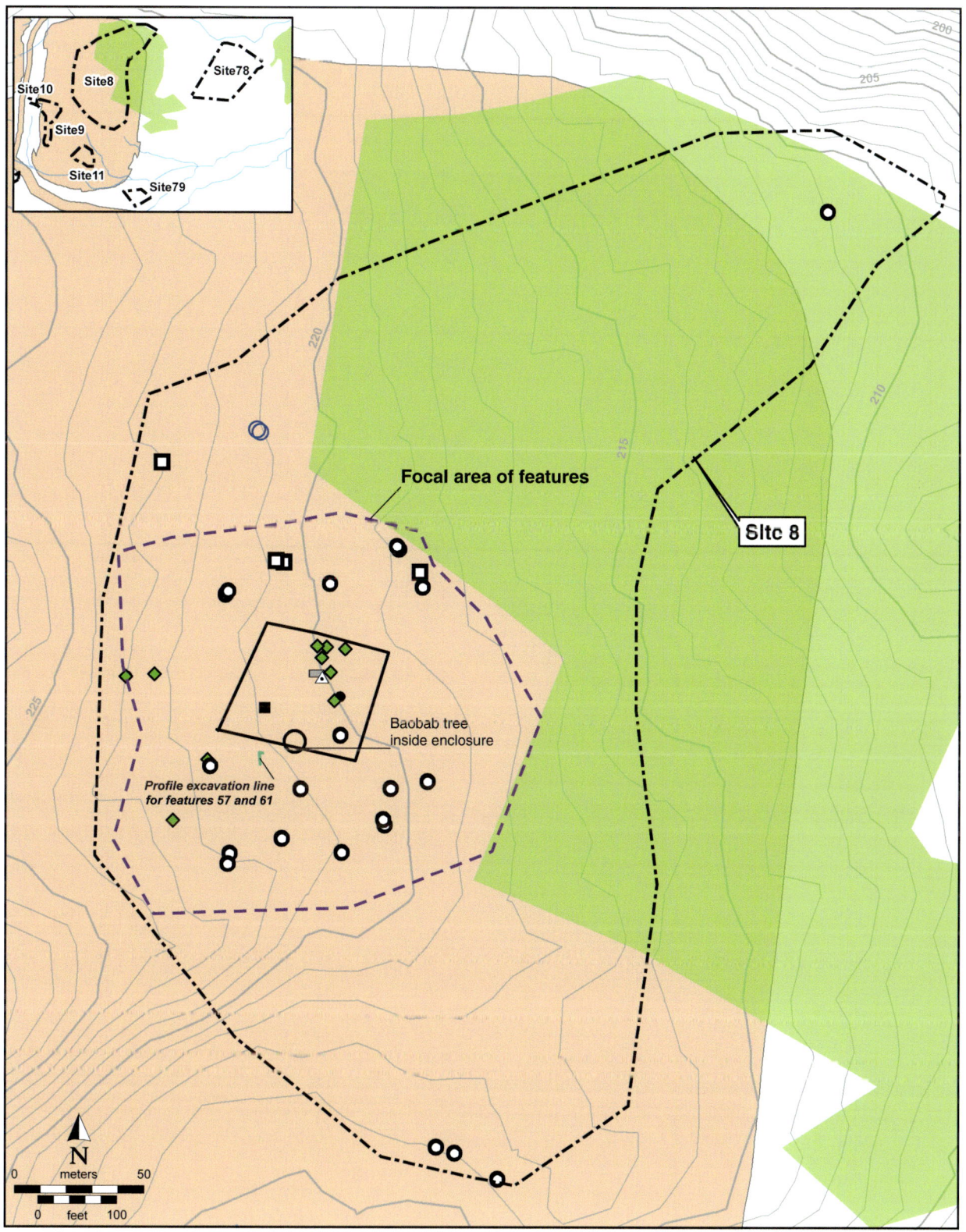

Figure 5.86. GIS-generated map of Site 8. Inset shows Sites 9, 10, 11, 78, and 79 in relation to Site 8. All five sites are probably all part of the 'polity center.' The scatter of pottery across the five sites is continuous.

Excavation revealed that the lines of stones interpreted as a foundation were only one stone deep and partially buried in topsoil (no construction trench, if there was one, was visible). The excavation results are consistent with a stone foundation for wooden-framed walls and a roof. The excavations contained very small fragments of painted plaster, which may be from interior walls. The stone feature is shown in plan in Figure 5.90, a photograph of the feature after surface cleaning is provided in Figures 5.94 and 5.95, and a view of the

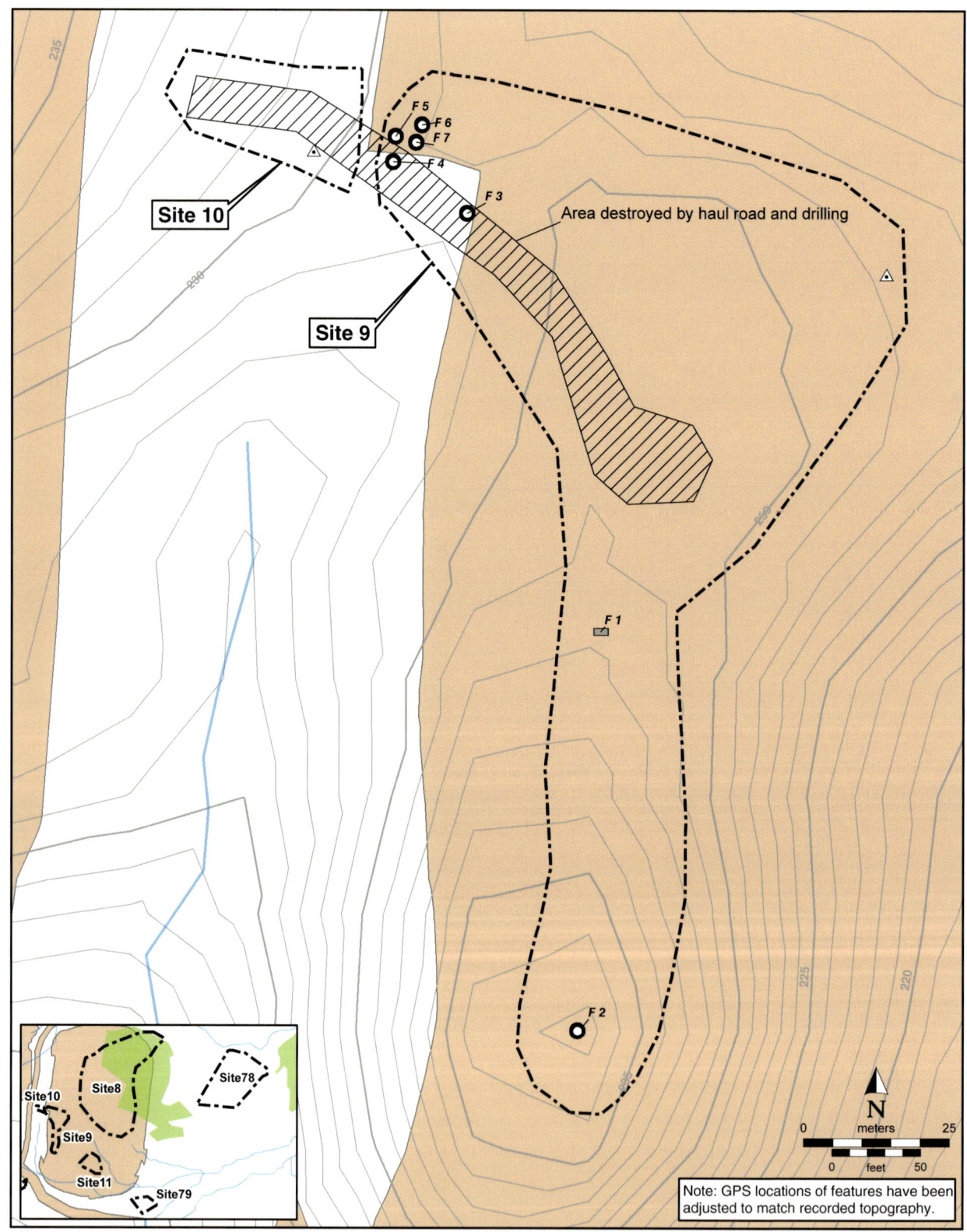

FIGURE 5.87. GIS-GENERATED MAP OF SITES 9 AND 10.

excavated test pit through the feature is provided in Figure 5.96.

Adjacent to this test pit, a sample excavation trench measuring 1 m by 2 m was excavated (Figures 5.97–5.99) across the line of the enclosure wall. This excavation confirmed that the linear ridge enclosing the site is made up of tumbled, mostly large laterite blocks. These stones were not found to be placed in any regular arrangements but instead appeared to be either random or fallen. The basal layer of stones was resting upon the subsoil B horizon, but no construction trench was visible. A quick attempt at stacking the excavated stones onsite suggested that the tumbled stones would have been sufficient to construct a wall, pyramidal in section, to about 80–100 cm in height. Such a wall would have sufficed as a visible marker or separator of space, or, perhaps more likely, could have served as a stone foundation for a wooden superstructure or stockade. This structure is reminiscent of local strongholds, referred to in the Senegambia as *tata*. They were made either of mud or of simple piles of rocks (Thiaw 1999).

Elsewhere on Sites 8 and 9, there were many stone-circle features. We excavated two of these circles; Figures 5.100–5.103 show Feature 5 at Site 9 and Feature 7 at Site 8, before and after excavation.

The sample excavation of the putative mosque and the enclosure wall produced a good collection of ceramics. These included fragments of tobacco pipes that included both locally manufactured materials and European imports. The excavated ceramics showed rim types and decoration motifs suggestive of a nineteenth-century assemblage.

FIGURE 5.88. 2009 PANORAMA OF THE SOUTHWEST CORNER OF THE ENCLOSURE AT SITE 8.

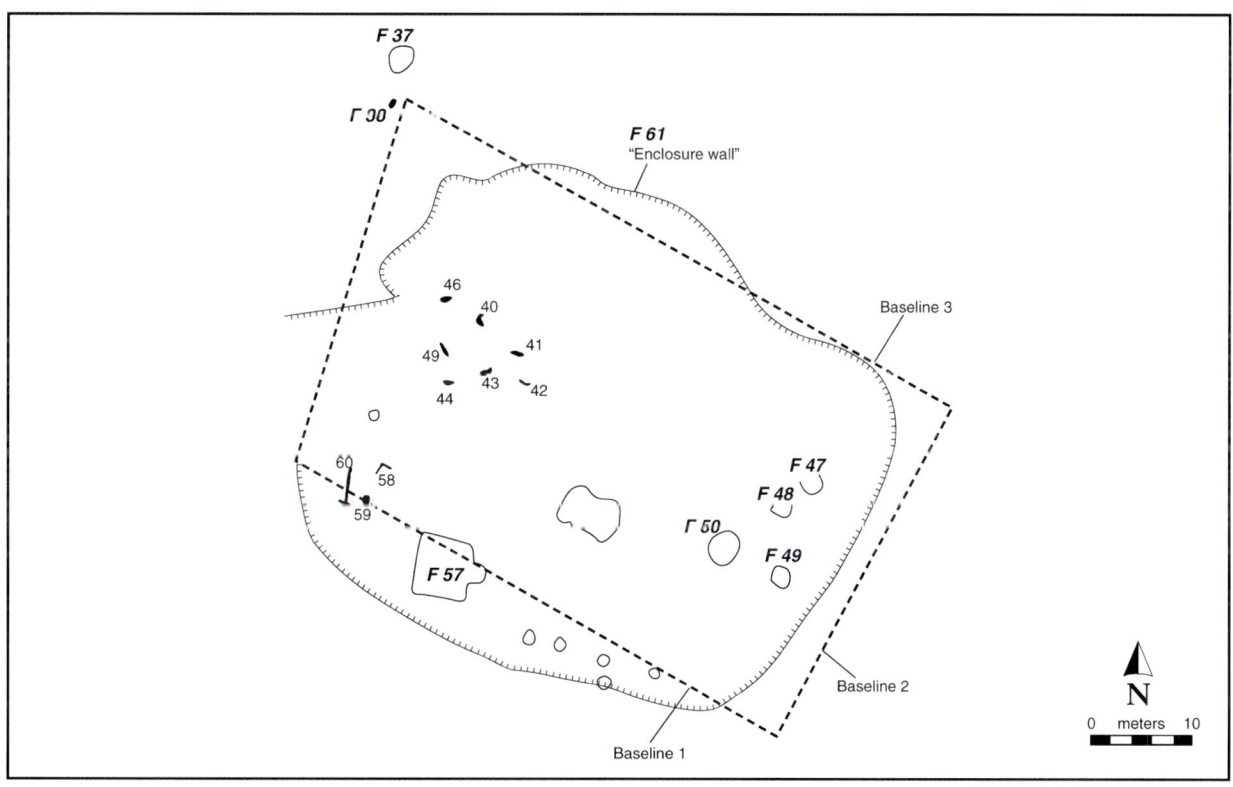

FIGURE 5.89. OVERALL MAP OF ENCLOSURE AT SITE 8 SHOWING BASELINES FOR OFF-SET MAPPING OF FEATURES. SOME PRINCIPAL FEATURES MARKED.

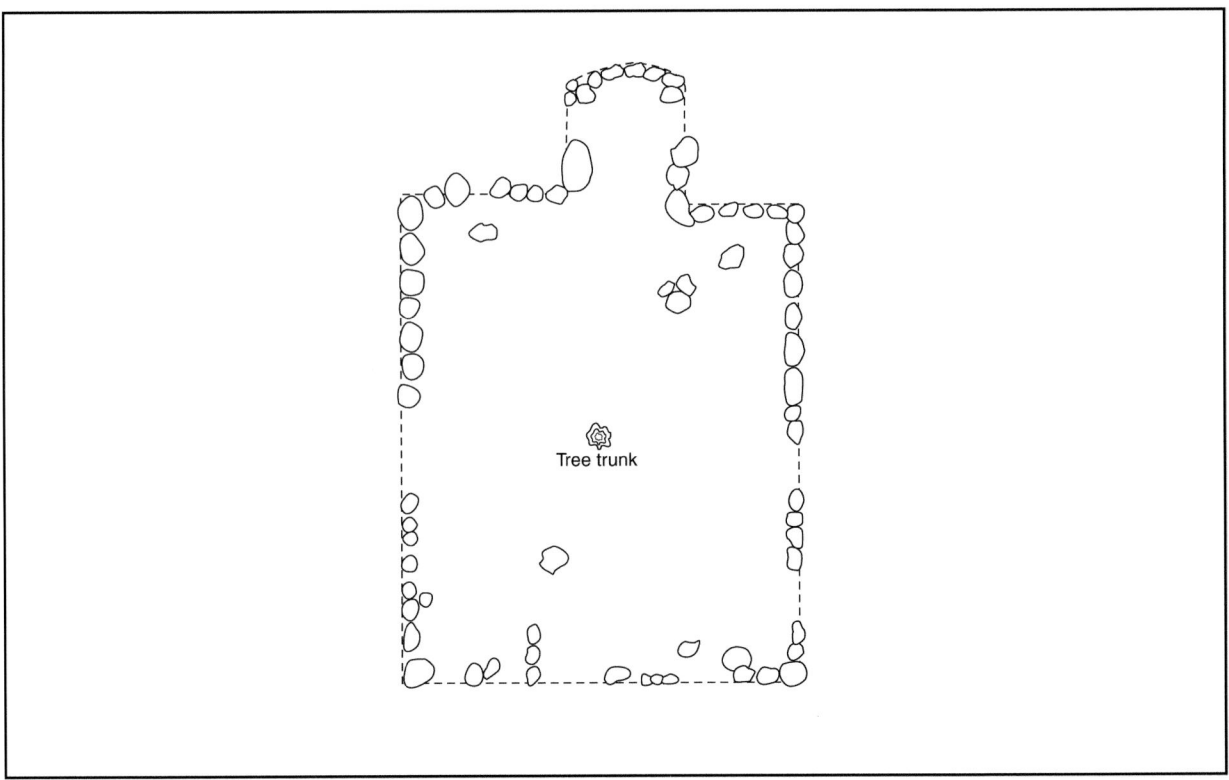

FIGURE 5.90. MAP OF FEATURE 57 AT SITE 8, THE PUTATIVE MOSQUE.

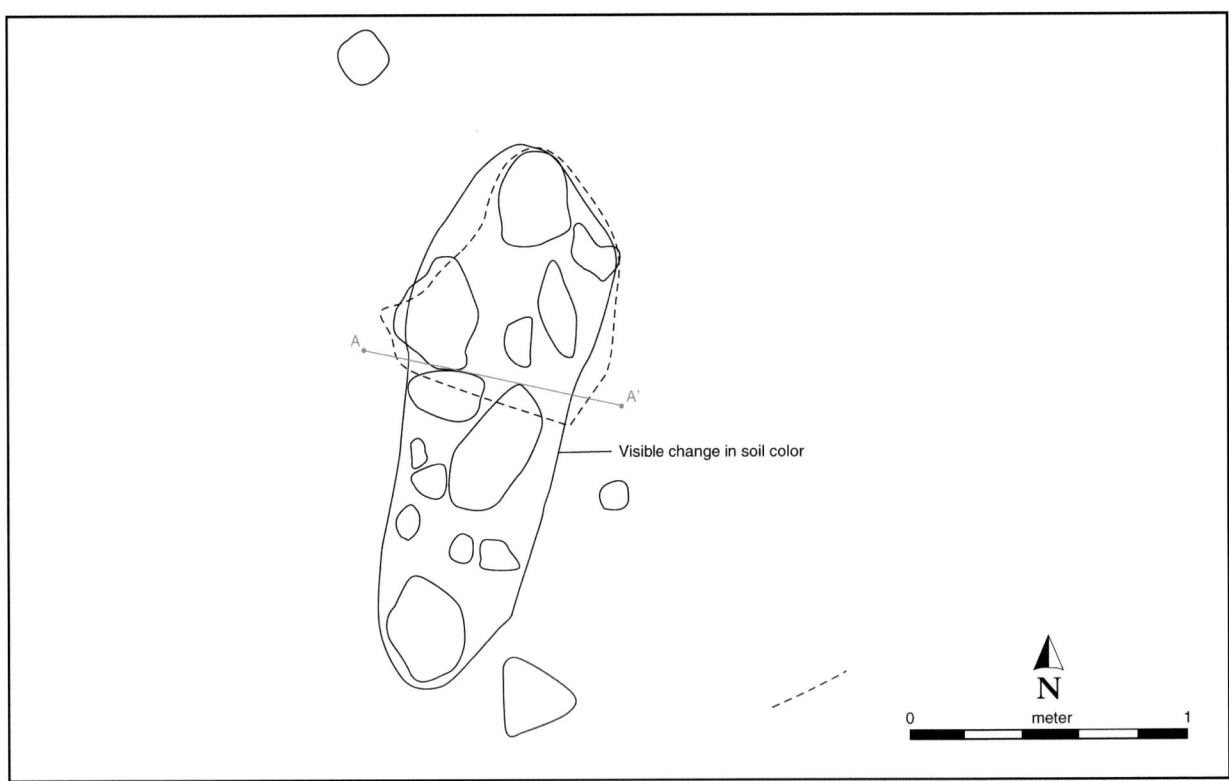

FIGURE 5.91. MAP OF FEATURE 49 AT SITE 8, A PUTATIVE BURIAL. PROFILE A-A NOT REPRODUCED HERE.

Archaeological Survey and Test-Excavation Results

Figure 5.92. Feature 49 at Site 8, a putative burial, prior to excavation.

Figure 5.93. Feature 62 at Site 8, a putative burial.

Figure 5.94. Feature 61, the enclosure wall in foreground with putative mosque Feature 57 in the background, prior to cleaning and sample excavation.

Figure 5.95. Putative mosque Feature 57 after cleaning.

Figure 5.96. Excavated section through west wall of putative mosque Feature 57.

Archaeological Survey and Test-Excavation Results

Figure 5.97. Enclosure wall Feature 61 in process of excavation.

Figure 5.98. Enclosure wall Feature 61 during course of excavation.

Figure 5.99. Excavated section through the enclosure wall of Feature 61 at Site 8

Figure 5.100. Feature 5 at Site 9 prior to excavation.

Archaeological Survey and Test-Excavation Results

Figure 5.101. Feature 7 at Site 8, a stone circle, prior to excavation.

Figure 5.102. Feature 5 at Site 9 after excavation.

FIGURE 5.103. FEATURE 7 AT SITE 8 AFTER CLEANING, WITH RAMMED CLAY FLOOR CLEARLY VISIBLE.

Ideological/Sacred Sites

Seven ideological/sacred sites were found throughout the OJVG concession. These sites differ from sacred sites documented during the ethnographic survey in that no residents that we interviewed mentioned these sites. It is possible that other members of the community knew of these sites or that our informants chose not to disclose their locations. We note that the locals who were part of the archaeological survey had no knowledge of these sites.

The seven ideological/sacred sites are an eclectic mix of possible burial cairns/graves, *tumuli*, and collections of cupules. The sites are not residential in nature, and none appeared to have an economic focus. Several ideological or sacred archaeological sites are located near residential sites. However, no information was obtained that would link these sites directly. Further, no information obtained about the function of the sacred/ideological sites. Two of these sites, Sites 1 and 157, are described below.

Site 1

Location in concession: This site is located on the top of a small laterite hill in Niakifiri, south of Sabodala.

Topographic setting: Hilltop, on laterite.

Vegetation: A few trees have taken root on the hilltop; otherwise, the site is barren laterite rock.

Hydrology: There is no water in the vicinity; the nearest is a few hundred meters to both the north and the south.

Modern disturbances: The site has been disturbed by the creation of flat drilling platforms for mining exploration. It is located within the proposed Niakifiri mine pit.

Site description: The site consists of 66 'cups,' or deep oval/circular hollows ground into the hard laterite crust that tops the hill. The cups vary in size from approximately 20 cm in diameter and 1 m in depth to large hollows, 50–80 cm across and 40–50 cm deep. The cups on the top of the hill were filled with soil and leaf litter, but the cups to the north and east were notably free of fill, suggesting they have been maintained in this condition. There was no spatial patterning in the distribution of sizes.

Artifacts: The only artifacts consisted of a small collection of round glass beads, which appeared to be relatively recent (second half of the twentieth century) in date.

Site interpretation: The site is interpreted as an ideological/sacred site. The cups seem to have no ordinary function, although in the souh-western USA

ARCHAEOLOGICAL SURVEY AND TEST-EXCAVATION RESULTS

they might be interpreted as bedrock-mortars for grinding grain or other produce. The location is on bare, hard laterite and is unsuitable for domestic use. The nearest modern settlement is the village of Sabodala, and in the ethnographic interviews, the villagers identified a number of sacred or traditional cultural properties that they said had been damaged by mining exploration but whose exact locations they would not divulge.

Site 1 was originally recorded, in 2009, as a small, sparse scatter of pottery on the northwest slope of this hill (Figure 5.104). In 2010, during the survey of the

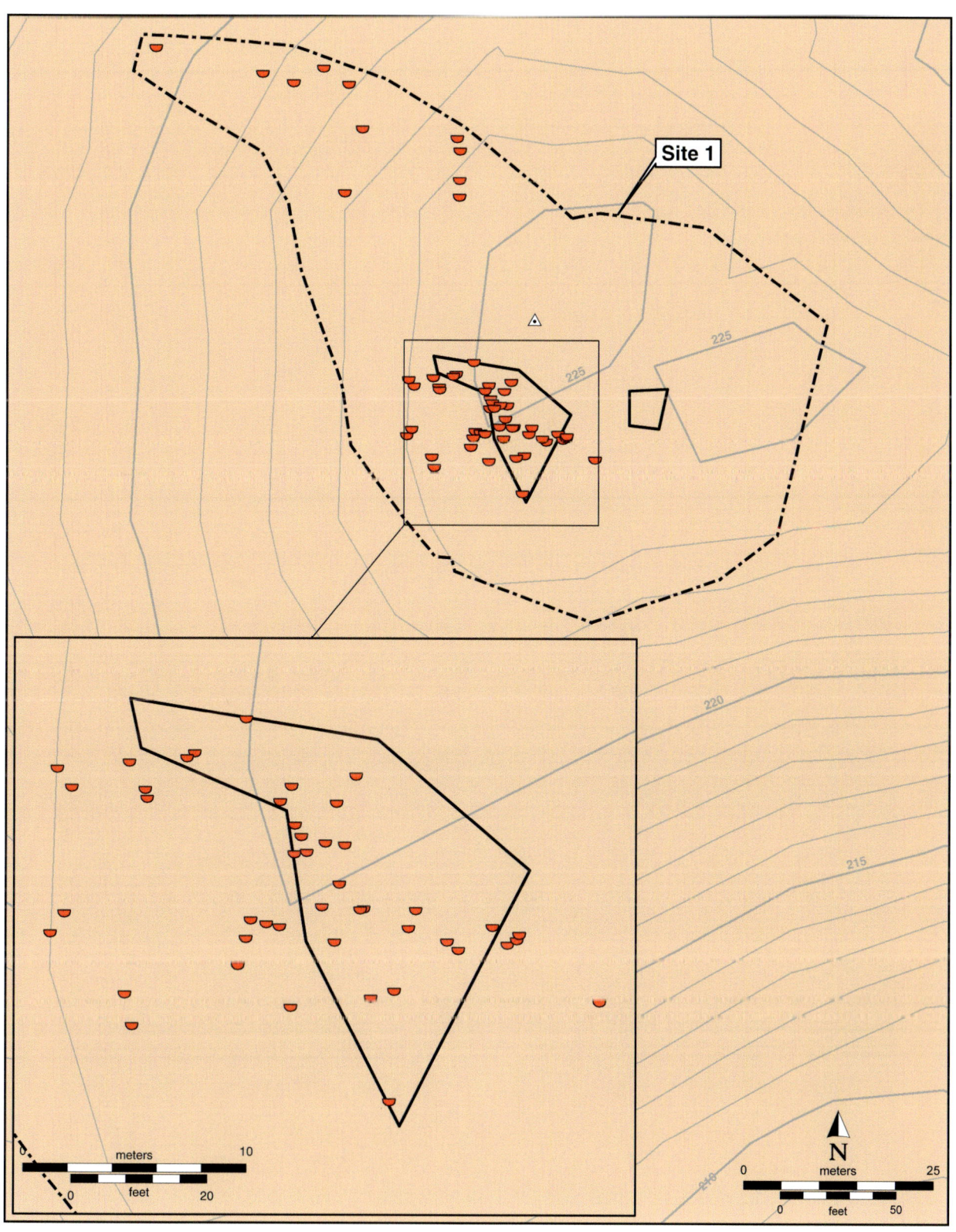

FIGURE 5.104. GIS-GENERATED MAP OF SITE 1.

119

proposed Niakafiri mine pit, the hill was traversed again, and this time, the summit of the hill was traversed, and a small, dense cluster of about 25 cups or 'bowls' ground into the laterite sheet that forms the summit plateau were

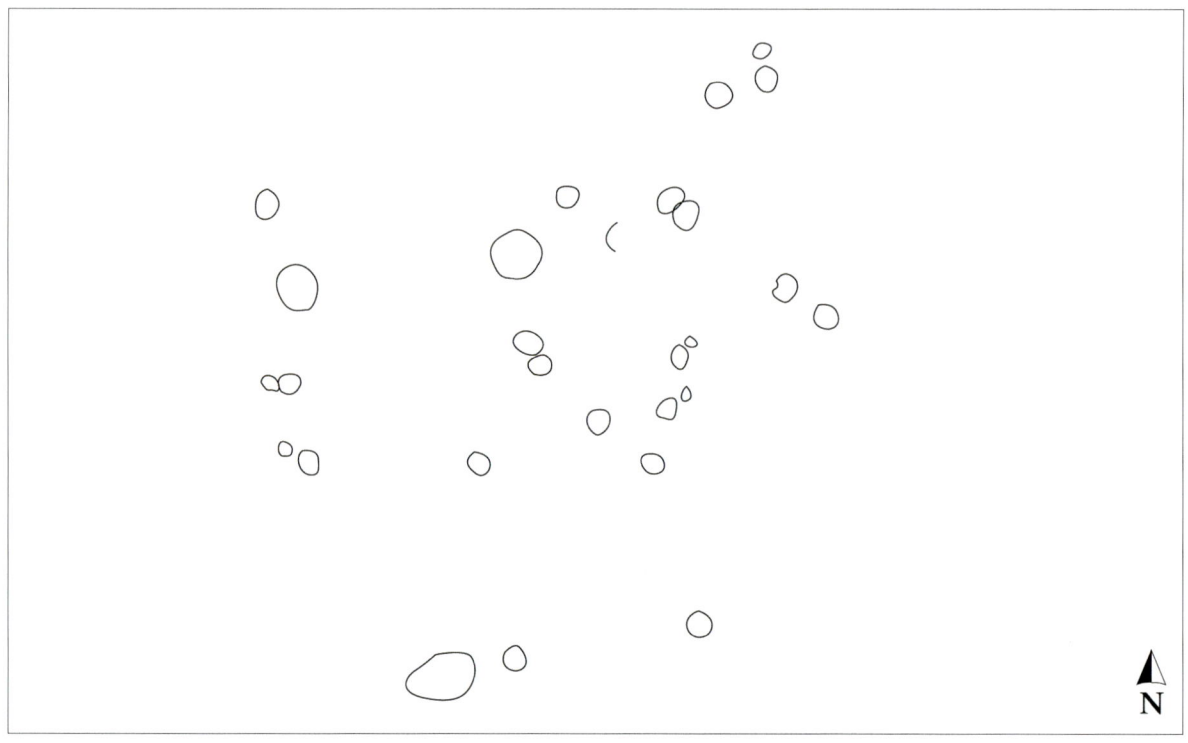

Figure 5.105. Scale drawing of the initial cluster of cup/cupules at Site 1.

Figure 5.106. The cup marks at Site 1 on the summit of the hill.

Archaeological Survey and Test-Excavation Results

FIGURE 5.107. FEATURES 9–11 AT SITE 1.

observed. These were largely filled with soil and leaf detritus and were excavated (but included no artifacts) and recorded with a measured plan (Figure 5.105) and photographs (Figures 5.106–5.108). Then, more cups were found to the west, and ultimately 66 were excavated, recorded, and photographed. There were probably more present; to the west of the main cluster on the map, a platform for a geological core has been terraced into the hillside, and the terracing would have destroyed any cups present. The excavation of the 40 or so cups to the west of the initial cluster revealed that very few had any significant fill of soil or detritus, except what might have blown in during the past season, and one pair of cups contained a small assemblage of multicolored glass beads. The beads and the lack of soil fill suggest that these cups have been kept clear in the recent past—in short, this may be a very recent or current sacred site. The nearest villages are Maka Madina and Sabodala. In 2009, interviews were held in Maka Madina, and a number of sacred sites were discussed and located but did not include this site. By contrast, the meetings in Sabodala were much less revealing, and the chief there recounted how a number, perhaps as many as 20, of their sacred traditional sites had been damaged or destroyed in the recent past by mining and exploration activities. Site 1 may be an example.

FIGURE 5.108. FEATURE 47. NOTE THE SIZE OF THE 'CUP MARK.'

Site 157

Location in concession: Site 157 is located south of Mamakhono, along the route of the proposed haul road.

Topographic setting: A broad plain of second terrace, with two small but steep-sided laterite hills, the larger of which is encompassed by Site 156.

Vegetation: Generally open bush, the northeastern part extending into arable fields of Mamakhono (the green polygons in the map extract).

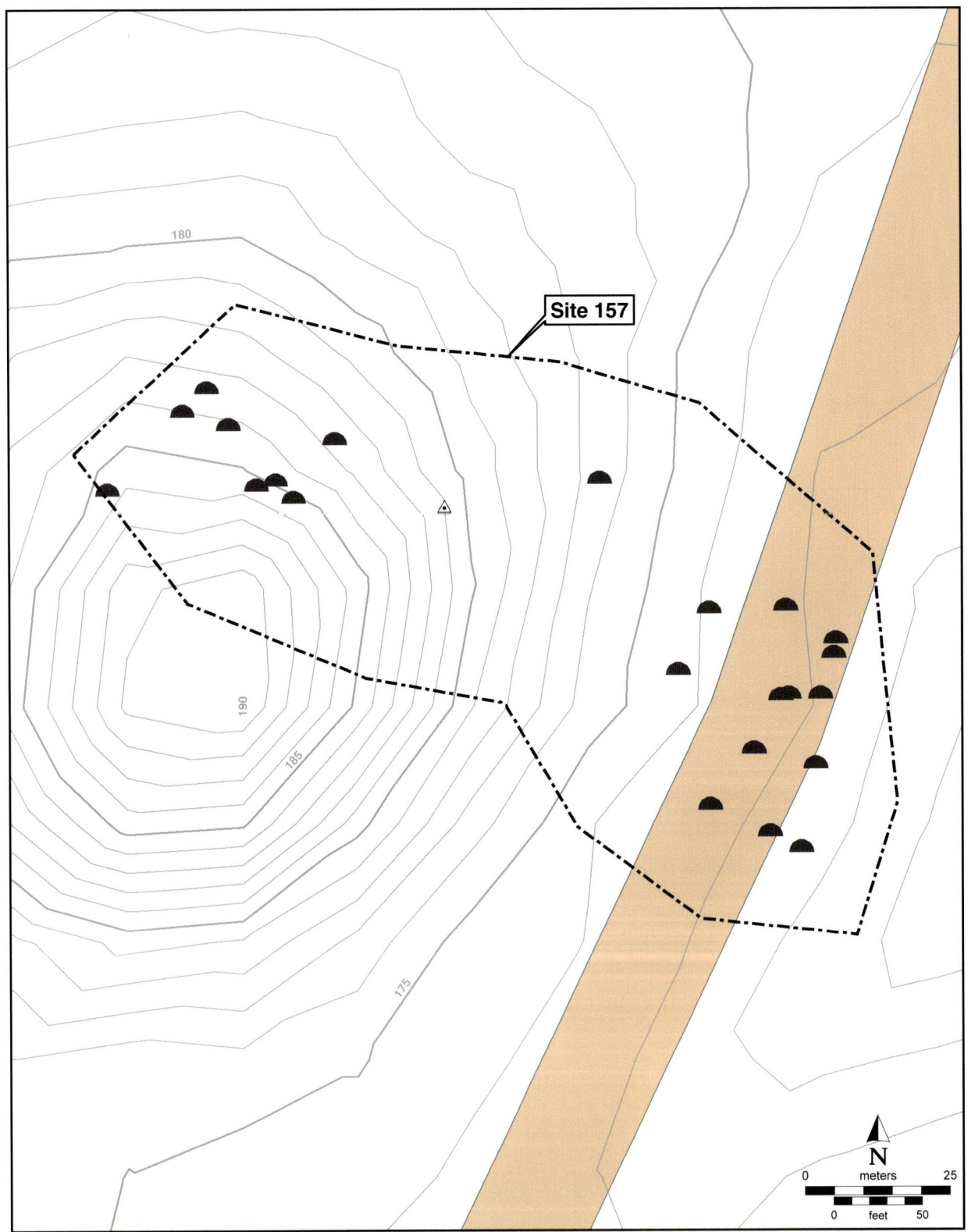

FIGURE 5.109. GIS-GENERATED MAP OF SITE 157.

Archaeological Survey and Test-Excavation Results

Hydrology: There are no stream courses in the immediate vicinity.

Modern disturbances: None.

Site description: The site consists of 22 *tumuli pierre*, or circular stone cairns. They are located on the flat plain southwest of Site 156, in two clusters, one directly in the route of the proposed haul road and the second at a higher elevation, on the northern slopes of a small hill (see Figure 5.108). The stone cairns or *tumuli* average 4–5 m in diameter and stand up to 1 m above the local ground surface.

Artifacts: Only two sherds of thin-walled pottery wares with fine paste and a deep red slip combined with twine were collected here. One was a vessel with a simple rim and a relief motif showing a possible snake. The other was a short, everted rim. Both show drastic differences from most of the pottery collected in the Sabodala region.

Site interpretation: The site is interpreted as a cemetery consisting of *tumuli pierre*. Features of this type were previously unknown in eastern Senegal but are known from the eastern region of the megalith zone, along the Gambia River system.

Site 157 was discovered during the course of survey along the line of the proposed road from the proposed processing plant and the village of Mamakhono. Site 157 is located only 200 m from a large village, Site 156, but there are no direct archaeological links between the two sites.

Site 157 consists of 22 stone, built mounds—*tumuli pierre*. This type of feature was previously unknown in this region of Eastern Senegal. The mounds appear to be in two clusters—the first on the lower, eastern slopes of a hill adjacent to a broad, shallow valley to the east and the second cluster on the upper, north-facing slopes (Figure 5.109). The mounds are essentially constructed mounds of stones averaging 4 m in diameter and between 80 cm and 1 m in height. The mounds were recorded with a GPS device and photographed (Figures 5.110–5.114).

Two mounds were selected for sample excavation; these were Feature 1 and Feature 3. Test excavations at Arch 157 (along the proposed road from the plant to the reservoir dam between Mamakhono and Dindifa) were based on the discovery at this site of large, domed-shaped rock rings that showed significant differences from the most commonly encountered stone features in the area. Their relatively large size and domed

Figure 5.110. Feature 1 at Site 157, *tumulus pierre*.

shape were reminiscent of stone monuments in the Senegambian megalith zone, where they are referred to as '*cercles pierrers*' (Thilmans et al. 1980). According to the investigators, these monuments represent a different megalithic tradition, one they referred to as the *oriental faciès*, characteristic of the eastern section of the Gambia River and its catchments. The presence of similar monuments in the Sabodala region is a major discovery, as it would extend the Senegambian megalith zone farther east, toward the Falémé River.

Excavation of Feature 1

Feature 1 is a rock ring with a big stone pile in the middle that gave it a dome-shaped aspect. The feature was divided into four quadrants and the northeast part was chosen as the excavation unit. The area covered by Feature 1 is almost 50 m². The test unit was excavated to a maximum depth of 108.5 m. Although excavations allowed us to gain insights as to the disposition of the rocks that were circular and the foundations of the rocks that were directly laid on the ground surface, no cultural remains were uncovered during the excavation of Feature 1. Three major stratigraphic horizons could be delineated from the wall profiles. The upper horizon was characterized by gravelly silt loam. The second horizon was gravelly silty clay. Finally, the lower, third horizon was silty clay loam. Like the first horizon, neither of the last two yielded cultural remains as might have been expected.

Excavation of Feature 3

Feature 3 is large rock ring that was domed-shaped, like Feature 1 (Figure 5.115). We initially delineated a trench of 3 by 1 m, oriented east-west (Figure 5.116). The top of the feature was covered with large blocks of rock that we first had to remove to reach soil underneath for excavations. No cultural debris was recovered at the end of Level 1, which was closed at about 58 cm below the datum. We were able to define the outline of the feature that defined a perfect rock-ring foundation in the eastern and western sides of the unit. Level 2 was excavated to a maximum depth of 75 cm. It is in this level that the possible ritual pottery of Arch 157 was uncovered. They were probably two vessels that must have been complete and deposited in the eastern part of the unit. One of them was a simple vessel with a very narrow mouth, above which was applied a relief decoration possibly representing a snake. The pots were directly on top of a second rock pile that appeared underneath the one excavated in Level 1. This second layer of rock pile seems to extend toward the north, where the pottery was collected, and toward the south and west. We

Figure 5.111. Feature 9 at Site 157, *tumulus pierre*.

ARCHAEOLOGICAL SURVEY AND TEST-EXCAVATION RESULTS

FIGURE 5.112. FEATURE 3 AT SITE 157, *TUMULUS PIERRE*.

FIGURE 5.113. FEATURE 5 AT SITE 157, *TUMULUS PIERRE*.

Figure 5.114. Feature 6 at Site 157, *tumulus pierre*.

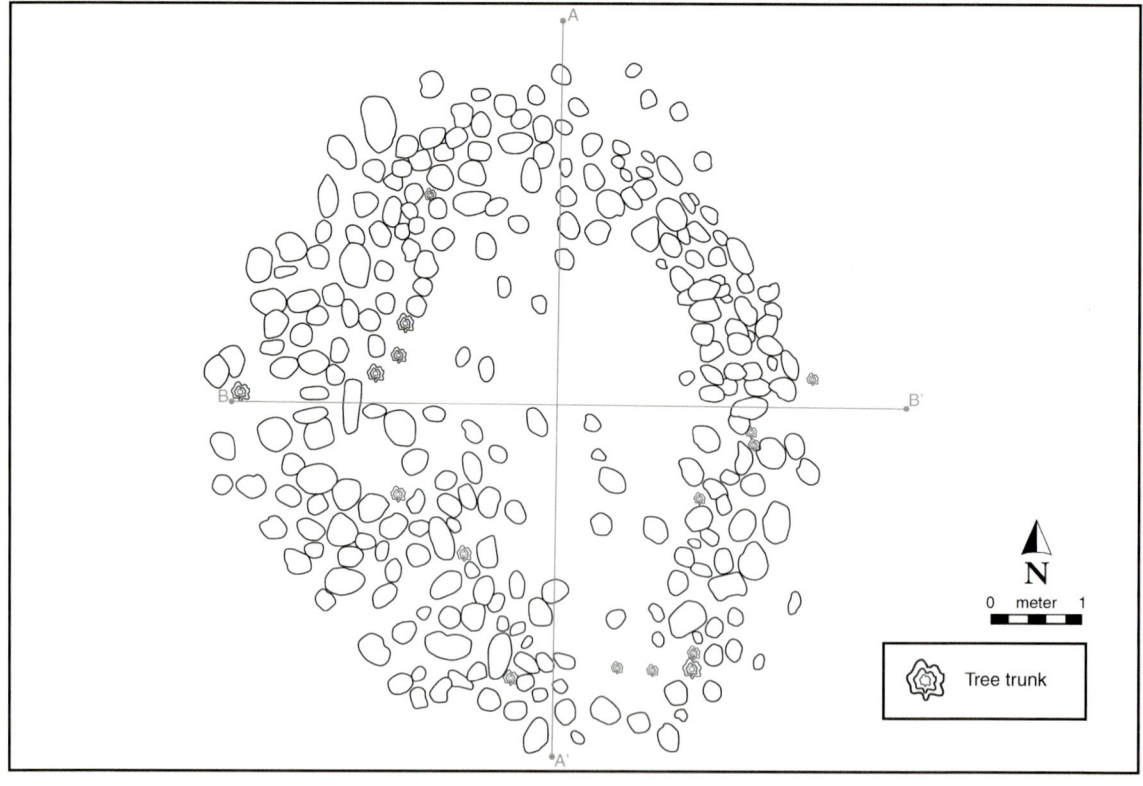

Figure 5.115. Scale map of Feature 1, pre-excavation.

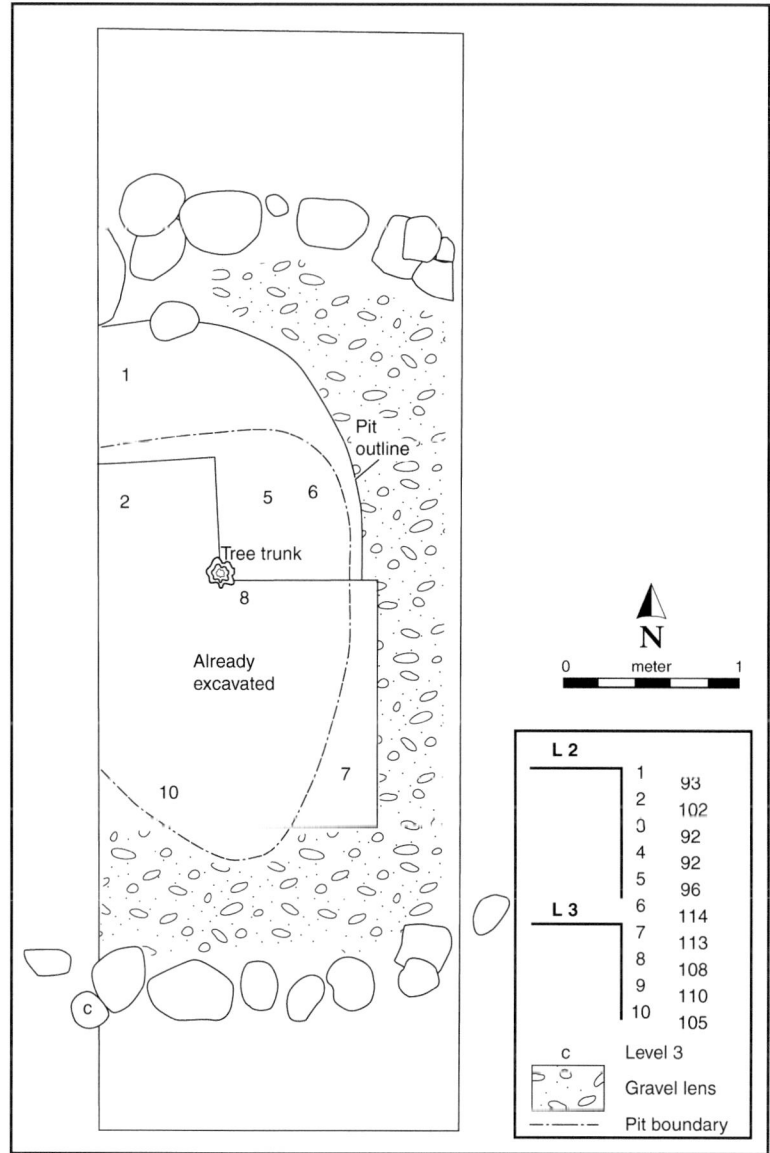

FIGURE 5.116. SCALE DRAWING OF FEATURE 3 DURING EXCAVATION.

then decided to extend the unit to define the rock pile. With these successive extensions, the excavation unit expanded to 4 by 2 m. In trying to delineate the outline of the rock pile in the middle of Feature 3, we noted that there were several layers of rocks that were culturally structured. At about 1 m in depth, the rocks were still oriented east-west and outlined a perfect body size of about 2 m in length and 50 cm in width. Underneath this layer, the rock pile began to fade away, mainly appearing in the western part of the unit, where it seemed to dive into the ground, almost reaching the outer rim of the feature. Excavations were taken down to a depth 1.20 m, allowing us to remove most of the rocks. At this level, the soil underneath the rock pile outlined a pit, which extended from east to west, less than 2 m in length and about 1.5 m in width. Interestingly, the pit was bounded by a gravel layer, particularly in its western, southern, and eastern parts. Inside the outline of the pit that we now refer to as a putative burial, the soil had a grayish color. The final level excavated reached a maximum depth of 1.62 m. The grayish sediment that seemed to outline a burial and that was bounded by a gravel layer turned into silty clay loam that coincided with sterile soil. To better understand this intriguing feature, we performed a pH analysis of soil samples taken at different levels (7 cm, 38 cm, 89 cm, and 1.39 m). The results yielded an optimal pH of 7.88. According to Jeff Homburg (personal communication 2010), bone preservation is not the best under these conditions, and when the variable of time is added, the chances of finding bone remains are quite limited.

Discussion of Site Settlement Types and Distribution

A review of Table 5.1 reveals that there is sufficient information in the field records (plus professional judgments) to categorize 251 sites, as shown in raw numbers in the left column and as percentages of the total to the right. This is graphically represented in Figure 5.117.

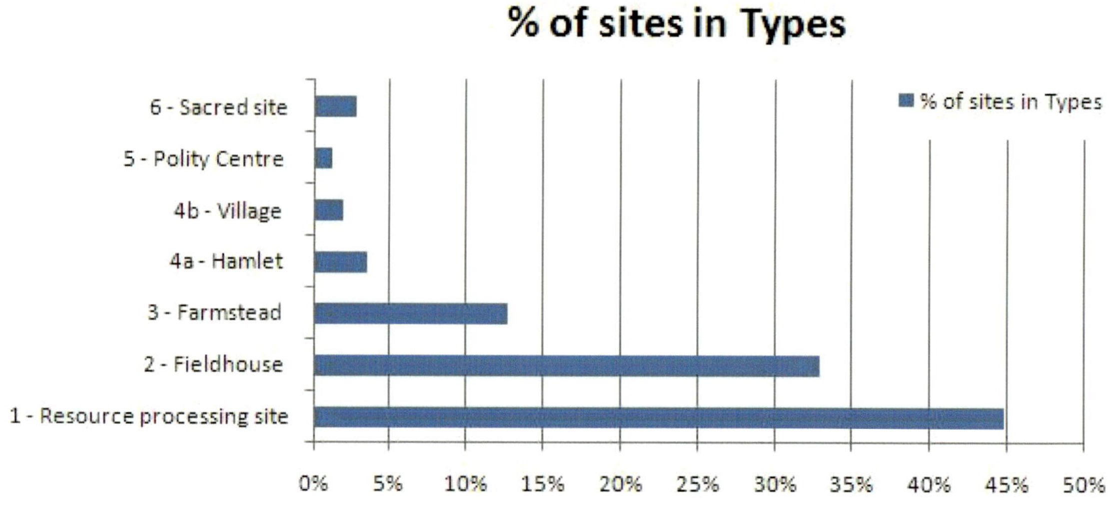

% of sites in Types

- 6 - Sacred site
- 5 - Polity Centre
- 4b - Village
- 4a - Hamlet
- 3 - Farmstead
- 2 - Fieldhouse
- 1 - Resource processing site

FIGURE 5.117. GRAPHICAL PRESENTATION OF PERCENTAGES OF THE SITE IN EACH SITE TYPE.

This indicates that only 8 percent of the sites identified were year-round domestic sites, and 92 percent of sites were either resource-processing places or temporary/seasonal occupations. The intensity of habitation is reflected in the number of stone rings representing structures on each type of site. The 30 farmsteads contained 143 documented rings, or an average of 4.8 per site. The 13 hamlets had 116 rings, an average of 8.9 per site, and the 4 villages had 261 rings, an average of 65 per site. As for the polity centers, the number of stone rings at Makhana Site 24 is unknown, whereas at Masato Sites 8 and 9 the number of rings is clearly more than 75.

The various archaeological investigations recorded sites across the whole of the OJVG concession. Field houses and farmsteads are located in areas similar to those favored by modern farmers. The placement of residential sites is somewhat more complex. In certain respects, such as topographic position and proximity to agricultural land, the archaeological hamlets and villages mimic their modern analogues. They differ, in that modern villages are found adjacent to reliable water sources, whereas their archaeological counterparts are at some distance. The polity center at Masato shows that a defensive position may have been more important in the past, and it is worth pursuing this line of inquiry to determine whether other habitations were also so inclined (see Chapters 8 and 9).

If nothing else, the survey of the OJVG concession has demonstrated that the archaeological record of the upper Senegal and upper Gambia River drainages is much more complicated than previously thought. Sites were found literally everywhere we looked. Most date to the later part of prehistory and history, but a fair number were also dated to the lower and upper Palaeolithic periods.

These data may give a false impression about the numbers and densities of settlements, because chronological information about these sites is very limited. It is likely that the majority of the sites (or, perhaps, the majority of the occupation evidence for the majority of the sites) belong to the last two or three centuries. The number and the size of sites that were occupied and in use at any one time was probably much smaller than these numbers might suggest. In short, these sites may represent no more than a couple of communities settled in villages of perhaps a few hundred individuals, at most. These populations would, at the peak agricultural times of planting and harvesting, split apart and occupy the many farmsteads and field houses, while the inhabitants were engaged in the labor-intensive work. If this line of reasoning is accurate, the population would, by comparison with the present, seem quite small and dispersed and perhaps more mobile than is common today.

Chapter 6

Artifact Analyses

Archaeological work associated with the SCHP has resulted in the collection of a large number of artifacts. Most of this material was recovered as part of the survey and test excavations in the ADI, although some were collected as part of reconnaissance surveys and monitoring activities. Pottery is by far the dominant artifact class in the collection, followed by lithics. The rest of the collection was grouped into a category termed 'small finds,' which included spindlewhorls, tobacco pipes, gunflints, beads, and glass and metal artifacts.

Most sites encountered had pottery. Surface collections of ceramics were made at most of the sites, as well as at a few locations termed 'isolated occurrences' (n = 148). Surface collection, however, was not always performed at sites found during the opportunistic archaeological reconnaissance survey and during the ethnographic survey. Even so, we believe that the ceramics collected are representative of all parts of the OJVG concession and of all site types. Far fewer sites (n = 49) and isolated occurrences contained lithic material and stone tools, and still fewer (n = 20) had other types of materials, classified as small finds. Accordingly, the bulk of our analytical effort was devoted to ceramic analysis. We turn our attention in this chapter to ceramics first, followed by a discussion of small finds, and then close with our analysis of the lithic artifacts.

Ceramic Sampling and Analysis Procedures

Archaeological assemblages in the upper Senegal region are poorly understood, and no ceramic sequence exists. The closest regions with ceramic typologies and culture history sequences are the middle Senegal (McIntosh 1991) and lower Falémé River Valleys (Thiaw 1999). To facilitate comparison with these regions, we used the same terminology for identical categories of artifacts and patterns. We also meticulously recorded new types that could result from regional, chronological, stylistic and/or cultural differences.

In general, rim types found in the Sabodala region are also known in the lower Falémé and middle Senegal River Valleys. Although similarities were noted in decorative motifs, significant differences were also observed. This section describes the collection and recording procedures for ceramics and situates them in regional and interregional prehistory and history.

More than 200 kg of pottery were collected during survey and test excavations. The bulk of the material was recovered from survey; test excavations revealed mostly shallow and sparse deposits. Although most of the sites encountered in the study area yielded pottery, the density and frequency of sherds were extremely variable from one site to another. To ensure collections of an adequate size, sampling procedures varied—from the collecting all ceramics on a site if it had less than 20 surface sherds to collecting a sample of mostly rim and decorated sherds.

Prior to analysis, all pottery was washed and air-dried. It was then sorted into body sherds and feature sherds. The latter category was composed mainly of rim sherds, but also included bases, handles, and special items, such as spindlewhorls and fragments of tobacco pipes, censers, and steamers. Most sites lacked feature sherds, only yielding body sherds. Analysis was carried out in the IFAN archaeology lab in Dakar.

Method for Analyzing Body Sherds

In all, 4,246 body sherds from the survey and test excavations were examined. Only decorative motif was recorded and analyzed for body sherds. The analysis consisted of sorting the collection from each site into decorative classes, which were then counted and recorded. Sherds with a body surface of less than 4 cm2 were considered too small for decorative motifs to be determined; these were counted and jettisoned. Multiple sherds from the same vessel were counted as one.

Body sherds were grouped into three broad decorative categories: plain (nondecorated), slipped, and plastic-decorated. Plastic decoration was subdivided into two major subclasses: subtractive and additive, each of which included a wide variety of motifs. Many sherds had more than one motif; these were grouped in the category 'multiple attributes.' Although decoration can be found on different parts of a ware body, vessel position was not recorded.

The different decorative motifs that were identified and recorded in the collection are briefly described below. We hasten to point out that identification of decorative motifs on archaeological ceramic is far from standardized in the Senegambia. In many cases, decoration patterns are described indiscriminately on the basis of the implement or tool employed to produced a particular kind of design. In other cases, decoration is described in terms of the technique used or shape obtained. As much as possible, we described decoration on the basis of the implement used to produce it.

Plain Sherds

Plain sherds are nondecorated. Although generally considered nondiagnostic, in the Sabodala region—just as elsewhere in northern (Guèye 1998, McIntosh 1991), northwestern, and eastern (Thiaw 1999) Senegal—high percentage of nondecorated sherds, when combined with other variables, such as temper and rim types, appears to be time sensitive.

Slip

Slip is a fluid, clayey coating applied to a vessel to produce lighter, clearer surface colors (Shepard 1974:191). The fine coat fills in the vessels' pores and improves surface texture, rendering the pottery less permeable.

Plastic Impression

Plastic impression is a very broad category that includes all decorative techniques exploiting the plasticity of clay. It can be subdivided into two major subclasses (Rice 1987). The first, referred to as subtractive motif, implies the use of a decorating implement that penetrates the clay. The second, additive motif, implies the application of additional clay of variable shape and size to parts of an existing manufactured ware. These subclasses can be further divided into smaller categories on the basis of either the shape, the motif, or the device or technique employed for the decoration.

Subtractive Motifs

All decorative techniques that result in the subtraction of clay during their application fall in this broad category. Subtractive decorative techniques include twine impressions, carved wooden roulette, incision, channeling, punctuate, and digital impressions (Figures 6.1–6.4). In Sabodala, as in many parts of Senegal, twine impression is the most popular subtractive motifs. It is also one of the most varied and complex subclasses of subtractive motifs. Because of its variability, we singled out twine impression from the rest of the plastic impressions as a separate class.

Twine Impressions

Three major roulettes—twisted and rolled twine corresponding in McIntosh's (1991) typology to braided twine 1 (Tw1), pleated twine 4 (Tw4), and twisted and rolled twine 6 (Tw6)—dominate this class (see Figure 6.1). Other motifs, including knotted twine and various cord-wrapped-stick techniques, are present in the collection, but in small numbers. Twine roulettes were probably designed to embellish ceramic wares, and the different motifs could reflect variation in cultural and aesthetic tastes. The roughened surface of a twine-impressed vessel ensures a more secure grip for lifting and carrying a pot (Rice 1987:232). In addition, the uneven surface produced by its application enhances cooking properties, as it absorbs heat more readily.

Tw1 is a braided twine roulette that produces chevron-shaped imprints when rolled across the surface of a vessel (McIntosh 1991). It is made of two or three cords that are pleated together. Tw4 is a pleated roulette that produces imprints of parallel rows of raised dashes or oval beads (McIntosh 1991). Most vessels with Tw4 roulette represented in the SCHP collections were made with a pleated fiber roulette, which produced patterns of oval or round beads similar to a maize-cob roulette without the grains. Tw6 is a twisted and rolled string that produces parallel, obliquely oriented rows of beaded depressions when applied to a vessel's body (McIntosh 1991).

Cord-Wrapped Stick

The cord-wrapped-stick roulette motifs encountered were generally made with twisted cordage (see Figure 6.2, middle and bottom). Other twine impressions were encountered, including knotted motifs, but these are extremely rare in the SCHP collection.

Carved Wood Roulette

A carved wood roulette is a wooden cylinder with a carved surface. The impression it leaves depends on the shape, size, and orientation of the carving. One major difference between the SCHP collection and those recovered in the lower Falémé and middle Senegal Valleys is the relatively high occurrence of carved wood roulette motifs. We recognized four types of carved wood roulettes, although more may exist (see Figures 6.3 and 6.4): two wavy types (CWR2 and CWR3), one geometrical type (CWR1), and one with a featherlike pattern (CWR4).

CWR1 yields a series of deep, squarish or lozenge designs imprinted on the vessel's body and separated by lines of raised clay (see Figure 6.3, middle). It corresponds to the carved wooden roulette R1, defined by Thiaw (1999) in the lower Falémé River Valley, where it is extremely rare. CWR2 is the most commonly found carved wooden roulette in the Sabadola region (see Figure 6.3, top). It corresponds to Thiaw's (1999) R3 carved wooden roulette in the lower Falémé Valley. As with CWR1, its incidence in the lower Falémé Valley is quite rare. It produces a pattern of deep imprints of wavy or zigzag impressions separated by similarly wavy or zigzag lines formed by the raised clay. Like other carved wooden roulette motifs encountered, it seems to be very diagnostic of the culture of this area. CWR3 is similar to CWR2, as both roulettes produce a zigzag pattern (see Figure 6.3, bottom). However, the CWR3 impressions are generally much deeper, outlining a series a parallel zigzag line. CWR4 is marked by a featherlike pattern defined by central impressions that look like spines, to which are attached, obliquely or perpendicularly, a pair of impressions (see Figure 6.4). This pattern is quite rare in the assemblage and is generally found in combination with other motifs.

FIGURE 6.1. SUBTRACTIVE DECORATIVE TECHNIQUES, TWINE IMPRESSION (TW): ***TOP,*** TW1; ***MIDDLE,*** TW4; ***BOTTOM,*** TW6.

FIGURE 6.2. SUBTRACTIVE DECORATIVE TECHNIQUES, SABOT AND CORD-WRAPPED STICK: ***TOP***, CARVED SPIKE OF ***BLEPHARIS*** SP. OR SABOT; ***MIDDLE AND BOTTOM,*** CORD-WRAPPED STICK.

Figure 6.3. Subtractive decorative technique: carved wooden roulette (CWR): *TOP,* CWR2; *MIDDLE,* CWR1; *BOTTOM,* CWR3.

Figure 6.4. Subtractive decorative techniques, carved wooden roulette (CWR) and incisions: *TOP LEFT AND MIDDLE,* CWR4 and incision; *TOP RIGHT,* CWR3; *BOTTOM LEFT,* incision and CWR1; *BOTTOM RIGHT,* straw punctuate and incision.

Incision

In general, an incised motif is obtained by pushing or dragging a sharp implement across the clay, creating an impression with a V-shaped cross-section. Because you can make the same or similar motifs using a variety of tools, it is extremely difficult to define types based on technology. Incised designs include continuous linear, wavy, and chevron, as well as discontinuous and zigzag motifs (Figure 6.5, top left). These can be single or multiple lines and can have various shapes.

Channeling

In contrast to incision, the tool used to obtain channeling is rather blunt and relatively large. It results in a U-shaped cross-section in the clay. Channeled motifs are marked by relatively wide and deep grooves (see Figure 6.5, bottom).

Other subtractive motifs

'Sabot' (hoof) roulette was defined in Senegal in 1964 by analogy to antelopes' hoofprints (Bessac 1964). Until recently, it was classified as twine roulette (see Figure 6.2, top). Most recent work suggests that it is a vegetal roulette made with a carved spike of Blepharis sp. In the lower Falémé and middle Senegal River Valleys, it is generally associated with Late Stone Age and, to some extent, early Iron Age assemblages. But it does occur in small numbers in more recent assemblages.

Punctuate is the pattern obtained by stabbing or punching the wet clay of a pot surface with a rigid implement, such as a straw or stick (Figure 6.6, upper). It is possible that some of the punctuate motifs found in our collection were produced using a carved wooden disc, as has been observed in some assemblages in Mali (Gosselain et al. 1996).

Fingernail and *digital impressions* are created by pressing the fingernail or the fingertip into the wet clay surface (see Figure 6.6, middle). Although present in the assemblage, this motif is poorly represented in the collection.

Additive Motifs

Two main types of additive motifs were identified in the SCHP collection: continuous linear cordon, generally applied around the circumference of the vessel, and discontinuous clay appliqués, modeled in various shapes and applied on the surface of the vessel. Several subclasses, depending on their shape, have been recognized in this later category; however, only three of these subclasses were present in the SCHP collection:

FIGURE 6.5. SUBTRACTIVE DECORATIVE TECHNIQUES: **TOP LEFT,** ZIGZAG INCISION; **TOP RIGHT,** CORD-WRAPPED STICK; **BOTTOM,** CHANNELING.

FIGURE 6.6. SUBTRACTIVE DECORATIVE TECHNIQUES: ***TOP,*** PUNCTUATE; ***MIDDLE,*** DIGIT IMPRESSIONS; ***BOTTOM,*** KNOTTED TWINE IMPRESSION.

FIGURE 6.7. SUBTRACTIVE DECORATIVE TECHNIQUES: ***TOP LEFT,*** TW6 AND INCISION; ***TOP RIGHT,*** INCISION AND CWR1; ***BOTTOM LEFT,*** INCISION AND CORD-WRAPPED STICK; ***BOTTOM RIGHT,*** CORDON, PUNCTUATE, AND SLIP.

téton (round and protruding appliqué with a pointed, teat-shaped end), button (protruding and round with a blunt rather than teat-shaped end), and pastille (flat, round, and slightly protruding).

Multiple Attributes and Unidentified Motifs

When more than one decoration motif was present on one sherd, it was recorded under the category 'multiple attributes' (Figure 6.7).

When identification of the motif on a sherd was impossible for some reason (unknown roulette and/or decorative technique, or simply because surface erosion prevented proper identification), the sherd was recorded as unidentifiable (Unid.).

Method for Analyzing Rim Sherds

We collected 336 rim sherds during the SCHP investigations. All were drawn and processed in a similar manner. The frequency of rim sherds varied greatly from site to site—some sites yielded plentiful rim

sherds, but the vast majority yielded very few or no rim sherds. Because rim morphology showed a high degree of similarity with other known and well-described assemblages in Senegal, formal description of most rim categories was straightforward. No new rim class was identified.

Most of the rim sherds collected during survey and test excavations were drawn and described using several formal and informal variables. Rim morphology, rim decoration, rim diameter, wall thickness, nonplastic inclusions, and core color were systematically recorded for each specimen. Description of the decorative elements used the same attribute classes that were used for body sherds. Because of the small sample size, certain diagnostic rim types that are elsewhere divided into subclasses were grouped together. Such was the case for collared rims, which in the ceramic sequence for the lower Falémé and middle Senegal Valleys are very diagnostic of Phases III and IV in the middle Senegal River Valley, dating to a.d. 900–1200 and marking increased exchange and interactions with the Sahara (McIntosh 1991; Thiaw 1999). Similarly, long everted rim types (types E6 and E7)—typical of a.d. 1300–1700 and perhaps later assemblages in the lower Falémé River Valley—were grouped into one type, and all short everted rim types, E1–E5, are collapsed into another (see below) (Figure 6.8).

Rim Attributes and Morphology

Two gross rim shape classes, simple and everted, represent more than 95 percent of the SCHP collection; the remaining 5 percent, including collared, vertical, carinated, and T-rim types, have a rather sporadic or low incidence that is quite variable in frequency from site to site (Figure 6.9). Certain rim classes, such as simple, everted, and collared, are broadly defined to include various subclasses (Figures 6.10 and 6.11; see Figure 6.8).

Simple Rims

The simple rim class includes two major subtypes: simple open (or unrestricted) and simple closed (also referred to as restricted). The morphology of the lip can vary, but it is not taken into account in the definition. Simple closed rims form angles less than 90° with the plane of the vessel mouth, which restricts access to the interior of the vessel. In contrast, simple open rims have angles greater than 90°, resulting in easy access to the interior of the vessel (see Figure 6.9).

Everted Rims

Everted rims form one of the most varied classes in the collection, as it comprises seven subclasses, defined on the basis of the shape of the angle and on the length of the rim measured between the lip and the inflection point. Depending on the shape of the angle (that is, either curved or angulated) and the length of the rim (defined as short when the rim is less than 2 cm and long when greater than 2 cm), known everted rims from the Sabodala region can be grouped into two major subclasses—short and long everted rims.

Short everted rims include all everted rims that measure less than 2 cm from the lip to the internal inflection point. These comprise 5 subclasses (see Figure 6.9):

E1 slightly everted; internal and external profiles curve parallel to each other
E2 angular rather than curved inflection point
E3 similar to E1 in shape, but inflection point is more marked, and the rim's length is generally close to or exactly 2 cm
E4 deep, sharp inflection point that differs from most from other everted rims; generally semicircular or round and flat in cross-section
E5 curved and deeply everted

Long everted rims are longer than 2 cm above the neck. This category includes two subclasses that we refer to as long-necked jars.

E6 longer version of the short everted E1 subclass, with a curved rim profile
E7 longer version of the short everted E2 subclass, with an angulated rim profile

Collared Rims

Collared rims are characterized by the addition of a collar to an already manufactured rim (McIntosh 1991).

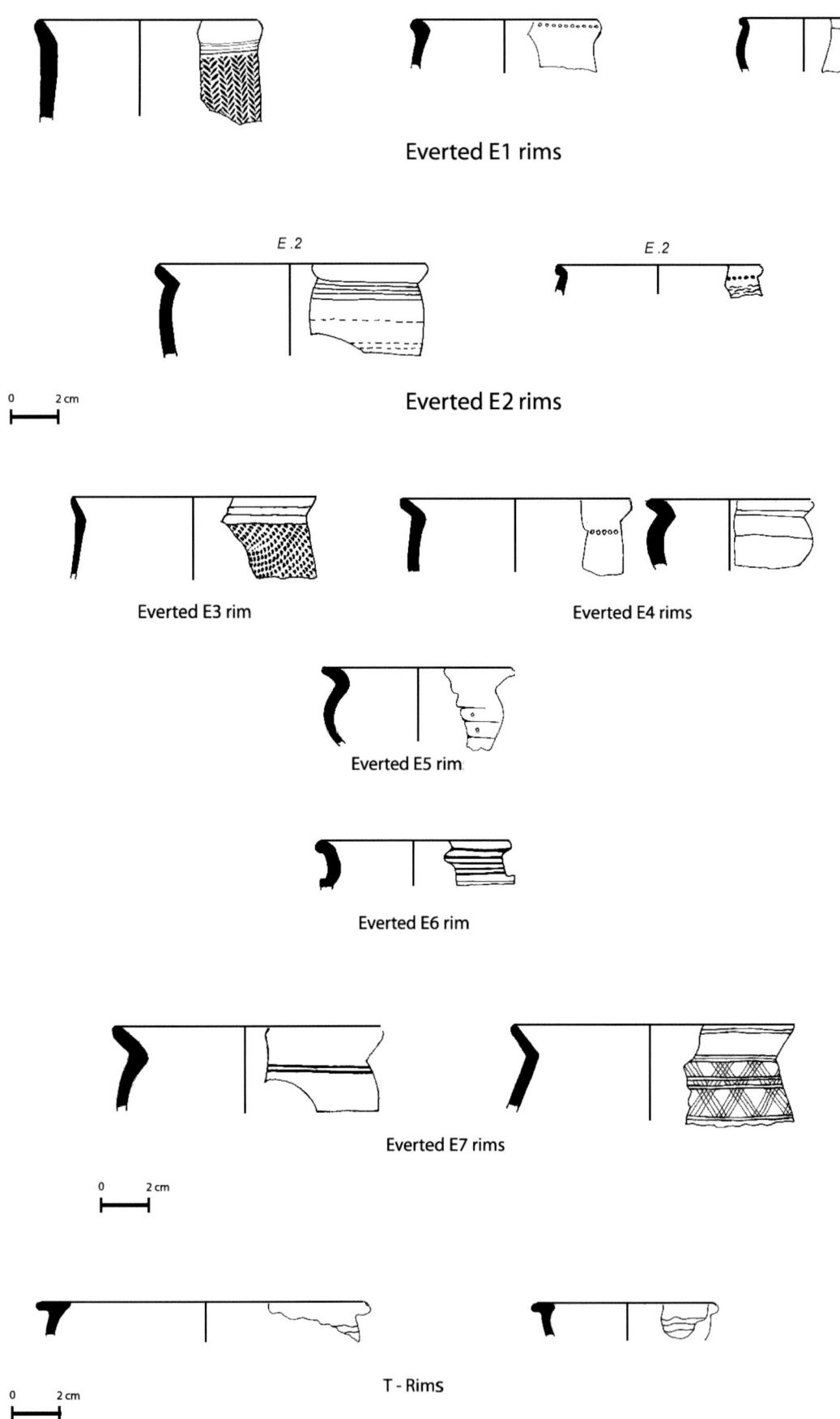

Figure 6.8. Everted rim types.

It is also possible that some collared rims were produced by completely folding out the rim of an already formed vessel (Thiaw 1999). According to Thilmans and Ravisé (1980), the collar or cordon was primarily functional and served as a handle.

Although a wide range of collared rims has been identified in the middle Senegal and lower Falémé River Valleys, only a few sites in the SCHP collection yielded this rim type. Because the sample of collared rims from the study area is small and includes only a few subclasses, we will only consider one gross class of collared rims (see Figure 6.9). The variability of collared rims is determined on the basis of the length of the rim measured from the vessel's lip to the center of the collar, but also on the shape of the collar, which can be squarish, subtriangular, or round in cross section. All these attributes are generally time sensitive (Thiaw 1999).

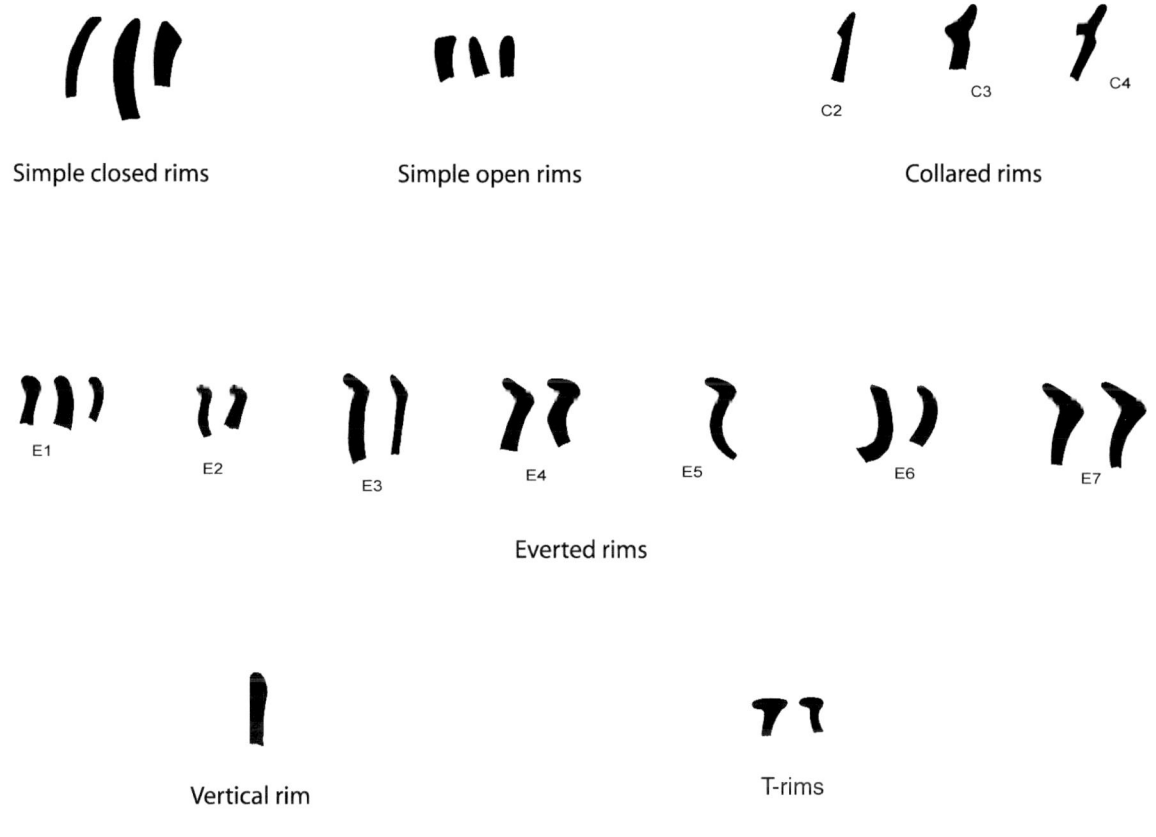

Figure 6.9. Major rim classes in the SCHP collection.

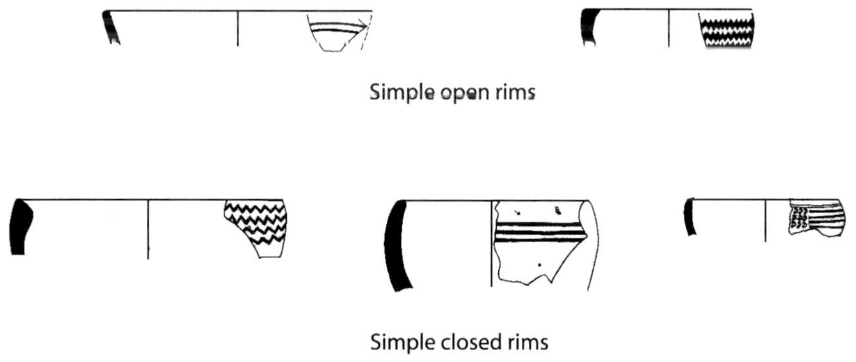

Figure 6.10. Simple rim types.

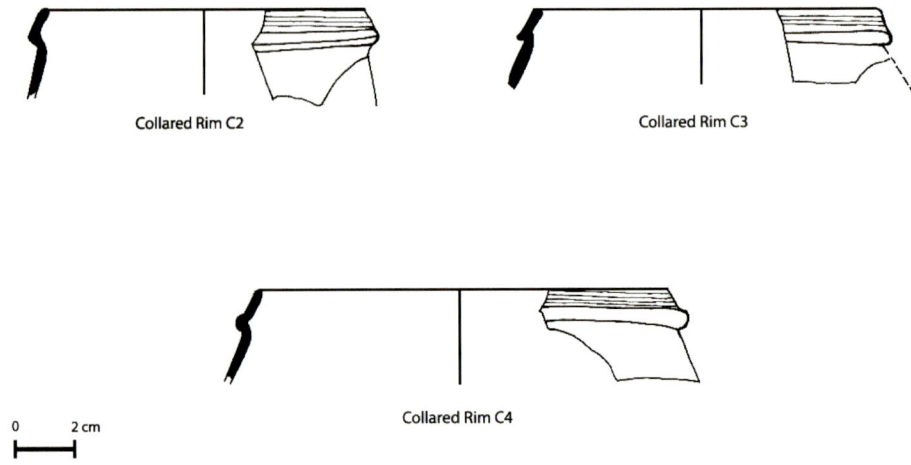

FIGURE 6.11. COLLARED RIM TYPES.

Other Rims

Only a handful of rim forms besides those enumerated above were identified in the SCHP: vertical rims, T-rims and, carinated rims. These were all poorly represented in most of the sites, and then only occurring in very small numbers (see Figure 6.9). Vertical rims are perpendicular to the plane of the vessel's mouth. T-rims, as the name indicates, have T-shaped profiles. Carinated rims are generally characterized by an in-turned rim at an angle to the body of the ware greater than 90°.

Results of Ceramic Analysis

Analysis of the ceramic collection yielded interesting patterns that allow us to offer cultural and historical interpretations with respect to regional archaeology. Analysis of the body sherds from most of the sites shows an overwhelming domination of plain sherds (Figure 6.12). This high incidence of plain sherds is known to characterize post-fifteenth-century assemblages in the Senegambia. Plain sherds are followed in popularity by slip, then by twine roulettes and other subtractive motifs, including incision, carved roulettes, and, more rarely, punctuate impressions. Full data on ceramic decoration

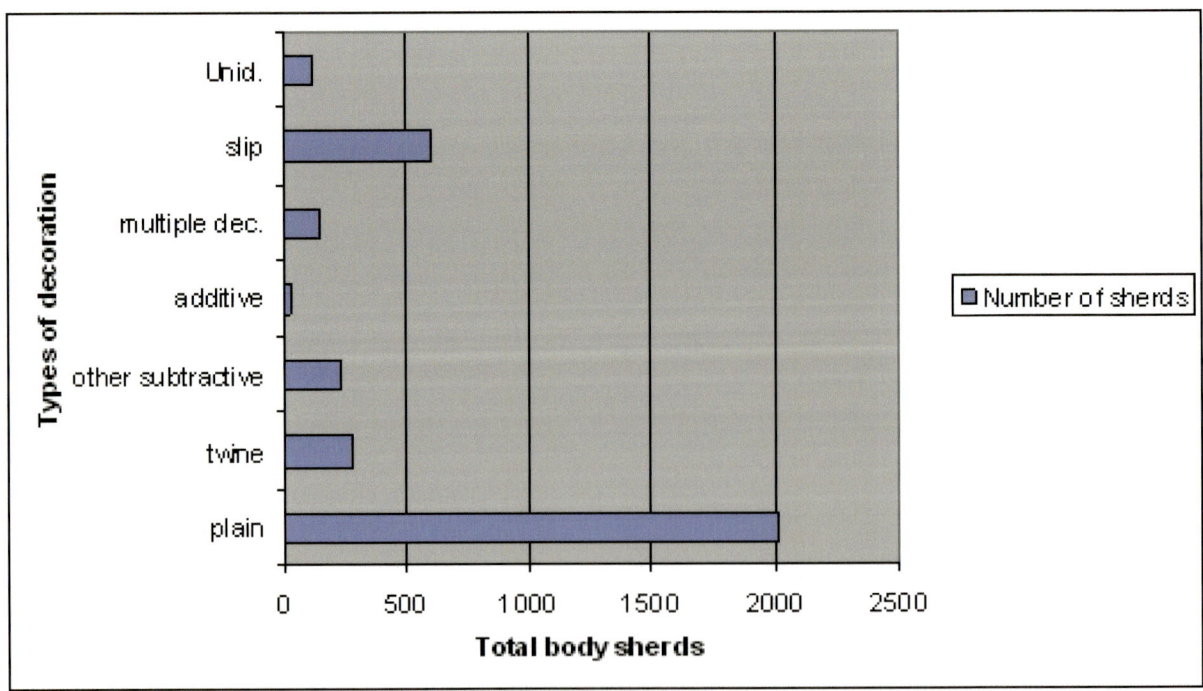

FIGURE 6.12. FREQUENCY OF PLAIN AND DECORATED BODY SHERDS IN THE SCHP COLLECTION.

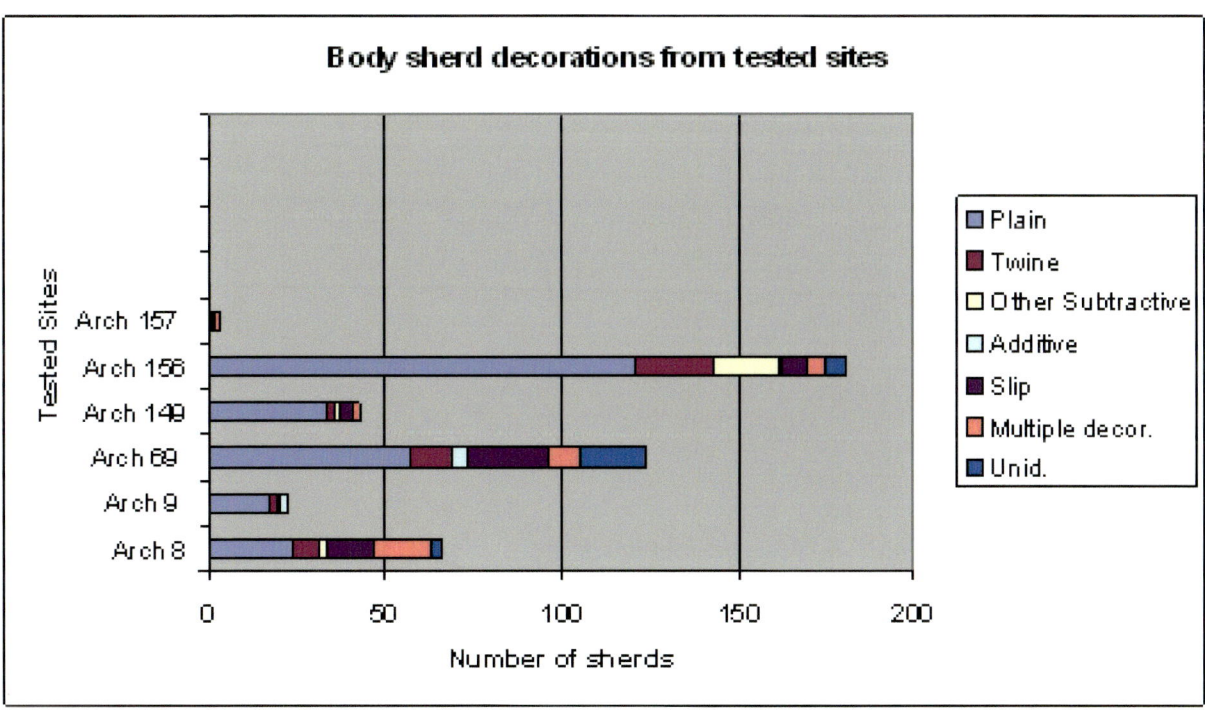

FIGURE 6.13. FREQUENCY OF PLAIN AND DECORATED BODY SHERDS FROM TEST EXCAVATIONS.

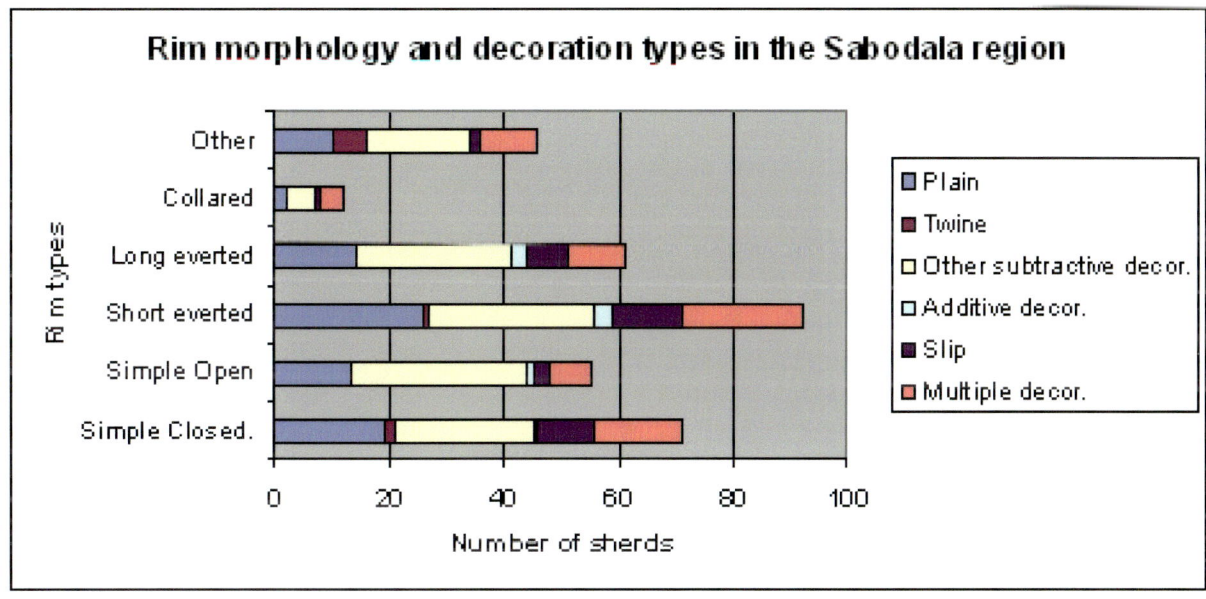

FIGURE 6.14. RIM MORPHOLOGY AND DECORATIVE TECHNIQUES DOCUMENTED IN THE SCHP COLLECTION.

is presented in Appendix 3, and data for rim morphology is presented in Appendix 4.

The high incidence of nondecorated sherds also characterizes material from tested sites. Most test excavations showed that the deposits were apparently very shallow. Examination of the ceramics from those test excavations further suggests that most sites had a single component. In general, material excavated shows no significant difference from the surface collections.

Analysis of rim morphology and decorations yielded critical information on the SCHP collection (Figures 6.13 and 6.14). Two major rim classes dominate the collection: simple and everted (see Figure 6.14). Everted rims are the most frequently found rim class in the study area, followed closely by simple rims. Short everted rims were found in significantly greater numbers than any other type, with simple closed following at a distant second. Long everted and simple open rims also were found in reasonably large numbers; all other types—

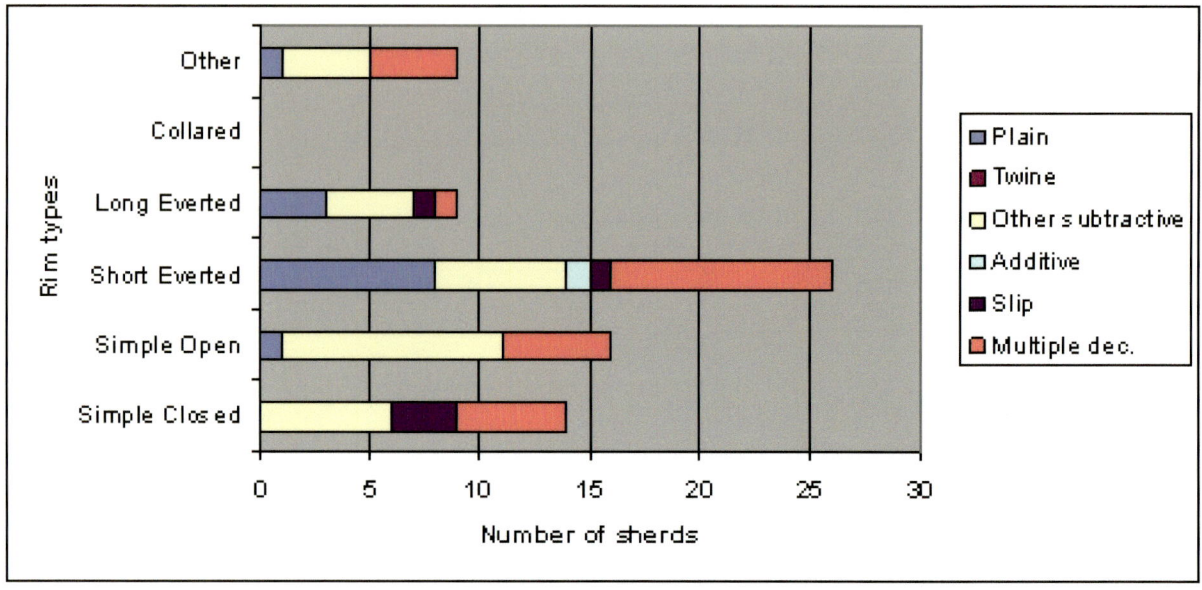

FIGURE 6.15. RIM MORPHOLOGY AND DECORATION TECHNIQUES DOCUMENTED AT SITE 8, MASATO.

collared rims, T-rims, and vertical rims—were poorly represented. Collared rims, for example, were recovered from six sites (see Figure 6.14).

Of these rims, two classes are time sensitive: the long everted vessels also referred to as long-necked jars, and the collared rims (see Figure 6.14). Both classes are well known in regions adjacent to the Sabodala area. Collared rims are first documented in the middle Senegal River Valley pottery sequence during Phase III, around A.D. 900. They are prevalent in these assemblages until A.D. 1200, evolving into various forms (McIntosh 1991). They are also documented elsewhere in the Senegambia, including the lower Falémé River Valley (Thiaw 1999). In the middle Senegal and lower Falémé River Valleys, the production of collared rims corresponds to a period of increased contact and interactions with the Sahara via trans-Saharan trade. About the same time, a number of trade items, including carnelian beads and copper, are found as prestige items in assemblages of the middle Senegal and lower Falémé River Valleys. These changes in the assemblages included technological innovations (e.g., spinning technology) that were spreading into these regions and perhaps beyond (McIntosh et al. 1992).

Although low in numbers, the incidence in the study area of collared rims could signify the incorporation of this remote region of Senegal into global trade about a thousand years ago. At two sites, 141 and 130, collared rims are associated with certain motifs, such as channeling, that also begin to develop elsewhere in Senegal during Phase IV, around A.D. 1200. At the other sites where collared rims are present, including Sites 13, 124, and 136, the numbers are too low to form much of an impression of associated decorative motifs.

The predominance of simple closed and simple open vessels and short and long everted rims is a pattern reminiscent of Phase IVC as defined in the lower Falémé River Valley and tentatively dated between A.D. 1300 and 1600 (Thiaw 1999). There are, however, several significant differences between the lower Falémé and Sabodala assemblages. First, large, beaded, collared rims are absent in the Sabodala region but are present in late Phase IVB and Phase IVC collections in the lower Falémé River Valley. Second, Unlike the Phase IVC assemblage as defined in the lower Falémé River Valley, the Sabodala pottery assemblage is characterized by a relatively low incidence of twine roulettes and a rise in frequency and variability of carved wood roulettes (along with other subtractive motifs).

The dominant ceramic types in the Sabodala region suggest that the bulk of the occupation dates to after A.D. 1300. Indeed, combining the ceramic collection with other lines of evidence suggests a much later occupation, perhaps in the late nineteenth and early twentieth centuries. Site 8, at Masato, for example, follows the general trend of a rim collection dominated by simple and everted forms (Figure 6.15).

The site also yielded European gunflints and tobacco pipe fragments, which clearly date no earlier than the nineteenth century. At Site 71, we also found a similar ceramic collection, this time together with a menthe alcohol glass bottle (rickless) that was popular in Senegal at the end of the nineteenth century and into the early part of the twentieth century.

Most of the pottery collected in the OJVG concession was utilitarian and was probably used for cooking, serving, and storage. Two pots excavated at Site 157, however, are best interpreted as ritual items. These two differ fundamentally from other vessels collected in the Sabodala region. They have deep red slip and polish and a fine paste that is reminiscent of material recovered from megalith and shell-mound sites in western and west central Senegambia (Thilmans et al. 1980). One of these pots is a short everted vessel with a red slip; the other vessel has a very restricted opening, above which there is a raised additive motif that could be a snake representation (Figure 6.16). To our knowledge, this is the first time this ware has been documented in Senegal, and its production and function deserve further investigation.

The collection also yielded a small vessel (from Site 142) of a type well known in the lower Falémé River Valley (Thiaw 1999) and which occurs generally in the same contexts as Phase III and IV vessels, dating to A.D. 900–1200 (Figure 6.16b). Thiaw (1999) speculated that, in the lower Falémé, these small, simple, open vessels were probably used as containers for facial make up.

Small Finds

Although many were fragments, we classified 169 artifacts as small finds (Figures 6.17 and 6.18; Table 6.1). Most of these were ceramic, including fragments of handles and bases of vessels, couscous steamers, bottle

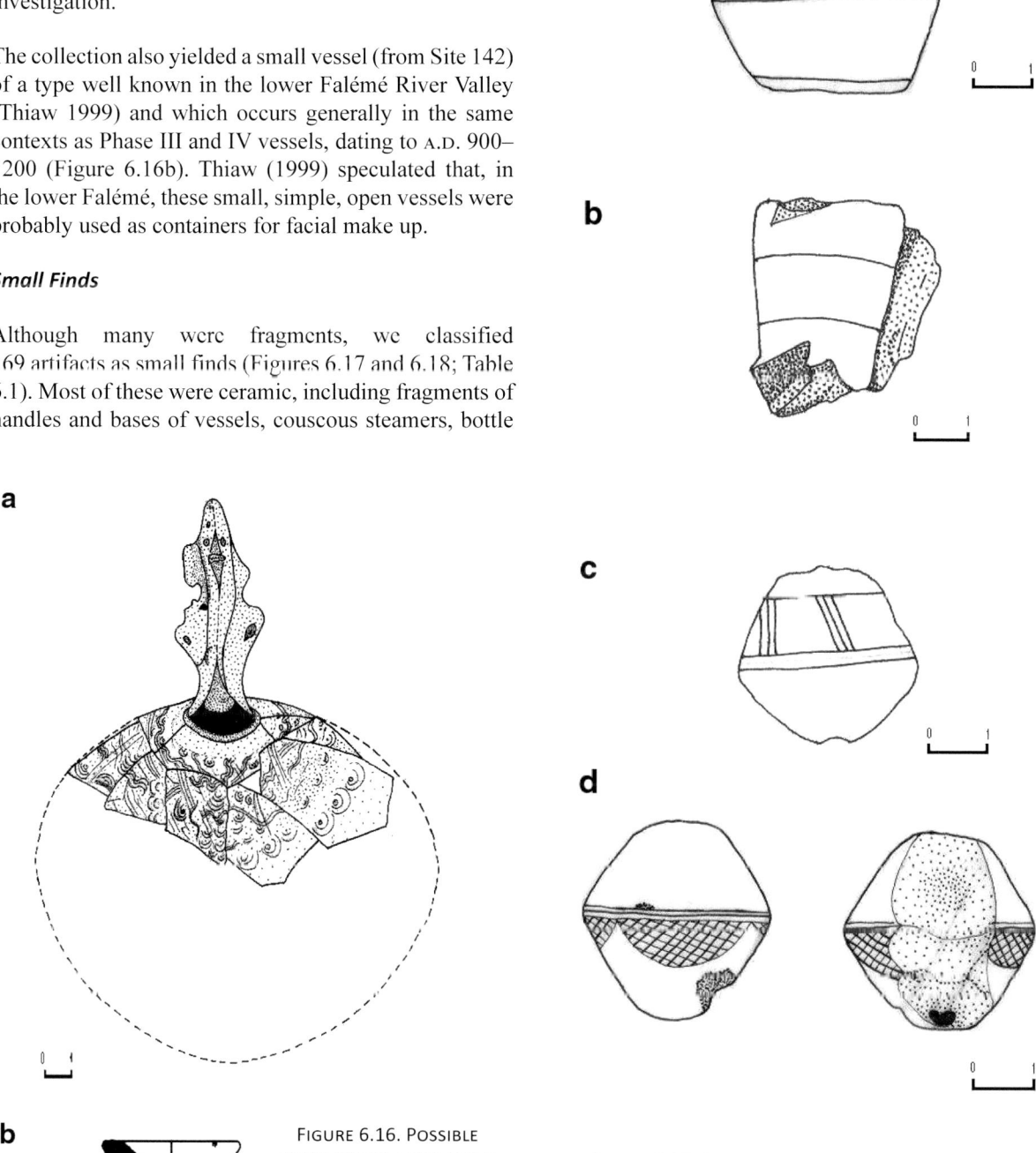

FIGURE 6.16. POSSIBLE RITUAL VESSEL FRAGMENTS: (**A**) POSSIBLE RITUAL/FUNERARY VESSEL, SITE 157; (**B**) SMALL, SIMPLE, OPEN VESSEL, SITE 142.

FIGURE 6.17. SMALL FINDS FROM THE SCHP COLLECTION: (**A**) TOBACCO PIPE FRAGMENT, SITE 139; (**B**) TOBACCO PIPE FRAGMENT, SITE 123; (**C**) SPINDLEWHORL FRAGMENT, UNIT A, LEVEL 02, FEATURE 29, SITE 08; (**D**) SPINDLEWHORL FRAGMENT, SITE 71.

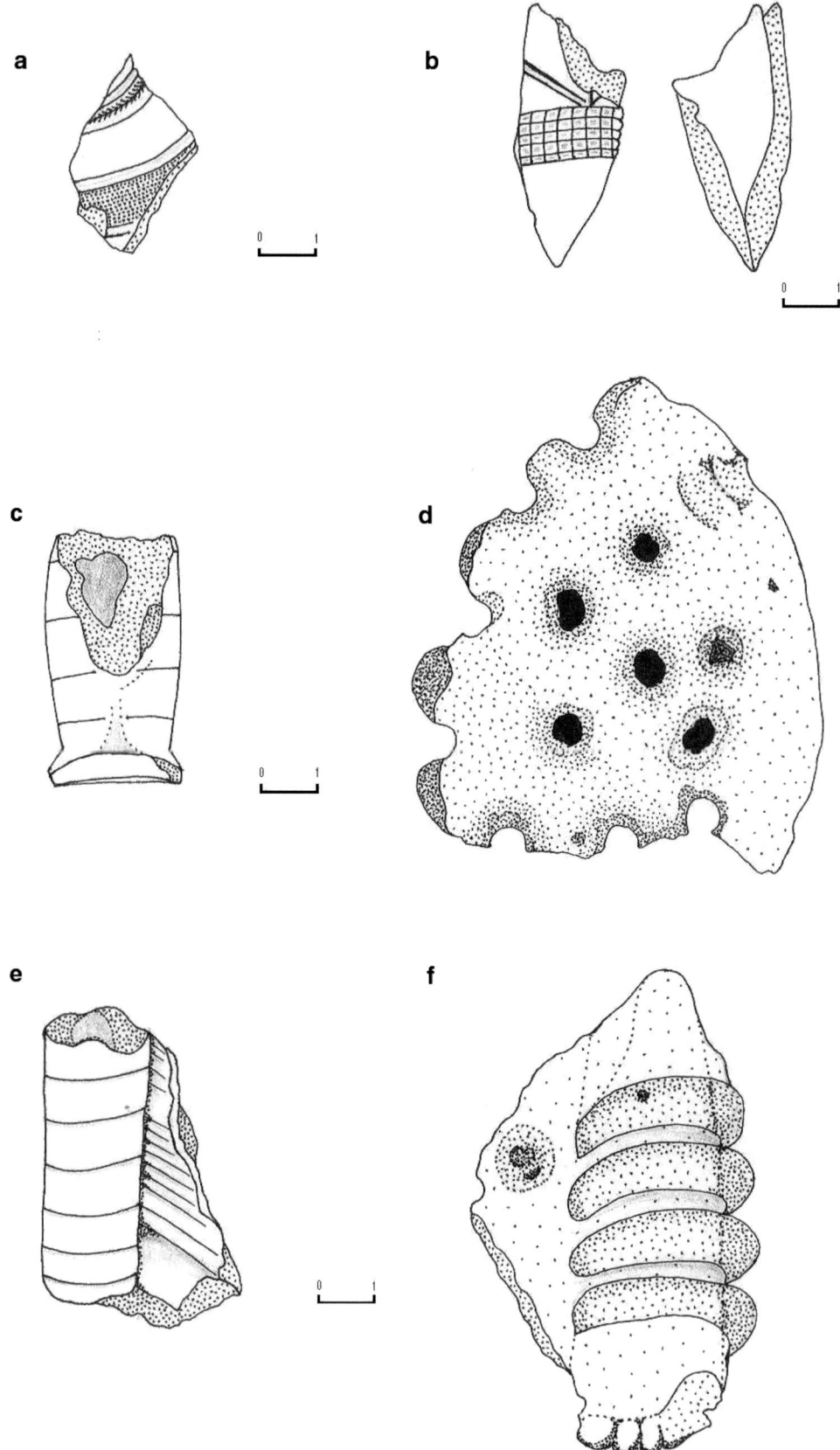

Figure 6.18. Small finds from the SCHP collection: (**A**) tobacco pipe fragment, Unit 2, Level 2, Site 08; (**B**) tobacco pipe fragment, Level 2 (10–20 cm), Feature A, Site 08; (**C**) tobacco pipe fragment, Unit 1A, Site 08; (**D**) fragment of *disque à cordeler*, Site 64; (**E**) tobacco pipe fragment, Level 0, Site 08; (**F**) potsherd with complex applique motif, Feature 21, Site 71.

stoppers, and spindlewhorls. One fragment each of a disque à cordeler and a net weight also were identified. Glass bottle fragments, tobacco pipe fragments, tuyère fragments, beads, and gunflints round out this category.

Tuyère fragments were extremely rare, and only 11 were recovered on sites in the OJVG concession. Tuyère fragments are an indicator that metalwork took place in the region. However, it is clear from the evidence that this was a poorly developed activity. Spindlewhorls are indicators of weaving, but this activity also seems to have been poorly developed in the area, as only two were collected. Thirty-four tobacco pipe fragments were collected. Part of the collection was clearly local, but a handful of thin-walled pipe fragments from Masato were European imports. The small finds in ceramic and baked clay suggest that, apart from pottery making, artisanal activities were in general poorly developed in the region.

Besides ceramic small finds, a handful of European imports were collected in the region—gunflints and glass bottle fragments. Some of the glass bottle fragments were containers of alcoholic beverages, including rickless and possibly wine (Site 71). Evian bottle fragments were also present at a few sites (Sites 123 and 09). A couple of glass bottle fragments collected at Site 77 could also be pharmaceutical. The three glass beads found in the entire survey contrast srrongly (despite problems with sampling) with the numbers found at similar contemporary sites in the Gambia (Gijanto 2011b) and the lower Faleme (DeCorse et al 2007).

Overall, these imports were extremely rare. The rarity of European imports perhaps indicates that in the recent historical past, the Sabodala area (an inland region away from the major waterways of the Senegal, Falémé, and Gambia Rivers) was only involved indirectly in the Atlantic networks.

Conclusion

The gross characteristics of Sabodala region pottery show some similarities with the lower Falémé and middle Sénégal River Valleys, but also significant differences. Fortunately for comparative analysis, our study of rim morphology revealed no rim type in Sabodala that is not known in the lower Falémé and middle Senegal. By contrasting the assemblages from the three regions, we can begin to define the culture history of the societies living in this part of the Senegambia.

TABLE 6.1. SMALL FINDS FROM SURVEY AND TEST EXCAVATIONS

Site	Handle	Base	Steamer Fragment	Tobacco Pipe Fragment	Spindlewhorl	Tuyère Fragment	Disque à Cordeler	Net Weight	Bottle Stopper	Gunflint	Glass Bottle Fragment	Bead	Total
Site 02	—	—	1	—	—	—	—	—	—	—	—	—	1
Site 07	—	—	1	—	—	—	—	—	—	—	—	—	1
Site 08	—	1	3	32	1	—	—	1	2	1	—	3	44
Site 09	—	—	—	—	—	—	—	—	—	—	49	—	49
Site 36	—	—	—	—	—	—	—	—	—	—	1	—	1
Site 57	—	—	1	—	—	—	—	—	—	—	5	—	6
Site 64	—	1	—	—	—	—	1	—	—	—	—	—	2
Site 69	1	—	—	—	—	—	—	—	—	—	—	—	1
Site 71	1	—	2	—	1	—	—	—	—	—	2	—	6
Site 77	—	—	—	—	—	—	—	—	—	—	4	—	4
Site 106	—	—	—	—	—	—	—	—	—	—	10	—	10
Site 111	—	—	—	—	—	—	—	—	—	1	—	—	1
Site 123	—	—	3	—	—	—	—	—	—	—	18	—	21
Site 130	—	—	—	—	—	—	—	—	1	—	—	—	1
Site 133	—	—	—	1	—	—	—	—	—	—	—	—	1
Site 139	—	—	—	1	—	—	—	—	—	—	—	—	1
Site 141	1	—	—	—	—	—	—	—	—	—	—	—	1
Site 142	—	1	—	—	—	—	—	—	—	—	—	—	1
Site 149	—	—	—	—	—	8	—	—	—	—	—	—	8
Site 156	2	3	1	—	—	—	—	—	—	—	—	—	6
Iso 02	—	—	—	—	—	3	—	—	—	—	—	—	3
Total	5	6	12	34	2	11	1	1	3	2	89	3	169

Although some of the assemblages could date to the Neolithic, the pottery of this period is poorly known in Senegal. Observations in the lower Falémé River Valley suggest that some of the assemblages with a high frequency of simple and short everted vessels could date to the Neolithic or the early Iron Age, the latter of which is dated approximately to the early first millennium A.D. (see Chapter 2). Decoration in these early assemblages generally includes a high percentage of twine roulette motifs and *sabot*. When associated with axes and milling stones (less often), these sites could tentatively be dated to the Neolithic.

A handful of sites in the study area could date to the late first and early second millennia A.D. An assemblage with collared rims and channeling characteristic of Phase IVB in the middle Senegal and lower Falémé River Valleys was documented in the study area. One site, Site 141, could be of particular importance. Although no evidence of long distance trade was recovered in the study area, Phase IVB assemblages are believed to reflect the development of trans-Saharan trade and its many corollaries, including elite formation, social differentiation, and political centralization. Although poorly documented archaeologically, there is abundant historical and oral evidence suggesting that the upper Senegal River Valley was central to the gold trade in the late first and early second millennia A.D. (Bathily 1989).

The prevalence of simple restricted and unrestricted vessels along with everted vessels is a common pattern in the region. A high incidence of long-necked jars (everted E6 and E7) is associated in the lower Falémé and middle Senegal River Valleys with early second millennium A.D. assemblages of Phase IVC (Thiaw 1999). Although mainly defined from surface collection, the Sabodala assemblage shares features of Phase IVC, which in the lower Falémé and middle Senegal is always associated with a thick beaded rim (referred to in the French literature as *bord ourlé*). This particular rim type is present in both Phase IVB and Phase IVC in the lower Falémé and middle Senegal but is absent in the Sabodala region. Could the absence of this particular beaded rim type in the Sabodala area indicate a cultural difference or chronological change? We suggest that assemblages with long-necked jars associated with simple closed and simple open vessels as well as short everted rims are more recent than Phase IVC as defined in the lower Falémé and dated A.D. 1300–1700.

Excluding the diagnostic presence of long-necked jars that is noted in eastern Senegambia and parts of Mali, the Sabodala assemblage shows striking similarities with '*subactuelle*' (recent historical-period) assemblages. It is characterized by a high frequency of nondecorated vessels, and we are tempted to define it as a local variant of *subactuelle* assemblages. In northern Senegambia, pottery assemblages dating after A.D. 1500, also known as *subactuelle* period, are characterized by rapid development of *subactuelle* pottery, with a high percentage of nondecorated vessels that are largely tempered with organic material. Although temper was not systematically recorded during analysis of the Sabodala material, we observed that large numbers of sherds were organically tempered. As in the lower Falémé River Valley, these long-necked jars are generally incised with a blunt object; there are also a few with multiple motifs. Application of decoration on the lip of ceramic wares becomes a rare but diagnostic feature on some *subactuelle* assemblages, both in the Falémé and the Sabodala area.

Most significantly, body sherds and rim decoration in the Sabodala region are marked by very diagnostic carved wooden roulettes. At least four different types were documented in the collection. Carved wooden roulettes are extremely rare in the known assemblages of northern Senegambia. Their relative importance and variety is a significant cultural signature that links this region of southeastern Senegal with other assemblages further east and upriver on the Senegal and Falémé River drainages (Thiaw 1999).

The small finds generally associated with the larger ceramic assemblages include locally manufactured steamers, incense burners, and tobacco pipes. These items are generally present in recent historical-period assemblages in the Senegambia. Often, they are also associated with European imports, including glass beads, tobacco pipes, and glass bottles. While a few sites in the study area produced similar European imports, they were particularly rare compared to sites documented along the Falémé River, the middle Senegal River Valley, and coastal Senegal.

Lithic Analysis

We recovered 121 lithic artifacts from all the different phases of the SCHP. Most of the collection came from the survey; only a few were found in excavations at Sites 08, 156B and, 157. Because sample size is very small, we opted for an analytic approach that was largely descriptive, and the complete data set is presented in Table 6.2.

Field Collection Strategy and Analytical Procedures

Lithic artifacts are generally poorly represented in most of the surface collections and test excavations. In the field, we collected all lithic artifacts from the surface save milling equipment. Milling implements were mostly metates and pestles, which were too cumbersome to carry during pedestrian survey.

Analysis of the lithic artifacts began with identification of raw material; then, the technology and typology of

ARTIFACT ANALYSES

TABLE 6.2. ALL LITHIC ARTIFACTS

Site	Flake	Debitage	Core	Handaxe	Axes	Metate W	Metate F	Pestle w	Pestle F	Misc. No.	Misc. Nature	Total
Site 1	1	—	—	—	—	—	—	—	—	—		1
Site 5	—	—	—	1	—	—	—	—	—	—		1
Site 8	1[a]	—	—	—	—	—	—	1	3[b]	—		5
Site 9	—	—	1	—	—	—	—	—	1	—		2
Site 36	—	—	—	—	1	—	—	—	—	—		1
Site 57	3	2	2	—	—	—	—	—	1	—		8
Site 61	3	—	—	1	—	—	1	—	—	—		5
Site 62	—	1	—	—	—	—	—	—	1	—		2
Site 64	4	—	1	—	—	—	2	1	—	—		8
Site 69	—	—	—	—	—	—	—	2	—	—		2
Site 71	—	—	—	—	—	—	—	—	—	1	pierre à cupules	1
Site 72	1	—	—	—	—	—	—	—	1	—		2
Site 79	1	—	—	—	—	—	—	—	—	—		1
Site 85	1	—	—	—	—	—	—	—	—	—		1
Site 96	—	—	—	—	—	—	—	—	1	—		1
Site 116	1	—	—	—	—	—	—	—	1	—		2
Site 120	1	—	—	—	—	—	—	—	2	1	pierre à cupules	4
Site 121	—	—	—	—	—	—	—	1	—	—		1
Site 122 B	1	—	—	—	—	—	—	—	—	—		1
Site 123	—	—	—	—	—	—	1	—	—	—		1
Site 124	4	—	—	—	—	—	—	—	—	—		4
Site 125	—	—	—	—	1	—	—	—	2	—		3
Site 133	1	—	—	—	1	—	—	—	—	—		2
Site 137	6	—	—	1	—	—	—	—	—	1	pierre à cupules	8
Site 139	4	—	—	1	—	—	—	—	2	—		7
Site 140	1	—	—	—	—	—	—	—	1	—		2
Site 142	1	—	1	—	—	—	—	—	—	—		2
Site 144	1	—	—	—	—	—	—	—	—	—		1
Site 145	—	—	—	—	—	—	—	—	—	1	hammerstone	1
Site 146	—	—	—	—	—	—	1	—	—	—		1
Site 156	1	—	—	1	1	—	1[a]	—	—	—		4
Site 156 B	5[c]	—	—	1	—	—	—	—	—	—		6
Site 157	1[a]	—	—	—	—	—	—	—	—	—		1
Site 222	—	—	—	—	—	—	1	—	—	—		1
Site 223	—	—	—	—	1	—	1	—	1	—		3
Site 225	—	—	—	—	1	—	—	—	—	—		1
Site 226	—	—	—	1	—	—	—	—	—	—		1
Site 227	—	—	—	—	—	—	—	1	—	—		1
Site 229	1	—	—	1	—	—	1	—	—	—		3
Site 230	1	—	—	1	—	—	—	—	—	—		2
Site 232	—	—	1	1	—	—	—	—	—	—		2
Site 233	—	—	—	—	—	—	—	—	—	1	hammerstone	1
Site 241	—	—	—	—	—	—	—	—	1	—		1
Site 248	—	—	—	1	—	—	—	—	1	—		1
Site 260	—	—	1	—	—	—	—	—	—	—		1
Site 265	—	—	—	—	—	—	—	—	—	1	strip	1
Site 279	—	—	—	—	—	—	1	—	—	—		1
Site 292	1	—	—	—	—	—	—	—	—	—		1
Site 294	—	—	—	—	2	—	—	—	—	—		2
Iso 6	—	—	1	—	—	—	—	—	—	—		1
Iso 7	—	—	—	—	—	—	—	—	—	1	rognon testé (tested cobble)	1
Iso 1	—	—	1	—	—	—	—	—	—	—		1
TR 05	1	—	—	—	—	—	—	—	—	—		1
S. Coord.	—	—	—	—	—	—	—	—	—	1	pierre à cupules	1
8132235 and 1455415	—	—	—	—	—	—	—	—	—	1	digging stick stone ball	1
Total	47	3	7	12	8	—	10	6	19	9		121

Key: W = whole; F = fragment.
[a] From test excavations.
[b] Two are from text excavations.
[c] Three are from test excavations.

each piece was classified. Each specimen was examined with the naked eye to determine the nature of the stones used, their texture, and their color. As different raw materials have different properties, they are not all equally suited for tool manufacture. Thus, the quality of the raw material is an important variable for a better understanding of tool manufacture technology.

Seven types of raw materials can be distinguished in the Sabodala lithics collection: greenstone (n = 67), quartz (n = 27), sandstone (n = 7), flint (n = 6), silexite (n = 4), granite (n = 3) and, schist (n = 1). These raw materials are often associated with the metamorphic formations of the Birimian, which offered multiple choices and possibilities for early hunter-gatherers of the Sabodala region.

The dominant raw material used by these early hunter-gatherers is a greenstone that we were unable to identify properly. This greenish stone predominates across all classes of stone artifacts. The stone is quite hard for knapping; not surprisingly, it was not the preferred raw material for small tools. There was a prevalence of quartz over greenstone among flakes and debris. In addition, greenstone is, in general, rarely used for axes. Greenstone, however, seems to be the ideal raw material for the manufacture of heavy milling equipment, such as metates and pestles.

The quartz in the Sabodala region has a smooth texture and is generally colorless. Although hard and not the best raw material, it is apt for knapping. It is abundant, outcropping from the Birimian and paleozoic formations. Sometimes, it can also be found in the form of cobbles that are rolled and available along drainages. Sandstone and sandstone quartzite are hard sedimentary stones with varied textures. They are found along drainages and are generally used for the production of hammerstones and axes. Sandstone easily alters, making it difficult to analyze.

The flint found in the Sabodala region is brown and fine grained. It is unlikely that this stone outcrops in the Sabodala region, which explains why flint tools are quite rare in the lithic collection. The flint pieces found in the OJVG concession could have resulted from short or long distance interaction among mobile hunter-gatherers whose territories covered wide regions.

Silexite found in the Sabodala region is fine grained. It differs from flint in that it is grayish or gray greenish with a dull vividness and irregular cracks. Like flint, silexite was rarely used in the production of lithic tools in the Sabodala region. Granites are hard, clear, colored stones. They are made of quartz minerals, feldspath, and mica. Granite outcroppings are abundant in the Sabodala region. The formation of schist is largely caused by tectonic stress. Strips of schist are present everywhere in the Sabodala region.

Although various raw materials were used in the Sabodala region to produce stone tools, the bulk of the lithic industry is made out of locally available raw materials. Most of the raw materials are volcanic and metamorphic stones that are abundant in the region. Greenstone is the most commonly used raw material and the one that knappers seem to have favored for most types of stone tools. However, stone tool makers also capitalized on the variety of raw material resources available within the region, and variations in the quality of stone reflect decisive technological choices. For instance, fine stones such as quartz, flint, and silexite were favored for the production of flakes, whereas heavy, voluminous stones like greenstone, sandstone, sandstone quartzite, and granite were preferred for large and heavy equipment like handaxes, metates, and pestles.

Once raw material was determined, each specimen was then either classified as a flaked stone or a milling implement. Flaked stone artifacts were divided into complete and fragmentary tools and then further divided by tool or debitage type. Tool types identified in the collection are flake tools, cores, handaxes, and axes. Flake tools were subdivided into notches, denticulates, side scrapers, and end scrapers. Cores, handaxes, and axes were found in small numbers and are described individually.

For each of the different classes of lithic artifacts, the criteria considered and described were morphometry (length, width, and thickness) and general morphology. Each piece was defined via diagrammatic analysis of the organization of old and recent removals. Technological analysis also examined the nature and character of the retouches (their morphology, orientation, and localization on the blanks). The importance of the cortex on the different faces of the piece was also examined. Surfaces without cortex were coded 0, whereas 100 percent cortex presence was coded 5.

Analysis of metates (grinding stones) and pestles used a nomenclature that mainly focused on their functional usage. In addition to their morphology, we also looked at traces of wear to try to determine their functions.

Results

Flaked stone products are largely dominated by flakes. The provenience of flaked stone was extremely variable, with no clear evidence of a workshop. Fifty out of the 121 lithic artifacts are flaked stone, or just over 40 percent of the collection (see Table 6.2). Of the 50 debitage pieces, 5 were collected from test excavations; the rest came from the survey.

Lithic Tools from Test Excavations

The five pieces from test excavations are flake tools—a broken scraper, a burin tip, an awl, and two pseudo-Levallois points. Most have no cortex and were manufactured either on quartz, flint, or greenstone. The scraper manufactured on quartz has a broken butt with a series of fine retouches resulting in a denticulate sharp edge. The burin had a beak in the proximal right angle.

The two pseudo-Levallois points were also made of quartz and are characterized by plain butts. Levallois points are defined as triangular flakes with butts; they are generally found in Mousterian assemblages but are rather rare in Levallois contexts. The retouch situated on the transverse proximal end consisted of two parallel and adjoining removals not on a retouched plane.

The awl is knapped on greenstone. It was the largest of the five pieces, with dimensions of 35 by 20 by 4 mm. A thin layer of clay ochre covers the arris of previous removals that are organized according to a longitudinal plan. Like the pseudo-Levallois points, its apex is broken, and it is difficult to determine the knapping technique.

Lithic Material from Surface Contexts

We collected 45 pieces from the surface—24 retouched flakes or debris and 21 pieces that were unmodified. The collection shows similarities with material from test excavations. The surface collection is largely dominated by blanks on flakes (93 percent of the collection), with just a few (7 percent) made on debris. Table 6.3 provides an overview of the nature of the collection according to the types of blanks that were used.

Debris

Only three pieces of debitage debris, all quartz, were collected. Two were manufactured on blanks without cortex; the other one is unmodified. Their average dimensions (31 by 24 by 9 mm) are in keeping with the rest of the debitage material.

Flakes

Flakes have the highest frequency of debitage material, representing 42 of 45 pieces. More than half the flaked stone collection is composed of retouched and unmodified flakes. As with the rest of the collection, greenstone is the predominant raw material, followed by quartz. Flint and schist flakes are present, but in low frequencies. Most flakes are slightly elongated (average 42 by 38 by 10 mm). They are generally very thin (around 10 mm), which may result from ample exploitation of the cores, as shown by the large number of anterior removals on the superior face. In fact, this knapping preference may explain why many flakes do not show cortex.

Overall, the average number of removals visible on the dorsal face is about three per flake. On both the unmodified and retouched flakes, the organization of initial removals is generally longitudinal and orthogonal. This pattern of removal suggests technical strategies that maximize exploitation and that are aimed at producing discoid cores.

Most flakes have smooth butt plans that are generally large and slightly inclined toward the inferior face of the flake. Dihedral and reduced butts are the most common type. Five flakes had missing butts because their proximal end was broken.

The analysis shows identical technical strategies across all sites where flakes were collected. Knapping is characterized by the production of flakes without cortex, with an average of three initial removals that are organized according to a mode of knapping that is either orthogonal or longitudinal. The absence of cortical flakes suggests that flakes are missing the initial phase of the debitage. This pattern implies that the initial debitage took place elsewhere and the products were brought to the sites at a later time. Because no workshops were found in the surveyed areas, it is plausible that prehistoric populations in the Sabodala region travelled for some distance to acquire raw materials or acquired them via trade or other forms of exchange. It must, however, be pointed out that very little interassemblage variability is noted in the debitage techniques employed. We were surprised by the degree of technical homogeneity from one site to another.

Tools

Tools are by far the predominant debitage product, with 53 percent of flakes (n = 24) being knapped into tools (Tables 6.3 and 6.4; Figure 6.19). Most tools (at least 22) were manufactured on an existing flake. Only 2 were manufactured on debris. The blanks are generally either in quartz (n = 10) or greenstone (n = 8) and more rarely in flint (n = 3) or silexite (n = 3).

The dominant types are notches and denticulates; there are also a few tools generally associated with Upper Paleolithic assemblages, such as end scrapers and burins.

Notches

The notch collection consists of 13 pieces, representing 54 percent of the flake tools. Tools with notches are generally manufactured on flakes. Their blanks show no cortical residues, and their dimensions (average 40 by 37 by 10 mm) are generally smaller than most flakes. The retouch of the denticulates generally forms large notches. Two techniques were observed on these tools: (1) notches obtained via an invasive removal that is either deep or shallow and (2) notches obtained via thick stepped removals that are repeated on a ridge. In both cases, the retouch changes the morphology of the

Table 6.3. Distribution of Lithic Surface Collection, by Type of Blank

Site	Retouched Flake	Retouched Debris	Total	Unmodified Flake	Unmodified Debris	Total
Site 1	1	—	1	—	—	—
Site 57	2	1	3	1	1	2
Site 61	3	—	3	—	—	—
Site 62	—	1	1	—	—	—
Site 64	3	—	3	1	—	1
Site 72	1	—	1	—	—	—
Site 79	—	—	—	1	—	1
Site 85	1	—	1	—	—	—
Site 116	—	—	—	1	—	1
Site 120	1	—	1	—	—	—
Site 122B	—	—	—	1	—	1
Site 124	2	—	2	2	—	2
Site 133	—	—	—	1	—	1
Site 137	3	—	3	3	—	3
Site 139	1	—	1	3	—	3
Site 140	—	—	—	1	—	1
Site 142	—	—	—	1	—	1
Site 144	1	—	1	—	—	—
Site 156B	1	—	1	2	—	2
Site 229	1	—	1	0	—	—
Site 230	1	—	1	0	—	—
Site 292	—	—	—	1	—	1
Trench 05	—	—	—	1	—	1
Total	22	2	24	20	1	21

Table 6.4. Lithic Tools per Site

| Site | Flake | | | | Debris | Total |
	Notch	Denticulate	Side Scraper	End Scraper	Denticulate	
Site 1	1	—	—	—	—	1
Site 57	1	1	—	—	1	3
Site 61	2	—	—	1	—	3
Site 62	—	—	—	—	1	1
Site 64	3	—	—	—	—	3
Site 72	1	—	—	—	—	1
Site 79	—	—	—	—	—	—
Site 85	—	1	—	—	—	1
Site 116	—	—	—	—	—	—
Site 120	—	—	—	1	—	1
Site 122B	—	—	—	—	—	—
Site 124	1	1	—	—	—	2
Site 133	—	—	—	—	—	—
Site 137	2	1	—	—	—	3
Site 139	1	—	—	—	—	1
Site 140	—	—	—	—	—	—
Site 142	—	—	—	—	—	—
Site 144	—	—	1	—	—	1
Site 156B	—	1	—	—	—	1
Site 229	1	—	—	—	—	1
Site 230	—	—	1	—	—	1
Site 292	—	—	—	—	—	—
Trench 05	—	—	—	—	—	—
Total	13	5	2	2	2	24

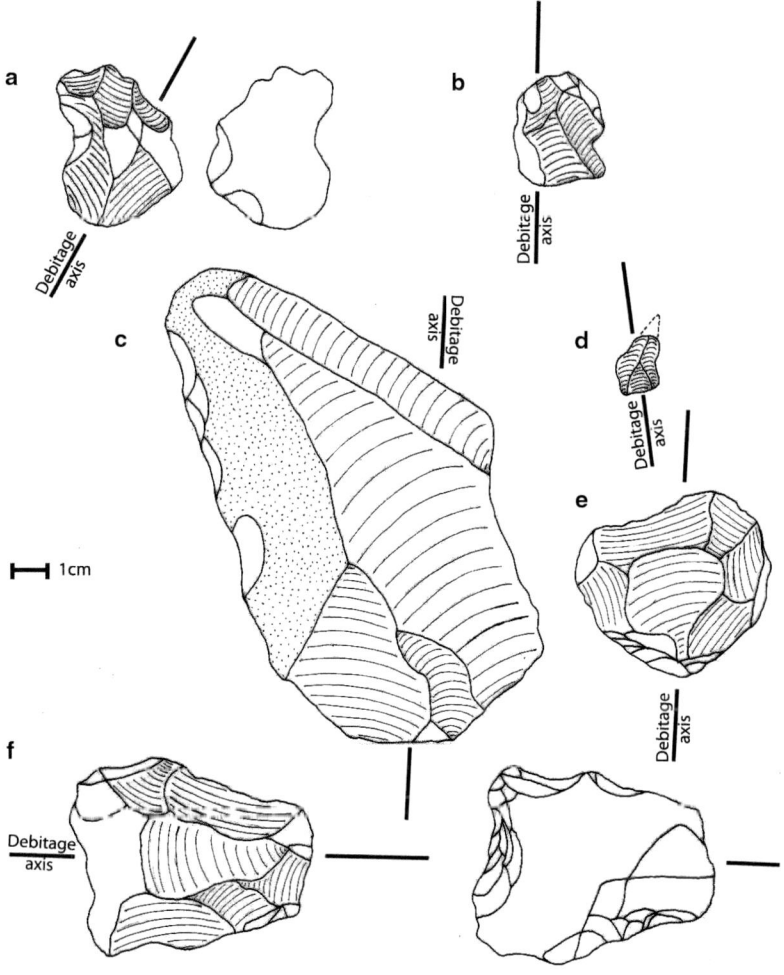

FIGURE 6.19. LITHIC TOOLS FROM THE SCHP COLLECTION: (**A**) END SCRAPER, SITE 137; (**B**) NOTCH, SITE 61; (**C**) SIDE SCRAPER, SITE 230; (**D**) PSEUDO LEVALLOIS POINT, SITE 156B; (**E**) PSEUDO-LEVALLOIS FLAKE, SITE 137; (**F**) NOTCH, SITE 01.

edge on which it was applied, producing notches with a sinuous or concave cutting edge.

Denticulates

Seven denticulates, representing 29 percent of the flake tools, were collected as part of the SCHP. Five were manufactured on flakes, the remaining two on debris. The blanks on which these were manufactured show little variability. The debris pieces are both quartz; the flakes are made of greenstone (3) and flint (2). Unlike the other tools in the collection, some denticulates show cortical residues on their dorsal faces that are in some cases invasive but generally situated on the edges. Except in one case, the retouch is applied on cutting edges without cortex. This finding suggests cortex removal on the edges prior to the retouch. Most denticulates in the collection are characterized by a fine denticulate retouch applied on a cutting edge that is either convex or rectilinear. The average dimensions are 33 by 32 by 9 mm, slightly smaller than those of notches. Butts are generally smooth, although two pieces show prepared butts that are faceted.

Side Scrapers

Two flakes, one of flint and the other of silexite, were transformed into side scrapers (8 percent of the flake tools). One has a large cortical surface. Both are lateral types. Interestingly, one may have served a different function. It shows a Clactonian notch developed on the proximal cross edge, which resulted in a removed butt. Overall, however, the side scrapers are characterized by a thick, stepped retouch generally straight and applied on a convex cutting edge.

End Scrapers

End scrapers are poorly represented (8 percent of flake tools). They are made of either quartz or greenstone and show no cortex. One piece has a dihedral butt; the second is broken on its proximal end and has a thick stepped retouch that develop on the upper face of its cross-distal edge.

Cores

Cores represent only 6 percent of the entire lithic collection and are made of either quartz or flint. Their relatively small dimensions (average 56 by 48 by 35 mm) suggest that prehistoric populations in this region selected small pebbles to produce their tools. Their morphology is generally oval or cubic and may have affected the techniques developed to manufacture tools. The goal for manufacturing centripetal core debitage bifaces is to produce flakes that are larger than they are long, with a smooth but nonprepared butt and a large number of scars (five in average) (Figures 6.20 and 6.21).

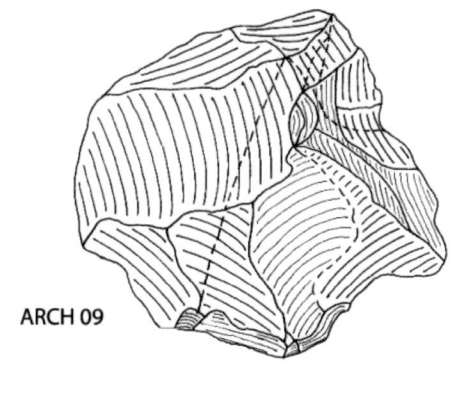

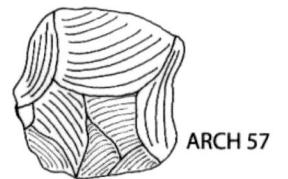

FIGURE 6.21. CENTRIPETAL UNIFACIAL CORES FROM THE SCHP COLLECTION.

Handaxes

There are 12 handaxes in the lithic collection, representing 10 percent of the entire collection (Figure 6.22). They are composed of 5 small oval handaxes, 6 fractured handaxes, and 1 rough-out handax. They are generally manufactured on greenstone or quartz cobbles and always appear as small strips of stone that are relatively thick. Like cores and flakes, a number of handaxes show ferrous inlay, whereas others only exhibit ferrous traces. It is likely that those with ferrous inlay have been trapped in a gravel layer.

Three possible Acheulean handaxes were collected during the survey (Figure 6.23; see Figure 6.22; c.f. Chapter 5). All three of these artifacts were made on local greenstone, with edge margins that had been worked along both sides. In addition, they all exhibit a heavy geological varnish, indicating that they are very old. Each item was associated with the highest terrace on the laterite bedrock (or on a nearby slope). The literature suggests that it takes at least 300,000 years for laterite deposits to form, providing a *terminus ante quem* of 300,000 years for these artifacts.

Camara and Duboscq (1984) have argued that gravel terraces that contain Acheulean artifacts on the Falémé River date to ca. 200,000–300,000 years ago. The Sabodala artifacts were probably associated with a stable land surface, whereas the Falémé examples are heavily waterworn and come from an alluvial deposit. This

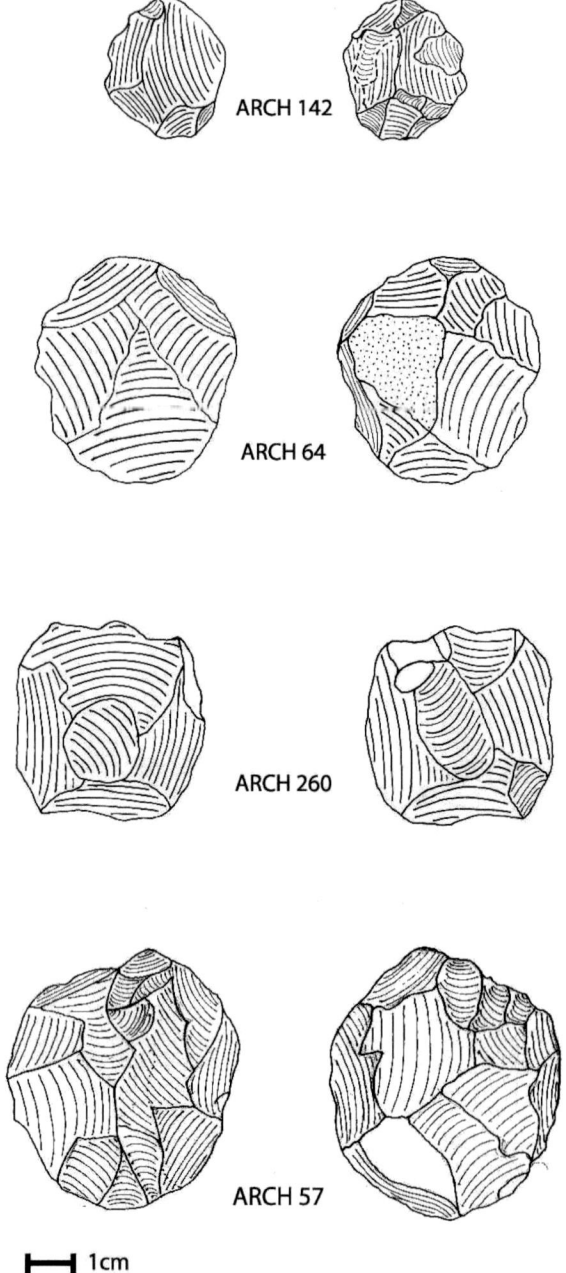

FIGURE 6.20. CENTRIPETAL BIFACIAL CORES FROM THE SCHP COLLECTION.

ARTIFACT ANALYSES

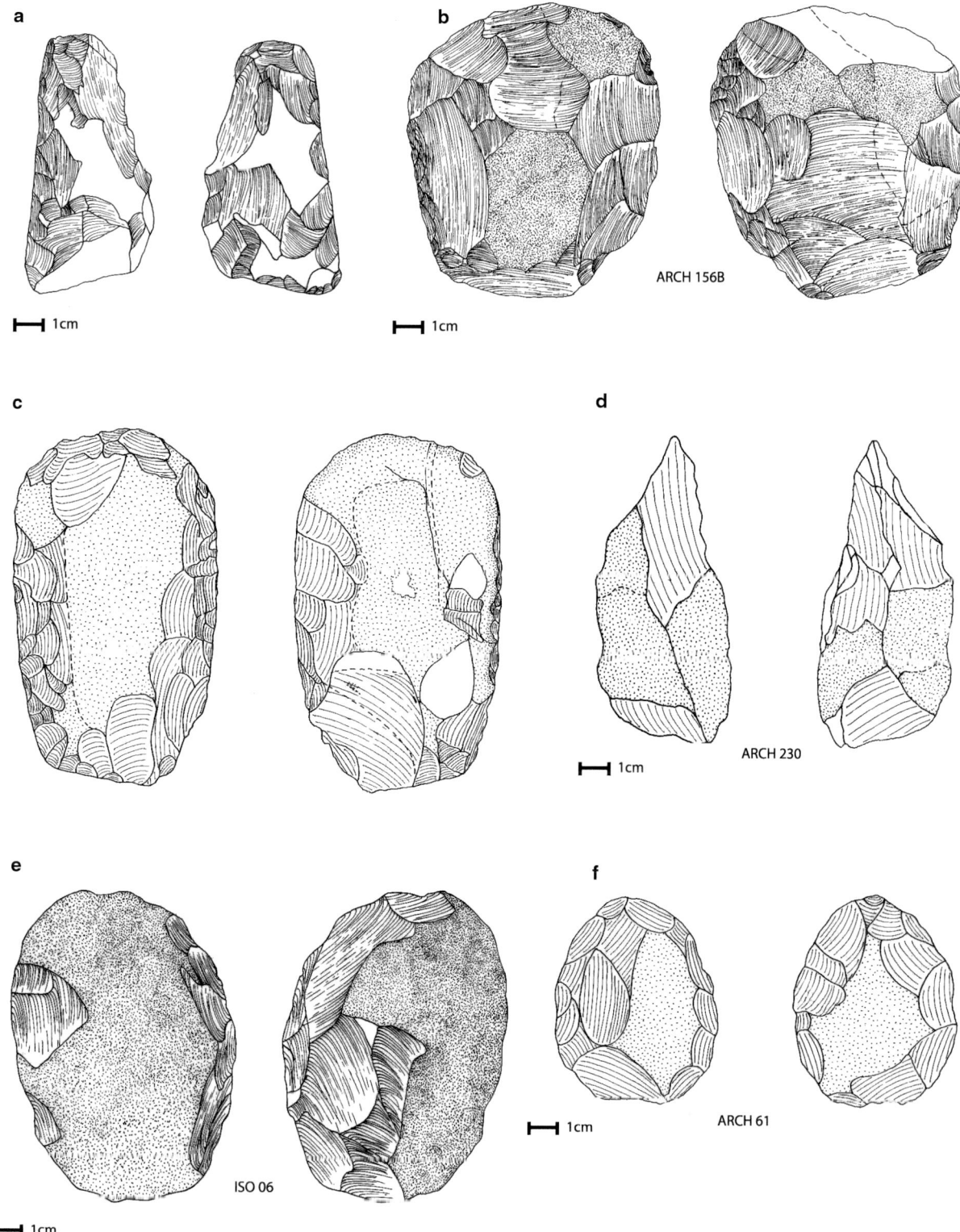

FIGURE 6.22. HANDAXES FROM THE SCHP COLLECTION: (**A**) FRACTURED, SITE 137; (**B AND C**) OVAL WITH A LARGE TRANSVERSE CUTTING (ACHEULEAN), SITE 156B; (**D**) OVAL WITH POINTED DISTAL END, SITE 230; (**E**) OVAL WITH A LARGE TRANSVERSE CUTTING (ACHEULEAN), ISO 6; (**F**) OVAL WITH A ROUND UP DISTAL END, SITE 61.

dichotomy between alluvial and inland contexts may suggest that Acheulean stone tool makers followed an opportunistic strategy, making tools from materials that were locally available and modifying their tool objectives as necessary. That is, typical handaxes from areas with large gravel materials versus marginally worked bifaces from inland areas poor in lithic resources. An intensive surface reconnaissance of these upper terraces may provide more examples of this rare stone tool technology.

FIGURE 6.23. ACHEULEAN HANDAXES.

TABLE 6.5. RAW MATERIAL DISTRIBUTION WITHIN DIFFERENT CLASSES OF GRINDING EQUIPMENT

Raw Material	Surface Collection			Test Excavations		Total
	Grinding Slabs	Pestle	Pierre à Cupules	Grinding Slabs	Pestle	
Granite	2	1	—	—	—	3
Greenstone	5	19	3	1	2	30
Sandstone	2	3	1	—	—	6
Total	9	23	4	1	2	39

Morphotechnical analysis of handaxes revealed two manufacturing techniques. In the first technique, handaxes are shaped on the faces by invasive removals. In contrast, the second technique is characterized by short removals that form eccentric arrangements of the edge. The frequent application of this latter technique produces a rather large cortical surface on one or two faces. Overall, the handaxes from the Sabodala region show very little technical variability.

The technical choices presiding over the manufacture of these handaxes seem to follow one goal: the production of a cutting chisel by short removals. Either natural or developed, this chisel almost always bears a nonintentional retouch, which may have resulted from intense utilization of the piece. We can speculate that, in producing handaxes, prehistoric populations in the Sabodala region sought to obtain cutting edges that could work on most materials. Using such tools, however, required intense physical effort.

Milling Implements

Thirty-nine pieces of milling equipment were recovered—10 grinding slabs, 25 pestles, and 4 pierres à cupules. Most specimens were collected from the surface; only 3 pieces were recovered from excavated contexts (Table 6.5). Most milling implements were made from greenstone; only a few are made of sandstone or granite. Greenstone was the first choice for grinding stones, pestles, and pierres à cupules, probably because of its abundance in the region. This pattern was already noted for other classes of artifacts, including debitage products and handaxes.

Grinding Slabs

Grinding slabs were abundant on many sites in the Sabodala region. Because of their bulk and weight, we only collected 10 specimens for analysis. Most of the pieces collected were fractured, which made it difficult to describe the contours and morphology of their used faces. A close examination of the collection, however, indicates that 9 out of 10 pieces had used faces, in the form of a slightly curved platforms (Figure 6.24).

Pestles

Pestles are the predominant milling implement in the SCHP collection. Twenty five were collected, of which

FIGURE 6.24. MILLING IMPLEMENTS FROM THE SCHP COLLECTION: (**A**) GRINDING SLAB FRAGMENT, SITE 223; (**B**) ELONGATED PESTLE, SITE 227; (**C**) OVAL PESTLE, SITE 64.

two were recovered during test excavations. Two types of pestles can be distinguished in the collection (see Figure 6.24). The first is an oval pestle (n = 5) that has rather small average dimensions (97 by 80 by 49 mm) and whose length is barely superior to its width. Most pieces in this group show a polished face opposed to the other face, which is often variable. The second type, by far the more frequent of the two (n = 20), is an elongated pestle. Most of these are fractured, this being largely a function of the blank on which they are manufactured. They are generally long cobbles with oval or quadrangular cross sections and one or multiple ridges. Both faces of these pestles were regularly used. In addition, the ends could have also been used as millers.

Pierres à Cupules

In addition to grinding stones, the collection from the Sabodala area also includes milling implements known in French as pierres à cupules (Figures 6.25 and 6.26). Like the rest of the collection, most of these tools are manufactured on greenstone. Compared to grinding stones, their dimensions are much smaller (average 91 by 74 by 48 mm) and they are lighter, rarely exceeding 1,000 g. They are generally manufactured either on a strip of stone, a small oval block, or a quadrangular cobble. Without regard to their shape, these pieces are characterized by the presence on their faces of shallow, cup-shaped holes. Both their diameter and their depth vary according to the length of time they were in use. Considering the small size of the cup, it is likely that most of these pieces were used for small-scale grinding of such items as medicinal plants, ochre, or tobacco when found on recent historical sites. They could have also been used to make fire. One piece within the collection is of particular interest. Its form is oval and it probably had a double usage: its flat and polished faces possibly served for grinding, whereas the shallow cup shaped surface was used as a miller (see Figure 6.26).

Traces of Wear on Milling Implements

Traces of wear were readily visible on the milling equipment. Three types of wear could be distinguished: picketing, polish, and striations (Table 6.6). Because of continuous use, milling stones wear out and require maintenance. Picketing with a hammerstone served to even out the active face of a grinding stone or a pestle. Polish occurs on the active surface of a piece and is produced by continuous rubbing of the pounder against

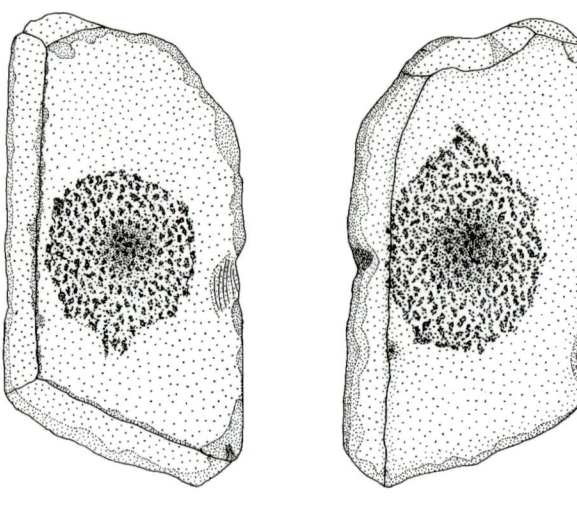

FIGURE 6.25. *Pierre à cupules* from Site 137.

FIGURE 6.26. *Pierre à cupules* from Site 71.

the miller. In contrast, striations are the linear traces resulting from abrasion. The relative high frequency of picketing in the collection suggests that many milling implements (including grinding stones, pestles, and pierres à cupules) were probably still in use as sites were abandoned. If correct, this inference may affect our evaluation of site activities and occupation patterns.

TABLE 6.6. DISTRIBUTION OF WEAR TYPES ON DIFFERENT CLASSES OF MILLING STONES

Traces of Wear	Metate Fragment	Pestle Fragment	Pestle Complete	*Pierres à Cupules*	Total
Picketing					
Face A	—	7	—	3	10
Face B	1	3	2	3	9
Edge	—	2	2	2	6
Picketing and polish					
Face A	—	2	2	1	5
Face B	7	4	3	—	14
Edge	—	1	—	—	1
Picketing and striation					
Face A	—	—	—	—	—
Face B	—	—	—	—	—
Edge	—	—	1	—	1
Polish					
Face A	—	2	1	—	3
Face B	1	3	2	—	6
Edge	—	—	—	—	—
Polish and striation					
Face A	—	1	—	—	1
Face B	—	1	—	—	1
Edge	—	—	—	—	—
Striation					
Face A	—	—	—	—	—
Face B	—	1	—	—	1
Edge	—	1	1	—	2
Total	9	28	14	9	60

Hammerstones

Only two hammerstones were collected from the surface. Both were manufactured on greenstone. Like most hammerstones, traces of wear can be noted on the angles, edges, and/or ridges (Figure 6.27). These wear patterns are either removals or the result of crushing or abrasion of the protruding sections of the hammer. These hammerstones could have been used either for the production of milling equipment or as part of the knapping kit to make flaked stone tools.

Axes

Eight axes were collected from seven sites (6 percent of the lithics) (Figure 6.28; see Table 6.2). Two axes have missing butts; the rest are complete. The initial production of axes is generally believed to have taken place in the Neolithic period and is largely associated with agricultural populations. It is likely, however, that the use of axes was highly variable, as they could be used as weapons, agricultural implements, and even charms.

The variety of raw materials used was large, considering the number of axes collected: five were made of greenstone, one of sandstone quartzite, one of quartz, and one of schist (Table 6.7). Axes were grouped based on their degree of polishing and general morphology, as well as the form of the edge, butt, and cutting edge. Three types

FIGURE 6.27. HAMMERSTONE FROM SITE 233.

were identified: polished axes (4), partially polished axes (2), and nonpolished axes (2). Polished axes generally derive from roughout knapping and later polishing on a grooved stone (Figure 6.29; see Figure 6.28). The two nonpolished axes can be considered roughouts that were prepared for polishing. The presence of retouches on one

FIGURE 6.28. EXAMPLES OF AXES FROM THE SCHP COLLECTION: (**A**) NONPOLISHED, SITE 133; (**B**) NONPOLISHED, SITE 225; (**C**) POLISHED, SITE 36; (**D**) POLISHED, SITE 223; (**E**) POLISHED, SITE 156.

Table 6.7. Raw Materials Used to Manufacture Axes

Axe Type	Raw Material				Total
	Greenstone	Quartz	Schist	Sandstone Quartzite	
Polished	3	1	—	—	4
Polished and nonpolished	1	—	1	—	2
Nonpolished	1	—	—	1	2
Total	5	1	1	1	8

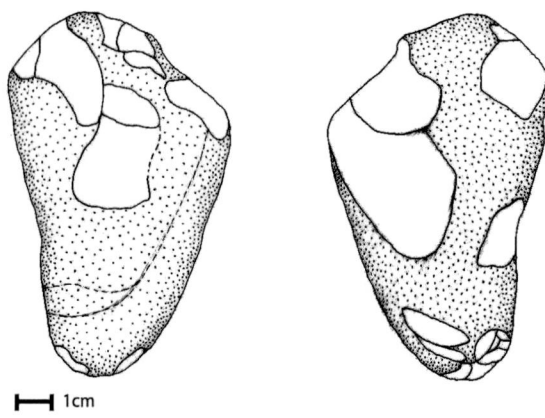

Figure 6.29. Partially polished axe from Site 294.

suggests that they may have been used. It is not clear that either polishing technique was well mastered. We can also speculate on the differential uses of polished versus nonpolished axes. Absence of polish could also indicate more archaic pieces, although this is not certain. Besides polish, almost all the axes in the collection bear pecking on the butt or on the edges that are the most suited for shafting.

Analysis of the morphology shows very little variation between the different types of axes. Although oval axes dominate slightly, quadrangular and triangular forms are also present.

Most (4) of the pieces have an asymmetrical cutting. Only one rectilinear and one convex cutting edge were observed. These two cases were polished axes and are characteristic of greater mastery of knapping techniques. In general, however, the width of the cutting edge is about the same size as the piece, which implies a more efficient cutting edge. A utilization retouch marked by scars, microscars and, more rarely, traces of crushing was noted on the cutting edge of the axes. This pattern most likely indicates their uses as tools rather than charms.

Asymmetrical chisels (4) are more numerous than symmetrical ones (2). In both cases, the chisels are double and generally associated with a line of convex cutting that is asymmetrical. However, the morphology of the axes remains variable and includes oval, triangular, and quadrangular pieces. The development of a simple chisel plan on two axes brings them close to being adzes. Both are slightly inclined toward the face bearing the chisel.

Miscellaneous

Two pieces were grouped into a miscellaneous category: a broken digging stick stone ball and a strip of stone in schist. The digging stick is a spheroid sandstone ball with a biconic perforation that weighed 450 g. No trace of hammering was noted on it. It appeared to have been made smaller and rounder before being polished. This kind of tool is believed to have been used to give weight to lighter wooden implements. Finally, the collection includes a strip of schist that is biplan with a trapezoidal shape. This strip shows no trace of knapping, but similar ones may have been used to manufacture axes and handaxes.

Conclusions

The sample of lithic artifacts is relatively small. Yet technological and typological analyses reveal variations that could be time sensitive, as well as possibly reflecting signatures of hunting-and-gathering cultures in this part of the Senegambia.

The lower Paleolithic is possibly represented by three handaxes found on higher laterite terraces in the OJVG concession. We are on much firmer ground with the middle Paleolithic. A Mousteroid assemblage that probably dates to the middle Paleolithic is revealed by the presence of cores and small tools. The cores are generally centripetal, which suggests flakes that are neither Levallois nor blade shaped. The manufacturing technique appears to be a variant of discoid debitage, which is often associated with the Mousterian complex.

Although small in number, the small tool collection also shows a Mousteroid aspect, as evidenced by the presence of notches and denticulates. These latter seem to be more prevalent than side scrapers, which are the most typical tools of the Middle Paleolithic period. This Mousteroid character is supported by the incidence of pseudo-Levallois points in the collection.

Material pertaining to the Upper Paleolithic is rare in the collection, comprising only two end scrapers, one burin, and one awl. It must be pointed out that these tools were known during the Acheulean, but their occurrence in such industries is generally very small. Blade debitage generally characterizes Upper Paleolithic assemblages, but blades were not exclusive to the Upper Paleolithic. No blade core was recovered in the OJVG concession, which accords with our hypothesis of a predominantly Middle Paleolithic assemblage of lithic material.

The presence of eight axes, of which some were polished, suggests Neolithic occupation of the study area. Milling stones are abundant in the region, but not as time sensitive; their use ranges from the Neolithic to the recent historical period.

Chapter 7

Geoarchaeological Investigations

Jeffrey A. Homburg and Massal Diagne

Introduction

As part of the SCHP, we completed a geoarchaeological study that was conducted in March 2010 and spearheaded by Dr. Jeffrey Homburg, with the assistance of IFAN graduate students Massal Diagne and Amy Colle Seck, Dr. Masamba Lamb (semiretired archaeologist), and seven local laborers: Mamadou Cisse, Sadio Daniokho, Amadou Cissokho, Pathe Diallo, Mamadou Latine Cissokho, Mamoudou Diallo, and Sorry Diarra. The research objectives of this study included (1) modeling the potential for buried archaeological sites in the areas of direct impact (ADIs) and (2) evaluating the associations of archaeological sites with geomorphic surfaces. This analysis was conceived from the outset as being integral to the SCHP, and therefore the discussion is presented below rather than in an appendix. A map of buried site sensitivity was produced for the different landforms, based on interpretations of soil development and geomorphic processes associated with various landforms and landscape positions. Buried-site probability was determined to be highest for the floodplains, but the site types located there are most likely dominated by agricultural fields, which leave few archaeological traces.

Preliminary Buried-Site Model

A preliminary model of buried-site probability was created for the OJVG concession prior to the field investigation to assist with the mine development plan (see Chapter 8). This model is based on slope elements and associated landforms that could be inferred from topographic maps with a 1-m contour interval. Figure 7.7 shows the buried-site model for the proposed freshwater-reservoir area, and Figure 7.8 shows an aerial photograph of this same area. The buried-site probability model is based primarily on Ruhe's (1975) descriptive slope elements: summits, shoulder slopes, back slopes, foot slopes, and toe slopes (Figure 7.9). Because these slope elements are associated with geomorphic processes that occur in different landscape positions, they are useful for predicting the likelihood of buried archaeological sites for different landform settings. The dominant geomorphic processes for each slope element are as follows: (1) summits—water infiltration and soil formation, (2) shoulder slopes—erosion, (3) back slopes—transportation of eroded sediment, (4) foot slopes—deposition of colluvial and slope-wash sediments, and (5) toe slopes—deposition of alluvial sediment (Table 7.1). At the outset, buried archaeological sites were predicted as most likely occurring in the lower landscape positions, in fill deposits associated with foot slopes and toe slopes, whereas surficial sites were expected to be concentrated on summits, foot slopes, and relict toe slopes (alluvial terraces) below foot slopes. High-, medium-, and low-probability areas were drawn by hand on the topographic maps and then digitized. High-probability areas include the toe slopes of floodplains and alluvial terraces that are less than about 1 m above the active floodplain. Medium-probability areas are defined as the junctures of foot slopes and toe slopes in valley-margin positions (mainly colluvial foot slopes and alluvial fans) and alluvial terraces more than about 1 m above the active floodplain. Low-probability areas consist of the elevated landforms of summits, shoulder slopes, and back slopes, places where archaeological deposits are most likely surficial. Because small pockets of colluvium that cannot be distinguished on the topographic maps may occur in the medium- and low-probability areas, it is possible that sites may be buried in these localities.

Methods

Field Methods

The first field task involved selecting, excavating, and documenting 13 backhoe trenches placed in different parts of the ADIs. The locations of the 13 backhoe trenches are shown in Figure 7.10, and Table 7.2 summarizes the locational data and landform associations for these trenches. Six backhoe trenches were excavated in the proposed freshwater-reservoir area (on the northeastern part of the map), 5 were excavated in the proposed tailings-reservoir area (on the south-central part of the map), and 2 were excavated on the proposed haul road (on the west-central part of the map). Trenches were mainly excavated to a depth of 3 m below the surface, using an excavator—a backhoe on tracks (also called a trackhoe) (Figure 7.11). A series of backhoe trenches were excavated in order to (1) document soil morphological properties (e.g., topsoil thickness, soil color, texture, horizons, structure, consistence, and other properties) in

Geoarchaeological Investigations

Figure 7.1. Laterite exposed on an old geomorphic surface in the western part of the Oromin Joint Venture Group concession, near the road west of Maka Madina.

Figure 7.2. Laterite exposed on an old geomorphic surface in the northern part of the Oromin Joint Venture Group concession, near the road to Branson.

Figure 7.4. Close-up of laterite exposed in a road cut on a road south-southwest of Maka Madina, showing inclusion of milky-quartz gravel.

Figure 7.3. Road cut showing laterite on a road south-southwest of Maka Madina.

Figure 7.5. Hilly terrain in the Masato area.

Figure 7.6. Hilly terrain in the southern portion of the concession, south-southeast of Kunemba.

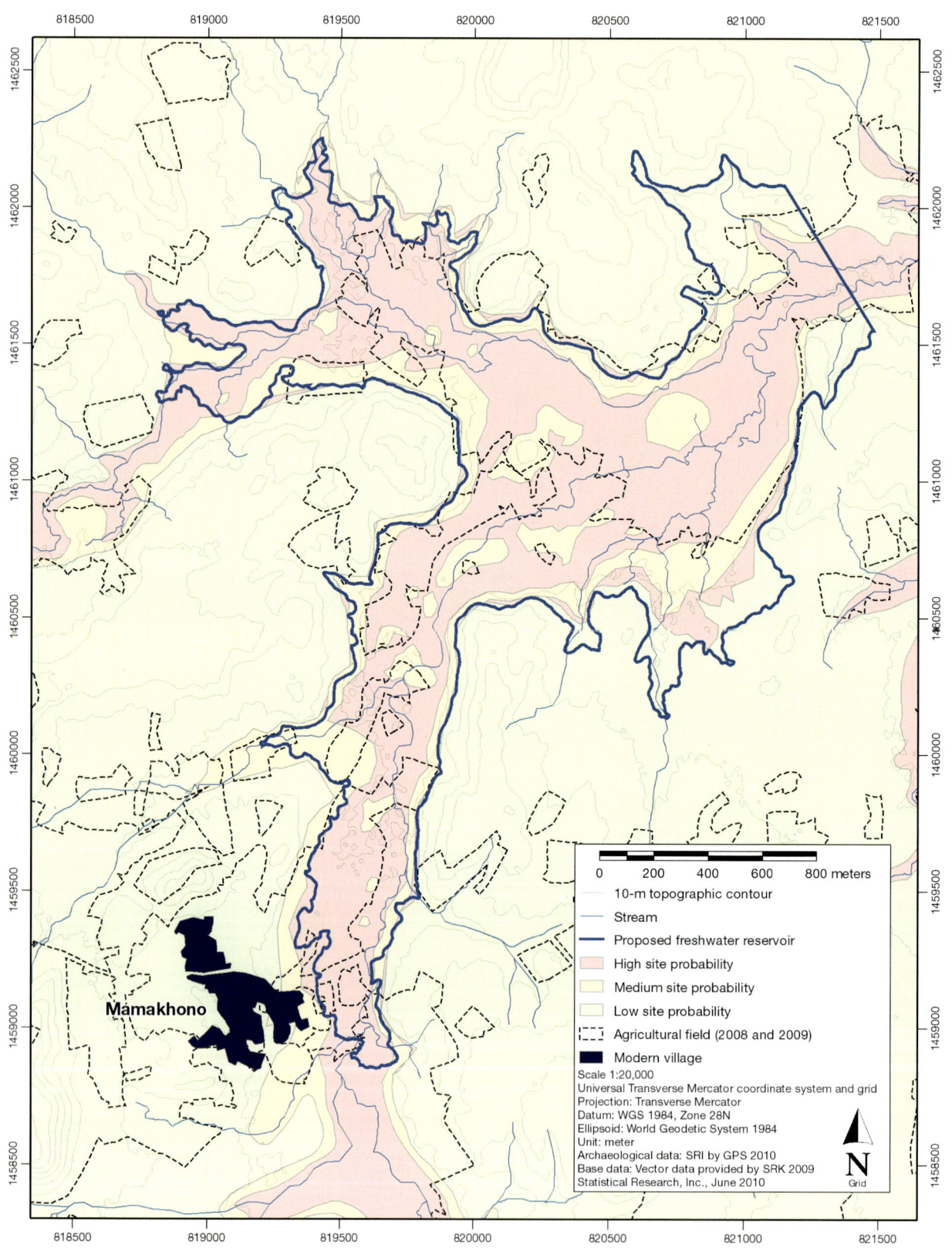

Figure 7.7. Buried-site-probability map for the proposed freshwater-reservoir area.

Figure 7.8. Aerial photograph of the proposed freshwater-reservoir area taken during the summer rainy season. The village of Mamakhono is in the southwest corner.

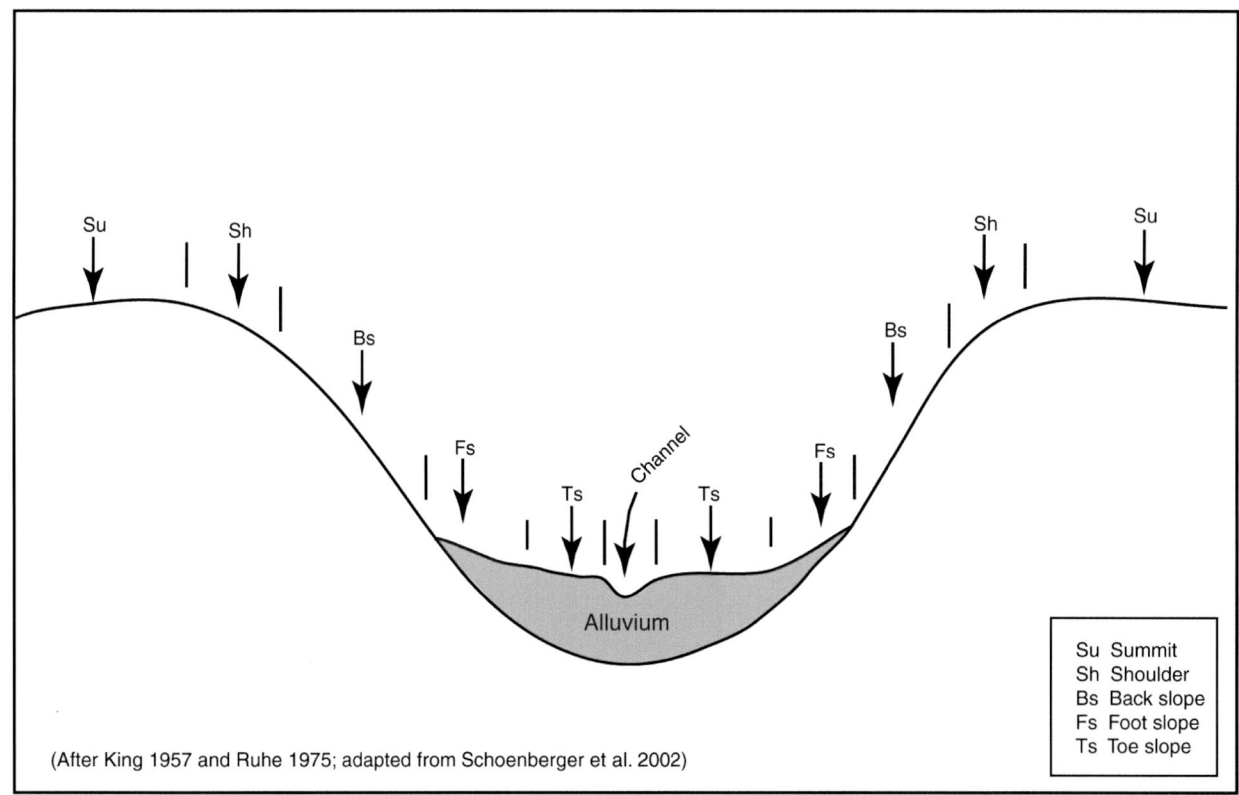

FIGURE 7.9. IDEALIZED VALLEY CROSS SECTION SHOWING RUHE'S SLOPE ELEMENTS.

TABLE 7.1. DOMINANT GEOMORPHIC PROCESSES AND
EXPECTED ARTIFACT DENSITIES FOR DIFFERENT SLOPE ELEMENTS

Dominant Geomorphic Processes, by Slope Element	Expected Artifact Density and Site Integrity
Summit	
Sheetwash erosion	high artifact visibility
Seepage	patchy intact deposits
Pedogenesis	artifacts concentrated on the surface
Shoulder slope	
Heavy sheetwash erosion	moderate artifact density
Soil creep	artifacts subject to erosion
Back slope	
Sediment transport	low artifact density
Mass movement by flow, slide, slump, and creep	artifacts subject to erosion and transport
Foot slope	
Colluvial deposition	moderate artifact density and integrity
Redeposition by mass movement and slopewash	artifacts subject to burial by colluvium
Pedogenesis	
Toe slope	
Alluvial deposition	low artifact density; artifacts subject to burial by alluvium

accordance with the conventions of modern soil survey (Soil Survey Division Staff 1993; Soil Survey Staff 1999), (2) assess the probability of buried archaeological sites for different landforms, and (3) collect soil samples from different landforms. The backhoe and operator were supplied by OJVG, as availability allowed between normal mining-exploration and earthmoving activities.

Soil samples for physical and chemical soil tests were collected from each soil horizon in the upper 1.5 m of the profiles for Backhoe Trenches 1–6, in the proposed freshwater-reservoir area.

Each backhoe trench was excavated in 30-cm levels, and the fill from each level was placed in a separate pile next

GEOARCHAEOLOGICAL INVESTIGATIONS

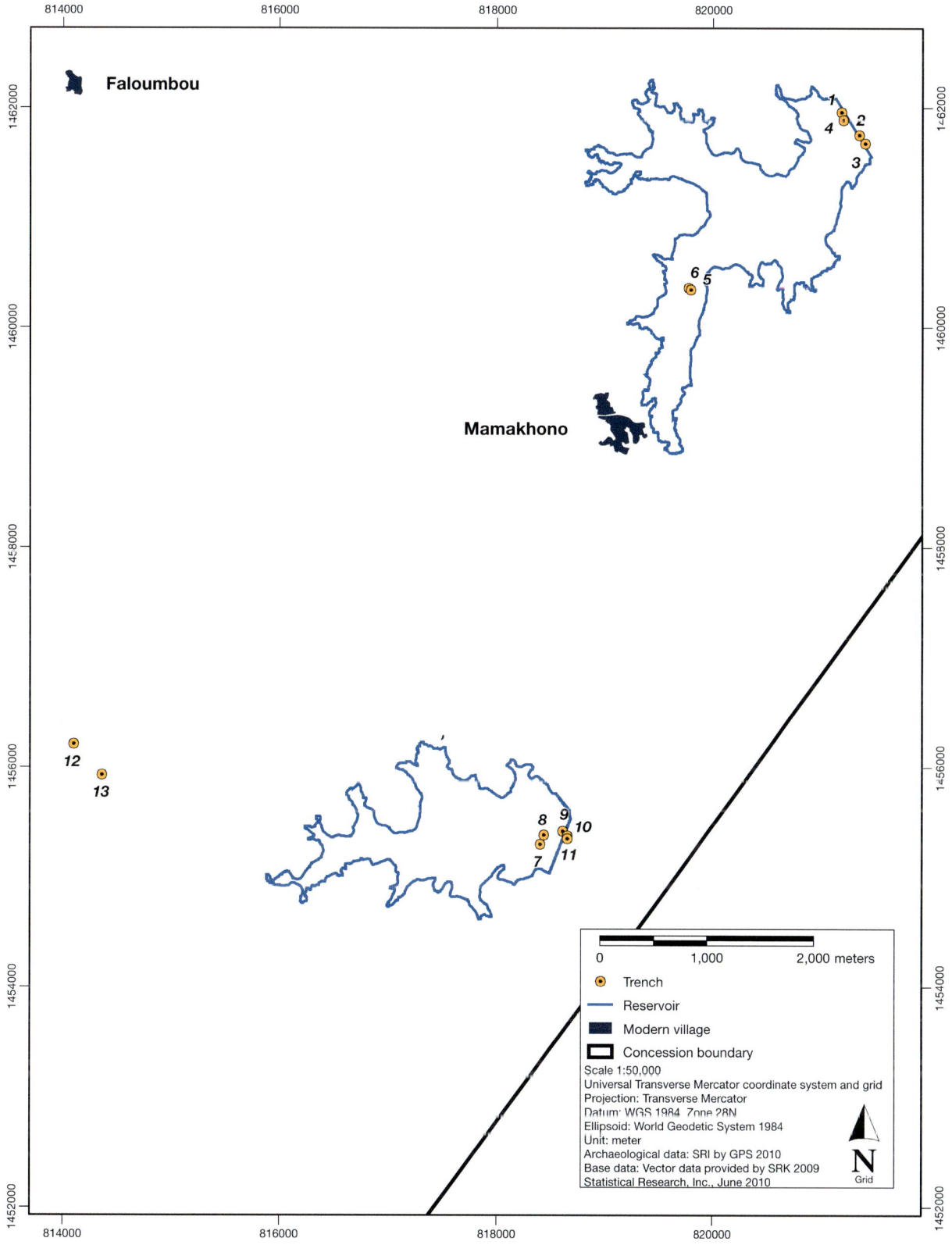

FIGURE 7.10. LOCATIONS OF BACKHOE TRENCHES IN THE PROPOSED FRESHWATER-RESERVOIR AREA (BACKHOE TRENCHES 1–6), THE TAILINGS-RESERVOIR AREA (BACKHOE TRENCHES 7–11), AND THE HAUL-ROAD ALIGNMENT (BACKHOE TRENCHES 12 AND 13) (NOTE: THE RESERVOIR TO THE NORTH IS THE PROPOSED FRESHWATER RESERVOIR; THE RESERVOIR TO THE SOUTH IS THE TAILINGS RESERVOIR).

TABLE 7.2. SUMMARY OF LOCATIONAL AND GEOMORPHOLOGICAL INFORMATION FOR BACKHOE TRENCHES

Trench No.	Location	UTM Coordinates		Elevation (MAMSL)	Trench Length (m)	Trench Orientation (degrees)	Slope Aspect	Slope Gradient (%)	Landform and Geomorphic Surface	Geomorphic Surface[a]	ARCH Site No.
		Easting	Northing								
1	freshwater-reservoir dam	821200	1461962	149	11.0	WNW (294)	SW (232)	2	erosion terrace capped by Pleistocene alluvium	T2	206
2	freshwater-reservoir dam	821366	1461754	142	10.0	NW (320)	ESE (110)	2	Holocene floodplain	T0	
3	freshwater-reservoir dam	821423	1461676	141	8.5	WSW (249)	NNW (340)	4	Holocene floodplain	T0	
4	freshwater-reservoir dam	821217	1461887	150	8.7	N (0)	NNE (20)	6	colluvial foot slope–Holocene floodplain juncture	T1	207
5	freshwater reservoir	819769	1460360	161	11.0	WSW (261)	E (81)	1	Pleistocene terrace	T1	208
6	freshwater reservoir	819792	1460344	179	9.0	SSW (190)	ESE (165)	2	Holocene floodplain	T0	
7	tailings reservoir	818402	1455300	184	7.2	SSW (212)	NE (67)	4	Pleistocene terrace	T1	209
8	tailings reservoir	818435	1455384	183	10.0	ENE (69)	NE (45)	2	Pleistocene terrace	T1	210
9	tailings reservoir	818610	1455421	185	9.2	NE (62)	SSW (165)	3	Holocene floodplain	T0	
10	tailings reservoir	818653	1455376	184	9.3	NW (318)	NW (305)	6	Pleistocene terrace	T1	
11	tailings reservoir	818653	1455352	185	9.8	W (269)	W (269)	11	Pleistocene terrace	T2	
12	haul road	814100	1456212	210	10.8	WNW (295)	NNE (17)	4	quaternary alluvial fan, medial fan	AF	
13	haul road	814363	1455932	222	9.6	E (101)	NW (308)	5	quaternary alluvial fan, proximal fan	AF	212
Creek bank	C14 sampling area	819920	1460703	145					Holocene floodplain	T0	

[a] T0 = floodplain; T1 = first terrace above the floodplain; T2 = second terrace above the floodplain; AF = alluvial fan.
Key: E = east; MAMSL = meters above mean sea level; N = north; S = south; UTM = Universal Transverse Mercator; W = west.

to the trench (Figure 7.12). Five 5-gallon buckets were filled for each level and screened for buried artifacts through ¼-inch- (6.35-mm-) mesh hardware cloth (Figure 7.13).

In addition to the work involving backhoe trenches, a geoarchaeological survey was conducted. This survey was a reconnaissance of areas spread across the OJVG concession. The geoarchaeology crew drove along roads throughout much of the project area, stopping to walk along stream channels that crossed or paralleled the road and examining other subsurface exposures (e.g., borrow pits and artificial exposures on the edges of well pads) for evidence of buried sites. Landforms adjacent to creek banks and other exposures were also examined for the presence of archaeological materials, such as artifacts and cultural features. Archaeological sites were briefly recorded, which involved taking GPS readings, keeping notes regarding artifacts and the numbers and types of cultural features, and making a small collection of artifacts, mainly decorated sherds and lithic tools.

Laboratory Methods

Some soil properties, such as soil pH and gravel content, were analyzed in a field lab. Gravel content was measured on a gravimetric basis (i.e., the weight of gravel relative to the weight of the entire bulk sample of soil). Initial sample preparation involved air-drying samples, lightly grinding the samples with a mortar and pestle to disaggregate the finer-fraction gravel, and screening the samples through a 2-mm sieve to remove gravel, roots, and other coarse, undecomposed, organic debris. Gravel content was then determined by weighing the gravel and expressing that weight as a percentage of the total sample weight.

Subsamples of the less-than-2-mm fraction were then weighed and analyzed for pH, particle-size, organic-matter, total-carbon (which is essentially organic carbon, in this case, because of the acidic pH of almost all the soil samples), nitrogen, and available-phosphorus analyses, which were divided, as needed, between two outside soil laboratories. Calcium, magnesium, potassium, sodium, and available-phosphorus analyses were completed by Mary Jo Schabel at the Milwaukee Soil Laboratory. Particle-size, total-carbon, and nitrogen analyses were completed by the Department of Geography Soil Analysis Laboratory at Northern Illinois University, under the direction of Dr. Michael Konen.

Available-phosphorus analysis was completed for 10-g subsamples that were mechanically ground to pass through a No. 100 sieve. Available phosphorus was measured using the Bray-1 extractant (Bray and Kurtz 1945). Soil pH was measured in the field by

Figure 7.11. Backhoe excavation of Backhoe Trench 6 on the floodplain (T0 terrace) in the proposed freshwater-reservoir area.

Figure 7.12. Backhoe excavation of Backhoe Trench 11 in the proposed haul-road alignment, with piles of soil excavated in 30-cm levels placed next to the trench, in preparation for screening.

FIGURE 7.13. PHOTOGRAPH OF GEOARCHAEOLOGY CREW MEMBERS SCREENING FILL FROM A BACKHOE TRENCH.

colorimetry, with a Hellige-Truog soil-reaction tester, and electrochemically, in a 1:1 (by weight) suspension of soil and distilled/deionized water, using a portable Hanna pH meter (model no. HI 991301) (Thomas 1996). Total-carbon and nitrogen concentrations were determined using an Elementar CN analyzer. Calcium, magnesium, potassium, and sodium were all measured using extraction techniques described by Mehlich (1953). Particle-size distributions were measured using the sieve-and-pipette method (Gee and Or 2002:Methods 2.4.3.2 and 2.4.3.4), with samples pretreated with 30 percent hydrogen peroxide for organic-matter digestion and a sodium hexametaphosphate solution for clay dispersion.

Results

Backhoe Trenching

As noted previously, 13 backhoe trenches were excavated in the ADIs (Backhoe Trenches 1–6 in the proposed freshwater-reservoir area, Backhoe Trenches 7–11 n the proposed tailings-reservoir area, and Backhoe Trenches 12 and 13 in the alignment of the proposed haul road between the Masato and Galouma (see Table 7.2) mining areas. Data on the alluvial terrace, soil-horizon sequence, length and orientation, and slope aspect and gradient for each trench are summarized in Tables 7.2 and 7.3.

Proposed Freshwater-Reservoir Area

The dam for the proposed freshwater reservoir is planned for about halfway between Mamakhono and Dindifa to the northeast (see Figures 7.7 and 7.10). There are two arms in the proposed reservoir, one extending southwest, nearly to Mamakhono, and the other northwest, where it will cover extensive areas of agricultural land, as indicated in Figure 7.7. The channel and bank of the trunk drainage in the valley are shown in Figures 7.14 and 7.15. The soils in the stream bank are characterized by an approximately 1-m-thick, brown A horizon over an oxidized, yellowish-brown to strong-brown C horizon. Redoximorphic features are visible in the C horizon and clearly indicate that oxidation is dominant but that flooding for significant periods of the year has caused reduction of iron.

Backhoe Trenches 1–4 were placed in the area of the proposed reservoir, on the alignment of the dam. Backhoe Trenches 5 and 6 were placed about halfway between the proposed dam and Mamakhono. Chemical and physical soil data for these backhoe trenches are presented in Tables 7.4 and 7.5, respectively. Soil pH

Geoarchaeological Investigations

TABLE 7.3. SUMMARY OF LOCATIONAL AND GEOMORPHOLOGICAL INFORMATION FOR BACKHOE TRENCHES

Trench No.	Location	Wall Profiled	Location of Profile in Trench Wall	Gemorphic Surface[a]	Soil-Horizon Sequence	Soil Order	Diagnostic Subsurface Horizon
1	freshwater-reservoir dam	east	2 m south of north end	T2	A-Bt1-Bt2-Bt3-Cr1-Cr2-Cr3-Cr4	Ultisol	argillic (strong)
2	freshwater-reservoir dam	east	3 m north of south end	T0	A-AC-C1-C2-C3-C4	Entisol	none
3	freshwater-reservoir dam	east	3 m north of south end	T0	A-CA-C1-C2-C3-C4-C5	Entisol	none
4	freshwater-reservoir dam	west	3 m east of west end	T1	A-Bt-BC-C1-C2-C3-C4	Alfisol	argillic (weak)
5	freshwater reservoir	north	5 m west of east end	T1	A-Bt1-Bt2-BCt1-BCt2-C1-C2	Alfisol	argillic (weak)
6	freshwater reservoir	east	3 m east of west end	T0	A-Bw1-Bw2-C1-C2-C3-C4	Inceptisol	cambic
7	tailings reservoir	west	2 m south of north end	T1	A-Bt1-Bt2-BC1-BC2-C1-C2	Ultisol	argillic (weak)
8	tailings reservoir	north	2 m west of east end	T1	A-Bw1-Bw2-C1-C2-C3-C4	Inceptisol	cambic
9	tailings reservoir	north	2 m east of west end	T0	A-Bw1-Bw2-BC-C1-C2-C3	Inceptisol	cambic
10	tailings reservoir	south	2 m west of east end	T1	A-Bw1-Bw2-BC-C1-C2-C3-2C4	Inceptisol	cambic
11	tailings reservoir	south	3 m west of east end	T2	A-Bt1-Bt2-BCt-C1-C2-2C3	Ultisol	argillic (strong)
12	haul road	west	3 m north of south end	AF	A-ABt-Bt-2C1-2C2-3C3-3C4	Ultisol	argillic (moderate)
13	haul road	north	4 m east of west end	AF	A-ABt-Bt-2Bt1-2Bt2-3C1-3C2	Ultisol	argillic (moderate)
Creek bank	C14 sampling area			T0	A-C		

[a] T0 = floodplain; T1 = first terrace above the floodplain; T2 = second terrace above the floodplain; AF = alluvial fan.

FIGURE 7.14. CHANNEL OF AN INTERMITTENT STREAM DURING THE DRY SEASON IN THE PROPOSED FRESHWATER-RESERVOIR AREA.

levels are mainly slightly acidic, with an average of 6.4, a standard deviation of 0.4, and a range of about 5.6–7.3. Because slightly acidic pH levels are poor for bone preservation, bone is not expected to be preserved in most of the archaeological sites in the proposed freshwater-reservoir area, if it is preserved in any. But slightly acidic pH levels are very productive for agriculture, because of their nutrient availability for many kinds of crops, including the dominant crops of sorghum and maize. Rock fragments are mainly

FIGURE 7.15. STRATIGRAPHY OF THE T0 TERRACE FILL EXPOSED IN THE CREEK BANK IN THE PROPOSED FRESHWATER-RESERVOIR AREA.

TABLE 7.4. SOIL CHEMICAL PROPERTIES FOR SOIL PROFILES IN BACKHOE TRENCHES 1–6

Trench/ Geomorphic Surface[a]	Soil Horizon	Depth (cmbs)	pH	C (g/kg)	N (g/kg)	C:N Ratio	Organic Matter (%)	Ca (mg/kg)	K (mg/kg)	Mg (mg/kg)	Na (mg/kg)	Available P (mg/kg)
Trench 1 T2	A	0–12	6.26	28.6	2.1	13.6	4.9	1314	270	361	10.2	16.1
	Btv1	12–43	6.79	4.3	0.5	8.1	0.7	1023	49	344	10.6	0.2
	Btv2	43–66	6.60	3.7	0.6	6.2	0.6	872	57	319	12.0	0.5
	Btv3	66–114	6.64	3.8	0.6	6.1	0.6	1223	49	466	12.8	0.5
	Cr1	114–131	6.41	3.2	0.5	7.0	0.6	1267	42	502	12.6	0.3
	Cr2	131–180	6.37	3.7	0.5	7.9	0.6	1357	47	590	18.8	0.3
Trench 2 T0	A	0–46	6.15	16.2	0.8	19.8	2.8	2484	30	763	14.9	0.9
	AC	46–98	5.95	12.7	0.5	26.6	2.2	2234	32	701	15.7	0.9
	C1	98–160	6.23	9.3	0.5	19.9	1.6	2005	32	704	13.0	0.5
Trench 3 T0	A	0–24	6.47	7.8	0.5	14.5	1.3	1058	28	276	6.8	0.9
	CA	24–56	6.33	4.5	0.4	10.7	0.8	926	30	279	8.5	0.9
	C1	56–101	6.29	2.4	0.3	8.5	0.4	1057	29	289	8.6	0.5
	C2	101–151	6.57	2.8	0.3	8.9	0.5	1209	29	321	14.5	0.3
Trench 4 T1	A	0–39	7.04	7.7	0.8	9.3	1.3	770	23	309	6.5	0.7
	Bt	39–50	6.22	5.7	0.7	8.5	1.0	801	20	365	9.7	0.7
	BC	50–81	6.63	2.8	0.4	7.5	0.5	843	25	375	12.7	0.3
	C1	81–150	6.82	3.3	0.5	7.2	0.6	870	23	395	13.4	0.5
Trench 5 T1	A	0–22	6.61	10.9	0.9	12.6	1.9	1013	70	153	3.6	5.0
	Bt1	22–64	6.78	4.5	0.4	10.8	0.8	857	46	119	4.5	0.9
	Bt2	64–110	6.57	2.0	0.3	7.5	0.3	683	22	175	9.3	0.3
	BCt1	110–177	7.26	1.3	0.2	6.5	0.2	524	18	186	8.1	0.2
Trench 6 T0	A	0–21	6.07	25.7	1.3	19.8	4.4	2348	42	574	13.8	4.6
	Bw1	21–34	5.82	14.7	0.6	22.6	2.5	1912	28	611	12.1	1.6
	Bw2	34–120	5.84	9.7	0.4	21.8	1.7	1614	17	600	16.3	0.5
	C1	120–199	5.58	6.8	0.4	17.2	1.2	1359	11	454	13.0	0.9

[a] T0 = floodplain; T1 = first terrace above the floodplain; T2 = second terrace above the floodplain.
Key: cmbs = centimeters below the surface.

GEOARCHAEOLOGICAL INVESTIGATIONS

TABLE 7.5. PARTICLE-SIZE DISTRIBUTIONS, TEXTURAL CLASS, AND GEOMETRIC MEANS FOR SOIL PROFILES IN BACKHOE TRENCHES 1–6

Trench/Geomorphic Surface[a]	Soil Horizon	Depth (cm)	Gravel (%)	Wentworth Geometric Progression												U.S. Department of Agriculture			Textural Class	Geometric Mean (2–0 mm) (mm)
				Sand (mm)					Silt (μm)					Clay (mm)	Sand (mm)	Silt (μm)	Clay (mm)		
				VCS (2–1)	CS (1–0.5)	MS (0.5–0.25)	FS (0.25–0.125)	VFS (0.125–0.063)	TS (2–0.063)	VCSi (63–32)	CSi (32–16)	MSi (16–8)	FSi (8–4)	VFSi (4–2)	TSi (63–2)	TC (<2)	TS (2–0.053)	TSi (53–2)	TC (<2)		
Trench 1 T2	A	0–12	79	13.3	11.3	8.2	7.2	6.6	46.6	8.2	13.1	8.9	4.2	5.7	40.0	13.4	48.7	37.9	13.4	extremely gravelly loam	53
	Btv1	12–43	62	10.6	4.5	1.3	1.4	3.3	21.2	3.8	7.7	6.6	6.6	7.2	32.0	46.8	22.3	30.9	46.8	very gravelly clay	8
	Btv2	43–66	70	11.3	3.5	1.1	1.4	3.5	20.8	3.4	3.8	14.6	5.8	7.1	34.7	44.5	21.8	33.7	44.5	extremely gravelly clay	9
	Btv3	66–114	75	8.7	4.3	1.2	1.3	2.4	17.9	4.0	6.6	10.9	11.8	6.7	40.2	41.9	18.9	39.2	41.9	extremely gravelly clay	8
	Cr1	114–131	70	8.4	4.8	1.7	2.2	4.2	21.3	4.5	7.0	15.1	10.4	8.8	45.9	32.8	22.9	44.2	32.8	extremely gravelly clay loam	11
	Cr2	131–180	74	5.6	4.2	2.6	3.1	7.4	22.9	8.0	10.0	13.4	12.0	8.5	51.8	25.2	25.0	49.8	25.2	extremely gravelly loam	14
Trench 2 T0	A	0–46	40	0.3	0.6	0.5	1.6	4.5	7.5	8.3	16.2	16.7	10.0	10.3	61.5	31.0	9.5	59.5	31.0	very gravelly silty clay loam	7
	AC	46–98	39	0.1	0.4	0.6	1.6	4.9	7.6	9.2	16.9	18.3	9.0	8.5	61.8	30.6	10.0	59.4	30.6	very gravelly silty clay loam	7
	C1	98–160	44	0.0	0.2	0.4	1.4	5.3	7.3	7.8	16.9	20.1	9.8	7.7	62.3	30.5	9.2	60.3	30.5	very gravelly silty clay loam	7
Trench 3 T0	A	0–24	48	6.4	6.2	5.5	5.9	7.8	31.7	11.5	13.0	8.2	4.7	2.1	39.6	28.6	35.2	36.2	28.6	very gravelly clay loam	21
	CA	24–56	52	3.3	7.4	7.7	7.5	8.3	34.0	9.5	11.4	7.0	3.1	3.1	34.0	32.0	37.2	30.8	32.0	very gravelly clay loam	19
	C1	56–101	57	2.3	7.4	8.8	9.0	8.8	36.3	10.6	10.0	7.0	2.9	6.1	36.6	27.1	39.7	33.2	27.1	very gravelly clay loam	22
	C2	101–151	70	6.5	10.7	7.4	5.7	7.6	37.9	10.0	10.4	6.7	3.0	5.4	35.4	26.7	40.3	33.0	26.7	extremely gravelly loam	26
Trench 4 T1	A	0–39	39	4.4	4.0	2.6	3.4	7.0	21.4	10.2	15.0	10.3	3.6	6.2	45.3	33.3	24.9	41.9	33.3	very gravelly clay loam	12
	Bt	39–50	36	0.9	1.2	1.6	2.5	7.0	13.3	2.0	17.3	11.9	4.1	4.5	49.9	36.8	17.0	46.2	36.8	very gravelly silty clay loam	8
	BC	50–81	66	1.1	1.3	0.8	1.3	5.7	10.1	5.7	18.1	11.8	5.9	6.3	57.8	32.1	14.6	53.3	32.1	extremely silty clay loam	9
	C1	81–150	61	1.4	1.2	0.7	1.2	7.0	11.4	3.5	17.1	13.7	4.4	7.1	55.9	32.7	15.9	51.4	32.7	very gravelly silty clay loam	9
Trench 5 T1	A	0–22	55	24.3	24.1	11.9	4.3	3.1	68.2	3.9	6.9	4.7	2.8	4.0	22.3	9.6	69.4	21.1	9.6	very gravelly sandy loam	157
	Bt1	22–64	66	18.7	23.0	11.9	2.9	2.0	60.5	1.7	2.8	2.7	1.8	3.5	12.5	27.0	60.9	12.1	27.0	very gravelly sandy clay loam	71
	Bt2	64–110	68	15.5	23.0	11.2	3.6	2.0	65.3	2.0	3.5	1.9	1.9	3.4	12.7	22.0	65.8	12.2	22.0	very gravelly sandy clay loam	103
	BCt1	110–177	58	15.7	20.8	8.0	2.7	1.6	68.8	1.5	3.0	5.1	0.3	3.9	13.8	17.4	69.3	13.3	17.4	very gravelly sandy loam	149
Trench 6 T0	A	0–21	2	0.3	0.4	0.3	1.1	2.5	4.7	5.9	20.9	17.5	13.4	11.1	68.8	26.5	6.0	67.4	26.5	silt loam	7
	Bw1	21–34	2	0.1	0.1	0.3	1.3	2.8	4.6	7.8	15.8	20.0	14.1	9.2	66.9	28.5	6.2	65.3	28.5	silty clay loam	7
	Bw2	34–120	3	0.7	0.9	1.1	2.3	5.4	10.5	6.5	18.3	13.8	11.6	9.1	59.6	29.9	12.2	57.9	29.9	silty clay loam	8
	C1	120–199	5	0.9	3.9	4.9	10.0	9.4	29.1	10.6	15.7	13.2	3.7	5.1	48.3	22.5	32.6	44.9	22.5	loam	19

[a] T0 = floodplain; T1 = first terrace above the floodplain; T2 = second terrace above the floodplain.

Key: CS = coarse sand; CSi = coarse silt; FS = fine sand; FSi = fine silt; MS = medium sand; MSi = medium silt; TC = total clay; TS = total sand; TSi = total silt; VCS = very coarse sand; VCSi = very coarse silt; VFS = very fine sand; VFSi = very fine silt.

very gravelly on the T0 and T1 terraces and extremely gravelly on the T2 terrace. The gravel consists mainly of fine to course, angular to subangular laterite gravels, indicating short-distance transport and redeposition from older, more-elevated landforms in the watershed. Soil textures are mainly loamy on the T0 and T1 terraces (sandy clay loams dominant on the T0 terrace and silty clay loams dominant on the T1 terrace) and clayey (clays and clay loams) on the T2 terrace. Loamy soils are the best textures for agriculture, because these soils tend to have good nutrient- and moisture-holding properties and they are well aerated, as long as they are not flooded.

Backhoe Trenches 2, 3, and 6 were placed on the floodplain (T0 terrace). Each of these trenches is characterized by fill deposits with A-C or A-Bw-C horizon soil profiles, with thick (approximately 0.5–1-m-thick), organic-rich A horizons. A Bw horizon (a cambic horizon, and an incipient B horizon marked by some soil structure and a color change from the C horizon) was found at Backhoe Trench 6, indicating that the floodplain in that part of the valley is geomorphically more stable than the area of the proposed dam, probably as a result of less flooding and sediment aggradation than areas downstream. The C subhorizons were differentiated based on (1) stratification of deposits that mark episodic aggradation of flood deposits and (2) variations in the expression of redoximorphic features caused by differences in the lengths of time that different subhorizons at different levels were waterlogged (Figures 7.16–7.18). Colors in the fill of the T0 terrace range from brown to yellowish brown to strong brown; darker colors reflect the masking of yellowish and reddish colors indicative of oxidation by organic-matter coatings on mineral grains. Coring, for the purpose of geotechnical work on and near the proposed dam location, indicated that the alluvium is about 9 m thick above the bedrock.

Backhoe Trenches 4 and 5 were placed on the T1 terrace, a geomorphic surface about 2–3 m above the elevation of the floodplain. This terrace often occurs as a terrace remnant within the floodplain, as shown in Figure 7.19, or as a bench flanking the floodplain. These trenches have A horizons that range in thickness from about 20 to 40 cm and overlie Bt horizons—illuvial horizons that qualify as cambic horizons if they have less than a 20 percent increase in clay relative to the overlying horizon or as argillic horizons if they have more than a 20 percent increase in clay (Figure 7.20). The presence of Bt horizons, as in Backhoe Trench 6, indicates greater pedogenic (or soil-forming) development and greater geomorphic stability (that is, neither aggraded at a rate too rapid to permit much soil development, such as in A-C horizon profiles, nor eroded to the degree that traces of soil formation have been erased).

FIGURE 7.16. PROFILE OF BACKHOE TRENCH 2 IN THE PROPOSED FRESHWATER-RESERVOIR AREA, SHOWING THE STRATIGRAPHY OF THE T0 TERRACE FILL.

Figure 7.17. Profile of Backhoe Trench 3 in the proposed freshwater-reservoir area, showing the stratigraphy of the T0 terrace fill.

Figure 7.18. Profile of Backhoe Trench 6 in the proposed freshwater-reservoir area, showing the stratigraphy of the T0 terrace fill.

Figure 7.19. West view of a remnant of T1 terrace in the proposed freshwater-reservoir area, west of Backhoe Trench 5.

Figure 7.20. Profile of Backhoe Trench 4 in the proposed freshwater-reservoir area, showing the stratigraphy of the T1 terrace fill.

GEOARCHAEOLOGICAL INVESTIGATIONS

FIGURE 7.21. PROFILE OF BACKHOE TRENCH 1 IN THE PROPOSED FRESHWATER-RESERVOIR AREA, SHOWING THE STRATIGRAPHY OF THE T2 TERRACE FILL OVER SOFT BEDROCK.

Backhoe Trench 6 was placed on the T2 terrace in the northern part of the proposed dam. The T2 terrace is characterized by an approximately 10-cm-thick A horizon over a well-developed Bt (argillic) horizon (Figure 7.21). Underlying the soil is soft, weathered metamorphic rock (or saprolite). The trench was placed on the edge of an archaeological site (Site 206) with an artifact scatter of plain and decorated ceramics and milky-quartz, blocky debris and a rock ring of laterite cobbles that mark the foundation of an agricultural field house or a structure used to store crops. Ceramic artifacts were recovered from the A horizon when the upper fill of the backhoe trench was screened. Angular to subangular laterite (or plinthite) gravel is abundant, measured at 62–79 percent by weight (very gravelly to extremely gravelly). We interpret the laterite as material redeposited from the weathering of laterite on older landforms in the watershed, not as plinthite formed in situ, by weathering.

Proposed Tailings-Mine Facility

The terrain of the proposed tailings mine facility (TMF) varies dramatically from that of the proposed freshwater-reservoir area (Figure 7.22). The valley of the TMF is narrower and more dissected, the floodplain is narrower, the trunk stream is smaller and less incised, and the relative elevations between the T0, T1, and T2 terraces are greater, but soil development is similar to comparable terrace fills in the freshwater-reservoir area. Figure 7.23 shows the location of Backhoe Trench 9 on the floodplain, which is next to the trunk-stream channel (Figure 7.24). The landforms for the trenches in the TMF are as follows: (1) Backhoe Trench 9—T0 terrace (Figure 7.25); (2) Backhoe Trenches 7, 8, and 10—T1 terrace (Figures 7.26–7.29); and (3) Backhoe Trench 11—T2 terrace (Figure 7.30). Soil development is similar to that of comparable geomorphic surfaces in the freshwater-reservoir area, but with slightly more development. The T0 terrace is associated with cambic subsurface horizons, the T1 terrace is associated with cambic or weakly developed argillic horizons, and the T2 terrace is associated with strongly developed argillic horizons.

Soil textures are loamy in all trenches, mainly silty clay loams or clay loams. The pH levels vary among the soils developed in the fill of the different terraces: (1) neutral in all horizons of the T0 terrace; (2) neutral, slightly acidic, and slightly alkaline in the A, B, and C horizons of the T1 terrace; and (3) neutral in the A horizon and moderately acidic in the B and C horizons of the T2 terrace. The T0 terrace horizon is relatively unweathered and good for bone preservation. The T2 terrace horizon is more heavily leached, with many of

Figure 7.22. East overview of the proposed tailings reservoir area from a hilltop.

Figure 7.23. Location of Backhoe Trench 9 on the T0 terrace (floodplain), in the proposed tailings-reservoir area.

Geoarchaeological Investigations

Figure 7.24. Channel of an intermittent stream in the proposed tailings-reservoir area (near Backhoe Trench 9).

Figure 7.25. Profile of Backhoe Trench 9 in the proposed tailings-reservoir area, showing the stratigraphy of the T0 terrace fill.

Figure 7.26. Profile of Backhoe Trench 7 in the proposed tailings-reservoir area, showing the stratigraphy of the T1 terrace fill.

Figure 7.27. Location of Backhoe Trench 8 on the T1 terrace, in the proposed tailings-reservoir area.

Figure 7.28. Profile of Backhoe Trench 8 in the proposed tailings-reservoir area, showing the stratigraphy of the T1 terrace fill.

Figure 7.29. Profile of Backhoe Trench 10 in the proposed tailings-reservoir area, showing the stratigraphy of the T1 terrace fill.

FIGURE 7.30. PROFILE OF BACKHOE TRENCH 11 IN THE PROPOSED TAILINGS-RESERVOIR AREA, SHOWING THE STRATIGRAPHY OF THE T2 TERRACE FILL.

its base nutrients (calcium, potassium, and magnesium) stripped, and bone preservation is poor in this soil. The T1 terrace is intermediate, with little weathering at the surface and the C horizon, both having suitable to excellent pH conditions for bone preservation, but the B horizon is moderately leached and poor for bone preservation.

Proposed Haul-Road Alignment

Backhoe Trenches 12 and 13 were placed on an alluvial fan next to an existing road in the location of the proposed haul road between the proposed Masato and Golouma mining areas. Moderately well-developed argillic (Bt) horizons were documented in both trenches. A buried channel deposit composed of angular gravel and cobbles was recorded in Backhoe Trench 12 (Figure 7.31). The soils in Backhoe Trench 13 are more oxidized in appearance, in all likelihood because of the deposition of more-heavily weathered sediment from the nearby hills in the upper alluvial fan (Figure 7.32).

Summary and Discussion

The associations of diagnostic soil horizons for the fill deposits of the respective alluvial terraces are summarized in Table 7.6, along with the approximate age and elevation of each terrace above the floodplain. Soils formed in fill deposits of the oldest terraces have the greatest degree of soil development, marked by the formation of argillic or oxic horizons (with argillic diagnostic subsurface horizons defined by the accumulation of significant amounts of translocated clay in the subsoil and oxic horizons defined by a high degree of weathering, concentrations of iron and aluminum oxides [i.e., sesquioxides], and a low percentage [less than 10 percent] of weatherable minerals). Younger fill deposits on the floodplain have soils with either no B horizon (as in the A-C horizon profiles on the floodplain) or incipient Bw horizons, known as cambic subsurface horizons (soils with a formation of soil structure or a color change that differentiates them from the underlying, relatively unweathered parent material, the C horizon, but with little or no translocated clay).

Although we can reconstruct relative ages for the three lowermost alluvial surfaces based on their landscape positions, there is no geochronological control; so, the true ages of these terraces are uncertain. Charcoal is absent in the fill deposits of the T1 and T2 terraces, and it is rare, often heavily degraded by repeated oxidation-reduction cycles, in the fill of the T0 terrace.

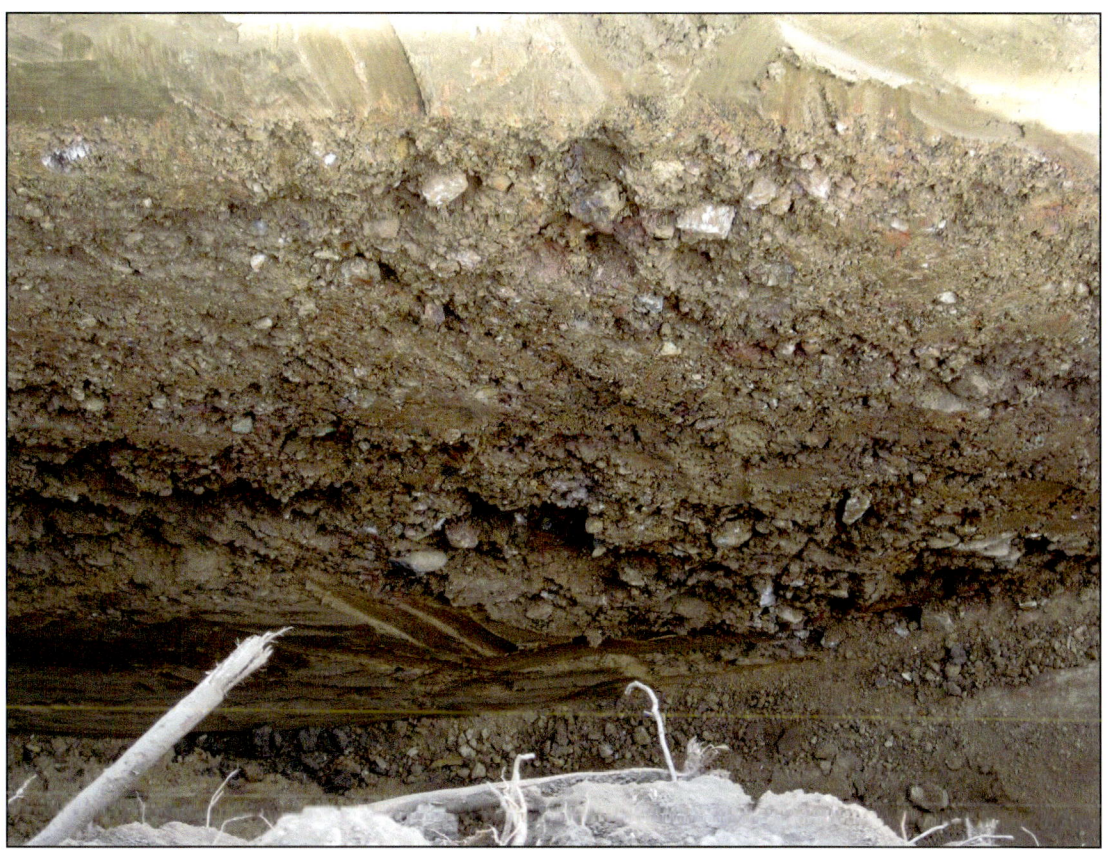

FIGURE 7.31. PROFILE OF BACKHOE TRENCH 12 IN THE ALIGNMENT OF THE PROPOSED HAUL ROAD, SHOWING THE STRATIGRAPHY OF FAN ALLUVIUM IN THE MEDIAL PART OF THE FAN.

FIGURE 7.32. PROFILE OF BACKHOE TRENCH 13 IN THE ALIGNMENT OF THE PROPOSED HAUL ROAD, SHOWING THE STRATIGRAPHY OF FAN ALLUVIUM IN UPPER PART OF THE FAN.

TABLE 7.6. ASSOCIATION OF DIAGNOSTIC SUBSURFACE HORIZONS FOR DIFFERENT GEOMORPHIC SURFACES IN THE PROPOSED FRESHWATER-RESERVOIR AND TAILINGS-RESERVOIR AREAS

Geomorphic Surface[a], by Reservoir Area	Approximate Elevation above the Floodplain (m)	Diagnostic Subsurface Horizon
Freshwater reservoir		
T0	—	none/cambic
T1	2–3	argillic (weak)
T2	4–6	argillic (strong)
Tailings reservoir		
T0	—	cambic
T1	3–5	cambic/argillic (weak)
T2	10–12	argillic (strong)

[a] T0 = floodplain; T1 = first terrace above the floodplain; T2 = second terrace above the floodplain; AF = alluvial fan.

Consequently, no charcoal could be collected for dating. Furthermore, unless a large number of radiocarbon dates could be obtained, there would be little basis for determining which charcoal deposits represent redeposited material and which are in situ and, therefore, interpretable. Humates are present in the A horizon of the T0 terrace, and there is promise for using them to date the upper floodplain deposits and to determine a sedimentation-accumulation rate for this most recent deposit. Six radiocarbon samples were collected from the approximately 1-m-thick A horizon, from the bank shown in Figure 7.15, but analysis of these samples is pending and subject to the availability of funding.

At this point, we assume that the T0 terrace dates to the late Holocene period (approximately 0–4,000 calendar years ago), the T1 terrace dates to the early to middle Holocene period (approximately 12,700 years ago), and the T2 dates to the late Pleistocene period (approximately 12,700–126,000 years ago). These estimates seem reasonable, given the degree of soil development, but they must be regarded as hypotheses that are in need of further testing. It is likely that downcutting events that account for the formation of terraces are correlated to regional climatic changes in the past. Unfortunately, no previous studies that could serve to further refine the age estimates based on the degree of soil development were identified in the literature for nearby regions with similar climatic conditions. Consequently, we are certain only of the relative ages of the terraces and lack both a geochronological control and a soil chronosequence that is based on cross correlation to soil morphological (that is, pedological) studies in other places.

Buried-Site Probability

The preliminary model of buried-site probability (see Figure 7.7) is supported by the field investigations, but there are important refinements in the interpretations. We still consider the T0 terrace, the floodplain, to have the highest probability of buried sites. But the sites most likely to occur on the floodplain—a landform that is typically flooded for significant periods annually, during the rainy season—would likely leave few archaeological traces. Furthermore, the floodplain is likely too young to have buried Paleolithic period sites.

Consideration of how the floodplain is used today could probably be very helpful in forming archaeological interpretations of how it was used by farming groups in the past. The floodplain is useful for cultivating certain crops, mainly rice and root crops adapted to prolonged periods of flooding, but it is not good for building agricultural field houses and storage structures, because it is flooded so frequently. The only noteworthy agricultural features we have observed on the present floodplain are drying racks, made of nine cobbles placed in a three-by-three pattern, that once supported wood and bamboo, forming a platform used for drying harvested crops. Drying racks are mainly made of perishable materials, and it is unlikely that cobbles from a buried drying rack would be identifiable as part of a cultural feature.

Agricultural activities, especially planting and weeding, are virtually invisible in the archaeological record. Wooden hoes and digging sticks are used for these activities, but these tools today have iron blades (on hoes) and iron tips (on digging sticks). These kinds of artifacts are probably buried in the alluvium, probably in low densities, and they are subject to degradation by rapid oxidation (i.e., rusting). If harvesting tools, such as metal scythes or lithic cutting implements, were used, they may be preserved in the alluvium, but it is significant that no such tools or other artifact types were recovered from the trench fill of any of the 13 trenches during our screening operation.

In short, we still regard the floodplain as a setting with a high potential for buried sites. But the agricultural sites likely to be buried there are virtually unidentifiable because of their very low visibility. If such sites could be identified, they would be significant, if only because of their overall invisibility and apparent rarity. The probability that settlements are buried in the floodplain is extremely low, simply because this is an unsuitable landform for building permanent or seasonal houses or short-term field houses.

The preliminary buried-site model identified pockets of the T1 terrace within the floodplain and the T1 and T2 terraces and colluvial foot slopes flanking the valleys as areas with medium probability for buried sites. This assessment is still supported, but mainly because these landforms likely predate agricultural use of the area and the shifting camps of previous hunting-and-gathering groups are likely sparse and widely scattered. It is possible that archaeological sites are buried there, but it would likely be a case of searching for a needle in a haystack to find such sites. We would add alluvial fans with moderately developed soils (such as in Backhoe Trenches 12 and 13) as places with medium probability for buried sites. In contrast, surface sites are concentrated on these alluvial and colluvial landforms, especially on the T1 terrace, which is in close proximity to water sources and is regarded by farmers today as the best setting for agriculture in the project area. Overall, the T1 terrace is less fertile than the T0 terrace, in terms of soil nutrients, but it is both well watered and well drained, unlike the poorly drained T0 terrace. Consequently, it is more productive for agriculture, and fields today are concentrated on it.

Elevated landforms away from alluvial valleys are dominated by laterite. These areas, other than perhaps small pockets of colluvium, are those we regard as having low to no probability for buried sites.

Association of Landforms and Archaeological Sites

The geoarchaeological survey successfully identified 95 archaeological sites spread across the concession. A summary of these sites is provided in Table 7.7. Only 1 buried site (Site 146) was found while searching subsurface exposures—a light ceramic scatter located about 1 km northeast of Kunemba. One plain sherd was found about 50–60 cm below the surface at Site 146, eroding out of the bank of an ephemeral-stream channel (Figures 7.33 and 7.34), and a decorated sherd had eroded out of the bank into the channel below. The finding of only a single buried site during the entire geoarchaeological investigation shows that buried sites, although rare, are present in the project area.

Sites found during the geoarchaeological survey are dominated by resource-processing sites and field houses. For the purposes of this study, we divided resource-processing sites into descriptive categories: artifact scatters (sites that contain both lithic and ceramic artifacts), ceramic scatters, lithic scatters, agricultural fields (sites with traces of agricultural features, such as drying racks), farmsteads/hamlets, and ideological/sacred sites (a large, oval-shaped rock pile) (Figure 7.35). These sites are concentrated on the T1 and T2 terraces but also occur on the T0 terrace and more-elevated landforms (Figure 7.36). Figure 7.37 graphically illustrates the frequency of different site types for the different landforms. The concentration of sites on the T1 and T2 terraces, combined with the kinds of sites they represent, is a clear indicator of the importance of these landforms for agricultural production. In addition to the field houses and small, seasonal agricultural

FIGURE 7.33. BURIED SHERD IN THE BANK OF A SMALL, EPHEMERAL STREAM NORTHWEST OF KUNEMBA.

FIGURE 7.34. CLOSE-UP VIEW OF THE BURIED SHERD
(SEE FIGURE 7.33) IN THE BANK OF A SMALL, EPHEMERAL STREAM.

settlements on the T1 and T2 terraces, ceramic and artifact scatters appear to reflect broad, agricultural use of these landforms. The distribution of these and other sites identified during the project, plus interpretations of the settlement patterns represented by their spatial patterns, are treated in much more detail in the chapter of this report that discusses archaeological predictive modeling (Chapter 8).

Conclusions

Buried-site probability is interpreted as having (1) the highest probability on floodplains (T0 terrace), although the sites expected there likely reflect agricultural activities, which leave few to no lasting archaeological traces; (2) medium probability in the T1 and T2 terraces, alluvial fans, and colluvial foot slopes, although buried sites in these settings likely reflect preagricultural camps associated with hunting and gathering or possibly pastoralism, which probably left widely scattered and sparse archaeological remains; and (3) low to no probability on more-elevated landforms dominated by laterite. These interpretations are supported by the lack of artifact recovery from the screened fill of backhoe trenches, combined with interpretations of modern land-use activities (assuming there is continuity in land-use practices to the present).

TABLE 7.7. SUMMARY OF SITES FOUND DURING GEOARCHAEOLOGICAL SURVEY OF STREAM CHANNELS, SUBSURFACE EXPOSURES, AND ADJACENT LANDFORMS

SRI Site No.	ARCH Site No.	Location	UTM Coordinates Easting	UTM Coordinates Northing	Elevation (M AMSL)	Site Type	Features	Artifacts	Landform[a]
100	201	near road west of Maka Madina	821238	1461781	206	sparse lithic scatter (100 × 30 m)		milky-quartz debitage and blocky debris	Pleistocene terrace (T3)
101	202	near road to Kunamba	811333	1452258	195	ceramic and lithic scatter	5 rock rings, several rock alignments, earthen berm, thermal feature (hearth?)	plain and decorated ceramics	Pleistocene terrace (T3)
102	203	near road south of Kunamba	812338	1447160	61	upper Paleolithic lithic scatter (according to Masamba Lamb)		basalt debitage, flaked stone axe, pestle, cores, and hammerstone	Pleistocene terrace (T2?), gravel bar
103	204	near road south of Kunamba	812249	1448051	204	upper Paleolithic lithic scatter (according to Masamba Lamb)		basalt- and andesite mano, hammerstones, mano/hammerstone, broken lithic tools (during manufacture)	colluvial foot slope at base of hill
104	205	near road to Kunamba	811170	1450545	not taken	agricultural clearings of surficial laterite cobbles	4 large rock piles, clearings in agricultural area (?)	none observed	Pleistocene terrace (T3)
105	206	freshwater-reservoir dam	815920	1461871	not taken	ceramic and lithic scatter	rock ring (burned)	plain and decorated ceramics, milky-quartz debitage	Pleistocene terrace (T2)
106	207	freshwater-reservoir dam	821418	1461705	not taken	light lithic scatter		milky-quartz and greenstone debitage and blocky debris	Pleistocene terrace (T1)
107	208	freshwater reservoir	819739	1460377	not taken	light lithic scatter		cores, hammerstone	Pleistocene terrace (T1)
108	209	tailings-reservoir dam	818402	1455301	184	light ceramic scatter		plain ceramics	Pleistocene terrace (T2)
109	210	tailings-reservoir dam	818426	1455382	183	ceramic scatter		plain ceramics	Pleistocene terrace (T1)
110	211	Masato area	818663	1455347	187	ceramic scatter		plain ceramics	colluvial foot slope in hills
111	212	haul road	814123	1456251	205	ceramic scatter		plain and decorated ceramics, hammerstone	alluvial fan
112	213	Galouma	814872	1452985	211	rock-pile field	approximately 20 rock piles (field-clearing features)	plain ceramics	colluvial foot slope in hills
113	214	freshwater-reservoir area	819520	1461000	167	ceramic scatter		plain ceramics	Pleistocene terrace (T3)
114	215	freshwater-reservoir area	819437	1461264	172	ceramic scatter		plain ceramics	Pleistocene terrace (T3)
115	216	freshwater-reservoir area	819420	1461370	155	light lithic scatter		plain ceramics, quartz blocky debris	Pleistocene terrace (T2)
116	217	freshwater-reservoir area	818826	1462509	173	light lithic scatter	rock ring (field house?)	plain ceramics, large biface	Pleistocene terrace (T2)
117	218	freshwater-reservoir area	819475	1461711	159	ceramic scatter		plain ceramics	colluvial foot slope
118		freshwater-reservoir area	UTM not recorded	UTM not recorded		ceramic scatter		plain ceramics	Holocene floodplain (T0)
119	220	freshwater-reservoir area	820949	1458811	178	ceramic and lithic scatter	rock ring (field house?)	plain ceramics, milky-quartz blocky debris	Pleistocene terrace (T2)

SRI Site No.	ARCH Site No.	Location	UTM Coordinates Easting	UTM Coordinates Northing	Elevation (MAMSL)	Site Type	Features	Artifacts	Landform[a]
120	221	freshwater-reservoir area	819106	1458424	159	lithic scatter		greenstone core and debitage	Pleistocene terrace (T2)
121	222	hilltop in tailings-reservoir area	818550	1455790	204	ceramic scatter		plain and decorated ceramics	summit of hill
122	223	hilltop in tailings-reservoir area	818835	1455593	202	ceramic and lithic scatter		plain ceramics, basin-metate fragment, hammerstone	summit of hill
123	224	mango orchard near camp	818709	1455581	206	ceramic and lithic scatter		plain and decorated ceramics, one biface	Holocene terrace (T1)
124	225	mango orchard near camp	813237	1455310	195	ceramic scatter		plain and decorated ceramics	Holocene terrace (T1)
125	226	road west of Maka Madina	810711	1455737	163	ceramic scatter		plain ceramics	Holocene terrace (T1)
									continued on next page
126	227	road west of Maka Madina	809633	1455316	170	ceramic and lithic scatter	rock ring (field house?), rock drying rack	plain ceramics, two-handed mano, white glass bead	Holocene terrace (T1)
127	228	road west of Maka Madina	807850	1455453	164	ceramic scatter		plain ceramics	Holocene terrace (T1)
128	229	road west of Maka Madina	807948	1455439	167	ceramic and lithic scatter		plain and decorated ceramics, metate and mano fragments, hammerstone	Holocene terrace (T1)
129	230	road west of Maka Madina	807715	1455276	167	ceramic and lithic scatter		plain and decorated ceramics, biface, milky-quartz debitage and blocky debris	Holocene terrace (T1)
130	231	road west of Maka Madina	807393	1455366	169	ceramic scatter		plain and decorated ceramics	Pleistocene terrace (T2)
131	232	road west of Maka Madina	807449	1455381	169	ceramic scatter		plain and decorated ceramics	Pleistocene terrace (T2)
132	233	road west of Maka Madina	807209	1455238	170	ceramic and lithic scatter		plain ceramics, hammerstone, milky-quartz blocky debris	Pleistocene terrace (T2)
133		road west of Maka Madina	806915	1455259	175	ceramic and lithic scatter		plain and decorated ceramics, basin-metate fragment	foot slope at base of hill
134	36	road west of Maka Madina	806031	1454674	160	village (or hamlet?)	approximately 10 rock rings (many burned), oven (?) (kiln?) feature	plain and decorated ceramics (several dense ceramic concentrations), stone axe	Pleistocene terrace (T2)
135	236	road west of Maka Madina	805353	1454224	153	ceramic scatter		plain and decorated ceramics	Holocene terrace (T1)

GEOARCHAEOLOGICAL INVESTIGATIONS

SRI Site No.	ARCH Site No.	Location	UTM Coordinates Easting	UTM Coordinates Northing	Elevation (MAMSL)	Site Type	Features	Artifacts	Landform[a]
136	237	road west of Maka Madina	812317	1455002	180	ceramic scatter		plain and decorated ceramics	Holocene terrace (T1)
137	238	road from Maka Madina to Kunamba	811937	1454214	182	ceramic scatter	rock ring (incomplete)	plain and decorated ceramics	Holocene terrace (T1)
138	239	road from Maka Madina to Kunamba	811934	1454285	184	ceramic scatter		plain and decorated ceramics	Holocene terrace (T1)
139	240	road from Maka Madina to Kunamba	811883	1453728	186	ceramic scatter	possible rock ring, rock alignment (agricultural?)	plain and decorated ceramics	Holocene terrace (T1)
140	241	road from Maka Madina to Kunamba	811471	1452505	198	ceramic and lithic scatter		plain and decorated ceramics, mano fragment	Holocene terrace (T1)
141	242	road from Maka Madina to Kunamba	811271	1451665	188	ceramic scatter		plain and decorated ceramics	Holocene terrace (T1)
142	243	road from Maka Madina to Kunamba	811155	1451620	192	village (formerly Kobokoto; chief was Mamadou Kaita)	approximately 10 rock rings, 3 baobab trees, and 1 mango tree; abandoned about 10 years ago, according to Sadio Daniokho of Sabodala	plain and decorated ceramics	Pleistocene terrace (T2)
143	244	road from Maka Madina to Kunamba	811018	1450991	198	ceramic scatter		plain and decorated ceramics	Pleistocene terrace (T3)
144	245	road from Maka Madina to Kunamba	810958	1450611	191	ceramic scatter		plain and decorated ceramics	back slope with laterite lag deposits
145	246	road from Maka Madina to Kunamba	811692	1450112	204	ceramic scatter		plain and decorated ceramics	Holocene terrace (T1)
146	247	road north of Kunamba	810884	1448863	197	ceramic scatter		plain and decorated ceramics	buried approximately 50–60 cm in Holocene terrace (T1) fill
147	248	road north of Kunamba	810312	1448048	189	ceramic and lithic scatter	rock ring	plain ceramics, milky-quartz blocky debris	Holocene terrace (T1)
148	249	road north of Kunamba	809721	1447131	184	ceramic scatter		plain ceramics	Holocene terrace (T1)
149	250	road north of Kunamba	812854	1445731	168	ceramic scatter	5 rock rings, 4 rock piles (hearths?), 3 rock alignments (approximately 1.2–1.5-m-long check dams)	plain ceramics, ceramic cous cous cooker, metal basin-shaped cooking pan with handles	Holocene terrace (T1)
150	251	road north of Kunamba	812742	1445970	178	ceramic scatter		plain and decorated ceramics	Pleistocene terrace (T2)
151	252	road north of Kunamba	812601	1446334	171	ceramic scatter		plain and decorated ceramics, metal hoe	foot slope at base of hill
152	253	road north of Kunamba	812452	1446493	177	ceramic scatter	2 rock rings (1 burned)	plain and decorated ceramics	Pleistocene alluvial fan
153	254	road north of Kunamba	812368	1447471	214	ceramic scatter	rock ring	decorated ceramics	Pediment at base of hill
154	255	road north of Kunamba	812272	1448084		ceramic scatter	rock ring	plain ceramics	foot slope at base of hill
155	256	road north of Kunamba	812088	1448194	218	ceramic and lithic scatter	2 rock rings (both burned)	plain ceramics, biface	Holocene terrace (T1)

SRI Site No.	ARCH Site No.	Location	UTM Coordinates Easting	UTM Coordinates Northing	Elevation (MAMSL)	Site Type	Features	Artifacts	Landform[a]
156	257	road north of Kunamba	808645	1448879	201	ceramic scatter		plain and decorated ceramics	Holocene terrace (T1)
157	258	road north of Kunamba	808013	1448540	201	ceramic scatter	rock ring, rock drying rack	decorated ceramics	Holocene terrace (T1)
158	259	road northeast of Kunamba	806903	1448588	202	rock rings	3 rock rings	no ceramics observed	foot slope at base of hill
159	260	road from freshwater dam to Dindifa	821454	1462041	147	ceramic and lithic scatter		plain ceramics, milky-quartz blocky debris	Holocene terrace (T1)
160	261	road from freshwater dam to Dindifa	821888	1462309	150	ceramic scatter		plain and decorated ceramics	Pleistocene terrace (T2)
161	262	road from freshwater dam to Dindifa	822128	1462299	143	ceramic scatter		plain and decorated ceramics, iron hoe with wooden shaft	Holocene terrace (T1)
162	263	road south of Mamakhono	822293	1458292	176	ceramic scatter	rock alignment (approximately 2-m-long check dam), 2 rock drying racks	plain and decorated ceramics	Pleistocene terrace (T2)
163		road south of Mamakhono	822042	1458376	172	ceramic scatter		decorated ceramics, iron knife	Pleistocene terrace (T2)
164	265	road south of Mamakhono	821702	1458487	167	ceramic and lithic scatter	approximately 20 rock drying racks	plain ceramics, stone axe	Pleistocene terrace (T2)
165	266	road south of Mamakhono	820067	1459171	176	ceramic scatter		plain ceramics, milky-quartz blocky debris	Pleistocene terrace (T3)
166	267	road northeast of Mamakhono	817629	1460011	191	ceramic scatter		decorated ceramics, iron axe	rock hilltop
167	268	road northeast of Mamakhono	817051	1460300	188	ceramic scatter		plain and decorated ceramics	foot slope at base of hill
168	269	road northeast of Mamakhono	816473	1460472	186	ceramic scatter	4 rock rings	plain and decorated ceramics	Pleistocene terrace (T2)
169	270	road northeast of Mamakhono	811914	1450155	206	ceramic scatter	2 rock rings (both burned)	plain and decorated ceramics	Holocene terrace (T1)
170	271	road northeast of Kunamba	811919	1450396	206	ceramic scatter		plain and decorated ceramics	Holocene terrace (T1)
171	272	road northeast of Kunamba	812060	1450448	212	ceramic scatter		plain and decorated ceramics	summit of low hill
172	273	road northeast of Kunamba	812855	1450306	214	ceramic scatter	rock ring (burned)	plain and decorated ceramics	Pleistocene terrace (T2)
173	274	road northeast of Kunamba	813129	1450410	206	ceramic scatter	rock alignment (function undetermined)	plain and decorated ceramics	Pleistocene terrace (T2)
174	275	road northeast of Kunamba	813100	1450520	207	ceramic scatter	rock ring (burned), burned circular structure without rocks	plain and decorated ceramics	Pleistocene terrace (T2)
175	276	road northeast of Kunamba	813409	1450512	208	ceramic scatter		plain and decorated ceramics	Pleistocene terrace (T2)
176	277	road northeast of Kunamba	813641	1450610	204	ceramic scatter	4 rock rings, 2 burned circular structures without rocks	plain and decorated ceramics	Pleistocene terrace (T2)

GEOARCHAEOLOGICAL INVESTIGATIONS

SRI Site No.	ARCH Site No.	Location	UTM Coordinates Easting	UTM Coordinates Northing	Elevation (MAMSL)	Site Type	Features	Artifacts	Landform[a]
177	278	road northeast of Kunamba	813897	1450536	213	ceramic scatter	rock ring (burned), burned circular structure without rocks	plain and decorated ceramics	colluvial foot slope at base of low hill
178	279	road northeast of Kunamba	814125	1450525	217	ceramic scatter	2 agricultural rock alignments (approximately 1–2.5 m and 1–1.5 m long)	plain and decorated ceramics, metate fragment	colluvial foot slope at base of hill
179	280	road northeast of Kunamba	814670	1450677	203	ceramic scatter		plain and decorated ceramics	finger ridge (interfluve) in hills
180	281	road northeast of Kunamba	814803	1450863	200	ceramic scatter		plain ceramics	juncture of colluvial foot slope and Holocene terrace (T1)
181	282	road northeast of Kunamba	816823	1452207	219	ceramic scatter	2 rock drying racks	plain and decorated ceramics	Pleistocene terrace (T2)
182	283	road northeast of Kunamba	817039	1452376	223	ceramic scatter		plain and decorated ceramics	Pleistocene terrace (T2)
183	284	road northeast of Kunamba	817423	1452418	226	ceramic scatter	rock drying rack	plain ceramics	Holocene terrace (T1)
184	285	road northeast of Kunamba	817598	1452389	233	rainy-season farming village of former MaMakano chief (Musa Cissokho)	8 rock rings (all burned); village abandoned 6–7 years ago, according to Sadio Daniokho of Sabodala	plain and decorated ceramics, metal spoon/fork fragment, metal ring for planting crops (?), tin-can top, palm stool	
185	286	road northeast of Kunamba	818042	1452589	220	ceramic scatter		plain and decorated ceramics	pediment at base of hill and summit of small hill
186	287	road northeast of Kunamba	818217	1452799	216	ceramic scatter	rock ring (only approximately 2 m in diameter)	plain and decorated ceramics	pediment
187	288	road northeast of Kunamba	818486	1454143	203	ceramic scatter	rock drying rack	no artifacts observed	pediment
188	289	road south of Bransan	814078	1467360	200	ceramic scatter	rectangular rock pile (approximately 3 × 2 m; possible burial)	plain and decorated ceramics	Pleistocene terrace (T4)
189		road south of Bransan	814157	SRI 189	181	ceramic scatter		plain and decorated ceramics	Pleistocene terrace (T4) at possible former spring head
190	291	road south of Bransan	814487	1466259	164	ceramic scatter		plain and decorated, milky-quartz debitage and blocky debris	Pleistocene terrace (T3)
191	292	road south of Bransan	814721	1465462	168	ceramic scatter		plain ceramics, milky-quartz debitage	Pleistocene terrace (T2)
192	293	road south of Bransan	814859	1465314	169	ceramic scatter		plain and decorated ceramics	Pleistocene terrace (T2)

continued on next page

SRI No.	Site ARCH Site No.	Location	UTM Coordinates Easting	UTM Coordinates Northing	Elevation (MAMSL)	Site Type	Features	Artifacts	Landform[a]
193	294	road south of Bransan	814883	1465222	172	ceramic scatter		decorated ceramics, ground axe fragment, flaked stone axe, milky-quartz blocky debris	Pleistocene terrace (T2)
194	295	road south of Bransan	815705	1463284	216	ceramic scatter	2 rock rings (both unburned, 1 incomplete)	plain and decorated ceramics	saddle of high ridge, approximately 25 m above surrounding terrain
195	296	road south of Bransan	815901	1463149	216	ceramic scatter		plain and decorated ceramics	pediment on foot slope below high hill
196	297	road south of Bransan	816152	1462461	211	farmstead (former village of Bangouraya)	1–2 rock rings (unburned and incomplete rings; others may be present); inhabitants moved to Faloumbou, according to Sadio Daniokho of Sabodala	plain and decorated ceramics (abundant)	colluvial foot slope at base of hill
197	298	road south of Bransan	816238	1461443	210	ceramic scatter		plain and decorated ceramics	Holocene floodplain (T0) to Holocene terrace (T1)
									continued on next page
198	299	road south of Bransan	816222	1461298	209	ceramic scatter		plain ceramics	Holocene terrace (T1)
199	300	road south of Bransan	816564	1460402	191	ceramic scatter		plain and decorated ceramics	Holocene terrace (T1)
200	301	road south of Bransan	816390	1460262	192	ceramic scatter	rock drying rack	plain ceramics	Holocene floodplain (T0)

[a] T0 = floodplain; T1 = first terrace above the floodplain; T2 = second terrace above the floodplain.

Key: MAMSL = meters above mean sea level; SRI = Statistical Research, Inc.; UTM = Universal Transverse Mercator.

Geoarchaeological Investigations

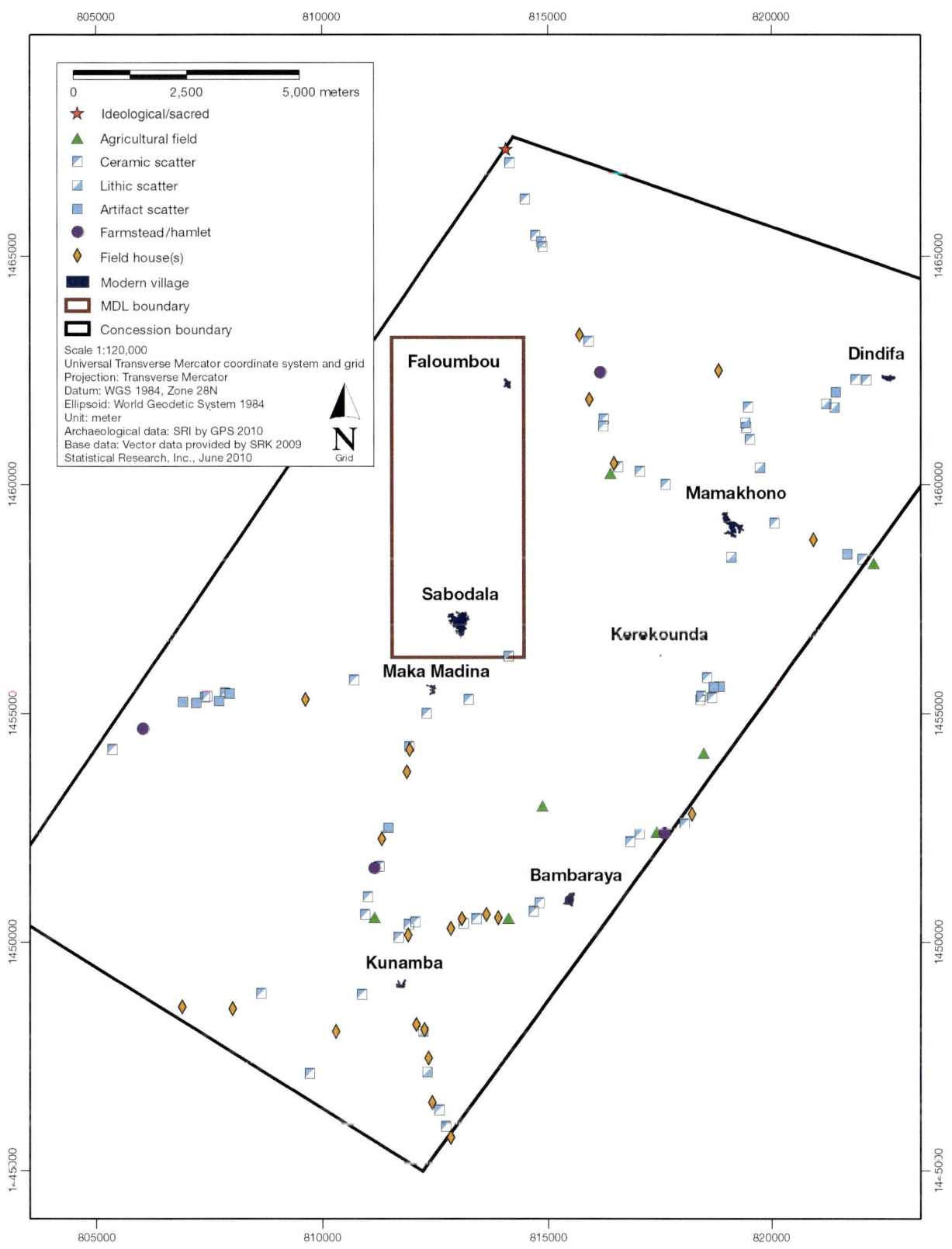

Figure 7.35. Distribution of sites, differentiated by site type, for archaeological sites identified during the geoarchaeological survey (MDL = Mineral Deposits Limited).

A Slave Who Would Be King

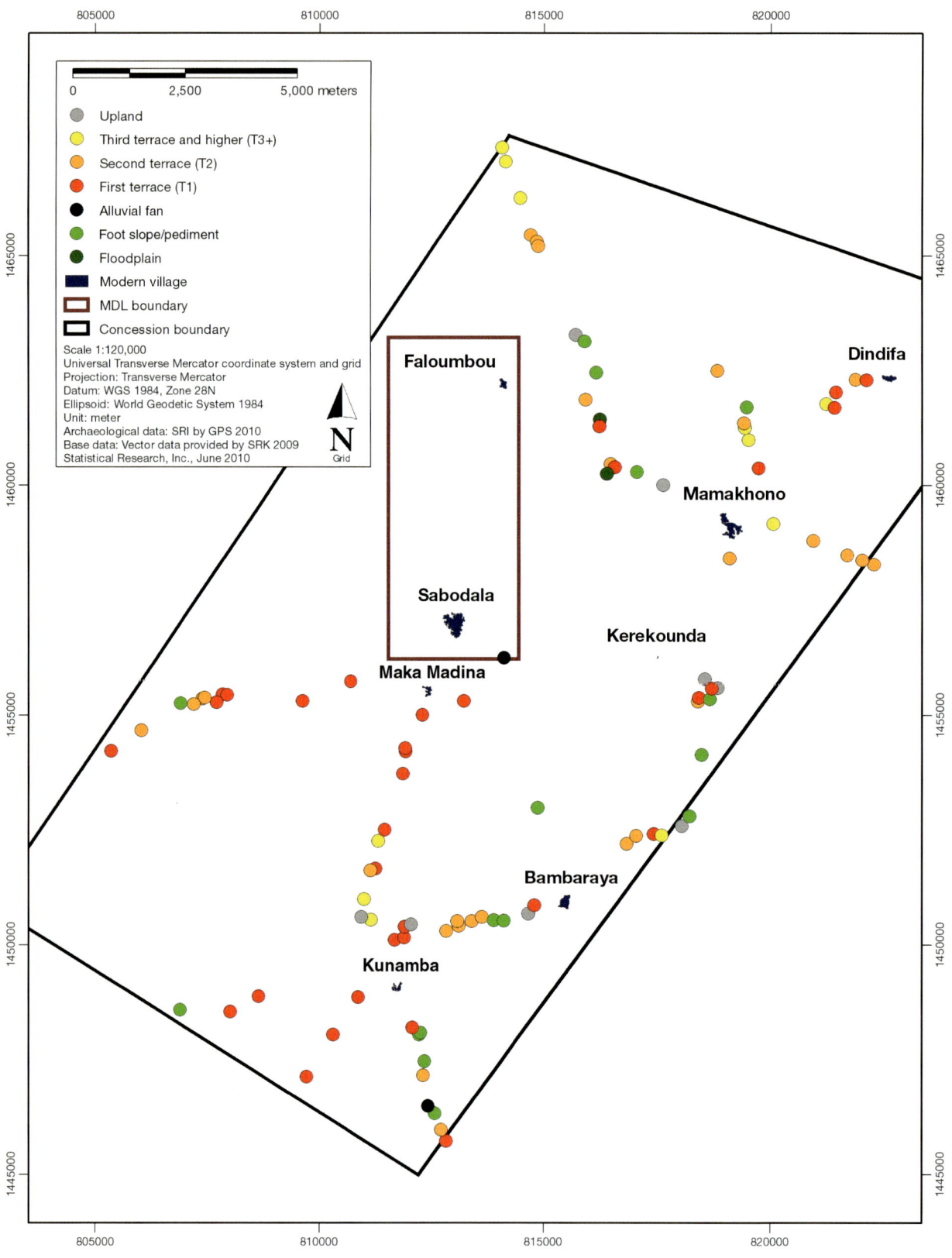

Figure 7.36. Distribution of sites, differentiated by landform, for archaeological sites identified during the geoarchaeological survey (MDL = Mineral Deposits Limited).

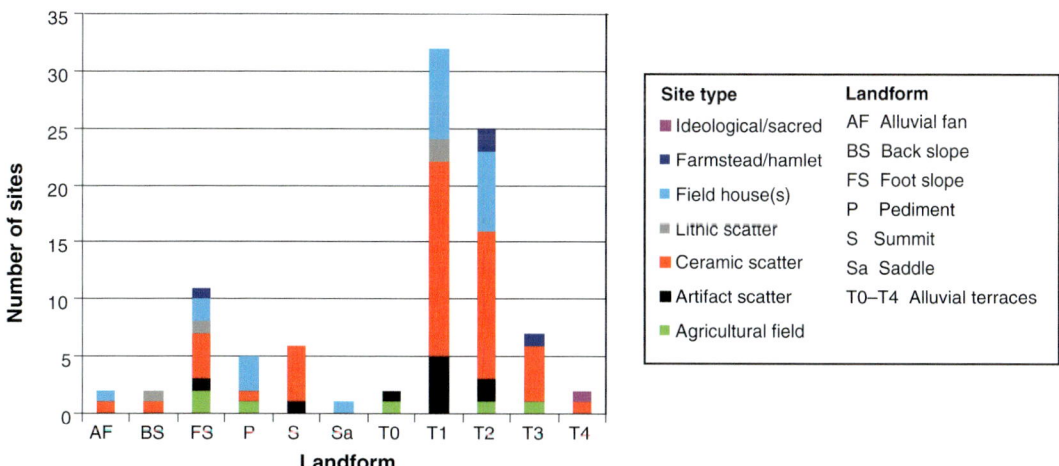

FIGURE 7.37. BAR GRAPH OF SITE FREQUENCY AND SITE TYPE FOR DIFFERENT LANDFORMS FOR ARCHAEOLOGICAL SITES IDENTIFIED DURING THE GEOARCHAEOLOGICAL SURVEY.

Chapter 8

Where Are the Sites, and Why Are They There?
A Methodological Exercise in Archaeological Predictive Modeling

The SCHP covers a portion of the upper Senegal River valley where there have been no previous archaeological investigations. This type of situation is fairly common in developing countries and poses a particular challenge to CRM. Put simply, how do we provide useful input for development plans (in this case, the mine plan) when we know next to nothing about the nature and distribution of archaeological resources? In this chapter, we examine our use of predictive models of archaeological site locations as a tool for addressing just this problem.

Like all sciences, archaeology is cumulative. Prior knowledge is used to predict the nature of past human occupation and how that occupation will be reflected in the archaeological record. Without specific information from the OJVG concession or the surrounding Sabodala region, we were forced to look more broadly. From work elsewhere in the Senegambia region, we formed general ideas about the cultural sequence, the types of resources that we would encounter, and the research questions that could be investigated as part of the SCHP (presented in Chapter 2).

Basic questions remained about the archaeology of the OJVG concession. How many, if any, sites exist in the concession? Where are they located? Which ones are important enough to protect? Cursory examination by drilling personnel who are knowledgeable about archaeology led some to speculate that no archaeological sites existed in the OJVG concession. A reconnaissance survey by Drs. Altschul and Thiaw quickly put an end to such speculation, replacing the purported absence of archaeological sites with a surprising abundance. Armed with this knowledge, the discussion shifted from whether we needed to do any archaeological investigations as part of the Environmental and Social Impact Assessment (ESIA) to how best to incorporate archaeology into the mine development plan.

In other parts of the world, particularly industrialized countries, the planning process begins with a series of alternative development plans that are assessed for archaeological resources through complete or sample surveys. The results are provided to decision makers, who then combine archaeological information with other types of environmental, economic, and social data to select the best alternative.

In Senegal, the process is different. A development plan is proposed, the ESIA baseline studies are performed, and the plan, perhaps refined based on the results of the study, is accepted. In this case, a premium is placed on 'getting the plan right' at the outset—that is, developing a plan that meets the needs of the mine and, at the same time, minimizes adverse impacts to the environment and society. But how do you minimize the impact of a mine plan on archaeological sites if you do not know what types of sites exist and where they are located?

Archaeologists working in CRM have struggled for decades with the problem of minimizing the impact of development on archaeological resources in areas that have not been inventoried for such resources. Expert knowledge is often relied upon, with archaeologists who are familiar with a general area providing their opinions about what will or will not be found. The problem with expert knowledge is that it is largely subjective; there is no way to assess its adequacy or accuracy prior to construction. Often the results are disastrous, with either important resources destroyed or construction delayed at tremendous cost while emergency excavations go forward.

The field of predictive modeling emerged in the late 1970s as a response to this situation (see Judge and Sebastian 1988; Kohler and Parker 1986; Kvamme 1983). Emerging from academic studies designed to explain settlement location, predictive models became a mainstay in CRM, particularly in the United States, throughout the 1980s. Modeling as a tool for compliance was largely discarded in the 1990s, only to re-emerge in the last decade as part of the planning process. To understand our use of predictive modeling in the SCHP, it is useful to briefly examine its history.

The History of Predictive Modeling

One of the precepts of anthropology as a social science is that human behavior is patterned and that, by isolating and then studying these patterns, we can achieve an understanding of why humans behave in the ways they do. Such an understanding provides us with greater insight into and edification of not only the human condition but also the tools by which we may be able to improve society.

Archaeologists throughout the latter half of the twentieth century capitalized on the assumption that humans conduct their activities on the landscape in patterned and predictable ways. Though not the first study of settlement patterns, perhaps the seminal investigation that demonstrated the utility of regional analysis was Gordon Willey's analysis of settlement in the Virú Valley in Peru (Willey 1953). Willey argued that sites were associated with particular environmental features and that change in subsistence patterns and sociopolitical conditions could be discerned from the distribution of sites and site types in the river valley. Willey's work was followed by a host of settlement-pattern studies in the 1950s and 1960s, spurred on, in large part, by the efforts of K. C. Chang (1967, 1968), through his research in China and his influence with students and colleagues around the world.

Most early settlement-pattern studies were descriptive; surveys were completed, and patterns were sought between settlement locations and environmental features, leading to ad hoc and largely untested conclusions about cultural evolution. Quantitative methods emerged as an important component of archaeological studies in the late 1960s. Issues of sampling, economic models, and spatial analysis were keenly discussed. Nowhere were these debates more intense than in the American Southwest. One outgrowth of particular relevance to predictive modeling was the Southwest Anthropological Research Group (SARG). Dedicated to the investigation of why archaeological sites are located where they are (Plog and Hill 1971), one of SARG's lasting legacies is a strong interest among Southwest archaeologists in developing objective measures of environmental variables.

In the early 1970s, Green (1973) advanced predictive modeling in an analysis of prehistoric period Mayan site location in northern British Honduras. Previously, archaeologists had related site location to environmental variables on a bivariate basis. Site locations were correlated with one environmental variable and then another. For example, archaeologists might assess the importance of the distance to water from sites. Next, they evaluated elevation and site location, then vegetation and site location, and so on. The result was a series of descriptive statements, such as *Sites tend to be found near water, on land with slopes less than 2 percent, and within boreal forests*.

Statistically, these statements are not very powerful, because they do not provide a means of measuring the independent effect of each environmental variable on site location. Most environmental variables are strongly intercorrelated; for example, certain soils and vegetation are found in areas that are well watered. Therefore, it is misleading to suggest that, because more variables are included in descriptive analysis, one can better predict site location in this manner. Statistically, the same variability in site location is being explained over and over again by the different variables, giving the impression of a very strong model, when in fact the predictive statement is much weaker.

Recognizing this problem, Green (1973) used multiple linear regression to incorporate a series of environmental variables into predicting the probability that a particular location would contain a site. Multivariate statistics, such as multiple linear regression, factor analysis, and principal-components analysis, are designed to eliminate the problem of highly correlated predictor variables, termed *multicollinearity*, that plagued early settlement-pattern studies. Green's study led the way to a host of statistical modeling techniques that have become the foundation of predictive modeling. But as we shall discuss below, fixing one problem, such as multicollinearity, often produces another set of problems that can prove equally difficult or even more daunting to address.

With Green's (1973) study having laid the foundation, predictive modeling in CRM began in earnest in the late 1970s. Many of these studies were performed in the United States, fueled by large land-holding agencies that found themselves in a dilemma. Intensive survey of entire project areas (e.g., a 300,000-acre shale-coal lease or a 1,000,000-acre military reservation) was economically prohibitive. Predictive modeling—by which a small fraction of a project area could be surveyed, with the results generalized for the rest of the project area—offered tremendous promise. The outcome of such modeling was a map of 'sensitivity zones.' Each zone was portrayed in a series of polygons, and together, the polygons representing all the zones completely encompassed the project area. Generally, three zones were defined: a low-probability zone, in which the probability of encountering a site was below a specified probability (e.g., $p \leq 0.3$); a medium-probability zone, in which the likelihood of finding a site bracketed random chance (e.g., $0.3 < p < 0.7$); and a high-probability zone, in which the probability of encountering a site was reasonably good (e.g., $p \geq 0.7$). Initially, land managers were attracted to predictive models by the promise that survey intensity would vary by probability zone; in other words, one could do less survey in low-probability zones and more in high-probability zones. By the mid 1980s, CRM was flooded with predictive models (see Thoms 1988).

Because of the wide variability in quality, the U.S. Department of the Interior Bureau of Land Management (BLM) sponsored the creation of a comprehensive text on predictive modeling that remains a seminal study of the subject (Judge and Sebastian 1988). The BLM volume is impressive in scope and reflects the diversity of issues that archaeologists were trying to simultaneously address. The theoretical and historical foundations of modeling were thoroughly discussed in this text. A variety of chapters were devoted to the methodological issues engrained in modeling, including statistical methods, sampling, remote sensing, and, as a last minute add-on, geographic information systems (GISs). The volume concluded with practical advice regarding the use of predictive models in the management of cultural resources. Though dated, the text remains the authoritative statement on the wide spectrum of topics involved in predictive modeling.

Almost as soon as the BLM text was published, the field of predictive modeling was revolutionized, not by advances in archaeological methods or by legislation, but by computer science. The late 1980s witnessed the advent of GIS technology in archaeology. At its core, GIS technology allows the manipulation and display of spatially related phenomena. A GIS allows users to store geographically referenced data as separate 'layers.' These layers often originate from different sources, many of which might have different projections, formats, and scales. GIS applications allow users to analyze the spatial relationships between variables, stored as layers, and to display the results (Allen et al. 1990; Wescott and Brandon 2000).

At the same time that GIS technology made predictive modeling affordable and accessible to land-managing agencies in the United States, archaeologists began questioning the efficacy of using model predictions to manage resources. Such qualms had long existed among archaeologists. Predictive models might be useful as heuristic devices, but few archaeologists believed we knew enough about prehistoric period behavior to be confident that the models could accurately predict the locations of all important sites. Regulators generally felt uncomfortable substituting model results for inventory. Finally, academic archaeologists launched a major broadside covering sample surveys that reinforced the need to continue the practice of 100 percent survey coverage for compliance (Fish and Kowalewski 1990).

By the mid-1990s, the debate over predictive modeling had spread from the United States to Europe. Just as land-managing agencies in the United States had to confront the reality that they could not inventory their entire holdings, so, too, did their counterparts in other countries. Various industrialized countries began experimenting with predictive modeling, and although the models behaved the same, different countries reacted differently to the new tool. Predictive modeling took root in Canada and the Netherlands, and to a lesser extent in Germany, Australia, and the Czech Republic. The Netherlands, in particular, embraced predictive modeling, with a substantial effort placed into developing a predictive model for the entire country that the government required archaeologists to consult as part of the planning process at the national, regional, and local levels (Deeben and Groenewouldt 2005). Elsewhere, though, modeling did not win favor; in England, for example, models were largely dismissed and were considered neither an interesting intellectual enterprise nor a useful management tool.

Inductive versus Deductive Models

The role of predictive modeling in CRM continues to be hotly debated, particularly in Europe (see Deeben and Groenwouldt 2005). Archaeologists have rightly pointed out that inductive models—in which environmental variables that are correlated with site locations in areas that have been surveyed are used to predict site locations in nonsurveyed areas—do not necessarily help us understand how people used available resources and why they chose particular places on the landscape to perform specific behaviors. Correlation, after all, is not explanation. For the latter, we need to have theories that are consistent with empirical results and can posit why and how humans make decisions about land use. Short of developing such theories and having them accepted by the discipline, many archaeologists continue to argue that, for development contexts in which archaeological resources are at risk, there is no substitute for 100 percent inventories of project areas.

Unfortunately, it has become increasingly clear that data alone have not led to greater understanding of prehistory. What good is 100 percent survey if the results are merely a descriptive list of sites? Understanding subsistence and settlement decisions and how these decisions are reflected in the archaeological record requires considerable analysis (see Heilen 2005). What are needed are not fewer models but more models, models of greater complexity and explanatory power.

As the debate about the proper role of predictive modeling went forward in CRM, considerable progress was made in methodological and theoretical issues associated with human settlement. Landscape theory emerged from its postprocessual roots (see Tilley 1993, 1994) and entered mainstream CRM (Whittlesey 1998; Zedeño 1997; Zedeño et al. 1997). In many ways, landscape theory, with its focus on the spatial relationships between human behaviors and the manifestation of these behaviors in the natural and archaeological records, is ideally suited for CRM. Compliance requires evaluating the scientific and cultural values of resources drawn from project areas that are, from an archaeological and cultural perspective, arbitrarily drawn. Evaluating the significance of a resource requires placing that resource in its proper context: *What behaviors took place here? How are they related to other behaviors in the region? Is the archaeological manifestation unique? Rare? Common?*

The problem with early attempts to incorporate landscape theory into CRM projects was the lack of a rigorous methodology. Landscape analyses became whatever archaeologists said they were. Everything from a traditional settlement-pattern investigation to a GIS-based simulation to an ethnographic account was passed off as a cultural landscape study. With landscape theory meaning all things to all people, it rapidly became less and less meaningful.

Landscape theory did leave its mark in one area that greatly affected predictive modeling: agency theory. As opposed to processual settlement-pattern studies—in which cultural dynamics are best understood as the result of the interplay or changing relationship between a benign, but malleable, environment and one or more cultural systems—landscape theory places the focus on human actors as the agents that drive cultural evolution. Because it is nearly impossible to study individual agents in the archaeological record, the purpose of archaeological interpretation shifted, for some, from knowledge to narrative, with the concomitant shift from a scientific paradigm to an artistic exploration (Tilley 2004:225).

Others remained within the scientific fold. Agency theory has become the driving force behind agent-based modeling in archaeology, which has recently been combined with complexity theory to create very sophisticated and comprehensive models of prehistoric settlement dynamics in the American Southwest and of the origins of civilization and urbanism in southern Mesopotamia (see Kohler and van der Leeuw 2007). Agency theory also lies behind recent attempts to develop 'cognitive predictive models.' One of the intriguing aspects of these models is that they use the same types of environmental and cultural data that regression-based predictive models use, but instead of mechanically linking these data in a deterministic mathematical fashion, cognitive models transform the environmental data into resource patches and allow 'agents' to make settlement decisions based on resource availability (Whitley 2005). The result, then, is a map of where sites 'should' be located, based on certain conditions and cultural choices, that can then be checked against the archaeological record.

Deductive-based predictive models, albeit of methodological and theoretical interest, have not generated strong interest in CRM for two basic reasons. First, their predictions do not coincide with management needs. Agent-based models test general trends in settlement: *Do villages form? How large are the villages? How long before they are abandoned?* These models do not provide probabilistic statements about the likelihood that any particular location will contain a site. For the most part, land managers are less concerned with why sites are located in particular locations than they are with whether a particular location will or will not contain a site. Second, agent-based models do not provide a unique and final solution. The results of agent-based models depend on the initial environmental (e.g., climate, flora, fauna, etc.) and cultural conditions (e.g., population size, settlement size, technology, birth rate, death rate, etc.), as well as assumptions about how individual agents will make settlement decisions. Changing one or more of a model's parameters changes the distribution and nature of the settlement pattern and, ultimately, the archaeological record. Agent-based models are ideal for testing different hypotheses about decision making in regard to land use, but because we can never know the exact set of conditions that prevailed in the past, these models will never yield the type of results desired for making CRM decisions.

In addition to deductive-based modeling efforts, substantial improvements also were made to inductive modeling techniques. Most early predictive models were based on statistical techniques derived from general linear regression. Regression assumes that there is a dependence relationship between a dependent variable—in the case of predictive modeling, archaeological site locations—and one or more independent variables—environmental features, such as elevation, aspect, and/or slope. All one has to do to create a predictive model is determine the mathematical relationship between the chosen environmental variables and known archaeological site locations from a sample of the project area and then use the equation to calculate the probability that a site will be found in an area that has not yet been surveyed, by putting the values for the independent environmental variables into the regression equation.

General linear regression, as is suggested by its name, assumes that the relationship between independent and dependent variables is linear, that a given change in the independent variable will always produce a corresponding change in the dependent variable. Although linearity is assumed between the independent and dependent variables, it is also assumed, when multiple independent variables are used, that no such relationship exists among the explanatory variables; as discussed above, this condition is known as multicollinearity. The multicollinearity assumption—along with the related independent error term's assumption, focused on spatial autocorrelation—is frequently violated, because environmental variables tend to be related.

Violating the multicollinearity assumption will not actually affect the predictive power of the model, but strongly correlated independent environmental variables can and often do lead to misinterpretations of the model results. Archaeologists tend to assume that the environmental variables used in the regression equation are actually the ones that are most closely related to the dependent variable of site location. Commonly, archaeologists also assume that the regression weights are measures of an environmental feature's importance in settlement decisions. Both assumptions are wrong;

here is why: vegetative communities and soils, for example, tend to be closely related because plants are adapted to certain soil conditions. Most software packages use stepwise algorithms, in which independent variables enter the regression equation based on the amount of variance in the archaeological site location they are explaining. If both vegetative communities and soils are used in a multiple-regression model, it is quite likely that one variable, but not both, will be entered into the equation. The reason is that, by the time the second variable enters the equation, most of the variation between that variable and archaeological site location has already been explained by the first variable. Even if the second variable enters the regression equation, it will be given much less weight as a predictor. A common mistake made by archaeologists is interpreting that, because vegetative communities, for example, entered the equation, and not soils, human decisions about how to use the landscape were based more on the distribution of plants than on soils. In truth, we can never know which variables were used by prehistoric period people, but we can assuredly avoid mistaking statistical explanation for theoretical explanation of land use.

There are series of other assumptions associated with the general linear regression (see Rose and Altschul 1988:213–216). None is perhaps more troubling than the one that requires continuous variables. Although some environmental variables related to archaeological site locations are measured on interval or ratio scales (e.g., elevation, slope, distance to water, etc.), many are not. Some variables measured on nominal or ordinal scales, such as landform, vegetation, and soil, are closely related to archaeological site locations. Traditionally, nominal- and ordinal-scale variables have been related to archaeological site locations in pairwise fashion, through tests of association. Archaeologists typically show, for instance, that sites are found on loamy soil in frequencies greater than would be expected by chance, but that is where the analysis ends; they do not incorporate these variables into multivariate models.

Logistic regression provides a solution to this problem. In this form of predictive modeling, the dependent variable is categorical—the probability that a site is present in a particular area or that a site is absent (Rose and Altschul 1988:215–216). Linear regression will not work in this situation, because a solution requires the violation of the constant-error-variance assumption. Additionally, expected values are expressed as probabilities that must fall between 1 and 0 and not, as is the case for linear regression, between infinity and negative infinity. A logistic model circumvents these problems by using nonlinear equations to arrive at dependent variables, expressed as probabilities.

Logistic regression has emerged as the preferred modeling technique, in large part because it allows the incorporation of nominal-scaled variables, particularly geomorphic variables. One of the major problems with early modeling techniques was that they were not very good at predicting buried sites. Regression equations were most often based solely on environmental variables whose scores could be calculated from surface maps, such as digital elevation models (DEMs). Variables commonly used included elevation, slope, and distance to water—interval- or ratio-scaled variables whose scores could easily be derived through GIS software. These variables tend to be associated with archaeological sites discovered on the surface via pedestrian survey or near the surface via shovel tests. Buried sites, in contrast, are best predicted by paleo–land surfaces, which are categorical in nature. By excluding geomorphic variables, buried sites were largely misidentified in the early models as 'nonsite' areas. Logistic regression had the potential to remedy this situation, and in areas with good geomorphic maps of paleo–land surfaces associated with site locations, these models were impressively strong (see Altschul et al. 2005).

The basic problem with logistic-regression models is their 'black box' nature. Evaluating why a logistic model works (i.e., which variables are the most important) is not straightforward. Most logistic-regression models in archaeology, therefore, tend to be probability maps that depict where sites are likely to be found and where they are likely to be absent, with little rationale for why this should be the case. Yet, at the same time, logistic regression is a common module of statistical software packages, thereby making the technique widely available, if not well understood.

Currently, there is interest in exploring inductive methods beyond logistic regression. Random forest, for example, is an ensemble-learning technique in which classification or regression 'trees' are aggregated into a 'forest' that is empirically proven to be better than the individual trees (Breiman 2001). Side-by-side evaluation of logistic-regression and random-forest modeling has shown the latter to be a significantly better predictor (Peters et al. 2007). Random-forest modeling, which has been applied primarily in ecological studies, has not been fully evaluated with archaeological data. Currently, SRI is performing such a study with data from Eglin Air Force Base, Florida (Michael Heilen, personal communication 2010).

Regardless of the outcome, random-forest modeling suffers the same liability as logistic-regression modeling: one cannot easily understand why the model works, only that it works. Some have argued that continued work on inductive modeling is counterproductive. As these techniques become more powerful, they become less interpretable. Without theoretical underpinnings to explain settlement behavior, some contend that inductive predictive modeling should be abandoned. But it is important to point out that much the same criticism—that the models are so complex that it is impossible to know exactly why they work—has been applied to agent-based models founded on complexity theory (Altschul 2009).

Claiming that one brand of modeling is superior to another misses the point. Both inductive and deductive predictive models are needed in CRM—one to assist in day-to-day management decisions, the other as a tool to understand past behavior and, ultimately, to help guide decisions about which resources to protect. Marrying inductive and deductive modeling in CRM contexts, therefore, remains an important, yet elusive, goal.

The SCHP Predictive Models

The use of predictive models for the SCHP was designed to assist us with answering two different, but related, questions:

1. Where are sites located?
2. Why are sites located where they are?

An answer to the first question was needed right away. OJVG was in the process of designing their mine development plan. Understandably, the company was reluctant to proceed with an archaeological survey if the boundaries of improvements and facilities were likely to change. At the same time, the company and regulators needed to know where sites, particularly important sites that would require significant investments in time and money to excavate, were likely to be located.

How to move forward was not entirely clear. No archaeological research had been performed in or around the OJVG concession since the French surveys for Paleolithic period sites in the 1930s, and those studies were poorly documented. During a brief reconnaissance survey and a month-long ethnographic study, we were able to document 49 archaeological sites (Wait et al. 2009). These sites represented chance finds that were encountered as we were performing other tasks. Other than knowing that sites existed in the OJVG concession, we really had no idea how many sites we should expect, where they might be located, what time periods they might represent, or what types of sites we would encounter.

We had two choices: we could either provide no input into the mine development plan, or we could use the data we had to offer predictions about what we might encounter in areas under consideration for development. We chose the latter alternative, on the grounds that failing to offer any advice was tantamount to forsaking our professional responsibility. But in giving advice, we wanted to make sure that others could follow our logic and replicate the results. Providing 'seat-of-the-pants' advice, no matter how well intentioned, had the potential of being given more weight, because of our status as 'experts,' than we thought it warranted.

We divided the task into two categories: buried sites and surface sites. A predictive model for each category was created, through very different means. The buried-sites model was largely a 'desktop' study based on published and unpublished topographic maps that applied knowledge about site-formation processes from other regions to the OJVG concession. The surface-sites model was a statistical projection based on the scanty knowledge collected from archaeological sites while pursuing other tasks. Each is described below.

Buried-Sites Model

The buried-sites model, developed by Jeff Homburg and described in more detail in Chapter 7, is based on slope elements and associated landforms that could be inferred from topographic maps (1-m contour interval). This model utilizes descriptive slope elements: summits, shoulder slopes, back slopes, foot slopes, and toe slopes. Buried archaeological sites are most likely in the lower landscape positions (that is, foot slopes and toe slopes), and surficial sites are most likely on summits, shoulder slopes, and back slopes. High-, medium-, and low-sensitivity areas were drawn by hand on the topographic maps and then digitized. High-sensitivity areas include the toe slopes of floodplains and alluvial terraces that are less than about 1 m above the active floodplain. Medium-sensitivity areas are defined as the juncture of foot slopes and toe slopes in valley-margin positions (mainly colluvial foot slopes and alluvial fans) and alluvial terraces that are more than about 1 m above the active floodplain. Low-sensitivity areas consist of the elevated landforms of summits, shoulder slopes, and back slopes—places where archaeological deposits are most likely surficial. Small pockets of colluvium that cannot be distinguished on the topographic maps may occur in the medium- and low-sensitivity areas; so, it is possible that sites may be buried in these localities.

Figure 7.7 presents the preliminary buried-sites predictive model. High-sensitivity areas lie along the larger watercourses. It is interesting that the two areas with the highest buried-site potential are the major streams flowing into the Gambia and Senegal Rivers, in the southwest and northeast portions of the project area, respectively. Not surprisingly, the sites we found on the surface are not located in high-sensitivity zones for buried sites, a reminder that the surface is often a poor predictor of the subsurface. Traditionally, reliance on predictive models based on surface observations has led to a false sense of security that oftentimes gets broken by 'discoveries' during construction.

Surface-Sites Model

Using GIS technology, we created a series of environmental and cultural themes. Each theme consisted of one environmental variable, such as elevation, slope, or aspect, or a cultural variable, such as archaeological site boundaries, ethnographic-village locations, or wells. Each theme was georeferenced and divided into 10-by-10-m cells, termed pixels. The site layer proved somewhat problematic. The locations of the 49 chance-find sites were recorded with a single GPS point; in the GIS, archaeological site locations were represented by a single pixel. But most sites are larger than a single pixel, and characterizing the environmental setting of a site by a single pixel has the distinct possibility of grossly misrepresenting it. Accordingly, we buffered the GPS site center with a 25-m radius. All pixels that touched this circle were defined as sites. Each site, therefore, was represented by approximately 20 pixels.

We performed pairwise tests of association between a dozen or so environmental variables and the 49 sites documented in the OJVG concession. Five variables—slope, aspect, runoff accumulation, soil type, and elevation—were associated (directly or indirectly) with site location. Four of these variables—slope, aspect, soil, and elevation—followed relatively standard definitions that are used in many predictive models. Runoff accumulation is a measure of water availability. It is defined as the distance in meters from the center of a pixel to the nearest 'sink' (i.e., a place where rainwater would accumulate). The concept of a sink is more useful for the Sabodala region than the more conventional measure of distance to water (defined as the shortest distance from a pixel to a 'blueline' feature on a topographic map), because water tends to pond in the rainy season, as opposed to flowing in streams year-round. Villagers rely on wells that are located in areas with high water tables, which in turn are often correlated with sinks. Thus, runoff accumulation can be viewed as a proxy for distance to water. A large runoff-accumulation score indicates a pixel far from reliable water, and a low score means that the pixel is close to standing water, at least seasonally.

The next step in a regression model would have been to produce logistical equations for sites and nonsites, based on survey data. Because we had not performed a systematic survey, we could not distinguish areas that contained sites from those that did not. Our site locations were areas we had stumbled across while driving or walking through the region on our way to someplace else. We had not identified any areas that did not have sites. Consequently, regression was not an option that we could use for modeling the OJVG concession.

Instead, we performed a cluster analysis on the five environmental variables associated with site locations. We used the ISO cluster algorithm in the ArcGIS Spatial Analyst module, which is a form of K-means cluster analysis (Esri 2010). Our goal was to end up with three clusters representing high, medium, or low sensitivity for site location, respectively. After specifying a three-cluster solution, the algorithm randomly selected three mean values, with each pixel in the OJVG concession assigned to the group for which it was closest to the mean, using Euclidean distance. A new mean was calculated for each of the three groups, and the processes were repeated until the groups stabilized.

Before we could perform the cluster analysis, we needed to transform all the variables so that they were measured on interval scales. Slope, elevation, and runoff accumulation already existed in this format, with slope measured in degrees, elevation in MAMSL, and runoff accumulation in meters. The remaining two variables were originally nominal categories and therefore had to be converted to dummy variables. For example, aspect was divided into four variables—north (316–45°), east (46–135°), south (136–225°), and west (226–315°)—with each pixel coded either '0', if it did not have this aspect, or '1', if it did. At the time of the statistical analysis, we had only soil information derived from engineering studies. Although these categories were used in the initial statistical tests, we—in consultation with Jeff Homburg, after his work on agricultural soils used by traditional farmers in Mamakhono (Homburg and Bèye 2010)—decided that the categories were not measuring anything of importance with regard to human settlement behavior, and they were deleted from the predictive model.

Three 'environmental' groups were defined and are shown in Figure 8.1. One was positively associated with site locations (gold—high-sensitivity zone), one had very few sites (green—low-sensitivity zone), and one was not strongly correlated with sites (brown—medium-sensitivity zone). High-sensitivity areas account for 33 percent of the OJVG concession and 52 percent of the sites. A strong predictive model is generally considered one that predicts 85 percent of the sites in 33 percent of the area. To start off at about 50 percent with no survey is reasonably good, suggesting that human settlement is highly correlated with resource location.

Our next step was to determine the environmental variables statistically most responsible for the clusters. Each pixel had been classified to one of the three environmental groups. These designations were used as input for a discriminant-function analysis. The purpose of this step was not to 'test' the cluster results—which would be tautological, because the discriminant groups are based on the same variables used to define the clusters—but instead to determine which variables were statistically the most important for defining the sensitivity classes. Based on the covariance and correlation matrices, it is clear that many of the variables are highly intercorrelated. Consequently, the classification-function coefficients are largely meaningless. In this case, the best approach to interpreting the statistical results is simply to compare the means and standard deviations of the groups

Where Are the Sites, and Why Are They There?

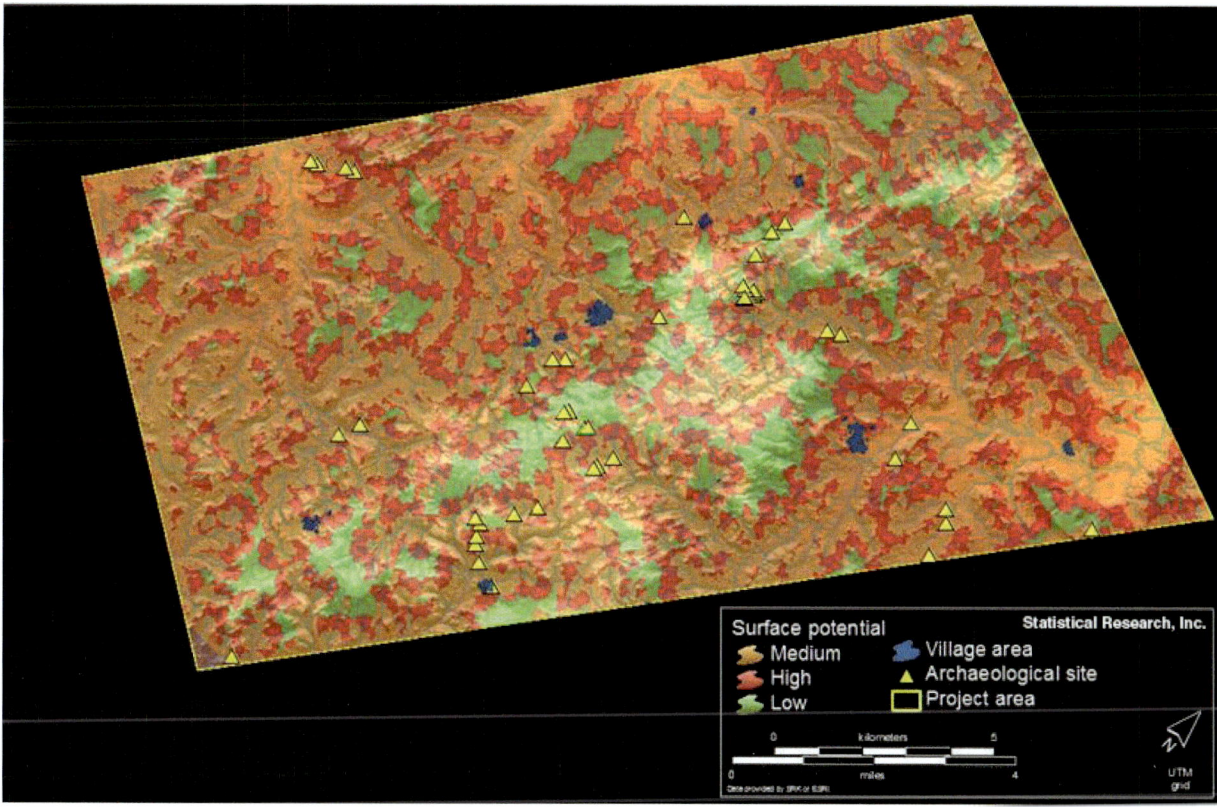

FIGURE 8.1. SURFACE-SITES PREDICTIVE MODEL.

TABLE 8.1. MEANS AND STANDARD DEVIATIONS OF ELEVATION, SLOPE, AND RUNOFF ACCUMULATION, BY SENSITIVITY CLASS

Sensitivity Class	Number of Site Pixels	Elevation (m)		Slope (degrees)		Runoff Accumulation (m)	
		Mean	SD	Mean	SD	Mean	SD
High	8,501	176.7	10.7	4.2	4.4	179.5	86.9
Medium	6,721	182.3	8.0	3.6	3.8	490.9	119.2
Low	1,161	189.9	8.7	2.5	1.9	851.6	77.4

Key: SD = standard deviation.

(Cowgill et al. 1984:186). In Table 8.1, we present the means and standard deviations for the three-interval-scale environmental variables for 'site' pixels found in each of the sensitivity zones.

The results show that sites in high-sensitivity areas are at lower elevations and closer to water than sites in medium-sensitivity areas, which, in turn, are lower and closer to water than sites in low-sensitivity areas. Surprisingly, this trend is reversed for slope, with high-sensitivity sites on the steepest slopes and low-sensitivity sites on the flattest ground, but slope has the highest standard deviation of all the variables, suggesting that, at least statistically, slope is not a strong predictor of site location.

Combined-Sensitivity Map

To aid in the design of the mine development plan, we overlaid the high-sensitivity zones of the surface-sites and buried-sites models and created a map that showed all high-sensitivity areas. Although we were not confident that sites were absent from medium- and low-sensitivity zones, we were comfortable offering the opinion that significant numbers of sites would be found in high-sensitivity zones. We then superimposed the proposed mine plan onto the predictive model, to get a rough feel for how important an issue archaeology might be (Figure 8.2). It turned out that 47.2 percent of the direct-impact zones lay in high-sensitivity zones for archaeological sites. This is a higher percentage than expected by chance alone (only 37 percent of the concession area is high sensitivity). Of particular concern was the proposed location of the reservoir dam, which was originally on a broad toe slope. Based on the archaeological predictive model, the location was moved downstream.

Model Testing

How well did we do? In light of the geoarchaeological and archaeological investigations reported herein, we

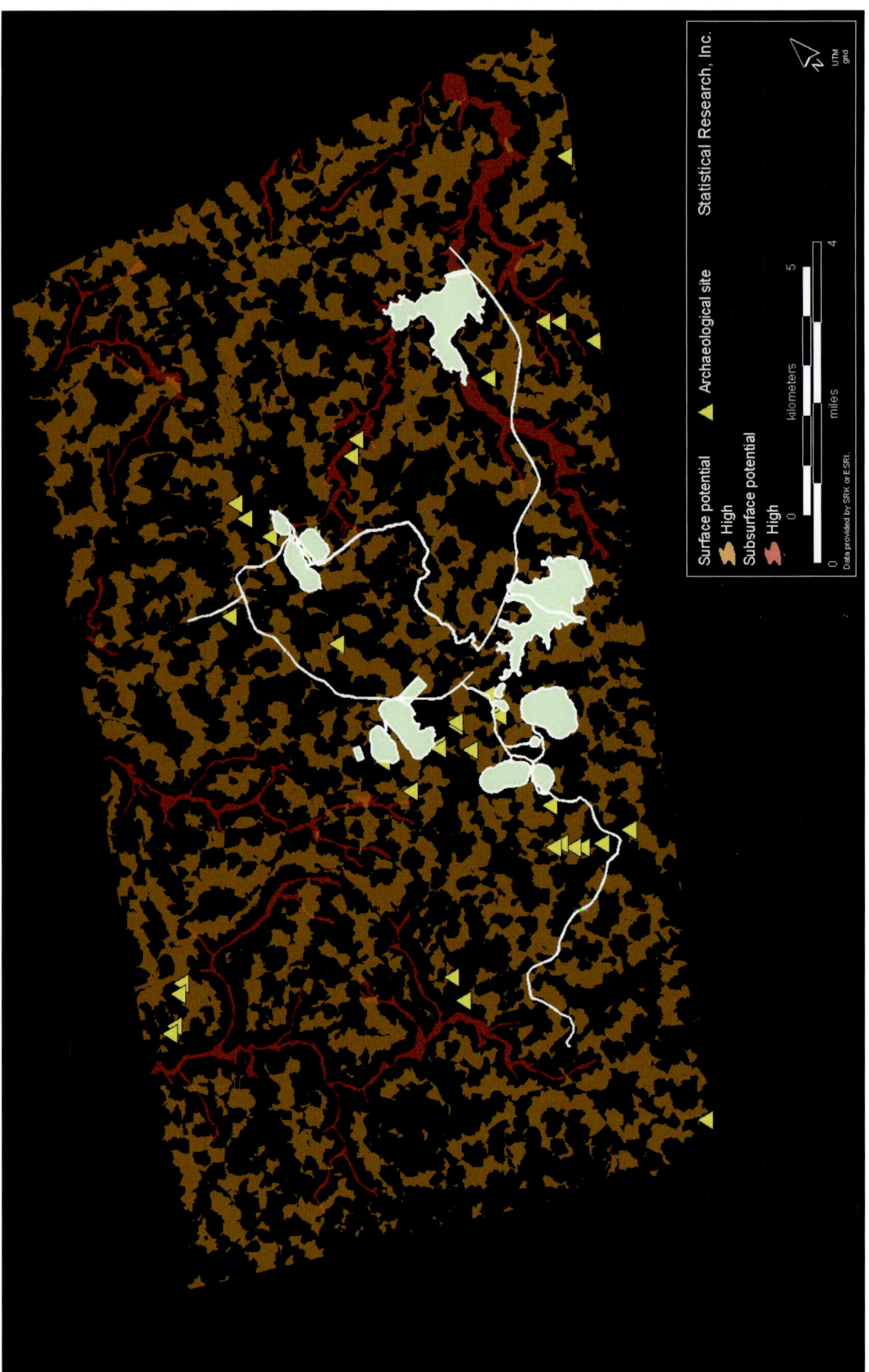

Figure 8.2. Mine development plan superimposed on the combined high-sensitivity zones of the surface-sites and buried-sites predictive models.

are in a position to evaluate the preliminary models. In Chapter 7, Homburg synthesized the stratigraphic, soils, geomorphic, hydrologic, and other data collected during the geoarchaeological study. He also evaluated the locations of archaeological sites in relation to the paleo–land surfaces. He concluded that the preliminary predictive model worked reasonably well (the interested reader is referred to Chapter 7 for a more detailed discussion).

The surface model performed about as well as expected, based on its original design (Table 8.2). The model performed slightly poorer during the survey, which is not surprising, given that the model was fitted to its source data. The major shifts are that slightly fewer sites fell into the high-sensitivity zone and somewhat more sites were found in the medium- and low-sensitivity zones than was the case with data used for the model development. The basic conclusion is that the model, though not very strong, made predictions in the right directions.

But that is not the whole story. Not all sites have equal scientific potential or traditional value. Residential sites—farmsteads, hamlets, villages, and polity centres—are of particular interest, because they can tell archaeologists the most about the past and because modern villagers are likely to have the greatest attachment to them. With the exception of farmsteads, the model performs better for residential sites than it does for sites as a whole (Table 8.3). Even so, there is major variation in model performance, particularly when comparing villages with hamlets and polity centres.

To explore these variations, we examined the means and standard deviations for the seven archaeological site types on the three-interval-scale environmental variables. We present the same data for modern villages in Table 8.4. A number of revealing observations can be offered. First, sites as a group are relatively heterogeneous. The poor predictive power of the model, therefore, is in part a consequence of grouping all sites together. Second, resource-processing sites tend to be located in the hills, relatively far from water, suggesting that most of these sites are nonagricultural in character. Their environmental signature is consistent with such activities as hunting and wild-plant gathering. Third, ideological and sacred sites are located in environmental settings similar to those of major residential sites, but on much steeper slopes. Although the association of ideological and sacred sites with hamlets, villages, and polity centres is speculative and needs much more survey data to be confirmed, it is certainly the case today that most sacred sites associated with particular villages are located nearby. Fourth, field houses and farmsteads are located in areas conducive to traditional agriculture. Sites of these two types are located significantly closer to water than sites in any other group. Their relatively low elevation is consistent with their placement on terraces overlooking drainages. On the whole, people do not appear to have been overly concerned with slope in locating these sites, suggesting a primary focus on economic activities.

The last set of observations relate to major residential sites. Archaeological hamlets and villages are found in similar environmental settings: at relatively low elevations, on flat ground, and surprisingly far from water. It is in this last characteristic that hamlets and villages differ from modern villages, which are generally located close to water. Water sources might have changed in the last few hundred years. Alternatively, the placement of villages during the chaotic late-nineteenth and early-twentieth centuries may have been influenced by noneconomic factors. In this regard, it is interesting to examine the locations of polity centres.

Although there are two polity centres defined in the OJVG concession, in the GIS, the polity-centre category is swamped by pixels from Masato (approximately 780 pixels). Three large sites, all of which were mapped, are consolidated in the Masato complex. In contrast, the polity at Makhana has not been mapped, although field observations suggest it is of comparable size to Masato. In the GIS, Makhana is represented by only 20 or so pixels.

Masato is located on a high, relatively flat terrace that backs into the hills that form the divide between the Gambia and Senegal River drainages. The complex overlooks an alluvial valley to the northeast that is ringed by mountains. It would be extremely difficult to approach Masato from any direction but the northeast, and from that direction, lookouts could track visitors from great distances. Masato is relatively far from water and good agricultural land but highly defendable—a characteristic that may have overridden economic interests in the volatile social and political climate in which it existed.

In assessing how well the SCHP predictive models performed, we need to evaluate both the model's overall performance and its ability to predict 'red flags.' The term 'red flag' refers to a site that is so costly in time, money, or both that missing it during the planning stages of a project can jeopardize the entire undertaking (Altschul 1990). Although solely cast in terms of their value to a project sponsor, red flags also tend to be the most important archaeological sites, in terms of scientific and/or traditional value (see also the discussion of 'magnet' sites in Altschul and Nagle 1988:258).

In the OJVG concession, the polity centre of Masato and possibly the one in Makhana represent red flags (see the discussion of World Heritage Listing, Chapter 9). It is worth asking, then, would these sites have been identified in the predictive model? The answer is, 'Maybe, maybe not.' The polity-centre site category had the highest percentage of high-sensitivity-zone pixels of all site types. Unfortunately, this percentage, 58 percent, is still relatively low.

Some may view the result as an indictment of predictive modeling, because it did not produce results adequate to the task. It is true that the model was not adequate for predicting red flags. But it is also true that the red flags we found were not anticipated by archaeologists. The modeling results reinforce what archaeologists have long argued: for areas, like the upper Senegal River, in which we know very little about the archaeology, nothing short of a complete inventory of the ADI is sufficient.

But a more complete evaluation of the models requires us to ask, 'Were the models useful planning tools?' Here, the answer is, 'Yes.' The combined subsurface-and-surface model correctly identified potential areas of high site density near the reservoir. Relatively minor changes in the dam configuration eliminated as many as 12 sites from the reservoir, or about 15 percent of the total number of sites in the ADI.

Summary

Correlative models, like the one we created for the OJVG concession, are based on the assumption that human behavior is patterned. Human decisions about what resources to exploit and how to procure and process them represent adaptations that are embedded in a cultural system that shapes all aspects of its members' lives. Because individual actions tend to be consistent with cultural proscriptions and norms, in the aggregate they follow patterns that are recognizable. The residues of these actions are recognizable in the archaeological record as phenomena that archaeologists term sites, features, artifacts, etc.

These phenomena often can be associated with modern environmental features, creating the 'environmental signatures' of locations that contain archaeological materials. Sometimes we can learn a lot just by examining these signatures. Sites may be found close to potable water, on flat land, *and* near arable land. Inferences can

TABLE 8.2. COMPARISON OF MODEL PREDICTIONS FOR THE TEST SAMPLE AND SURVEY RESULTS

Sensitivity Zone	Sites		Concession Model (%)
	Test Sample (%)	Survey Results (%)	
High	52	46	33
Medium	41	45	54
Low	7	9	13
Total	100	100	100

TABLE 8.3. COMPARISON OF MODEL PREDICTIONS FOR RESIDENTIAL SITE TYPES AND SURVEY RESULTS

Sensitivity Zone	Residential Site Types				Survey Results (All Sites) (%)
	Farmstead (%)	Hamlet (%)	Village (%)	Polity Centre (%)	
High	30	53	49	58	46
Medium	69	26	50	29	45
Low	1	21	1	13	9
Total	100	100	100	100	100

TABLE 8.4. MEANS AND STANDARD DEVIATIONS OF ELEVATION, SLOPE, AND RUNOFF ACCUMULATION FOR ARCHAEOLOGICAL SITE TYPES AND MODERN VILLAGES

Site Type	Number of Site Pixels	Elevation (m)		Slope (degrees)		Runoff Accumulation (m)	
		Mean	SD	Mean	SD	Mean	SD
Resource processing	1,549	222.2	16.6	6.0	4.5	299.1	195.5
Field house	2,159	169.2	31.1	4.3	3.0	227.0	213.5
Farmstead	3,024	182.4	15.6	4.1	2.9	266.2	173.3
Hamlet	1,421	174.7	10.8	3.6	2.0	447.6	219.1
Village	1,486	175.5	5.5	3.7	3.5	350.1	172.2
Polity centre	802	220.2	5.0	2.7	1.4	509.5	200.5
Ideological/sacred	132	197.0	26.2	7.4	3.3	409.0	246.9
Modern village	4,072	182.3	20.2	3.0	1.7	227.4	206.3

Key: SD = standard deviation.

be drawn about why people chose certain places, some of which can be tested with further study.

What is often lost in discussions of correlative models is people: people of the past, of the present, and of the future. Debate swirls around how strong a predictive model must be before its predictions can be trusted and when and how to use predictions in the ESIA process. Less is said about what we are saving the past for and how we can incorporate archaeological studies into decisions about resource development. These are much more difficult issues and require a completely different approach to modeling.

Why Are Sites Located Where They Are?
The Case for Agent-Based Modeling

A common failure in CRM predictive modeling is to assume that simply knowing the locations of sites is sufficient to manage them. But CRM is about managing conflicting objectives—the development of land and resources and the protection of cultural heritage. To find a balance between these objectives, one needs to be able to evaluate the costs and benefits of favoring one over the other in any particular situation. Moving a road alignment may protect an artifact scatter, but at a significant cost. Failing to move the road as it crosses an abandoned village may release spirits that harm the descendant communities.

CRM is about more than simply protecting the past; it is also about shaping the future. The OJVG gold mine will pose challenges, just as it creates opportunities for the residents of the villages of the concession and the region. Jobs will be created, outsiders will move into the old villages and perhaps create new ones, restrictions will be placed on artisanal mining, and agricultural lands will be lost, as new technologies and crops are brought in as compensation. How the villagers adapt to the new conditions will depend, in large part, on how well these changes are incorporated into the existing cultural framework. Can the past serve as a guide?

Many aid projects are based on the assumption that individuals will endeavor to maximize their returns. But many indigenous cultures in arid environments are adapted to minimize risk. The disconnect leads not only to the failure of development projects but, at times, to the collapse of traditional culture. The switch from a traditional to a cash economy in Nigeria, for example, which was supposed to lead to prosperity, led to the collapse of traditional relationships and resulted in the population's increasing dependence on government subsidies (Legge 1989). The construction of irrigation facilities in the middle Senegal River Valley was designed to ameliorate the devastation caused by periodic droughts and to increase agricultural productivity but, instead, concentrated power in the hands of already wealthy families and impoverished an already stressed underclass to the point of rebellion (Park et al. 1993).

To avoid these mistakes in Sabodala, we need to recognize that a fundamental assumption of many mitigation plans—that members of the affected populations have equal access to new opportunities—will not be met. As is the case in many parts of West Africa, society in the Sabodala villages is stratified into three main classes: nobles, 'castes', and slave descendants. The lion's share of opportunities for jobs, education, access to health care, and so forth, will fall to members of the noble classes, with other members of the population receiving fewer benefits derived from economic development.

One approach to expanding the reach of these benefits is to increase the productivity of traditional economic practices. There are three pillars of the traditional economy in Sabodala: agriculture, pastoralism, and gold mining. All three will be affected by the OJVG gold mine. Agricultural lands will be lost, particularly in the area covered by the reservoir. Pastoralists, who pass through the region, will be affected, as the increase in population decreases access to pasture land. Finally, artisanal gold mining will likely be restricted to specific areas or denied access altogether to lands within the concession.

To compensate for these losses, new economic opportunities will be developed. Many of these enhancements will be in agriculture. New crops and fertilizers may be introduced, allowing fields to become more abundant and more productive. But the question remains: will such changes be experienced by all or just reserved for a few?

Combining the results of the cultural heritage investigations with agent-based modeling provides a unique approach to addressing this question. As befits the difficulty of the questions we are trying to address, agent-based modeling is an involved and complicated process. Unlike correlative modeling, it requires a tremendous amount of knowledge about environmental and cultural variables and their interrelationship. Whereas correlative modeling can be conducted early in a project, agent-based modeling generally requires a long-term commitment. Not surprisingly, the SCHP agent-based model is just beginning and will be completed as part of the mitigative package of actions.

Even though we are at the early stages of the modeling process, we can outline our general approach. The program we are using is a beta version of Agent Analyst (see Argonne National Laboratory and University of Redlands 2010). The program requires that, first, we set the parameters, or rules, that will govern the model. The rules specify how agents, or actors, interact with environmental variables. Agents can be individuals or groups of individuals who act as a unit; a lineage, for example, may be the most appropriate agent for a model of the upper Senegal River Valley. The behavior of the agents is then linked to a set of environmental variables whose conditions may or may not change with each interval of the model. The interval represents a time period—in our case, a year—and the model works in an iterative manner. In Year 1, for example, there may be sufficient rain and moderate temperatures, allowing actors to plant and harvest 10 fields. In Year 2, rainfall may diminish so that crops are harvested from only 5 of the 10 fields. Each year, agents also buy or sell cattle and goats, depending on the number of people in the lineage and their perception of the upcoming harvest (modeled, for example, on the size of the previous year's harvest), allocating so many lineage members to the care of livestock. These members will then leave the region (i.e., stop consuming lineage foodstuffs) in search of pasture, for a length of time determined by current climatic conditions. If the lineage still has excess labor, some members will be tasked to mining gold or raiding lineages outside the model for slaves.

Second, we need to specify the consequences of these events for each interval. What happens if food is abundant (birth rates increase, death rates decrease, etc.) or inadequate (death rates increase, migration outside the model area occurs, etc.)? How large can villages become before a set of people leave and form a new village (e.g., if 20 percent or more of a lineage's fields are located more than 8 hours from a village, the lineage splits in two, with one half staying in the village and the other half forming a new village)? How much disposable cash is earned per unit of gold mining performed? What is the expected success (gaining slaves) or failure (loss of raiders) of raiding? And so forth. These results will then influence agent behavior the following year, in terms of the number of people each agent will have available for agricultural, pastoral, and mining pursuits. By running the model numerous times according to one set of rules and then again under slightly different sets of rules, we can home in on the set of parameters most consistent with the archaeological record.

As should be apparent, agent-based modeling can be exceedingly complex. One always has to balance the objectives that make the model realistic but also understandable. If there are too many rules governing the system, then our ability to determine why the model works is nearly impossible. If there are too few rules, then the model has little explanatory power. In negotiating these competing objectives, we have taken a middle road. Our modeling efforts focus on two cultural systems, one based on a hierarchical social structure and one based on an egalitarian social structure.

Archaeology and ethnography allow us to discern the key elements of an adaptation that was sustainable in the upper Senegal River Valley for at least the last millennium. These elements include (1) an economy based on agropastoralism, supplanted by the trade of gold and, at times, slaves; (2) a region where good agricultural land is highly restricted and generally not sufficient for village populations; (3) a land-tenure system in which favored agricultural land is held corporately by lineages and access to this land is determined by lineage elders; (4) a highly mobile population whose movement is not greatly restricted and whose range covers large areas of West Africa; and (5) a hierarchical society in which power and wealth are highly concentrated. We are confident that we can create an agent-based model from rules founded on these elements that is consistent with the archaeological record. Such a model will be very useful in providing answers to such questions as *How many years we would expect a typical traditional village to last? What is the average size of a traditional village? Does village size change over the life cycle of a village?* and *What is the long-term average population of the Sabodala region, and how is it distributed?*

Although we believe that such a model will provide useful baseline information regarding population size and settlement dynamics, we also are cognizant that this model is of limited use going forward. Aspects of traditional society, particularly the existence of a slave class, are no longer morally or socially acceptable. Is it possible that an adaptation based on traditional agropastoralism and artisanal mining is viable if the social structure is more egalitarian and access to economic opportunities is more open? To test this notion, we are in the process of creating a second model, using rules more in line with family-based farming communities. Inspired by the agent-based SWARM model developed by Kohler and his colleagues at the Santa Fe Institute for portions of the Colorado Plateau of the American Southwest (see Kohler et al. 2007), the agents in the SCHP egalitarian model represent individual nuclear families. Each agent has access to all types of agricultural land. We plan to run the model with pastoralism as a secondary economic focus that is largely in the hands of outsiders (as it is today). Each agent will also be able to allocate a certain amount of human resources to gold-mining activities, which will be redeemed by outside agents (i.e., agents not in the simulation) for cash, which, in turn, will be used in times of shortages to purchase food (measured in calories).

The outcomes of the two models will be helpful in visualizing what traditional settlement dynamics were like prior to industrialized mining and what they might have looked like under a different social system. As the mine develops and pressure is placed on social institutions to allow greater access to all members of society, planners and government officials should be in a better position to monitor the trajectories of population and social changes and to influence these trajectories in positive directions.

Conclusions

We have used predictive models for the SCHP to address two different situations that confront all development projects. The first is assisting in the design of a development when little or no archaeology has been conducted in the project area or region. Our task was to develop objective and replicable tools that could predict the locations of archaeological sites. We split this task into two components. Using topographic maps, we created a model for buried sites that was tested as part of the geoarchaeological investigations. The model was found to be largely accurate, although the likelihood of buried sites anywhere in the OJVG concession was deemed to be rather small. The second model, designed to predict surface sites, generalized the association to the entire concession of a small set of environmental variables with sites discovered as chance finds. Although weak, the model's predictions, based on a small and biased sample, were found to be reasonably accurate.

The second problem common not only to development but to all archaeological projects goes beyond prediction to explanation: why are archaeological sites located where they are? Answering this question is fundamental to evaluating the scientific and traditional importance of sites and, therefore, critical to developing appropriate mitigative measures. We have chosen to address this topic through agent-based modeling. By combining archaeological, ethnographic, and historical data, we are in the process of developing a hierarchical and an egalitarian model that simulates settlement and population dynamics for the Sabodala region.

We view our use of modeling as neither innovative nor controversial. Others have developed these techniques; we have refined them to fit our needs. We recognize, though, that predictive modeling is not universally accepted. Much of the criticism, we believe, is misdirected. Those who would argue that only 100 percent survey and 100 percent excavation will ensure protection of the past are mistaking the collection of data for interpretation. Interpretation requires a theoretical framework, a model of reality. Predictive models are neither good nor bad, although they may be put to good or bad use. We believe, ultimately, that good CRM decisions require a sound framework, one whose measurements are objective, whose logic is transparent, and whose results are replicable. It is our job as archaeologists to ensure that those who use predictive models to make resource decisions understand their underlying assumptions and the limitations of their predictions, as well as their potential to highlight aspects of heritage that otherwise might be lost.

Chapter 9

Settlement Dynamics in Beledougou in the Second Millennium A.D.

This chapter presents a synthetic summary of the key outcomes from the work presented in the preceding chapters. This is a highly selective synthesis that revolves around two deceptively simple questions: *What has happened in the Sabodala region in the last thousand years?* and *What did we learn from doing all this work?* The first question falls into the realm of culture history—the who, what, and when of prehistory and history. Our answer to the second question is a first attempt at addressing the question of why these events occurred.

We have focused on the last thousand years for several reasons. Although human—and indeed hominid—use of the region may extend back as far as 300,000 years, more than 95 percent of the sites found in the OJVG concession either firmly or probably date to this period. This evidence, and the story it can be made to tell, forms a bridge in the ESIA process between the identification of archaeological, historical, and traditional sites that might be adversely impacted by the development of the mine (discussed in Chapters 3 and 5) and the evaluation of those resources in terms of their regional, national, and local significance (discussion of which follows, in Chapter 10).

Beledougou in Context

The social and agricultural histories of Beledougou, the sociopolitical entity that has encompassed the Sabodala region for last few centuries, forms the geographic context for interpreting the archaeological record of the OJVG concession (Figure 9.1). Beledougou has been shaped by local and regional historical events and processes, which include, among others:

- The rise and fall of the Mali empire (the 'fall' was a process that began ca. A.D. 1560 and was completed by about 1625).
- The floruit of the trans-Saharan trade routes, especially for gold that originated in the upper Senegal River area (including Beledougou) over the last 500 years, with Beledougou near the crossing of east-west and north-south routes. The trans-Saharan routes that flourished under the Mali Empire were gradually replaced. East-west routes to the coast gained prominence as the Songhai Empire replaced the Mali Empire.
- The appearance of Europeans on the Atlantic coast, first in the fifteenth century and, by the seventeenth and eighteenth centuries, pushing inland, up the rivers. The shifts in foci of the European trade entrepôt, from ca. A.D. 1600 forward, also had consequential effects for repeated dislocations of trading routes.
- The spread of Islam, in several waves, beginning at the start of the second millennium but, in some instances—locally most noticeably in the eighteenth and nineteenth centuries—involving major social upheavals and conversion by jihad.
- Colonial rule and the attendant, European-dominated slave trade, with endemic, locally based slavery. In the twentieth century, the gradual abolition of slavery also set in motion significant social changes. Over the last century, there has also probably been significant population movement of freed and escaped slaves who formed communities in rural/marginal districts, including Beledougou.
- Inward migration of peoples, in several waves, beginning with Tenda groups (the first group that we know of—for example, the Bassari) and followed by Soninke lineages from Soumare; then the Peul of the Pulaar/Halpulaar family, with connections to the theocratic polities of Boundou and Fouta Djallon from the eighteenth and nineteenth centuries; and eventually the Malinké, dominated by Cissokho lineages (probably in the last 150 years or so).
- Climatic change from the 1400s led to drier conditions and relief from the endemic tsetse fly, allowing cattle pastoralists (or at least pastoralism) to appear in the upper Senegal River region. With some short-term reversions to wetter conditions, this drying trend has continued to the present.
- The presence of gold in the geologic strata in eastern Senegal, which has been known and exploited for millennium, was prominent in European motivations in the sixteenth through twentieth centuries and was always exploited at varying levels of intensity—including in the context for the SCHP.

Throughout this litany of 'big-picture' events, the upper Senegal and Falémé River basins and their hinterlands—including Beledougou—appear as recipients of changes originating elsewhere, rather than as places from whence change occurred and then rippled outward. In the sense of the insights that arise form a careful consideration of the fundamental ideas of Kopytoff's (1987) 'internal frontier' it is clear that Beledougou may be usefully considered as just such an internal frontier zone.

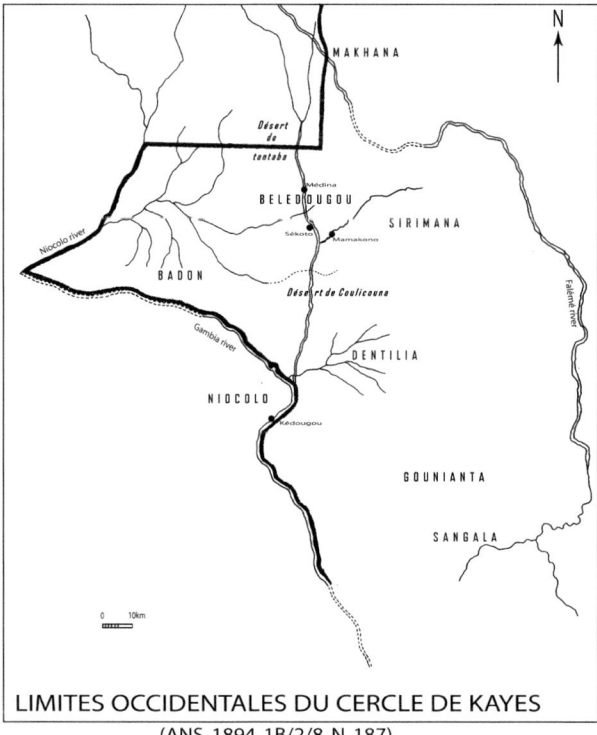

FIGURE 9.1. THE GEOPOLITICAL CONTEXT OF BELEDOUGOU.

Settlement and Subsistence

The history of Beledougou is one of successive groups, beginning with the Bassari and ending with the Malinké. The reasons behind group movements are complex mixtures of economic, social, political, and religious causes, some specific to individual groups and others following regional trends affecting much of West Africa. Regardless of why each group came to Beledougou, what did they do once they arrived? Did they follow the same economic practices? Were settlements placed in the same or similar locations? Was a village-based settlement characteristic of all occupations? Or did polities emerge that altered the settlement hierarchy and pattern?

The archaeological surveys document a distributional pattern that, for the most part, indicates that sites of particular types are located on the landscape in similar settings, presumably for similar reasons. It is clear from the ethnographic studies that folk memory places availability of water and availability of fertile land as two of the most frequently named reasons for the placement of the present villages. Likewise, archaeological hamlets and villages favor terraces adjacent to areas of fertile soils (this is discussed again, below).

The ethnographic settlement pattern up until the recent past (say, the last 25 years or so) has been one of mainly quite small settlements with few larger agglomerations. There is also a history of frequent fissioning and fusing of settlements caused by complex, small-scale social tensions, as family and lineage groups dispute, split, and regroup. Many small and medium-sized settlements seem to have been occupied for fairly short periods of time—perhaps a single or a few generations.

This pattern is consistent with most of the archaeological record. The hamlet and village sites all contained modest ceramic assemblages, and few exhibited either very large or very diverse assemblages; modest sizes and relatively homogeneous collections are consistent with fairly short-lived occupations, for most of the sites.

The exception to this statement may be Mamakhono. Archival maps and documents, along with oral history, indicate that Mamakhono was the first settlement in the region, some 670 years ago. If oral traditions are correct, the village should have been settled by Bassari or Soninke groups. If so, this 'ethnic' origin is now lost, and the newer peoples have usurped their predecessors' roles in settlement creation. Ethnoarchaeological investigations of Mamakhono would be necessary to determine when the village was established and how its population has waxed and waned over the centuries.

Although we know little of the village of Mamakhono, the study of present agricultural systems at Mamakhono by Homburg and Bèye (2010) may prove to be a powerful analogue of the archaeological record, not only of this village system, but of others in Beledougou. They documented that the dispersal of agricultural fields around villages is largely limited by daily travel time to and from the settlement. Proximity is especially important through the later parts of the growing (rainy) season, when farmers need to protect their maturing crops from animal damage. More-distant fields are provided with field houses, where farmers, and often their families, may stay for longer periods leading up to the harvest, when the site may take on the very short-term character of a farmstead.

Homburg and Bèye (2010) also examined the effectiveness of recent agricultural regimes. They noted a clear and explicit preference for Pleistocene first-terrace (T1) locations and gravelly soils, a preference they linked to a strategy of minimizing risk in dry years, rather than one of maximizing crop yields in good years. White sorghum, beans, peanuts, maize, and rice are the principal crops. They noted that farmers crop a field for about 7 years and then let it lie fallow for 5 or 6 years, during which time the field begins to revert to bush. Agriculture is based on hand-planting, using digging sticks and hoeing by hand rather than ploughing. After harvest, fields may be grazed by cattle/sheep or goats (with their attendant manuring) and the residue burned off. Gradual soil degradation is well understood, and early warning signs are known and used for making decisions about returning a field to fallow and shifting crops elsewhere. The appearance of cattle cannot be documented archaeologically yet (because of the soil acidity where investigations have been made) but must have occurred since about A.D. 1500, when conditions became dry enough to make the tsetse fly less of a barrier to animal husbandry. Their conclusions are important—that the system is very well adapted, based upon centuries of embedded knowledge, and is sustainable, even under current population sizes.

It is important to remember that modern subsistence relies on more than agricultural and pastoral pursuits. Wong et al. (2010) have shown that forest resources are used extensively. Some of the use is fairly obvious; the use of timber and bamboo for building materials and grass for thatching are ubiquitous. Forest plants are also used regularly for their medicinal properties. The extent to which forest products are used to supplement agricultural produce as foodstuffs, especially in the dry season, is especially noteworthy (Wong et al. 2010).

Continuity in Settlement

We can draw morphological parallels between present sites and archaeological sites to illustrate the apparent continuity of settlement types over the last few centuries.

Field houses known archaeologically include Sites 149 and 155; these consist of a few huts (five at Site 149 and three at Site 155) placed on the floodplain or along the interfaces of the T1 and T2 terraces. At both sites, evidence for extensive domestic occupation is missing. Each site has one or two structures with fired-clay-daub walling, suggestive of plain, woven walls. The artifact collections are small in size and restricted in range. These may be compared to the field house and adjacent drying platforms, threshing areas, and 'ramadas' recorded by Homburg (see Chapter 7) among the Mamakhono fields and by the authors at Ouassa/Wassa in 2009 and illustrated in Figure 9.2.

It is less easy to compare archaeological hamlets or small villages with modern settlements, as there were no 'hamlets' occupied in 2009–2010, but the small village of Bambarayading, to the east-northeast of Bambaraya, may serve as a proxy (Figure 9.3). Archaeologically, the best examples of small villages are Sites 71 and 156. The numbers of recorded huts range from about 65 (at Site 156) to over 100 (at Site 71). At each site, the volume of artifactual material is considerable, and the diversity is high. Consistent elements of hamlets/villages are the large, ground stone milling stones for grinding grain; these are too large to be easily transported on a routine basis (e.g., to seasonal field houses) and are considered a marker of more-permanent settlements.

Bambarayading has a population of about 200, consisting of 14 families occupying about 150 structures (including huts, granaries, armadas, privies, etc., as counted from aerial photographs). Residents now use wooden, rather than stone, grinding/pounding basins for sorghum, but otherwise, the material culture is large and diverse, although noticeably less so than at the large villages of Sabodala and Mamakhono.

On the basis of this comparison, it is not difficult to see Site 71, for example, as a small village about two-thirds the size of Bambarayading.

Settlement Dynamics

Using modern village sizes and populations as analogues suggests that, throughout the 'archaeological past' (i.e., prior to A.D. 1900), the population of the OJVG concession was considerably less than it is today (even discounting the well-understood, very recent influx of people drawn by the prospect of employment in the existing mine of the OJVG exploration). Village and hamlet sites are relatively few, well dispersed, and short-lived, all of these traits suggesting low population numbers and density. We might characterize the population for much of the first millennium as 'Bassari,' followed by the Soninke (perhaps ca. the fourteenth to fifteenth century?) and then, in the eighteenth to nineteenth century (or earlier?), by the Peul, as climates became drier. Two forces were probably at play: a background trajectory of slow, organic population growth impacted by occasional influxes of ethnically new groups. The net result was to push older groups into more marginal areas and/or to simply subsume them. In the mid- to late-nineteenth century, in part replacing the influences of the Peul theocracies in Boundou and Fouta Djallon, came the Malinké, loosely contemporaneous with inward movements of escaped/freed slaves.

The last period was marked by turbulence, emanating from the 'big-picture' events discussed at the outset of this chapter. At that time, the earliest of the other known settlements in the area appeared: Bambaraya, Nion Madina (south of Bransan), Dindifa, Maka Madina (from Makhana, the putative polity in the south of the concession), Sabodala, and Khossanto. These all claim foundation by Cissokho Malinkés. These Malinké-Cissokho communities are essentially those documented in Chapter 3—settled agriculturalists mixed with partially displaced Peul (who traditionally placed a greater emphasis on pastoralism). The Mali Empire had collapsed, and the Malinké diaspora had begun. A claimed origin in Tomara, in Mali, was a regular feature of our interviews; even today, these communities all maintain close social and familial links to Mali.

The late-nineteenth century is also when Beledougou was effectively converted to Islam. Certainly Islam was present earlier, and conversion to the new religion was occurring at a slow but steady pace when the region

FIGURE 9.2. (*A–B*) ABANDONED FIELD HOUSES AND (*C*) STONE-CIRCLE FOUNDATIONS FOR AN 'ARCHAEOLOGICAL' HUT AT WASSA IN 2009.

Figure 9.3. Bambarayading, from the approach road.

got caught up in broader historical events. In the mid-nineteenth century, El Hadj Umar Tall swept through the upper Senegal River area on a jihad aimed at forcibly converting all 'nonbelievers' to Islam that may have had consequences in Beledougou. Folklore recounted to us as part of the ethnographic survey links the site and area of Makhana to Sheikh Umar. This episode involved massive population movements among the middle Senegal River, upper Senegal River, and Mali areas, with Beledougou likely to have been swept across on numerous occasions. The Halpulaar jihad of Umar precipitated major conflicts with settled agriculturalists (Malinké) who practiced traditional African religions.

The jihad of Umar was not simply or solely an Islamic movement; it was also anticolonial in nature. France had assumed colonial hegemony, with consequent impacts on local societies and polities and also with serious dislocations of previous trade routes (especially impacting the gold trade). Although not abolished until later, slavery was increasingly frowned upon. Meanwhile, slavery was an intrinsic part of the Malinké-Peul social system, with society divided into three classes: aristocracy and freemen, caste-griots, and slaves. In Beledougou, Peul communities and, subsequently, the Malinkés had weak political structures in which political chiefs and freemen-merchants both maintained standing 'armies' of slave-warriors. On occasions, these 'armies' staged coups d'état to replace chieftains. This system was increasingly in opposition to the French colonial administrations, initially based in Kayes and later in the Cercle de Kédougou.

This paints a picture of a concatenation of events reaching a crescendo of change in the period from ca. 1850 to 1900. Beledougou was not an active participant in this but was, apparently a more passive recipient of influences from elsewhere. Beledougou could be called a 'refugium,' pressed by the spread of Islam and wrapped up with ethnic tensions, French colonial effects, the demise of the Malinké Empire of Mali and the slightly later theocracies of the Peul in Boundou and Futa Djallon, and, throughout, the exploitation and trade of gold. This period is one of social stresses and instability, and of rapid changes.

These events are all contemporaneous with the inward movement of peoples during a period of great social turbulence. It is, therefore, hardly surprising that the folk history accounts for the present villages' foundations, occurring during this period, do not accord in detail with these wider-historical processes, even when supported, as they are, by some archaeological evidence.

This period of instability is echoed in one of the most intriguing stories we were told by the ethnographic informants, which takes us back to the archaeological evidence for this specific period (see also Conrad 2008 for the value of oral tradition). This is the story of Tobri Sidibe.

The context of the story is interesting; it has no overtly Islamic elements and, therefore, should date to before the mid-nineteenth-century forced conversions. The established elite at the time were the Soninke Soumare.

The patronymic, *Sidibe*, indicates he was a Peul. In the story, Sidibe was a slave who somehow acquired great powers and became a king. Was he a mercenary slave warrior who assumed the status of his noble/merchant owner? In any case, according to the narratives collected among the Malinké Cissokho who claimed to be the descendants of those who defeated him, Tobri Sidibe took despotic power, probably linked to controlling access to water and/or gold. The Soumare sought assistance from the Malinké Cissokho lineages at Tomara Mali. There, Chief Sora Moussa sent his sons, Dan Moussa and Dan Sirima, with their sister, Dan Manian, to rid the Soumare of Sidibe's control. Through some form of manipulation, in which the sister seems to have married Tobiri Sidibe only to understand the source of his power, the brothers succeeded in killing Sidibe. Some versions of the story also involve the sacrifice of a griot by the brothers, as part of their coup. Dan Moussa then took the chieftainship of Beledougou, and Dan Sirima, that of nearby Sirimana. From one perspective, this folktale is an origin or foundation story that explains how and why the Cissokho lineages from Tomara ousted the Soninke and Peul and assumed political domination.

This story would have been merely of quaint interest had it not been for its direct resonance with one of the more intriguing archaeological finds—Site 8 (and the area encompassing Sites 09, 10, and 11) at Masato. According to one informant from the village of Sabodala, the complex of archaeological sites at Masato was the seat of Sidibe's realm. We have used the widespread folktale involving Sidibe, along with local residents' belief that Masato was the seat of the 'slave-king's' realm, combined with the complexity of the archaeological complex and its placement for seemingly defensive purposes, as the basis for hypothesizing that Masato is an archaeological example of the small West African polities that emerged in the late-nineteenth and twentieth centuries at a time of consolidation of French colonial rule in the region. In parallel, a similar connection between Site 24 at Makhana and Sheikh Umar is the basis for the attribution of 'polity' to that site, although this inference is much weaker and needs corroboration from archival records.

These processes illustrate the discussions in Kopytoff (1987) about the origins and functioning of 'internal frontier' settlements, and even more clearly are examples of a history in the past being created, maintained and elaborated in present events (Stahl 2001).

Masato: The Archaeology of a West African Polity Centre

The story of Tobri Sidibe and his possible link to Masato allows us to ask, *What did a nineteenth-century West African polity centre look like?* The SCHP provides a rare opportunity to apply the archaeological evidence toward developing a set of answers. We also need to consider that French colonial rule was already established in the region at this time but that their control over local affairs was still very loose. The French colonial administration appointed local chiefs who often acted on their own will. In this sense, the detailed interpretation that we put on the definition of 'polity,' as a centre functioning with as much local autonomy as feasible in the interstices of a very broad-based colonial power, is different from the more-normal use of 'polity' to mean a more truly independent power.

A prominent aspect of Site 8 is the walled enclosure, encompassing an area of about 2,000 m^2. The enclosure wall is interesting. There is not enough stone present to make a truly defensible barrier; so, it must always have been largely a symbolic barrier or division. The enclosure is, clearly, in part residential, with a handful of stone circles, most likely hut foundations, at the eastern edge. Outside the enclosure wall are at least scores of stone circles that easily number more than 100 when those at Sites 09, 10, and 11 are added to the features at Site 8. One of the functions of the enclosure walls, then, appears to have been to separate the chiefly, political, and religious elites from common freemen and slaves.

In the southwest sector of the enclosure is the foundation of the putative mosque, with what appear to be public spaces to the north and west. There may even be the remains of the public washing place for worshipers entering the mosque. The presence of a possible mosque is interesting for many reasons. Among these is the apparent non-Islamic nature of the Sidibe story. It is possible, though by no means certain, that the mosque was added to the Sidibe site sometime after his reign. It would be equally useful to ask about the nature and character of a mosque in a society undergoing tremendous social upheaval, in which the population may be a mixture of Muslim and traditional African religions. In many instances, Islam cohabited peacefully with local African religions. Initial conversion concerned mainly the elites and the merchant class, who used it to tap into the trans-Saharan trade. It was only in the nineteenth century that it became militant. Test excavations of the possible mosque at Site 8 provided clues about the manner in which the structure was built, but not about the building's function or nature. These are left to future investigations.

Another intriguing aspect of the 'Sidibe polity' at Site 8 is, quite simply, its small size. Compared to modern villages, such as Mamakhono or Sabodala, an enclosure of 2,000 m^2 and a settlement of about 100 huts is, frankly, very small. We do not have the evidence to speak about Makhana, but the ceramic evidence at Masato does not suggest a long-lived settlement. This inference is consistent with the folk history. The small size and limited lifespan of such a settlement is indicative of a fluid settlement system and of political power based on personal charisma/power as the basis for social dominance. If the personal basis for social power was disrupted—as by the death of Sidibe—then the system should have fragmented and the settlements dispersed. Our assumption is that the settlers at Masato were Soumare (or people who were at least led by the Soumare, with other groups included in the population) who split off from their parent community in Mamakhono. According to folk history, these lineages eventually moved back to Mamakhono, when the reasons for the split had been resolved. Was this upon the demise of Sidibe at the hands of the incoming Cissokho warriors?

Sabodala and Internal Frontiers

The ethnography (see Chapter 3) suggested that the Sabodala area presents a case study for the testing of the explanatory power of Kopytoff's 'internal African frontier'. The convergence of the archaeology at Masato, and the sidelights shone on other sites like 24 at Makhana reinforces this potential. Unfortunately, the archaeological data is limited to survey alone, and subsequent ethnographic work was likewise never required by the government in advance of the mining works. In some senses, the potential remains, but our ability to draw conclusions is thwarted.

Certainly the stories we received about the origins of the Cissokho and their predecessors, and the relations between the groups (and the even older, even more aboriginal Bassari) – and the whole of the story of Sidibe, fits neatly and without a ripple into the sequence postulated by Kopytoff (1987, 16-17) for the movements of groups, adherents as kinsman (1987 40-52) and/or subjects, patrimonialism and so on. The harkening to Mali is likewise typical (Kopytoff 1987, 77) and the tensions between Sidibe and the Soumare illustrates tensions of the authority of firstcomers over latecomers (52-54) and the resolution by legitimating (or not!) an usurper (Kopytoff 1987, 65). There are however aspects that do not fit Kopytoff's model – such as the absence of griot, the lack of restrictions upon music-making etc – so there are clearly discordant notes that remain unexplained.

It is clear that several histories have been created by the different social groups within the OJVG concession, and that these histories have been critical in the formation and continuation of social identities into the present. Following Stahl (2001) we were able to structure interviews to enable us to get beyond the initial layers of historical narratives. However, we are also fully aware that our work, and perhaps more than anything else producing this final report, will in some senses be made to serve in affirming or reifying some aspects of the various histories by some of the social groups in Sabodala. However, other aspects of our narrative will equally be used to support some more subversive histories.

The parallel applications of ethnography and archaeology were deliberate and if unusual it was not unique – Anne Stahl implemented a more thoughtful and self-reflective programme among the Banda over several decades (2001). The investigations continued by using local men as labourers, who then served as yet more informants – creating a highly unusual self-reflexive 'community approach' to all forms of heritage within the studies of the OJVG concession. This bore fruit even within the limited field seasons that we were able to undertake, and would have been far more valuable had the pre-mining mitigation investigations that we had anticipated been required by the government of Senegal and undertaken.

While this cuts across historical accounts and allowed us to record competing and over-lapping narratives, the potential ethical implications were clear at the time and remain unresolved. The American Anthropological Association's maxim to 'do no harm' is not wrong, but felt totally inadequate to us when what the diverse specialists undertaking an environmental impact assessment wanted to achieve as an outcome was 'to do good'.

Perhaps the best that we could achieve in the end was this account of the various histories that are current, and are currently being deployed and built-upon in Sabodala, tempered by our thoughts of the interplay between those histories and set along-side the interpretations were have been able to offer concerning the 'lived history' (Stahl 2001, 17) of the last few centuries in Sabodala.

The Past Living in the Present

The story recounts that, upon the death of Sidibe, the Cissokho did not return power to the former chiefs (the Soumare) but assumed political dominance, which they hold still. The chieftainship in 10 of the 11 villages (all except Bambarayading) is still held by the Cissokho. This reality belies internal divisions, rivalries, and tensions; the Cissokho Malinké sociopolitical dominance is not monolithic. There are multiple aspects that may contribute to the present-day situation. First, the means by which the Cissokho gained power may have involved the sacrifice of a griot. Even today, there is a lingering edict against griots in Mamakhono and a near-total absence of griots in all the villages of the OJVG concession. Second, variations in the stories explain the complicated, indeed fictive, relationships necessary to keep multiple Cissokho lineages in power and from turning on each other. Whereas some lineages can trace ancestry to the clan homeland in Mali, others may have origins with slave ancestors and/or may, perhaps, descend from (griot?) blacksmiths. The variations in folktales draw in the very atypical aspects of the societies in the concession that make them so unlike the

Malinké norm—the absence of griots, the ability of most young men to play drums and make music in public, the *dansa* itself, and the presence of Peul-speaking people practicing the *Kankourang*, which should be very strictly reserved for Malinké. Alongside these cultural variants must be placed the continued contest of some village chieftainships due to alleged origins from slave individuals or, in other versions, from blacksmiths in the relatively recent past.

Combining ethnographic and archaeological data yields a picture of a period of intense social change that occurred at the end of the nineteenth century and extended well in to the mid twentieth century. This involved the overturning of previous norms by social groups of mixed ethnicity, who proceeded to create new social work-arounds for previous ethnic prohibitions. It also probably involved the final end to slavery, but possibly only within living memory.

It seems likely that some sites—archaeological as well as traditional sacred properties—provide tangible links between the current villages and a highly contested and emotionally charged past. To paraphrase the American novelist, William Faulkner, the past in Sabodala is never dead; in fact, it's not even past.

Chapter 10

Summary

The specialist baseline study for the OJVG Sabodala Gold Mine Project ESIA for archaeology and cultural heritage required the following:

- Description of the baseline archaeological and cultural environment of the study area;
- Description of the significance of any finds in a national context;
- Summary of the relevant legal framework (national legal standards and World Bank guidelines) for archaeology sites in Senegal that could affect compliance of the project design; and
- Provide suggestions for dealing with any new archaeology sites that may be discovered during the proposed mining project.

To achieve these objectives, the ToR specified that the SCHP include background research on the regional culture and environment, field surveys to identify cultural resources, and analysis and synthesis of the fieldwork results. In Chapter 2, we presented the results of the background research, including preliminary research questions to guide the evaluation of archaeological sites.

Based on the background research, we identified three major field studies to perform. An ethnographic survey was performed to identify sacred and traditional sites, as well as to provide baseline information regarding social, political, and economic relationships and institutions upon which society and culture in the 10 villages of the OJVG concession are based (see Chapter 3). Next, we performed archaeological investigations consisting of survey and test excavation in areas proposed for mine development and improvements (the ADI). These investigations took the form of reconnaissance and intensive survey, along with the monitoring and test excavations (see Chapters 4–6). The third field study was devoted to geoarchaeology, particularly to determining the likelihood that mine development would encounter buried sites (see Chapter 7). A corollary field study on traditional farming in the Mamakhono area (Homburg and Bèye 2010) was performed, in conjunction with a separate baseline ESIA study called for in the ToR. We also created predictive models of archaeological site locations, because the design of the mine plan preceded archaeological field studies, and the mine engineers wanted to know whether there were specific areas of concern (see Chapter 8). Both the study of traditional farming and the modeling efforts greatly enhanced our understanding of past and present land use and subsistence systems, as synthesized in Chapter 9.

Significance Evaluations

In the OJVG concession, we documented two types of cultural resources: sacred/traditional resources and archaeological resources. The significance of each type at the regional (West Africa), national (Senegal), and local (Sabodala region) levels is considered below.

Sacred and Traditional Resources

UNESCO conventions recognize two categories of traditional resources: tangible and intangible. Tangible resources are those with physical attributes; they can be located on a map, they have boundaries, and they have integrity. Such resources include burial sites (either in general or of people important to the affected community), natural features that are sacred (e.g., trees, rock formations, springs, etc., included in creation stories), or traditional-use areas (e.g., plant-gathering areas, clay sources for ceramic vessels, hunting grounds, etc.). From a management perspective, tangible resources are relatively straightforward; either a development avoids and protects them or its actions disturb them. Disturbance may be minimized through a variety of actions, such as movement of an object, prayers, or compensation.

In contrast, intangible resources have no physical characteristics. They are nonetheless essential to the well-being of a society. Intangible resources cover a wide range of cultural actions and items, including language, songs and prayers, public speech and oral histories, rituals and ceremonies, and traditional knowledge about farming and hunting. Safeguarding intangible heritage is a major concern of UNESCO, and the 2003 convention urged countries to list representative intangible heritage (in what is known as the Representative List of Intangible Cultural Heritage of Humanity), as well as to list those resources that require international support (the List of Intangible Heritage in Need of Urgent Safeguarding). In 2005, the *Kankourang* was placed on the Representative List by Senegal and The Gambia, requiring the two countries to actively promote the resource's practice and transmission.

We documented 46 sacred sites in the OJVG concession, although this number should be considered a minimal figure. We were told of another 20 sites but could not verify their existence. Further, we suspect that, as the SCHP continues and we build trust with villagers of the OJVG concession, we will learn of many more places of sacred and traditional importance.

Most sacred sites were located near modern villages and include features of the natural environment (e.g., water sources, hills, trees, forests, and caves), locations of initiations, and places where spirits dwell. Residents are taught from a young age not to disturb these places. If they are disturbed, then special rituals and prayers need to be invoked, to ward off sickness and bad luck.

The sacred sites documented in the OJVG concession are not significant at either a regional or a national level. They are not known outside the Sabodala region and often not beyond the boundaries of particular villages. But to the villagers, these sites are sacred, reflecting the values, beliefs, and traditions of the village residents. To these people, all 46 sacred sites are important.

In addition to sacred places, we also documented a number of ceremonies and festivals that are part of the social fabric of the villages in the OJVG concession. Festivals include the harvest festival, which currently is not being conducted, because the villages are too poor, but likely will be resurrected in the future. Another ritual that takes place during marriage and circumcision ceremonies is the *dansa*, a competition between generations that can be considered a rite of passage.

Some traditional West African ceremonies no longer take place in the villages of the OJVG concession. These include initiation ceremonies involving the *Kankourang*, which traditionally accompanied the circumcision of boys or the excision of girls. The *Kankourang* is the Malinké equivalent of the *Kankurang*, the Manding initiation rite that has been listed on the UNESCO Representative List of Intangible Cultural Heritage of Humanity. The modern rite in Sabodala bears little relation to the traditional *Kankurang* and now is performed more as entertainment than as an essential element of the cultural fabric.

No intangible resources documented in the villages of the OJVG concession appear to meet the criteria for listing on either UNESCO's Representative List of Intangible Cultural Heritage of Humanity or the List of Intangible Heritage in Need of Urgent Safeguarding. That does not mean that intangible cultural resources are not significant. Our ethnographic research documented a fluid and dynamic cultural environment in which many of the traditional institutions common to Malinké and Peul society have been altered in response to historical events. Village life in the Sabodala region is a unique amalgamation and an integration of traditional economic practices, social structures, and political organizations that are tied together by a distinctly West African form of Islam. Industrial mining will be yet another outside influence that shapes the direction of the local culture.

Archaeological Sites

Archaeological sites are considered significant based on their aesthetic, scientific, and/or traditional value. In the upper Senegal River Valley, archaeological sites do not contain monumental architecture or other features that would draw attention to their aesthetic qualities. These sites, therefore, must be judged on their scientific potential to provide new insights into the past and on their traditional value to local communities, national interests, and pan-regional cultures.

At the outset of the SCHP, we had few expectations of what we would encounter in the OJVG concession. So little work had been done in the upper Senegal River basin that anything we found, or did not find, was of interest. During the course of our investigations, we documented 251 archaeological sites. Even now, it is hard to determine what this number represents. How many sites should we have found? How old should they be? What types of sites are there, and what behaviors do they represent?

One method of estimating the number of sites in the OJVG concession is to calculate the site density of a representative area and apply it to the rest of the concession. As is common in development projects, we did not perform a random sample of the concession but, instead, systematically surveyed the entire ADI. Consequently, we cannot calculate parameter estimates, such as site density, with statistical confidence. Yet we have no reason to suspect that the areas surveyed have any systematic bias that would preclude generalizing the results of the ADI survey as a first approximation of site density for the OJVG concession.

Of the 251 archaeological sites, 66 were encountered as part of the intensive survey of the ADI. The ADI consists of about 872 ha. The site density of the ADI, therefore is 0.076 sites per hectare. Assuming the site density of the ADI is representative of the concession as a whole, the best estimate of the total number of sites in the 230-km^2 OJVG concession is 1,748.

A large number to be sure, but are they all significant? To determine significance, we need to know what types of sites are represented and what they can tell us about the past. We need to know what time periods are represented and what site types belong to each period.

Africa has supported human life longer than any other continent on the planet. We expected to find evidence of early human occupation, and we were not disappointed. The lithic collection included three possible Acheulean bifaces made on local greenstone and exhibiting heavy geological varnish. These artifacts were associated with the highest terrace on the laterite bedrock or nearby slope. The presence of this rare and ancient tool technology (possibly 200,000–300,000 years old) in the Sabodala areas extends our knowledge of the very earliest human inhabitants of West Africa. We also found a small number of sites that contain artifacts dating to the middle and upper Paleolithic. All Paleolithc artifacts were surface finds, and as Homburg points out in Chapter 7, there is little likelihood of finding intact Paleolithic features or deposits within the OJVG concession.

The vast majority of sites relate to agriculturalists and pastoralists. Some of these date to the Neolithic, or the first millennium A.D., but by far, most of the sites were occupied toward the end of the Iron Age and into the historical period. The dominant material class collected from these sites is ceramic. The SCHP collection, by far the largest ceramic collection in the upper Senegal River basin, has some similarities to collections from the better-known lower Falémé and middle Senegal River Valleys but also differs in significant ways from these riverine collections. The ceramics of the Sabodala region by the end of the first millennium A.D. conform well enough to regional collections to suggest that the area participated in trans-Saharan trade. Pottery collections from the period between A.D. 1300 and 1700 diverge from those of the riverine areas, suggesting that Sabodala was cut off from regional events and that cultural isolation became the norm for its residents. By A.D. 1500, this pattern again shifted, with Sabodala ceramics showing similarities to the subactuelle collections in the Senegambia.

The collection also includes tuyere and slag fragments, markers of iron production. Although the Sabodala pieces are small and confined to a few sites, they nonetheless point to small-scale, local blacksmithing and possibly smelting from the iron-rich laterites. The Sabodala area does not appear to have been a vibrant center for the production of iron. Most iron artifacts collected date to the recent-historical period and are mainly farming implements. These include axe heads (yendo), digging-stick tips (sombe), and hoes (dabo), plus small knives and an array of small fragments that probably represent a plethora of metal fittings, including nails, hinges, and straps.

Finally, the collection contains a few trade imports, including glass, gunflints, and tobacco-pipe fragments. Although relatively small, this part of the collection points to regional and international connections of the Sabodala area with other regions and with European powers. Future research may place this collection into a more specific chronological context and thereby show how Sabodala was linked into trade and colonial relationships westward to the Atlantic, as well as eastward via Mali and the trans-Saharan trade routes.

Based on material culture, site size, topographic location, and features, we classified each of the SCHP sites into one of seven functional site classes: resource-processing sites, field houses, ideological/sacred sites, farmsteads, hamlets, villages, and polity centres. We have assessed the significance of archaeological resources by site class, as opposed to individual resource evaluations. We have chosen this method because both the scientific value and the traditional value of resources are largely driven by context. From a scientific perspective, the archaeology of the OJVG concession can inform in two research domains. The first is culture history—the who, what, when, and where of prehistory.

Our work suggests that, although Paleolithic occupation of the region occurred, the likelihood of finding sites with intact deposits is poor. Chance finds from this period are important to collect and study but hardly represent a major research avenue. We have a much greater ability to study the last two thousand years, or from the Neolithic to the historical period, most particularly the last portion of prehistory and the early-historical period. Fixing the cultural sequence is still an important task. Although the artifact collections are an immense step forward, we still have no absolute dates for the region. All dating, therefore, is relative cross-dating with better-known regions, some of which are at considerable distances from Sabodala. We still cannot answer basic questions: Who were the first farmers/herders of the region? How are they related to the Bassari? When did Peul-speaking people move in? Malinké speaking people? How are these movements related to world events, such as the spread of Islam and European exploration and settlement?

In addition to culture history, the other major archaeological research domain that seems most appropriate to the OJVG concession relates to the 'how' of prehistory: How did people make a living? How were they organized? How did the events of the outside world affect the upper Senegal River region? Most of these questions fall under the rubric of settlement and subsistence of the late-prehistoric and early-historical periods. Preserved in the archaeological record are the constituent parts of relatively small, but complete, village systems—the villages, hamlets, and farmsteads that together constituted a community, as well as the places the people farmed and extracted wild resources from the environment. In addition to understanding village-based life just prior to and during European contact in West Africa, we also encountered the remains of what appears to be the central village of one small West African polity, and possibly a second. Few such polity centres have been found, and fewer still have been systematically studied.

Archaeological sites also may have traditional values, particularly sites that can be associated with famous personages in the past or direct ancestors of the living. Ancestral villages to modern ones are often places where family members are buried and their spirits live. In many parts of the world, archaeological sites are often used as shrines, where passersby place offerings for safe travels or ask gods and spirits to intervene on their behalf to cure illness, win favor for a marriage proposal, or invoke witchcraft.

In Table 10.1, we provide an assessment of the significance of site classes encountered in the OJVG concession. The scores for scientific and traditional value range from 1 (not important) to 10 (extremely important). It is important to point out that these site classes refer to Neolithic and later occupations of the OJVG concession; all Paleolithic materials, whether intact sites or surface finds, should be considered highly significant at a local, national, and regional level.

Although generally of limited research potential, *resource-processing sites* provide insight into behaviors otherwise lost in the archaeological record. Which wild plants and animals people actually targeted, where they went to obtain these resources, and how they processed them are all important and often can be studied by investigating a relatively small sample of resource-processing sites.

Field houses are critical elements of an agropastoral landscape. They refer to locations that served as logistical nodes in a subsistence and settlement system. Primarily used in farming, field houses also served as hunting camps, wild-plant-procurement and -processing sites, and temporary storage, or for a variety of task-specific activities. Because of the diversity of activities associated with field houses, a relatively large number will need to be investigated to ensure that the subsistence system is adequately characterized.

Ideological or sacred sites contain features that are best interpreted as having spiritual or ideological value. These features include burial cairns and tumuli, as well as sets of cupules that may have been used in a variety of rituals and ceremonies. These sites are distinguished from 'sacred' sites in that they were not identified during ethnographic interviews, although they contain similar characteristics. It is possible that the interviewees did not know about these sites or that they choose not to tell us about them. The scientific potential of these sites depends on our ability to study mortuary remains. Consultation with the local villages is needed to determine if restrictions will be placed on such studies. Regardless, these sites are likely to be considered of tremendous traditional importance to the local population.

Farmsteads, hamlets, and *villages* represent the primary types of residential sites. Although the distinction may seem one of scale—a farmstead as the home of a single family, a hamlet as home to two to five families, and a village as the residence of many more families—the sites differ more in character than in sheer size. Villages and hamlets are places with several ethnic groups where all social classes are evident and where the full range of

TABLE 10.1. SIGNIFICANCE OF ARCHAEOLOGICAL SITE CLASSES FOR THE OJVG CONCESSION

Site Class	Level of Significance	Scientific Value	Traditional Value
Resource processing	local	3	1
Field house	local	5	5
Ideological/sacred	local	6	10
Farmstead	local	7	5
Hamlet	local	8	6
Village	local	9	8
Polity centre	local, national, and regional	10	10

economic activities takes place. Farmsteads, in contrast, are socially and ethnically more homogeneous; they are tied socially, economically, and politically to a particular village or hamlet.

Archaeologically, all residential sites are potentially important, because they can best address questions of culture history and settlement dynamics. Residential sites will have the best preservation of foodstuffs, the widest diversity of material culture, and the full array of storage and residential features. They also may contain burials. Modern villagers may have personal attachments to particular residential sites, as well as more-general feelings about them, associated with spiritual beliefs based on real or purported events that took place there (e.g., villages that were abandoned during epidemics may be considered dangerous because of evil spirits that remained behind).

One of the interesting elements of the investigations was the documentation of circular stone features. These features were found at all types of residential sites. Many of the stone features appear to be supports for raised floors of huts, although others appear to have been used as storage features, hearths, and roasting pits. Some stone circles may have been used for burials. The stone features of the upper Senegal River region bear little in common with the Stone Circles of Senegambia—a group of sites inscribed in the World Heritage List and located on the Gambia River, about 250 km to the west (UNESCO 2010)—but this inference is far from secure, and more research on the features in the upper Senegal River area is required and would be best carried out as part of a larger institutional research project.

We recorded two site complexes that we interpreted as centers of early-historical-period West African polities. One polity (ARCHs 08 and 09), located near Masato, is possibly associated with the historical figure Tobri Sidibe. The site is composed of an enclosure surrounded by many stone features (probably huts and storage facilities). Within the enclosure are larger stone circles (perhaps the chief's residences), a mosque, stone features that may be burials, and a plaza. The second polity is located at Makhana (ARCH 24). Archaeologically, the Makhana complex is composed of a large village site,

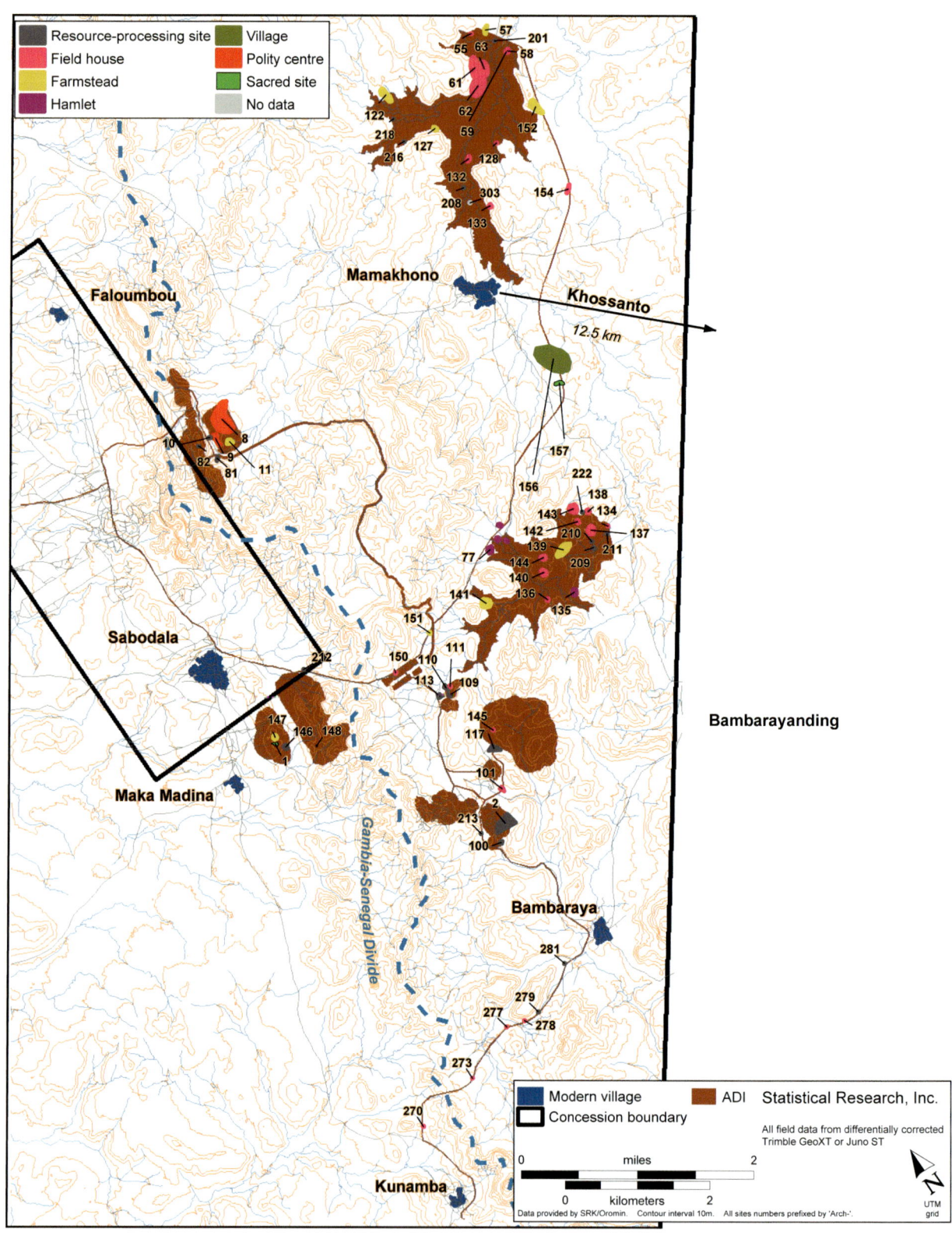

Figure 10.1. Archaeological sites within the areas of direct impact (ADI).

and burials are reported to be present in several localities (likely cemeteries). This site complex is also in good shape and may be associated with the well-known Sheikh Umar, who led a jihad throughout this region in the mid-nineteenth century to convert the local populations to Islam.

The polities are rare archaeological phenomena; both are in good condition, with strong site integrity. The sites have unique potential to address many questions concerning culture history and settlement dynamics, as well as those related to specific historical events. Peul-speaking people, in particular, may place a high value on one site because of its association with their last 'king' in the region. Of all the sites in the OJVG concession, the complexes of Masato and Makhana are the only ones that could meet the criteria for inscription in the World Heritage List.

Impact Analysis

The footprint of the OJVG Sabodala gold mine is presented in Figure 10.1, along with the archaeological sites identified in the ADI. Table 10.2 presents the archaeological sites located in the ADI by site type and the proposed level of disturbance caused by mining activities. We estimated the percentage of each site that will be disturbed. These estimates are best viewed as relative classes that span the range from complete, to near-complete, to more-than-half, to less-than-half, to small disturbances. Because boundaries of improvements and sites are likely to change on the ground, these estimates should only be used for planning purposes.

Forty-four, or two-thirds, of the 66 sites will be completely destroyed under the current mine development plan. Another 6 sites will have more than half their cultural deposits disturbed. Sixteen sites, or roughly 25 percent, will have less than half the site area disturbed.

Three sacred sites identified during the ethnographic survey lie in the ADI (Table 10.3; Figure 10.2). Two are sacred trees, and one is a location of prayer between two trees. Sacred Sites 13 and 21 lie on roads and could probably be avoided, but sacred Site 5 lies in the proposed reservoir area and will be covered by water.

TABLE 10.2. ARCHAEOLOGICAL SITES IN THE AREAS OF DIRECT IMPACT (ADI)

Site Number	Site Type	Location in the ADI	Level of Disturbance
1	ideological/sacred	Golouma pit shell	complete
2	resource processing	Golouma pit shell	complete
8	polity centre	Masato waste dump	nearly complete (>90%)
9	polity centre	Masato waste dump	complete
10	resource processing	Masato waste dump	complete
11	farmstead	Masato waste dump	complete
55	field house	reservoir	complete
57	farmstead	reservoir	partial (>50%)
58	field house	reservoir	complete
59	field house	reservoir	complete
61	field house	reservoir	partial (<25%)
62	field house	reservoir	partial (>50%)
63	field house	reservoir	complete
77	hamlet	tailing-mine facility/ road—processing plant to dam	partial (>50%)
81	resource processing	road—Masato to processing plant	partial (<10%)
82	resource processing	Masato pit shell	complete
100	resource processing	Golouma pit shell	complete
101	field house	road—Golouma South	partial (<50%)
109	resource processing	Kerekounda waste dump	complete
110	resource processing	Kerekounda waste dump	complete
111	field house	Kerekounda waste dump	partial (<10%)
113	resource processing	Kerekounda waste dump	partial (<10%)
117	resource processing	road—Golouma South	partial (<50%)
122	farmstead	reservoir	partial (<25%)
127	farmstead	reservoir	partial (>50%)
128	field house	reservoir	complete
132	field house	reservoir	complete
133	field house	reservoir	partial (<25%)
134	field house	tailing-mine facility	complete
135	hamlet	tailing-mine facility	complete
136	field house	tailing-mine facility	complete
137	field house	tailing-mine facility	complete

Site Number	Site Type	Location in the ADI	Level of Disturbance
138	field house	tailing-mine facility	complete
139	farmstead	tailing-mine facility	complete
140	field house	tailing-mine facility	complete
141	farmstead	tailing-mine facility	complete
142	field house	tailing-mine facility	complete
143	field house	tailing-mine facility	partial (<10%)
144	field house	tailing-mine facility	complete
145	field house	Golouma South waste dump	complete
146	resource processing	Golouma pit shell	complete
147	farmstead	Golouma pit shell	complete
148	ideological/sacred	Golouma West waste dump	complete
150	field house	processing plant	complete
151	farmstead	road—processing plant to dam	complete
152	farmstead	road—processing plant to dam	partial (<50%)
154	field house	road—processing plant to dam	partial (<10%)
156	village	road—processing plant to dam	partial (<10%)
157	ideological/sacred	road—processing plant to dam	partial (<25%)
201	resource processing	reservoir	complete
208	resource processing	reservoir	complete
209	resource processing	tailing-mine facility	complete
210	resource processing	tailing-mine facility	complete
211	resource processing	tailing-mine facility	complete
212	resource processing	road—Golouma West to processing plant	partial (<50%)
213	resource processing	road–Golouma	complete
216	resource processing	reservoir	complete
218	resource processing	reservoir	complete
222	resource processing	tailing-mine facility	complete
270	field house	southern road	complete
273	field house	southern road	complete
277	field house	southern road	complete
278	field house	southern road	complete
279	resource processing	southern road	complete
281	resource processing	southern road	complete
303	resource processing	reservoir	complete

TABLE 10.3. SACRED SITES IN THE AREAS OF DIRECT IMPACT

Site No.	Village	Type	Description
SACR-5	Mamakhono	sacred tree	Approximately 80 years old; where women pray concerning problems with children and fertility; an old man accompanies a woman to the tree, and if she has a child, it will be the man's namesake.
SACR-13	Kunamba	sacred place	Sacred place between two trees where one goes to pray.
SACR-21	Bambaraya	sacred tree	

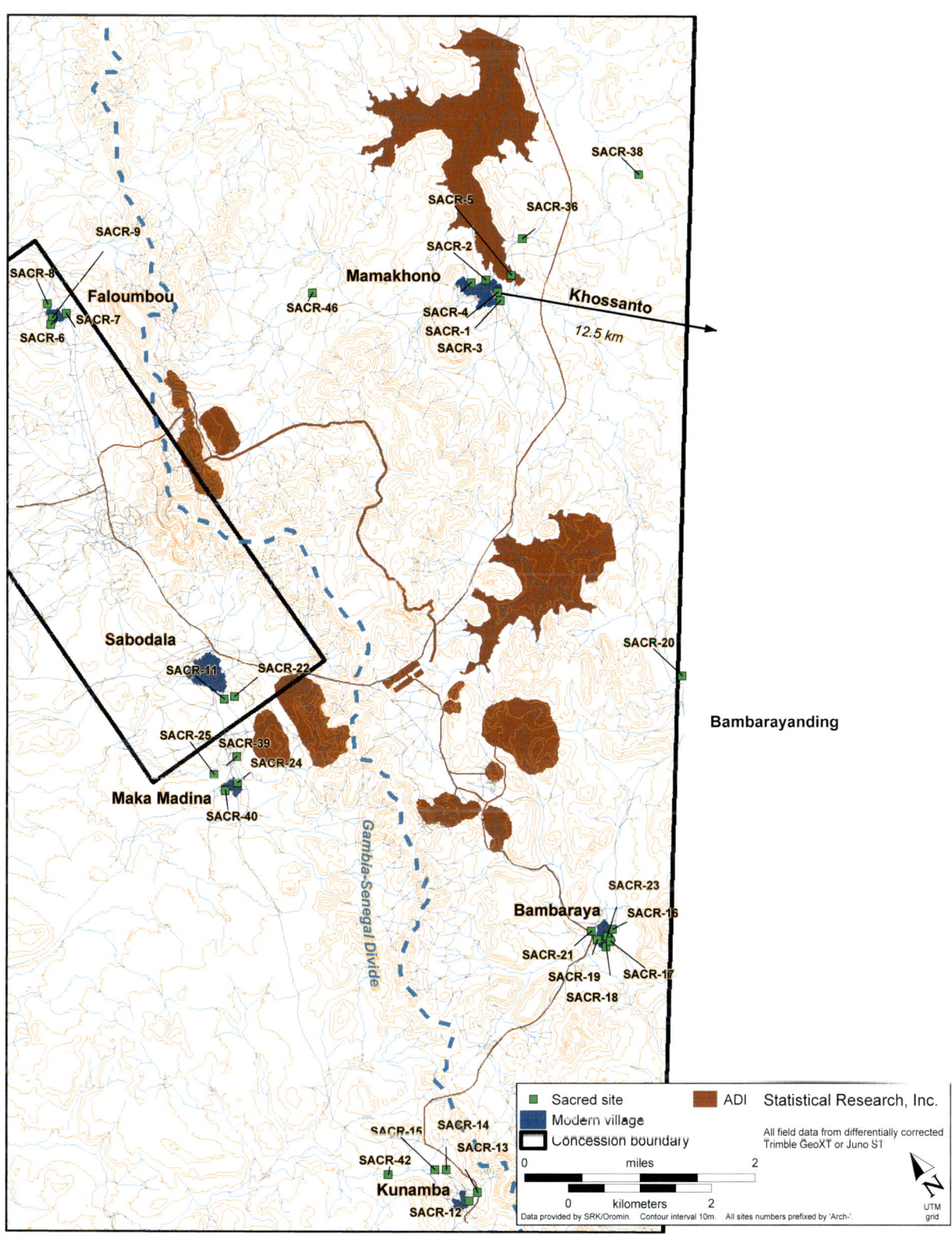

Figure 10.2. Traditional sacred properties within the areas of direct impact (ADI).

Appendix A

Gazetteer of Sites

Site No.	Size of Site	Topographic context	Elevation	Slope	Simple Aspect	Proximity to Water	Simplified Vegetation Types	Surface Artifacts	Surface Features	Interpretative Site Type	Comments Regarding Artifacts: Variety, Dating
1	small	elevated plateau/ hill-top; laterites	224.63	steep	SW	254.15	open laterite	glass beads	66 - cup/cupules	6 - Sacred site	
2	medium	Pleistocene terrace (T2) ?	222.61	shallow	SW	284.30	field	ceramics	1	1 - Resource-processing site	
3	small	Pleistocene terrace (T2) ?	210.25	shallow	S	58.12	wood	ceramics		1 - Resource-processing site	
4	small	Pleistocene terrace (T2) ?	261.84	shallow	SW	318.73	nd	ceramics		1 - Resource-processing site	
5	small	Pleistocene terrace (T2) ?	224.68	v steep	NE	151.21	wood	ceramics		1 - Resource-processing site	
6	small	Pleistocene terrace (T2) ?	0.00	flat		771.88	nd	ceramics		1 - Resource-processing site	
7	small	Pleistocene terrace (T2) ?	174.33	shallow	SW	159.17	nd	ceramics		1 - Resource-processing site	
8	v large	elevated plateau	217.61	shallow	E	153.72	mixed	ceramics and ground stone fragment	2	5 - Polity Centre	Part of Masato Polity complex.
9	v large	elevated plateau/ hill-top; laterites	218.50	moderate	SE	49.10	mixed	ceramics and ground stone fragments	7 stone circles	5 - Polity Centre	Part of Masato Polity complex.
10	small	Pleistocene terrace (T2)	231.65	shallow	SE	51.28	wood	ceramics		1 - Resource-processing site	Part of Masato Polity complex.
11	small	elevated plateau/ hill-top; laterites	214.65	flat	SW	28.99	wood	ceramics	11 stone circles	3 - Farmstead	Part of Masato Polity complex.
12	small	elevated plateau/ hill-top; laterites	228.20	v steep	NE	176.18	nd	ceramics		1 - Resource-processing site	
13	small	elevated plateau	259.03	moderate	SW	346.10	nd	ceramics		1 - Resource-processing site	
14	small	elevated plateau/ hill-top; laterites	216.64	shallow	NE	129.40	wood	ceramics		1 - Resource-processing site	

GAZETTEER OF SITES

Site No.	Size of Site	Topographic context	Elevation	Slope	Simple Aspect	Proximity to Water	Simplified Vegetation Types	Surface Artifacts	Surface Features	Interpretative Site Type	Comments Regarding Artifacts: Variety, Dating
15	small	elevated plateau/ hill-top; laterites	185.01	shallow	NW	425.86	wood	ceramics		2 - Field house	
16	small	Pleistocene terrace (T2–3)	237.42	shallow	NE	92.68	wood	ceramics		2 - Field house	
17	small	Pleistocene terrace (T2–3)	207.80	shallow	SW	25.18	field	ceramics		2 - Field house	
18	small	Pleistocene terrace (T2–3)	208.42	shallow	SE	162.18	field	ceramics		2 - Field house	
19	small	elevated plateau/ hill-top; laterites	282.34	v steep	SW	122.45	field + wood	ceramics		6 - Sacred Site	Tumulus, burial?
20	small	elevated plateau/ hill-top; laterites	279.34	shallow	SW	64.17	wood	ceramics		6 - Sacred Site	Tumulus, burial?
21	small	Holocene terrace (T1)	233.77	v steep	NE	11.99	wood	ceramics		2 - Field house	
22	small	Holocene terrace (T1)	228.85	shallow	SE	49.78	wood	ceramics		2 - Field house	
23	small	Pleistocene terrace (T2–3); hill-top	188.63	moderate	NW	231.73	wood	ceramics		2 - Field house	
24	small	Pleistocene terrace (T2)	178.75	moderate	SE	65.46	riverine	ceramics and ground stone fragments	>50 stone features	5- Polity Centre	Makhana
25	small	Pleistocene terrace (T2)	187.54	flat	SW	148.93	riverine	ceramics and ground stone fragments	>50 stone features	4b - Village	KhoboKhota
26	small	elevated plateau	0.00	flat		1156.43	nd	ceramics		1 - Resource-processing site	
27	small	Pleistocene terrace (T2)	0.00	flat		1595.63	nd	ceramics	3 - 5 stone features	2 - Field house	
28	small	Pleistocene terrace (T2)	172.11	shallow	NW	312.49	wood	ceramics and ground stone fragments		4a - Hamlet	
29	small	Pleistocene terrace (T2)	158.59	shallow	SE	5.58	wood	ceramics		1 - Resource-processing site	Sacred site SACR-42
30	small	Pleistocene terrace (T2)	159.35	flat	NE	144.59	wood	ceramics		1 - Resource-processing site	
31	small	Pleistocene terrace (T2)	156.96	flat	SW	32.54	field	ceramics		6 - Sacred site	Sacred site SACR-41

Site No.	Size of Site	Topographic context	Elevation	Slope	Simple Aspect	Proximity to Water	Simplified Vegetation Types	Surface Artifacts	Surface Features	Interpretative Site Type	Comments Regarding Artifacts: Variety, Dating
32	small	Pleistocene terrace (T2)	207.63	shallow	NW	197.41	ferro-etc	ceramics		1 - Resource-processing site	
33	small	Pleistocene terrace (T2)	170.30	moderate	NE	237.92	mixed	ceramics and ground stone fragments		2 - Field houses	
34	small	Pleistocene terrace (T2)	163.04	flat	NW	179.14	ferro-etc	ceramics and ground stone fragments		2 - Field houses	
35	small	Pleistocene terrace (T2)	153.19	flat	SW	245.62	grass + bamboo			2 - Field houses	
36	small	Pleistocene terrace (T2)	150.93	flat	NW	320.98	field	ceramics and ground stone fragments plain and decorated ceramics (several dense ceramic concentrations), stone axe	~10 rock rings (many burned), oven (?, kiln?) feature	3 - Farmstead	
37	small	Pleistocene terrace (T2)	154.78	flat	SW	520.38	nd	ceramics		2 - Field houses	
38	small	Pleistocene terrace (T2)	0.00	flat		648.22	nd	ceramics		2 - Field houses	
39	small	Pleistocene terrace (T2)	0.00	flat		859.28	nd	ceramics		2 - Field houses	
40	small	Pleistocene terrace (T2)	185.82	shallow	SE	70.61	field			1 - Resource-processing site 4b - Village	
41	small	Pleistocene terrace (T2)	198.35	flat	NW	233.46	field	ceramics			
42	small	elevated plateau/ hill-top; laterites	0.00	flat		896.45	nd	ceramics		1 - Resource-processing site	
43	small	elevated plateau/ hill-top; laterites	184.10	flat	NW	110.37	ferro-etc	ceramics		1 - Resource-processing site	
44	small	Pleistocene terrace (T2-3)	183.72	moderate	NE	136.07	wood	ceramics		3 - Farmstead	
45	small	Pleistocene terrace (T2-3)	192.42	shallow	S	147.26	riverine	ceramics		3 - Farmstead	Basari?
46	small	Pleistocene terrace (T2-3)	208.39	flat	SE	149.49	ferro-etc	ceramics		3 - Farmstead	Basari?
47	small	Pleistocene terrace (T2-3)	213.05	shallow	NE	133.20	bamboo = ferro-etc	ceramics		3 - Farmstead	Basari?

Gazetteer of Sites

Site No.	Size of Site	Topographic context	Elevation	Slope	Simple Aspect	Proximity to Water	Simplified Vegetation Types	Surface Artifacts	Surface Features	Interpretative Site Type	Comments Regarding Artifacts: Variety, Dating
48	small	Pleistocene terrace (T2–3)	229.03	flat	NE	90.54	bamboo	ceramics		3 - Farmstead	Basari?
49	small	Pleistocene terrace (T2–3)	242.37	shallow	SE	151.71	bamboo	ceramics		3 - Farmstead	Basari?
55	small	Pleistocene terrace (T2–3)	151.48	shallow	SE	80.57	wood	ceramics and ground stone fragments		2 - Field house	
56	small	elevated plateau	257.55	moderate	S	280.93	nd	ceramics		2 - Field house	
57	small	Pleistocene terrace (T1–T2)	148.80	flat	SE	134.01	wood	ceramics and ground stone fragments	6	3 - Farmstead	
58	small	Pleistocene terrace (T1–T2)	146.93	moderate	NE	48.86	field + bamboo	ceramics and ground stone fragments		2 - Field house	
59	small	plateau/slope - Pleistocene terrace (T2–3)	148.25	moderate	SW	73.05	field + bamboo	ceramics		2 - Field house	
60	small	plateau/slope - Pleistocene terrace (T2–3)	168.30	v steep	SW	137.97	bamboo	ceramics		2 - Field house	
61	medium	plateau/slope - Pleistocene terrace (T2–3)	156.64	moderate	SE	75.05	wood + field	ceramics and ground stone fragments		2 - Field house	
62	medium	Pleistocene terrace (T1–T2)	152.55	shallow	SE	53.28	field + bamboo	ceramics and ground stone fragments	>2	2 - Field house	
63	medium	Pleistocene terrace (T1–T2)	147.15	shallow	SE	38.13	field	ceramics and ground stone fragments		2 - Field house	
64	large	elevated plateau/hill-top	175.93	shallow	SE	271.66	bamboo + ferro-etc	ceramics and ground stone fragments	3	4a - Hamlet	
65	small	plateau/slope - Pleistocene terrace (T2–3)	143.23	flat	NE	28.62	riverine	ceramics	3	2 - Field house	
66	medium	plateau/slope - Pleistocene terrace (T2–3)	141.15	flat	SW	39.47	field	ceramics		2 - Field house	
67	small	plateau/slope - Pleistocene terrace (T2–3)	143.28	flat	S	76.33	field	ceramics		2 - Field house	
68	small	plateau/slope - Pleistocene terrace (T2–3)	149.01	moderate	SW	96.22	bamboo + field	ceramics		2 - Field house	

Site No.	Size of Site	Topographic context	Elevation	Slope	Simple Aspect	Proximity to Water	Simplified Vegetation Types	Surface Artifacts	Surface Features	Interpretative Site Type	Comments Regarding Artifacts: Variety, Dating
69	v large	plateau/slope - Pleistocene terrace (T2–3)	178.39	shallow	SE	72.57	wood	ceramics and ground stone fragments	1	3 - Farmstead	
70	small	plateau/slope - Pleistocene terrace (T2–3)	182.39	shallow	SE	14.08	field	ceramics	>2	2 - Field house	
71	medium	Pleistocene terrace (T2)	180.50	shallow	SE	115.10	mixed	ceramics and ground stone fragments	96	4b - Village	
72	medium	Pleistocene terrace (T1–T2)	178.91	shallow	SE	50.63	bamboo + field	ceramics and ground stone fragments		3 - Farmstead	
73	small	Pleistocene terrace (T1–T2)	211.45	flat	SE	60.77	riverine	ceramics		2 - Field house	
74	small	Pleistocene terrace (T1)	210.72	shallow	SE	105.16	riverine + wood	ceramics and ground stone fragments		1 - Resource-processing site	
75	small	Pleistocene terrace (T1)	207.16	shallow	SE	26.61	riverine	ceramics and ground stone fragments	>2	3 - Farmstead	
76	small	Pleistocene terrace (T1–T2)	214.37	shallow	SE	100.63	wood	ceramics and ground stone fragments		2 - Field house	
77a	small	Pleistocene terrace (T1–T2)	201.21	shallow	SE	40.04	mixed	ceramics and ground stone fragments	21	4a - Hamlet	
77b	small	Pleistocene terrace (T1–T2)	201.21	shallow	SE	40.04	mixed	ceramics and ground stone fragments	4	4a - Hamlet	
77c	small	Pleistocene terrace (T1–T2)	201.21	shallow	SE	40.04	mixed	ceramics and ground stone fragments	7	4a - Hamlet	
78	medium	elevated plateau below Arch 08	199.92	shallow	NE	135.35	mixed	ceramics	8	3 - Farmstead	
79	small	Floodplain	205.71	shallow	SE	52.07	riverine and open wood	ceramics	12	3 - Farmstead	
80	small	Pleistocene terrace (T1)	222.95	moderate	SE	155.41	wood	ceramics		1 - Resource-processing site	
81	small	Pleistocene terrace (T1)	225.90	v steep	NE	68.78	riverine + wood	ceramics		1 - Resource-processing site	
82	small	Pleistocene terrace (T1)	266.66	v steep	NW	137.69	wood	ceramics		1 - Resource-processing site	
83	small	Pleistocene terrace (T1)	221.82	moderate	SW	173.16	wood	ceramics		1 - Resource-processing site	
84	small	Pleistocene terrace (T1)	224.00	moderate	E	178.03	wood	ceramics and ground stone fragments	>1	2 - Field house	
85	medium	Pleistocene terrace (T1)	215.35	shallow	SW	54.74	wood + bamboo	ceramics and ground stone fragments		1 - Resource-processing site	

Gazetteer of Sites

Site No.	Size of Site	Topographic context	Elevation	Slope	Simple Aspect	Proximity to Water	Simplified Vegetation Types	Surface Artifacts	Surface Features	Interpretative Site Type	Comments Regarding Artifacts: Variety, Dating
86	small	Pleistocene terrace (T1)	223.85	moderate	SW	60.46	wood + bamboo	ceramics		1 - Resource-processing site	
87	small	Pleistocene terrace (T1)	222.84	moderate	SW	118.22	wood	ceramics	>1	2 - Field house	
88	small	Pleistocene terrace (T1)	227.21	v steep	NW	128.86	field	ceramics		1 - Resource-processing site	
89	small	Floodplain	217.74	shallow	S	198.40	wood	ceramics		1 - Resource-processing site	
90	small	Pleistocene terrace (T1)	220.96	moderate	SE	79.88	wood	ceramics		1 - Resource-processing site	
91	medium	Pleistocene terrace (T1)	233.39	v steep	SE	102.15	wood	ceramics		1 - Resource-processing site	
92	medium	Floodplain	221.77	shallow	E	114.19	wood	ceramics		1 - Resource-processing site	
93	small	Floodplain	223.44	moderate	NE	43.29	wood	ceramics	>1	2 - Field house	
94	small	Floodplain	225.82	flat	SE	20.92	wood	ceramics		1 - Resource-processing site	
95	small	Floodplain	239.42	shallow	NE	343.59	field	ceramics		1 - Resource-processing site	
96	small	Floodplain	232.88	shallow	SE	140.33	wood	ceramics and ground stone fragments		1 - Resource-processing site	
97	small	Floodplain	229.14	shallow	SE	72.97	wood	ceramics	9	3 - Farmstead	
98	small	Floodplain	220.66	shallow	E	58.19	field	ceramics	5	3 - Farmstead	
99	small	Floodplain	214.42	flat	SE	81.94	field	ceramics	>1	2 - Field house	
100	small	Floodplain	215.08	shallow	NW	75.90	field	ceramics		1 - Resource-processing site	
101	small	Pleistocene terrace (T1)	220.25	shallow	SW	84.47	wood	ceramics	4	2 - Field house	
102	small	Floodplain	219.84	shallow	SW	57.49	bamboo + wood	ceramics		1 - Resource-processing site	
103	medium	Pleistocene terrace (T1)	230.43	v steep	SW	153.77	ferro-etc + wood	ceramics		1 - Resource-processing site	
104	small	Floodplain	221.94	shallow	SW	152.46	field	ceramics	3	2 - Field house	
105	small	Floodplain	214.49	shallow	SE	73.30	field	ceramics		1 - Resource-processing site	
106	small	Floodplain	220.27	shallow	SE	32.75	wood + field	ceramics and ground stone fragments	8	3 - Farmstead	
107	small	Floodplain	222.00	flat	SE	94.63	field + wood	ceramics		1 - Resource-processing site	
108	small	Pleistocene terrace (T1)	215.57	moderate	SW	43.19	wood	ceramics		1 - Resource-processing site	

Site No.	Size of Site	Topographic context	Elevation	Slope	Simple Aspect	Proximity to Water	Simplified Vegetation Types	Surface Artifacts	Surface Features	Interpretative Site Type	Comments Regarding Artifacts: Variety, Dating
109	small	Pleistocene terrace (T1)	213.86	shallow	NW	164.08	wood	ceramics		1 - Resource-processing site	
110	small	Floodplain	208.63	shallow	NW	93.08	wood	ceramics		1 - Resource-processing site	
111	small	Pleistocene terrace (T1)	210.42	shallow	NW	107.68	wood	ceramics and ground stone fragments	2	2 - Field house	
112	small	Floodplain	204.47	shallow	SW	8.61	wood + field	ceramics		1 - Resource-processing site	
113	small	Pleistocene terrace (T1)	210.26	shallow	NW	57.26	wood	ceramics		1 - Resource-processing site	
114	small	Pleistocene terrace (T1)	221.66	shallow	SE	16.84	wood	ceramics	2	2 - Field house	
115	small	elevated plateau Pleistocene terrace (T2)	257.92	moderate	SW	90.77	nd	ceramics		1 - Resource-processing site	
116	small	elevated plateau Pleistocene terrace (T2)	235.29	v steep	SW	146.09	wood	ceramics and ground stone fragments		1 - Resource-processing site	
117	small	elevated plateau Pleistocene terrace (T2)	252.00	shallow	SW	358.20	wood + ferro-etc	ceramics		1 - Resource-processing site	
118	small	elevated plateau Pleistocene terrace (T2)	165.94	shallow	SW	424.75	bamboo	ceramics	>1	2 - Field house	
119	medium	elevated plateau Pleistocene terrace (T2)	175.77	moderate	SW	280.76	bamboo + field	ceramics	4	3 - Farmstead	
120	small	Pleistocene terrace (T2)	150.27	shallow	SW	101.66	bamboo		2	2 - Field house	
121	small	Holocene Terrace (T1)	155.60	flat	SE	78.65	grass + bamboo	ceramics	0	1 - Resource-processing site	
122	medium	Pleistocene terrace (T2)	157.77	shallow	SE	53.33	bamboo + grass	ceramics and ground stone fragments	9	3 - Farmstead	

Gazetteer of Sites

Site No.	Size of Site	Topographic context	Elevation	Slope	Simple Aspect	Proximity to Water	Simplified Vegetation Types	Surface Artifacts	Surface Features	Interpretative Site Type	Comments Regarding Artifacts: Variety, Dating
123	medium	Pleistocene terrace (T2)	157.50	shallow	SE	158.58	mixed	ceramics	19	4b - Village	Has enclosure wall with niches; therefore different status?
124	medium	elevated plateau/hill-top;	130.56	shallow	SW	120.93	mixed	ceramics and ground stone fragments	8	3 - Farmstead	
125	small	Pleistocene terrace (T2)	170.28	shallow	SE	372.88	bamboo	ceramics and ground stone fragments	6	3 - Farmstead	
126	small	Pleistocene terrace (T2)	158.53	moderate	SE	197.36	bamboo	ceramics and ground stone fragments	5	3 - Farmstead	
127	small	Holocene terrace (T1)	153.95	shallow	NE	174.97	field	ceramics	6	3 - Farmstead	
128	small	elevated plateau	153.07	flat	SE	44.81	riverine	ceramics	2	2 - Field house	
129	small	elevated plateau	166.43	shallow	SW	351.19	bamboo	ceramics and ground stone fragments	2	2 - Field house	
130	small	elevated plateau	162.87	shallow	SW	145.74	bamboo + ferro-etc	ceramics and ground stone fragments	30	4a - Hamlet	
131	small	Holocene terrace (T1); summit of small hill/terrace	169.54	shallow	SE	285.94	bamboo	ceramics	4	2 - Field house	
132	small	Holocene terrace (T1)	147.77	flat	S	76.36	riverine	ceramics	2	2 - Field house	
133	small	elevated plateau Pleistocene terrace (T2)	156.50	moderate	SE	149.17	bamboo	ceramics	1	2 - Field house	
134	small	Holocene terrace (T1)	176.10	flat	SE	21.41	riverine	ceramics	1	2 - Field house	
135	small	Holocene terrace (T1)	196.43	shallow	NW	106.33	wood	ceramics	14	4a - Hamlet	
136	small	elevated plateau	193.28	shallow	SE	28.03	wood + field	ceramics and ground stone fragments	2	2 - Field house	
137	small	elevated plateau	185.86	shallow	SE	170.29	bamboo + wood	ceramics and ground stone fragments	1	2 - Field house	
138	small	Holocene terrace (T1)	192.59	shallow	SW	201.83	wood	ceramics	1	2 - Field house	
139	medium	elevated plateau	188.56	moderate	SE	60.29	mixed	ceramics and ground stone fragments	7	3 - Farmstead	

Site No.	Size of Site	Topographic context	Elevation	Slope	Simple Aspect	Proximity to Water	Simplified Vegetation Types	Surface Artifacts	Surface Features	Interpretative Site Type	Comments Regarding Artifacts: Variety, Dating
140	small	elevated plateau	202.32	moderate	SE	115.78	mixed	ceramics	3	2 - Field house	
141	medium	elevated plateau	200.24	moderate	E	46.27	bamboo	ceramics	5	3 - Farmstead	
142	small	Pleistocene terrace (T2) elevated plateau	189.71	shallow	SE	168.86	wood	ceramics	1	2 - Field house	
143	medium	Pleistocene terrace (T2) elevated plateau	207.21	moderate	SE	103.05	wood + ferro-etc	ceramics and ground stone fragments	2	2 - Field house	
144	small	elevated plateau	203.94	shallow	SE	194.13	ferro-etc + bamboo	ceramics		2 - Field house	
145	small	elevated plateau	246.01	shallow	SW	183.41	ferro-etc	ceramics		2 - Field house	
146	small	Pleistocene terrace (T2-3)	209.41	moderate	S	107.69	field	ceramics	1	1 - Resource-processing site	
147	small	Pleistocene terrace (T2-3)	221.42	shallow	SE	241.25	field	ceramics	8	3 - Farmstead	
148	small	Pleistocene terrace (T2-3)	222.72	moderate	SW	73.78	field		3 funeral features	6 - Sacred Site	Funeral features?
149	small	Pleistocene terrace (T2-3)	225.35	flat	SE	99.44	open bush/wood	ceramics and ground stone fragments	5	3 - Farmstead	
150	small	Pleistocene terrace (T2-3)	222.15	flat	SE	45.45	wood	ceramics	4	2 - Field house	
151	small	Holocene terrace (T1)	216.28	flat	SE	35.18	open bush/grassland	ceramics	6	3 - Farmstead	
152	medium	Floodplain/Holocene terrace (T1)	155.87	flat	SE	196.24	wood	ceramics	6	3 - Farmstead	
153	small	Holocene terrace (T1)	204.62	shallow	SW	103.35	field	ceramics	4	2 - Field house	
154	small	Floodplain	170.78	flat	SE	275.94	field	ceramics	2	2 - Field house	
155	small	Holocene terrace (T1)	177.84	flat	NE	148.58	wood	ceramics	3	2 - Field house	
156	v large	Pleistocene terrace (T2)	174.30	shallow	SE	161.13	open bush/wood	ceramics and ground stone fragments	65	4b - Village	
157	small	Pleistocene terrace (T2)	181.06	moderate	SE	281.34	wood	ceramics	22 - *tumuli pierre*	6 - Sacred site	Burial ground?

Gazetteer of Sites

Site No.	Size of Site	Topographic context	Elevation	Slope	Simple Aspect	Proximity to Water	Simplified Vegetation Types	Surface Artifacts	Surface Features	Interpretative Site Type	Comments Regarding Artifacts: Variety, Dating
201	small	Pleistocene terrace (T3)	141.87	flat	NW	21.23	field	sparse lithic scatter (100 x 30 m)		1 - Resource-processing site	
202	small	Pleistocene terrace (T3)	204.74	flat	W	246.10	wood	ceramic and lithic scatter plain and decorated ceramics	5 rock rings, several rock alignments, earthen berm, thermal feature (hearth?)	3 - Farmstead	
203	small	Pleistocene terrace (T2?), gravel bar	193.14	v steep	SE	27.04	bamboo + field	upper paleolithic lithic scatter (according to Masamba Lamb) basalt debitage, flaked stone axe, pestle, cores, and hammerstone		1 - Resource-processing site	
204	small	Colluvial footslope at base of hill	210.38	moderate	SE	92.67	field	upper paleolithic lithic scatter (according to Masamba Lamb) basalt- and andesite mano, hammerstones, mano/hammerstone, broken lithic tools (during manufacture)		1 - Resource-processing site	
205	small	Pleistocene terrace (T3)	197.74	shallow	W	268.55	ferro-agric + ferro-etc	agricultural clearings of surficial laterite cobbles	4 large rock piles, clearings in agricultural area (?)	1 - Resource-processing site	
206	small	Pleistocene terrace (T2)	230.29	v steep	NW	30.50	wood + grass	ceramic and lithic scatter plain and decorated ceramics, milky quartz debitage	Rock ring (burned)	2 - Field house	
207	small	Pleistocene terrace (T1)	141.03	shallow	NW	4.82	field	light lithic scatter milky quartz and greenstone debitage and blocky debris		1 - Resource-processing site	
208	small	Pleistocene terrace (T1)	149.74	shallow	NW	67.56	riverine	light lithic scatter cores, hammerstone		1 - Resource-processing site	
209	small	Pleistocene terrace (T2)	178.22	shallow	SE	26.88	riverine	light ceramic scatter plain ceramics		1 - Resource-processing site	
210	small	Pleistocene terrace (T1)	177.19	shallow	NE	92.41	riverine	ceramic scatter plain ceramics		1 - Resource-processing site	

Site No.	Size of Site	Topographic context	Elevation	Slope	Simple Aspect	Proximity to Water	Simplified Vegetation Types	Surface Artifacts	Surface Features	Interpretative Site Type	Comments Regarding Artifacts: Variety, Dating
211	small	Colluvial footslope in hills	178.71	shallow	NW	47.93	riverine	ceramic scatter plain ceramics		1 - Resource-processing site	
212	small	Alluvial fan	205.43	flat	SW	57.77	field	ceramic scatter plain and decorated ceramics, hammerstone		1 - Resource-processing site	
213	small	Colluvial footslope in hills	216.35	shallow	SE	148.79	wood + field	rock pile field plain ceramics	~ 20 rock piles (field clearing features)	1 - Resource-processing site	
214	small	Pleistocene terrace (T3)	167.21	shallow	SE	383.46	bamboo	ceramic scatter plain ceramics		1 - Resource-processing site	
215	small	Pleistocene terrace (T3)	170.64	shallow	NW	278.70	wood	ceramic scatter plain ceramics		1 - Resource-processing site	
216	small	Pleistocene terrace (T2)	151.98	shallow	NW	184.69	field	plain ceramics, quartz blocky debris scatter		1 - Resource-processing site	
217	small	Pleistocene terrace (T2)	168.26	flat	NE	241.39	field	light lithic scatter plain ceramics, large biface	Rock ring (field house?)	2 - Field house	
218	small	Colluvial footslope	151.87	shallow	SW	49.85	field	ceramic scatter, plain ceramics		1 - Resource-processing site	
220	small	Pleistocene terrace (T2)	171.16	shallow	SE	130.15	field	ceramic and lithic scatter plain ceramics, milky quartz blocky debris	Rock ring (field house?)	2 - Field house	
221	small	Pleistocene terrace (T2)	163.29	shallow	SE	72.24	field	lithic scatter greenstone core and debitage		1 - Resource-processing site	
222	small	Summit of hill	205.36	v steep	SE	175.43	wood	plain and decorated ceramics		1 - Resource-processing site	
223	small	Summit of hill	199.63	moderate	SE	116.38	bamboo	plain ceramics, basin metate fragment, hammerstone		2 - Field house	
224	small	Holocene terrace (T1)	205.98	shallow	SE	137.33	bamboo	plain and decorated ceramics, one biface		2 - Field house	
225	small	Holocene terrace (T1)	203.20	shallow	SW	23.58	field	plain and decorated ceramics		1 - Resource-processing site	
226	small	Holocene terrace (T1)	165.33	shallow	SW	29.97	field	plain ceramics		1 - Resource-processing site	
228	small	Holocene terrace (T1)	161.83	shallow	SW	43.76	mixed	plain ceramics		1 - Resource-processing site	

GAZETTEER OF SITES

Site No.	Size of Site	Topographic context	Elevation	Slope	Simple Aspect	Proximity to Water	Simplified Vegetation Types	Surface Artifacts	Surface Features	Interpretative Site Type	Comments Regarding Artifacts: Variety, Dating
227	small	Holocene terrace (T1)	171.69	flat	SW	96.80	riverine	plain ceramics, two-handed mano, white glass bead	Rock ring (field house?), rock drying rack	2 - Field house	
229	small	Holocene terrace (T1)	165.17	flat	SW	138.82	field	plain and decorated ceramics, metate and mano fragments, hammerstone		2 - Field house	
230	small	Holocene terrace (T1)	159.28	flat	SE	45.86	riverine	plain and decorated ceramics, biface, milky quartz debitage and blocky debris		2 - Field house	
231	small	Pleistocene terrace (T2)	151.74	shallow	E	24.23	field	plain and decorated ceramics		1 - Resource-processing site	
232	small	Pleistocene terrace (T2)	162.51	shallow	SW	31.77	field	plain and decorated ceramics		1 - Resource-processing site	
233	small	Pleistocene terrace (T2)	164.05	shallow	NE	39.13	riverine	plain ceramics, hammerstone, milky quartz blocky debris		2 - Field house	
236	small	Holocene terrace (T1)	141.52	flat	SE	59.79	riverine	plain and decorated ceramics		1 - Resource-processing site	
237	small	Holocene terrace (T1)	183.82	flat	SW	33.90	field	plain and decorated ceramics		1 - Resource-processing site	
238	small	Holocene terrace (T1)	187.57	flat	NW	168.84	field	plain and decorated ceramics	Rock ring (incomplete)	2 - Field house	
239	small	Holocene terrace (T1)	187.50	flat	SW	198.12	field	plain and decorated ceramics		1 - Resource-processing site	
240	small	Holocene terrace (T1)	190.27	shallow	NE	96.97	wood	plain and decorated ceramics	Possible rock ring, rock alignment (agricultural?)	2 - Field house	
241	small	Holocene terrace (T1)	203.46	moderate	NW	190.44	wood	plain and decorated ceramics, mano fragment		2 - Field house	
242	small	Holocene terrace (T1)	190.36	flat	SW	50.27	field	plain and decorated ceramics		1 - Resource-processing site	
243	small	Pleistocene terrace (T2)	193.74	shallow	SE	124.32	wood	plain and decorated ceramics	~10 rock rings, 3 baobab trees and 1 mango tree; abandoned about 10 years ago according to Sadio Daniokho of Sabodala	4a - Hamlet	

235

Site No.	Size of Site	Topographic context	Elevation	Slope	Simple Aspect	Proximity to Water	Simplified Vegetation Types	Surface Artifacts	Surface Features	Interpretative Site Type	Comments Regarding Artifacts: Variety, Dating
244	small	Pleistocene terrace (T3)	199.05	shallow	SW	158.61	ferro-etc + ferro-agric	plain and decorated ceramics		1 - Resource-processing site	
245	small	Backslope with laterite lag deposits	188.47	shallow	SW	129.66	ferro-etc	plain and decorated ceramics		1 - Resource-processing site	
246	small	Holocene terrace (T1)	201.02	shallow	SE	6.78	wood	plain and decorated ceramics		1 - Resource-processing site	
247	small	Buried ~50–60 cm in Holocene terrace (T1) fill	192.93	shallow	SW	3.53	riverine	plain and decorated ceramics		1 - Resource-processing site	
248	small	Holocene terrace (T1)	183.16	flat	NE	8.80	field	plain ceramics, milky quartz blocky debris	Rock ring	2 - Field house	
249	small	Holocene terrace (T1)	176.47	flat	SE	49.91	grass	plain ceramics		1 - Resource-processing site	
250	small	Holocene terrace (T1)	169.34	flat	SE	263.06	nd	plain ceramics, ceramic couscous cooker, metal basin-shaped cooking pan with handles	5 rock rings, 4 rock piles (hearths?), 3 rock alignments (~1.2-1.5 m long check dams)	3 - Farmstead	
251	small	Pleistocene terrace (T2)	179.06	moderate	NE	41.97	riverine	plain and decorated ceramics		1 - Resource-processing site	
252	small	Footslope at base of hill	171.83	moderate	NE	33.41	field	plain and decorated ceramics, metal hoe		1 - Resource-processing site	
253	small	Pleistocene alluvial fan	177.14	shallow	SE	70.93	field	plain and decorated ceramics	2 rock rings (one is burned)	2 - Field house	
254	small	Pediment at base of hill	218.12	shallow	NE	112.68	bamboo + field	decorated ceramics	Rock ring	2 - Field house	
255	small	Footslope at base of hill	209.55	shallow	SE	69.77	field	plain ceramics	Rock ring	2 - Field house	
256	small	Holocene terrace (T1)	212.30	flat	SE	54.31	field	plain ceramics, biface	2 rock rings (both burned)	2 - Field house	
257	small	Holocene terrace (T1)	193.17	shallow	NE	33.44	field	plain and decorated ceramics		1 - Resource-processing site	
258	small	Holocene terrace (T1)	194.72	flat	NE	30.04	field	decorated ceramics	Rock ring, rock drying rack	2 - Field house	
259	small	Footslope at base of hill	185.65	shallow	NE	58.56	riverine + ferro-etc	no ceramics observed	3 rock rings	2 - Field house	
260	small	Holocene terrace (T1)	143.23	flat	SE	49.03	bamboo	plain ceramics, milky quartz blocky debris		1 - Resource-processing site	

Gazetteer of Sites

Site No.	Size of Site	Topographic context	Elevation	Slope	Simple Aspect	Proximity to Water	Simplified Vegetation Types	Surface Artifacts	Surface Features	Interpretative Site Type	Comments Regarding Artifacts: Variety, Dating
261	small	Pleistocene terrace (T2)	149.36	flat	SE	265.87	bamboo	plain and decorated ceramics		1 - Resource-processing site	
262	small	Holocene terrace (T1)	143.76	shallow	SE	217.20	field	plain and decorated ceramics, iron hoe and wooden shaft		1 - Resource-processing site	
263	small	Pleistocene terrace (T2)	178.32	flat	NW	571.91	nd	plain and decorated ceramics	Rock alignment (~2 m long check dam), 2 rock drying racks	1 - Resource-processing site	
265	small	Pleistocene terrace (T2)	155.59	flat	SE	41.52	field	plain ceramics, stone axe	~20 rock drying racks	1 - Resource-processing site	
266	small	Pleistocene terrace (T3)	176.28	shallow	NW	67.05	wood	plain ceramics, milky quartz blocky debris		1 - Resource-processing site	
267	small	Rock hill top	137.91	shallow	NW	272.15	wood	decorated ceramics, iron axe		1 - Resource-processing site	
268	small	Footslope at base of hill	183.74	moderate	SW	210.47	wood	plain and decorated ceramics		1 - Resource-processing site	
269	small	Pleistocene terrace (T2)	179.28	flat	SE	31.00	field	plain and decorated ceramics	4 rock rings	2 - Field house	
270	small	Holocene terrace (T1)	209.75	flat	SW	93.22	wood	plain and decorated ceramics	2 rock rings (both burned)	2 - Field house	
271	small	Holocene terrace (T1)	208.61	flat	NW	24.13	wood	plain and decorated ceramics		1 - Resource-processing site	
272	small	Summit of low hill	214.16	moderate	W	108.53	field	plain and decorated ceramics		1 - Resource-processing site	
273	small	Pleistocene terrace (T2)	219.08	flat	NE	156.01	field	plain and decorated ceramics	rock ring (burned)	2 - Field house	
274	small	Pleistocene terrace (T2)	211.03	shallow	SE	61.73	grass	plain and decorated ceramics	Rock alignment (function undetermined)	1 - Resource-processing site	
275	small	Pleistocene terrace (T2)	210.93	shallow	NE	77.87	field	plain and decorated ceramics	Rock ring (burned), burned circular structure w/o rocks	1 - Resource-processing site	
276	small	Pleistocene terrace (T2)	210.78	flat	NE	9.35	grass	plain and decorated ceramics		1 - Resource-processing site	
277	small	Pleistocene terrace (T2)	207.95	moderate	SW	101.83	field	plain and decorated ceramics	4 rock rings, 2 burned circular structures w/o rocks	2 - Field house	

Site No.	Size of Site	Topographic context	Elevation	Slope	Simple Aspect	Proximity to Water	Simplified Vegetation Types	Surface Artifacts	Surface Features	Interpretative Site Type	Comments Regarding Artifacts: Variety, Dating
278	small	Colluvial footslope at base of low hill	212.38	moderate	SE	50.16	field	plain and decorated ceramics	Rock ring (burned), burned circular structure w/o rocks	2 - Field house	
279	small	Colluvial footslope at base of hill	216.76	shallow	SE	16.53	field	plain and decorated ceramics, metate fragment	2 agricultural rock alignments (1 ~2.5 m and 1 ~1.5 m long)	1 - Resource-processing site	
280	small	Finger ridge (interfluve) in hills	198.64	shallow	NE	26.48	wood	plain and decorated ceramics		1 - Resource-processing site	
281	small	Juncture of colluvial footslope and Holocene terrace (T1)	194.69	shallow	SE	102.57	wood	plain ceramics		1 - Resource-processing site	
282	small	Pleistocene terrace (T2)	213.66	flat	NW	25.66	field	plain and decorated ceramics	2 rock drying racks	1 - Resource-processing site	
283	small	Pleistocene terrace (T2)	217.42	shallow	SE	91.55	field	plain and decorated ceramics		1 - Resource-processing site	
284	small	Holocene terrace (T1)	222.17	flat	SW	6.20	field + wood	plain ceramics	Rock drying rack	1 - Resource-processing site	
285	small	Holocene terrace (T1)	227.43	flat	NW	42.35	wood	plain and decorated ceramics, metal spoon/fork fragment, metal ring for planting crops (?), tin can top, palm stool.	8 rock rings (all burned); village abandoned 6–7 years ago according to Sadio Daniokho of Sabodala	3 - Farmstead	
286	small	Pediment at base of hill and summit of small hill	213.37	shallow	NE	219.55	nd	plain and decorated ceramics		1 - Resource-processing site	
287	small	Pediment	206.64	shallow	NW	119.41	nd	plain and decorated ceramics	Rock ring (only ~2 m in diameter)	2 - Field house	
288	small	Pediment	193.20	flat	NE	155.85	field	no artifacts observed	Rock drying rack	1 - Resource-processing site	
289	small	Pleistocene terrace (T4)	180.88	flat	SW	343.31	nd	plain and decorated ceramics	Rectangular rock pile (~3 by 2 m; possible burial)	6 - Sacred Site	Burial cairn.

Gazetteer of Sites

Site No.	Size of Site	Topographic context	Elevation	Slope	Simple Aspect	Proximity to Water	Simplified Vegetation Types	Surface Artifacts	Surface Features	Interpretative Site Type	Comments Regarding Artifacts: Variety, Dating
290	small	Pleistocene terrace (T4) at possible former spring head	179.31	shallow	SW	30.07	wood	ceramic scatter		1 - Resource-processing site	
291	small	Pleistocene terrace (T3)	161.64	moderate	SE	48.61	riverine	plain and decorated, milky quartz debitage and blocky debris		1 - Resource-processing site	
292	small	Pleistocene terrace (T2)	163.19	shallow	NE	53.18	wood	plain ceramics, milky quartz debitage		1 - Resource-processing site	
293	small	Pleistocene terrace (T2)	163.15	flat	NW	10.51	wood	plain and decorated ceramics		1 - Resource-processing site	
294	small	Pleistocene terrace (T2)	165.00	flat	NW	36.79	wood	decorated ceramics, ground axe fragment, flaked stone axe, milky quartz blocky debris		1 - Resource-processing site	
295	small	Saddle of high ridge, ~25 m above surrounding terrain	211.34	shallow	SW	200.82	wood	plain and decorated ceramics	2 rock rings (both unburned, one is incomplete)	2 - Field house	
296	small	Pediment on footslope below high hill	212.13	shallow	SW	61.15	wood	plain and decorated ceramics		1 - Resource-processing site	
297	small	Colluvial footslope at base of hill	204.88	shallow	E	55.20	field	farmstead (former village of Bangouraya) plain and decorated ceramics (abundant)	1–2 rock rings (unburned and incomplete rings; others may be present); inhabitants moved to Faloumbou according to Sadio Daniokho of Sabodala	4a - Hamlet	
298	small	Holocene floodplain (T0) to Holocene terrace (T1)	200.74	shallow	NE	37.88	wood	plain and decorated ceramics		1 - Resource-processing site	
299	small	Holocene terrace (T1)	198.76	flat	SE	100.54	wood	plain ceramics		1 - Resource-processing site	

Site No.	Size of Site	Topographic context	Elevation	Slope	Simple Aspect	Proximity to Water	Simplified Vegetation Types	Surface Artifacts	Surface Features	Interpretative Site Type	Comments Regarding Artifacts: Variety, Dating
300	small	Holocene terrace (T1)	177.55	flat	SE	50.85	field	plain and decorated ceramics		1 - Resource-processing site	
301	small	Holocene floodplain (T0)	178.78	flat	E	20.88	field	plain ceramics	Rock drying rack	1 - Resource-processing site	
302	small		176.94	shallow	SE	166.45	wood				
303	small		149.32	flat	SW	5.60	riverine			1 - Resource-processing site	

Note: This gazetteer of sites lists all the sites discovered in 2009 and 2010. The information recorded during the reconnaissance survey in 2009 contains only location point data and a very brief free-text comment. In 2010 all sites discovered were recorded in greater, but not uniform detail about the site as an entity and about its constituent parts (see Appendix B).

Appendix B

Gazetteer of Features and Sites

Feature No.	Feature Type Name	Interpretive Feature Type	Comment
		Site 1	
1	cup	cup	cup/cupules in laterite
2	cup	cup	cup
3	cup	cup	cup, 60-cm diameter
4	cup	cup	cup, 30-cm oval
5	cup	cup	cup, oval, 50 cm
6	cup	cup	cup, 25-cm circle
7	cup	cup	pit, 30 cm
8	cup	cup	cup, 40-cm oval
9	cup	cup	irregular oval, max 45 cm
10	cup	cup	cup, deep oval, 35 cm
11	cup	cup	cup, 25-cm oval
12	cup	cup	cup, 25 cm
13	cup	cup	irregular cup, max 40 cm
14	cup	cup	cup, 45-cm oval
15	cup	cup	cup pair?, 30 cm
16	cup	cup	cup pair, 40-cm max
17	cup	cup	small, 15-cm cup
18	cup	cup	small, 15-cm cup
19	cup	cup	pair cups, max 40 cm
20	cup	cup	small,15-cm cup
21	cup	cup	oval 45-cm cup
22	cup	cup	cup, 20 cm
23	cup	cup	oval cup, 20 cm
24	cup	cup	cup, 50 cm
25	cup	cup	shallow oval, 25 cm
26	cup	cup	deep oval cup, 40 cm by 20 cm deep
27	cup	cup	circle cup, 45-cm diameter by 25 cm deep
28	cup	cup	cup, 30-cm diameter by 15 cm deep
29	cup	cup	cup, 70-cm diameter by 40 cm deep
30	cup	cup	oval cup, 50 cm by 25 cm deep
31	cup	cup	cup, 40-cm diameter by 20 cm deep
32	cup	cup	cup, 20 cm by 10 cm deep
33	cup	cup	cup, 30-cm diameter by 25 cm deep
34	cup	cup	cup, 20-cm diameter by 15 cm deep
35	cup	cup	cup, 35-cm diameter by 20 cm deep
36	cup	cup	cup, 3 conjoined, max 50 cm by 25 cm deep
37	cup	cup	cup oval, 40 cm by 20 cm deep
38	cup	cup	cup, 40 cm by 15 cm deep
39	cup	cup	cup, 20-cm diameter by 10 cm deep
40	cup	cup	cup, 20-cm diameter by 10 cm deep
41	cup	cup	cup, 40-cm oval, 20 cm deep
42	cup	cup	cup, 15 cm by 10 cm
43	cup	cup	cup, 20 cm by 15 cm
44	cup	cup	cup, 40 cm by 25 cm
45	cup	cup	pair cups, 60 cm by 30 cm deep
46	cup	cup	oval, 40 by 30 by 30 cm deep
47	cup	cup	very large oval, 1,100 mm by 60 cm by 50 cm deep
48	cup	cup	circle cup, 50 cm by 30 cm deep
49	cup	cup	circle cup, 30 cm by 20 cm
50	cup	cup	cup, 60-cm diameter by 40 cm deep
51	cup	cup	oval cup, 40 cm by 30 cm by 25 cm deep
52	cup	cup	oval cup, 60 cm by 30 cm by 30 cm deep
53	cup	cup	cup, 50-cm diameter by 40 cm deep

Feature No.	Feature Type Name	Interpretive Feature Type	Comment
54	cup	cup	oval, 40 by 30 cm by 20 cm deep
55	cup	cup	pair conjoined, max 70 by 70 cm by 40 cm deep
56	cup	cup	pit, 33-cm diameter, 20 cm deep
57	cup	cup	small, 20-cm diameter by 10 cm deep
Site 8			
1	burial	burial	
2	burial	burial	
3	stone circle	stone circle	
4	stone circle	stone circle	
5	stone circle	stone circle	
6	stone circle	stone circle	
7	stone circle	stone circle	
8	stone circle	stone circle	
9	stone circle	stone circle	
10	stone circle	stone circle	
11	stone square	stone square	
12	burial	burial	
13	burial	burial	
14	stone circle	stone circle	
15	furnace?	stone circle	
16	stone circle	stone circle	
17	stone circle	stone circle	
18	stone circle	stone circle	
19	stone circle	stone circle	
20	stone circle	stone circle	
25	stone circle	stone circle	
26	burial	burial	
27	burial	burial	
28	burial	burial	
29	burial	burial	
30	burial	burial	
31	burial	burial	
32	stone square	stone square	
33	stone circle	stone circle	
35	stone square	stone square	
36	stone circle	stone circle	
51	stone circle	stone circle	
52	stone circle	stone circle	
53	stone circle	stone circle	
55	artifact concentration	artifact concentration	
56	stone square	stone square	
62	stone alignment	stone alignment	rock alignment/possible burial
63	artifact concentration	artifact concentration	
64	stone circle	stone circle	
Site 9			
1	stone alignment	stone alignment	rock alignment/possible burial
2	stone circle	stone circle	stone circle, 6.4-m diameter
3	stone circle	stone circle	stone circle full of daub, part destroyed by haul road
4	stone circle	stone circle	site of stone circle full of daub
5	stone circle	stone circle	stone circle full of daub
6	stone circle	stone circle	stone circle full of daub
7	stone circle	stone circle	stone circle full of daub
Site 11			
1	stone circle	stone circle	stone circle with daub, pot in situ
2	stone circle	stone circle	stone circle with daub
3	stone circle	stone circle	stone circle with daub
4	stone circle	stone circle	stone circle, no daub
5	stone circle	stone circle	stone circle with daub
6	stone circle	stone circle	stone circle, no daub

Gazetteer of Features and Sites

Feature No.	Feature Type Name	Interpretive Feature Type	Comment
7	stone circle	stone circle	stone circle, small, no daub
8	stone circle	stone circle	stone circle with daub
9	stone circle	stone circle	stone circle with daub
10	stone circle	stone circle	stone circle, 4-m diameter
11	stone circle	stone circle	stone circle, 2.5-m diameter
		Site 57	
1	stone circle	stone circle	rock ring
2	stone circle	stone circle	rock ring in brush
3	stone circle	stone circle	rock ring
4	stone circle	stone circle	250-cm-diameter rock ring
5	stone circle	stone circle	rock ring, 280-cm diameter
6	stone circle	stone circle	small rock ring, 120-cm
		Site 64	
1	stone circle	stone circle	rock ring, 260-cm diameter
2	stone circle	stone circle	rock pile, 190-cm diameter
3	stone circle	stone circle	possible ring, 310-cm diameter
		Site 65	
1	stone circle	stone circle	
2	stone circle	stone circle	
3	stone circle	stone circle	area of burned mud from walls
		Site 69	
1	stone circle	stone circle	rock ring, 270 cm
		Site 71	
1	stone circle	stone circle	rock ring, 320-cm diameter
4	stone circle	stone circle	stone circle, 2-m diameter
5	stone alignment	stone alignment	stone oval, 2 by 1 m
6	stone circle	stone circle	stone circle, 5-m diameter
7	stone circle	stone circle	stone circle, 2.5-m diameter
8	stone circle	stone circle	stone circle, 3-m diameter
9	stone circle	stone circle	stone circle, 1.8-m diameter
10	stone alignment	stone alignment	reverse L in rock lines, 4 m long
11	stone alignment	stone alignment	stone alignment, 2.5 m
13	stone circle	stone circle	stone-filled circle, 2-m diameter
15	stone circle	stone circle	stone-filled circle, 2-m diameter
16	stone cairn	stone alignment	stone oval, 1.2 m by 0.8 m
17	stone alignment	stone alignment	rock alignment, 2 m by 0.5 m
18	stone square	stone square	stone feature, 1-by-0.5-m rectangle
19	stone square	stone square	stone rectangle, 1 by 0.75 m
20	stone alignment	stone alignment	rock alignment, 2 by 1 m nw-se
21	stone cairn	stone alignment	stone oval, 1 by 2 m
23	stone alignment	stone alignment	stone alignment, 1.5 by 0.7 m
30	stone alignment	stone alignment	rock alignment, 2 by 0.5 m
32	stone alignment	stone alignment	rock alignment
33a	stone square	stone square	stone; 4 stones
33b	stone circle	stone circle	stone circle, 2.75-m diameter
34	stone circle	stone circle	stone circle, 3.5 m with daub
35	stone circle	stone circle	stone ring, 2-m diameter
36	stone circle	stone circle	stone ring, 2-m diameter
37	stone square	stone square	stone square, 1.8 by 2 m
38	stone circle	stone circle	stone ring, 3-m diameter
39	stone alignment	stone alignment	rock alignment, 1 by 2 m
40	stone circle	stone circle	rock ring, 3-m diameter
41	stone circle	stone circle	rock ring, 3-m diameter
42	stone circle	stone circle	rock ring, 3-m diameter
43	stone circle	stone circle	rock ring, 3-m diameter
44	stone circle	stone circle	rock ring, 2.5-m diameter, with daub
45	stone circle	stone circle	rock ring, 2.8-m diameter
46	stone circle	stone circle	rock ring, 2.5-m diameter
47	stone alignment	stone alignment	rock alignment, 1.2 by 0.8 m
48	stone cairn	stone alignment	rock cairn, 1.2 by 0.8 m

Feature No.	Feature Type Name	Interpretive Feature Type	Comment
49	stone cairn	stone alignment	rock cairn, 1.2 by 0.8 m
50	stone alignment	stone alignment	rock alignment a/arc, 2 by 0.9 m
51	stone circle	stone circle	rock ring, 4-m diameter
52	stone circle	stone circle	stone circle, 3-m diameter
53	stone circle	stone circle	rock ring, 3-m diameter
54	stone cairn	stone alignment	rock cairn, 1 by 0.8 m
55	stone cairn	stone alignment	rock cairn, 1 by 1 m
56	stone cairn	stone alignment	rock cairn, 2 by 1 m
57	stone cairn	stone alignment	rock cairn, 1.2 by 0.8 m
58	stone cairn	stone alignment	rock cairn, 1 by 1 m
59	stone cairn	stone alignment	rock cairn, 2 by 1 m
60	stone cairn	stone alignment	rock cairn, 1.5 by 0.8 m
61	stone square	stone square	rock rectangle, 1.2 by 2.5 m
62	stone circle	stone circle	rock ring, 3.8-m diameter
63	stone cairn	stone alignment	rock cairn, 1.2 by 0.8 m
64	stone circle	stone circle	rock ring, 3-m diameter
65	stone circle	stone circle	rock ring, 1.5-m diameter
66	stone alignment	stone alignment	rock cairn, 1 by 2 m
67	stone circle	stone circle	rock ring, 2.5-m diameter
68	stone circle	stone circle	rock ring, 2.75-m diameter
69	stone circle	stone circle	stone ring, 2-m diameter
70	stone circle	stone circle	rock ring, 3-m diameter
71	stone circle	stone circle	stone ring, 3-m diameter
72	stone circle	stone circle	stone ring, 1.5-m diameter
73	stone circle	stone circle	stone ring, 1.8-m diameter
74	stone circle	stone circle	stone ring, 2-m diameter
75	stone circle	stone circle	stone ring, 3-m diameter
76	stone circle	stone circle	stone ring, 3.2-m diameter
77	stone alignment	stone alignment	rock alignment, 1.5 by .5 m
78	stone circle	stone circle	rock ring, 1.8-m diameter
79	stone circle	stone circle	rock ring, 1.5-m diameter
80	stone circle	stone circle	rock ring, 2.8-m diameter
82	stone circle	stone circle	rock ring, 3.2-m diameter
83	stone circle	stone circle	rock circle pile, 2-m diameter
84	stone alignment	stone alignment	rock alignment, 1.5 by 1 m
85	stone alignment	stone alignment	rock alignment, 2 rows by 5 stones, 1.2 by 0.75 m
86	stone alignment	stone alignment	rock alignment/oval, 1.5 by 0.8 m
87	stone alignment	stone alignment	rock oval, 2 m by 1 m
88	stone alignment	stone alignment	2 by rock alignments, each 1.8 by 1 m
89	stone alignment	stone alignment	rock alignment, 2 by 0.8 m
91	stone square	stone square	rock square, 3 rows 5 stones
91a	stone alignment	stone alignment	rock alignment/oval, 2 by 0.9 m
92	stone alignment	stone alignment	rock line
93	stone circle	stone circle	rock ring, 3.5-m diameter
94	stone square	stone square	rock pavement 1 by 2 m
95	stone circle	stone circle	rock ring, 2-m diameter
96	stone alignment	stone alignment	rock oval, 2 by 1 m
97	stone square	stone square	rock rectangle, 2.5 by 1.2 m
98	stone cairn	stone alignment	rock cairn, 2 by 1 m
99	stone square	stone square	rock rectangle, 3 rows 5 stones
99	stone square	stone square	rock rectangle, 3 rows 5 stones
100	stone alignment	stone alignment	rock alignment, 2 by 1 m
101	stone square	stone square	square rock room, 3.5 m square
102	stone alignment	stone alignment	rock oval, 1 by 2 m
103	stone alignment	stone alignment	rock oval, 1 by 2 m
104	stone square	stone square	3 rows of 6, 4 and 5 stones
105	stone alignment	stone alignment	rock oval, 2 by 1.2 m
105	stone square	stone square	3 rows of stones: 5, 5, and 3
107	stone alignment	stone alignment	rock oval, 1.5 by 0.8 m

Gazetteer of Features and Sites

Feature No.	Feature Type Name	Interpretive Feature Type	Comment
108	stone alignment	stone alignment	rock ovals?, 2 by 3 m
Site 77			
1	stone circle	stone circle	rock ring, 300 cm
2	stone circle	stone circle	rock ring, 320 cm
3	stone circle	stone circle	rock ring, 290 cm
4	stone circle	stone circle	rock ring, 230 cm
5	stone circle	stone circle	rock ring, 300 cm
6	stone circle	stone circle	rock ring, 280 cm
7	stone circle	stone circle	rock ring, 280 cm
8	stone circle	stone circle	rock ring, 260 cm
9	stone circle	stone circle	rock ring, 310 cm
10	stone circle	stone circle	rock ring, 260 cm
11	stone circle	stone circle	rock ring, 260 cm
12	stone circle	stone circle	rock ring, 290 cm
13	stone circle	stone circle	rock ring, 285 cm
14	stone circle	stone circle	rock ring, 280 cm
15	stone circle	stone circle	ring w/o rocks only daub, 270 cm
16	stone circle	stone circle	rock ring, 370 cm
17	stone circle	stone circle	rock ring, 350 cm
18	stone circle	stone circle	rock ring, 280 cm
19	stone circle	stone circle	rock ring, 400 cm, another nearby
20	stone circle	stone circle	rock ring, 300 cm
21	stone circle	stone circle	circular feature, burnt daub
22	stone circle	stone circle	circular feature, burnt daub
23	stone circle	stone circle	stone circle, raised daub interior
24	stone circle	stone circle	stone circle near contemporary hut
25	stone circle	stone circle	stone circle near contemporary hut
26	stone circle	stone circle	stone circle with daub near contemporary hut
27	stone circle	stone circle	stone circle, 3-m diameter with daub.
28	stone circle	stone circle	stone circle with daub, 2.75-m diameter.
29	stone circle	stone circle	stone circle, 2.5-m diameter with daub
30	stone circle	stone circle	stone circle, 2.8-m diameter no daub
31	stone circle	stone circle	stone circle, 2.75-m diameter, no daub
32	stone circle	stone circle	
Site 78			
1	stone circle	stone circle	stone circles with daub
2	stone circle	stone circle	stone circle, 3.4 m with daub
3	stone circle	stone circle	stone circles no daub
4	stone circle	stone circle	stone circle, no daub 3.2-m diameter
5	stone alignment	stone alignment	rock alignment
6	stone alignment	stone alignment	rock alignment
7	stone alignment	stone alignment	rock alignment
8	stone alignment	stone alignment	rock alignment
9	stone alignment	stone alignment	rock alignment
10	stone alignment	stone alignment	rock alignment
11	stone alignment	stone alignment	rock alignment
12	stone alignment	stone alignment	rock alignment
13	stone alignment	stone alignment	rock alignment
14	stone alignment	stone alignment	rock alignment
15	stone alignment	stone alignment	rock alignment
16	stone alignment	stone alignment	rock alignment
17	stone alignment	stone alignment	rock alignment
18	stone alignment	stone alignment	rock alignment
19	stone alignment	stone alignment	rock alignment
20	stone alignment	stone alignment	rock alignment
21	stone alignment	stone alignment	rock alignment
22	stone alignment	stone alignment	rock alignment
Site 79			
1	stone circle	stone circle	daub but no stone circle
2	stone circle	stone circle	stone circle with daub, 2.8-m diameter

Feature No.	Feature Type Name	Interpretive Feature Type	Comment
3	stone circle	stone circle	stone circle with daub, 2.7-m diameter
4	stone circle	stone circle	stone circle
5	stone circle	stone circle	stone circle, 3-m diameter
6	stone circle	stone circle	stone circle, 3-m diameter
7	stone circle	stone circle	stone circle, 3-m diameter
8	stone circle	stone circle	stone circle with daub, 3.2-m diameter
9	stone circle	stone circle	stone circle, 2-m diameter
10	stone circle	stone circle	stone circle, 2.2-m diameter
11	stone circle	stone circle	stone circle, no daub 2 5-m diameter
Site 120			
1	stone circle	stone circle	
2	stone circle	stone circle	rock ring
Site 122			
1	stone circle	stone circle	rock ring, 2 m
2	stone circle	stone circle	rock ring, 180-cm diameter
3	stone circle	stone circle	rock ring, 230-cm diameter
4	stone circle	stone circle	rock ring, 180 cm
5	stone circle	stone circle	rock ring, 250 cm
6	stone circle	stone circle	rock pile, 170 cm
7	stone circle	stone circle	rock ring, 250 cm
8	stone circle	stone circle	rock pile, 140 cm
9	stone square	stone square	rock square, 230 by 160 cm
Site 123			
1	stone circle	stone circle	rock ring, 250 cm
2	stone circle	stone circle	rock ring, 250 cm
3	stone circle	stone circle	rock ring, 160-cm diameter
4	stone circle	stone circle	rock ring, 500-cm diameter
5	stone circle	stone circle	rock ring, 190 cm
6	stone circle	stone circle	rock ring, 240 cm
7	stone circle	stone circle	rock ring, 300 cm
8	stone circle	stone circle	rock ring, 240 cm
9	stone circle	stone circle	rock ring, 300 cm
10	stone circle	stone circle	rock ring, 300 cm
11	stone circle	stone circle	rock ring, 250 cm
12	stone circle	stone circle	rock ring, 300 cm
14	stone circle	stone circle	rock ring, 330 cm
14	stone circle	stone circle	rock ring, 310 cm
15	stone circle	stone circle	rock ring, 300 cm
16	stone circle	stone circle	rock ring, 330 cm
17	stone circle	stone circle	rock ring, 230 cm
18	stone alignment	stone alignment	stone alignment, 45 by 60 m
19	stone circle	stone circle	rock ring, 290 cm
20	stone circle	stone circle	rock ring, 270 cm
100	stone circle	stone circle	stone circle, 3.2-m diameter
101	artifact concentration	artifact concentration	granite grinding stone
102	stone circle	stone circle	stone circle, 3-m diameter
105	stone circle	stone circle	stone circle, 3.3-m diameter
106	stone circle	stone circle	stone circle, 3.4-m diameter
106	stone circle	stone circle	house debris, fired wattle and daub
107	stone circle	stone circle	stone circle, 3-m diameter
110	stone square	stone square	stone square, 5 m
111	stone circle	stone circle	dense 3-m diameter scatter, burnt wattle and daub
112	stone circle	stone circle	stone circle, 3-m diameter inside enclosure
113	stone circle	stone circle	stone circle, 3-m diameter inside enclosure
114	artifact concentration	artifact concentration	ground stone quern
116	stone circle	stone circle	stone circle, 2.8-m diameter
117	stone circle	stone circle	circle feature possible well
118	stone circle	stone circle	stone circle, 3-m diameter
119	stone circle	stone circle	hut circle of daub, no stones
121	stone circle	stone circle	stone set, 1-m diameter

Gazetteer of Features and Sites

Feature No.	Feature Type Name	Interpretive Feature Type	Comment
122	stone circle	stone circle	stone circle, 3-m diameter
123	stone square	stone square	stone set, 1.5 m
		Site 124	
1	burial	burial	possible grave, 310 by 210 cm
2	stone circle	stone circle	rock arch, 390 cm long
3	stone circle	stone circle	small rock arc, 170 cm long
4	stone circle	stone circle	large rock arc, 820 cm
5	stone square	stone square	rock 'floor,' 230 by 110 cm
6	stone circle	stone circle	rock arch, 520 cm
7	artifact concentration	artifact concentration	
8	artifact concentration	artifact concentration	
		Site 125	
1	stone alignment	stone alignment	rock feature
2	stone alignment	stone alignment	rock pile
3	stone alignment	stone alignment	rock pile, 180-cm diameter
4	stone circle	stone circle	rock ring, 220-cm diameter
5	stone alignment	stone alignment	rock pile, 180-cm diameter
6	stone circle	stone circle	rock ring, 520-cm diameter
		Site 126	
1	stone circle	stone circle	rock ring, 125-cm diameter
2	stone circle	stone circle	rock pile/ring, 125-cm diameter
3	stone circle	stone circle	rock ring, 260-cm diameter
4	stone circle	stone circle	rock ring, 380-cm diameter
5	stone circle	stone circle	rock ring, 250-cm diameter
		Site 127	
1	stone circle	stone circle	possible structure, mud remains, 440 cm
2	stone square	stone square	rectangle, 190 by 350
3	stone circle	stone circle	daub circle, 400-cm diameter
4	stone square	stone square	rock square, 250 by 250 cm
5	stone square	stone square	rock square, 270 by 250 cm
6	stone square	stone square	rock square, 250 by 250 cm
		Site 128	
1	stone square	stone square	rock square, 200 by 200 cm
2	stone square	stone square	rock square, 250 by 200 cm
		Site 129	
1	stone circle	stone circle	rock ring, 350-cm diameter
		Site 130	
1	stone circle	stone circle	rock ring, 300-cm diameter
2	stone square	stone square	stone square
3	stone circle	stone circle	rock ring, 200-cm diameter
4	stone circle	stone circle	rock ring and wall, 350 by 250 cm
5	stone circle	stone circle	stone circle, 250-cm diameter
6	stone circle	stone circle	stone circle, 3.5-m diameter
7	stone square	stone square	stone square
8	stone alignment	stone alignment	rock alignment/possible burial
9	stone alignment	stone alignment	rock alignment, 145 cm
10	stone alignment	stone alignment	rock alignments
11	stone alignment	stone alignment	rock alignment/possible burial
12	stone circle	stone circle	rock ring, 350-cm diameter
13	stone circle	stone circle	rock ring, 320-cm diameter
14	stone circle	stone circle	rock ring, 350-cm diameter, no photo
100	stone circle	stone circle	stone circle, 3-m diameter
101	stone circle	stone circle	stone circle, 3-m diameter
103	stone circle	stone circle	stone circle, 3.5-m diameter
105	stone alignment	stone alignment	rock alignment
106	stone alignment	stone alignment	rock alignment
107	stone alignment	stone alignment	rock alignment
108	stone alignment	stone alignment	rock features
109	stone circle	stone circle	rock circle
110	stone alignment	stone alignment	rock alignment

Feature No.	Feature Type Name	Interpretive Feature Type	Comment
111	stone circle	stone circle	stone circle
112	stone circle	stone circle	stone circle
114	stone alignment	stone alignment	rock alignment
115	stone circle	stone circle	stone circle, 2-m diameter
116	stone alignment	stone alignment	rock alignment/possible burial
116	stone alignment	stone alignment	rock alignment near Feature 2
118	stone alignment	stone alignment	rock alignment
Site 131			
1	stone circle	stone circle	330-cm diameter
2	stone circle	stone circle	rock ring, 140-cm diameter
3	stone circle	stone circle	370-cm diameter
4	stone circle	stone circle	rock ring, 270-cm diameter
Site 132			
1	artifact concentration	artifact concentration	ceramic scatter, 15 by 20 m
2	stone circle	stone circle	burned daub, 200 cm
Site 133			
1	stone circle	stone circle	rock ring, 230 cm
Site 134			
1	stone circle	stone circle	rock ring, 240 cm
Site 135			
1	stone alignment	stone alignment	rock pile, 150 by 130
2	stone circle	stone circle	rock pile, 100 cm
3	stone alignment	stone alignment	rock pile, disturbed, 210 by 130 cm
4	stone circle	stone circle	rock ring, 380 cm
5	stone circle	stone circle	rock pile, 150 cm
6	stone circle	stone circle	rock ring, 260 cm
7	stone circle	stone circle	rock pile, 100 cm
8	stone alignment	stone alignment	rock alignment, 170 by 130 cm
9	stone circle	stone circle	half rock ring, 170-cm diameter
10	stone circle	stone circle	half rock ring, 120-cm diameter
11	stone alignment	stone alignment	rock alignment, 260 cm
12	stone circle	stone circle	rock ring, 180 cm
13	stone alignment	stone alignment	rock alignment, 230 cm
14	stone circle	stone circle	rock ring, 480 cm
Site 136			
1	stone circle	stone circle	rock ring, 420 cm
2	stone circle	stone circle	rock pile, 140 cm
Site 137			
1	stone circle	stone circle	rock ring, 200 cm
Site 138			
1	stone circle	stone circle	rock ring, 500 cm
Site 139			
1	stone circle	stone circle	rock ring hearth, 100 cm
2	stone circle	stone circle	rock ring, 230 cm
3	stone circle	stone circle	rock ring, 150 cm
4	stone circle	stone circle	rock ring, 230 cm
5	stone circle	stone circle	rock ring, 310 cm
6	stone circle	stone circle	rock ring, 570 cm
7	stone circle	stone circle	rock ring, 140 cm
8	artifact concentration	artifact concentration	6–8 pieces of ground stone
Site 140			
1	stone circle	stone circle	rock ring, 280 cm
2	stone circle	stone circle	rock ring, 260 cm
3	stone circle	stone circle	rock ring, 200 cm
Site 141			
1	stone circle	stone circle	rock ring, 330-cm diameter
2	stone circle	stone circle	rock ring, 550-cm diameter
3	stone circle	stone circle	rock ring, 320 cm
4	stone circle	stone circle	rock ring, 330-cm diameter

Gazetteer of Features and Sites

Feature No.	Feature Type Name	Interpretive Feature Type	Comment
5	artifact concentration	artifact concentration	30 by 30 m
		Site 142	
1	stone circle	stone circle	rock ring, 200 m
		Site 143	
1	stone alignment	stone alignment	rock feature
2	stone alignment	stone alignment	rock feature
		Site 147	
1	stone circle	stone circle	rock ring, 280 cm
2	stone alignment	stone alignment	rock pile, 150 cm
3	stone alignment	stone alignment	rock pile, 100 cm
4	stone alignment	stone alignment	rock pile, 100 cm
5	stone circle	stone circle	rock ring, 250 cm
7	stone circle	stone circle	rock ring, 140-cm diameter
9	stone circle	stone circle	rock ring w/rocks inside, 175-cm diameter
10	stone square	stone circle	rock feature, 160 by 100 cm
		Site 148	
1	burial	burial	burial, 270 by 130 cm
2	burial	burial	burial, 360 by 130 cm
3	burial	burial	burial, 230 by 90 cm
		Site 149	
1	stone circle	stone circle	rock ring, 180 cm
2	stone circle	stone circle	rock ring, 270 cm
3	stone circle	stone circle	rock ring, 320 cm
4	stone alignment	stone alignment	rock pile, 150 cm
5	stone circle	stone circle	ring with daub, 320-cm diameter
		Site 150	
1	stone circle	stone circle	rock ring, 250 cm
2	stone circle	stone circle	rock ring, 250 cm
3	stone square	stone square	rock pile, 90 cm
4	stone square	stone square	rock square, 180 cm
		Site 151	
1	stone circle	stone circle	stone circle, 2.2-m diameter
2	stone circle	stone circle	stone circle, 3-m diameter
3	stone circle	stone circle	rock ring, 290 cm
4	stone circle	stone circle	stone circle with daub, 3-m diameter
5	stone circle	stone circle	stone circle, 2.75-m diameter
6	stone circle	stone circle	rock ring, 260 cm
		Site 152	
2	stone alignment	stone alignment	rock pile, 185-cm diameter
2	stone circle	stone circle	rock ring, 125-cm diameter
3	stone alignment	stone alignment	rock structure, 430 by 530 cm
4	stone circle	stone circle	3 rock rings, 600 by 800 cm
5	stone circle	stone circle	partial rock ring, 370 cm
6	stone circle	stone circle	rock ring, 125-cm diameter
		Site 153	
1	stone circle	stone circle	rock ring, 330 cm
2	stone circle	stone circle	stone circle with daub, 3.2-m diameter
3	stone circle	stone circle	rock ring, 290 cm
4	stone circle	stone circle	cluster burnt daub, no stone ring
		Site 154	
1	stone circle	stone circle	rock ring, 220-cm diameter
2	stone circle	stone circle	disturbed rock ring, 200 cm
		Site 155	
1	stone circle	stone circle	rock ring, 210 cm
2	stone circle	stone circle	rock ring, 130 cm
3	stone circle	stone circle	rock ring, 240 cm
		Site 156	
1	stone circle	stone circle	large stone circle, 4-m diameter
2	stone circle	stone circle	rock ring, 235 diameter
4	stone cairn	stone circle	rock alignment; oval cairn

Feature No.	Feature Type Name	Interpretive Feature Type	Comment
5	stone circle	stone circle	large stone circle, 4-m diameter
6	stone square	stone square	rock square, 120 by 120 cm
7	stone circle	stone circle	stone circle, 2-m diameter
8	stone alignment	stone alignment	stone alignment, 1.9 by 1.10 m
9	stone circle	stone circle	stone oval, 3 by 2 m
10	stone circle	stone circle	
11	stone circle	stone circle	stone circle, 4-m diameter
12	stone circle	stone circle	stone oval, 4 by 2.5 m
13	stone circle	stone circle	stone circle, 2.8-m diameter
14	stone circle	stone circle	stone circle, 2.8 m
15	stone circle	stone circle	stone oval, 3 by 2 m
16	stone alignment	stone alignment	rock alignment
17	stone circle	stone circle	stone circle, 4.5-m diameter
18	stone circle	stone circle	stone circle, 4.2-m diameter
19	stone circle	stone circle	stone circle, 3.5-m diameter
20	stone circle	stone circle	stone circle, 3.5-m diameter
21	stone circle	stone circle	stone circle, 3-m diameter
22	stone circle	stone circle	stone circle, 3-m diameter
23	stone circle	stone circle	stone circle, 3-m diameter
24	stone circle	stone circle	stone circles, 2.8-m diameter
25	stone circle	stone circle	stone circle, 2.75-m diameter
26	stone circle	stone circle	stone circle, 3-m diameter
27	stone circle	stone circle	stone circle, 3.5-m diameter
28	stone alignment	stone alignment	stone alignment, 1 by 2 m
29	stone circle	stone circle	stone circle, 3-m diameter
30	stone circle	stone circle	stone circle, 2.8-m diameter
31	stone circle	stone circle	stone circle, 3-m diameter
32	stone circle	stone circle	stone circle, 3.5-m diameter
33	stone circle	stone circle	stone circle, 3.5-m diameter
34	stone circle	stone circle	stone circle, 2.75-m diameter
35	stone circle	stone circle	stone circle, 2.75-m diameter
37	stone circle	stone circle	stone circle, 3.5-m diameter
38	stone circle	stone circle	stone circle, 3-m diameter
40	stone circle	stone circle	stone circle, 3.5-m diameter
41	stone circle	stone circle	stone circle, 3-m diameter
42	stone circle	stone circle	stone circle, 2.5-m diameter
43	stone circle	stone circle	stone circle, 2.5-m diameter, full of stones
44	stone alignment	stone alignment	stone alignment/oval, 2 by 1 m
45	stone alignment	stone alignment	stone alignment/oval, 2 by 1 m
48	stone alignment	stone alignment	stone alignment/oval, 1 by 2 m
49	stone alignment	stone alignment	stone alignment/oval, 1 by 2 m
50	stone square	stone square	stone square, 4 by 4 stones, 1.5 m square
51	stone alignment	stone alignment	stone alignment/oval, 1 by 2 m
52	stone circle	stone circle	stone circle filled with stones, 2.5 m
53	stone circle	stone circle	stone circle filled with stones, 2-m diameter
54	stone circle	stone circle	stone-filled circle, 2-m diameter
55	stone alignment	stone alignment	stone alignment/oval, 1 by 2.5 m
56	stone circle	stone circle	stone-filled circle, 2-m diameter
57	stone alignment	stone alignment	stone alignment, 1 by 2 m
58	stone alignment	stone alignment	stone alignment, 1 by 2 m NE-SW
59	stone alignment	stone alignment	stone alignment/oval, 1 by 2 m NE-SW
Site 157			
1	stone tumulus	stone tumulus	rock ring platform, 550 cm
2	stone tumulus	stone tumulus	rock ring platform, 630 cm
3	stone tumulus	stone tumulus	tumulus, 550 cm
4	stone tumulus	stone tumulus	tumulus, 200 cm
5	stone tumulus	stone tumulus	tumulus 340 cm
6	stone tumulus	stone tumulus	tumulus platform, 370 cm
7	stone tumulus	stone tumulus	tumulus 460 cm
8	stone tumulus	stone tumulus	tumulus 420 cm

Gazetteer of Features and Sites

Feature No.	Feature Type Name	Interpretive Feature Type	Comment
9	stone tumulus	stone tumulus	tumulus 480 cm
10	stone tumulus	stone tumulus	tumulus 420 cm
11	stone tumulus	stone tumulus	rock pile, 140 cm
12	stone tumulus	stone tumulus	tumulus 430 cm
13	stone tumulus	stone tumulus	tumulus 370 cm
14	stone tumulus	stone tumulus	tumulus, 350-cm diameter
15	stone tumulus	stone tumulus	tumulus, 430-cm diameter
16	stone tumulus	stone tumulus	tumulus, 320-cm diameter
17	stone tumulus	stone tumulus	tumulus, 400-cm diameter
18	stone tumulus	stone tumulus	tumulus, 440-cm diameter
19	stone tumulus	stone tumulus	tumulus, 490-cm diameter
20	stone tumulus	stone tumulus	tumulus, 420-cm diameter
21	stone tumulus	stone tumulus	tumulus, 470-cm diameter
22	stone tumulus	stone tumulus	tumulus, 450-cm diameter

Note: Many of the sites found in 2010 were recorded in greater detail in a deliberate sampling strategy, and the information about the features which make up these site is presented here. This greater level of information may stand in proxy for the remaining sites found in 2009 or 2010, and possibly even for sites as yet undiscovered.

Appendix C

Ceramic Decorative Techniques

TABLE C.1. BODY SHERD DECORATIVE TECHNIQUES FROM THE SCHP COLLECTION

Site	Plain	Twine	Other Subtractive Techniques	Additive Techniques	Multiple Attributes	Slip	Unidentified
Site 1	8	6	9	—	5	1	2
Site 2	7	5	3	—	3	12	—
Site 4	—	—	—	1	—	—	—
Site 7	—	—	—	—	1	1	—
Site 8	24	7	3	—	16	13	3
Site 9	17	2	1	2	—	—	—
Site 11	—	17	—	—	—	24	—
Site 13	—	—	—	1	—	—	—
Site 46	4	2	—	—	—	—	—
Site 55	10	—	1	—	—	16	—
Site 56	73	15	5	1	6	60	2
Site 57	55	—	6	—	—	47	—
Site 58	46	—	1	—	—	16	1
Site 59	3	1	—	—	—	5	—
Site 60	6	—	—	—	1	—	1
Site 61	24	4	6	—	—	—	—
Site.62	49	2	2	—	—	18	4
Site 63	24	—	—	—	—	—	—
Site 64	107	1	1	1	7	—	8
Site 65	—	—	—	—	1	—	—
Site 69	33	6	—	4	9	23	6
Site 71	369	25	54	2	22	101	13
Site 72	55	5	1	—	4	—	6
Site 73	7	—	—	—	—	—	—
Site 74	5	—	—	—	1	—	1
Site 75	10	3	1	1	1	6	3
Site 76	10	3	1	—	—	—	3
Site 77	28	—	16	—	—	23	—
Site 78	60	—	3	—	1	35	—
Site 79	18	—	2	—	—	5	1
Site 80	3	—	1	—	—	1	—
Site 81	—	8	—	—	4	3	—
Site 82	2	4	—	—	3	1	5
Site 83	1	—	—	—	—	5	—
Site 84	4	—	—	—	—	4	—
Site 85	25	—	5	—	3	9	2
Site 86	8	—	—	—	—	—	—
Site 87	17	—	1	—	—	4	—
Site 88	6	1	—	—	2	—	—
Site 89	6	—	—	—	—	2	—
Site 90	11	7	—	—	—	4	—
Site 91	17	—	—	—	—	3	—
Site 92	16	1	1	—	2	4	1
Site 93	12	—	—	—	—	—	—
Site 94	1	—	—	—	—	—	—
Site 95	6	—	—	—	—	3	—
Site 96	10	2	1	—	1	10	—
Site 97	—	1	—	—	—	3	—
Site 98	—	—	—	—	—	5	—
Site 100	2	—	2	—	—	6	—
Site 101	2	—	—	—	—	4	—
Site 102	2	—	—	—	2	11	—
Site 103	42	3	2	—	—	9	—

Ceramic Decorative Techniques

Site	Plain	Twine	Other Subtractive Techniques	Additive Techniques	Multiple Attributes	Slip	Unidentified
Site 104	13	1	—	—	1	2	—
Site 105	4	1	1	—	1	2	—
Site 106	8	—	—	—	—	—	—
Site 107	2	1	—	—	—	—	—
Site 108	8	—	1	—	1	1	2
Site 109	14	—	—	—	—	10	—
Site 110	6	—	—	—	—	13	1
Site 111	6	—	—	—	—	6	1
Site 112	10	—	—	—	—	—	—
Site 114	4	—	—	—	—	1	4
Site 115	20	2	2	—	2	2	—
Site 116	22	—	—	—	—	6	—
Site 117	7	—	—	—	—	—	1
Site 118	16	2	—	—	4	3	3
Site 119	18	—	1	1	—	2	5
Site 123	148	28	18	1	16	47	5
Site 137	18	2	12	1	5	1	—
Site 140	15	1	1	—	1	—	—
Site 141	—	8	4	—	—	1	—
Site 145	4	4	—	6	1	—	—
Site 146	55	24	—	1	1	—	3
Site 149	59	3	1	—	2	2	—
Site 155	30	8	5	—	2	4	3
Site 156	392	80	42	10	5	1	20
Site 168	5	—	—	—	—	—	—
Site 220	—	—	—	—	—	2	—
Site 222	1	1	1	—	—	—	—
Site 223	4	—	—	—	1	2	—
Site 224	3	—	—	—	—	—	—
Site 225	1	—	—	—	—	3	—
Site 226	—	—	—	—	1	1	—
Site 227	1	—	3	—	—	3	—
Site 228	1	—	—	—	—	—	—
Site 229	4	—	1	—	—	—	—
Site 230	1	—	—	—	—	2	—
Site 231	1	1	—	—	—	—	—
Site 232	1	—	—	—	—	—	—
Site 233	1	—	—	—	—	—	—
Site 234	1	7	—	—	—	—	—
Site 235	5	2	6	—	2	—	—
Site 236	1	—	—	—	2	—	—
Site 237	—	—	1	—	—	—	—
Site 238	2	1	3	—	3	—	1
Site 239	1	6	—	—	—	—	—
Site 240	—	1	—	—	—	—	—
Site 241	13	—	4	—	—	—	—
Site 242	4	—	1	—	—	—	—
Site 243	—	2	1	—	1	2	—
Site 244	1	2	2	—	—	—	—
Site 245	1	1	—	—	—	—	—
Site 246	2	?	1	—	—	—	—
Site 247	1	1	—	—	—	—	—
Site 248	—	1	—	—	—	—	—
Site 249	4	1	—	—	—	—	—
Site 255	1	—	—	—	—	—	—
Site 256	1	—	—	—	—	—	—
Site 257	1	—	1	—	1	—	—
Site 260	3	—	—	—	—	—	—
Site 261	1	2	—	—	—	—	—
Site 262	4	—	—	—	—	—	—
Site 263	1	2	1	—	—	—	—
Site 264	—	—	1	—	2	—	—

Site	Plain	Twine	Other Subtractive Techniques	Additive Techniques	Multiple Attributes	Slip	Unidentified
Site 265	2	—	—	—	—	—	1
Site 266	4	2	1	—	—	—	3
Site 267	1	—	1	—	—	—	—
Site 268	—	2	1	—	—	—	—
Site 269	—	1	—	—	—	1	—
Site 270	1	—	—	—	—	—	—
Site 271	1	—	—	—	—	1	—
Site 272	—	—	—	—	—	2	—
Site 273	1	—	—	—	—	—	—
Site 274	—	1	—	—	—	—	—
Site 275	2	—	1	—	—	1	—
Site 276	1	2	1	1	—	—	—
Site 277	—	3	—	—	—	1	—
Site 278	1	1	—	1	—	1	—
Site 279	4	—	—	—	—	—	—
Site 281	3	—	—	—	—	—	—
Site 282	3	—	—	—	—	—	—
Site 283	2	2	—	—	1	—	—
Site 284	1	—	—	—	—	—	—
Site 285	—	—	2	—	—	3	—
Site 286	1	—	—	—	—	—	—
Site 287	—	—	1	—	—	—	—
Site 289	—	—	1	—	—	—	—
Site 292	4	1	—	—	—	—	—
Site 293	—	—	—	—	—	—	1
Site 295	2	2	1	—	—	2	—
Site 296	3	1	1	—	—	—	—
Site 297	6	—	3	—	—	—	—
Site 298	4	—	1	—	—	—	—
Site 299	—	—	1	—	—	—	—
ISO 51	3	1	—	—	—	—	—
ISO 52	12	6	1	3	1	—	—
ISO 53	4	—	—	—	—	—	—
Total	2,262	354	261	38	152	628	116

TABLE C.2. BODY SHERD DECORATIVE TECHNIQUES FROM TESTED SITES

Site	Plain	Twine	Other Subtractive	Additive	Multiple Attributes	Slip	Unidentified
Site 8	24	7	3	—	16	13	3
Site 9	17	2	1	2	—	—	—
Site 69	57	12	—	4	9	23	19
Site 149	33	3	1	—	4	—	2
Site 156	77	11	7	1	5	1	3
Site 156B	18	—	1	—	—	—	3
Site 156C	26	9	10	—	—	6	—
Site 157	—	—	—	—	1	1	—
Total	252	44	23	7	35	44	30

Appendix D

Ceramic Rim Sherd Data

Table D.1. Rim Sherd Data from the SCHP Collection

Site/Type	S.Cl.	S.Op.	E1	E2	E3	E4	E5	E6	E7	C1	C2	C3	C4	C5	Carinated	T–rim	Unidentified
Site 2																	
Additive	—	—	—	—	—	—	—	—	1	—	—	—	—	—	—	—	—
Multiple attr.	1	—	2	—	2	—	—	1	—	—	—	—	—	—	—	—	—
Other subtractive	2	1	1	—	2	—	2	—	—	—	—	—	—	—	—	—	—
Plain	—	—	1	—	1	—	—	—	—	—	—	—	—	—	—	—	—
Slip	—	—	1	—	—	1	—	—	—	—	—	—	—	—	—	—	—
Twine	—	—	—	—	—	—	—	—	—	—	—	—	—	—	—	—	—
Unidentified	—	—	—	—	—	—	—	—	—	—	—	—	—	—	—	—	—
Site 4																	
Additive	—	—	—	—	—	1	—	—	—	—	—	—	—	—	—	—	—
Multiple attr.	—	—	—	—	—	—	—	—	—	—	—	—	—	—	—	—	—
Other subtractive	—	—	—	—	—	—	—	—	—	—	—	—	—	—	—	—	—
Plain	—	—	—	—	—	—	—	—	—	—	—	—	—	—	—	—	—
Slip	—	—	—	—	—	—	—	—	—	—	—	—	—	—	—	—	—
Twine	—	—	—	—	—	—	—	—	—	—	—	—	—	—	—	—	—
Unidentified	—	—	—	—	—	—	—	—	—	—	—	—	—	—	—	—	—
Site 7																	
Additive	—	—	—	—	—	—	—	—	—	—	—	—	—	—	—	—	—
Multiple attr.	—	—	—	—	—	—	—	1	—	—	—	—	—	—	—	—	—
Other subtractive	—	—	—	—	—	—	—	—	—	—	—	—	—	—	—	—	—
Plain	—	—	—	—	—	—	—	—	—	—	—	—	—	—	—	—	—
Slip	—	—	—	—	—	—	—	—	—	—	—	—	—	—	—	—	—
Twine	—	—	—	—	—	—	—	—	—	—	—	—	—	—	—	—	—
Unidentified	—	—	—	—	—	—	—	—	—	—	—	—	—	—	—	—	—
Site 11																	
Additive	—	—	—	—	—	—	—	—	—	—	—	—	—	—	—	—	—
Multiple attr.	—	—	—	—	—	—	—	—	—	—	—	—	—	—	—	—	—
Other subtractive	—	—	—	—	—	—	—	—	—	1	—	—	—	—	—	—	—
Plain	—	—	—	—	—	—	—	—	—	—	—	—	—	—	—	—	—
Slip	—	—	—	—	—	—	—	—	—	—	—	—	—	—	—	—	—
Twine	—	—	—	—	—	—	—	—	—	—	—	—	—	—	—	—	—
Unidentified	—	—	—	—	—	—	—	—	—	—	—	—	—	—	—	—	—
Site 13																	
Additive	—	—	—	—	—	—	—	—	—	—	—	—	—	—	—	—	—
Multiple attr.	—	—	—	—	—	—	—	—	—	—	—	—	—	—	—	—	—
Other subtractive	—	—	—	—	—	—	—	—	—	—	—	—	—	—	—	—	—
Plain	1	—	—	—	—	—	—	—	—	—	1	—	—	—	—	—	—
Slip	—	—	—	—	—	—	—	—	—	—	—	—	—	—	—	—	—
Twine	—	—	—	—	—	—	—	—	—	—	—	—	—	—	—	—	—
Unidentified	—	—	—	—	—	—	—	—	—	—	—	—	—	—	—	—	—
Site 18																	
Additive	—	—	—	—	—	—	—	—	—	—	—	—	—	—	—	—	—
Multiple attr.	—	—	—	—	—	—	—	—	—	—	—	—	—	—	—	—	—
Other subtractive	—	—	—	—	—	—	—	—	—	—	—	—	—	—	—	—	—
Plain	—	—	—	—	—	—	—	—	—	—	—	—	—	—	—	—	—
Slip	—	—	—	—	—	—	—	—	—	—	—	—	—	—	—	—	—
Twine	1	—	—	—	—	—	—	—	—	—	—	—	—	—	—	—	—
Unidentified	—	—	—	—	—	—	—	—	—	—	—	—	—	—	—	—	—
Site 36																	
Additive	—	—	—	—	—	—	—	—	—	—	—	—	—	—	—	—	—

Site/Type	S.Cl.	S.Op.	E1	E2	E3	E4	E5	E6	E7	C1	C2	C3	C4	C5	Carinated	T–rim	Unidentified
Multiple attr.	—	—	—	1	1	—	—	2	—	—	—	—	—	—	—	—	—
Other subtractive	—	—	—	—	—	—	—	—	—	—	—	—	—	—	—	—	—
Plain	—	—	—	—	—	—	—	—	1	—	—	—	—	—	—	—	—
Plain	—	3	—	1	—	—	—	—	—	—	—	—	—	—	—	—	—
Slip	—	—	1	—	—	—	—	—	1	—	—	—	—	—	—	—	—
Twine	—	—	—	—	—	—	—	—	—	—	—	—	—	—	—	—	—
Unidentified	—	—	—	—	—	—	—	—	—	—	—	—	—	—	—	—	—
Site 56																	
Additive	—	—	—	—	—	—	—	—	—	—	—	—	—	—	—	—	—
Multiple attr.	—	—	—	—	—	—	—	—	—	—	—	—	—	—	—	—	—
Other subtractive	1	1	—	—	—	—	—	—	—	—	—	—	—	—	—	1	1
Slip	—	—	—	—	—	—	—	—	—	—	—	—	—	—	—	—	—
Twine	—	—	—	—	—	—	—	—	—	—	—	—	—	—	—	—	—
Unidentified	—	—	—	—	—	—	—	—	—	—	—	—	—	—	—	—	—
Site 57																	
Additive	—	—	—	—	—	—	—	—	—	—	—	—	—	—	—	—	—
Multiple attr.	1	1	—	—	—	—	—	—	—	—	—	—	—	—	—	—	—
Other subtractive	—	—	—	—	—	—	—	—	—	—	—	—	—	—	—	—	—
Plain	—	—	—	—	—	—	—	—	—	—	—	—	—	—	—	—	1
Slip	—	—	—	—	—	—	—	—	—	—	—	—	—	—	—	—	—
Twine	—	—	—	—	—	—	—	—	—	—	—	—	—	—	—	—	—
Unidentified	—	—	—	—	—	—	—	—	—	—	—	—	—	—	—	—	—
Site 58																	
Additive	—	—	—	—	—	—	—	—	—	—	—	—	—	—	—	—	—
Multiple attr.	—	—	—	—	—	—	—	—	—	—	—	—	—	—	—	—	—
Other subtractive	—	—	—	—	—	—	—	—	—	—	—	—	—	—	—	—	—
Plain	—	—	1	—	—	—	—	—	—	—	—	—	—	—	—	—	—
Slip	—	—	—	—	—	—	—	—	—	—	—	—	—	—	—	—	—
Twine	—	—	—	—	—	—	—	—	—	—	—	—	—	—	—	—	—
Unidentified	—	—	—	—	—	—	—	—	—	—	—	—	—	—	—	—	—
Site 62																	
Additive	1	—	—	—	—	—	—	—	—	—	—	—	—	—	—	—	—
Multiple attr.	—	—	—	—	—	—	—	—	—	—	—	—	—	—	—	—	—
Other subtractive	—	—	—	—	—	—	—	—	—	—	—	—	—	—	—	—	1
Plain	—	—	—	—	1	—	—	—	—	—	—	—	—	—	—	—	—
Slip	—	—	—	—	—	—	—	—	—	—	—	—	—	—	—	—	—
Twine	—	—	—	—	—	—	—	—	—	—	—	—	—	—	—	1	—
Unidentified	—	—	—	—	—	—	—	—	—	—	—	—	—	—	—	—	—
Site 64																	
Additive	—	—	—	—	—	—	—	—	—	—	—	—	—	—	—	—	—
Multiple attr.	—	—	—	—	—	—	—	1	—	—	—	—	—	—	—	—	—
Other subtractive	1	—	—	—	—	—	—	—	—	—	—	—	—	—	—	—	—
Plain	1	—	—	—	—	—	—	—	—	—	—	—	—	—	—	—	—
Slip	—	—	—	—	—	—	—	—	—	—	—	—	—	—	—	—	—
Twine	1	—	1	—	—	—	—	—	—	—	—	—	—	—	—	—	—
Unidentified	—	—	—	—	—	—	—	—	—	—	—	—	—	—	—	—	—
Site 71																	
Additive	—	—	—	—	—	—	—	—	—	—	—	—	—	—	—	—	—
Multiple attr.	—	—	1	—	—	—	—	—	1	—	—	—	—	—	—	—	—
Other subtractive	—	—	1	—	—	1	—	—	2	—	—	—	—	—	—	—	—
Plain	3	—	—	—	1	—	2	—	—	—	—	—	—	—	—	—	—
Slip	1	—	—	1	—	—	—	—	—	—	—	—	—	—	—	—	—
Twine	—	—	—	—	—	—	—	—	—	—	—	—	—	—	—	—	—
Unidentified	—	—	—	—	—	—	—	—	—	—	—	—	—	—	—	—	—
Site 72																	
Additive	—	—	—	—	—	—	—	—	—	—	—	—	—	—	—	—	—
Multiple attr.	—	—	—	—	—	—	—	—	—	—	—	—	—	—	—	—	—

Site/Type	S.Cl.	S.Op.	E1	E2	E3	E4	E5	E6	E7	C1	C2	C3	C4	C5	Carinated	T–rim	Unidentified
Other subtractive	—	—	—	—	—	—	—	—	—	—	—	—	—	—	—	—	—
Plain	2	—	—	—	—	—	—	—	—	—	—	—	—	—	—	—	—
Slip	—	—	—	—	—	—	—	—	—	—	—	—	—	—	—	—	—
Twine	—	—	—	—	—	—	—	—	—	—	—	—	—	—	—	—	—
Unidentified	—	—	—	—	—	—	—	—	—	—	—	—	—	—	—	—	—
Site 78																	
Additive	—	—	—	—	—	—	—	—	—	—	—	—	—	—	—	—	—
Multiple attr.	—	—	—	—	—	—	—	—	1	—	—	—	—	—	—	—	1
Other subtractive	—	—	—	—	—	—	—	—	1	—	—	—	—	—	—	—	—
Plain	1	1	—	—	—	—	—	—	—	—	—	—	—	—	—	—	—
Slip	—	—	—	—	—	—	—	—	—	—	—	—	—	—	—	—	—
Twine	—	—	—	—	—	—	—	—	—	—	—	—	—	—	—	1	—
Unidentified	—	—	—	—	—	—	—	—	—	—	—	—	—	—	—	—	—
Site 79																	
Additive	—	—	—	—	—	—	—	—	—	—	—	—	—	—	—	—	—
Multiple attr.	—	—	—	—	—	1	—	—	—	—	—	—	—	—	—	—	—
Other subtractive	—	—	—	—	—	—	—	—	—	—	—	—	—	—	—	—	—
Plain	—	—	—	—	—	—	—	—	—	—	—	—	—	—	—	—	1
Slip	3	—	—	—	—	—	—	—	—	—	—	—	—	—	—	—	—
Twine	—	—	—	—	—	—	—	—	—	—	—	—	—	—	—	—	—
Unidentified	—	—	—	—	—	—	—	—	—	—	—	—	—	—	—	—	—
Site 81																	
Additive	—	—	—	—	—	—	—	—	—	—	—	—	—	—	—	—	—
Multiple attr.	—	—	—	—	—	—	—	—	—	—	—	—	—	—	—	—	—
Other subtractive	1	1	—	—	—	1	—	—	—	—	—	—	—	—	—	—	—
Plain	—	—	—	—	—	—	—	—	—	—	—	—	—	—	—	—	—
Slip	—	—	—	—	—	—	—	—	—	—	—	—	—	—	—	—	—
Twine	—	—	—	—	—	—	—	—	—	—	—	—	—	—	—	—	—
Unidentified	—	—	—	—	—	—	—	—	—	—	—	—	—	—	—	—	—
Site 83																	
Additive	—	—	—	—	—	—	—	—	—	—	—	—	—	—	—	—	—
Multiple attr.	—	—	—	—	—	—	—	—	—	—	—	—	—	—	—	—	—
Other subtractive	—	—	—	—	—	—	—	—	—	—	—	—	—	—	—	—	—
Plain	1	1	—	—	—	—	—	—	—	—	—	—	—	—	—	—	—
Slip	—	—	—	—	—	—	—	—	—	—	—	—	—	—	—	—	—
Twine	—	—	—	—	—	—	—	—	—	—	—	—	—	—	—	—	—
Unidentified	—	—	—	—	—	—	—	—	—	—	—	—	—	—	—	—	—
Site 87																	
Additive	—	—	—	—	—	—	—	—	—	—	—	—	—	—	—	—	—
Multiple attr.	—	—	—	—	—	—	—	—	—	—	—	—	—	—	—	—	—
Other subtractive	—	1	—	—	—	—	—	—	—	—	—	—	—	—	—	—	—
Plain	—	—	—	—	—	—	—	—	—	—	—	—	—	—	—	—	—
Slip	—	—	—	—	—	—	—	—	—	—	—	—	—	—	—	—	—
Twine	—	—	—	—	—	—	—	—	—	—	—	—	—	—	—	—	—
Unidentified	—	—	—	—	—	—	—	—	—	—	—	—	—	—	—	—	—
Site 89																	
Additive	—	—	—	—	—	—	—	—	—	—	—	—	—	—	—	—	—
Multiple attr.	—	—	—	—	—	—	—	—	—	—	—	—	—	—	—	—	—
Other subtractive	—	—	—	—	—	—	—	—	—	—	—	—	—	—	—	—	—
Plain	1	—	—	—	—	—	—	—	—	—	—	—	—	—	—	—	—
Slip	—	1	—	—	—	—	—	—	—	—	—	—	—	—	—	—	—
Twine	—	—	—	—	—	—	—	—	—	—	—	—	—	—	—	—	—
Unidentified	—	—	—	—	—	—	—	—	—	—	—	—	—	—	—	—	—
Site 91																	
Additive	—	—	—	—	—	—	—	—	—	—	—	—	—	—	—	—	—
Multiple attr.	—	—	—	—	—	—	—	—	—	—	—	—	—	—	—	—	—
Other subtractive	—	—	1	—	—	—	—	—	—	—	—	—	—	—	—	—	—

Site/Type	S.Cl.	S.Op.	E1	E2	E3	E4	E5	E6	E7	C1	C2	C3	C4	C5	Carinated	T–rim	Unidentified
Plain	—	—	—	—	—	—	—	—	—	—	—	—	—	—	—	—	—
Slip	—	—	—	—	—	—	—	—	—	—	—	—	—	—	—	—	—
Twine	—	—	—	—	—	—	—	—	—	—	—	—	—	—	—	—	—
Unidentified	—	—	—	—	—	—	—	—	—	—	—	—	—	—	—	—	—
Site 96																	
Additive	—	—	—	—	1	—	—	—	—	—	—	—	—	—	—	—	—
Multiple attr.	—	—	—	—	—	—	—	—	—	—	—	—	—	—	—	—	—
Other subtractive	—	—	—	—	—	—	—	—	—	—	—	—	—	—	—	—	—
Plain	—	—	—	—	—	—	—	—	—	—	—	—	—	—	—	—	—
Slip	—	—	—	—	—	—	—	—	—	—	—	—	—	—	—	—	—
Twine	—	—	—	—	—	—	—	—	—	—	—	—	—	—	—	—	—
Unidentified	—	—	—	—	—	—	—	—	—	—	—	—	—	—	—	—	—
Site 100																	
Additive	—	—	—	—	—	—	—	—	—	—	—	—	—	—	—	—	—
Multiple attr.	1	—	—	—	—	—	—	—	—	—	—	—	—	—	—	—	—
Other subtractive	—	—	—	—	—	—	—	—	—	—	—	—	—	—	—	—	—
Plain	—	—	—	—	—	—	—	—	—	—	—	—	—	—	—	—	—
Slip	1	—	—	—	—	—	—	—	—	—	—	—	—	—	—	—	—
Twine	—	—	—	—	—	—	—	—	—	—	—	—	—	—	—	—	—
Unidentified	—	—	—	—	—	—	—	—	—	—	—	—	—	—	—	—	—
Site 102																	
Additive	—	—	—	—	—	—	—	—	—	—	—	—	—	—	—	—	—
Multiple attr.	2	—	—	—	—	—	—	—	—	—	—	—	—	—	—	—	—
Other subtractive	—	—	—	—	—	—	—	—	—	—	—	—	—	—	—	—	—
Plain	—	—	—	—	—	—	—	—	—	—	—	—	—	—	—	—	—
Slip	—	—	—	—	—	—	—	—	—	—	—	—	—	—	—	—	—
Twine	—	—	—	—	—	—	—	—	—	—	—	—	—	—	—	—	—
Unidentified	—	—	—	—	—	—	—	—	—	—	—	—	—	—	—	—	—
Site 104																	
Additive	—	—	—	—	—	—	—	—	—	—	—	—	—	—	—	—	—
Multiple attr.	—	—	—	—	—	—	—	—	—	—	—	—	—	—	—	—	—
Other subtractive	—	—	—	—	—	—	—	1	—	—	—	—	—	—	—	—	—
Plain	—	—	—	—	—	—	—	—	—	—	—	—	—	—	—	—	—
Slip	—	—	—	—	—	—	—	—	—	—	—	—	—	—	—	—	—
Twine	—	—	—	—	—	—	—	—	—	—	—	—	—	—	—	—	—
Unidentified	—	—	—	—	—	—	—	—	—	—	—	—	—	—	—	—	—
Site 105																	
Additive	—	—	—	—	—	—	—	—	—	—	—	—	—	—	—	—	—
Multiple attr.	1	—	—	—	—	—	—	—	—	—	—	—	—	—	—	—	—
Other subtractive	—	1	—	—	—	—	—	—	—	—	—	—	—	—	—	1	—
Plain	—	—	—	—	—	—	—	—	—	—	—	—	—	—	—	—	—
Slip	—	—	—	—	—	—	—	—	—	—	—	—	—	—	—	—	—
Twine	—	—	—	—	—	—	—	—	—	—	—	—	—	—	—	—	—
Unidentified	—	—	—	—	—	—	—	—	—	—	—	—	—	—	—	—	—
Site 114																	
Additive	—	—	—	—	—	—	—	—	—	—	—	—	—	—	—	—	—
Multiple attr.	—	—	—	—	—	—	—	—	—	—	—	—	—	—	—	—	—
Other subtractive	1	—	—	—	—	—	—	—	—	—	—	—	—	—	—	—	—
Plain	—	—	—	—	—	—	—	—	—	—	—	—	—	—	—	—	—
Slip	—	—	—	—	—	—	—	—	—	—	—	—	—	—	—	—	—
Twine	—	—	—	—	—	—	—	—	—	—	—	—	—	—	—	—	—
Unidentified	—	—	—	—	—	—	—	—	—	—	—	—	—	—	—	—	—
Site 116																	
Additive	—	—	—	—	—	—	—	—	—	—	—	—	—	—	—	—	—
Multiple attr.	—	—	—	—	—	—	—	—	—	—	—	—	—	—	—	—	—
Other subtractive	—	—	—	—	—	—	—	1	—	—	—	—	—	—	—	—	—
Plain	—	—	—	—	—	—	—	—	—	—	—	—	—	—	—	—	—

Ceramic Rim Sherd Data

Site/Type	S.Cl.	S.Op.	E1	E2	E3	E4	E5	E6	E7	C1	C2	C3	C4	C5	Carinated	T–rim	Unidentified
Slip	—	—	—	—	—	—	—	—	—	—	—	—	—	—	—	—	—
Twine	—	—	—	—	—	—	—	—	—	—	—	—	—	—	—	—	—
Unidentified	—	—	—	—	—	—	—	—	—	—	—	—	—	—	—	—	—
Site 120																	
Additive	—	—	—	—	—	—	—	—	—	—	—	—	—	—	—	—	—
Multiple attr.	—	—	—	—	1	—	—	1	—	—	—	—	—	—	—	—	—
Other subtractive	—	—	—	—	—	—	—	1	—	—	—	—	—	—	—	—	—
Plain	—	—	—	—	—	—	—	1	—	—	—	—	—	—	—	—	—
Slip	—	—	1	—	1	1	—	—	—	—	—	—	—	—	—	—	—
Twine	—	—	—	—	—	—	—	—	—	—	—	—	—	—	—	—	—
Unidentified	—	—	—	—	—	—	—	—	—	—	—	—	—	—	—	—	—
Site 124																	
Additive	—	—	—	—	—	—	—	—	—	—	—	—	—	—	—	—	—
Multiple attr.	—	—	—	—	—	—	—	—	—	—	—	—	—	—	—	—	—
Other subtractive	5	1	1	—	—	—	—	—	—	—	—	—	1	—	—	—	—
Plain	—	1	—	—	—	—	—	—	—	—	—	—	—	—	—	—	—
Slip	—	1	—	—	—	—	—	—	—	—	—	—	—	—	—	—	—
Twine	—	—	—	—	—	—	—	—	—	—	—	—	—	—	—	—	—
Unidentified	—	—	—	—	—	—	—	—	—	—	—	—	—	—	—	—	—
Site 129																	
Additive	—	—	—	—	—	—	—	—	—	—	—	—	—	—	—	—	—
Multiple attr.	1	—	—	—	—	—	—	—	—	—	—	—	—	—	—	—	—
Other subtractive	—	—	—	—	—	—	—	—	—	—	—	—	—	—	—	—	—
Plain	—	—	—	—	—	—	—	—	—	—	—	—	—	—	—	—	—
Slip	—	—	—	—	—	—	—	—	—	—	—	—	—	—	—	—	—
Twine	—	—	—	—	—	—	—	—	—	—	—	—	—	—	—	—	—
Unidentified	—	—	—	—	—	—	—	—	—	—	—	—	—	—	—	—	—
Site 130																	
Additive	—	—	—	—	—	—	—	—	—	—	—	—	—	—	—	—	—
Multiple attr.	—	—	—	—	—	—	—	—	—	—	1	—	—	—	—	—	—
Other subtractive	—	2	—	—	—	—	—	—	—	—	1	—	—	—	—	—	—
Plain	1	1	—	1	—	1	—	—	—	—	—	—	—	—	—	—	—
Slip	—	—	—	—	—	—	—	—	—	1	—	—	—	—	—	—	—
Twine	—	—	—	—	—	—	—	—	—	—	—	—	—	—	—	—	—
Unidentified	—	—	—	—	—	—	—	—	—	—	—	—	—	—	—	—	—
Site 132																	
Additive	—	—	—	—	—	—	—	—	—	—	—	—	—	—	—	—	—
Multiple attr.	—	—	—	—	—	—	—	—	—	—	—	—	—	—	—	—	1
Other subtractive	—	—	—	—	—	—	—	—	—	—	—	—	—	—	—	—	—
Plain	—	—	—	—	—	—	—	1	—	—	—	—	—	—	—	—	—
Slip	2	—	—	—	—	—	—	—	—	—	—	—	—	—	—	—	—
Twine	—	—	—	—	—	—	—	—	—	—	—	—	—	—	—	—	—
Unidentified	—	—	—	—	—	—	—	—	—	—	—	—	—	—	—	—	—
Site 136																	
Additive	—	—	—	—	—	—	—	—	—	—	—	—	—	—	—	—	—
Multiple attr.	—	—	—	—	—	—	—	—	—	—	—	—	—	—	—	—	—
Other subtractive	1	1	—	—	—	—	—	—	—	—	—	—	1	—	—	—	—
Plain	—	—	1	—	—	—	—	—	—	—	—	—	—	—	—	—	—
Slip	—	—	—	—	—	—	—	—	—	—	—	—	—	—	—	—	—
Twine	—	—	—	—	—	—	—	—	—	—	—	—	—	—	—	—	—
Unidentified	—	—	—	—	—	—	—	—	—	—	—	—	—	—	—	—	—
Site 140																	
Additive	—	—	—	—	—	—	—	—	—	—	—	—	—	—	—	—	—
Multiple attr.	—	—	—	—	—	—	—	—	—	—	—	—	—	—	—	—	—
Other subtractive	—	1	—	—	—	—	—	—	—	—	—	—	—	—	—	—	—
Plain	—	—	—	—	—	—	—	—	—	—	—	—	—	—	—	—	—
Slip	—	—	—	—	—	—	—	—	—	—	—	—	—	—	—	—	—

Site/Type	S.Cl.	S.Op.	E1	E2	E3	E4	E5	E6	E7	C1	C2	C3	C4	C5	Carinated	T–rim	Unidentified
Twine	—	—	—	—	—	—	—	—	—	—	—	—	—	—	—	—	—
Unidentified	—	—	—	—	—	—	—	—	—	—	—	—	—	—	—	—	—
Site 141																	
Additive	—	—	—	—	—	—	—	—	—	—	—	—	—	—	—	—	—
Multiple attr.	—	1	—	—	—	—	—	—	—	1	1	1	—	—	—	—	—
Other subtractive	2	6	3	—	—	1	—	5	—	1	—	1	—	—	—	—	2
Plain	—	—	—	—	—	—	—	1	—	—	—	—	—	—	—	—	—
Slip	—	—	—	—	—	—	—	—	—	—	—	—	—	—	—	—	—
Twine	—	—	—	—	—	—	—	—	—	—	—	—	—	—	—	—	—
Unidentified	—	—	—	—	—	—	—	—	—	—	—	—	—	—	—	—	—
Site 146																	
Additive	—	1	—	—	—	—	—	—	—	—	—	—	—	—	—	—	—
Multiple attr.	—	—	—	—	—	—	—	—	—	—	—	—	—	—	—	—	—
Other subtractive	1	2	1	—	1	—	—	—	—	—	—	—	—	—	—	—	—
Plain	—	—	1	—	—	—	—	—	—	—	—	—	—	—	—	—	—
Slip	—	—	—	—	—	—	—	—	—	—	—	—	—	—	—	—	—
Twine	—	—	—	—	—	—	—	—	—	—	—	—	—	—	—	—	—
Unidentified	—	—	—	—	—	—	—	—	—	—	—	—	—	—	—	—	—
Site 154																	
Additive	—	—	—	—	—	—	—	—	—	—	—	—	—	—	—	—	—
Multiple attr.	—	—	—	—	—	—	—	—	—	—	—	—	—	—	—	—	—
Other subtractive	—	—	—	—	—	—	—	1	—	—	—	—	—	—	—	—	—
Plain	—	—	—	—	—	—	—	—	—	—	—	—	—	—	—	—	—
Slip	—	—	—	—	—	—	—	—	—	—	—	—	—	—	—	—	—
Twine	—	—	—	—	—	—	—	—	—	—	—	—	—	—	—	—	—
Unidentified	—	—	—	—	—	—	—	—	—	—	—	—	—	—	—	—	—
Site 242																	
Additive	—	—	—	—	—	—	—	—	—	—	—	—	—	—	—	—	—
Multiple attr.	1	—	—	—	—	—	—	—	—	—	—	—	—	—	—	—	—
Other subtractive	—	—	—	—	—	—	—	—	—	—	—	—	—	—	—	—	—
Plain	2	—	—	—	—	—	—	—	—	—	—	—	—	—	—	—	—
Slip	—	—	—	—	—	—	—	—	—	—	—	—	—	—	—	—	—
Twine	—	—	—	—	—	—	—	—	—	—	—	—	—	—	—	—	—
Unidentified	—	—	—	—	—	—	—	—	—	—	—	—	—	—	—	—	—
Site 243																	
Additive	—	—	—	—	—	—	—	—	—	—	—	—	—	—	—	—	—
Multiple attr.	—	—	—	—	1	—	—	—	—	—	—	—	—	—	—	—	—
Other subtractive	—	—	—	—	—	—	—	—	—	—	—	—	—	—	—	—	—
Plain	—	—	—	—	—	—	—	—	—	—	—	—	—	—	—	—	—
Slip	—	—	—	—	1	—	—	—	—	—	—	—	—	—	—	—	—
Twine	—	—	—	—	—	—	—	—	—	—	—	—	—	—	—	—	—
Unidentified	—	—	—	—	—	—	—	—	—	—	—	—	—	—	—	—	—
Site 244																	
Additive	—	—	—	—	—	—	—	—	—	—	—	—	—	—	—	—	—
Multiple attr.	—	—	—	—	—	—	—	—	—	—	—	—	—	—	—	—	—
Other subtractive	—	—	1	—	—	—	—	—	—	—	—	—	—	—	—	—	—
Plain	—	—	—	—	—	—	—	—	—	—	—	—	—	—	—	—	—
Slip	—	—	—	—	—	—	—	—	—	—	—	—	—	—	—	—	—
Twine	—	—	—	—	—	—	—	—	—	—	—	—	—	—	—	—	—
Unidentified	—	—	—	—	—	—	—	—	—	—	—	—	—	—	—	—	—
Site 248																	
Additive	—	—	—	—	—	—	—	—	—	—	—	—	—	—	—	—	—
Multiple attr.	—	—	—	—	—	—	—	—	1	—	—	—	—	—	—	—	—
Other subtractive	—	—	—	—	—	—	—	—	—	—	—	—	—	—	—	—	—
Plain	—	—	—	—	—	—	—	—	—	—	—	—	—	—	—	—	—
Slip	—	—	—	—	—	—	—	—	1	—	—	—	—	—	—	—	—
Twine	—	—	—	—	—	—	—	—	—	—	—	—	—	—	—	—	—

Site/Type	S.Cl.	S.Op.	E1	E2	E3	E4	E5	E6	E7	C1	C2	C3	C4	C5	Carinated	T–rim	Unidentified
Unidentified	—	—	—	—	—	—	—	—	—	—	—	—	—	—	—	—	—
Site 276																	
Additive	—	—	—	—	—	—	—	—	—	—	—	—	—	—	—	—	—
Multiple attr.	—	—	—	—	—	—	—	—	—	—	—	—	—	—	—	—	—
Other subtractive	—	—	—	—	—	—	—	—	—	—	—	—	—	—	—	—	—
Plain	1	—	—	—	—	—	—	—	—	—	—	—	—	—	—	—	—
Slip	—	—	—	—	—	—	—	—	—	—	—	—	—	—	—	—	—
Twine	—	—	—	—	—	—	—	—	—	—	—	—	—	—	—	—	—
Unidentified	—	—	—	—	—	—	—	—	—	—	—	—	—	—	—	—	—
Site 278																	
Additive	—	—	—	—	—	—	—	—	—	—	—	—	—	—	—	—	—
Multiple attr.	—	—	—	—	1	—	—	—	—	—	—	—	—	—	—	—	—
Other subtractive	—	—	—	—	—	—	—	—	—	—	—	—	—	—	—	—	—
Plain	—	1	—	—	—	—	—	—	—	—	—	—	—	—	—	—	—
Slip	—	—	—	—	—	—	—	—	—	—	—	—	—	—	—	—	—
Twine	—	—	—	—	—	—	—	—	—	—	—	—	—	—	—	—	—
Unidentified	—	—	—	—	—	—	—	—	—	—	—	—	—	—	—	—	—
Site 286																	
Additive	—	—	—	—	—	—	—	—	—	—	—	—	—	—	—	—	—
Multiple attr.	1	—	—	—	—	—	—	—	—	—	—	—	—	—	—	—	—
Other subtractive	—	—	—	—	—	—	—	—	—	—	—	—	—	—	—	—	—
Plain	—	—	—	—	—	—	—	—	—	—	1	—	—	—	—	—	—
Slip	—	—	—	—	—	—	—	—	—	—	—	—	—	—	—	—	—
Twine	—	—	—	—	—	—	—	—	—	—	—	—	—	—	—	—	—
Unidentified	—	—	—	—	—	—	—	—	—	—	—	—	—	—	—	—	—
Total	48	31	20	4	15	8	4	18	11	2	5	3	2	—	—	4	8

Key: S.Op. = simple open rim; S.Cl. = simple closed rim.

Table D.2. Rim Sherd Data from Tested Sites

Site/Type	Simple Closed	Simple Open	Short Everted	Long Everted	Collared	Other
Site 08						
Plain	—	1	8	3	—	1
Twine	—	—	—	—	—	—
Other subtractive	6	10	6	4	—	4
Additive	—	—	1	—	—	—
Slip	3	—	1	1	—	—
Multiple attributes	5	5	10	1	—	4
Site 09						
Plain	2	1	—	1	—	—
Twine	—	—	—	—	—	1
Other subtractive	1	1	1	3	—	1
Additive	—	—	—	—	—	—
Slip	1	—	1	4	—	—
Multiple attributes	—	—	—	—	—	—
Unid.	—	—	—	—	—	—
Site 69						
Plain	2	—	1	2	—	3
Twine	—	—	—	—	—	2
Other subtractive	1	1	1	3	—	2
Additive	—	—	—	—	—	—
Slip	—	—	—	—	—	2
Multiple attributes	—	—	—	—	—	2
Unid.						
Site 157						
Plain	—	—	—	—	—	—
Twine	—	—	—	—	—	—
Other subtractive	—	—	—	—	—	—
Additive	—	—	—	—	—	—
Slip	—	—	1	—	—	—
Multiple attributes	1	—	—	—	—	—
Site 156						
Plain	1	3	5	4	—	5
Twine	—	—	—	—	—	—
Other subtractive	1	1	4	4	—	3
Additive	—	—	—	2	—	—
Slip	—	1	1	—	—	—
Multiple attributes	—	—	—	—	—	2
Unid.	—	—	—	—	—	—
Total	24	24	41	32	—	32

References Cited

Allen, Kathleen M. S., Stanton W. Green, and Ezra B. W. Zubrow (editors)
1990 *Interpreting Space: GIS and Archaeology.* Taylor and Francis, London.

Altschul, Jeffrey H.
1990 Red Flag Models: The Use of Modeling in Management Contexts. In *Interpreting Space: GIS and Archaeology,* edited by Kathleen M. S. Allen, Stanton W. Green, and Ezra B. W. Zubrow, pp. 226–238. Taylor and Francis, London.

2008 Culture as an Applied Concept. In *Fragile Patterns: The Archaeology of the Western Papaguería,* edited by Jeffrey H. Altschul and Adrianne Rankin, pp. 631–637. SRI Press, Tucson.

2009 Review of *The Model-Based Archaeology of Socionatural Systems.* Timothy A. Kohler and Sander E. van der Leeuw, editors. *American Antiquity* 74(3):573–574.

Altschul, J., and Douglass, D. I.
2010 *Protocols for Archaeological Monitoring of the Oromin Joint Venture Group Concession, Sabodala, Senegal.* Sabodala Cultural Heritage Project Technical Report 1. Statistical Research, Tucson, Arizona, USA.

Altschul, Jeffrey H., Terry H. Klein, and Lynne Sebastian
2005 *A Workshop on Predictive Modeling and Cultural Resource Management on Military Installations.* Preservation Research Series 4, Legacy Project. SRI Foundation, Rio Rancho, New Mexico.

Altschul, Jeffrey H., and Christopher L. Nagle
1988 Collecting New Data for the Purpose of Model Development. In *Quantifying the Past and Predicting the Future: Theory, Method, and Application of Archaeological Predictive Modeling,* edited by W. James Judge and Lynne Sebastian, pp. 257–299. USDI Bureau of Land Management, Denver, Colorado.

Argonne National Laboratory and University of Redlands
2010 Agent Analyst: Agent Based Modeling Extension for ArcGIS Users. Electronic document, http://www.institute.redlands.edu/AgentAnalyst/, accessed July 28, 2010.

Barry, B.
1988 *La Sénégambie du XVe au XIXe siècle, traite négrière, Islam et Conquête.* Paris, l'Harmattan.

Bassot, J. P.
1966 Etudes Géologiques du Sénégal Oriental, et des ses conflits guinéo-maliens. *Mémoires du BRGM* Numéro 40. Editions BRGM, Paris.

Bathily, A.
1970 Mamadou Lamine et la Résistance Anti-Imperialiste Dans le Haut Sénégal (1885–1887). *Notes Africaines,* 125:20–30

1989 *Les Portes de l'or. Le Royaume de Galam (Sénégal) de l'Ere des musulmans au temps des négriers (VIII–XVIIIé siècle).* Éditions L'Harmattan, Paris.

Bessac, H.
1964 Fragments de potterie archéologique du Fouta sénégalais. *Notes Africaines* 103:65–70.

Bocoum, H.
1986 *La Métallurgie au Sénégal, approche archéologique, technologique et historique.* Thèse 3é cycle, Université de Paris I, Sorbonne.

2008 Aménagement du territoire et archéologie préventive au Sénégal: quels enjeux pour la recherche. In *L'archéologie Préventive En Afrique De L'ouest, Enjeux Et Perspectives,* by Baouba Ould Mohamed Naffé, Raymond Lanfranchi, and Nathan Schlanger, pp. 75–85. Actes du colloque de Nouakchott 1–3 février 2007. Editions Sépia, Saint-Maur-des-Fossés.

Boucard, Claude
1974 Relation du Bambouc (1729), edited by Philip Curtin and Jean Boulègue. In *Bulletin de l'Institut Fondamental d'Afrique Noire,* Série B, 36:246–276.

Boulègue, J.
1987 *Les Anciens Royaumes Wolof(Sénégal): Le Grand Jolof (XIIé-XIVé siècle).* Editions Façades, Paris.

Bray, R. H., and L. T. Kurtz
1945 Determination of total, organic, and available forms of phosphorus in soils. *Soil Science* 59:39–45.

Breiman, L.
2001 Random forests. *Machine Learning* 45:5–32.

Brooks, G. E.
1986 A Provisional Historical Schema for Western Africa Based on Seven Climate Periods (ca. 9000 B.C. to the 19th Century). *Cahiers d'Etudes Africaines* 101–102(XXVI-1-2):43–62.

1993 *Landlords and Strangers. Ecology, Society and, Trade in Western Africa, 1000–1630.* Westview Press, Boulder.

Camara, A., and B. Duboscq
1984 Le gisement préhistorique de Sansandé, basse vallée de la Falémé, Sénégal. Approche Typologique et Stratigraphique. *L'Anthropologie (Paris)* Tome 88, Numéro 3:377–402

1987 Contexte chronostratigraphique des outillages du Paléolithique évolué dans l'Est du Sénégal. *L'Anthropologie (Paris)* Tome 91, Numéro 2:511–520.

1990 La fouille d'un site Acheuléen à Djita (Basse vallée de la Falémé, Sénégal*). L'Anthropologie (Paris)* Tome 94, Numéro 2:293–304.

Chambonneau
1898 Relation du Sr Chambonneau, commis de la Compagnie du Sénégal, du voyage par luy fait en remontant le Niger (Juillet 1688). *Bulletin de géographie historique et descriptive,* Numéro 2:308–321.

Chang, Kwang-chih
1967 *Rethinking Archaeology.* Random House, New York.

1968 *Settlement Archaeology.* National Press Books, Palo Alto, California.

Charpentier
1984 *Mémoire de Sir Charpentier*, Comm. De St Joseph en Galam pendant l'année 1725. Edited by A. Bathily, avec le concours de C. Becker.

Chavane, B. A.
1985 *Villages de l'Ancien Tekrour. Recherches archéologiques dans la moyenne vallée du fleuve Sénégal.* Editions Karthala, Paris.

Clark, A. F.
1994 Internal Migrations and Population Movements in the Upper Senegal Valley (West Africa), 1890–1920. *Canadian Journal of African Studies* 28(3):399–420.

Conrad, D. C. (2008). From the 'Banan' Tree of Kouroussa: Mapping the Landscape in Mande Traditional History. *Canadian Journal of African Studies,* 42(2/3): 384-408.

Conrad, D. C., and B. E. Frank (editors)
1995 *Status and Identity in West Africa.* Indiana University, Bloomington and Indianapolis.

Consortium SNC-LAVAL/BCEOM
1996 *Étude des Impacts du Canal du Cayor sur l'environnement. Rapport A9: Rapport sur l'archéologie et le patrimoine.* For Ministère de l'Hydraulique, République de Sénégal.

Cowgill, George L., Jeffrey H. Altschul, and Rebecca S. Sload
1984 Spatial Analysis of Teotihuacán: A Mesoamerican Metropolis. In *Intrasite Spatial Analysis in Archaeology,* edited by H. J. Hietala, pp. 154–195. Cambridge University Press, Cambridge.

Curtin, Philip D.
1975 *Economic Change in Precolonial Africa: Senegambia in the Era of the Slave Trade.* University of Wisconsin Press, Madison.

Danfakha, M.
1992 Kédougou: Histoire et Culture. Colloque, premières journées de Kédougou, 13–15 février 1992. *ANS.*

Daveau, S.
1969 La découverte du climat d'Afrique tropicale au cours des navigations portugaises (XVè siècle et début XVIè siècle). *Bulletin de l'Institut Fondamental d'Afrique Noir*, Série B, Tome XXXI, Numéro 4.

David, N. (1998). The Ethnoarchaeology and Field Archaeology of Grinding at Sukur, Adamawa State, Nigeria. *African Archaeological Review,* 15(1): 13-63.

David, P.
1974 *Journal d'un voyage fait en Bambouc en 1744.* Publié par André Delcourt, Société Française d'Histoire d'Outre-Mer, Paris.

1980 *Les Navetanes: histoires des migrants saisonniers de l'arachide en Sénégambie des origines à nos jours.* NEA, Dakar-Abidjan.

DeCorse, C. R., Richard, F. G. and Thiaw, I. (2003). Toward a Systematic Bead Description System: A View from the Lower Falemme, Senegal. *Journal of African Archaeology,* 1(1): 77-110.

DeCorse, C. R., Gijanto, L. and Sanyang, B. (2010). An Archaeological Appraisal of Early European Settlement in The Gambia. *Nyame Akuma,* 73(1): 55-64.

Deeben, Jos, and Bert Groenewoudt
2005 The Expanding Role of Predictive Modeling in Archaeological Heritage Management in the Netherlands. In *Heritage of Value, Archaeology of*

Renown: Reshaping Archaeological Assessment and Significance, edited by Clay Mathers, Timothy Darvill, and Barbara J. Little, pp. 298–300. University Press of Florida, Gainesville.

Deme, A.
2003 Archaeological Investigations of settlement and long-term complexity in the Middle Senegal Valley (Senegal). Unpublished Ph.D. dissertation, Department of Anthropology, Rice University, Houston, Texas.

Deme, A. and McIntosh, S. K. (2006). Excavations at Walaldé: New Light on the Settlement of the Middle Senegal Valley by Iron-Using Peoples. *Journal of African Archaeology*, 4(2): 317-347.

De Sapir, O. L.
1971 Shell Middens of Lower Casamance and Problems of Joola Protohistory. *West African Journal of Archaeology* 1:23–54.

Descamps, C.
1972 Contribution à la Préhistoire de l'Ouest Sénégalais. Thèse, Université de Paris, Paris.

Descamps, C., and G. Thilmans
1979 Les tumulus coquilliers des îles du Saloum (Sénégal). *Bulletin de Liaison, ASEQUA*, Numéro 54–55:81–91.

2001 Fouille de tumulus à Djouta (îles du Saloum, Sénégal). *Xième Congrés UISPP*, Liège, Belgium.

Diagne, I.
1978 Le néolithique dans l'aire Sénégambienne et dans les régions adjacentes. Contribution à la Préhistoire de l'Ouest Africain. Thèse de 3è cycle, Paris.

Diallo, T.
1972 *Les institutions politiques du Fouta Dyalon au XIXe siècle*. Université de Dakar, IFAN, Dakar, Sénégal.

Dilley, R. M. (2004). *Islamic and Caste Knowledge Practices among Haalpulaar'en in Senegal: Between Mosque and Termite Mound*. Edinburgh: Edinburgh University Press.

Diop, A.
1980 Découverte d'un biface à biseau terminal à Djita (Sénégal Oriental). *Notes Africaines*, Numéro 167:68–70.

Diouf, S.
2006 Les chasseurs traditionnels du Sénégal: contribution à l'anthropologie politique et sociale. Unpublished manuscript.

Esri
2010 ArcGIS 9.2 Desktop Help: How Iso Cluster Works. Electronic document, http://webhelp.esri.com/arcgisdesktop/9.2/index.cfm?TopicName=How%20Iso%20Cluster%20works, accessed July 28, 2010.

Fish, Suzanne K., and Stephen A. Kowalewski (editors)
1990 *The Archaeology of Regions: A Case for Full-Coverage Survey*. Smithsonian Institution Press, Washington, D.C.

Gee, Glendon W., and Dani Or
2002 Particle-Size Analysis. In *Physical Methods*, edited by J. H. Dane and G. C. Topp, pp. 255–293. Methods of Soil Analysis, pt. 4. Book Series No. 5. Soil Science Society of America, Madison, Wisconsin.

Gelbert, A. (2001). Ethnoarchaeological Study of Ceramic Borrowings. A New Methodological Approach Applied in the Middle and Upper Valleys of the Senegal River. In: Beyries, S. and Pétrequin, P. eds. *Ethno-Archaeology and Transfers*. Oxford: Archaeopress, 81-94.

Gessain, R. (1963). Introduction à l'Étude du Sénégal Oriental (Cercle de Kédougou). *Cahiers du Centre de Recherches Anthropologiques*, 11(5): 5-85.

Gijanto, L. (2011a). Exchange, Interaction, and Change in Local Ceramic Production in the Niumi Commercial Center. *Journal of Social Archaeology*, 11(1): 21-48.

Gijanto, L. (2011b). Personal Adornment and Expressions of Status: Beads and the Gambia River's Atlantic Trade. *International Journal of Historical Archaeology*, 15(4): 637-668.

Girard, J.
1992 L'or du Bambouk. *Une Dynamique de civilisation ouest-africaine, Du Gabou à la Casamance*. Georg Editeur. SA, Genève.

Gokee, C. D. (2011). Practical Knowledge and Politics of Encounter along the Lower Falémé River, Senegambia (c. AD 1500-1925). *Azania*, 46(3): 269-293.

Gokee, C. D. (2012). *Daily Life in the Land of Bambuk: An Archaeological Study of Political Economy at Diouboye, Senegal*. Unpublished PhD Dissertation. University of Michigan.

Gomez, M. A.
1992 *Pragmatism in the Age of Jihad: The Precolonial State of Boundou*. Cambridge University Press, Cambridge.

Goodland, Robert, and Maryla Webb
1987 *The Management of Cultural Property in World Bank-Assisted Projects: Archaeological Historical Religious and Natural Unique Sites*. World Bank Technical Paper Number 62. World Bank, Washington, D.C.

Gosselain, Olivier P., Alexandre Livingstone Smith, Hélène Wallaert, Guy Williams Ewe, and Marc Vander Linden
1996 Preliminary classification of African rouletting tools. Proposed during the workshop held at the Royal Museum for Central Africa, Tervuren, Belgium, September 26, 1996. Documents of the Ceramic and Society Project 5, November 1996. Tervuren, Belgium.

Green, Ernestine L.
1973 Location Analysis of Prehistoric Maya Sites in Northern British Honduras. *American Antiquity* 38:279–293.

Guéye, N. S.
1998 Poteries et peuplements de la moyenne vallée du Fleuve Sénégal du XVIé au Xxé siècle: Approches ethnoarchéologiques et ethnohistoriques. Thèse de Doctorat, Départemente d'Ethnologie et de Sociologie comparative, Université de Paris X, Nanterre.

Guitat, R.
1970 Carte et répertoire des sites néolithiques du Sénégal. *Bulletin de l'Institut Fondamental d'Afrique Noire,* Série B, Numéro 4:1125–1135.

Guitat, R. (1972). Carte et Répertoire des Site Néolithiques du Mali et de la Haute-Volta. *Bulletin de l'Institut Fondamental d'Afrique Noire, Série B,* 34(4): 896-925.

Hamy, E. T.
1901 L'age de la pierre de la Falemme. *Bulletins du Musée d'Histoire Naturelle* 4:313.

1904 Quelques observations sur les tumulus de la vallée de la Gambie. Présentée a l'occasion d'une exploration récente de M. le capitaine Duchemin. *Comptes Rendus des Séances de l'Académie des Inscriptions et Belles-Lettres*:560–569.

Heilen, Michael P.
2005 An Archaeological Theory of Landscapes. Unpublished Ph.D. Dissertation, Department of Anthropology, University of Arizona. Tucson, Arizona.

Homburg, Jeffrey A., and Gora Béye
2010 *Agricultural Soil Productivity of the Oromin Concession, Senegal*. Sabodala Cultural Heritage Program Technical Report No. 5. Technical Report 10-62. Statistical Research, Redlands, California, and Institut Fondamental d'Afrique Noir, Dakar, Senegal.

Huysecom, E. (1990). *Fanfannyégèné I: Un Abri-Sous-Roche à Occupation Néolithique au Mali: La Fouille, le Matériel Archéologique, l'Art Rupestre*. Stuttgart: Steiner Verlag Wiesbaden.

Judge, James, and Lynne Sebastian (editors)
1988 *Quantifying the Present and Predicting the Past: Theory, Method, and Application of Archaeological Predictive Modeling*. USDI Bureau of Land Management, Denver, Colorado.

Klein, M.
1998 *Slavery and Colonial Rule in French West Africa*. Cambridge, Cambridge University Press.

Kohler, Timothy A., and Sandra C. Parker
1986 Predictive Models for Archaeological Resource Location. In *Advances in Archaeological Method and Theory*, vol. 9, edited by Michael B. Schiffer, pp. 397–452. Academic Press, New York.

Kohler, Timothy A., and Sander E. van der Leeuw (editors)
2007 *Model-Based Archaeology of Socionatural Systems*. School of American Research, Santa Fe, New Mexico.

Kohler, Timothy A., C. David Johnson, Mark Varien, Scott Ortman, Robert Reynolds, Ziad Kobti, Jason Cowan, Kenneth Kolm, Schaun Smith, and Lorene Yap
2007 Settlement Ecodynamics in the Prehispanic Central Mesa Verde Region. In *The Model-Based Archaeology of Socionatural Systems*, edited by Timothy A. Kohler and Sander E. van der Leeuw, pp. 61–104. School of Advanced Research, SAR Press, Santa Fe, New Mexico, USA.

Kopytoff, I.
1987 Introduction: The Internal African Frontier: The Making of African Political Culture. In *The African Frontier. The Reproduction of Traditional African Societies,* edited by I. Kopytoff, pp. 3–83. Indiana University Press, Bloomington and Indianapolis.

Kvamme, Kenneth L.
1983 *A Manual for Predictive Site Location Models: Examples from the Grand Junction District, Colorado.* USDI Bureau of Land Management, Grand Junction District, Grand Junction, Colorado.

Laforgue, P.
1923 Essai sur l'influence de l'Industrie saharienne en Afrique occidentale au cours de la période néolithique. *Bulletin de la Société Préhistorique Française*, Tome 20:61–166.

1924 L'outillage néolithique en Hématite de la Falemme (Sénégal). *Bulletin de la Société Préhistorique Française,* Tome 21:263–264.

1925 Etat actuel de nos connaissances sur la Préhistoire en Afrique Occidentale française. *Bulletin du Comité Historique et Scientifique de l'A.O.F.,* Tome 8, Numéro 1:105–171.

Lame, M. N.
1981 Le Néolithique microlithique dunaire dans la Presqu'île du Cap Vert et ses environs. Essai d'étude typologique. Thèse de Doctorat 3è cycle, Université Paris I, Panthéon Sorbonne.

Launay, R.
1995 The Dieli of Korhogo: Identity and Identification. In *Status and Identity in West Africa*, edited by D. C. Conrad and B. E. Frank, pp. 153–169. Indiana University Press, Bloomington and Indianapolis.

Lawson, A. (2003). *Megaliths and Mande States: Sociopolitical Change in the Gambia Valley over the Past Two Millennia.* Unpublished PhD Dissertation. University of Michigan.

Legge, Karen
1989 Changing Reponses to Drought Among the Wodaabe of Niger. In *Bad Year Economics: Cultural Responses to Risk and Uncertainty*, edited by Paul Halstead and John O'Shea, pp. 81–86. Cambridge University Press, Cambridge, England.

Lestrange, M. (1955). *Les Coniagui et les Bassari (Guinée Française).* Paris: Presses Universitaires de France.

Lezine, A. M.
1989 Late Quaternary Vegetation and Climate of the Sahel. *Quaternary Research* 32:317–334.

Manchuelle, F.
1997 *Willing Migrants. Soninke Labor Diasporas, 1848–1960.* Ohio University Press, Athens.

Martin, V., and C. Becker
1970 *Sites et Monument protohistorique de la Sénégambie. Données numériques concernant la zone des tumulus et la zone mégalithique.* Kaolack, ronéotype.

1974 *Répertoire des sites protohistorique du Sénégal et de la Gambie.* Kaolack, ronéotype.

1977a Sites protohistoriques de la Sénégambie. In *Atlas National du Sénégal*, edited by R. Van Chi, pp. 48–51. IGN, Paris.

1977b Les groupes ethniques. In *Atlas National du Sénégal,* edited by R. Van Chi, pp. 64–67. IGN, Paris.

Mauny, R.
1961 *Tableau Géographique de l'Ouest Africain au Moyen Age.* Mémoire de L'IFAN 61.

Mauny, R. (1963). Contribution à la Préhistoire et à la Protohistoire de la Région de Kédougou (Sénégal Oriental). *Cahiers du Centre de Recherches Anthropologiques,* 11(5): 113-122.

McIntosh, R. J.
1983 Floodplain Geomorphology and human occupation of the upper Inland Delta of the Niger. *The Geographical Journal* 149(2):182–201.

McIntosh, S. K.
1991 Analysis of the Cuballel pottery assemblage.

1994 Changing perceptions of West Africa's Past: Archaeological Research since 1988. *Journal of Archaeological Research* 2(2):165–198.

McIntosh, S. K. (editor)
1995 *Exacavations at Jenné-Jeno, Hambarketolo and Kaniana (Inland Niger Delta, Mali), 1981 Season.* University of California Publications in Anthropology Vol. 20. University of California Press, Berkeley.

McIntosh, S. K., and H. Bocoum
2000 New Perspectives on Sincu Bara, a First Millennium Site in the Senegal Valley *African Archaeological Review* 17(1).1–43.

2002 *Excavations at Sincu Bara, Middle Senegal Valley (Senegal).* CRIAA-University de Nouakchott/IFAN-Dakar.

McIntosh, S. K., and R. J. McIntosh
1980 *Prehistoric Investigations in the Region of Jenne, Mali.* 2 vol.Cambridge Monographs in African Archaeology No. 2. Oxford, BAR.

1988 From Stone to Metal: New Perspectives on the Later Prehistory of West Africa. *Journal of World Prehistory* 2(1).

1993 Field Survey in the Tumulus Zone of Senegal. *African Archaeological Review* 11:73–107.

McIntosh, S. K., R. J. McIntosh, and H. Bocoum
1992 The Middle Senegal Valley Project: Preliminary Results from the 1990–91 Field Season. *Nyame Akuma* 38:47–61.

Mehlich, A.
1953 *Short Test Methods Used in Soil Testing Division*. Department of Agriculture, North Carolina State University, Raleigh, North Carolina.

Michel, P.
1973 *Les Bassins des Fleuves Sénégal et de Gambie. Etude Géomorphologique*. 2 tomes. Mémoires ORSTOM, Paris, France.

Monroe, J. C. and Ogundiran, A., eds. (2012). *Power and Landscape in Atlantic West Africa: Archaeological Perspectives*. Cambridge: Cambridge University Press.

Moreau, J. L. M.
1900 Notes sur les haches polies provenant de la vallée de la Haute-Falémé (Sénégal). *Bulletins du Musée d'Histoire Naturelle* 6:94–96.

Naffé, B. O. M., R. Lanfranchi, and N. Schlanger
2008 *L'archéologie Préventive En Afrique De L'ouest, Enjeux Et Perspectives*. Institut National de Recherches Archéologiques Preventives. Actes du colloque de Nouakchott 1–3 février 2007. Editions Sépia, Saint-Maur-des-Fossés.

Niane, D. T.
1960 *Soundjata ou l'épopée mandingue*. Présence Africaine, Paris, Dakar.

1989 *Histoire des Mandingues de l'Ouest*. Le Royaume du Gabou. Karthala, Paris.

Nicholson, S. E.
1978 Comparison of historical and recent African rainfall anomalies with late Pleistocene and early Holocene. *Palaeoecology of Africa and The Surrounding Islands* 10:99–123.

Oromin Explorations, Ltd.
2010 Senegal Sabodala Project. Electronic document, http://www.oromin.com/s/Senegal_Sabodala.asp, accessed June 21, 2010.

Ogundiran, A. (2002). Of Small Things Remembered: Beads, Cowries, and Cultural Translations of the Atlantic Experience in Yorubaland. *International Journal of African Historical Studies,* 35(2/3): 427-457.

Park, Thomas K., Mamadou Baro, and Tidiane Ngaid
1993 Crisis in Nationalism in Mauritania. In *Risk and Tenure in Arid Lands: The Political Ecology of Development in the Senegal River Basin*, edited by Thomas K. Park, pp. 87–121. University of Arizona Press, Tucson, Arizona, USA.

Peters, Jan, Bernard De Baets, Niko E. C. Verhoest, Roeland Samson, Sven Degroeve, Piet De Becker, and Willy Huybrechts
2007 Random Forests as a tool for ecohydrological distribution modeling. *Ecological Modelling* 207:304–318.

Petit-Maire, N.
1991 Tableau D'Ensemble. In *Paléoenvironnements du Sahara. Lacs holocènes à Taoudenni (Mali)*. Editions du CNRS, Paris.

Petite-Maire, N. et al.
1991 Contexte Archéologique. In *Paléoenvironnements du Sahara. Lacs holocènes à Taoudenni (Mali)*. Sous la direction de N. Petit-Maire, Editions du CNRS Paris.

Plog, Fred T., and James N. Hill
1971 Explaining Variability in the Distribution of Prehistoric Population Aggregates. In *The Distribution of Prehistoric Population Aggregates*, edited by George J. Gumerman, pp. 7–36. Prescott College Anthropological Reports No. 1. Prescott, Arizona.

Pruneau, J.
1983 *Mémoire sur le commerce de la concession du Sénégal (1752)*. Publié et commenté par C. Becker. Kaolack, Senegal.

Rançon, A.
1894 Le Boundou: Étude de géographie et d'histoire soudaniennes de 1681 à nos jours. *Bulletin de la société de géographie de Bordeaux* 7:433–463.

Ravisé, A.
1970 Industrie néolithique en os dans la région de Saint Louis (Sénégal). *Notes Africaines* 128:97–102.

1975 Recensement des sites Paléolithiques et Néolithiques du Sénégal. *Bulletin de l'Institut Fondamental d'Afrique Noire,* Série B, Tome 37:234–245.

Rice, P. M.
1987　*Pottery Analysis. A Sourcebook*. The University of Chicago Press, Chicago.

Richard, F. G. (2010). Recharting Atlantic Encounters: Object Trajectories and Histories of Value in the Siin (Senegal) and Senegambia. *Archaeological Dialogues,* 17(1): 1-27.

Roberts, R.
1987　*Warriors, Merchants and, Slaves. The State and the Economy in the Middle Niger Valley, 1700–1914*. Stanford University Press, Stanford.

Robinson, D.
1985　*The Holy War of Umar Tal: The Western Sudan in the mid-nineteenth Century*. Clarenton Press, Oxford.

Rose, Martin R., and Jeffrey H. Altschul
1988　An Overview of Statistical Method and Theory for Quantitative Model Building. In *Quantifying the Present and Predicting the Past*, edited by W. J. Judge and L. Sebastian, pp. 173–255. U.S. Department of the Interior, Bureau of Land Management, Denver.

Ruhe, Robert V.
1975　*Geomorphology: Geomorphic Processes and Surficial Geology*. Houghton Mifflin Harcourt, Boston, Massachusetts.

Sanneh, L. O. (1989). *The Jakhanke Muslim Clerics: A religious and historical study of Islam in Senegambia*. Lanham: University Press of America.

Sarnethein, M.
1978　Sand deserts during glacial maximum and climatic optimum. *Nature* 272:43–46.

Schoenberger, P. J., D. A. Wysocki, E. C. Benham, and W. D. Broderson
2002　Field Book for Describing and Sampling Soils (version 2.0). Natural Resources Conservation Service, National Soil Survey Center, Lincoln, Nebraska.

Searing, J. F.
2001　*God alone is king: Islam and emancipation in Senegal, the Wolof kingdoms of Kajoor and Bawol, 1859–1914*. Heinemann, Porthsmouth.

Shepard, O. A.
1974　*Ceramics for the Archaeologists*. Carnegie Institution of Washington, Washington D.C.

Singleton, M.
1982　De l'intendance indigene du gibier à une gestion endogène de la faune. In *Environnement Africain: Gestion de la faune sauvage, facteur de développement*, edited by P. P. Vinkie and M. Singleton, pp. 69–106. Études et Recherches Numéro °71–72. ISFENDA-MAB/UNESCO, Paris.

Smith, Laurajane, and Natsuko Akagawa
2009　*Intangible Heritage*. Routledge, London.

Soil Survey Division Staff
1993　*Soil Survey Manual*. USDA Handbook No. 18. U.S. Government Printing Office, Washington, D.C.

Soil Survey Staff
1999　*Soil Taxonomy: A Basic System of Soil Classification for Making and Interpreting Soil Surveys*. Agriculture Handbook 436. USDA Natural Resources Conservation Service, Washington, D.C.

Stahl, A. B. (2001). *Making History in Banda: Anthropological Visions of Africa's Past*. Cambridge: Cambridge University Press.

Stahl, A. B. (2002). Colonial Entanglements and the Practices of Taste: An Alternative to Logocentric Approaches. *American Anthropologist,* 104(3): 827-845.

Szumowski, G. (1956). Fouilles de l'Abri Sous Roche de Kourounkorokalé (Soudan Français). *Bulletin de l'Institut Français d'Afrique Noire, Série B,* 18(3-4): 462-508.

Tamari, T.
1991　The Development of Caste Systems in West Africa. *Journal of African History* 32:221–250.

Thiam, M.
1991　La céramique au Sénégal: Archéologie et Histoire. Thèse de Doctorat 3è cycle, Université de Paris I, Sorbonne.

Thiam, M. (2010). Poterie et Identité: Les Bassari et Bedik du Sénégal Oriental. *In:* Thiaw, I. ed. *Espaces, Culture Matérielle et Identités en Sénégambie*. Dakar: CODESRIA, 68-84.

Thiaw, I.
1999　An Archeological Investigation of Long-Term Culture Change in the Lower Falemme (Upper Senegal Region) A.D. 500–1900. Unpublished Ph.D. Dissertation. Department of Anthropology, Rice University, Houston, Texas.

2003 Archaeology and the Public in Senegal: Reflections on doing Fieldwork at Home. *Journal of African Archaeology* 9(2):215–225.

2007 Grands chantiers et destruction de notre patrimoine culturel: le Cri de cœur d'un archéologue. *Le Quotidien*, jeudi 5 juillet, pp. 9.

2008 Développement touristique et mal gestion des ressources culturelles archéologiques dans le Delta du Saloum (Sénégal). In *L'archéologie Préventive En Afrique De L'ouest, Enjeux Et Perspectives,* by Baouba Ould Mohamed Naffé, Raymond Lanfranchi, and Nathan Schlanger, pp. 86–96. Actes du colloque de Nouakchott 1–3 février 2007. Editions Sépia, Saint-Maur-des-Fossés.

Thiaw, I., M. Diagne, and J. Altschul
2010a *Report on Archaeological Monitoring of Proposed Drill Sites and Other Mine-Related Activities in the Mining areas of the Proposed Reservoir and Mining Areas of Kerekounda and, Korolo, Sabodala, Senegal.* Sabodala Cultural Heritage Project Technical Report 2. Statistical Research, Tucson, Arizona, USA.

2010b *Report on Archaeological Monitoring of Proposed Drill Sites and Other Mine-Related Activities in the Mining Areas of Masato, Golouma, and Kerekounda, Sabodala, Senegal.* Sabodala Cultural Heritage Project Technical Report 3. Statistical Research, Tucson, Arizona, USA.

Thilmans, G., and C. Descamps
1982 *Amas et tumulus du delta du Saloum. Recherches Scientifiques dans les Parcs nationaux du Sénégal.* Mémoires de l'Institut Fondamental d'Afrique Noire, Numéro 92. IFAN, Dakar.

Thilmans, G., C. Descamps, and B. Khayat
1980 *Protohistoire du Sénégal. Recherches archéologiques.* Tome 1, Les sites mégalithiques. Mémoires de l'Institut Fondamental d'Afrique Noire, Numéro 91. IFAN, Dakar.

Thilmans, G., and A. Ravisé
1980 *Protohistoire du Sénégal. Recherches archéologiques.* Tome 2, Sincu Bara et les sites du Fleuve. Mémoires de l'Institut Fondamental d'Afrique Noire, Numéro 91. IFAN, Dakar.

Thomas, Grant W.
1996 Soil pH and Soil Acidity. In *Chemical Methods*, edited by D. L. Sparks, pp. 475–490. Methods of Soil Analysis, pt. 3. Book Series No. 5. Soil Science Society of America and the American Society of Agronomy, Madison, Wisconsin.

Thoms, Alston V.
1988 Survey of Predictive Locational Models: Examples from the Late 1970s and Early 1980s. In *Quantifying the Present and Predicting the Past: Theory, Method, and Application of Archaeological Predictive Modeling,* edited by James Judge and Lynne Sebastian. Appendix, pp. 581–645. U.S. Department of the Interior, Bureau of Land Management, Denver, Colorado.

Tilley, Christopher
1993 Art, Architecture, Landscape [Neolithic Sweden]. In *Landscape, Politics and Perspectives,* edited by B. Bender, pp. 49–84. Berg, Providence.

1994 *A Phenomenology of Landscape: Places, Paths and Monuments*. Berg, Oxford.

2004 *The Materiality of Stone. Explorations in Landscape Phenomenology I*. Berg, Oxford.

Togola, T.
1996 Iron Age occupation in the Méma Region, Mali. *African Archaeological Review* 13(2):91–110.

United Nations Educational, Scientific and Cultural Organization (UNESCO)
1995–2010 The Intangible Heritage Lists. Electronic document, http://www.unesco.org/culture/ich/index.php, accessed July 24, 2010.

2010 Stone Circles of Senegambia. Electronic document, http://whc.unesco.org/en/list/1226, accessed July 28, 2010.

Vendrig, Mark, and Christina James
2008 *Terms of Reference: Specialist Baseline Studies*. ESIA for the Proposed Oromin Mine: Sabodala, Senegal. Prepared for the Oromin Joint Venture Group. SRK. Project Number 2CO003.003. SRK Consulting, Vancouver, B.C.

Wait, G., I. Thiaw, and J. Altschul
2009 *Prefeasibility Report: Cultural Heritage Component of the Economic and Social Impact Assessment, Oromin Gold Mine Project, Sabodala, Senegal.* Technical Report 09-28. Statistical Research, Tucson, Arizona, USA.

Wait, Gerald, Ibrahima Thiaw, Jeffrey A. Homburg, and Jeffrey H. Altschul
2010 *Report on Archaeological Investigations Sabodala, Senegal, March–April 2010.* Sabodala Cultural Heritage Project Technical Report 4. Statistical Research, Tucson, Arizona, USA.

Wescott, K. L., and R. J. Brandon
2000 *Practical Applications of GIS for Archaeology: A Predictive Modeling Toolkit*. Taylor and Francis, Philadelphia.

Whitley, T. G.
2005 A Brief Outline of Causality-Based Cognitive Archaeological Probabilistic Modeling. In *Predictive Modelling for Archaeological Heritage Management: a research agenda,* edited by M. van Leusen and H. Kamermans, pp. 123–138. Rijksdienst voor het Oudheidkundig Bodemonderzoek, Amersfoort.

Whittlesey, Stephanie M.
1998 Archaeological Landscapes: A Methodological and Theoretical Discussion. In *Overview, Synthesis, and Conclusions*, edited by Stephanie M. Whittlesey, Richard Ciolek-Torrello, and Jeffrey H. Altschul, pp. 17–28. Vanishing River: Landscapes and Lives of the Lower Verde Valley: The Lower Verde Archaeological Project. SRI Press, Tucson, Arizona.

Willey, Gordon Randolph
1953 *Prehistoric Settlement Patterns in the Virú Valley, Perú*. Bureau of Ethnology Bulletin No. 155. Smithsonian Institution, Washington, D.C.

Wong, Jenny, Mathieu Gueye, Sognibe N'Danikou, Ababacar Cisse, Salif Sankhere, and Moussa Diallo
2010 *Medicinal plants and other forest products baseline report*. Specialist Study 15. Sabodala Environmental and Social Impacts Statement. Submitted to SRK Consulting, Vancouver, Canada by Wild Resources, Ltd., Gwynedd, Wales.

Zedeño, María Nieves
1997 Landscapes, Land Use, and the History of Territory Formation: An Example from the Puebloan Southwest. *Journal of Archaeological Method and Theory* 4(1):67–103.

Zedeño, María Nieves, Diane Austin, and Richard Stoffle
1997 *Landmark and Landscape: A Contextual Approach to the Management of American Indian Resources*. Bureau of Applied Research in Anthropology, University of Arizona, Tucson.

Zeltner, F.
1916 Quelques Gisements Préhistoriques de la Vallée du Sénégal. *Extrait des Bulletins et Mémoires de la Société d'Anthropologie de Paris*: 238–244.

Agricultural-Soil Productivity of the Oromin Joint Venture Group Concession, Senegal

Jeffrey A. Homburg and Gora Bèye

Introduction

Statistical Research, Inc. (SRI), conducted an agricultural-soil-productivity study for SRK Consulting (SRK) as part of the baseline studies for the Environmental and Social Impact Assessment for the Sabodala Gold Mine Operation in southeast Senegal. As stated in the Terms of Reference for the baseline studies, 'the main objective of this study (soils) is to describe and map soil resources within the concession area and to characterize the soil condition in terms of nutrient status, agricultural potential, erodibility and rehabilitation potential' (Vendrig and James 2008:44). To meet this objective, SRI proposed a study focused on soil productivity and based on observations of soil properties in profiles (e.g., topsoil thickness, depth to diagnostic soil horizons, structure, etc.) and tests of soil quality, such as pH, soil nutrients, particle-size analysis, and infiltration rates, to compare the soil quality of fields with that of fallow areas. SRI compiled soil maps scaled to the project area from previously published soil maps and assessed the productivity for agriculture and agroforestry, as well as soil erodibility, based on these soil maps. With the help of SRK's Geographic Information System (GIS) staff, we combined field observations with remote-sensing data to assess land-use capability at a general level. Finally, we offer recommendations for improving agricultural sustainability.

The evaluation of agricultural-soil productivity for the Oromin Joint Venture Group (OJVG) concession was based on soil map units identified in a published soil map (Stanicoff et al. 1986). Because of the large scale of the map, we aimed to refine this general evaluation with a complementary study to assess the effects of agriculture on soil productivity for one community, Mamakhono, the oldest village in the OJVG concession. The goals of this study were to (1) interview local farmers in order to document and record their soil-management and -conservation techniques and the Malinké classifications of different soil types, landforms, and other terms of agricultural significance; (2) characterize and measure anthropogenic effects on agricultural-soil quality; (3) assess the impact of the proposed mining activities on agriculture; and (4) recommend measures that might mitigate potentially negative impacts of the mining project.

The SRI study was spearheaded by Dr. Jeffrey Homburg, soil scientist and geoarchaeologist at SRI, in collaboration with Mr. Gora Bèye, an agricultural specialist at the Centre de Suivi Écologique (CSE) in Dakar. Field investigations for this agricultural-soil study were conducted in conjunction with geoarchaeological research that was directed by Dr. Homburg. This work complements a previous agricultural study of the OJVG concession by Bèye et al. (2010).

This report is divided into three sections. The first section outlines our field and analytical methods. The second section presents our results for the OJVG concession and for the more limited Mamakhono study. The third, and final, section assesses the effects of mining activities on agricultural practices for the OJVG concession as a whole and, at a more refined level, for Mamakhono.

Methods

Testing for human-caused soil change is predicated on the validity of the methods for detecting such changes. There are a number of potential problems and uncertainties in evaluating the long-term effects of agriculture on soils. Examples of these issues center on (1) the availability of appropriate uncultivated ('control') soils to use as references for assessing soil change from agriculture, as well as the kinds of control soils, their validity, and what can be inferred from them; (2) the sampling design—the number, depth, and types of samples and sample sites needed to test for soil differences; and (3) the appropriate physical, chemical, and biological assays of soil properties and how to interpret results (see Holliday 2004; Homburg et al. 2005; Sandor et al. 1986).

This soil-quality evaluations is based on the soil criteria summarized in Table 1 (all but bulk density and total phosphorus). Although we consider all of the properties listed in Table 1 to be important for measuring soil quality, it is important to note that there is no universally accepted method for assessing soil degradation in all agricultural soils. Furthermore, there is no consensus on how soil quality should be defined and measured. The utility of the soil-quality concept, itself, has even come under attack (Sojka and Upchurch 1999). As noted by Mausbach and Seybold (1998:33), soil-quality definitions range from simply 'the capacity of a soil to function' (Pierce and Larson 1993) to more-inclusive ones, such as

TABLE 1. SOIL PROPERTIES THAT MAY INDICATE SOIL DEGRADATION CAUSED BY CULTIVATION
(ADAPTED FROM HOMBURG AND SANDOR 2005).

Soil Property	Criteria for Recognizing Degradation: Typical Causes and Consequences
A horizon thickness	Decreased thickness caused by water or wind erosion. Reduces important organic matter-enriched surface layer that can be exploited by plants for water, nutrients, and oxygen. Shallower depth to possible root-limiting subsurface layers such as strongly developed argillic horizons.
Soil structure	Macromorphology: lowered grade of granular or subangular blocky structure, trend toward massive state, especially in surface horizons. Commonly results from compaction and organic matter decline.
Bulk density	Compaction (increase in bulk density above that of natural condition) associated with soil structure degradation. Compaction and structure degradation commonly retard seed germination and root growth, reduce root access to water, oxygen, and nutrients, reduce diffusion of gases, and decrease water infiltration and available water capacity.
Organic carbon	Decrease in organic C is common under conventional cultivation. Results from accelerated microbial oxidation of organic matter in disrupted, exposed soil aggregates, and other effects of agriculture. Numerous benefits of organic matter for soil physical, chemical, and biological properties important to plant growth are well documented.
Nitrogen	Decrease in total N accompanies declining organic matter in agricultural soils, though C:N ratio tends to decrease. Nitrate and ammonium are plant available forms of N, which is commonly a key limiting factor for plant growth in all regions, including arid regions.
Phosphorus	P (both total and available) is another macronutrient that has been shown to decrease due to cultivation in some cases. P is a key ecological and soil indicator because of its low mobility, low availability to plants, and long-term stability of its forms in soils.
pH	Very high soil pH can indicate salt accumulation (which is measured by electrical conductivity). Sodic soil conditions (recognized by high exchangeable sodium) can be prevalent in agricultural soils of arid and semiarid regions. Detrimental effects on many plants, including crop species, occur both through direct chemical effects and through soil structural deterioration. pH is also an indicator of the availability of nutrients to crops.

'the capacity of a specific kind of soil to function, within natural or managed ecosystem boundaries, to sustain plant and animal productivity, maintain or enhance water and air quality, and support human health and habitation' (Karlen et al. 1997). In selecting a suite of soil tests, it is therefore necessary to consider such local factors as climate, topography, hydrology, soil type, native vegetation, crop type and variety, agricultural technology, and the duration and intensity of cultivation. Although there is controversy about the concept of soil quality and how it should be measured, there is a consensus that the properties summarized in Table 1 are all key indicators of soil quality and agricultural sustainability (Arshad and Coen 1992; Larson and Pierce 1991, 1994; Papendick and Parr 1992), and so we consider our approach to be valid for this study.

Field Methods

The overall design and field methods for this study build on previous research conducted by Dr. Homburg and his colleagues (especially Dr. Jonathan Sandor, Soil Science professor at Iowa State University) in the North American Southwest, the Peruvian Andes, and East Africa (see Homburg 1992, 1994, 2000, 2002, 2003, 2005a, 2005b; Homburg and Casey 2007; Homburg and Palacios-Fest 2010; Homburg and Sandor 1997; Homburg et al. 2004, 2005; Sandor 1995, 2006; Sandor and Eash 1991; Sandor and Gersper 1988; Sandor et al. 1986, 1990, 2005, 2007; Sutton and Homburg 2002).

Before initiating the field investigation, we compiled and reviewed existing regional soil and geologic maps. The field phase of our work extended from March 1 to March 28, 2010. Dr. Homburg was assisted in the field by Mr. Massal Diagne and Ms. Amy Colle Seck (Institut Fondamental d'Afrique Noire graduate students), Dr. Masamba Lamb (semiretired archaeologist), and seven local laborers (Mr. Mamadou Cisse, Mr. Sadio Daniokho, Mr. Amadou Cissokho, Mr. Pathe Diallo, Mr. Mamadou Lamine Cissokho, Mr. Mamoudou Diallo, and Mr. Sorry Diarra). The field phase of this investigation focused on agricultural soils in the Mamakhono farming community. The agricultural fields near Mamakhono and others in the OJVG concession are shown in Figure 1. The first field task involved selecting, excavating, and

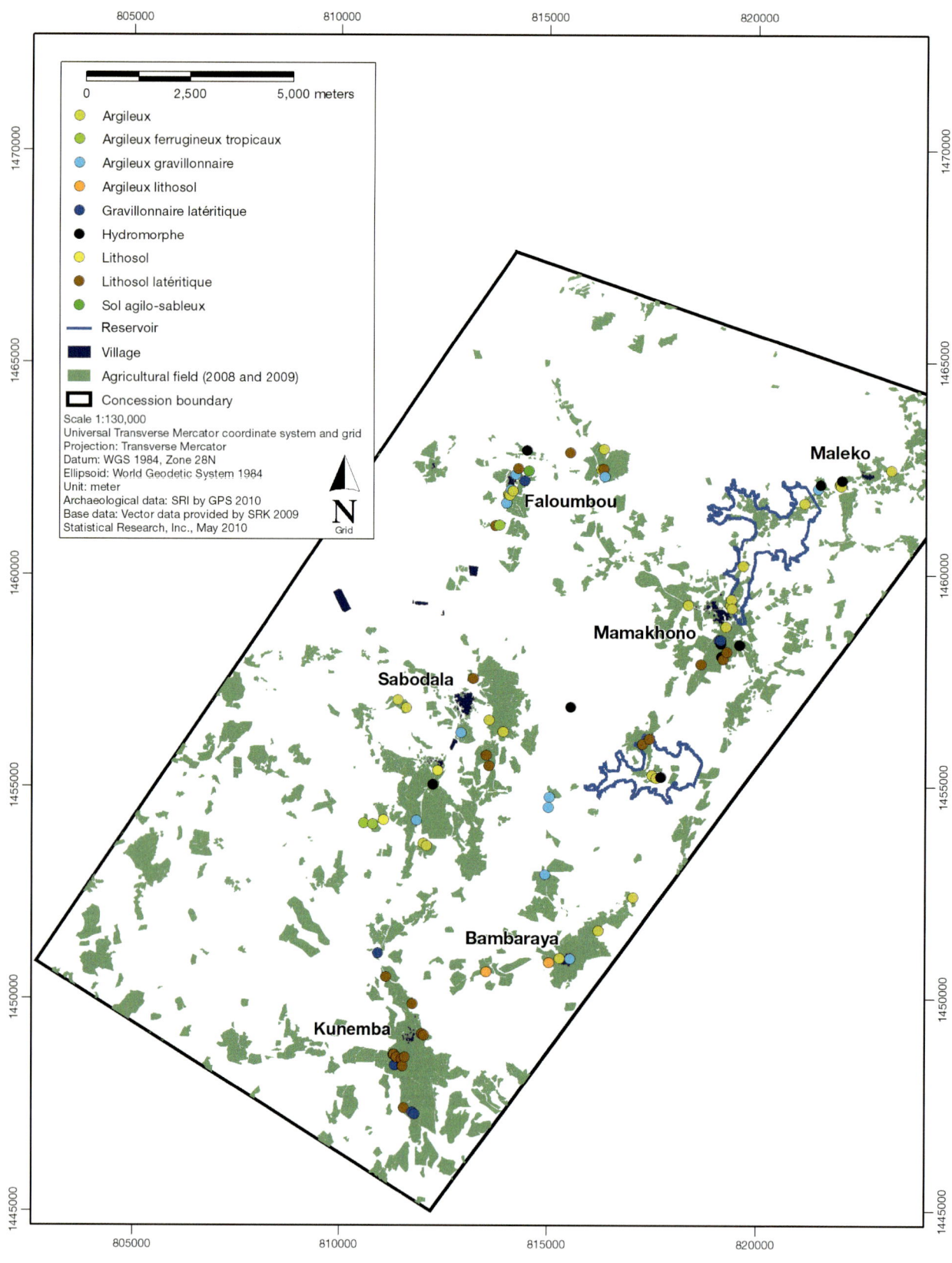

Figure 1. Map of agricultural fields for a 2-year period (2008–2009) in the Oromin Joint Venture Group concession and the locations of agricultural fields documented by Gora Bèye (2010) and their soil types.

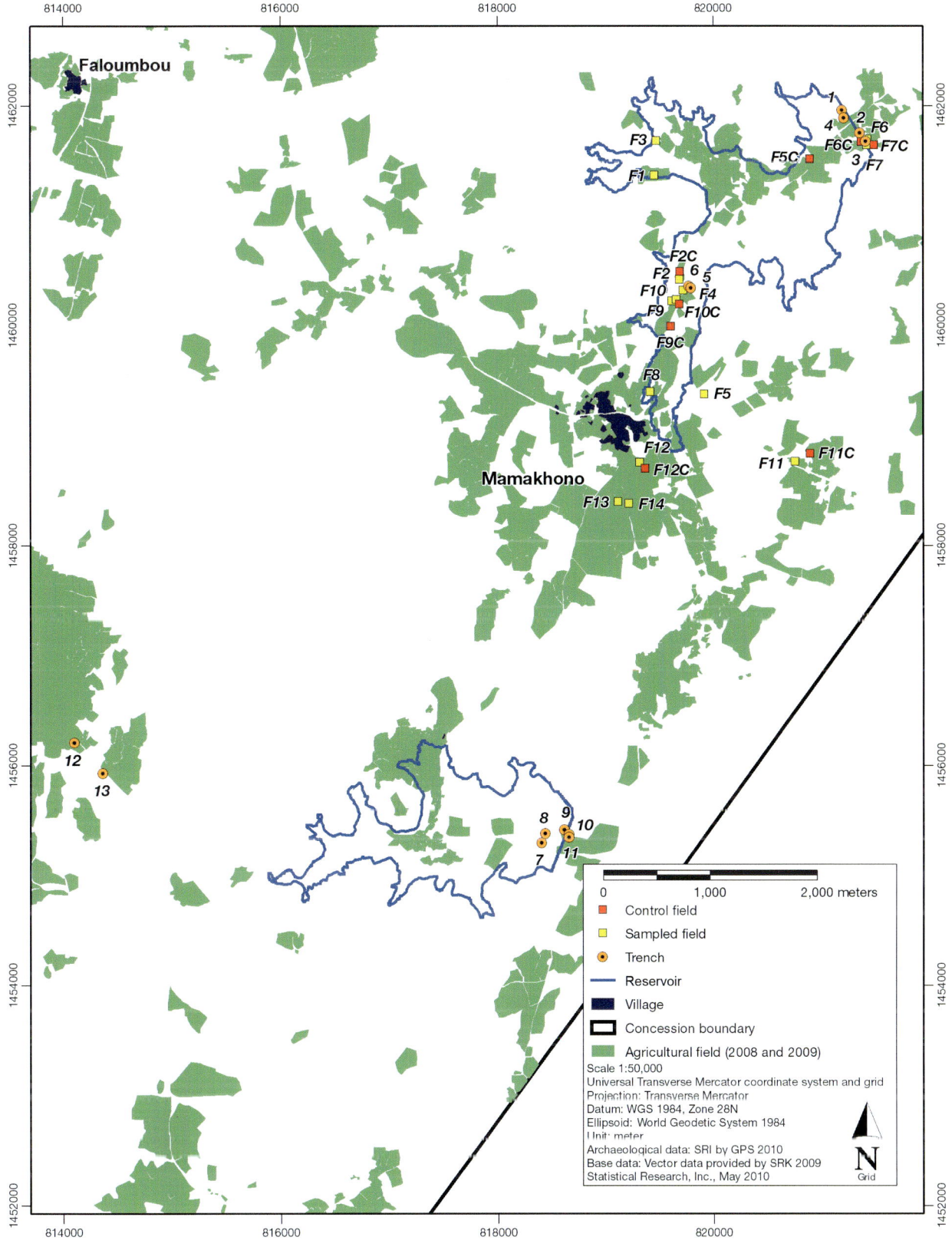

FIGURE 2. LOCATIONS OF AGRICULTURAL FIELDS AND FIELD CONTROLS IN THE MAMAKHONO AREA AND GEOARCHAEOLOGICAL BACKHOE TRENCHES IN THE PROJECT AREA.

A Slave Who Would Be King

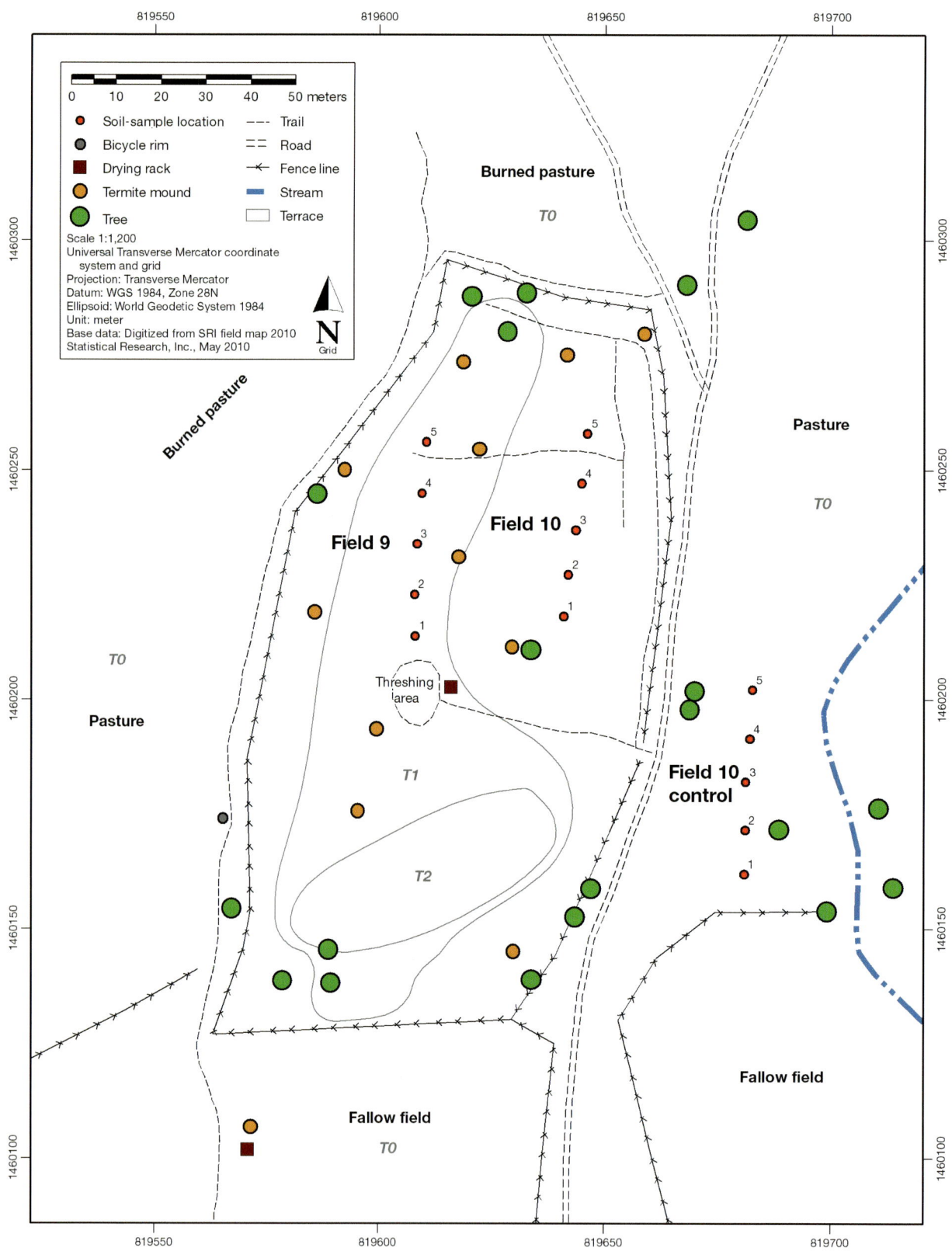

FIGURE 3. MAP OF FIELDS 9/10 AND THE FIELD 10 CONTROL,
SHOWING THE LOCATIONS WHERE SOIL SAMPLES WERE COLLECTED AND THE GEOMORPHIC SURFACES.

Figure 4. Mamadou Cisse (*left*) and Amy Colle Seck (*right*) collecting soil samples from an agricultural field.

Figure 5. Massal Diagne collecting unsaturated hydraulic-conductivity data from an agricultural field, using a tension infiltrometer.

FIGURE 6. MAMAKHONO CHIEF BOUCARY CISSOKHO (*HOLDING THE BABY*) WITH FAMILY AND LOCAL FARMERS, LATINE CISSOKHO (*NEPHEW OF BOUCARY, WITH A HAT, KNEELING ON THE LEFT*), AND INTERVIEWER JEFFREY HOMBURG (*TO THE RIGHT OF BOUCARY*).

documenting 13 backhoe trenches placed in proposed impact areas (6 in the proposed freshwater-reservoir area, 5 in the proposed tailings reservoir, and 2 on the proposed haul road) (Figure 2). Trenches were mainly excavated to a depth of 3 m below the surface, using an excavator—a backhoe on tracks (also called a trackhoe). Soil morphological properties (e.g., depth and thickness of soil horizons, color, texture, structure, etc.) were described for all profiles.

The backhoe trenches were used to (1) document soil morphological properties (e.g., topsoil thickness, soil color, texture, horizons, structure, consistence, and other properties) in accordance with the conventions of modern soil survey (Soil Survey Division Staff 1993; Soil Survey Staff 1999), (2) assess the probability of buried archaeological sites for different landforms, and (3) collect soil samples from different landforms, most of which were ones used for agricultural production. The backhoe and operator were supplied by OJVG, as availability allowed between their normal mining-exploration activities. Backhoe Trenches 1–6 were all excavated in the proposed freshwater-reservoir area. All soil horizons in the upper 1.5 m of the profile were analyzed for the physical and chemical soil tests described below.

After the backhoe trenching was complete, 14 agricultural fields and 8 field controls in the Mamakhono area (see Figure 2) were visited. Representative digital photographs were documented for each site, including agricultural features, such as crop-drying racks, bamboo/mud field houses, and any noteworthy observations. Five approximately 300-g soil samples were collected from the upper 15 cm of soil from each field/control, with samples collected at 10-m intervals from a transect across a representative part of each field/control (Figures 3 and 4). Samples were numbered consecutively (that is, 1–5) within each field/control. In all, 110 soil samples were collected from the 22 fields/controls. Soil pH and gravel analyses were completed for all samples from each field/control, and equal subsamples from the five samples from each field/control were combined into a single sample for particle-size and other chemical analyses. Figure 3 shows how soil-sampling locations were placed in the fields and controls (note: Fields 9 and 10 are actually part of a single field, but soil samples were collected from two different geomorphic surfaces within the field; so, the two sections of the field were designated as Field 9 and Field 10, to distinguish them) and in a control area from the same geomorphic surface (the floodplain) as that of Field 10. Unsaturated-hydraulic-conductivity tests were completed next to the No. 3 soil sample for each field/control (Figure 5), the middle point of each soil-sampling transect. Global Positioning System (GPS) readings were recorded for the No. 3 soil sample of each field/control, and the orientation of the soil-sampling transect was measured using a Sunto compass. The slope aspect and gradient representative of each field/control were measured using a compass and clinometer. None of the fields were being cultivated at the time of our fieldwork, as our work was conducted during March, in the dry season. Information on recently cultivated crops was recorded and was based on traces of crop residues observed for each field. The natural vegetation of each control was also documented.

During the course of fieldwork on this agricultural-soil study, we arranged to interview Mamakhono farmers to document their agricultural-management and -conservation techniques and to record a number of Malinké terms important to agriculture. Two translators were used in the interviews. Mr. Diagne translated dialogue from English to Wolof, and Mr. Latine Cissokho (an OJVG worker and the nephew of Chief Boucary Cissokho, chief of Mamakhono) translated dialogue from Wolof to Malinké. The farmers interviewed included Chief Cissokho, Mr. Ibrahima Cissokho and Mr. Boubacar Cissokho (sons of the chief), Mr. Kama Keito, Mr. Saraba Diallo, Mr. Seyni Toure, Mr. Aliou Diallo, and Mr. Tagotango Diallo (Figure 6).

Analytical Methods

Evaluations of anthropogenic effects on agricultural-soil quality were based on comparisons of soil samples from fields now under cultivation with the uncultivated controls. Differences between the fields and the controls served as the yardstick for measuring the effects of cultivation. A concerted effort was made to search for suitable controls for each field; that is, nearby soils in similar landscape positions (defined as the same geomorphic surfaces of respective alluvial terraces) and soils. But in six cases, no suitable controls were found. Consequently, different types of comparisons were made: (1) all fields versus all controls, (2) the eight fields paired with their controls, and (3) all fields versus controls for each respective landform on which they occur (that is, the T0 [or floodplain], T1 [first terrace above the floodplain], and T2 [second terrace above the floodplain]). These comparisons were made graphically with a series of histograms and statistically using t-tests; paired t-tests were completed for the eight fields paired with controls.

Some soil properties were analyzed in a field lab, such as soil pH analyses, to obtain data regarding nutrient availability to plants, and gravel-content analyses. Gravel content was measured on a gravimetric basis (that is, the weight of gravel relative to the weight of the entire bulk sample of soil). Gravel content was measured by air-drying the bulk soil samples collected from the field, grinding the air-dried samples with a mortar and pestle so that natural soil particles larger than 2 mm in size (the size boundary between gravel and sand) could be separated in a sieve, and then weighing the gravel.

Particle size, bulk density, organic matter, total carbon (essentially organic carbon, in this case, because of the acid pH of almost all soils), nitrogen, total and available phosphorus, pH, and electrical conductivity were analyzed. Initial sample preparation involved air-drying and sifting samples through a 2-mm sieve to remove gravel, roots, and other coarse, undecomposed, organic debris. Subsamples were then taken for the various soil analyses at two soil laboratories. Calcium, magnesium, potassium, sodium, and available-phosphorus analyses were conducted by Mary Jo Schabel at the Milwaukee Soil Laboratory. Particle-size, total-carbon, and nitrogen analyses were conducted by the Department of Geography Soil Analysis Laboratory at Northern Illinois University, under the direction of Dr. Michael Konen.

Available-phosphorus analysis was completed for 10-g subsamples that were mechanically ground to pass through a No. 100 sieve. Available phosphorus was measured using the Bray 1 extractant (Bray and Kurtz 1945). Soil pH was measured in the field by colorimetry, with a Hellige-Truog soil-reaction tester, and electrochemically, in a 1:1 (by weight) suspension of soil and distilled/deionized water, using a portable Hanna pH meter (model no. HI 991301) (Thomas 1996). Total-carbon and nitrogen concentrations were determined using an Elementar CN analyzer. Calcium, magnesium, potassium, and sodium were all measured using extraction techniques described by Mehlich (1953). Particle-size distributions were measured using the sieve-and-pipette method (Gee and Or 2002: Methods 2.4.3.2 and 2.4.3.4), with samples pretreated with 30 percent hydrogen peroxide for organic-matter digestion and a sodium hexametaphosphate solution for clay dispersion.

A minidisk tension infiltrometer with a 45-mm-diameter baseplate made by Decagon Devices was used to measure unsaturated infiltration rates for all 24 of the field and control soils. Infiltration rates were measured at a pressure head (ψ): -2. The surface of the soil was leveled, to ensure good hydraulic contact between the infiltrometer disk and the soil surface, by placing the base plate of the infiltrometer on a thin layer of clean contact sand (medium quartz sand used in swimming-pool filters). Infiltration proceeded until a steady-state infiltration rate was reached, with infiltration volumes recorded every 60 seconds.

Hydraulic conductivity (K) was determined using a method proposed by Logsdon and Jaynes (1993), in which Gardner's (1958) expression for the exponential relation between K and ψ was substituted into Wooding's (1968) solution for unconfined steady-state infiltration from a disk. The exponential relation between K and ψ is as follows (Gardner 1958), in Equation 1:

$$\frac{q(\psi)}{(\pi R^2)} = K_{sat}\, e^{\alpha\psi} + \frac{4K_{sat}\, e^{\alpha\psi}}{\pi R \alpha}$$

$$K(\psi) = K_{sat} e^{\alpha\psi}$$

where $K(\psi)$ is the unsaturated hydraulic conductivity [cm min^{-1}] at the specified pressure head (ψ), K_{sat} is the saturated hydraulic conductivity, and α is a constant [cm^{-1}] that reflects the slope of the exponential function (White and Sully 1987). Logsdon and Jaynes (1993) assumed α to be constant for $\psi \leq 0$ and derived a method to estimate α and K_{sat} using a nonlinear regression technique to fit the following expression to measured data (Equation 2):

In Equation 2, q is the measured steady-state infiltration rate [cm min^{-1}], and R is the base radius (4 cm) of the infiltrometer. Experimental parameters of α and K_{sat} were estimated using a nonlinear regression technique, by plotting steady-state fluxes (= q/πR^2; nothing appears before the equals sign, as this equation refers to how α and K_{sat} were estimated) versus the pressure-head values at which they were measured (i.e., ψ = -2, -10, and -15 cm). The α and K_{sat} values were iteratively changed so that an optimized fit of Equation 2 to the measured data was achieved. Plant available water and other soil hydraulic properties (e.g., field capacity, permanent wilting point, and saturated hydraulic conductivity) were modeled using the regression coefficients of Saxton et al. (1986), based on sand and clay content.

Results

Evaluation of Agricultural-Soil Productivity for the OJVG Concession

A 1:500,000-scale soil map published by Stanicioff et al. (1986) covers the OJVG concession. Figure 7 shows part of this soil map for the project area. This map has five soil map units, each of which was classified in accordance with the Food and Agriculture Organization (FAO) system. The key for Figure 7 is elaborated in Table 2 to provide information on the approximate association of the FAO soil types with the U.S. Department of Agriculture (USDA) soil taxonomy. Soil map units in the OJVG concession are composed of (1) alluvial-floodplain and alluvial-terrace soils (unit Aa3); (2) Lithosols and Regosols formed in residuum weathered from basic rocks (M1a); (3) Vertisols and vertic soils on floodplains (M1c); (4) 30 percent Lithosols (soils armored with laterite), 40 percent Regosols formed in gravelly material, and 20 percent leached, tropical ferruginous soils formed in material derived from migmetites (M2b); and (5) 60 percent Lithosols and 25–40 percent Regosols (M3a2). Each of these soils is described in more detail in Table 2, along with information on the areal extent of each soil and the amount of each soil cultivated in 2008–2009, as indicated by GIS analysis of aerial photographs compiled by SRK. About 21 percent (or 5,277 ha of the 25,161-ha area of the OJVG concession) was cultivated during this 2-year period. On average, fields are cultivated for 7 years before being left fallow; so, the amount of farmland in any year is about one-seventh less than the 21 percent figure, or about 18 percent (in all, approximately 4,523 ha). Fields in the OJVG concession are left fallow for periods ranging from 4 to 7 years (Bèye et al. 2010); so, the total amount of agricultural land is substantially greater than that farmed in any given year. The total amount of farmland is estimated at 8,077 ha, or just under one-third (32 percent) of the OJVG concession.

Agricultural fields are found on all five soil map units, although they vary substantially in productivity. No data exist on the agricultural yield for each soil map unit, but it is possible to assess their general agricultural productivity based on the descriptions of each unit, combined with information learned from local farmers during interviews; the information from these interviews is reviewed in more detail in the next section of this report. Before evaluating the general agricultural productivity of each soil map unit, it is important to understand the limitations of the soil map on which this evaluation is based. The map was prepared at a scale of 1:500,000, which qualifies it as a fifth-order soil survey, the grossest resolution recognized by the Natural Resources Conservation Service of the USDA is 1:250,000–1,000,000 or smaller (Soil Survey Division Staff 1993:Table 2-1). Field procedures for fifth-order soil surveys involve mapping representative areas by remotely sensed data, with limited on-site verification or field traversing. The kinds of map units in fifth-order soil surveys are chiefly associations, consociations, and undifferentiated groups, and complexes in the USDA system). The minimum size delineation for a 1:500,000-scale soil map is 1,000 ha, a scale that is insufficient for delineating and differentiating pockets of farmland at the scale of agricultural fields or smaller parcels. Contrasting inclusions of differing soils can vary dramatically in size and extent for soil maps at such scales. The primary use of fifth-order surveys is to select areas for more-intensive study: 'Fifth-order surveys are made to collect soils information in very large areas at a level of detail suitable for planning regional land use and interpreting information at a high level of generalization' (Soil Survey Division Staff 1993:55).

Although we recognize the limits of the soil map of the OJVG concession, we consider it suitable for making broad assessments of agricultural productivity for the purposes of this study. Tables 2 and 3 summarize our evaluation of the agricultural productivity for each unit. Productivity for these soils, from the highest to lowest, follows this trend: Aa3 > M1c > M1a > M3a2 > M2b.

Agricultural-Soil Productivity of the Oromin Joint Venture Group Concession, Senegal

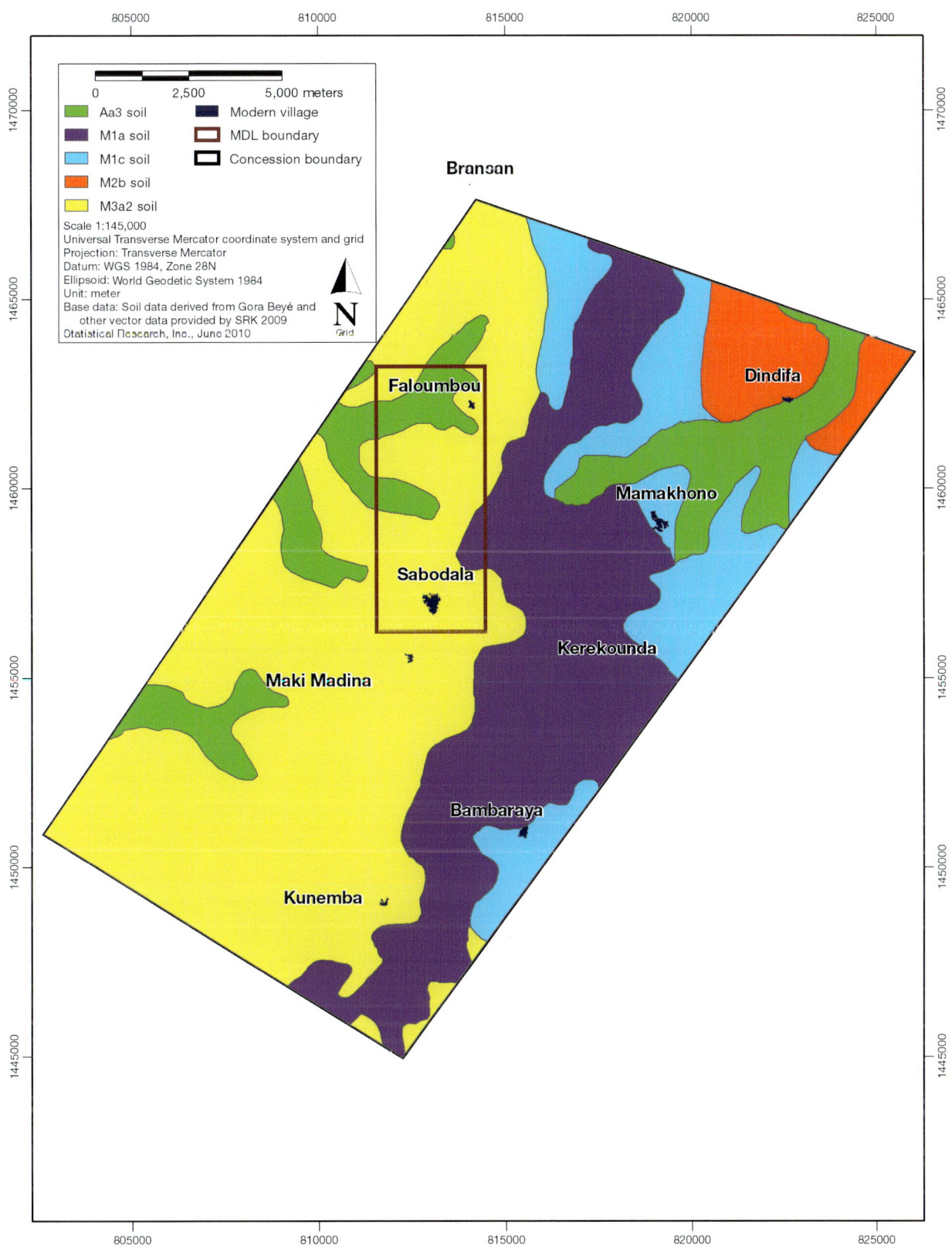

Figure 7. Map of soil types in the Oromin Joint Venture Group concession.

TABLE 2. GENERAL CHARACTERISTICS OF SOILS IN THE OROMIN CONCESSION (KEY FOR FIGURE 4).

Soil Map Unit	FAO and USDA Soil Order, General Descriptions, and Associated Landforms[1]		Area of Concession		Area Cultivated (2008-2009)		General Agricultural Productivity	
	(English)	(French)	(ha)	(%)	(ha)	(%)	Description	Rank
Aa3	Alluvial soils of terraces and colluvial footslopes in valleys, parts of which are flooded during the rainy season; mainly Entisols in the USDA soil taxonomy, but also includes Inceptisols, Alfisols, and Ultisols. Entisols are mainly on T0 (floodplain), Inceptisols and Alfisols on the T1, and Ultisols on the T2 terrace.	Terrasse colluvio-alluviales, vallons fonctionnels, sols hydromorphes sur matériau alluvial	3158	13	624	20	Most productive agricultural soil in the Concession; fine very gravelly soils on the first terrace of this soil are regarded by local farmers as the best of all agricultural soils.	1
M1a	Lithosols on basic rocks and various Regosols (brown eutrophic soils) on various basic rock fragments in hilly terrain; Lithosols are soils in humid climates in which soluble salts and minerals are leached out of the upper layers and are cemented or compacted at a lower level; Lithosols have no equivalent in USDA soil taxonomy, but occur in lithic subgroups of many soil orders; Regosols are characterized by shallow, medium- to fine-textured, unconsolidated parent material that may be of alluvial origin and by the lack of a significant soil horizon formation; Regosols are equivalent to Orthents, Psamments, and other secondary map units in USDA soil taxonomy.	Colline, Lithosols sur roches basiques diverses et régosols bruns eutrophes sur débris de roches basiques diverses	6433	26	1426	22	Intermediate productivity; productivity is limited by thin soils above shallow lithic contact and low water availability, but pockets of suitable agricultural land occur in unit M1a.	3
M1c	Vertic soils formed on alluvial floodplains with abundant smectite clay (high shrink-swell soils that develop large cracks during most dry seasons); mainly Vertisols or vertic Entisols in USDA soil taxonomy.	Valons, sols vertiques sur matériau argileux gonflant	2983	12	685	23	Productive agricultural soil with a very high cation exchange capacity, but the high shrink-swell capacity can disrupt crop root growth.	2
M2b	30% Lithosols (soils armored with laterite), 40% Regosols formed in gravelly material, 20% leached tropical ferruginous soils formed in material derived from migmetites; Lithosols are soils in humid climates in which soluble salts and minerals are leached out of the upper layers and are cemented or compacted at a lower level; Lithosols have no equivalent in USDA soil taxonomy, but occur in lithic subgroups of many soil orders; Regosols are characterized by shallow, medium- to fine-textured, unconsolidated parent material that may be of alluvial origin and by the lack of a significant soil horizon formation; Regosols are equivalent to Orthents and Psamments in the Entisols soil order, and other secondary map units in USDA soil taxonomy.	Glacis étagé, Lithosols sur cuirasse, Régosols sur matériau gravillonnaire, sols férrugineux tropicaux lessivés sur matériau dérivé des migmatites	1189	5	62	5	Least productive agricultural field in the Concession, but comprises less than 5% of the Concession, all near Dindifa.	5
M3a2	Similar to above, but 60% Lithosols and 25 to 40% Regosols, and no tropical ferruginous soils.	Glacis étagés, lithosols sur cuirasse et régosols sur matériau gravillonnaire	11398	45	2480	22	Second least productive soils, but it still accounts for nearly half (47%) of agricultural land in the Concession.	4
		Total	25161	100	5277	21		

1- FAO : Food and Agriculture Organization; USDA : United States Department of Agriculture
Source map from: DAT, USAID, RSI (1984). Cartographie et télédétection des ressources du Sénégal: étude de la géologie, de l'hydrologie, des sols, de la végétation et des potentiels d'utilisation des sols (scale: 1:500,000). Projet SDSU-RSI-86-01, 653 pages.

TABLE 3. AREA (HECTARES) OF SOIL MAP UNITS AND AGRICULTURAL LAND (YEARS 2008 AND 2009) FOR EACH VILLAGE.

Modern Village	Village Area	Soil Map Unit	Land Use Type			Land Use Type	Soil Map Unit					
			Cultivated	Uncultivated	Total		Aa3	M1a	M1c	M2b	M3a2	Total
	(ha)		(ha)	(ha)	(ha)		(ha)	(ha)	(ha)	(ha)	(ha)	
Bambaraya	5.1	Aa3	-	-	-	Cultivated	-	379	139	-	0	519
		M1a	379	811	1190	Uncultivated	-	811	322	-	6	1138
		M1c	139	322	461							
		M2b	-	-	-							
		M3a2	0	6	6							
		Subtotal (ha)	519	1138	1657	Subtotal (ha)	0	1190	461	0	6	1657
		Subtotal (%)	31	69	100	Subtotal (%)	0	72	28	0	0	100
Bransan	0.1	Aa3	0	6	6	Cultivated	0	21	48	-	34	102
		M1a	21	102	123	Uncultivated	6	102	223	-	545	876
		M1c	48	223	271							
		M2b	-	-	-							
		M3a2	34	545	578							
		Subtotal (ha)	102	876	978	Subtotal (ha)	6	123	271	0	578	978
		Subtotal (%)	10	90	100	Subtotal (%)	1	13	28	0	59	100
Dindifa	3.0	Aa3	251	544	795	Cultivated	251	15	36	62	-	364
		M1a	15	218	233	Uncultivated	544	218	563	1127	-	2452
		M1c	36	563	599							
		M2b	62	1127	1189							
		M3a2	-	-	-							
		Subtotal (ha)	364	2452	2816	Subtotal (ha)	795	233	599	1189	0	2816
		Subtotal (%)	13	87	100	Subtotal (%)	28	8	21	42	0	100
Faloumbou	2.4	Aa3	56	655	711	Cultivated	56	77	60	-	187	380
		M1a	77	758	835	Uncultivated	655	758	228	-	1633	3273
		M1c	60	228	288							
		M2b	-	-	-							
		M3a2	187	1633	1819							
		Subtotal (ha)	380	3273	3653	Subtotal (ha)	711	835	288	0	1819	3653
		Subtotal (%)	10	90	100	Subtotal (%)	19	23	8	0	50	100
Kerekounda	0.1	Aa3	-	-	-	Cultivated	-	187	58	-	10	255
		M1a	187	1540	1727	Uncultivated	-	1540	228	-	12	1781
		M1c	58	228	286							
		M2b	-	-	-							
		M3a2	10	12	22							
		Subtotal (ha)	255	1781	2035	Subtotal (ha)	0	1727	286	0	22	2035
		Subtotal (%)	13	87	100	Subtotal (%)	0	85	14	0	1	100
Kunemba	2.3	Aa3	8	28	36	Cultivated	8	474	10	-	916	1408
		M1a	474	636	1111	Uncultivated	28	636	12	-	3273	3950
		M1c	10	12	22							
		M2b	-	-	-							
		M3a2	916	3273	4189							
		Subtotal (ha)	1408	3950	5357	Subtotal (ha)	36	1111	22	0	4189	5357
		Subtotal (%)	26	74	100	Subtotal (%)	1	21	0	0	78	100
Maki Madina	2.3	Aa3	94	367	461	Cultivated	94	53	-	-	1005	1152
		M1a	53	189	242	Uncultivated	367	189	-	-	2258	2814
		M1c	-	-	-							
		M2b										
		M3a2	1005	2258	3263							
		Subtotal (ha)	1152	2814	3966	Subtotal (ha)	461	242	0	0	3263	3966
		Subtotal (%)	29	71	100	Subtotal (%)	12	6	0	0	82	100
Mamakhono	10.9	Aa3	183	522	705	Cultivated	183	196	334	-	-	712
		M1a	196	448	644	Uncultivated	522	448	723	-	-	1693
		M1c	334	723	1056							
		M2b	-	-	-							
		M3a2	-	-	-							
		Subtotal (ha)	712	1693	2405	Subtotal (ha)	705	644	1056	0	0	2405
		Subtotal (%)	30	70	100	Subtotal (%)	29	27	44	0	0	100

Modern Village	Village Area	Soil Map Unit	Land Use Type			Land Use Type	Soil Map Unit					
			Cultivated	Uncultivated	Total		Aa3	M1a	M1c	M2b	M3a2	Total
Sabodala	14.8	Aa3	33	411	444	Cultivated	33	23	-	-	328	385
		M1a	23	305	328	Uncultivated	411	305	-	-	1192	1908
		M1c	-	-	-							
		M2b	-	-	-							
		M3a2	328	1192	1521							
		Subtotal (ha)	385	1908	2293	Subtotal (ha)	444	328	0	0	1521	2293
		Subtotal (%)	17	83	100	Subtotal (%)	19	14	0	0	66	100
All Villages		Aa3	624	2534	3158	Cultivated (ha)	624	1426	685	62	2480	5277
		M1a	1426	5007	6433	Cultivated (%)	20	22	23	5	22	21
		M1c	685	2298	2983	Uncultivated (ha)	2534	5007	2298	1127	8918	19884
		M2b	62	1127	1189	Uncultivated (%)	80	78	77	95	78	79
		M3a2	2480	8918	11398							
		Total (ha)	5277	19884	25161	Total (ha)	3158	6433	2983	1189	11398	25161
		Total (%)	21	79	100	Total (%)	13	26	12	5	45	100

Unit Aa3 occurs in alluvial valleys and colluvial foot slopes that flank the valleys. The productivity of this unit can be further differentiated based on landform, as the T1 terrace is considered by local farmers to be the most productive, followed by the T2 terrace and the floodplain (T0). This assessment is covered in more detail in the following section discussing the agricultural field study. For reasons elaborated in this later section, the T1 terrace is so gravelly that the gravel functions as a mulch to increase the depth of wetting into the root zone after storm events and to reduce evaporative losses and sheetwash and rill/gully erosion. Soils on the T1 terrace are well watered, and they retain plant available moisture in the root zone, but they drain relatively quickly and prevent the damaging effects that could be caused by waterlogging. Furthermore, they are dominated by Alfisols, a soil with an argillic horizon (a zone where translocated clay accumulates) that slows infiltrating water and conserves it in the subsoil, but it is not so heavily leached, so most plant nutrients have not been stripped from the root zone. Floodplain soils are actually more fertile than alluvial-terrace soils in terms of plant nutrients, but they are subject to long periods of flooding during the growing season, which limits the kinds of crops that can be cultivated to those adapted to aquic conditions, such as rice.

Unit M1c consists of Vertisols or vertic soils. Vertisols are a soil order defined by the presence of less than 35 percent smectite clay and the development of soil cracks wider than 1 cm, deeper than 50 cm, and longer than 30 cm that are open to the surface in the dry season during most years. Vertic soils are also high in smectite, and they also develop cracks, though not as large or as frequent as those of Vertisols. These clayey soils are very fertile in terms of their nutrient status, because smectite clay has a high surface area (approximately 800 m^2/g) and a high cation exchange capacity. Also, because these soils are not highly weathered, base nutrients such as calcium and magnesium are loosely held in the lattice structure of this 2:1 clay (defined by one octahedral sheet sandwiched between two tetrahedral sheets) and are therefore easily exchanged in soil solution when in contact with clay-mineral surfaces and plant roots. Vertisols and vertic soils have the highest cation exchange capacity of all soils, but the large quantities of smectite can cause physical problems for agricultural production. Propagation of soil cracks can severe the roots of crops and other plants, especially if cracks form during the growing season. Furthermore, smectite has a high water-holding capacity, but the water is held so tightly in the interlayer of these clay minerals that the amount of water held at the permanent wilting point is also high in comparison to soils higher in silt and sand. Consequently, the amount of water available to plants is not as great as it is in loamy soils, especially loams, silt loams, and clay loams. Although there are potential problems with Vertisols and vertic soils, if managed properly, they are among the most productive agricultural soils, both in the project area and on a worldwide basis.

The other three soil map units (M1a, M2b, and M3a2) are dominated by laterite, a heavily weathered soil cemented by iron. These soil map units vary in the percentage of Lithosols, Regosols, and tropical ferruginous soil (see Table 2). Laterite soils commonly have such high iron contents that they function much like geologic bedrock in terms of how they can block water infiltration. Most importantly for agriculture, cemented laterite soils are poorly suited as anchors for roots and for root growth. Furthermore, they are so heavily weathered that most nutrients required by plants have been stripped away by leaching and erosion. Laterite serves as a 'caprock' that is exposed at or near the surfaces of hilltops and older alluvial terraces. Unconsolidated soil is often so thin that there is not enough soil for cultivating crops.

Pockets of soil within each of the three map units are suitable for agriculture, especially the gravelly Regosols of units M1a and M3a2. M1a has an intermediate agricultural-soil productivity, and it accounts for over one-quarter of all farmland (26 percent) in the OJVG concession. Overall, M3a2 is lower in agricultural productivity than M1a, but it accounts for nearly one-half (45 percent) of the farmland in the concession. Pockets of land within these three units can be farmed successfully, but they are less resilient and sustainable than units Aa3 and M1c, and so, they require a longer period of fallowing to maintain crop productivity. One major problem with these relatively thin soils is that, because they occur in more-elevated areas—areas that have greater slope gradients and less natural vegetation than the alluvial valleys—they can be severely affected by erosion when cleared for agriculture. They are therefore more difficult to manage.

Given the superiority of units Aa3 and M1c for agriculture, it is remarkable that such a similarly large fraction of four of the five soil map units (all but M2b) is cultivated (see Table 3). The percentage of land cultivated in these four soil map units in 2008–2009 is in a remarkably narrow range, from 20 to 23 percent. Limited access to the best farmland for many villages has pressure farmers to cultivate land that less well suited for agriculture than units Aa3 and M1c. The fact that only 5 percent of unit M2b was cultivated in 2008–2009 is a clear indicator that this soil is substantially less productive than all other soils.

Agricultural Management in Mamakhono

Assessing agricultural-soil productivity is not simply a matter of soil science. Agriculture, by definition, is a human activity. How this activity is embedded in local culture is every bit as important for assessing agricultural productivity as is knowledge of the soil properties. Studies of agricultural-soil productivity associated with contemporary, small-scale agricultural systems are helpful for illuminating long-term human-environmental relationships, land-use sustainability, and indigenous knowledge about farming.

Studies of indigenous, small-scale agricultural systems from an integrated soil science and anthropological perspective are part of an emerging discipline known as ethnopedology (for other examples of this kind of research in Africa, see Birmingham 2003; Carney 1991; Gobin et al. 2000a, 2000b; Gray and Morant 2003; Mairura et al. 2007; Mapfumo et al. 2005; Osbahr and Allan 2003; Osunade 1992; Oudwater and Martin 2003; Payton et al. 2003; Sanchez 2002; Warren et al. 2003). Ethnopedology involves a 'bottom-up' approach that values local knowledge and involves working in partnership with local farmers, rather than operating from the pervasive 'top-down' transfer of knowledge that typically comes from agricultural experts aiming to help local farmers. Ethnopedologic research is a collaborative effort with local farmers whereby scientists learn from local farmers about their agricultural management and conservation practices while, at the same time, making practical recommendations, that might improve agriculture. In particular, we seek to explore ways in which the effects of proposed mining activities on the farming systems can be mitigated.

The field phase of our ethnopedological investigation focuses on agricultural soils in the Mamakhono farming community. The agricultural fields near Mamakhono and others in the OJVG concession are shown in Figure 1, along with the locations of particular fields investigated by Bèye et al. (2010) and their soil types. The rationale for concentrating on this particular community is threefold. First, the village of Mamakhono will be the one most directly affected by the proposed mining operations, as a broad expanse of their farmland will be inundated by construction of the freshwater reservoir downstream from their village. Second, Mamakhono, the oldest village in the project area, at nearly 700 years in age, was undoubtedly established in its location to take advantage of large expanses of well-watered and productive agricultural land, much of the best agricultural land in the entire Sabodala project area. Third, statistical comparisons are stronger for comparisons of fields in a more circumscribed area, such as a single valley, as there is better control when landforms and soils are similar and because soil-forming factors other than anthropogenic effects are more analogous. If the study had been spread over the entire concession, it is more likely that statistical differences would be identified that could not be explained satisfactorily. A substantial increase in the soil-sampling effort and the scope of this investigation would be necessary to evaluate and compare soil quality for agricultural systems spread over a broader area.

Soil changes caused by cultivation can be inferred by comparing soils in agricultural fields with uncultivated areas in similar soil and landscape settings. Variability in soil-response trajectories can be caused by differences in initial ecosystem conditions, agricultural methods, the mix of crops and cropping intensity, and environmental sensitivity to alteration (varying resistance and resilience). Agricultural diversification, such as coupled floodwater-and-runoff systems, is a key component of the risk-management strategies used by Mamakhono farmers. Likewise, diversity contributes to the stability and resilience of soil resources and ecosystems, which is crucial for subsistence farmers, such as those in Mamakhono. Although the trajectories of soil change are complex, they can be interpreted on a gradient, from enhancement of soil quality to soil degradation, with neutral, mixed, or uncertain outcomes in between.

The goals of the ethnopedological study were to document (1) traditional agricultural-management practices for the farming systems (e.g., rain-fed, runoff, and floodwater-recession systems), (2) indigenous classification of agricultural soils and landforms, and (3) strategies that farmers use to recognize and head off soil degradation. To accomplish these objectives, we begin with a discussion of traditional agriculture as practiced by the Malinké in the vicinity of the OJVG concession. This section is based on interviews with traditional farmers from Mamakhono. We then turn to the analytical results of the field study.

Traditional Malinké Agriculture

Mamakhono farmers plant most crops at the beginning of the rainy season, which typically starts around May 25, and harvest in September. The rainy season normally ends in late October. Farmers in larger families usually have five to six agricultural fields, and smaller families have one or two fields. Their slash-and-burn agricultural system typically involves cultivating fields for about seven years and then leaving them fallow for five or six years. Vegetation in fields is burned in November after it dries out, following the rainy season.

Malinké terms for crops, soils, and landforms, as well as other terms, are listed in Table 4. The most common cropping rotation consists of white sorghum (*nio*) (Figure 8) intercropped with beans (*soso*), alternating with years of peanuts (*tigo*). Sorghum is dried, stored, and then ground before it is consumed (Figure 9). Other main crops include maize (*mako*) (Figure 10) and rice (*malo*) (Figure 11), and minor crops include okra (*hanjo*) (Figure 12, which also shows peanuts), onion (*jabo*), squash (*fe*), tomato (*mantengo*), red sorghum (*kruto*), cassava (*banteara*), hibiscus (*bissap*) (see Figure 12), and other root crops, such as *jabero* and *wusso*. Cotton (*cotondo*) is not cultivated by Mamakhono farmers but is grown in the fields of neighboring villages. Mango (*mango*) is the most important tree crop. It is grown in orchards near Mamakhono (Figures 13 and 14) and scattered in a number of the fields away from the village, with young trees placed in basketlike structures made of bamboo (see Figure 12) to protect them from cattle and goats. Rice is planted before the start of the rainy season on the floodplain (*faro*) (the T0 geomorphic surface), as part of a floodwater-recession type of farming system. Most other crops are cultivated on the first terrace above the floodplain (*tinto*) (the T1 geomorphic surface), which is regarded locally as the best overall landform for agriculture. These fields are part of a rain-fed type of agricultural system. Fields are especially concentrated on colluvial foot slopes, the lower scarps of the junctures of the T1-T2 terrace and the T0-T2 terrace, a landscape position that is called *fouloungo*. These fields are watered by runoff water combined with direct rainfall. Farmers clearly know the importance of *fouloungo*, a place they define as where runoff water accumulates and is concentrated but drains quickly. This landscape position is particularly important in dry years, when there are fewer or more-poorly spaced rainfall events. Some fields are placed on the second terrace (T2) and occasionally on more-elevated hill slopes and pediments, but these landforms typically have thinner and more-erodible topsoils and are considered marginal for agriculture, compared to the T1 and T0 surfaces.

Harvested crops are stored in granaries made of bamboo, wood, and thatch, with raised floors made of bamboo supported by rocks (mainly laterite cobbles) placed in a circle ranging from about 3 to 5 m in diameter. Crops are stored for varying amounts of time. Beans are stored for about 2–3 months, rice and maize for 3–4 months, peanuts for 4–5 months, and sorghum for 6–7 months. Stored crops are depleted before the harvest in the following year, which means that the people must rely on the availability of wild plant and animal foods to carry them to the next season. Wild foods are also important supplements during the growing season. Domesticated animals, such as cows (*niso*), goats (*bah*), sheep (*sakho*), and chickens (*cise*), serve as important protein sources, although cattle are rarely consumed and are eaten mainly only during feasts associated with special occasions, such as wedding ceremonies. Meat is not consumed during most meals, although that is not by choice, as Mamakhono residents would like to have access to more of it. Agricultural crops clearly supply most of the caloric intake, supplemented by wild plants and wild and domesticated animals.

Soil fertility is rejuvenated by leaving fields fallow; ash from the slash-and-burn process (such ash is referred to as *segelibougouto*); cultivating crops that fix nitrogen (mainly beans); manure additions from domesticated animals, especially cows; and additions of natural, organic debris, in the runoff from the decomposition of plants. Cattle are commonly allowed into fields after the harvest to eat the stalks and other crop residue. Some farmers use inorganic fertilizers (mainly NPK—a mix of nitrogen, phosphorus, and potassium—and urea) in their fields, but because of the high expense, especially the transportation costs, few farmers can afford them. Urea ($CO(NH_2)$) is a nitrogen fertilizer containing 46 percent nitrogen that, once applied to moist soil, quickly undergoes chemical changes to form ammonium (NH_4^+), a cation that provides readily available nitrogen to plants.

Because most fields are placed in naturally wooded areas, trees have to be thinned from the fields. Trees are normally cut about 50 cm above the ground so they will continue to live and produce leaves to provide supplemental food for livestock.

Use rights of fields are passed down within families. If a farmer wants to establish a field in an uncultivated parcel

Table 4. Malinke terms for soils, crops, other agricultural terms, landforms, and animals.

English	Malinke	English	Malinke	English	Malinke	English	Malinke
Crops		**Soil Colors, Texures, and Other Terms**		**Agricultural Tools**		**Animals that Consume Crops**	
Beans	Soso	Soil	Bankho	Axe	Yendo	Baboon	Maro, woulengo
Maize	Mako	Black soil	Bankho fima	Axe handle wood	Faro	Birds	Jobo
Peanuts	Tigo	Brown	Kouna	Digging stick	Somengo	Black monkey	Manganfimgo
Rice	Malo	Gray	Toukho	Hoe	Dabo	Chimpanzee	Gongo
White sorghum[1]	Nio	Red	Come	Metal tip	Sombe	Porcupine	Ballo
Casava	Bantearo	White	Touhahoyo	digging stick		Small wild dog	Watto
Cotton	Cotondo	Yellow	Haran harango	Plow	Machine seno	Squirrel	Kerengo
Okra	Hanjo	Clay soil	Noumon bankho	**Agricultural Features**		Warthog	Le
Onion	Jabo	Sandy soil	Bankhomoungo	Bamboo fence	Bo suto	**Domesticated Animals**	
Red sorghum	Kinto	Gravelly soil	Kouroundounga	Drying rack	Niobento	Bull	Tura
Squash	Fe	Ash from slash and burn	Segelibougouto	Fieldhouse	Bugo	Chicken	Cise
Tomato	Mantengo	Ash-like leached soil	Dougou khoto khouno	Ramada	Bire	Cow	Niso
	Wusso[2]	Black gravelly soil, most fertile soil	Kouroundounga fingo	Agricultural Water		Cow with calf	Hango
	Jabero[2]	Fertile ashy soil, richer than others areas within fields	Tanokhonia	First runoff event	Woyo	Cow without calf	Niere
Hibiscus[3]	Bissap	Rocky soil on hills, unproductive	Bayango	Rain ('sky water')	Sandjo	Dog	Woulo
Fruit trees		Clay for making pottery	Dakho			Donkey	Falo
Banana	Banano	Red or white clay from hills; type of clay consumed by humans, especially women	Foukhola			Goat	Bah
Date palm	Tamaro	**Landforms**				Sheep	Sakho
Mango	Mango	Colluvial footslope	Fouloungo				
Tamarind	Tamarengo	Floodplain	Faro				
Baobab (or monkey bread tree)	Baobab	Terrace	Tinto				
	Dugoto[2]						
	Neto[2]						

1 - White sorghum Is referred to incorrectly as millet by the Malinke farmers in Mamakhono. True millet is not cultivated locally.
2 - English terms for these not identified.
3 - Outer leaves of hibiscus flowers are used to make tea mixed with mint and sugar, and to make jam.

of land, he will either plant some small mangos or mark some trees to delineate a claim of ownership. For cases in which two farmers try to claim the same parcel, the chief of the village will resolve the dispute. New fields are placed where the natural grassy vegetation grows tallest, a clear indicator of the best-watered, fertile land.

The main farming implements are a hoe (*dabo*) (Figure 15) for weeding, a digging stick *(somengo)* with a conical iron tip *(sombe)* (Figure 16) for planting, and an axe *(yendo)* for clearing trees and shrubs. Seeds are planted about 5 cm deep in the holes created by poking the digging stick into the ground. Most farmers practice minimum tillage (that is, without using a plow). Some farmers plow their fields with plows pulled by draft animals, but most farmers cannot afford this method. Plowing is mainly done to aid in weed control and to loosen the soil; such loosening can improve tilth, but in the long run, the soil structure can be made worse, as organic matter declines. Minimum tillage is effective in minimizing erosion, reducing organic-matter losses by limiting the surface area of soil aggregates exposed to the sun (thereby reducing oxidation), and maintaining soil structure, which favors higher rates of infiltration and aeration). A few farmers have mechanical planting devices pulled by draft animals, but most cannot afford them.

Figure 8. White sorghum in gravelly soil at Field 13.

Figure 9. Ground white sorghum in a calabas (or gourd) bowl..

Figure 10. Maize in Fields 9/10 in 2009.

Figure 11. Rice field in the northeast arm of the proposed freshwater reservoir.

Figure 12. Common crops in the project area: peanuts (*upper left*), okra (*upper right*), hibiscus. (*bissap*) (*lower left*), and a young mango tree in a bamboo protective structure (*lower right*).

Figure 13. Field 8, a mango orchard near Mamakhono.

Figure 14. Close-up view of abundant mangos growing in Field 8.

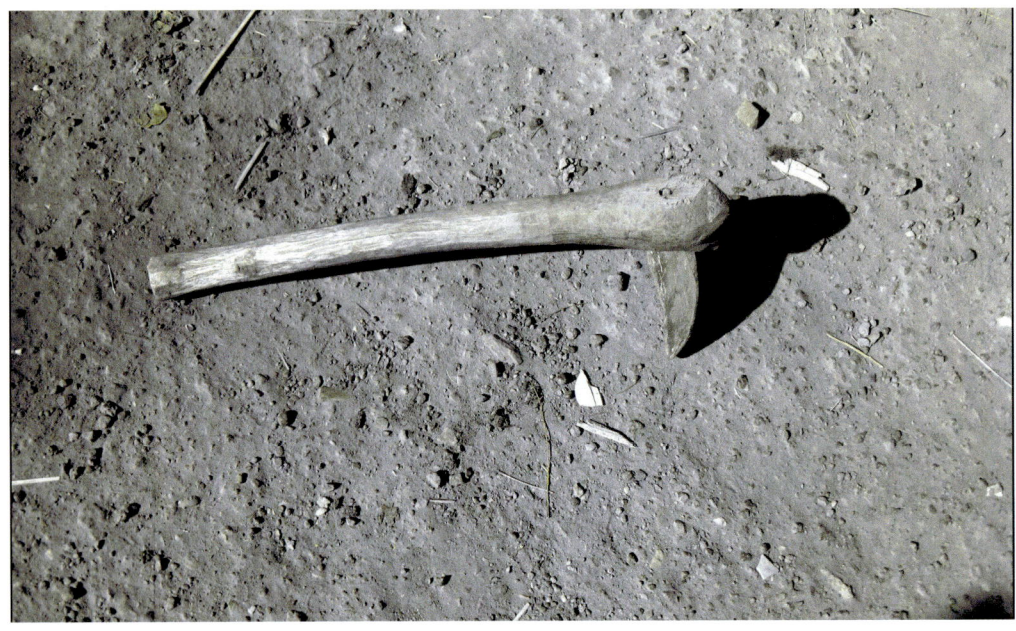

FIGURE 15. A HOE (DABO) SUCH AS THIS IS ONE OF THE MAIN FARMING IMPLEMENTS.

FIGURE 16. CONICAL IRON TIP OF A DIGGING STICK USED IN PLANTING

Harvested crops are dried in the fields on drying racks. Drying racks are made of bamboo and wood poles and built into elevated platforms (Figure 17) or on low platforms placed on rocks in a three-by-three pattern of nine rocks (Figure 18; see Figure 3 for the location of this feature next to a grain-threshing area in the center of Field 9/10). Field houses are common in agricultural fields place farther from the village (Figure 19). Some are used for sleeping and cooking, and others are used for storing dried crops before they are transported back to the village. Farmers spend time in their fields every day during the growing season, but they can easily walk to fields near the village. After the crops are planted, fields require continual weeding until the harvest. As the harvest nears, farmers spend substantial amounts of time to ensure that wild animals that might consume their crops are kept out of their fields. Farther fields require farmers to build field houses where they will stay for significant periods of time during the growing season, sometimes trading off with other family members who help tend the fields. Today, donkeys, bicycles, and motorcycles permit farmers to travel from the village to more distant fields on a daily basis.

Mamakhono farmers have developed a number of techniques for recognizing early stages of degradation that would prompt them to shift the locations of their slash-and-burn fields. These techniques rely on observations of (1) a weed, known as *lanlango*, that is the first plant to grow and die in fields; (2) growth of a grass, known as *tenengene kotio*, that migrates into fields and quickly becomes dominant over the crops; (3) formation of a gray, acidic soil, known as *dougou khoto khouno*; and (4) stunted crop growth and a failure

Figure 17. Elevated drying rack made of wooden posts, bamboo, and thatch.

Figure 18. Drying rack made of wooden poles and bamboo and built on top of nine cobbles placed in a three-by-three pattern.

FIGURE 19. TYPICAL AGRICULTURAL FIELD HOUSE MADE OF BAMBOO AND THATCH.

TABLE 5. GPS COORDINATES, SUMMARY OF LAST CROPS IN EACH AGRICULTURAL FIELD, AND VEGETATION IN FIELD CONTROLS.

Field/control	UTM Coordinates		Crop(s) Last Cultivated and
	Easting	Northing	Vegetation of Controls
Field 1	819448	1461367	Maize, okra
Field 2	819681	1460419	Maize, okra, squash
Field 2 control	819685	1460493	Bamboo, grass
Field 3	819464	1461679	White sorghum, peanuts, okra, squash
Field 4	819717	1460321	Maize
Field 5	819914	1459378	White sorghum, peanuts, okra
Field 5 control	820900	1461515	Bamboo, trees
Field 6	821434	1461693	Maize
Field 6 control	821379	1461671	Grass
Field 7	821430	1461645	White sorghum, peanuts, okra
Field 7 control	821499	1461643	Bamboo, trees
Field 8	819404	1459398	Mangos
Field 9	819609	1460225	White sorghum, peanuts
Field 9 control	819601	1459992	Trees, misc. forbs, bamboo
Field 10	819650	1460239	White sorghum
Field 10 control	819681	1460194	Grass, trees (including acacia), bamboo
Field 11	820762	1458763	White sorghum, peanuts, okra, squash
Field 11 control	820899	1458835	Grass, scattered trees
Field 12	819309	1458755	White sorghum, mangos
Field 12 control	819360	1458699	Grass, scattered trees
Field 13	819106	1458401	White sorghum, okra
Field 14	819205	1458385	White sorghum, okra

of a crop to produce mature fruits or viable seeds. Early recognition of these signs of degradation, combined with shifting field locations regularly, help ensure that soil quality is maintained and that agricultural production is sustained.

Agricultural Field Study

The most recently cultivated crops for each field and the vegetation of each field control are summarized in Table 5. Observations of crop residues in the fields indicate that the dominant crops are sorghum, maize, and peanuts. Dominant vegetation in the field controls range from bamboo to thick grass to mixed grass and woodlands. We found that the crop residue of fenced fields, those fields nearest to Mamakhono, is commonly left in the fields after harvest, a practice that helps to slow erosion and to protect the soil from organic-matter loss (Figure 20). Bamboo fencing is common in many fields, to keep out such animals as goats and cattle (Figure 21). Representative examples of agricultural fields and their controls on the T1 terrace, the most productive

FIGURE 20. FIELD 10 ON THE T0 TERRACE (FLOODPLAIN), WITH MAIZE-CROP RESIDUE AND TREE STUMPS.

FIGURE 21. BAMBOO-AND-POST FENCING AROUND FIELD 10.

geomorphic surface for agriculture, are shown in Figures 22–25. A floodplain (T0) field with numerous tree stumps and its control in the adjacent grassy patch to the north are shown in Figures 26 and 27. A field on a colluvial foot slope (*fouloungo*), the landscape position where runoff is concentrated, is shown in Figure 28, and its adjacent control in bamboo to the south is shown in Figure 29.

Figure 22. Field 9 on the T1 terrace, with maize residue.

Figure 23. Field 9 control in a grassland-woodland vegetation community.

Figure 24. Field 5, a field on the T1 terrace with numerous tree stumps; sorghum, peanuts, and okra were the most-recent crops cultivated in this field.

Figure 25. Field 5 control on the T1 terrace, in an area dominated by bamboo.

Figure 26. Field 6 on the T0 terrace (floodplain), with sorghum-crop residue and numerous tree stumps.

Figure 27. Field 6 control, with thick, grassy vegetation.

Figure 28. Field 7 on a T1 foot slope, a landscape position where runoff is concentrated.

Figure 29. Field 7 control on a similar T1 foot slope (see Figure 28), south of Field 7.

The chemical and particle-size soil data for the fields are presented in Tables 6 and 7, respectively, and the chemical and particle-size soil data for the backhoe trenches are presented in Tables 8 and 9, respectively. The means and standards for the soil-chemistry data for the fields are presented graphically in Figures 30 and 31. These histograms show comparisons of all fields versus all controls and the paired fields and controls on the graphs to the left and fields versus controls for each geomorphic surface on the graphs to the right.

Figures 30 and 31 clearly illustrate that there is little difference between the cultivated and uncultivated fields, in terms of soil fertility. This assessment is supported by the t-tests, as no statistical differences were identified in any of these comparisons. This finding indicates that (1) cultivation has not caused soil quality to decline, (2) agricultural fields are well managed by the Mamakhono farmers, and (3) agricultural production under the current climatic conditions is sustainable for the existing population size of the village. Centuries of knowledge embodied in the Mamakhono farming practices have resulted in a highly sustainable agricultural system. This situation stands in stark contrast to that of many other parts of Africa, especially agricultural regions with significantly dryer climates and sandier and less-resilient soils.

Soil pH levels are mainly slightly acidic, with an average of 6.6 (ranging from approximately 6.3 to approximately 7.2) in the cultivated fields, which is only about 0.1 pH units less than the 6.7 (ranging from 6.4 to 7.0) average of the controls. Slightly acidic pH levels are very productive, in terms of cation exchange capacity and nutrient availability. For example, the ideal level for maize production is pH 6.5. Organic-carbon and nitrogen levels are about 7–10 times higher than that of other farming systems in the region, such as one documented by Owens (2008) at Gourel Yoba, an agricultural village between Tambacounda and Kedougou. Although organic carbon is not a nutrient that plants access from the soil, high levels of organic carbon impart numerous biological, chemical, and physical properties to the soil that are favorable to agriculture. Ratios of carbon to nitrogen are relatively large compared to many agricultural systems, a property that apparently is caused by continual additions of fresh organic material to the soil due to the practice of slash-and-burn agriculture. The result is that microbial decomposition is incomplete, but nitrogen levels are high enough that plant availability is great, beyond the levels required by soil bacteria that compete with plants for access to nitrogen. Available-phosphorous levels required by crops in the project area are unknown, but it is likely that levels above about 5 mg/kg are sufficient and levels below about 2 mg/kg

TABLE 6. CHEMICAL SOIL PROPERTIES OF FIELDS AND FIELD CONTROLS.

Field/Control	Geomorphic Surface	pH	C (g/kg)	N (g/kg)	C:N Ratio	OM (%)	Ca (mg/kg)	K (mg/kg)	Mg (mg/kg)	Na (mg/kg)	Avail. P
Field 1	T1	6.75	18.7	1.2	15.6	0.21	1777	151	291	13.0	11.1
Field 2	T0	6.49	35.2	1.9	18.5	0.33	2567	178	539	13.1	27.5
Field 2 control	T0	7.02	34.4	2.6	13.5	0.44	3187	183	362	13.1	29.0
Field 3	T0	6.62	39.0	1.9	20.6	0.33	3157	146	652	9.2	37.5
Field 4	T1	6.56	32.4	1.8	18.2	0.31	2981	83	912	6.3	12.8
Field 5	T2	6.77	19.4	1.4	14.2	0.24	1277	106	197	6.8	4.9
Field 5 control	T2	6.60	11.1	0.7	15.9	0.12	461	94	163	6.1	3.6
Field 6	T0	6.37	20.7	1.4	14.8	0.24	930	134	200	6.9	7.1
Field 6 control	T0	6.81	14.5	0.9	15.5	0.16	1430	149	313	6.7	4.0
Field 7	T1	6.96	27.3	1.4	19.3	0.24	2473	59	697	8.4	6.8
Field 7 control	T1	6.62	21.2	1.2	17.2	0.21	1440	130	244	4.7	8.4
Field 8	T0	6.36	25.6	1.3	19.1	0.23	1138	79	304	3.5	4.4
Field 9	T1	7.16	11.2	0.7	16.1	0.12	1495	78	347	12.7	2.5
Field 9 control	T1	6.62	12.2	0.8	14.5	0.15	1179	70	166	12.3	2.4
Field 10	T0	6.96	25.4	1.5	17.5	0.25	2579	36	523	11.7	10.3
Field 10 control	T0	6.72	24.9	1.5	17.1	0.25	2391	62	503	8.8	13.9
Field 11	T2	6.27	13.3	0.9	14.7	0.16	629	39	168	7.4	3.3
Field 11 control	T2	6.42	29.3	1.7	16.9	0.30	1670	107	561	3.2	5.8
Field 12	T0	6.48	20.9	1.5	14.2	0.25	2492	85	580	7.6	6.1
Field 12 control	T0	6.77	33.7	2.1	15.8	0.37	2499	84	470	16.6	5.6
Field 13	T1	6.39	26.1	1.5	17.5	0.26	3107	89	833	6.8	4.7
Field 14	T2	6.46	27.6	1.9	14.4	0.33	2258	60	440	6.7	4.0

TABLE 7. PARTICLE-SIZE DISTRIBUTIONS, TEXTURAL CLASS, AND GEOMETRIC MEANS OF FIELDS AND FIELD CONTROLS.

Field/Control	Geomorphic Surface	Gravel (%)	Wentworth Geometric Progression														USDA				Geometric Mean (2-0 mm) (mm)
			Sand (mm)						Silt (µm)						Clay TC <2 mm	Sand TS 2-0.053 mm	Silt TSi 53-2 mm	Clay TC <2 mm	Texural Class	
			VCS 2-1	CS 1-0.5	MS 0.5-0.25	FS 0.25-0.125	VFS 0.125-0.063	TS 2-0.063	VCSi 63-32	CSi 32-16	MSi 16-8	FSi 8-4	VFSi 4-2	TSi 63-2						
Field 1	T1	33	15.4	14.2	8.8	7.4	5.2	51.0	6.9	12.8	6.5	4.2	4.3	34.8	14.3	52.6	33.1	14.3	gravelly sandy loam	65
Field 2	T0	34	4.2	5.4	3.6	3.6	6.9	23.7	8.5	17.9	14.3	6.5	8.5	55.7	20.5	26.3	53.2	20.5	gravelly silt loam	17
Field 2 control	T0	41	0.8	1.0	1.1	3.1	11.0	17.1	11.8	17.3	14.4	12.2	5.5	61.2	21.7	20.7	57.6	21.7	very gravelly sandy clay loam	12
Field 3	T0	29	0.2	0.5	0.5	1.3	3.5	6.0	8.4	22.5	15.7	13.4	11.8	71.8	22.3	7.8	70.0	22.3	gravelly silt loam	8
Field 4	T1	28	0.8	1.5	1.3	1.9	3.2	8.8	5.9	22.5	16.2	11.3	9.1	65.0	26.2	10.2	63.6	26.2	gravelly silt loam	8
Field 5	T2	41	19.9	14.4	9.4	6.3	5.3	55.2	5.3	11.3	5.3	1.4	5.4	28.6	16.2	56.7	27.1	16.2	very gravelly sandy loam	74
Field 5 control	T2	52	17.1	9.2	5.7	5.8	9.5	47.2	12.8	16.7	6.5	1.2	2.8	40.0	12.8	51.8	35.4	12.8	very gravelly loam	64
Field 6	T0	58	16.8	9.0	6.9	5.6	8.2	46.5	11.3	17.3	5.0	3.3	4.2	41.1	12.4	49.9	37.7	12.4	very gravelly loam	61
Field 6 control	T0	21	1.8	3.9	6.2	8.1	9.4	29.4	16.1	20.8	7.2	2.8	6.7	53.5	17.0	34.5	48.5	17.0	gravelly loam	24
Field 7	T1	25	0.2	0.6	0.6	1.5	5.2	8.1	6.7	13.5	17.3	13.4	12.4	63.2	28.7	10.3	61.1	28.7	gravelly sandy clay loam	7
Field 7 control	T1	43	11.4	8.4	7.7	6.6	9.8	43.6	8.5	10.9	8.2	4.1	2.7	34.4	22.0	46.2	31.8	22.0	very gravelly loam	37
Field 8	T0	53	13.0	11.2	10.2	8.0	10.3	52.6	8.8	5.4	7.7	3.1	6.0	30.9	16.6	55.5	27.9	16.6	very gravelly silt loam	54
Field 9	T1	41	12.5	10.8	8.2	5.7	5.3	42.6	7.4	9.9	6.0	4.7	1.5	29.4	28.0	44.4	27.6	28.0	very gravelly clay loam	33
Field 9 control	T1	37	10.4	11.1	11.8	9.5	9.2	52.0	9.2	10.6	5.3	2.7	1.8	29.7	18.3	55.1	26.6	18.3	very gravelly silt loam	55
Field 10	T0	37	1.5	1.5	1.6	2.8	4.7	12.0	9.7	15.5	14.9	12.2	8.6	61.0	27.0	14.1	58.9	27.0	very gravelly sandy clay loam	9
Field 10 control	T0	32	3.7	3.4	2.4	3.8	7.2	20.6	9.0	15.7	14.1	8.7	6.9	54.6	24.8	23.8	51.4	24.8	gravelly sandy clay loam	14
Field 11	T2	45	17.4	10.1	7.6	8.4	9.1	52.3	7.5	14.2	8.1	3.8	1.6	35.1	12.5	55.2	32.3	12.5	very gravelly silt loam	70
Field 11 control	T2	65	13.1	5.7	4.4	9.5	10.0	42.7	7.0	10.5	6.4	6.2	6.3	36.4	20.8	44.6	34.5	20.8	very gravelly silt loam	33
Field 12	T0	56	4.2	5.7	5.2	5.7	9.5	30.4	12.3	12.5	7.6	3.5	6.0	41.8	27.8	34.0	38.1	27.8	very gravelly clay loam	18
Field 12 control	T0	41	5.7	7.9	5.0	4.3	6.8	29.7	9.3	14.3	8.9	5.1	7.3	44.9	25.4	32.4	42.2	25.4	very gravelly loam	20
Field 13	T1	42	13.2	9.2	6.0	6.7	7.8	42.9	7.1	5.3	5.2	6.1	7.8	31.6	25.4	45.6	28.9	25.4	very gravelly loam	64
Field 14	T2	50	15.5	9.5	6.9	7.1	7.0	46.3	6.9	6.3	7.1	2.7	9.6	30.7	25.6	48.1	28.9	25.6	very gravelly loam	62

Table 8. Chemical soil properties for soil profiles in backhoe trenches 1-6.

Trench/ Geomorphic Surface	Soil Horizon	Depth (cm)	pH	C (g/kg)	N (g/kg)	C:N Ratio	Organic matter (%)	Ca	K	Mg (mg/kg)	Na	Avail. P
Trench 1 T2	A	0-12	6.26	28.6	2.1	13.6	4.9	1314	270	361	10.2	16.1
	Btv1	12-43	6.79	4.3	0.5	8.1	0.7	1023	49	344	10.6	0.2
	Btv2	43-66	6.60	3.7	0.6	6.2	0.6	872	57	319	12.0	0.5
	Btv3	66-114	6.64	3.8	0.6	6.1	0.6	1223	49	466	12.8	0.5
	Cr1	114-131	6.41	3.2	0.5	7.0	0.6	1267	42	502	12.6	0.3
	Cr2	131-180	6.37	3.7	0.5	7.9	0.6	1357	47	590	18.8	0.3
Trench 2 T0	A	0-46	6.15	16.2	0.8	19.8	2.8	2484	30	763	14.9	0.9
	AC	46-98	5.95	12.7	0.5	26.6	2.2	2234	32	701	15.7	0.9
	C1	98-160	6.23	9.3	0.5	19.9	1.6	2005	32	704	13.0	0.5
Trench 3 T0	A	0-24	6.47	7.8	0.5	14.5	1.3	1058	28	276	6.8	0.9
	CA	24-56	6.33	4.5	0.4	10.7	0.8	926	30	279	8.5	0.9
	C1	56-101	6.29	2.4	0.3	8.5	0.4	1057	29	289	8.6	0.5
	C2	101-151	6.57	2.8	0.3	8.9	0.5	1209	29	321	14.5	0.3
Trench 4 T1	A	0-39	7.04	7.7	0.8	9.3	1.3	770	23	309	6.5	0.7
	Bt	39-50	6.22	5.7	0.7	8.5	1.0	801	20	365	9.7	0.7
	BC	50-81	6.63	2.8	0.4	7.5	0.5	843	25	375	12.7	0.3
	C1	81-150	6.82	3.3	0.5	7.2	0.6	870	23	395	13.4	0.5
Trench 5 T1	A	0-22	6.61	10.9	0.9	12.6	1.9	1013	70	153	3.6	5.0
	Bt1	22-64	6.78	4.5	0.4	10.8	0.8	857	46	119	4.5	0.9
	Bt2	64-110	6.57	2.0	0.3	7.5	0.3	683	22	175	9.3	0.3
	BCt1	110-177	7.26	1.3	0.2	6.5	0.2	524	18	186	8.1	0.2
Trench 6 T0	A	0-21	6.07	25.7	1.3	19.8	4.4	2348	42	574	13.8	4.6
	Bw1	21-34	5.82	14.7	0.6	22.6	2.5	1912	28	611	12.1	1.6
	Bw2	34-120	5.84	9.7	0.4	21.8	1.7	1614	17	600	16.3	0.5
	C1	120-199	5.58	6.8	0.4	17.2	1.2	1359	11	454	13.0	0.9

may be deficient. Available-phosphorus levels average nearly twice the sufficient level, in both the fields and the controls. Base nutrients (calcium, magnesium, and potassium), especially potassium, are provided by the ash produced by the slash-and-burn process, and the levels of the Mamakhono fields are sufficient for agricultural production. Fallowing permits base nutrients to be restored for crops to use when fields are brought back into production.

Soil textures are all loamy, ranging, in order of abundance, from loams to silt loams, sandy clay loams, clay loams, and sandy loams. Loamy soils are the best textures for agriculture, because they tend to have good nutrient- and moisture-holding properties and they are well aerated, as long as they are not flooded. All fields are gravelly (15–35 percent gravel) to very gravelly (35–65 percent gravel). Mamakhono farmers regard fields with abundant gravel (smaller than 7.5 cm in diameter, with cobbles being larger than this size), especially when the soil is dark colored, as the best farmland. They refer to this kind of soil as *kouroundounga fingo* (black, gravelly soil) (see Table 4). Although the gravel essentially just takes up space in the soil, contributing very little in terms of supplying nutrients and storing soil moisture, it does provide a number of properties favorable for agriculture. Gravel causes infiltrating water to move between the gravel, which increases the depth of wetting into the root zone after a rainfall event. Furthermore, gravel armors the soil, slowing erosion and protecting organic matter in the soil from being rapidly oxidized. Gravelly to very gravelly soils are more difficult to plow, but few Mamakhono farmers plow their fields, and the gravel does not cause significant problems for planting with a digging stick.

The main differences in soil chemical properties in the study area are among the different geomorphic surfaces, not between cultivated and uncultivated fields (see Figures 30 and 31). Soil organic carbon, nitrogen, calcium, and potassium, and especially available phosphorus, all tend to have the highest concentrations on the floodplain. And because the floodplain has thicker topsoils than other geomorphic surfaces, with A horizons that average 35 cm in thickness (and some reaching thicknesses up to 1 m), there are significantly more nutrients available to crops on the floodplain; in contrast, topsoil thicknesses of the T1 and T2 terraces average 30 cm and 12 cm, respectively. But because the floodplain is flooded for significant periods during the growing season, the crops that may be cultivated there are limited to those that can tolerate flooding, such as

TABLE 9. PARTICLE-SIZE DISTRIBUTIONS, TEXTURAL CLASS, AND GEOMETRIC MEANS FOR SOIL PROFILES IN BACKHOE TRENCHES 1-6.

Trench/ Geomorphic Surface	Soil Horizon	Depth (cm)	Gravel (%)	Wentworth Geometric Progression														USDA						Geometric Mean (2-0 mm)
				Sand (mm)						Silt (mm)							Clay	Sand		Silt		Clay	Textural Class		
				VCS 2-1	CS 1-0.5	MS 0.5-0.25	FS 0.25-0.125	VFS 0.125-0.063	TS 2-0.063	VCSi 63-32	CSi 32-16	MSi 16-8	FSi 8-4	VFSi 4-2	TSi 63-2		TC <2 mm	TS 2-0.053 mm		TSi 53-2 mm	TC <2 mm	Class		
Trench 1 T2	A	0-12	79	13.3	11.3	8.2	7.2	6.6	46.6	8.2	13.1	8.9	4.2	5.7	40.0		13.4	48.7		37.9	13.4	extremely gravelly loam		53
	Btv1	12-43	62	10.6	4.5	1.3	1.4	3.3	21.2	3.8	7.7	6.6	6.6	7.2	32.0		46.8	22.3		30.9	46.8	very gravelly clay		8
	Btv2	43-66	70	11.3	3.5	1.1	1.4	3.5	20.8	3.4	3.8	14.6	5.8	7.1	34.7		44.5	21.8		33.7	44.5	extremely gravelly clay		9
	Btv3	66-114	75	8.7	4.3	1.2	1.3	2.4	17.9	4.0	6.6	10.9	11.8	6.7	40.2		41.9	18.9		39.2	41.9	extremely gravelly clay		8
	Cr1	114-131	70	8.4	4.8	1.7	2.2	4.2	21.3	4.5	7.0	15.1	10.4	8.8	45.9		32.8	22.9		44.2	32.8	extremely gravelly clay loam		11
	Cr2	131-180	74	5.6	4.2	2.6	3.1	7.4	22.9	8.0	10.0	13.4	12.0	8.5	51.8		25.2	25.0		49.8	25.2	extremely gravelly loam		14
Trench 2 T0	A	0-46	40	0.3	0.6	0.5	1.6	4.5	7.5	8.3	16.2	16.7	10.0	10.3	61.5		31.0	9.5		59.5	31.0	very gravelly silty clay loam		7
	AC	46-98	39	0.1	0.4	0.6	1.6	4.9	7.5	9.2	16.9	18.3	9.0	8.5	61.8		30.6	10.0		59.4	30.6	very gravelly silty clay loam		7
	C1	98-160	44	0.0	0.2	0.4	1.4	5.3	7.3	7.8	16.9	20.1	9.8	7.7	62.3		30.5	9.2		50.3	30.5	very gravelly silty clay loam		7
Trench 3 T0	A	0-24	48	6.4	6.2	5.5	5.9	7.8	31.7	11.5	13.0	8.2	4.7	2.3	39.6		28.6	35.2		36.2	28.6	very gravelly clay loam		21
	CA	24-56	52	3.3	7.4	7.7	7.5	8.3	34.0	9.5	11.4	7.0	3.1	3.1	34.0		32.0	37.2		30.8	32.0	very gravelly clay loam		19
	C1	56-101	57	2.3	7.4	8.8	9.0	8.8	36.3	10.6	10.0	7.0	2.9	6.1	36.6		27.1	39.7		33.2	27.1	very gravelly clay loam		22
	C2	101-151	70	6.5	10.7	7.4	5.7	7.6	37.9	10.0	10.4	6.7	3.0	5.4	35.4		26.7	40.3		33.0	26.7	extremely loam		26
Trench 4 T1	A	0-39	39	2.4	4.0	2.6	3.4	7.0	21.4	10.2	15.0	10.3	3.6	6.2	45.3		33.3	24.9		41.9	33.3	very gravelly clay loam		12
	Bt	39-50	36	0.9	1.2	1.6	2.5	7.0	13.3	12.0	17.3	11.9	4.1	4.6	49.9		36.8	17.0		46.2	36.8	very gravelly silty clay loam		8
	BC	50-81	66	1.1	1.3	0.8	1.3	5.7	10.1	15.7	18.1	11.8	5.9	6.3	57.8		32.1	14.6		53.3	32.1	extremely silty clay loam		9
	C1	81-150	61	1.4	1.2	0.7	1.2	7.0	11.4	13.5	17.1	13.7	4.4	7.1	55.9		32.7	15.9		51.4	32.7	very gravelly silty clay loam		9
Trench 5 T1	A	0-22	55	21.8	24.1	11.9	4.3	3.1	68.2	3.9	6.9	4.7	2.8	4.0	22.3		9.6	69.4		21.1	9.6	very gravelly sandy loam		157
	Bt1	22-64	66	13.7	25.0	11.9	2.9	2.0	60.5	1.7	2.8	2.7	1.8	3.5	12.5		27.0	60.9		12.1	27.0	very gravelly sandy clay loam		71
	Bt2	64-110	68	25.6	23.0	11.2	3.6	2.0	65.3	2.0	3.5	1.9	1.9	3.4	12.7		22.0	65.8		12.2	22.0	very gravelly sandy clay loam		103
	BCt1	110-177	58	35.7	20.8	8.0	2.7	1.6	68.8	1.5	3.0	5.1	0.3	3.9	13.8		17.4	69.3		13.3	17.4	very gravelly sandy loam		149
Trench 6 T0	A	0-21	2	0.3	0.4	0.3	1.1	2.5	4.7	5.9	20.9	17.5	13.4	11.1	68.8		26.5	6.0		57.4	26.5	silt loam		7
	Bw1	21-34	2	0.1	0.1	0.3	1.3	2.8	4.5	7.8	15.8	20.0	14.1	9.2	66.9		28.5	6.2		55.3	28.5	silty clay loam		7
	Bw2	34-120	3	0.7	0.9	1.1	2.3	5.4	10.5	6.5	18.3	13.8	11.6	9.3	59.6		29.9	12.2		57.9	29.9	silty clay loam		8
	C1	120-199	5	0.9	3.9	4.9	10.0	9.4	29.1	10.6	15.7	13.2	3.7	5.1	48.3		22.5	32.6		44.9	22.5	loam		19

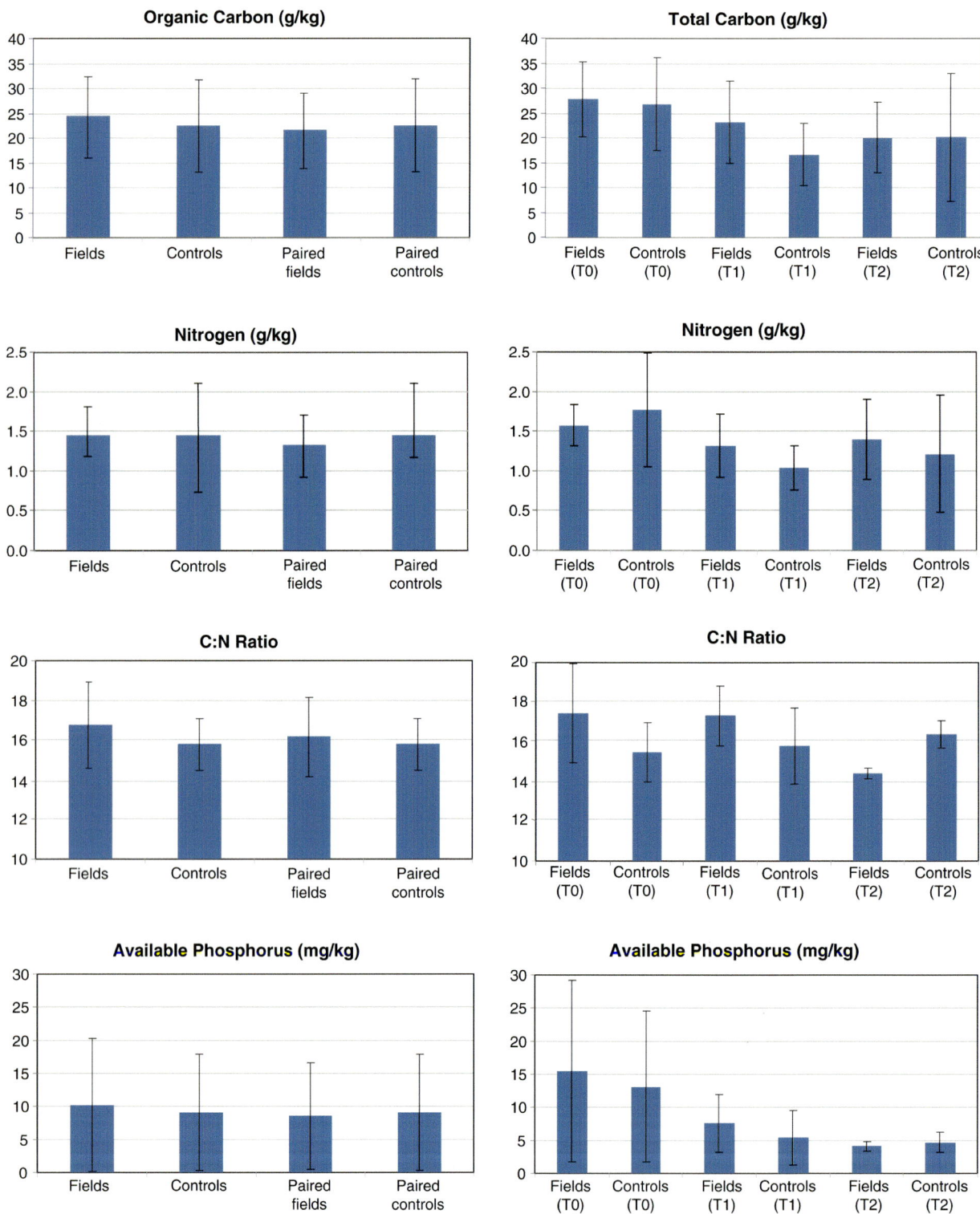

Figure 30. Histograms of organic carbon, nitrogen, carbon-to-nitrogen ratios, and available phosphorus for all fields versus all controls and field/control pairs (*left*) and fields versus controls for each landform (T0 [floodplain], T1 [first terrace above the floodplain], and T2 [second terrace above the floodplain]) (*right*).

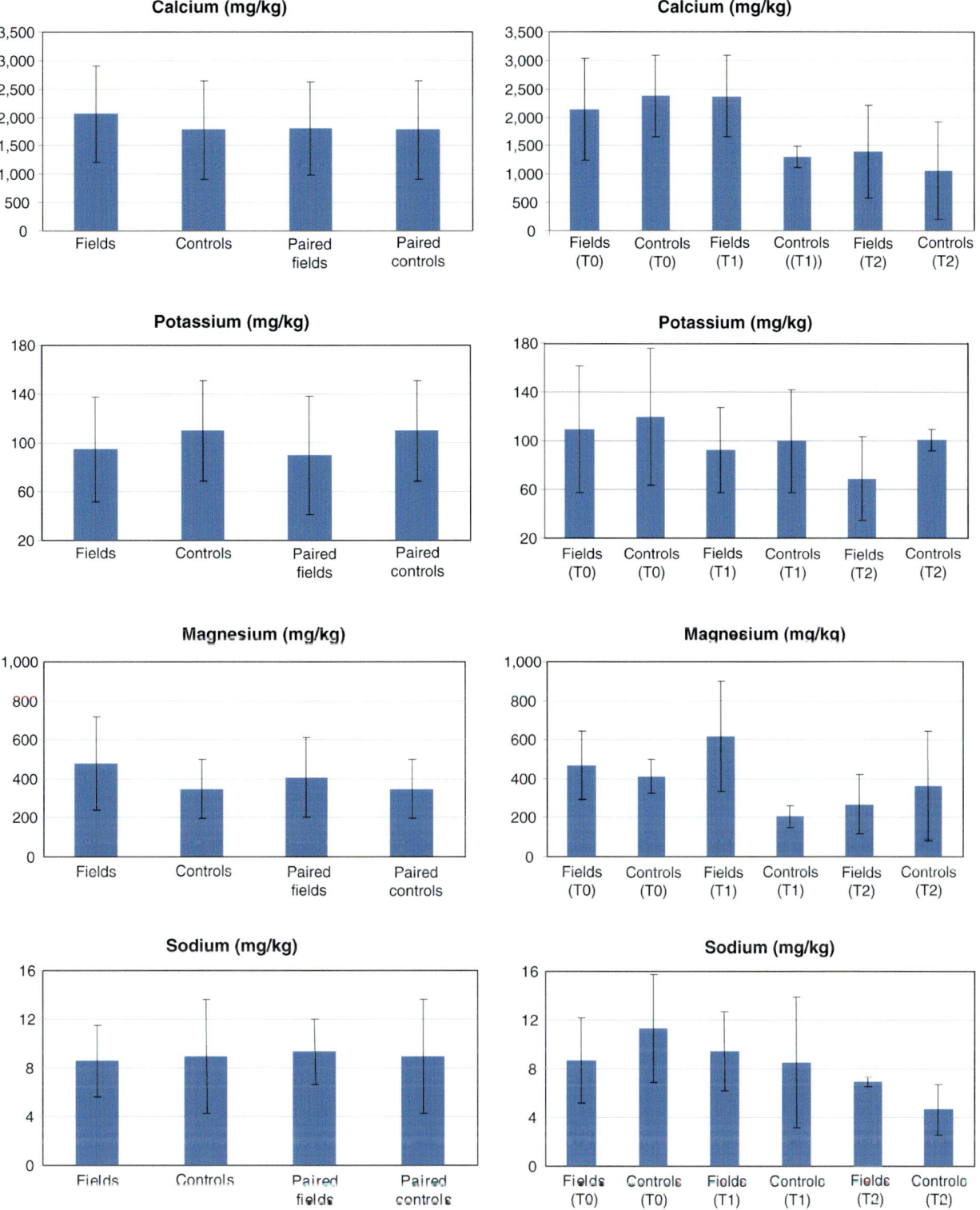

FIGURE 31. HISTOGRAMS OF CALCIUM, POTASSIUM, MAGNESIUM, AND SODIUM FOR ALL FIELDS VERSUS ALL CONTROLS AND FIELD/CONTROL PAIRS (*LEFT*) AND FIELDS VERSUS CONTROLS FOR EACH LANDFORM (T0 [FLOOD- PLAIN], T1 [FIRST TERRACE ABOVE THE FLOODPLAIN], AND T2 [SECOND TERRACE ABOVE THE FLOODPLAIN]) (*RIGHT*).

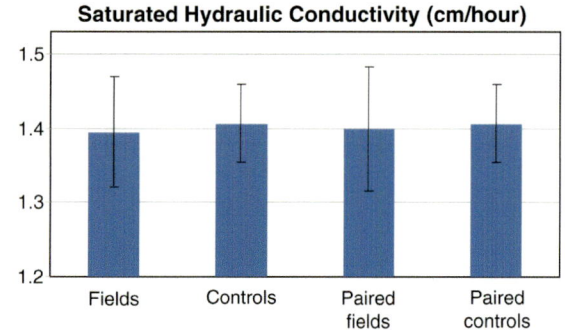
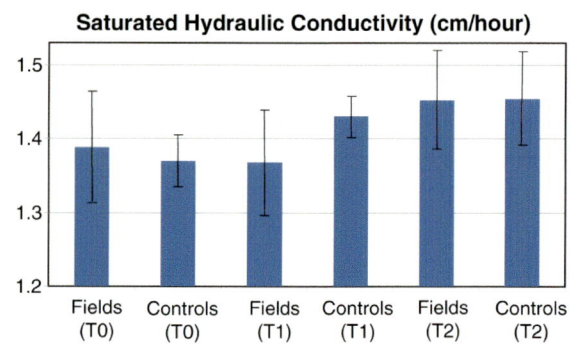
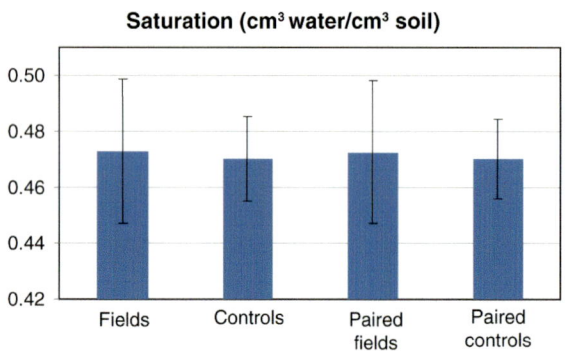
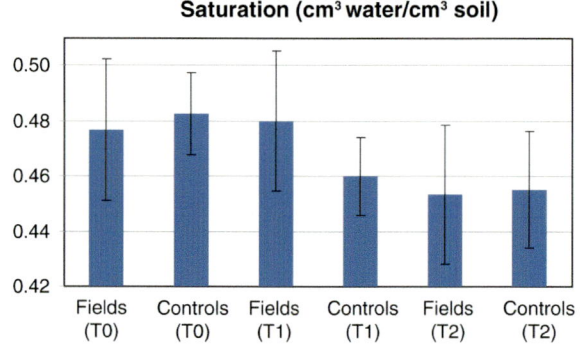
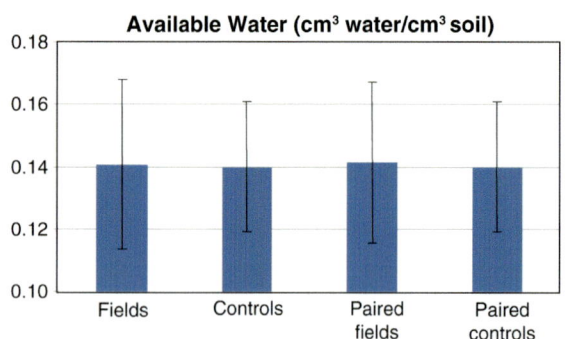
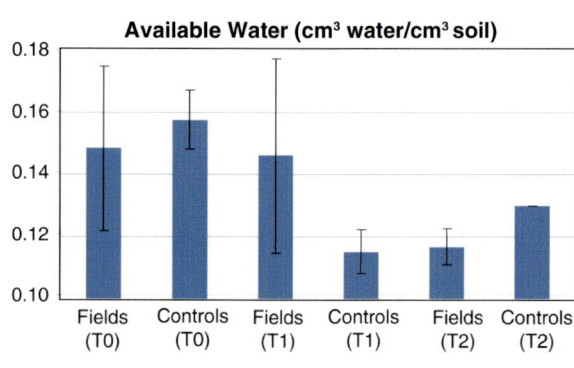
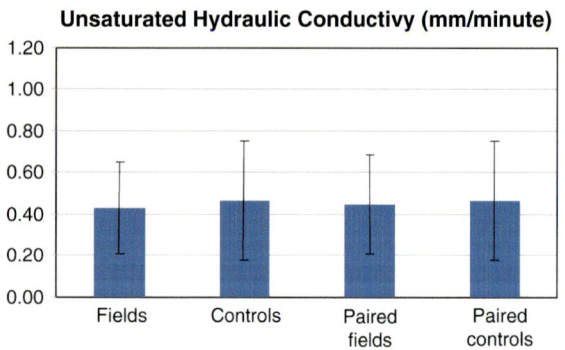
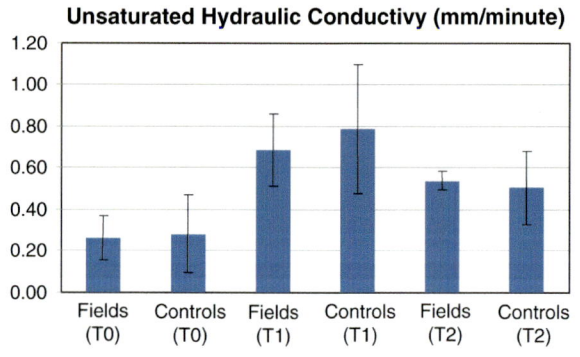

FIGURE 32. HISTOGRAMS OF SOIL HYDRAULIC PROPERTIES.

TABLE 10. UNSATURATED HYDRAULIC CONDUCTIVITY AND MODELED HYDRAULIC SOIL PROPERTIES FOR FIELDS AND FIELD CONTROLS.

Field/Control	Geomorphic Surface	Bulk Density g/cm3	Saturated Hydraulic Conductivity cm/hr	Saturation	Field Capacity	Permanent Wilting Point	Plant Available Water	Unsaturated Hydraulic Conductivity mm/min
				------------------ cm3 water/cm3 soil ------------------				
Field 1	T1	1.48	1.52	0.44	0.23	0.11	0.12	0.82
Field 2	T0	1.38	0.99	0.48	0.29	0.12	0.16	0.13
Field 2 control	T0	1.36	0.96	0.49	0.30	0.13	0.17	0.44
Field 3	T0	1.33	1.13	0.50	0.31	0.13	0.18	0.32
Field 4	T1	1.31	0.78	0.49	0.33	0.15	0.18	0.44
Field 5	T2	1.47	1.17	0.45	0.23	0.11	0.11	0.51
Field 5 control	T2	1.50	1.85	0.44	0.23	0.10	0.13	0.63
Field 6	T0	1.50	1.96	0.44	0.23	0.11	0.13	0.25
Field 6 control	T0	1.42	1.28	0.46	0.26	0.11	0.15	0.19
Field 7	T1	1.30	0.64	0.51	0.34	0.16	0.18	0.79
Field 7 control	T1	1.41	0.66	0.47	0.26	0.13	0.12	1.01
Field 8	T0	1.46	1.12	0.45	0.23	0.11	0.11	0.25
Field 9	T1	1.37	0.38	0.48	0.28	0.16	0.12	0.69
Field 9 control	T1	1.45	0.92	0.45	0.23	0.12	0.11	0.57
Field 10	T0	1.31	0.68	0.50	0.33	0.15	0.17	0.19
Field 10 control	T0	1.34	0.69	0.49	0.30	0.14	0.16	0.44
Field 11	T2	1.51	1.90	0.43	0.22	0.10	0.12	0.57
Field 11 control	T2	1.41	0.76	0.47	0.26	0.13	0.13	0.38
Field 12	T0	1.35	0.45	0.49	0.30	0.16	0.14	0.44
Field 12 control	T0	1.36	0.57	0.49	0.29	0.15	0.15	0.06
Field 13	T1	1.38	0.49	0.48	0.27	0.14	0.13	0.25
Field 14	T2	1.38	0.46	0.48	0.27	0.15	0.12	0.38

rice. Consequently, the T1 terrace has the best overall agricultural productivity.

Soil hydraulic properties are presented in Table 10 and summarized graphically in Figure 32. As with the soil chemical properties, there are no significant differences in hydraulic properties between the cultivated fields and their controls, but there are strong contrasts among the hydraulic properties of the different geomorphic surfaces. Unsaturated hydraulic conductivity (which models infiltration when there are air-filled soil pores, as there are during virtually all rainfall events on landforms above the floodplain) is highest for the T1 terrace. Such high levels are favorable to agriculture, because roots are wetted quickly after a rainfall event. Available water is greatest in the T0 soils and the T1 field soils (note: available water is the water available to plants, defined as the amount of water held in the soil, between the amount held at the permanent wilting point and the amount at field capacity; field capacity is the amount of water held for a couple of days after a soil has been saturated and gravitational water has been allowed to drain).

Assessment of Mining Effects on Agricultural Systems

OJVG Concession

In order to evaluate the distribution of soil map units for villages practicing agriculture in the OJVG concession, and therefore the general agricultural-soil productivity for each village, we calculated the approximate territory of each village, using ArcGIS to delineate Thiessen polygons. Thiessen polygons essentially enclose the space around each village, using an algorithm in the thematic mapper of ArcGIS to calculate the location of a boundary midway between villages. For the purposes of this study, the area of both the OJVG and Mineral Deposits Limited (MDL) concessions are included in the analysis. Because one village (Branson) occurs just outside the OJVG concession, we included its location, in order to more realistically define the territory of each village. The Thiessen polygons for each village are shown in Figure 33. We used these polygons to calculate the amount of cultivated land for each soil unit in each village territory (see Table 3).

The analysis clearly shows that Mamakhono and Dindifa are best positioned, in terms of proximity to the largest amount of available, prime agricultural land (units Aa3 and M1c). Kerekounda, Bambaraya, and Kunemba have access to substantial areas of farmland of intermediate quality (unit M1a). Sabodala is poorly positioned, relative to the best agricultural land; so, the growth of this community, the largest in the project area, must be related to other factors, most notably the availability of jobs for mining, mining exploration, and support roles, funded by OJVG and MDL. It appears that polygons that separate Sabodala from Maki Madina are not as

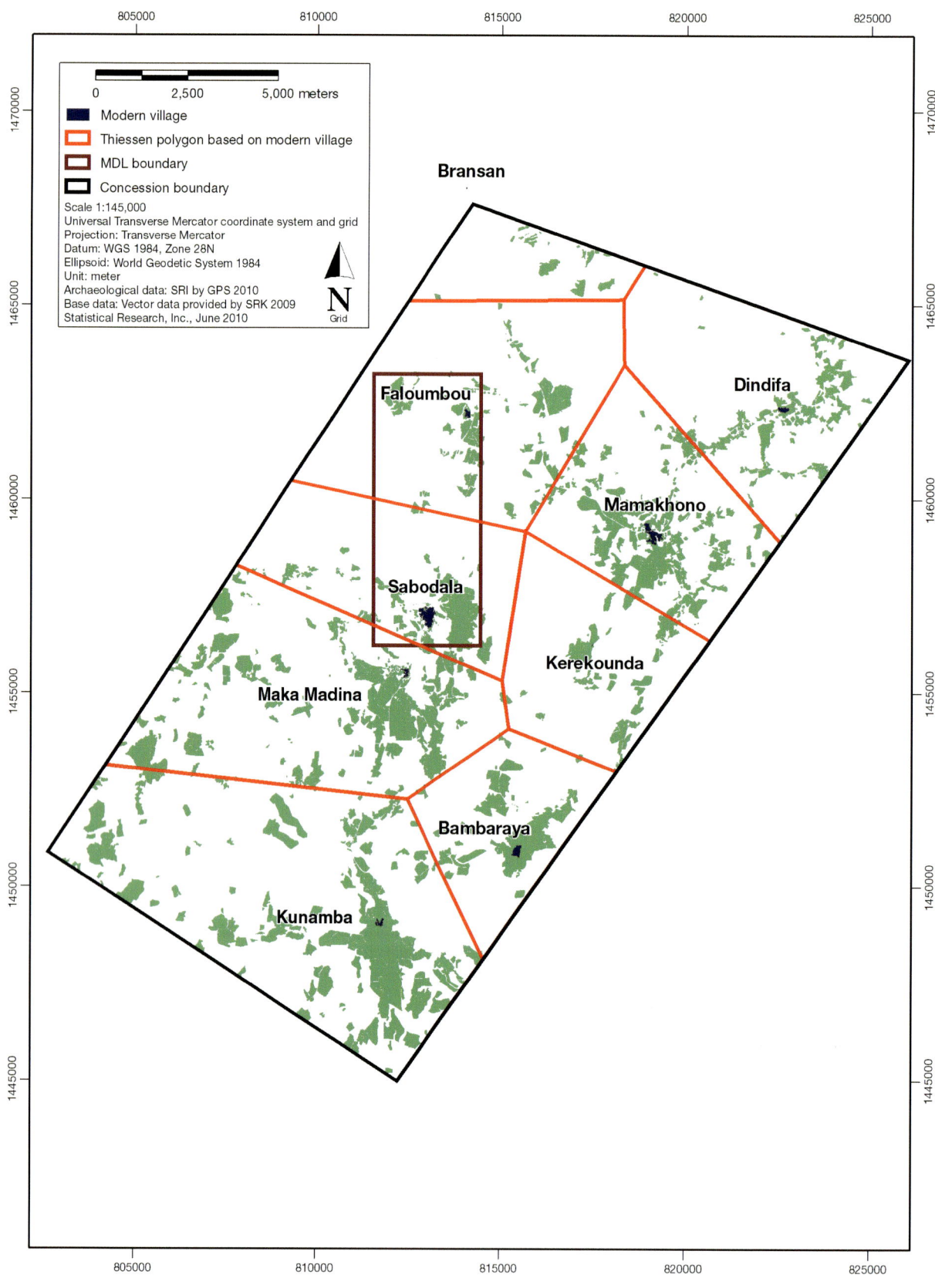

Figure 33. Map of the Oromin Joint Venture Group concession with agricultural land (2008 and 2009) for Thiessen polygons of each village territory.

realistic as those of other villages. These two are so close, and the territory of Maki Madina is shown so large, relative to the much larger population of Sabodala, that, for practical purposes, the agricultural land of these two nearby villages should be merged. It is likely that many fields included within Maki Madina's territory are actually cultivated by Sabodala farmers.

Mamakhono

Construction of the proposed freshwater reservoir will have a direct effect on the agricultural yield of Mamakhono farmers. Depending on the precise upper boundary of the reservoir, it appears that about 15 percent of the Mamakhono fields will be subject to inundation (see Figure 1). Most of this farmland is concentrated on the floodplain and low terraces east and northeast of Mamakhono, in the north arm of the proposed reservoir, and within about 500 m upstream of the proposed dam. Of course, the total amount of farmland that will be inundated is substantially more than that depicted in Figure 2, as the agricultural fields shown are limited to the years 2008–2009 and fallow fields are not shown.

The most-productive land that will be inundated, assuming that the reservoir boundary depicted in Figure 2 is not changed, is the area immediately east and northeast of Mamakhono (within about 500 m of the village). This area is intensively cultivated, and substantial effort has been expended to build bamboo fencing around these fields to keep goats and other animals out of the fields and to clearly mark field ownership. The most valuable of these fields are mango orchards that have large and highly productive mango trees. If the proposed lake level is reduced enough so that the fields nearest to Mamakhono are not inundated, then the potential negative effects on the local farmers will be greatly lessened.

Of course, there are likely to be positive effects for inhabitants of Mamakhono, as well, if they are permitted to use water from the reservoir for watering their livestock and for other purposes and if the reservoir produces fish that the locals can use. Furthermore, the reservoir may make areas immediately around the lake more productive for cultivating rice in the high water table.

Summary and Recommendations

Statistical Research, Inc. (SRI) conducted an agricultural soil productivity study for SRK Consulting (SRK) as part of the baseline studies for Environmental and Social Impact Assessment for the Sabodala Gold Mine Operation in southeast Senegal. The study's primary objective was to describe and map soil resources within the concession area, followed by characterizing soil conditiosn in terms of nutrient status, agricultural potential, erodibility and rehabilitation potential. SRI used a soil map published in 1984 to accomplish the first task and then field studies to characterize existing soil conditions. This section summarizes our results and provides recommendations for mitigating the loss of agricultural land that will occur due to development of the mine.

The only soil map published for the area is rather broad, at a scale of 1:500,000, which is sufficient for assess the general agricultural-soil productivity of the project area. This map identifies these five soil map units in the Oromin Joint Venture Group (OJVG) concession (1) alluvial-floodplain and alluvial-terrace soils (unit Aa3); (2) Lithosols and Regosols formed in residuum weathered from basic rocks (M1a); (3) Vertisols and vertic soils on floodplains (M1c); (4) 30 percent Lithosols (soils armored with laterite), 40 percent Regosols formed in gravelly material, and 20 percent leached, tropical ferruginous soils formed in material derived from migmetite (M2b); and (5) 60 percent Lithosols and 25–40 percent Regosols (M3a2). The alluvial soils of unit Aa3 and the clay-rich soils of M1c are by far the most productive agricultural soils of the OJVG concession. Significant quantities are cultivated in pockets of the other three units (especially M1a and M3a2), but these soils are less resilient to perturbations caused by agriculture and so they require longer periods of fallowing in order to maintain agricultural sustainability. The overall trend in agricultural productivity for the five soils in the OJVG concession is as follows: Aa3 > M1c > M1a > M3a2 > M2b.

Although agriculture in all villages will be affected by the mine development and operations, there is little doubt that the greatest impacts will be felt by Mamakhono farmers compared to those of other villages. Currently, these farmers enjoy some of the best agricultural land in the concession, but much of this land will be covered by the freshwater reservoir.

The ethnopedology investigation of this study documented how agricultural soils and landforms are classified by local farmers. The agricultural field study provide data for evaluating the anthropogenic effects of agriculture on soil quality. Measures of soil quality indicate that agriculture has not degraded the Mamakhono fields, which suggests that their farming system is sustainable at the current population level and under the existing climatic conditions. Floodplains have the highest nutrient status, but because they are poorly aerated during the growing season due to flooding, the gravelly and loamy soils of the first terrace are regarded as as the prime agricultural land in the project area.

Mitigating the loss of agricultural land to construction of the proposed freshwater reservoir will require careful consideration of alternatives that consider their indigenous crops and management practices. If farmers are forced to move fields to areas outside the portions of the alluvial valley that will be inundated, then soil-degradation risks will be increased. That is because areas away from the bottomlands have thinner topsoils that are less fertile, less resilient, and more erodible. The lake will also have some positive effects for the village, in terms of supplying water and fish. But it is unlikely that the positive effects will outweigh the loss of a significant amount of their best agricultural land, and that is especially true for their most valuable land, that of their mango orchards.

The current fallow system appears to be sufficient for rejuvenating soil fertility for the Mamakhono community. Increasing the length of the fallow is not a real option, as it is usually ineffective in the semitropics of Africa, because the long dry season limits nitrogen-fixation potential.

Soil data compiled by this study provide a baseline for monitoring soil quality for Mamakhono fields in the future. We recommend that ethnopedological studies of agricultural soils and management practices be expanded to other farming communities in the OJVG concession. In particular, we recommend that a study be undertaken to interview Sabodala farmers and the farmers of other villages and to test the soil quality of their fields. The population of Sabodala is significantly larger than that of Mamakhono and it is growing faster than other communities in the concession because of the increased job opportunities to work for OJVG and MDL there. Increased population means increased competition for agricultural land; so, young, prospective farmers will have increasingly more difficulty obtaining access to agricultural land. Consequently, there is greater pressure on these agricultural soils, pressures likely to cause soil quality to decline in the coming years.

Any recommendations to improve agricultural productivity should only be carried out in partnership with local farmers, who would serve as decision makers in experimenting with new and potentially more-productive crops. Increasing reliance on inorganic fertilizers is not a real option for the Mamakhono and other local farmers, because of the high costs and the difficulties in transporting inorganic fertilizers to remote farming villages, such as those in the concession area. But soil fertility might be increased by planting nitrogen-fixing, leguminous trees in fallowed fields, a practice that has been promoted successfully in East Africa, where researchers have found that the amount of nitrogen captured by leguminous trees is comparable to, but much less costly than, the amount provided by artificial nitrogen fertilizer.

Agriculture is always an experiment, and it is inevitable that there will be changes in agriculture in the concession as populations rise and job opportunities increase. Climatic changes, in particular, will likely require changes in agricultural practices in the future. In seeking ways to solve problems that farmers are likely to face in the future, agricultural experts should work in partnership with the local farmers, so that all may take full advantage of the knowledge that both groups hold.

References Cited

Arshad, M. A., and G. M. Coen
1992 Characterization of Soil Quality: Physical and Chemical Criteria. *American Journal of Alternative Agriculture* 7:25–31.

Bèye, Gora, R. Macina, and B. Diop
2010 *Situation de Référence de l'Agriculture dans la Concession d'Oromin.* Draft. Centre de Suivi Écologique, Dakar, Senegal. Submitted to SRK Consulting, Vancouver, Canada.

Birmingham, Deirdre M.
2003 Local Knowledge of Soils: The Case of Contrast in Côte d'Ivoire. *Geoderma* 111:481–502.

Bray, R. H., and L. T. Kurtz
1945 Determination of Total, Organic, and Available Forms of Phosphorus in Soils. *Soil Science* 59:39–45.

Carney, Judith
1991 Indigenous Soil and Water Management in Senegambian Rice Farming Systems. *Agriculture and Human Values* 8:37–48.

Stancioff, A., M. Staljanssens, and G. Tappan
1986 Mapping and Remote Sensing of the Resources of the Republic of Senegal: A Study of the Geology, Hydrology, Soils, Vegetation and Land Use Potential. Project SDSU-RSI-86-01. Remote Sensing Institute, South Dakota State University, Brookings.

Gardner, W. R.
1958 Some Steady-State Solutions of the Unsaturated Moisture Flow Equation with Application to Evaporation from a Water Table. *Soil Science* 85:228–232.

Gee, Glendon W., and Dani Or
2002 Particle-Size Analysis. In *Physical Methods*, edited by J. H. Dane and G. C. Topp, pp. 255–293. Methods of Soil Analysis, part 4. Book Series No. 5. Soil Science Society of America, Madison, Wisconsin.

Gobin, Ann, Paul Campling, Jozef Deckers, and Jan Feyen
2000a Quantifying Soil Morphology in Tropical Environments: Methods and Application in Soil Classification. *Soil Science Society of America Journal* 64:1423–1433.

2000b Integrated Toposequence Analyses to Combine Local and Scientific Knowledge Systems. *Geoderma* 97:103–123.

Gray, Leslie C., and Philippe Morant
2003 Reconciling Indigenous Knowledge with Scientific Assessment of Soil Fertility Changes in Southwestern Burkina Faso. *Geoderma* 111:425–437.

Holliday, Vance T.
2004 *Soils and Archaeological Research.* Oxford University Press, Oxford, England.

Homburg, Jeffrey A.
1992 Soil Fertility Study. In *Archaeological Investigations at Lee Canyon: Kayenta Anasazi Farmsteads in the Upper Basin, Coconino County, Arizona*, edited by Stephanie M. Whittlesey, pp. 145–161. Technical Series 38. Statistical Research, Tucson.

1994 Soil Fertility and Prehistoric Agriculture in the Tonto Basin. In *Changing Land Use in the Tonto Basin*, edited by Richard Ciolek-Torrello and John R. Welch, pp. 253–295. The Roosevelt Rural Sites Study, vol. 3. Technical Series 28. Statistical Research, Tucson.

2000 Agricultural Potential of Soils and Landforms near the Pistol Hill Site. In *Archaeological Investigations at the Pistol Hill Site*, edited by Stephanie M. Whittlesey and C. Riggs, pp. 21–31. Technical Report 00-62. Statistical Research, Tucson.

2002 Soil and Environmental Studies Recommended for the Ancient Engaruka Fields of Tanzania. Paper presented at the 2nd PLATINA Workshop, October 17–19, sponsored by the British Institute in Eastern Africa and the Department of Human Geography, Stockholm University, MS-TCDC, Usa River, Arusha, Tanzania.

2003 Soil Productivity of a Suspected Prehistoric Agricultural Field in Round Valley. In *Analyses of Prehistoric Remains*, edited by Eric E. Klucas, Richard Ciolek-Torrello, and Rein Vanderpot, pp. 295–312. From the Desert to the Mountains: Archaeology of the Transition Zone, The State Route 87–Sycamore Creek Project, vol. 2. Technical Series 73. Statistical Research, Tucson.

2005a   Agricultural Soil Quality in the Carrizo Wash Drainage System. In *Environmental Studies*, edited by Edgar K. Huber and Carla R. Van West, pp. 28.1–28.47. Draft. Technical Series 84. Statistical Research, Tucson.

2005b   Archeology in Relation to Soils. In *Encyclopedia of Soils in the Environment, Vol. 1 (A–Fa)*, edited by Daniel Hillel, pp. 95–102. Elsevier, Oxford, England.

Homburg, Jeffrey A., and Francis X. M. Casey
2007   Agricultural Soil Productivity in the Santa Rosa Valley. In Ak Chin Farmers of the Desert: Archaeological and Historical Investigations at the Ak Chin Site (TO:GA:6 [TO]), Gu Achi District of the Tohono O'odham Nation, Arizona, edited by Jeffrey A. Homburg, pp. 403–422. Technical Series 89. Statistical Research, Tucson.

Homburg, Jeffrey A., and Manuel Palacios-Fest
2010   Soil Productivity of an Ancient Agricultural System Near Middle Queen Creek. In *Queen Valley to Queen Creek Prehistoric Analyses*, edited by Robert M. Wegener, Michael P. Heilen, and Richard Ciolek-Torrello, pp. 12.1–12.33. The U.S. 60 Archaeological Project: Early Agricultural, Formative, and Historical-Period Use of the Upper Queen Creek Region, vol. 4. Draft. Technical Report 10-01. Statistical Research, Tucson. Submitted to Arizona Department of Transportation, Phoenix, Project No. 02-62.

Homburg, Jeffrey A., and Jonathan A. Sandor
1997   An Agronomic Study of Two Classic Period Agricultural Fields in the Horseshoe Basin. In *Agricultural, Subsistence, and Environmental Studies*, edited by Jeffrey A. Homburg and Richard Ciolek-Torrello, pp. 127–147. Vanishing River: Landscapes and Lives of the Lower Verde River: The Lower Verde Archaeological Project, vol. 2. CD-ROM. SRI Press, Tucson.

Homburg, Jeffrey A., Jonathan A. Sandor, and Dale R. Lightfoot
2004   Soil Investigations. In *The Safford Valley Grids: Prehistoric Cultivation in the Southern Arizona Desert*, edited by William E. Doolittle and J. A. Neely. Anthropological Papers No. 70. University of Arizona Press, Tucson.

Homburg, Jeffrey A., Jonathan A. Sandor, and Jay B. Norton
2005   Anthropogenic Influences on Zuni Agricultural Soils. *Geoarchaeology: An International Journal* 20:661–693.

Karlen, D. L., M. J. Mausbach, J. W. Doran, R. G. Kline, R. F. Harris, and G. E. Schuman
1997   Soil Quality: Concept, Rationale, and Research Needs. *Soil Science Society of America Journal* 60:4–10.

Larson, W. E., and F. J. Pierce
1991   Conservation and Enhancement of Soil Quality. In *Evaluation for Sustainable Land Management in the Developing World*, edited by J. Dumanski, H. Eswaren, E. Pushparajah, and A. Smyth, pp. 175–203. Proceedings No. 12, vol. 2. International Board for Soil Research Management, Bangkok.

1994   The Dynamics of Soil Quality as a Measure of Sustainable Management. In *Defining Soil Quality for a Sustainable Environment*, edited by J. W. Doran, D. C. Coleman, D. F. Bezdicek, and B. A. Stewart, pp. 37–51. Soil Science Society of America and the American Society of Agronomy, Madison, Wisconsin.

Logsdon, S. D., and D. B. Jaynes
1993   Methodology for Determining Hydraulic Conductivity with Tension Infiltrometers. *Soil Science Society of America Journal* 57:1426–1431.

Mairura F. S., D. N. Mugendi, J. I. Mwanje, J. J. Ramisch, P. K. Mbugua, and J. N. Chianu
2007   Integrating Scientific and Farmers' Evaluation of Soil Quality Indicators in Central Kenya. *Geoderma* 139:134–143.

Mapfumo P., F. Mtambanengwe, K. E. Giller, and S. Mpeperekia
2005   Tapping Indigenous Herbaceous Legumes for Soil Fertility Management by Resource-Poor Farmers in Zimbabwe. *Agriculture, Ecosystems & Environment* 109:221–233.

Mausbach, M. J., and C. A. Seybold
1998   Assessment of Soil Quality. In *Soil Quality and Agricultural Sustainability*, edited by R. Lal, pp. 33–43. Ann Arbor Press, Chelsea, Michigan.

Mehlich, A.
1953   *Short Test Methods Used in Soil Testing Division*. Department of Agriculture, North Carolina State University, Raleigh.

Osbahr, Henny, and Christie Allan
2003   Indigenous Knowledge of Soil Fertility Management in Southwest Niger. *Geoderma* 111:457–479.

Osunade, M. A. A.
1992   Identification of Crop Soils by Small Farmers of South-Western Nigeria. *Journal of Environmental Management* 35:193–203.

Oudwater, Nicoliene, and Adrienne Martin
2003 Methods and Issues in Exploring Local Knowledge of Soils. *Geoderma* 111:387–401.

Owens, C. C.
2008 Exploring Indigenous Soil Knowledge in Gourel Yoba, Senegal: Two Years as a Peace Corps Volunteer. *Soil Survey Horizons* 49:31–35.

Papendick, R. I., and J. F. Parr
1992 Soil Quality: The Key to a Sustainable Agriculture. *American Journal of Alternative Agriculture* 7:2–3.

Payton R. W., J. J. F. Barr, A. Martin, P. Sillitoe, J. F. Deckers, J. W. Gowing, N. Natibu, S. B. Naseem, M. Tenywa, and M. I. Zuberi
2003 Contrasting Approaches to Integrating Indigenous Knowledge about Soils and Scientific Soil Survey in East Africa and Bangladesh. *Geoderma* 111:355–386.

Pierce, F. J., and W. E. Larson
1993 Developing Criteria to Evaluate Sustainable Land Management. In Proceedings of the Eighth International Soil Management Workshop: Utilization of Soil Survey Information for Sustainable Land Use, edited by J. M. Kimble, pp. 7–14. USDA Soil Conservation Service, Lincoln, Nebraska.

Sanchez, Pedro A.
2002 Soil Fertility and Hunger in Africa. *Science* 295:2019–2020.

Sandor, Jonathan A.
1995 Searching Soil for Clues about Southwest Prehistoric Agriculture. In *Soil, Water, Biology, and Belief in Prehistoric and Traditional Southwestern Agriculture*, edited by H. W. Toll, pp. 119–137. Special Publication 2. New Mexico Archaeological Council, C & M Press, Denver, Colorado.

2006 Ancient Agricultural Terraces and Soils. In *Footprints in the Soil: People and Ideas in Soil History*, edited by B. Warkentin, pp. 505–534. Elsevier, Amsterdam.

Sandor, Jonathan A., Charles L. Burras, and Michael Thompson
2005 Factors of Soil Formation: Human Impacts. In *Encyclopedia of Soils in the Environment, Vol. 1 (A–Fa)*, edited by Daniel Hillel, pp. 520–532. Elsevier, Oxford, England.

Sandor, Jonathan A., and Neal S. Eash
1991 Significance of Ancient Agricultural Soils for Long-Term Agronomic Studies and Sustainable Agriculture Research. *Agronomy Journal* 83:29–37.

Sandor, Jonathan A., and Paul L. Gersper
1988 Evaluation of Soil Fertility in Some Prehistoric Agricultural Terraces in New Mexico. *Agronomy Journal* 80:846–850.

Sandor, Jonathan A., Paul L. Gersper, and John W. Hawley
1986 Soils at Prehistoric Agricultural Terracing Sites in New Mexico: I. Site Placement, Soil Morphology, and Classification; II. Organic Matter and Bulk Density Changes; III. Phosphorus, Selected Micronutrients, and pH. *Soil Science Society of America Journal* 50:166–180.

1990 Prehistoric Agricultural Terraces and Soils in the Mimbres Area, New Mexico. *World Archaeology* 22:70–86.

Sandor, Jonathan A., Jay B. Norton, Jeffrey A. Homburg, Deborah A. Muenchrath, Carl S. White, Stephen E. Williams, Celeste I. Havener, and Peter D. Stahl
2007 Biogeochemical Studies of a Native American Runoff Agroecosystem. *Geoarchaeology: An International Journal* 22:359–386.

Saxton, K. E., W. J. Rawls, J. S. Romberger, and R. I. Papendick
1986 Estimating Generalized Soil-Water Characteristics from Texture. *Soil Science Society of America Journal* 50:1031–1036.

Soil Survey Division Staff
1993 *Soil Survey Manual*. USDA Handbook No. 18. U.S. Government Printing Office, Washington, D.C.

Soil Survey Staff
1999 *Soil Taxonomy: A Basic System of Soil Classification for Making and Interpreting Soil Surveys*. Agriculture Handbook 436. USDA Natural Resources Conservation Service, Washington, D.C.

Sojka, R. E., and D. R. Upchurch
1999 Reservations Regarding the Soil Quality Concept. *Soil Science Society of America Journal* 63:1039–1054.

Sutton, John E. G., and Jeffrey A. Homburg
2002 Testing the Ancient Engaruka Fields of Tanzania: Ideas and Methods from the American Southwest. Poster presented at the 16th Biennial Conference of the Society of Africanist Archaeologists, May 18–24, University of Arizona, Tucson.

Thomas, Grant W.
1996 Soil pH and Soil Acidity. In *Chemical Methods*, edited by D. L. Sparks, pp. 475–490. Methods of Soil Analysis, part 3. Book Series No. 5. Soil Science

Society of America and the American Society of Agronomy, Madison, Wisconsin.

Vendrig, Mark, and Christina James
2008 ESIA for the Proposed Oromin Mine, Sabodala, Senegal. Terms of Reference: Specialist Baseline Studies. Prepared for the Oromin Joint Venture Group by SRK Consulting, Vancouver, Canada.

Warren, Andrew, Henny Osbahr, Simon Batterbury, and Adrian Chappell
2003 Indigenous Views of Soil Erosion at Fandou Béri, Southwestern Niger. *Geoderma* 111:439–456.

White, I., and M. J. Sully
1987 Macroscopic and Microscopic Capillary Length and Time Scales from Field Infiltration. *Water Resources Research* 23:1514–1522.

Wooding, R. A.
1968 Steady Infiltration from a Shallow Circular Pond. *Water Resources Research* 4:1259–1273.